FOR THE
LOVE OF GOD
VOLUME TWO

FOR THE
LOVE
OF GOD

VOLUME TWO

*A Daily Companion for Discovering
the Treasures of God's Word*

D. A. CARSON

CROSSWAY BOOKS • WHEATON, ILLINOIS
A DIVISION OF GOOD NEWS PUBLISHERS

For the Love of God, Volume Two

Copyright © 1999 by D. A. Carson

Published by Crossway Books
          a division of Good News Publishers
          1300 Crescent Street
          Wheaton, Illinois 60187

Cover design: Cindy Kiple

First printing, 1999

Printed in the United States of America

ISBN 1-58134-118-0

Unless otherwise noted, Scripture is from the *Holy Bible: New International Version®*. Copyright © 1973, 1978, 1984 by International Bible Society. Used by permission of Zondervan Publishing House. All rights reserved.

The "NIV" and "New International Version" trademarks are registered in the United States Patent and Trademark Office by International Bible Society. Use of either trademark requires the permission of International Bible Society.

Scripture references marked RSV are from the *Revised Standard Version*. Copyright © 1946, 1953 1971, 1973 by the Division of Christian Education of the National Council of the Churches of Christ in the U.S.A.

Scripture references marked NEB are from *The New English Bible* © The Delegates of the Oxford University Press and The Syndics of the Cambridge University Press, 1961, 1970.

Scripture references marked JB are from *The Jerusalem Bible*. Copyright © 1966, 1967, 1968 by Darton, Longman & Todd Ltd. and Doubleday & Co., Inc.

Scripture references marked KJV are from the King James Version.

Library of Congress Cataloging in Publication Data

Carson, D. A.
    For the Love of God, Volume Two : a daily companion for discovering
the treasures of God's Word / D. A. Carson.
      p.   cm.
    Includes bibliographical references and index.
    ISBN 1-58134-008-7 (v. 1 hardcover : alk. paper)
    ISBN 1-58134-118-0 (v. 2 hardcover : alk. paper)
    1. Bible—Devotional use.   2. Devotional calendars.
3. Bible—Reading.   I. Title.
BS617.8.C37 1999
220'.071—dc21   99-26484
                                                      CIP

15	14	13	12	11	10	09	08	07	06	05	04	03	02	01	00	99
15	14	13	12	11	10	9	8	7	6	5	4	3	2	1		

This book is gratefully dedicated

to my dear wife

Joy

who is to me as her name.

CONTENTS

∾

PREFACE

∾

This book is for Christians who want to read the Bible, who want to read all the Bible. It is the second of two volumes that share the same end.

At their best, Christians have saturated themselves in the Bible. They say with Job, "I have treasured the words of his mouth more than my daily bread" (Job 23:12). That comparison was something the children of Israel were meant to learn in the wilderness: we are told that God led them into hunger and then fed them with manna, to teach them "that man does not live on bread alone but on every word that comes from the mouth of the Lord" (Deut. 8:3)—words quoted by the Lord Jesus when he himself faced temptation (Matt. 4:4). Not only for the book of Revelation may it properly be said, "Blessed is the one who reads the words of this prophecy, and blessed are those who hear it and take to heart what is written in it" (Rev. 1:3). On the night he was betrayed, Jesus Christ prayed for his followers in these terms: "Sanctify them by the truth; your word is truth" (John 17:17). The means by which God sanctifies men and women, setting them apart as his own people, is the Word of truth.

The challenge has become increasingly severe in recent years, owing to several factors. All of us must confront the regular sins of laziness or lack of discipline, sins of the flesh and of the pride of life. But there are additional pressures. The sheer pace of life affords us many excuses for sacrificing the important on the altar of the urgent. The constant sensory input from all sides is gently addictive— we become used to being entertained and diverted, and it is difficult to carve out the space and silence necessary for serious and thoughtful reading of Scripture. More seriously yet, the rising biblical illiteracy in Western culture means that the Bible is increasingly a closed book, even to many Christians. As the culture drifts away from its former rootedness in a Judeo-Christian understanding of God, history, truth, right and wrong, purpose, judgment, forgiveness, and community, so the Bible seems stranger and stranger. For precisely the same reason, it becomes all the more urgent to read it and reread it, so that at least confessing Christians preserve the heritage and outlook of a mind shaped and informed by holy Scripture.

This is a book to encourage that end. Devotional guides tend to offer short, personal readings from the Bible, sometimes only a verse or two, followed by several paragraphs of edifying exposition. Doubtless they provide personal help for believers with private needs and fears and hopes. But they do not provide the *framework* of what the Bible says—the "plotline" or "story line"—the big picture that makes sense of all the little bits of the Bible. Wrongly used, such devotional guides may ultimately engender the profoundly wrong-headed view that God exists to sort out my problems; they may foster profoundly mistaken interpretations of some Scriptures, simply because the handful of passages they treat are no longer placed within the framework of the big picture, which is gradually fading from view. Only systematic and repeated reading of the whole Bible can meet these challenges.

That is what this book encourages. Here you will find a plan that will help you read through the New Testament and Psalms twice, and the rest of the Bible once, in the course of a year—or, on a modification of the plan, in the course of two years. Comment is offered for each day, but this book fails utterly in its goal if you read the comment and not the assigned biblical passages.

The reading scheme laid out here is a slight modification of one first developed a century and a half ago by a Scottish minister, Robert Murray M'Cheyne. How it works, and why this book is "Volume Two" (even though it goes through the entire calendar year), are laid out in the Introduction.

I am deeply grateful to my doctoral assistant Tom Wood, assisted by Lesley Kim, for the extraordinary work they put into the indexes. The indexes make it possible to trace entire biblical themes through the canon. In that way these two volumes may contribute to helping readers develop biblical theology.

"Like newborn babies, crave pure spiritual milk, so that by it you may grow up in your salvation, now that you have tasted that the Lord is good" (1 Peter 2:2-3).

Soli Deo gloria.

—D. A. Carson,
Trinity Evangelical Divinity School

INTRODUCTION

∿

Robert Murray M'Cheyne was born in Edinburgh on May 21, 1813. He died in Dundee on March 25, 1843—not yet thirty years of age. He had been serving as minister of St. Peter's, Dundee, since 1836. Though so young, he was known throughout Scotland as "the saintly M'Cheyne"; nor was his remarkable influence limited to the borders of Scotland.

His friend and colleague in ministry, Andrew Bonar, collected some of M'Cheyne's letters, messages, and miscellaneous papers, and published them, along with a brief biography, in 1844 under the title *Robert Murray M'Cheyne: Memoir and Remains.* That work has been widely recognized as one of the great spiritual classics. Within twenty-five years of its initial publication, it went through 116 British editions, quite apart from those in America and elsewhere. Contemporary believers interested in Christian living under the shadow of genuine revival could scarcely do better than to read and reflect on this collection of writings.

One of M'Cheyne's abiding concerns was to encourage his people, and himself, to read the Bible. To one young man he wrote, "You read your Bible regularly, of course; but do try and understand it, and still more to feel it. Read more parts than one at a time. For example, if you are reading Genesis, read a Psalm also; or if you are reading Matthew, read a small bit of an Epistle also. Turn the Bible into prayer. Thus, if you were reading the First Psalm, spread the Bible on the chair before you, and kneel and pray, 'O Lord, give me the blessedness of the man'; 'let me not stand in the counsel of the ungodly.' This is the best way of knowing the meaning of the Bible, and of learning to pray." This was not some quaint or escapist pietism, for at the same time, M'Cheyne was himself diligent in the study of Hebrew and Greek. While a theological student, he met regularly for prayer, study, and Hebrew and Greek exercises with Andrew Bonar, Horatius Bonar, and a handful of other earnest ministers-in-training. They took the Bible so seriously in their living and preaching that when the eminent Thomas Chalmers, then

Professor of Divinity, heard of the way they approached the Bible, he is reported to have said, "I like these literalities."

In line with his desire to foster serious Bible reading, M'Cheyne prepared a scheme for daily reading that would take readers through the New Testament and Psalms twice each year, and through the rest of the Bible once. It is reproduced, in slightly modified form, at the end of this Introduction.[1] Some explanation of the chart may be helpful.

The first column is self-explanatory: it lists the date, for every day of the year. The following points explain the other features of this chart and the way this book is laid out.

(1) Originally M'Cheyne listed two columns labeled "Family" and two labeled "Secret." He intended that, with some exceptions, the Scripture listings in the "Family" columns be read in family devotions, and those in the "Secret" columns be read privately, in personal devotions. The choice of the word *secret* was drawn from Matthew 6:6, and was in common use in M'Cheyne's day. I have labeled the two pairs of columns "Family" and "Private" respectively.

(2) For those using the chart for purely private devotions, the headings are of little significance. Over the last century and a half, many, many Christians have used this chart in just this way, as a guide and a schedule for their own Bible reading.

(3) That there are two columns for "Family" readings and two columns for "Private" readings reflects M'Cheyne's view that Christians should read from more than one part of the Bible at a time. Not only will this help you link various passages in your mind, but it will help carry you through some of the parts of the Bible that are on first inspection somewhat leaner than others (e.g., 1 Chronicles 1—12).

(4) If you read through the four passages listed for each date, in the course of a year you will, as I have indicated, read through the New Testament and the Psalms twice, and the rest of the Bible once. But if for any reason you find this too fast a pace, then read the passages listed in the first two columns (headed "Family") in the first year, and the passages listed in the last two columns (headed "Private") in the second year. Obviously this halves the rate of progress.

(5) One page of this book is devoted to each day. At the top of the page is the date, followed by the references to the four readings. The second pair, corresponding to the entries in the "Private" columns, are in italics; the first two, correspon-

---

[1] The original can be found in many editions of the book already referred to: Andrew A. Bonar, ed., *Robert Murray M'Cheyne: Memoir and Remains.* My copy is from the 1966 reprint, published by Banner of Truth, taken from the 1892 edition, pp. 623-628. Some popular editions, such as the two-volume paperback edition published by Moody Press (n.d.), omit the chart. The principal changes in substance I have introduced are four places where I have changed the break in the passage by two or three verses.

ding to the entries in the "Family" columns, are in Roman type. The "Comment" that occupies the rest of the page is occasionally based on some theme that links all four passages, but more commonly is based on some theme or text found in the italicized passages. In other words, this second volume complements the first, which focused on the readings of the first two columns; here the concentration is on the second two columns. In this volume, I have not restricted comment to passages in only one column (e.g., the third), because, in agreement with M'Cheyne, I suppose that focus on only one part of Scripture will not be as helpful as a broader exposure to Scripture. So I have normally commented on a passage of Scripture in one of the last two columns. The first time I refer to the passage on which I am commenting I put the reference in boldface type.

(6) In no way do these pages pretend to be a commentary as that word is commonly understood. My aim is much more modest: to provide edifying comments and reflections on some part of the designated texts, and thus to encourage readers to reflect further on the biblical passages they are reading. If there is something unusual about these comments, it is that I have tried to devote at least some of them to helping the reader keep the big picture of the Bible's "story line" in mind, and to see what relevance this has for our thinking and living. In other words, although I want the comments to be edifying, this edification is not always of a private, individualized sort. My aim is to show, in however preliminary a way, that reading the whole Bible must stir up thoughtful Christians to thinking theologically and holistically, as well as reverently and humbly.

Finally, I should venture a few practical suggestions. If you must skip something, skip this book; read the Bible instead. If you fall behind, do not use that as an excuse for giving up the effort until next January 1. Either catch up (by an afternoon of diligent reading, perhaps some Sunday), or skip ahead to where you should be and take up there. If your schedule allows it, set a regular time and place for your Bible reading. M'Cheyne himself wrote, "Let our secret reading prevent [i.e., precede] the dawning of the day. Let God's voice be the first we hear in the morning." Whether that is the best time of day for you is of little consequence; regular habits are of more importance. When you read, remember that God himself has declared, "This is the one I esteem: he who is humble and contrite in spirit, and trembles at my word" (Isaiah 66:2). Learn to distill what a passage is saying, and pray it back to the Lord—whether in petition, thanksgiving, praise, or frank uncertainty. In time your Bible reading will so be linked with your praying that the two will not always be differentiable.[2]

---

[2] I have tried to offer some practical pointers in this respect in *A Call to Spiritual Reformation: Priorities from Paul and His Prayers* (Grand Rapids, Mich.: Baker, 1992).

M'Cheyne Chart of Daily Bible Readings

DATE	FAMILY	FAMILY	PRIVATE	PRIVATE
Jan 1	Gen 1	Matt 1	Ezra 1	Acts 1
Jan 2	Gen 2	Matt 2	Ezra 2	Acts 2
Jan 3	Gen 3	Matt 3	Ezra 3	Acts 3
Jan 4	Gen 4	Matt 4	Ezra 4	Acts 4
Jan 5	Gen 5	Matt 5	Ezra 5	Acts 5
Jan 6	Gen 6	Matt 6	Ezra 6	Acts 6
Jan 7	Gen 7	Matt 7	Ezra 7	Acts 7
Jan 8	Gen 8	Matt 8	Ezra 8	Acts 8
Jan 9	Gen 9-10	Matt 9	Ezra 9	Acts 9
Jan 10	Gen 11	Matt 10	Ezra 10	Acts 10
Jan 11	Gen 12	Matt 11	Neh 1	Acts 11
Jan 12	Gen 13	Matt 12	Neh 2	Acts 12
Jan 13	Gen 14	Matt 13	Neh 3	Acts 13
Jan 14	Gen 15	Matt 14	Neh 4	Acts 14
Jan 15	Gen 16	Matt 15	Neh 5	Acts 15
Jan 16	Gen 17	Matt 16	Neh 6	Acts 16
Jan 17	Gen 18	Matt 17	Neh 7	Acts 17
Jan 18	Gen 19	Matt 18	Neh 8	Acts 18
Jan 19	Gen 20	Matt 19	Neh 9	Acts 19
Jan 20	Gen 21	Matt 20	Neh 10	Acts 20
Jan 21	Gen 22	Matt 21	Neh 11	Acts 21
Jan 22	Gen 23	Matt 22	Neh 12	Acts 22
Jan 23	Gen 24	Matt 23	Neh 13	Acts 23
Jan 24	Gen 25	Matt 24	Est 1	Acts 24
Jan 25	Gen 26	Matt 25	Est 2	Acts 25
Jan 26	Gen 27	Matt 26	Est 3	Acts 26
Jan 27	Gen 28	Matt 27	Est 4	Acts 27
Jan 28	Gen 29	Matt 28	Est 5	Acts 28
Jan 29	Gen 30	Mark 1	Est 6	Rom 1
Jan 30	Gen 31	Mark 2	Est 7	Rom 2
Jan 31	Gen 32	Mark 3	Est 8	Rom 3

M'Cheyne Chart of Daily Bible Readings

DATE	FAMILY	FAMILY	PRIVATE	PRIVATE
Feb 1	Gen 33	Mark 4	Est 9-10	Rom 4
Feb 2	Gen 34	Mark 5	Job 1	Rom 5
Feb 3	Gen 35–36	Mark 6	Job 2	Rom 6
Feb 4	Gen 37	Mark 7	Job 3	Rom 7
Feb 5	Gen 38	Mark 8	Job 4	Rom 8
Feb 6	Gen 39	Mark 9	Job 5	Rom 9
Feb 7	Gen 40	Mark 10	Job 6	Rom 10
Feb 8	Gen 41	Mark 11	Job 7	Rom 11
Feb 9	Gen 42	Mark 12	Job 8	Rom 12
Feb 10	Gen 43	Mark 13	Job 9	Rom 13
Feb 11	Gen 44	Mark 14	Job 10	Rom 14
Feb 12	Gen 45	Mark 15	Job 11	Rom 15
Feb 13	Gen 46	Mark 16	Job 12	Rom 16
Feb 14	Gen 47	Lu 1:1-38	Job 13	1 Cor 1
Feb 15	Gen 48	Lu 1:39-80	Job 14	1 Cor 2
Feb 16	Gen 49	Lu 2	Job 15	1 Cor 3
Feb 17	Gen 50	Lu 3	Job 16-17	1 Cor 4
Feb 18	Ex 1	Lu 4	Job 18	1 Cor 5
Feb 19	Ex 2	Lu 5	Job 19	1 Cor 6
Feb 20	Ex 3	Lu 6	Job 20	1 Cor 7
Feb 21	Ex 4	Lu 7	Job 21	1 Cor 8
Feb 22	Ex 5	Lu 8	Job 22	1 Cor 9
Feb 23	Ex 6	Lu 9	Job 23	1 Cor 10
Feb 24	Ex 7	Lu 10	Job 24	1 Cor 11
Feb 25	Ex 8	Lu 11	Job 25–26	1 Cor 12
Feb 26	Ex 9	Lu 12	Job 27	1 Cor 13
Feb 27	Ex 10	Lu 13	Job 28	1 Cor 14
Feb 28	Ex 11:1–12:20	Lu 14	Job 29	1 Cor 15

M'Cheyne Chart of Daily Bible Readings

DATE	FAMILY	FAMILY	PRIVATE	PRIVATE
Mar 1	Ex 12:21-50	Lu 15	Job 30	1 Cor 16
Mar 2	Ex 13	Lu 16	Job 31	2 Cor 1
Mar 3	Ex 14	Lu 17	Job 32	2 Cor 2
Mar 4	Ex 15	Lu 18	Job 33	2 Cor 3
Mar 5	Ex 16	Lu 19	Job 34	2 Cor 4
Mar 6	Ex 17	Lu 20	Job 35	2 Cor 5
Mar 7	Ex 18	Lu 21	Job 36	2 Cor 6
Mar 8	Ex 19	Lu 22	Job 37	2 Cor 7
Mar 9	Ex 20	Lu 23	Job 38	2 Cor 8
Mar 10	Ex 21	Lu 24	Job 39	2 Cor 9
Mar 11	Ex 22	John 1	Job 40	2 Cor 10
Mar 12	Ex 23	John 2	Job 41	2 Cor 11
Mar 13	Ex 24	John 3	Job 42	2 Cor 12
Mar 14	Ex 25	John 4	Prov 1	2 Cor 13
Mar 15	Ex 26	John 5	Prov 2	Gal 1
Mar 16	Ex 27	John 6	Prov 3	Gal 2
Mar 17	Ex 28	John 7	Prov 4	Gal 3
Mar 18	Ex 29	John 8	Prov 5	Gal 4
Mar 19	Ex 30	John 9	Prov 6	Gal 5
Mar 20	Ex 31	John 10	Prov 7	Gal 6
Mar 21	Ex 32	John 11	Prov 8	Eph 1
Mar 22	Ex 33	John 12	Prov 9	Eph 2
Mar 23	Ex 34	John 13	Prov 10	Eph 3
Mar 24	Ex 35	John 14	Prov 11	Eph 4
Mar 25	Ex 36	John 15	Prov 12	Eph 5
Mar 26	Ex 37	John 16	Prov 13	Eph 6
Mar 27	Ex 38	John 17	Prov 14	Phil 1
Mar 28	Ex 39	John 18	Prov 15	Phil 2
Mar 29	Ex 40	John 19	Prov 16	Phil 3
Mar 30	Lev 1	John 20	Prov 17	Phil 4
Mar 31	Lev 2–3	John 21	Prov 18	Col 1

M'Cheyne Chart of Daily Bible Readings

DATE	FAMILY	FAMILY	PRIVATE	PRIVATE
Apr 1	Lev 4	Ps 1–2	Prov 19	Col 2
Apr 2	Lev 5	Ps 3–4	Prov 20	Col 3
Apr 3	Lev 6	Ps 5–6	Prov 21	Col 4
Apr 4	Lev 7	Ps 7–8	Prov 22	1 Thess 1
Apr 5	Lev 8	Ps 9	Prov 23	1 Thess 2
Apr 6	Lev 9	Ps 10	Prov 24	1 Thess 3
Apr 7	Lev 10	Ps 11–12	Prov 25	1 Thess 4
Apr 8	Lev 11–12	Ps 13–14	Prov 26	1 Thess 5
Apr 9	Lev 13	Ps 15–16	Prov 27	2 Thess 1
Apr 10	Lev 14	Ps 17	Prov 28	2 Thess 2
Apr 11	Lev 15	Ps 18	Prov 29	2 Thess 3
Apr 12	Lev 16	Ps 19	Prov 30	1 Tim 1
Apr 13	Lev 17	Ps 20–21	Prov 31	1 Tim 2
Apr 14	Lev 18	Ps 22	Eccles 1	1 Tim 3
Apr 15	Lev 19	Ps 23–24	Eccles 2	1 Tim 4
Apr 16	Lev 20	Ps 25	Eccles 3	1 Tim 5
Apr 17	Lev 21	Ps 26–27	Eccles 4	1 Tim 6
Apr 18	Lev 22	Ps 28–29	Eccles 5	2 Tim 1
Apr 19	Lev 23	Ps 30	Eccles 6	2 Tim 2
Apr 20	Lev 24	Ps 31	Eccles 7	2 Tim 3
Apr 21	Lev 25	Ps 32	Eccles 8	2 Tim 4
Apr 22	Lev 26	Ps 33	Eccles 9	Titus 1
Apr 23	Lev 27	Ps 34	Eccles 10	Titus 2
Apr 24	Num 1	Ps 35	Eccles 11	Titus 3
Apr 25	Num 2	Ps 36	Eccles 12	Philem
Apr 26	Num 3	Ps 37	Song 1	Heb 1
Apr 27	Num 4	Ps 38	Song 2	Heb 2
Apr 28	Num 5	Ps 39	Song 3	Heb 3
Apr 29	Num 6	Ps 40–41	Song 4	Heb 4
Apr 30	Num 7	Ps 42–43	Song 5	Heb 5

M'Cheyne Chart of Daily Bible Readings

DATE	FAMILY	FAMILY	PRIVATE	PRIVATE
May 1	Num 8	Ps 44	Song 6	Heb 6
May 2	Num 9	Ps 45	Song 7	Heb 7
May 3	Num 10	Ps 46-47	Song 8	Heb 8
May 4	Num 11	Ps 48	Isa 1	Heb 9
May 5	Num 12-13	Ps 49	Isa 2	Heb 10
May 6	Num 14	Ps 50	Isa 3-4	Heb 11
May 7	Num 15	Ps 51	Isa 5	Heb 12
May 8	Num 16	Ps 52-54	Isa 6	Heb 13
May 9	Num 17-18	Ps 55	Isa 7	James 1
May 10	Num 19	Ps 56-57	Isa 8:1–9:7	James 2
May 11	Num 20	Ps 58-59	Isa 9:8–10:4	James 3
May 12	Num 21	Ps 60-61	Isa 10:5-34	James 4
May 13	Num 22	Ps 62-63	Isa 11-12	James 5
May 14	Num 23	Ps 64-65	Isa 13	1 Peter 1
May 15	Num 24	Ps 66-67	Isa 14	1 Peter 2
May 16	Num 25	Ps 68	Isa 15	1 Peter 3
May 17	Num 26	Ps 69	Isa 16	1 Peter 4
May 18	Num 27	Ps 70-71	Isa 17-18	1 Peter 5
May 19	Num 28	Ps 72	Isa 19-20	2 Peter 1
May 20	Num 29	Ps 73	Isa 21	2 Peter 2
May 21	Num 30	Ps 74	Isa 22	2 Peter 3
May 22	Num 31	Ps 75-76	Isa 23	1 John 1
May 23	Num 32	Ps 77	Isa 24	1 John 2
May 24	Num 33	Ps 78:1-39	Isa 25	1 John 3
May 25	Num 34	Ps 78:40-72	Isa 26	1 John 4
May 26	Num 35	Ps 79	Isa 27	1 John 5
May 27	Num 36	Ps 80	Isa 28	2 John
May 28	Deut 1	Ps 81-82	Isa 29	3 John
May 29	Deut 2	Ps 83-84	Isa 30	Jude
May 30	Deut 3	Ps 85	Isa 31	Rev 1
May 31	Deut 4	Ps 86-87	Isa 32	Rev 2

M'Cheyne Chart of Daily Bible Readings

DATE	FAMILY	FAMILY	PRIVATE	PRIVATE
Jun 1	Deut 5	Ps 88	Isa 33	Rev 3
Jun 2	Deut 6	Ps 89	Isa 34	Rev 4
Jun 3	Deut 7	Ps 90	Isa 35	Rev 5
Jun 4	Deut 8	Ps 91	Isa 36	Rev 6
Jun 5	Deut 9	Ps 92–93	Isa 37	Rev 7
Jun 6	Deut 10	Ps 94	Isa 38	Rev 8
Jun 7	Deut 11	Ps 95–96	Isa 39	Rev 9
Jun 8	Deut 12	Ps 97–98	Isa 40	Rev 10
Jun 9	Deut 13–14	Ps 99–101	Isa 41	Rev 11
Jun 10	Deut 15	Ps 102	Isa 42	Rev 12
Jun 11	Deut 16	Ps 103	Isa 43	Rev 13
Jun 12	Deut 17	Ps 104	Isa 44	Rev 14
Jun 13	Deut 18	Ps 105	Isa 45	Rev 15
Jun 14	Deut 19	Ps 106	Isa 46	Rev 16
Jun 15	Deut 20	Ps 107	Isa 47	Rev 17
Jun 16	Deut 21	Ps 108–109	Isa 48	Rev 18
Jun 17	Deut 22	Ps 110–111	Isa 49	Rev 19
Jun 18	Deut 23	Ps 112–113	Isa 50	Rev 20
Jun 19	Deut 24	Ps 114–115	Isa 51	Rev 21
Jun 20	Deut 25	Ps 116	Isa 52	Rev 22
Jun 21	Deut 26	Ps 117–118	Isa 53	Matt 1
Jun 22	Deut 27:1–28:19	Ps 119:1-24	Isa 54	Matt 2
Jun 23	Deut 28:20-68	Ps 119:25-48	Isa 55	Matt 3
Jun 24	Deut 29	Ps 119:49-72	Isa 56	Matt 4
Jun 25	Deut 30	Ps 119:73-96	Isa 57	Matt 5
Jun 26	Deut 31	Ps 119:97-120	Isa 58	Matt 6
Jun 27	Deut 32	Ps 119:121-144	Isa 59	Matt 7
Jun 28	Deut 33–34	Ps 119:145-176	Isa 60	Matt 8
Jun 29	Josh 1	Ps 120–122	Isa 61	Matt 9
Jun 30	Josh 2	Ps 123–125	Isa 62	Matt 10

M'Cheyne Chart of Daily Bible Readings

DATE	FAMILY	FAMILY	PRIVATE	PRIVATE
Jul 1	Josh 3	Ps 126–128	Isa 63	Matt 11
Jul 2	Josh 4	Ps 129–131	Isa 64	Matt 12
Jul 3	Josh 5	Ps 132–134	Isa 65	Matt 13
Jul 4	Josh 6	Ps 135–136	Isa 66	Matt 14
Jul 5	Josh 7	Ps 137–138	Jer 1	Matt 15
Jul 6	Josh 8	Ps 139	Jer 2	Matt 16
Jul 7	Josh 9	Ps 140–141	Jer 3	Matt 17
Jul 8	Josh 10	Ps 142–143	Jer 4	Matt 18
Jul 9	Josh 11	Ps 144	Jer 5	Matt 19
Jul 10	Josh 12–13	Ps 145	Jer 6	Matt 20
Jul 11	Josh 14–15	Ps 146–147	Jer 7	Matt 21
Jul 12	Josh 16–17	Ps 148	Jer 8	Matt 22
Jul 13	Josh 18–19	Ps 149–150	Jer 9	Matt 23
Jul 14	Josh 20–21	Acts 1	Jer 10	Matt 24
Jul 15	Josh 22	Acts 2	Jer 11	Matt 25
Jul 16	Josh 23	Acts 3	Jer 12	Matt 26
Jul 17	Josh 24	Acts 4	Jer 13	Matt 27
Jul 18	Judg 1	Acts 5	Jer 14	Matt 28
Jul 19	Judg 2	Acts 6	Jer 15	Mark 1
Jul 20	Judg 3	Acts 7	Jer 16	Mark 2
Jul 21	Judg 4	Acts 8	Jer 17	Mark 3
Jul 22	Judg 5	Acts 9	Jer 18	Mark 4
Jul 23	Judg 6	Acts 10	Jer 19	Mark 5
Jul 24	Judg 7	Acts 11	Jer 20	Mark 6
Jul 25	Judg 8	Acts 12	Jer 21	Mark 7
Jul 26	Judg 9	Acts 13	Jer 22	Mark 8
Jul 27	Judg 10	Acts 14	Jer 23	Mark 9
Jul 28	Judg 11	Acts 15	Jer 24	Mark 10
Jul 29	Judg 12	Acts 16	Jer 25	Mark 11
Jul 30	Judg 13	Acts 17	Jer 26	Mark 12
Jul 31	Judg 14	Acts 18	Jer 27	Mark 13

M'Cheyne Chart of Daily Bible Readings

DATE	FAMILY	FAMILY	PRIVATE	PRIVATE
Aug 1	Judg 15	Acts 19	Jer 28	Mark 14
Aug 2	Judg 16	Acts 20	Jer 29	Mark 15
Aug 3	Judg 17	Acts 21	Jer 30–31	Mark 16
Aug 4	Judg 18	Acts 22	Jer 32	Ps 1–2
Aug 5	Judg 19	Acts 23	Jer 33	Ps 3–4
Aug 6	Judg 20	Acts 24	Jer 34	Ps 5–6
Aug 7	Judg 21	Acts 25	Jer 35	Ps 7–8
Aug 8	Ruth 1	Acts 26	Jer 36, 45	Ps 9
Aug 9	Ruth 2	Acts 27	Jer 37	Ps 10
Aug 10	Ruth 3–4	Acts 28	Jer 38	Ps 11–12
Aug 11	1 Sam 1	Rom 1	Jer 39	Ps 13–14
Aug 12	1 Sam 2	Rom 2	Jer 40	Ps 15–16
Aug 13	1 Sam 3	Rom 3	Jer 41	Ps 17
Aug 14	1 Sam 4	Rom 4	Jer 42	Ps 18
Aug 15	1 Sam 5–6	Rom 5	Jer 43	Ps 19
Aug 16	1 Sam 7–8	Rom 6	Jer 44	Ps 20–21
Aug 17	1 Sam 9	Rom 7	Jer 46	Ps 22
Aug 18	1 Sam 10	Rom 8	Jer 47	Ps 23–24
Aug 19	1 Sam 11	Rom 9	Jer 48	Ps 25
Aug 20	1 Sam 12	Rom 10	Jer 49	Ps 26–27
Aug 21	1 Sam 13	Rom 11	Jer 50	Ps 28–29
Aug 22	1 Sam 14	Rom 12	Jer 51	Ps 30
Aug 23	1 Sam 15	Rom 13	Jer 52	Ps 31
Aug 24	1 Sam 16	Rom 14	Lam 1	Ps 32
Aug 25	1 Sam 17	Rom 15	Lam 2	Ps 33
Aug 26	1 Sam 18	Rom 16	Lam 3	Ps 34
Aug 27	1 Sam 19	1 Cor 1	Lam 4	Ps 35
Aug 28	1 Sam 20	1 Cor 2	Lam 5	Ps 36
Aug 29	1 Sam 21–22	1 Cor 3	Ezek 1	Ps 37
Aug 30	1 Sam 23	1 Cor 4	Ezek 2	Ps 38
Aug 31	1 Sam 24	1 Cor 5	Ezek 3	Ps 39

M'Cheyne Chart of Daily Bible Readings

DATE	FAMILY	FAMILY	PRIVATE	PRIVATE
Sep 1	1 Sam 25	1 Cor 6	Ezek 4	Ps 40–41
Sep 2	1 Sam 26	1 Cor 7	Ezek 5	Ps 42–43
Sep 3	1 Sam 27	1 Cor 8	Ezek 6	Ps 44
Sep 4	1 Sam 28	1 Cor 9	Ezek 7	Ps 45
Sep 5	1 Sam 29–30	1 Cor 10	Ezek 8	Ps 46–47
Sep 6	1 Sam 31	1 Cor 11	Ezek 9	Ps 48
Sep 7	2 Sam 1	1 Cor 12	Ezek 10	Ps 49
Sep 8	2 Sam 2	1 Cor 13	Ezek 11	Ps 50
Sep 9	2 Sam 3	1 Cor 14	Ezek 12	Ps 51
Sep 10	2 Sam 4–5	1 Cor 15	Ezek 13	Ps 52–54
Sep 11	2 Sam 6	1 Cor 16	Ezek 14	Ps 55
Sep 12	2 Sam 7	2 Cor 1	Ezek 15	Ps 56–57
Sep 13	2 Sam 8–9	2 Cor 2	Ezek 16	Ps 58–59
Sep 14	2 Sam 10	2 Cor 3	Ezek 17	Ps 60–61
Sep 15	2 Sam 11	2 Cor 4	Ezek 18	Ps 62–63
Sep 16	2 Sam 12	2 Cor 5	Ezek 19	Ps 64–65
Sep 17	2 Sam 13	2 Cor 6	Ezek 20	Ps 66–67
Sep 18	2 Sam 14	2 Cor 7	Ezek 21	Ps 68
Sep 19	2 Sam 15	2 Cor 8	Ezek 22	Ps 69
Sep 20	2 Sam 16	2 Cor 9	Ezek 23	Ps 70–71
Sep 21	2 Sam 17	2 Cor 10	Ezek 24	Ps 72
Sep 22	2 Sam 18	2 Cor 11	Ezek 25	Ps 73
Sep 23	2 Sam 19	2 Cor 12	Ezek 26	Ps 74
Sep 24	2 Sam 20	2 Cor 13	Ezek 27	Ps 75–76
Sep 25	2 Sam 21	Gal 1	Ezek 28	Ps 77
Sep 26	2 Sam 22	Gal 2	Ezek 29	Ps 78:1-39
Sep 27	2 Sam 23	Gal 3	Ezek 30	Ps 78:40-72
Sep 28	2 Sam 24	Gal 4	Ezek 31	Ps 79
Sep 29	1 Ki 1	Gal 5	Ezek 32	Ps 80
Sep 30	1 Ki 2	Gal 6	Ezek 33	Ps 81–82

M'Cheyne Chart of Daily Bible Readings

DATE	FAMILY	FAMILY	PRIVATE	PRIVATE
Oct 1	1 Ki 3	Eph 1	Ezek 34	Ps 83-84
Oct 2	1 Ki 4–5	Eph 2	Ezek 35	Ps 85
Oct 3	1 Ki 6	Eph 3	Ezek 36	Ps 86
Oct 4	1 Ki 7	Eph 4	Ezek 37	Ps 87–88
Oct 5	1 Ki 8	Eph 5	Ezek 38	Ps 89
Oct 6	1 Ki 9	Eph 6	Ezek 39	Ps 90
Oct 7	1 Ki 10	Phil 1	Ezek 40	Ps 91
Oct 8	1 Ki 11	Phil 2	Ezek 41	Ps 92–93
Oct 9	1 Ki 12	Phil 3	Ezek 42	Ps 94
Oct 10	1 Ki 13	Phil 4	Ezek 43	Ps 95–96
Oct 11	1 Ki 14	Col 1	Ezek 44	Ps 97–98
Oct 12	1 Ki 15	Col 2	Ezek 45	Ps 99–101
Oct 13	1 Ki 16	Col 3	Ezek 46	Ps 102
Oct 14	1 Ki 17	Col 4	Ezek 47	Ps 103
Oct 15	1 Ki 18	1 Thess 1	Ezek 48	Ps 104
Oct 16	1 Ki 19	1 Thess 2	Dan 1	Ps 105
Oct 17	1 Ki 20	1 Thess 3	Dan 2	Ps 106
Oct 18	1 Ki 21	1 Thess 4	Dan 3	Ps 107
Oct 19	1 Ki 22	1 Thess 5	Dan 4	Ps 108–109
Oct 20	2 Ki 1	2 Thess 1	Dan 5	Ps 110–111
Oct 21	2 Ki 2	2 Thess 2	Dan 6	Ps 112–113
Oct 22	2 Ki 3	2 Thess 3	Dan 7	Ps 114–115
Oct 23	2 Ki 4	1 Tim 1	Dan 8	Ps 116
Oct 24	2 Ki 5	1 Tim 2	Dan 9	Ps 117–118
Oct 25	2 Ki 6	1 Tim 3	Dan 10	Ps 119:1-24
Oct 26	2 Ki 7	1 Tim 4	Dan 11	Ps 119:25-48
Oct 27	2 Ki 8	1 Tim 5	Dan 12	Ps 119:49-72
Oct 28	2 Ki 9	1 Tim 6	Hosea 1	Ps 119:73-96
Oct 29	2 Ki 10–11	2 Tim 1	Hosea 2	Ps 119:97-120
Oct 30	2 Ki 12	2 Tim 2	Hosea 3–4	Ps 119:121-144
Oct 31	2 Ki 13	2 Tim 3	Hosea 5–6	Ps 119:145-176

M'Cheyne Chart of Daily Bible Readings

DATE	FAMILY	FAMILY	PRIVATE	PRIVATE
Nov 1	2 Ki 14	2 Tim 4	Hosea 7	Ps 120–122
Nov 2	2 Ki 15	Titus 1	Hosea 8	Ps 123–125
Nov 3	2 Ki 16	Titus 2	Hosea 9	Ps 126–128
Nov 4	2 Ki 17	Titus 3	Hosea 10	Ps 129–131
Nov 5	2 Ki 18	Philem	Hosea 11	Ps 132–134
Nov 6	2 Ki 19	Heb 1	Hosea 12	Ps 135–136
Nov 7	2 Ki 20	Heb 2	Hosea 13	Ps 137–138
Nov 8	2 Ki 21	Heb 3	Hosea 14	Ps 139
Nov 9	2 Ki 22	Heb 4	Joel 1	Ps 140–141
Nov 10	2 Ki 23	Heb 5	Joel 2	Ps 142
Nov 11	2 Ki 24	Heb 6	Joel 3	Ps 143
Nov 12	2 Ki 25	Heb 7	Amos 1	Ps 144
Nov 13	1 Chr 1–2	Heb 8	Amos 2	Ps 145
Nov 14	1 Chr 3–4	Heb 9	Amos 3	Ps 146–147
Nov 15	1 Chr 5–6	Heb 10	Amos 4	Ps 148–150
Nov 16	1 Chr 7–8	Heb 11	Amos 5	Lu 1:1-38
Nov 17	1 Chr 9–10	Heb 12	Amos 6	Lu 1:39-80
Nov 18	1 Chr 11–12	Heb 13	Amos 7	Lu 2
Nov 19	1 Chr 13–14	James 1	Amos 8	Lu 3
Nov 20	1 Chr 15	James 2	Amos 9	Lu 4
Nov 21	1 Chr 16	James 3	Obadiah	Lu 5
Nov 22	1 Chr 17	James 4	Jonah 1	Lu 6
Nov 23	1 Chr 18	James 5	Jonah 2	Lu 7
Nov 24	1 Chr 19–20	1 Peter 1	Jonah 3	Lu 8
Nov 25	1 Chr 21	1 Peter 2	Jonah 4	Lu 9
Nov 26	1 Chr 22	1 Peter 3	Micah 1	Lu 10
Nov 27	1 Chr 23	1 Peter 4	Micah 2	Lu 11
Nov 28	1 Chr 24–25	1 Peter 5	Micah 3	Lu 12
Nov 29	1 Chr 26–27	2 Peter 1	Micah 4	Lu 13
Nov 30	1 Chr 28	2 Peter 2	Micah 5	Lu 14

M'Cheyne Chart of Daily Bible Readings

DATE	FAMILY	FAMILY	PRIVATE	PRIVATE
Dec 1	1 Chr 29	2 Peter 3	Micah 6	Lu 15
Dec 2	2 Chr 1	1 John 1	Micah 7	Lu 16
Dec 3	2 Chr 2	1 John 2	Nahum 1	Lu 17
Dec 4	2 Chr 3–4	1 John 3	Nahum 2	Lu 18
Dec 5	2 Chr 5:1–6:11	1 John 4	Nahum 3	Lu 19
Dec 6	2 Chr 6:12-42	1 John 5	Hab 1	Lu 20
Dec 7	2 Chr 7	2 John	Hab 2	Lu 21
Dec 8	2 Chr 8	3 John	Hab 3	Lu 22
Dec 9	2 Chr 9	Jude	Zeph 1	Lu 23
Dec 10	2 Chr 10	Rev 1	Zeph 2	Lu 24
Dec 11	2 Chr 11–12	Rev 2	Zeph 3	John 1
Dec 12	2 Chr 13	Rev 3	Hag 1	John 2
Dec 13	2 Chr 14–15	Rev 4	Hag 2	John 3
Dec 14	2 Chr 16	Rev 5	Zech 1	John 4
Dec 15	2 Chr 17	Rev 6	Zech 2	John 5
Dec 16	2 Chr 18	Rev 7	Zech 3	John 6
Dec 17	2 Chr 19–20	Rev 8	Zech 4	John 7
Dec 18	2 Chr 21	Rev 9	Zech 5	John 8
Dec 19	2 Chr 22–23	Rev 10	Zech 6	John 9
Dec 20	2 Chr 24	Rev 11	Zech 7	John 10
Dec 21	2 Chr 25	Rev 12	Zech 8	John 11
Dec 22	2 Chr 26	Rev 13	Zech 9	John 12
Dec 23	2 Chr 27–28	Rev 14	Zech 10	John 13
Dec 24	2 Chr 29	Rev 15	Zech 11	John 14
Dec 25	2 Chr 30	Rev 16	Zech 12:1–13:1	John 15
Dec 26	2 Chr 31	Rev 17	Zech 13:2-9	John 16
Dec 27	2 Chr 32	Rev 18	Zech 14	John 17
Dec 28	2 Chr 33	Rev 19	Mal 1	John 18
Dec 29	2 Chr 34	Rev 20	Mal 2	John 19
Dec 30	2 Chr 35	Rev 21	Mal 3	John 20
Dec 31	2 Chr 36	Rev 22	Mal 4	John 21

Genesis 1; Matthew 1; *Ezra 1*; *Acts 1*

∾

THE FIRST STEPS TOWARD ISRAEL'S RETURN from exile and their rebuilding of the temple (**Ezra 1**) are full of interest:

(1) A person without much knowledge of history might be forgiven for thinking that Israel was the only national group released from the bondage of exile. Historically, that is not true. When the Persians took over from the Babylonians (who had sent Judah into exile), King Cyrus of Persia reversed the Babylonian policy. The Babylonians (and the Assyrians before them) transported the aristocracy and leading citizens of subjugated territories. Rebellion in the ancient world was often suspended on the threefold cord of people, land, and religion. If one of these three strands could be removed, there was less likelihood of revolt. By transporting all the leaders of every branch of a culture to some new territory far removed from their own land (thereby disconnecting people and land), these empires secured a kind of peace. Obviously they also introduced enormous dislocation, which must have had many negative effects, not least economic. Whatever the reasons, Cyrus not only stopped this policy, but permitted exiles—including the Jews—to return home.

(2) But Ezra is right in understanding this to be the work of God: "The LORD moved the heart of Cyrus king of Persia" (1:1). At another time, the Lord would cause a census to be taken of the entire Roman world, to bring a pregnant woman to Bethlehem—once again to fulfill an ancient Scripture (Luke 2).

(3) The prophecy in this case, according to Ezra, is that of Jeremiah (Ezra 1:1), probably referring to Jeremiah 25:11-12; 29:10-14; 51. It would be a mistake to read Ezra 1:1 as if God were somehow bound by Jeremiah's word, instead of the other way around. The point is that the prophecy of Jeremiah is nothing other than the word of God. God is bound by his own word. When Daniel understood that the prescribed time of exile was coming to an end, he set himself to seek the face of God for his people (Dan. 9)—which of course was exactly the right thing to do. And here we find the answers both to Daniel's prayers and to God's promises.

(4) As usual, when God works decisively, there are no loose ends. On the one hand, he moves Cyrus the King to make his proclamation; on the other hand, he moves in the hearts of many Jews to return home (1:5). After all, we are dealing now with a generation that had grown up entirely in the Tigris-Euphrates valleys. It would be like asking the second or third generation of immigrants to the United States from, say, Japan or Germany, to return "home." But God's people become willing in the day of his power.

∾

Genesis 2; Matthew 2; *Ezra* 2; *Acts* 2

∾

THE SHEER PRECISION OF THE REPORTS of return (**Ezra 2**) is one of the first things to strike the casual reader of this chapter. Not only are the numbers of the people accurately reported, along with the names of their clans, but even the numbers of their animals—horses, mules, camels, donkeys (2:66). One remembers the response of the old Puritan who was being berated for insisting on precision when talking about God and the teachings of the Bible. "Sir," he replied, "I serve a precise God."

That is only one side of the story, of course. This same God delights in the spontaneous praise of children, who are not known for precision. The Bible he has given us uses evocative imagery as well as precise reports. Yet our age is so committed to vague feelings that precision in matters divine is often despised. We want to follow our intuitions, not our instructions; we elevate feelings, not facts; we ingest treacle, not truth.

In this case there are several reasons for the precision of the report. For a start, such precision gives the account authority: this is not some distant hearsay, but the close reportage of someone who had intimate knowledge of the details. Further, naming these individuals and their families bestows on them an implicit approval. Countless tens of thousands of Israelites never returned to the Promised Land; they were too settled where they were, and the restoration of Jerusalem and the temple was of too little importance to them to warrant such dislocation. Their names have been lost; they are of little consequence in the sweep of redemptive history. But *these* names are remembered and written down in sacred Scripture. Read them slowly; they call forth our respect and gratitude.

But there is another element in the precision. Some of the returning clans could not show that they were descended from Israel (2:59); some of those who claimed priestly lineage were in the same predicament (2:62). The problem was taken seriously, and Zerubbabel the governor ordered that they be excluded from priestly service until the ancient way of divine guidance, the Urim and Thummim, could be reinstituted and their claims checked (2:63). Here were a people serious about observing the stipulations of the Mosaic covenant, serious about preserving the purity not only of the covenant community in general but of the priesthood in particular, serious about following all of God's words. The seriousness with which they undertook the massive enterprise of the return is attested even by the gifts that they gave toward rebuilding the house of God (2:68-69).

The fact that this fledgling postexilic community soon stumbled into a new generation of fresh problems and old sins should not diminish the power of their example for believers today.

∾

Genesis 3; Matthew 3; *Ezra 3*; Acts 3

∾

THE SHEER INTENSITY OF THE experiences of God's people during the first few months of their return to the Promised Land (**Ezra 3**) shines through the lines of the text.

(1) They are afraid (3:3). This is the first hint of the dangers that they face, the source of which becomes clearer in the following chapters. The Persian king Cyrus has granted permission to the Jews to return to their homeland, and even sanctioned certain payments for their support and for the rebuilding of the temple. But the frontiers of the empire are a long way from the center, and in the rough politics of the real world, possession is nine-tenths of the law. These Jews are, after all, a minority surrounded by foes much stronger than they.

(2) They are resolute (3:3). The opposition understands that the erection of the temple is not only a religious sign but a sign of growing political strength. The Jews therefore would have had some incentive to keep quiet and maintain a low profile. But their resolution at this juncture is admirable: despite their understandable fear, they build the altar of the Lord and re-institute the sacrificial system prescribed by the "Law of Moses the man of God" (3:2-6), and then proceed with the first steps of constructing a new temple.

(3) They are full of joy and praise (3:10-11). The laying of the foundation of the new temple elicits worship and adoration of God himself, who transparently is blessing the endeavors of his chastened covenant community. Here is hope not only for a temple, but for a restoration of the Davidic dynasty, the fulfillment of the glorious promises of hope delivered by the prophets during Israel's darkest hours of exile.

(4) Many weep (3:12-13). These tend to be the older ones who can still remember the contours of Solomon's magnificent temple. The foundations of the new structure seem piddling in comparison. Doubtless these people are grateful for days of small things; after all, they, too, have elected to return. But days of small things are still small, and the intensity of their emotional response is elicited by long memories of things past.

At least these people are alive, and getting on with God's business. Their responses may sometimes be wrenching, full of lows and highs, but they are real, vital, human, charged with life and engagement. Here there is no glum despondency, no cynical reserve, no emotionally flat withdrawal. Here are the emotions of a group of people committed, in difficult circumstances, to doing God's will.

∾

Genesis 4; Matthew 4; *Ezra 4; Acts 4*

∾

IN THIS BROKEN WORLD, THERE WILL ALWAYS be people who try, in one way or another, to discourage and defeat the people of God. Add such people to the discouragements and failures that surface from within, and circumstances can appear desperately bleak and foreboding.

In **Ezra 4**, the enemies of the returned exiles try three distinct approaches, all of them aimed at defeating this small community of God's people.

The *first* is to make common cause with them. It sounds so good: "Let us help you build because, like you, we seek your God and have been sacrificing to him since the time of Esarhaddon king of Assyria, who brought us here" (4:2). Unwary people might have been taken in. There is always a place for genuine unity, of course, but unbridled ecumenism inevitably results in redefining the Gospel in terms of the lowest possible denominator. One of the best ways to divert a committee is to pack it with your own supporters. Pretending support, you take something over and deploy its energies in some innocuous direction, like a cancerous growth that usurps the body's energies for its own aggrandizement. The strategy does not work in this case, because the leaders of God's people, far from congratulating themselves that help has arrived, refuse to be taken in. They turn down the offer. This precipitates a different strategy from the opponents, one that unmasks their true colors.

The *second* approach is "to discourage the people of Judah and make them afraid to go on building" (4:4). Some of their plan is disclosed in the book of Ezra; even more of it surfaces in Nehemiah. So committed are these opponents to the failure of God's people that they even hire "counselors to work against them and frustrate their plans" (4:5). Rumors, threats, shortages of supply, energy-sapping diversions—all are concocted by strategists-for-hire, clever people who think of themselves as wise, influential, and powerful, but who have no spiritual or moral perception of the situation at all.

The *third* attack is directly political. In a carefully crafted letter filled with half-truths, these opponents of God's people manage to convince King Xerxes to shut down the building project. The ban remains in force for decades. What begins as a seemingly insurmountable political barrier settles down into a way of life, the Jews themselves accepting the status quo until the powerful preaching of Haggai and Zechariah (5:1) shake them out of their lethargy.

How have these three instruments of discouragement been deployed in the twentieth century?

∾

Genesis 5; Matthew 5; *Ezra 5*; Acts 5

MORE YEARS OF DELAY AND DISAPPOINTMENT go by before God raises up the prophets Haggai and Zechariah (**Ezra 5**), who encourage the people to restart the building of the temple. The temple's foundations have been laid, but nothing more has been done. Now, under the revitalizing ministry of the two prophets, the building starts again.

This precipitates a new crisis. Tattenai, governor of Trans-Euphrates (from the Persian perspective Trans-Euphrates means everything in the Persian Empire to the west of the Euphrates, including the strip of land we know as Israel), questions the authority of the Jews to engage in this building project. Tattenai writes to Darius, the new king, and in the next chapter Darius responds positively: the Jews are not only permitted to rebuild, but should be supported by the treasury.

One can see why, humanly speaking, imperial policy has reversed itself. For a start, we are dealing with a new emperor. More importantly, a careful reading of Tattenai's letter (5:7-17) shows it to be a remarkably even-handed missive, setting out the facts of the case without prejudice and simply wanting to know the right way forward. How different was the remarkably perverse letter of Rehum and Shimshai (4:11-16). As Scripture comments, that was really a letter "against Jerusalem" (4:8), a nasty piece of work that only the most astute monarch would have penetrated, and Artaxerxes was not that kind of monarch. So in the peculiar providence of God, the letter in Ezra 4 shuts the project down, while the letter in Ezra 5, written by pagans no less than the first, not only wins authorization for the building project, but money as well.

It is important for believers to remember that God sovereignly controls countless elements over which we have little sway. I recall speaking at a Cambridge college chapel more than twenty years ago on the assigned topic of death and judgment. What frightened me was the obligatory discussion that would follow. I preached as simply and as faithfully as I could, and after the meeting we settled down for the discussion. The chaplain was sure there would be "questions arising." In that interesting but mixed crowd, I waited with some trepidation for the first shot. Then a mathematics "don" (a college teacher) I had never met quietly commented, "If we heard more sermons like that, England would not be in her mess." That comment established the tone of the rest of the meeting. Everyone was serious, and I spent the time explaining the Gospel. But the fact that it was that question which set the tone, and not some taunting sneer, was entirely in the hand of God.

∾

ALTHOUGH THE SEVEN MEN WHO ARE appointed to certain responsibilities in **Acts 6:1-7** are not explicitly called "deacons," few doubt that this is the beginning of what came to be called the diaconate. Several points call for comment:

(1) What precipitates this step is a problem—a particular kind of problem. The Greek-speaking Jewish Christians are dissatisfied with the level of support being received by their widows, compared with the support received by the widows of Aramaic-speaking Jewish Christians. Whether the charge is justified or not—and, if it is, whether it is an intentional slight or an accidental one because the Aramaic-speakers were on home turf and probably in the ascendancy—cannot at this point be determined. In any case, the divisiveness is at least as potentially dangerous for this large, fledgling church as the perceived injustice that precipitated it. Note: (a) The church ran its own welfare system for the indigent and the unsupported. (b) It is mildly reassuring, in a wry way, to discover that the earliest church faced problems of alleged inequity, injustice, and consequent divisiveness. (c) More telling is the fact that it addressed those problems. (d) Moreover, it is obvious that the size of a church, not to say its rising problems of equity and communication, may demand improvements in organization and the appointment of new officers.

(2) The reasoning of the Twelve is stunningly focused: "It would not be right for us to neglect the ministry of the word of God in order to wait on tables" (6:2). Again, they lay down some criteria and insist that they themselves will give their attention "to prayer and the ministry of the word" (6:4). We may not have the Twelve today, but pastors/elders/overseers have inherited this ministry of the word and prayer. That includes not only teaching others, but doing the serious study and preparation and intercession that stand behind good teaching and preaching. There will always be a hundred things to distract you. Do not be distracted from what is central.

(3) The criteria presented by the Twelve for the church to use in their choice of seven men are not managerial prowess and gifts of diplomacy. The men are to be known as full of the Holy Spirit and wisdom and faith (6:4, 5). Of course, these criteria include managerial savvy: if a person is full of the Holy Spirit, he or she will exercise care in relationships; and "wisdom" can include practical, godly skill in some defined area. But at bottom, these seven men are appointed because they are judged to be mature and godly Christians as well as gifted for the tasks assigned them.

∾

Genesis 7; Matthew 7; *Ezra 7*; *Acts 7*

∾

EZRA 7 RECOUNTS THE MISSION OF Ezra in the postexilic community in Jerusalem and Judah. Obviously it was part of imperial policy that if exiled groups were permitted to return to their homeland, they should be supported by their priests. From the perspective of pagan superstition, the rulers would not want any of the regional gods angry with them (7:23); from the perspective of the covenant community, this was formidable evidence that the good hand of God was upon them, that he was able to rule the affairs of the mightiest empires so as to preserve his own people.

The nature of Ezra's task could easily be taken as a model of the privileges and responsibilities of all whose duty it is to teach the Word of God to the people of God: "For Ezra had devoted himself to the study and observance of the Law of the LORD, and to teaching its decrees and laws in Israel" (7:10).

(1) Ezra devoted himself to the study of the Law. There is no long-range effective teaching of the Bible that is not accompanied by long hours of ongoing study of the Bible. Effectiveness in teaching the Bible is purchased at the price of much study, some of it lonely, all of it tiring. If you are not a student of the Word, you are not called to be a teacher of the Word.

(2) Ezra devoted himself to the observance of the Law. For some people, study is an end in itself, or perhaps a means to the end of teaching. But even though the subject matter is Scripture, for these people there is no personal commitment to living under its precepts—to ordering their marriage, their finances, their talk, their priorities, their values, by the Word of God. They do not constantly ask how the assumptions of their age and culture, assumptions that all of us pick up unawares, are challenged by Scripture. The study of Scripture, for such people, is an excellent intellectual discipline, but not a persistent call to worship; the Bible is to be mastered like a textbook, but it does not call the people of God to tremble; its truths are to be cherished, but it does not mediate the presence of God. Ezra avoided all these traps and devoted himself to observing what Scripture says.

(3) Ezra devoted himself to the teaching of the Law. He was not a hermit-scholar; he was a pastor-scholar. What he learned in study and obedience he also learned how to pass on. Whether in large, solemn assemblies, in family or clan settings, or in one-on-one studies, Ezra committed himself to teaching the Word of God to the people of God. It is difficult to imagine a higher calling.

∾

JANUARY 8

Genesis 8; Matthew 8; *Ezra 8; Acts 8*

OUR VISION IS MYOPIC AND OUR understanding patchy. We rarely "read" really well the events going on around us. Consider the immediate aftermath of the martyrdom of Stephen (**Acts 8:1-5**). "On that day a great persecution broke out against the church at Jerusalem" (8:1). That situation probably was not very comfortable for the believers undergoing it. Nevertheless:

(1) "[A]nd all except the apostles were scattered throughout Judea and Samaria" (8:1). Doubtless it was easier to hide twelve men than the thousands of people who now constituted the church. Moreover, to keep the Twelve at Jerusalem was to keep them at the center, and therefore to maintain some oversight of the rapid developments.

(2) "Those who had been scattered preached the word wherever they went" (8:4). This signaled far more rapid extension of the Gospel than if the apostles had all gone out on missions while the rest of the church stayed home. Here was a force of thousands and thousands, most of them simply "gossiping the Gospel," others highly gifted evangelists, disseminated by persecution.

(3) "Philip went down to a city in Samaria and proclaimed the Christ there" (8:5). Often in the book of Acts, Luke makes a general statement and then gives a concrete example of it. For example, in 4:32-36, Luke tells how believers regularly sold property and put the proceeds into the common pot for the relief of the poor. He then tells the story of one particular man, Joseph, nicknamed Barnabas by the apostles, who did just that. This simultaneously provides a concrete example of the general trend Luke had just described, and introduces Barnabas (who will be a major player later on), who in turn provides a foil for Ananias and Sapphira, who lie about the proceeds of their own sale (Acts 5). Thus the account is carried forward. So also here in Acts 8: Luke describes the scattering of believers, observing that they "preached the word wherever they went," and then relates one particular account, that of Philip. He was one of the seven men appointed to the nascent "diaconate" (Acts 6); now he becomes a strategic evangelist in bringing the Gospel across one of the first social-cultural hurdles: from Jews to Samaritans.

(4) "Godly men buried Stephen and mourned deeply for him. But Saul began to destroy the church. Going from house to house, he dragged off men and women and put them in prison" (8:2-3). The contrast is stunning. Saul thinks he is doing God's work; in reality, the really godly mourn for and bury the first Christian martyr. Yet in God's peculiar providence, this Saul will become one of the greatest cross-cultural missionaries of all time and the human author of about one-quarter of the New Testament.

Genesis 9—10; Matthew 9; *Ezra 9*; Acts 9

∾

IT MAY BE DIFFICULT FOR SOME CHRISTIANS, immersed in the heritage of individualism and influenced by postmodern relativism, to find much sympathy for Ezra
and his prayer (**Ezra 9**). A hundred or so of the returned Israelites, out of a population that by this time would have been at least fifty or sixty thousand, have
married pagan women from the surrounding tribes. Ezra treats this as an unmitigated disaster and weeps before the Lord as if really grievous harm has been done.
Has religion descended to the level where it tells its adherents whom they may
marry? Moreover, the aftermath of this prayer (on which we shall reflect tomorrow) is pretty heartless, isn't it?

In reality, Ezra's prayer discloses a man who has thought long and hard about
Israel's history.

First, he understands what brought about the exile, the formal destruction
of the nation, the scattering of the people. It was nothing other than the sins of
the people—and terribly often these sins had been fostered by links, not least
marital links, between the people of the covenant and the surrounding tribes.
"Because of our sins, we and our kings and our priests have been subjected to
the sword and captivity, to pillage and humiliation at the hand of foreign kings,
as it is today" (9:7).

Second, he understands that if this community has been permitted to return
to Judah, it is because "for a brief moment, the LORD our God has been gracious
in leaving us a remnant and giving us a firm place in his sanctuary, and so our
God gives light to our eyes and a little relief in our bondage" (9:8).

Third, he understands that in the light of the first two points, and in the light
of Scripture's explicit prohibition against intermarriage, what has taken place is
not only singular ingratitude but concrete defiance of the God who has come to
Israel's relief not only in the Exodus but also in the exile.

Fourth, he understands the complex, corrosive, corporate nature of sin. Like
Isaiah before him (Isa. 6:5), Ezra aligns himself with the people in their sin (9:6).
He grasps the stubborn fact that these are not individual failures and nothing
more; these are means by which raw paganism, and finally the relativizing of
Almighty God, are smuggled into the entire community through the back door.
How could such marriages, even among some priests, have been arranged unless
many, many others had given their approval, or at least winked at the exercise?
Above all, Ezra understands that the sins of the people of God are far worse than
the punishment they have received (9:13-15).

How should these lines of thought shape our thinking about the sins of the
people of God today?

∾

Genesis 11; Matthew 10; *Ezra 10; Acts 10*

∾

BROADLY SPEAKING, EZRA 10 is understood in two different ways:

According to the *first* view, what takes place is something akin to revival. Ezra's tears and prayer prove so moving that the leaders of the community, though they too have been compromised by these intermarriages, enter into a pact to divorce their pagan wives and send them home to their own people, along with whatever children have sprung up from these marriages. Those who disagree with this decision will be expelled from the assembly of the exiles (10:8), henceforth to be treated like foreigners themselves. The appropriate councils are set up, and the work is discharged. This is remarkably courageous, a sure sign of God's blessing, ringing evidence that these people love God even more than they love their own families. The purity of the postexilic community is maintained, and the wrath of God is averted. The lesson, then, is that one must deal radically with sin.

According to the *second* view, although Ezra's prayer (Ezra 9) is exactly right, the steps that flow from it are virtually all wrong. Marriage, after all, is a creation ordinance. In any case, one cannot simply undo a marriage; if the Law prohibits marriage with a pagan, it also prohibits easy divorce. What about all those children? Are they to be banished to their pagan grandparents, without any access to the covenant community and the one God of all the earth—quite apart from the psychological damage that doubtless will befall them? Could not other steps be taken instead? For example, all further mixed marriages could be proscribed and rigorously prevented, under the sanction of being expelled from the assembly. Priests who have intermarried could be stripped of priestly rights and duties. The kind of widespread repentance that is evident could be channeled toward faithful study of the Law, not least by these mixed families. What sanction is there for so inhumane an action as that in this chapter?

Strictly speaking, the text itself does not adjudicate between these two interpretations, though the first of the two is slightly more natural within the stance of the book. But is it more natural within the stance of the entire canon or of the Old Testament canon?

Without meaning to avoid the issue, I suspect that in large measure both views are correct. There is something noble and courageous about the action taken; there is also something heartless and reductionistic. One suspects that this is one of those mixed results in which the Bible frankly abounds, like the account of Gideon, or of Jephthah, or of Samson. Some sins have such complex tentacles that it is not surprising if solutions undertaken by repentant sinners are messy as well.

∾

Genesis 12; Matthew 11; *Nehemiah 1; Acts 11*

॰

IN THE COMPLEX HISTORY OF THE postexilic community in Judah, Nehemiah plays a singular role. He was not part of the original party that returned to Judah, but before long he was sent there by the emperor himself. In two separate expeditions, Nehemiah served as *de facto* governor of the remnant community and was largely responsible for rebuilding Jerusalem's walls, not to mention other reforms. His work overlapped that of Ezra.

The book of Nehemiah is often treated as a manual on godly leadership. I wonder if this does justice to the book. Did Nehemiah intend to write a manual on leadership? Is the book included in the canon for that purpose—as if we turn, say, to Acts to discover the history of the early church and to Nehemiah to discover the principles of leadership?

This is not to say that there is nothing about leadership to be learned from Nehemiah—or, for that matter, from Moses, David, Peter, and Paul. Yet a reading of this book that focuses on the theme of leadership is bound to be skewed; it is in line neither with authorial intent nor with canonical priorities.

Nehemiah is a book about God's faithfulness and about the agents God used in reestablishing his covenant people in the Promised Land at the end of the exile—about the first steps taken to secure their protection and identity as God's people and to assure their covenantal faithfulness. Canonically, this part of the Bible's story-line establishes chunks of postexilic history that take us on to the Lord Jesus himself.

But perhaps we can profitably focus on one or two elements of **Nehemiah 1**, trailing on to Nehemiah 2.

Early reports of the sorry condition of the returned remnant community in Judah (1:3) elicit from Nehemiah profound grief and fervent intercession (1:4). The substance of his prayer occupies most of the first chapter (1:5-11). Nehemiah addresses the "great and awesome God" in terms of the covenant. God had promised to send his people into exile if they were persistent in their disobedience; but he had also promised, if they repented and returned to him, to gather them again to the place he had chosen as a dwelling for his name (1:8-9; see Deut. 30:4-5). Yet Nehemiah is not praying for others while avoiding any role for himself. He prays that he might find favor in the eyes of the emperor, whom he serves as cupbearer (1:11), when he approaches him about this great burden. Even Nehemiah's "bullet prayer" in the next chapter (2:4) is the outcropping of sustained intercessory prayer in secret.

॰

Genesis 13; Matthew 12; *Nehemiah 2; Acts 12*

∾

IT IS WORTH COMPARING THE TWO italicized passages (**Neh. 2; Acts 12:1-19**).

The same God is behind both situations, of course. In both situations, a lone servant of God faces the challenge of building up and strengthening God's people in the teeth of opposition from some pretty hostile customers. Both men are in danger, in part for political reasons, though Peter's danger is the more immediate. Both are unflinching in their loyalty to the living God and to the mission to which each is called.

Thereafter the stories diverge. Having won the ear of the emperor, Nehemiah finds himself on the imperial frontier. He has a certain paper authority, but the locals are set on giving him a hard time. He proceeds step by step, wisely, winning the support of the local Jewish leaders, securing the supplies needed for building the wall, dismissing the opponents and all their wiles. For Nehemiah there are no miracles, no mighty displays of power, no angels in the night. There is only a great deal of risky and courageous work.

By contrast, Peter's situation is much more restricted. He has been arrested and is in prison awaiting execution. Since James has already been killed, Peter has no reason to think he will escape the executioner's sword. In a strange apparition that he mistakes for a dream, Peter is rescued by an angel; the chains fall away from him, the doors open of their own accord. Finding himself outside the prison walls, Peter comes to his senses and presents himself at the home of John Mark's mother, where people have gathered to pray for him. Eventually he secures entrance, and in due course leaves for "another place" (12:17). In Peter's case, to escape death is a triumph, and the faith of the church has been strengthened by what has happened. And it all happened because of a miraculous display of angelic help.

The lesson of these radically different experiences is one that we must learn again and again: God's servants do not have the same gifts, the same tasks, the same success, or the same degree of divine intervention. It is partly a matter of gifts and calling; it is partly a matter of where we fit into God's unfolding redemptive purposes. Has he placed us in times of declension, for example, or of revival; of persecution, or of major advance? Let God be God; let all his servants be faithful.

∾

Genesis 14; Matthew 13; *Nehemiah 3; Acts 13*

∾

IT IS ALWAYS WORTH ASKING WHY the summary of a particular sermon is included in Acts. Sometimes the answer is immediately obvious, at least in part. For example, Peter's sermon on the day of Pentecost, reported in Acts 2: whatever its distinctive features, it is above all the first post-resurrection Christian evangelistic sermon, the first Christian sermon after the descent of the Holy Spirit. The sermon Paul preaches in Pisidian Antioch (**Acts 13:13-52**) has many interesting features that help explain why Luke records it:

(1) It is preached in a synagogue, and thus to people whom Paul views as biblically literate—Jews, proselytes, God-fearers. He does not have to explain basic categories the way he does to the Athenians, who are biblically illiterate (Acts 17).

(2) Preaching to the biblically literate, Paul begins with a selective recitation of Israel's history—obviously a standard approach in some Christian preaching, for Stephen does the same thing (Acts 7).

(3) More importantly, this selective history is directed toward establishing one central point: God had promised the coming of a king in the Davidic line. That provides Paul with the base from which he springs forward to Christian witness: the Messiah, that Davidic king, has arrived, and his name is Jesus.

(4) With this line of thought, and to this biblically-literate crowd, Paul devotes part of his sermon to exposition of particular texts in order to demonstrate his major points.

(5) Paul makes it clear that the purpose and focus of Christ's coming is the forgiveness of sins. He compares and contrasts the nature and scope of this forgiveness with what the Law of Moses provided. Paul is interested in the salvation-historical developments that have taken place with the coming of the Messiah (13:39). Further, the salvation Paul announces assigns a central role to justification.

(6) The following verses (13:42-52) explain how Paul's popularity incites jealousy, which generates various results—including Paul's move away from the synagogue to the broader Gentile population. This is a concrete demonstration of something that characterizes Paul's evangelistic ministry in every new place he visits: he begins with Jews and all those gathered in the synagogue—a matter of theological conviction for him; but he eventually turns, or is forced to turn, to the biblically illiterate pagans—a matter of calling for him, for he knows he is called to be the apostle to the Gentiles (Gal. 2:8).

(7) As on other occasions, Paul's preaching causes both a riot and a revival.

∾

Genesis 15; Matthew 14; *Nehemiah 4; Acts 14*

∾

THE DRAMA OF NEHEMIAH 4 ABOUNDS with lessons and illustrations of various truths. But we must not forget that what to us is a dramatic narrative was to those experiencing it days of brutally hard work, high tension, genuine fear, insecurity, rising faith, dirt and grime. Nevertheless, some lessons transcend the ages:

(1) Among the hardest things to endure is derisory contempt. That is what Nehemiah and the Jews faced from Sanballat, Tobiah, and the rest (4:1-3). The Judeo-Christian heritage of Western nations was until recent decades so strong that many Christians were shielded from such scorn. No more. We had better get used to what our brothers and sisters in Christ in other lands and centuries handle better than we.

(2) Although God sometimes works through spectacular and supernatural means, he commonly works through ordinary people who take responsibility for themselves and seek to act faithfully even in difficult circumstances. So the Jews "prayed to [their] God and posted a guard day and night" (4:9). They armed themselves and divided their number between fighters and builders, but were also exhorted to, "Remember the Lord, who is great and awesome, and fight for . . . your homes" (4:14). Jews living near the enemy heard of the plots to demolish the building project and reported it to Nehemiah, who took appropriate action— but God gets the credit for frustrating the plot (4:15).

(3) Practical implications flow from this outlook. (a) It presupposes a God-centered outlook that avoids naturalism. If God is God, if he has graciously made himself known in the great moments of redemptive history and in visions and words faithfully transmitted by prophets he has raised up, why should we not also think of this God as operating in the so-called "natural" course of events? Otherwise we have retreated to some myopic vision in which God works only in the spectacular and the miraculous, but otherwise is absent or asleep or uncaring. The God described in the Bible is never so small or distant. (b) That is why God can be trusted. Nehemiah is not resorting to mere psychological puffery, nor to shameless religious rhetoric. His faith is properly grounded in the God who is always active and who is working out his redemptive-historical purposes in the ending of the exile and the rebuilding of Jerusalem—just as today our faith is properly grounded in the God who is always active and who is working out his redemptive-historical purposes in the calling and transformation of the elect and the building and purifying of his church.

∾

Genesis 16; Matthew 15; *Nehemiah 5*; Acts 15

∾

WHEN I WAS A HIGH SCHOOL STUDENT IN CANADA, I heard a story told by our history teacher. He related it with deadly anger. He had just returned from the battlefields of World War II, where he had seen many of his friends killed. Furloughed home because of a war wound, he was riding a bus in a major Canadian city. Seated behind two prosperous-looking women, he overheard one of them say to the other, "I hope this war doesn't end soon. We've never had it so good."

There are almost always people who profit from the disasters of others, not least from war. So it was in Nehemiah's day (**Neh. 5**). Even while there was a disciplined effort to rebuild the city, in the surrounding countryside the fiscal pressures of the times, coupled with famine conditions, made the rich richer and the poor poorer. In an effort to keep going, the poor mortgaged their land and then lost it; they sold themselves or their families into slavery. From Nehemiah's perspective, slavery was slavery; to be a slave to a fellow Jew was still to be a slave. In some ways it was worse: Nehemiah was concerned not only with the slavery itself, but with the moral hardness of the rich who were profiting from the bankruptcy of others—the want of compassion, the failure to obey the Mosaic code that forbade usury, the sheer covetousness and greed. Transparently they did not need more. Nor was this a question of buying off the lazy. What conceivable justification could they offer for such profiteering?

Yet, mercifully, the consciences of these rich people were tender enough that they did not rebel when they were rebuked. "They kept quiet, because they could find nothing to say" (5:8). Indeed, in due course they repented, returned what had been taken, and stopped charging interest to their brothers.

Clearly one of the factors that enhanced Nehemiah's credibility as he labored to bring about these reforms was his own conduct. Doubtless the vast majority of governors at the time used their positions of power to accumulate considerable wealth for themselves. Nehemiah refused to do so. He received, presumably from the central treasury, an ample stipend and sufficient support for himself and his staff, and he therefore declined to use his power to demand additional material support from the local population. Indeed, he ended up supporting many of them (5:14-18).

Obedience to God, compassion toward one's fellows, consistency in the leadership, covenantal faithfulness that extends to one's pocketbook, repentance and restoration where there has been either corruption or rapacity—these were values more important than the building of the wall. If the wall had been rebuilt without rebuilding the people, the triumph would have been small.

∾

Genesis 17; Matthew 16; *Nehemiah 6; Acts 16*

IT IS COMMON FOR GREAT ENTERPRISES OF FAITH to be surrounded by extremely difficult relationships.

William Carey, the father of modern Protestant missions, may be a hero to us, but in his own day he was viewed as eccentric and had more than his share of personal and familial sorrow. The great magisterial reformers did not battle for mere ideas; they were enmeshed in a great controversy that included not only "enemies" but countless people who were "friends" in some arenas and foes in others. In any great controversy there is bound to be a spectrum of viewpoints and a considerable diversity of degrees of integrity. One cannot read a detailed and candid biography of any Christian leader without observing the kinds and frequency of the difficult, painful, and sometimes deceptive debates in which they were called to participate. Consider, for example, Arnold Dallimore's *George Whitefield* or Iain Murray's *D. Martyn Lloyd-Jones*. I cannot think of an exception.

Where sufficient information is provided, the same thing must be said regarding leaders of the faith whose cameos appear in Scripture. Despite the long list of physical sufferings inflicted on him by unbelievers and by his calling as a church-planting apostle (2 Cor. 11), doubtless Paul's most anguished moments come to him from closer to home—from Christians behaving in sub-Christian ways, from false brothers and false apostles undermining his work with innuendo and half-truths.

These are the kinds of things Nehemiah now faces (**Neh. 6**). Failing to succeed by ridicule, threat, and direct opposition, Sanballat, Tobiah, and their colleagues embark on subterfuge and personal pressure. In this chapter there are lies, false prophets, and accusations of rebellion. Indeed, even some of the Jews, Nehemiah's own people, owe allegiance through political and marriage alliances to Tobiah, and use their compromised positions to try to influence the governor away from a policy that is good for the Jews and honoring to God. In all these machinations, Nehemiah steers a straight course, asks God for help, and shows himself to be a discerning and far-seeing leader.

Similar problems assail genuine Christian leaders today, and similar quiet resolve and fearless discernment are required to meet them. This is certainly true in pastoral ministry. The most difficult challenges will erupt not from direct opposition or from problems with a building or the like, but from deceivers, liars, those committed to some other agenda but whose smooth talk is so superficially "spiritual" that many are deceived. Expect such difficulties; they will surely come. It is the price of godly leadership in a fallen world.

Genesis 18; Matthew 17; *Nehemiah 7; Acts 17*

∿

WHEN A LARGE BUILDING PROJECT IS FINISHED, or when an important goal has been reached, often there is a tendency to slack off. Many a congregation has devoted considerable energy to building a new facility, only to retreat into lethargy for months or even years afterward.

Nehemiah perceives that the building of the wall is not the climax of the return, after which relaxation should be the order of the day. The rest of the book makes this point clearly enough. The rebuilding of the wall is scarcely more than preparation for a number of more far-reaching political and religious reforms. In ministry, it is vital always to distinguish means and ends.

With the wall finished, Nehemiah stays on for a while as governor of the entire region of Judah, but appoints two men to be in charge of Jerusalem—his brother Hanani (apparently a man he could trust), and a military man, Hananiah, chosen "because he was a man of integrity and feared God more than most men do" (**Neh. 7:2**—compare meditation for January 6). There is something refreshing and fundamental about such leaders. They are not sycophants or mercenaries; they are not trying to "find themselves" or prove their manhood; they are not scrambling up the mobile ladder to success. They are men of integrity, who fear God more than most.

Nehemiah then gives instructions regarding the opening and closing of the gates—instructions designed to avoid any traps set between the dangerous hours of dusk and dawn (7:3). Thus the administration and defense of Jerusalem are settled.

The sheer emptiness of the city is what now confronts Nehemiah (7:4). The walls have been rebuilt more or less along their original lines. Jerusalem is a substantial city, and yet the vast majority of the returned Jews are living in the countryside. What takes place in the following chapters, then, is something that can only be called a revival, followed by the determination of the people to send one-tenth of their number into Jerusalem to become the fledgling kernel of a new generation of Jerusalemites. As a first step, Nehemiah digs out the now aging records of those exiles who had first returned from exile in order to determine whose genealogical records demonstrated them to be part of the covenant people, and especially those who could legitimately serve as priests. The steps Nehemiah pursues seem to be part of a careful plan, one which, as Nehemiah himself insists, "my God put . . . into my heart" (7:5).

∿

Genesis 19; Matthew 18; *Nehemiah 8; Acts 18*

∾

SOMETHING IS TO BE GAINED BY bringing today's two readings, **Nehemiah 8** and **Acts 18**, into juxtaposition.

Much of Acts 18 is devoted to preaching and teaching the Word of God and to the issue of how to understand God's revelation aright. When Silas and Timothy arrive in Corinth from Macedonia (18:5), presumably bringing with them some support money, Paul is set free to devote himself "exclusively to preaching, testifying to the Jews that Jesus was the Christ" (18:5). Eventually the heat of opposition drives him to spend more time with Gentiles. No longer free to use the synagogue, he uses the house of Titius Justus next door. Soon the synagogue ruler himself is converted (18:8). Some Jews mount a legal challenge against Paul, but the local magistrate perceives that the dispute essentially involves controverted interpretations of Scripture (18:12-16). The end of the chapter introduces Apollos, learned in the Scriptures and a powerful speaker, but still somewhat ill-informed regarding Jesus. He "knew only the baptism of John" (18:25). He may well have known enough of John the Baptist's teaching to announce the coming of Jesus and perhaps even details of Jesus' life, death, and resurrection; but like the "believers" at the beginning of the next chapter, he might not have known of Pentecost and the gift of the Spirit. After all, many Jews from around the empire visited Jerusalem at the time of the feasts and then returned home. If Apollos and others had left Jerusalem after the resurrection but before Pentecost, it was not impossible that years could have elapsed before they became better informed. And information is precisely what Priscilla and Aquila provide Apollos, explaining to him "the way of God more adequately" (Acts 18:26).

In Nehemiah 8, Ezra begins a seven-day Bible conference. He carefully reads "the Law" to the assembled crowd. The Levites join in; they "instructed the people in the Law. . . . They read from the Book of the Law of God, making it clear and giving the meaning so that the people could understand what was being read" (8:7-8). The expression "making it clear" could be rendered "translating it"; after all, the Law was written in Hebrew, and by this time most of the people spoke Aramaic. The Bible had become a closed book to them. Whether through translation or exposition or both, the people are understanding it again. Joy dawns "because they now understood the words that had been made known to them" (8:12).

Whether under the old covenant or the new, nothing is more important for the growth and maturation of God's people than a heart hungry to read and understand what God says, and people to make it plain.

∾

Genesis 20; Matthew 19; *Nehemiah 9; Acts 19*

∾

CROWD PSYCHOLOGY IS EASILY EXPLAINED after the fact, but difficult to predict. I recall at a raucous campus election at McGill University thirty-five years ago, one student heckler made a couple of telling points that embarrassed the candidate in question. The crowd was instantly on his side, cheering him on. Thus emboldened, he attempted another sally, but this one was anemic and pointless. The candidate looked at him disdainfully and asked, "Is there some point you are trying to make?" Unable to reply with a quick and direct barb, the student immediately found the crowd hissing and booing him and telling him to shut up and sit down. In two minutes the crowd had turned from avid support to dismissive scorn. It was easy enough to analyze after the fact; it was difficult to predict.

Demetrius the silversmith learned this lesson the hard way (**Acts 19:23-41**). In the face of Paul's effective evangelism, and therefore the threat of a diminution of his business as an artisan producing silver figurines of the goddess Artemis (her Latin name was Diana), Demetrius tries to stir up enough opposition to stop the Christian movement. Planned or otherwise, the result is a full-fledged riot. Paul sees this as a glorious opportunity to articulate the Gospel to a huge crowd; his friends, however, see this crowd as so dangerous that they succeed, with whatever difficulty, in persuading him to stay away.

Eventually the "city clerk" (more or less equivalent to a mayor) quiets the crowd. Ephesus is a free city; it is trusted by Rome to govern itself and remain loyal to the empire. The city clerk well knows that reports of riots in Ephesus could prompt an inquiry that might result in a change of status. Roman troops could be imposed and a governor commissioned by either the senate or the emperor himself. The Christians, says the mayor, are not guilty of desecrating the temple of Artemis. So why the riot? If Demetrius and his friends have a grievance, there are courts, or they can await the calling of the next properly constituted city "assembly" (19:39—interestingly, the word is *ekklesia,* from which we derive "church"). So the city clerk quells the crowd and dismisses it.

Some of the lessons are obvious. (1) It is usually very foolish to whip up a crowd. The results are unpredictable. (2) God remains in charge. Despite some desperate moments, the results in this case are wonderful: the Christian cause has been exonerated, Demetrius and his cronies have lost face, no one has suffered harm. (3) God can use strange economic and political pressures, including, in this case, a pagan artisan and a mayor, to bring about his good purposes.

Genesis 21; Matthew 20; *Nehemiah 10; Acts 20*

∾

NEHEMIAH 9 AND **NEHEMIAH 10** NEED to be read together. Nehemiah 9 finds the Israelites confessing "their sins and the wickedness of their fathers" (9:2). Yet the scene is not of individualistic repentance and confession. There is a large-scale corporate dimension, organized yet powerfully empowered by the Spirit of God, that is wonderful to contemplate. For a quarter of the day the people hear the Scriptures translated and explained; for another quarter of the day they commit themselves to confession and worship. In this they are led by the Levites.

The corporate prayer in which they are led is in large measure a review of Israelite history. It highlights the repeated cycles of declension into which the people have fallen, and the repeated visitations of God to restore them. The heart of the confession is found in 9:33: "In all that has happened to us, you have been just; you have acted faithfully, while we did wrong."

"In view of all this" (9:38), then, the people enter into a covenant with God (Neh. 10). More precisely, this is a renewal of the old Mosaic covenant. Since the prayer is led by the priests, it is not surprising that many of its elements focus on the temple. Nevertheless, there are broader issues regarding marriage (to preserve the people from pagan contamination), Sabbath observance, and a generalized commitment "to follow the Law of God given through Moses the servant of God and to obey carefully all the commands, regulations and decrees of the LORD our Lord" (10:29).

Of course, had the feasts and rites of ancient Israel functioned the way they were designed to function, this covenant renewal would not have been necessary. For strictly speaking, the great feasts were to be occasions of covenant renewal. For instance, Passover was designed to recall the Exodus and restore to the people's consciousness the Lord's mercy and faithfulness in rescuing them, while providing an opportunity for a renewed pledge of allegiance.

No less than the ancient Israelites, Christians are called to covenant renewal. That is one of the large purposes of the Lord's Supper. It is a time for self-examination, confession of sin, remembering what the Lord Jesus endured to secure our redemption, and, together with the people of God in local assembly, a time to remember and proclaim his death until he comes. Thereby we renew our pledge of allegiance. If we permit the Lord's Supper to descend to the level of meaningless rite, all the while hardening our hearts against the living God, we face grave danger. It will do us good, in solemn assembly, to review our sins and confess them, to grasp anew the Lord's faithfulness, and to pledge fresh loyalty to the new covenant.

∾

Genesis 22; Matthew 21; *Nehemiah 11*; *Acts 21*

∾

IN ACTS 21 WE FIND PAUL AND THE CHURCH in Jerusalem trying to be as accommodating as possible, but nothing will avail. Paul is arrested, in line with the prophecies to the effect that he would be seized and bound (21:4, 11). Note:

(1) This is one of the "we" passages in Acts (21:1, 17). On the face of it, Luke the author is at this point traveling with Paul and is a witness to the events described here. That is worth noting, because many critics find these events completely unbelievable.

(2) The church and its leaders warmly receive Paul and his reports of gospel fruitfulness among the Gentiles. This is entirely in line with their earlier delight when Paul reported many Gentile conversions (e.g., Acts 15). In other words, experiences in Samaria (Acts 8) and Peter's visit with Cornelius and his household (Acts 10—11) have prepared the church to delight in the manifest progress of the Gospel among the Gentiles.

(3) Nevertheless, the leaders are painfully aware that substantial numbers of conservative Jews are out to get Paul. They have heard that he is counseling "all" the Jews in the Diaspora not to circumcise their children or follow the Law of Moses (21:21). So they devise a plan to help him regain a reputation for observing conservatism (21:23-24). "Then everybody will know there is no truth in these reports about you, but that you yourself are living in obedience to the law" (21:24).

It is this passage that is especially controverted, for does not Paul himself say that he is flexible on such matters (1 Cor. 9:19-23; Gal.)? Yet before we write off the Jerusalem elders and Paul himself for massive inconsistency, or Luke for making up stories, observe: (a) The initial charge is that Paul exhorts all Jews in the Diaspora to abandon circumcision and the Law of Moses. That he does not do. He refuses to allow circumcision and kosher observance to become a test of spirituality, but he does not advocate universal abandonment of the Law. He himself circumcised Timothy to advance the communication of the Gospel. (b) One suspects that the biggest fear of some conservative Jews was that Paul would desecrate the temple (21:27-29). The elders therefore sought to show that *while he was in Jerusalem* Paul was a carefully observant Jew, even paying for the temple purification rites of others. After all, neither Paul nor the Jerusalem leaders imposed full observance on all Christian believers (21:25; cf. Acts 15; see vol. 1, meditation for July 28).

So in the providence of God, Paul is arrested. Thus he arrives, for the first time, in Rome, and the Gospel is heard in Caesar's courts.

∾

Genesis 23; Matthew 22; *Nehemiah 12*; Acts 22

∾

READING PAUL'S IMPROMPTU DEFENSE to the crowd (**Acts 22**), one is struck by the sparse simplicity of the narrative. But two details urge reflection here:

First, we must ask why the crowd turns nasty when it does. When Paul starts to address the people in their mother tongue, Aramaic, initially "they became very quiet" (22:2). They listen to the entire account of his conversion and call to ministry without breaking out in anger. But when Paul says that the Lord himself told Paul, "Go; I will send you far away to the Gentiles" (22:21), the unleashed malice of the mob will be satisfied with nothing less than his death. Why?

Inevitably, the answers are complex. Some of the pressures Jews felt to remain distinctive from the Gentiles were doubtless sociological: their self-identity was bound up with kosher food laws, Sabbath observance, circumcision, and the like, and a man like Paul, who was perceived to be reducing those barriers, was threatening their self-identity. But the heat of their passion cannot be explained by merely horizontal analysis. At least two other factors must be acknowledged. (1) For devout, conservative, Jerusalemite Jews, what was at issue was the Law of God, the exclusive primacy of the temple, their understanding of Scripture. From their perspective, Paul was destroying what God himself had set up. He was entangling the people of God in compromises with pagans. Not only was he jeopardizing their identity, he was blaspheming the Almighty, whose people they were and whose revelation they were appointed to obey and preserve. (2) At the same time, it is hard to miss the element of ownership: these people were acting as though God was so exclusively the property of ancestral Jews that Gentiles could not get a look in. From Paul's perspective, this entailed a profoundly mistaken and even perverse reading of the Old Testament, and a sadly tribal vision of a domesticated God. Of course, their error is often repeated today, with less justification, by those who so tie their culture to their understanding of Christian religion that the Bible itself becomes domesticated and the missionary impulse frozen.

Second, we must ask why Paul stands on his Roman citizenship here, avoiding a flogging, while on occasion he simply takes the beating. At least one of the reasons is that he tends to appeal to his legal status when doing so is likely to establish a precedent that will help to protect Christians. One of Luke's arguments in these chapters is that Christianity is not politically dangerous; rather, it is repeatedly legally vindicated. Paul, thinking of his brothers and sisters, acts, as usual, for their benefit.

∾

Genesis 24; Matthew 23; *Nehemiah 13; Acts 23*

∾

ONE OF THE MOST STRIKING EVIDENCES of sinful human nature lies in the universal propensity for downward drift. In other words, it takes thought, resolve, energy, and effort to bring about reform. In the grace of God, sometimes human beings display such virtues. But where such virtues are absent, the drift is invariably toward compromise, comfort, indiscipline, sliding disobedience, and decay that advances, sometimes at a crawl and sometimes at a gallop, across generations.

People do not drift toward holiness. Apart from grace-driven effort, people do not gravitate toward godliness, prayer, obedience to Scripture, faith, and delight in the Lord. We drift toward compromise and call it tolerance; we drift toward disobedience and call it freedom; we drift toward superstition and call it faith. We cherish the indiscipline of lost self-control and call it relaxation; we slouch toward prayerlessness and delude ourselves into thinking we have escaped legalism; we slide toward godlessness and convince ourselves we have been liberated.

That is the sort of situation Nehemiah faces toward the end of his leadership in Jerusalem (**Neh. 13**). He has been away for a time, required by his responsibilities toward the Emperor Artaxerxes to return to the capital. When he comes back to Jerusalem for a second term as governor, he finds that commercial interests have superseded Sabbath discipline, that compromise with the surrounding pagans has displaced covenantal faithfulness, that greed has withheld some of the stipend of the clergy, and therefore their numbers and usefulness have been reduced, and that some combination of indiscipline and sheer stupidity has admitted to the temple and to the highest councils of power men like Tobiah and Sanballat, who have no interest in faithfulness toward God and his Word.

By an extraordinary combination of exhortation, command, and executive action, Nehemiah restores covenantal discipline. Doubtless many of the godly breathe a sigh of relief and thank God for him; no less certainly, many others grumble that he is a busybody, a killjoy, a narrow-minded legalist. Our permissive and relativizing culture fits more comfortably into the latter group than the former—but that says more about our culture than about Nehemiah.

Genuine reformation and revival have never occurred in the church apart from leaders for whom devotion to God is of paramount importance. If, absorbing the values of the ambient culture, the Western church becomes suspicious of such leaders, or else reacts with knee-jerk cultural conservatism that is as devoid of biblical integrity as the compromise it opposes, we are undone. May God have mercy on us and send us prophetic leaders.

Genesis 25; Matthew 24; *Esther 1; Acts 24*

∾

IN THE TRIAL OF PAUL BEFORE FELIX (**Acts 24**), the governor comes across as a man in authority who has no moral vision authorizing him to take decisive action. He is, in short, a moral wimp. He also represents the many powerful people who are disturbed by the Gospel, and at some deep level know that it is true, yet who never become Christians. Note:

(1) Judging by his approach and oratory, Tertullus is an orator trained in the Greek tradition and thus well able to represent the Jewish leaders in this quintessentially Hellenistic setting. The charge against Paul of temple desecration (24:6) is serious, punishable by death. When Tertullus encourages Felix to "examine" Paul (24:8), he means more than that Felix should ask a few probing questions. Roman "examination" of a prisoner was open-ended beating until the prisoner "confessed." Roman officers did not have the right to "examine" a Roman citizen like Paul, but a governor like Felix could doubtless manage to waive the rules now and then.

(2) Paul's response, no less courteous than that of Tertullus, denies the charge of temple desecration (24:12-13, 17-18) and provides a plausible explanation of the uproar by describing the actions of "some Jews from the province of Asia" (24:19). Paul also seizes the opportunity to acknowledge that he is a follower of "the Way"—a delightful expression referring to first-century Christianity, bearing, perhaps, multiple allusions. Christianity is more than a belief system; it is a way of living. Moreover, it provides a way to God, a way to be forgiven and accepted by the living God—and that Way is Jesus himself (as John 14:6 explicitly avers).

(3) Paul insists that he believes "everything that agrees with the Law and that is written in the Prophets" (24:14). This expression does not make the Law the final arbiter, yet nevertheless insists that the "everything" Paul believes agrees with the Law. The Law is thus a critical test that points to the "everything" Paul believes, but it is not the substance of everything he believes. Compare Matthew 5:17-20; Romans 3:21 (see meditation for January 31).

(4) And Felix? Owing to his Jewish wife Drusilla (24:24), he has some acquaintance with "the Way" (24:22). Yet here he ducks a decision between justice and his desire to placate Paul's opponents, appealing to the need to hear from Lysias the commander. It is all pretense. He enjoys talking with Paul, and even trembles before his message, but always dismisses the apostle at the critical moment. For two years he is torn between a desire to repent and a desire for a bribe. In eternity, how will Felix assess those two years?

∾

Genesis 26; Matthew 25; *Esther 2; Acts 25*

THE CHANGE IN GOVERNOR FROM FELIX to Porcius Festus (Acts 24:27) brings no immediate improvement in Paul's condition. Yet God remains in control, and in this chapter, **Acts 25**, under God's providence Paul takes a decisive step. How was this brought about?

(1) New to the area and still relatively ignorant of its political and religious dynamics, Festus is determined to get off on the right foot. A mere three days after arriving at the regional Roman capital of Caesarea, he travels up to Jerusalem to meet the local Jewish authorities. He could have summoned them; he could have delayed his visit. But off he goes, and is promptly informed what a terrible man Paul is. The Jewish authorities see the accession of Festus as an opportunity to do away with Paul. They express their desire to have him brought to Jerusalem for trial, but in reality they plan an ambush that would ensure his demise (25:1-3). Festus replies that Paul is being held in Caesarea and insists that his interlocutors press their case there.

(2) In the next round of legal maneuverings the charges against Paul and his responses to them (25:6-8) provide Festus with no clear idea of what to do. Still trying to make a good impression on the Jewish authorities (and thus far more likely to listen to them than to a solitary man already in jail for two years), Festus asks Paul if he is willing to stand trial before the Roman court, *but in Jerusalem.*

(3) There is no hint that Paul is tipped off as to the planned ambush. Nevertheless, two years earlier he had been warned of a similar plot (23:16), and it would not take much to figure out that such a plot was likely being hatched again. If he agrees with Festus's suggestion, he will be murdered; if he declines, he will appear obstreperous and arrogant. So he exercises the right of every Roman citizen in the first century: he appeals to Caesar. That was the judicial equivalent of appealing to the Supreme Court. Humanly speaking, this was a desperate move. Emperor Nero did not take kindly to frivolous suits, and he was already known to be corrupt and intoxicated by his own power.

(4) Yet by that means, as the rest of the book shows, Paul finally arrives in Rome. As Joseph was brought to Egypt's palaces by way of slavery and prison, so Paul is brought to testify for King Jesus before the mightiest human authorities by way of prison and corrupt justice. Indeed, how did Jesus gain his place at the Father's right hand?

Genesis 27; Matthew 26; *Esther 3; Acts 26*

∾

IN ACTS 26, LUKE PROVIDES THE third account in this book of Paul's conversion (compare Acts 9 and 22). Each has a different aim, of course. Here Paul is defending himself before the Roman Governor Porcius Festus and Herod Agrippa II of Galilee. Important highlights include the following:

(1) As in earlier defenses, Paul stresses his continuity with his past in conservative Judaism: he shares with unconverted Jews a "hope" for what God promised to their fathers and an anticipation of the final resurrection (e.g., 24:15; 26:6-7).

(2) Paul's remarkable rhetorical question in 26:8 therefore accomplishes several things at once. He asks: "Why should any of you consider it incredible that God raises the dead?" To Jews who are in the court, the question establishes Paul's agreement at this point with the Pharisaic strand of Jewish tradition. Implicitly, it also hints that if they have a category for God raising the dead at the end, why should it be thought so impossible that God raised Jesus from the dead in anticipation of the end? To a man like King Agrippa, well acquainted with Jewish beliefs, the question was reinforcing categories with which he was already familiar. To a man like Festus, the question aimed at lessening the skepticism of his sophisticated pagan background. To people with naturalistic outlooks today, the same question remains a challenge: dismissal of the category of resurrection stems from an earlier dismissal of the God of the Bible. Granted the God of the Bible, why is the category of resurrection so difficult?

(3) Paul addresses himself primarily to King Agrippa (26:2, 13, 19), that is, to the ruler most familiar with the Jewish heritage and the Bible. For his part, Festus acknowledges he is at sea (25:26-27); and for all that he recognizes Paul's learning, he judges Paul's claims so bizarre that they only demonstrate he must be insane (26:24). Had Paul addressed himself most immediately to Festus, perhaps he would have used an approach like that in Acts 17:16-31, the Mars Hill address.

(4) Paul's direct appeal to King Agrippa (26:25-29) is openly evangelistic and wonderfully direct while remaining perfectly respectful. Paul's "defense" is not at all defensive; his address reads more like an evangelistic offensive attack than the plea of a frightened or cowed prisoner. Yet just as his "defense" is not defensive, so this "offense" never becomes offensive.

(5) Both Festus and Agrippa perceive that, whatever they make of him, Paul has done nothing worthy of death or imprisonment (26:31). Had this taken place before the events of 25:1-12, Paul would have been released. As it is, appeals to Caesar cannot be undone, so in God's providence Paul is transported to Rome.

∾

Genesis 28; Matthew 27; *Esther 4; Acts 27*

∾

FOR NARRATIVE SIMPLICITY AND POWER, the book of Esther readily captures the imagination. Though by now we are three chapters into it, we can pick up something of both its flavor and its message by reflecting on selected elements of **Esther 4**.

(1) The book makes its profound theological points by the shape of its restrained narrative. Commentators never fail to observe that not once does the book explicitly mention God. Nevertheless, it says a great deal about God and his providence, about his protection of his covenant people (even when they are far from the land, learning to survive during the exile and throughout the Diaspora), and about their faith in him, even when they are horribly threatened.

(2) The book thus gradually leads us to reflect on the strange circumstances that bring Esther to succeed Vashti as queen, as the consort of the Emperor Xerxes. If the point is overlooked by the careless reader, the chapter before us makes it pretty obvious to all but the most obtuse. "And who knows but that you have come to royal position for such a time as this?" (4:14), Mordecai asks Esther by the hand of Hathach. Mordecai is not appealing to impersonal fate; he is a devout and pious Jew. But the form of his utterance emphasizes God's sovereign providence even while implicitly acknowledging that providence is hard to read. God's people must act responsibly, wisely, strategically in light of the circumstances that play out around them, knowing that God is in control.

(3) Even while Mordecai mourns and wails deeply when he discovers Haman's plot (4:1-3), he neither descends into fatalism nor loses his faith. Having had time to mull over the wretched threat to his people, he reaches the conclusion (as he puts it to Esther) that, "For if you remain silent at this time, relief and deliverance for the Jews will arise from another place, but you and your father's family will perish" (4:14). Granted that God is faithful to his covenant promises, Mordecai cannot conceive that he would permit the people of God to be destroyed.

(4) True to her upbringing by Mordecai, Esther simultaneously expresses confidence in the living God and avoids the presumption that God's purposes for her life are easy to infer. She knows that God is there and that he hears and answers importunate prayer. "Go, gather together all the Jews who are in Susa [the capital city], and fast for me. Do not eat or drink for three days, night or day. I and my maids will fast as you do. . . . And if I perish, I perish" (4:16). While she resolves to do what is right, she acknowledges that she cannot see her own future and commits herself to the grace of God.

∾

Genesis 29; Matthew 28; *Esther 5*; Acts 28

∾

THREE OBSERVATIONS THAT SPRING from **Esther 5**:

First, the pace of the story prompts a cultural observation. There is much in our culture that demands instantaneous decision. That is as true in the ecclesiastical arena as in the political. We observe what we judge to be an injustice and immediately we get on the phone, fire off E-mails, or huddle in small groups at the local coffee shop to talk over the situation. Of course, some situations require speed. Endemic procrastination is not a virtue. But a great many situations, especially those that involve people relations, could benefit from extra time, a slower pace, a period to reflect. We have already seen that the news of Haman's plot has been disseminated throughout the empire. Considerable time therefore elapsed before Mordecai approached Esther and challenged her to act. Even then, she did not barge into the king's presence. She allowed three days for preparation and prayer. Now she is in the presence of the king. Her unauthorized entrance has been accepted. But instead of laying out the problem immediately, she calmly invites the king and Haman to a private banquet. When they get there, she slows the pace even more and builds anticipation by proposing a further banquet, when she will tell all.

Second, Haman represents a man lusting for power. He is in high spirits because only the king and he have been invited to Esther's banquet (5:9, 12). His boast is his wealth and his public elevation above the other nobles (5:11). It is not enough for him to be rich and powerful; he must be richer and more powerful than others. Doubtless some readers suppose that such temptations do not really afflict them, because they do not have access to the measures of wealth and power that might make them vulnerable. This is naive. Watch how often people, Christian people, become unprincipled, silly, easily manipulated, when they are in the presence of what they judge to be greatness. One of the great virtues of genuine holiness, a virtue immaculately reflected in the Lord Jesus, is the ability to interact the same way with rich and poor alike, with strong and weak alike. Beware of those who fawn over wealth and power and boast about the powerful people they know. Their spiritual mentor is Haman.

Third, Haman represents a man sold out to hatred. All of his strengths and advantages, by his own admission, mean nothing to him when he thinks of Mordecai, "that Jew" (5:13). The only thing that can restore his delight is the prospect of Mordecai's death (5:14). Here is self-love, the heart of all sin, at its social worst: unrestrained, it vows that it will be first and wants the death of all who stand in the way of fulfilling that vow.

∾

Genesis 30; Mark 1; *Esther 6; Romans 1*

∞

"THAT NIGHT THE KING COULD NOT SLEEP" (**Esther 6:1**). What a great dramatic line! Are we supposed to think this is an accident?

Both the Bible and history offer countless "coincidences" brought about in the providence of God, the significance of which is discerned only in hindsight. Even in this chapter, Haman chooses this particular morning to present himself early in the court—to obtain sanction for Mordecai's execution, at that!—and that makes him the man to whom the king puts his fateful question (6:4-6). In the meditation for January 25 we observed that the peculiar timing of Agrippa II's visit to Porcius Festus meant that Paul was forced to appeal to Caesar—and that brought him to Rome. Likewise, in God's providence, Caesar Augustus, more than half a century earlier, had decreed that the Roman world face a census, and under the local rules that decree brought Joseph and Mary to Bethlehem just in time for the birth of Jesus, fulfilling the biblical prophecy that the Messiah would be born in Bethlehem (Micah 5:2).

History entirely removed from the canon provides numerous circumstances where the tiniest adjustment would have changed the course of events. Suppose Britain had not broken the "Enigma" code machines. Would the Battle of Britain, and even World War II, have gone another way? Suppose Hitler had not held back his panzers at Dunkirk, sending in his planes instead. Would 150,000 British soldiers have been captured or killed, once again changing the face of the war? Is it not remarkable that Hitler's persecution of Jews drove some of the best scientific minds out of Germany and into the United States? Had he not done so, is it not entirely possible that Hitler would have invented an A-bomb before America did? What then would the history of the past fifty years have looked like? Suppose Khrushchev had not blinked at the Cuba missile crisis, and a nuclear exchange had followed. What would be the state of the world today? Suppose the bullet aimed at Kennedy had missed. Suppose the bullet aimed at Martin Luther King had missed. Suppose the bullet that took out the Archduke in Sarajevo had missed. Christians cannot possibly suppose that any of these events and billions more, small and great, were outside of God's control.

So the first verse of Esther 6 sets the reader up for the dramatic developments in this chapter, plunging us into many useful reflections on the matchless wisdom and peculiar providence of God. Then, at the end of the chapter, comes a line scarcely less dramatic: "While they were still talking with him, the king's eunuchs arrived and hurried Haman away to the banquet Esther had prepared" (6:14). What profit should readers gain from reflecting on this turning point?

∞

Genesis 31; Mark 2; *Esther 7*; Romans 2

∾

SO HAMAN IS HANGED (ESTHER 7). The details of how this point in the narrative is reached simultaneously attest to the providential hand of God and the narrative skills of the author of this little book. Esther's second garden party leaves Haman completely exposed and utterly defenseless. A few minutes later he falls over himself on Esther's couch, begging for his life, only to find that his actions have been interpreted by the enraged King Xerxes as a crass attempt to molest the queen. Moreover, that seventy-five-foot gallows prepared for Mordecai—the Mordecai whom Haman was forced to honor—now becomes the site for his own execution. The man who wanted to commit genocide is killed.

In hindsight, how easy the operation has been. Despite Mordecai's agonized tears, despite Esther's uncertainty and her call for three days of fasting and prayer, from this vantage point the result seems almost inevitable. Nevertheless, observe:

First, in most of the conflicts in which we find ourselves, not least conflicts about the Gospel and the life and health of God's people, we do not know the outcome as we grimly enter the fray. That knowledge is reserved for God alone. Yet Christian faith is never to be confused with fatalism; the intervention of Mordecai and Esther demanded soul-searching, faith, prayer, and obedience. In retrospect, even their presence in the court and on the fringes of the court was God's preparation, and certainly the outcome was God's doing; but never should our confidence in God's ultimate victory dilute our own passionate involvement, intercession, and insertion into the affairs that touch God's covenant people.

Second, this singular victory does not mean that all the problems of the Jews are over. Rapid perusal of the rest of Esther shows how much farther there is to go. That is utterly realistic. Sometimes we enjoy decisive moments, but even these usually turn out to be mere steps in a much more complicated endeavor. Paul gives his decisive address to the Ephesian elders (Acts 20), but he is realistic enough to recognize the ongoing dangers that await that church (Acts 20:29-31). We have just seen how, under Nehemiah, the wall could be built around Jerusalem, and its completion viewed as a success, and how, under Ezra, revival broke out as the ancient feasts of the covenant were re-instituted—but immediately there were fresh challenges, dangers from new compromises, and hard decisions to be made.

It is ever so. Satan takes no vacations. The moment we are content in this fallen world, the dangers return—not least the danger of over-contentment. Without being contentious, prepare for conflict; without being combative, equip yourself for the "good fight" (2 Tim. 4:7). It will last at least as long as you live.

∾

Genesis 32; Mark 3; *Esther 8; Romans 3*

∾

ALMOST EVERYTHING IN ROMANS **3:21-26** is disputed. There is no space for justifying a particular exegesis. But in my view, these are some of the more important conclusions to be drawn:

(1) "But now" (3:21): the expression is temporal, not merely logical. Paul has devoted 1:18—3:20 to demonstrating that all of the human race, Jews and Gentiles alike—i.e., those who have the Mosaic Law and those who do not—are guilty before God. But now, at this point in redemptive history, something new has happened. A "righteousness from God" has been made known.

(2) The phrase "apart from law" probably modifies "has been made known"— i.e., "a righteousness from God has been made known *apart from law*."

(3) "The law" does not here mean "legalism," as if Paul were saying that now a righteousness has been made known apart from legalism. Paul's point, rather, is that now, with the death and resurrection of Jesus, a righteousness from God has been made known *apart from the law-covenant,* the Law of Moses. This does not mean that such righteousness was unanticipated. Far from it: "the Law and the Prophets" (i.e., holy Scripture) had testified to it, had borne witness to it. In other words, "the righteousness of God" that has come to us through Jesus appeared independently from the law-covenant, but nevertheless the old law—indeed, the entire Hebrew Bible—bore witness to it and anticipated it.

(4) This "righteousness from God" comes to all who believe (3:22-24). It cannot come to those who are good, for Paul has just spent two chapters proving that all are bad. It comes therefore to those who believe, and it comes freely by the grace of God "through the redemption that came by Christ Jesus" (3:24).

(5) This redemption was achieved by God setting forth Christ Jesus as "a sacrifice of atonement" (3:25) or, more precisely, as "a propitiation" (KJV). God so brought about Jesus' death that, in his crucifixion, Jesus died "the just for the unjust" (1 Pet. 3:18, KJV) and thereby made God favorable or "propitious" to those who would otherwise face only his wrath. Thus Christ's death is not only an "expiation" (it cancels our sin) but a "propitiation" (it thereby makes God propitious). Of course, since it is God himself who provides the sacrifice, there is a profound sense in which God propitiates himself—i.e., he graciously provides the sacrifice that pacifies his own wrath.

(6) Stated otherwise, God offers up Christ not only to justify ungodly sinners such as ourselves, who have faith in Jesus, but also to maintain his own justice, to be just, in the face of all the sins ever committed (3:25-26).

∾

Genesis 33; Mark 4; *Esther 9—10; Romans 4*

∽

HISTORY LOOKS DIFFERENT IN different cultures. I do not simply mean that different cultures interpret the same past differently (though that is often the case), but that the understanding of what history is may vary from culture to culture. Indeed, even within one culture there are often competing notions as to what history is.

This issue has become ever more complex during the past several decades, owing to the advance of postmodernism and its innovative ideas about what history is. As important as that debate is, I do not wish to explore it here. At the moment I am painting on a larger canvas.

Many ancient Greeks thought that history went around in circles. This does not mean that each cycle repeats itself exactly, but that there is an unending repetition of patterns, with no end, no ultimate climax, no *telos*. A great deal of contemporary naturalism thinks that our sun will finally burn out, and life on earth will come to an end. Some hold that the universe itself will eventually settle into a more or less even distribution of energy, and die; others think that somehow it will rejuvenate itself by collapsing and exploding again to repeat a cycle something like the present one. By contrast, in university history departments events on such a scale are irrelevant. History—whether this refers to what happened, or to our reconstruction of it—covers the period of human writing. Everything before that is "prehistoric."

The Bible has its own perspectives on history, and some of them are non-negotiable: if we lose sight of them or deny them, we can no longer understand the Bible on its own terms. Certainly the Bible sometimes retells "what happened" in parabolic categories (compare 2 Sam. 11 and 12), or in highly selective condensations (e.g., Acts 7), or in poetic form (Ps. 78). But more importantly, we cannot rightly understand the Bible unless we grasp several key elements of its sequence. On the largest scale, history begins at Creation and ends at the supreme *telos*, the final judgment and the new heaven and new earth. We are not simply going around in circles. In Galatians 3 (see vol. 1, meditation for September 27), Paul's argument turns on the fact that the Mosaic Law came *after* the promises to Abraham. Somewhat similarly here (**Romans 4**), Abraham's faith was credited to him as righteousness *before* he was circumcised, so circumcision cannot be made a condition of righteousness. Under Semitic notions of sonship, Abraham becomes the father of all who believe, circumcised or not (4:1-12). Something similar can be said of Abraham's relation to the Law of Moses (4:13-17). The sequence of the biblical history is critical.

∽

Genesis 34; Mark 5; *Job 1*; Romans 5

∿

THE BIBLE DEALS WITH THE REALITY of evil in many different ways. Sometimes justice is done, and is seen to be done, in this life. Especially in the New Testament, the final recompense for evil is bound up with judgment to come. Sometimes suffering has a humbling role, as it challenges our endless hubris. War, pestilence, and famine are sometimes God's terrible weapons of judgment. These and many more themes are developed in the Bible.

But the book of Job is matchless for causing us to reflect on the question of *innocent* suffering. That is made clear in **Job 1**, which in some ways sets up the rest of the book. Job "was blameless and upright; he feared God and shunned evil" (1:1). Although Job was blessed with wealth and a large family, he took nothing for granted. He even engaged in what might be called preemptive intercession on behalf of his grown children: he prayed and offered sacrifices on their behalf, fearful that perhaps at an otherwise innocent gathering, one of his children had sinned and cursed God (1:5).

Job does not know, as the reader knows, that another drama is playing out in the throne room of God. Little is said about these "sons of God," these angels, who approach the Almighty; little is said about Satan, though transparently he is evil and lives up to his name, "Accuser." The exchange between Satan and God accomplishes three things. *First,* it sets up the drama that unfolds in the rest of the book. *Second,* implicitly it establishes that even Satan himself has restraints on his power and cannot act outside God's sanction. *Third,* it discloses that Satan's intention is to prove that all human loyalty to God is nothing more than crass self-interest, while God's intention is to demonstrate that a man like Job is loyal and faithful regardless of the blessings he receives or does not receive.

Job, of course, knows nothing of these arrangements. He couldn't, for the drama that follows would be vitiated if he did. In short order Job loses his wealth and his children, all to "natural" causes that Job knows full well remain within God's sway. When the last bit of bad news reaches him, Job tears his robe and shaves his head (both signs of abasement) and worships, uttering words that become famous: "Naked I came from my mother's womb, and naked I will depart. The LORD gave and the LORD has taken away; may the name of the LORD be praised" (1:21).

The narrator comments, "In all this, Job did not sin by charging God with wrongdoing" (1:22)—which of course means, in the context of this chapter, that God's assessment of the man was right and Satan's was wrong.

∿

Genesis 35—36; Mark 6; *Job 2*; *Romans 6*

∿

IT IS ONE THING TO ENDURE WITH steadfast loyalty when the losses, however painful, are all external; it is quite another thing to endure when one loses one's health (**Job 2**). Some reflections:

(1) We are still dealing with innocent suffering. God himself declares of Job, "There is no one on earth like him; he is blameless and upright, a man who fears God and shuns evil. And he still maintains his integrity" (2:3).

(2) Up to this point, God has proved Satan wrong: Job's loyalty to God is not conditioned by crass, self-serving bartering. Here is a man who is upright and faithful when all his wealth and even all his children are stripped away from him. That is what makes Satan up the ante: "Let me take away his health," Satan says in effect, "and he will surely curse you to your face" (2:4-5). So a new level of entirely innocent suffering is introduced, and the stage is set for the rest of the book.

(3) At this point believers must ask painful questions. Doesn't this sound as if God is using Job in some fantastic experiment? Why should the poor chap have to lose his wealth, his family, his health, and (as we shall see) his reputation, merely to prove God right in a challenge God might well have ignored?

That question could call forth a very long book. I have no final, exhaustive answers. But some things should be borne in mind. (a) We belong to God. He may do with us as he wishes. There is something deep within us that rebels at being reminded of that elemental truth. But truth it is. Indeed, our rebellion in the face of it is a reminder of how much we still want to be at the center of the universe, with God serving us. That is the heart of all idolatry. (b) Suppose Job had known of the arrangement between God and Satan. A lesser man might have protested violently, but it is at least plausible to think that Job would have used such information to invest his suffering with profound significance, thus making it easier to endure. Indeed, he might have seen his suffering as bound up somehow in a larger cosmic struggle between good and evil. (c) Other factors to be borne in mind must await the conclusion of the book of Job—indeed, the conclusion of the Book, the Bible. But I shall return to some of these matters in the devotional for March 13.

(4) So Job now faces painful and degrading physical breakdown, emotional abandonment by his wife, and the arrival of the three miserable comforters. Innocent suffering is immeasurably difficult to endure; it is still worse when every emotional support proves to be a broken reed.

∿

Genesis 37; Mark 7; *Job 3; Romans 7*

∽

FROM JOB 3 UNTIL THE FIRST PART of the last chapter of the book, with a small exception at the beginning of chapter 32, the text is written in Hebrew poetry. The book is a giant drama, like a Shakespearean play. Speech follows speech, the movement of the drama carried forward on the sustained argument between Job and his three "friends." Eventually another character is introduced, and finally God himself responds.

The opening speech belongs to Job. The burden of his utterance is unmistakable: he wishes he had never been born. He is not ready to curse God, but he is certainly prepared to curse the day that brought him to birth (3:1, 3, 8). Everything about that day he wishes he could blot out. If he could not have been stillborn (3:11, 16), then why couldn't he have just starved to death (3:12)?

Implicitly, of course, this is criticism of God, however indirect. "Why is life given to a man whose way is hidden, whom God has hedged in?" (3:23). What Job is experiencing is what he feared throughout his years of plenty (3:25). He has no peace, no quietness, no rest, but only turmoil (3:26).

Four reflections will put this first address in perspective:

(1) This is the rhetoric of a man in deep anguish. So many of the things about which we complain are trivial. Even our most serious grounds for complaint are usually only some fraction of what Job faced.

(2) Before we condemn Job, therefore, we must listen attentively, even fearfully. When we come across those who for good reason are in terrible despair, we must cut them some slack. It would have been wonderful if one of the "friends" had put an arm around Job's shoulder and wept with him, saying, "We love you, Job. We do not pretend to understand. But we love you, and we'll do whatever we can for you."

(3) Job is transparently honest. He does not don a front of feigned piety so that no one will think he is letting down the side. The man hurts so much he wishes he were dead, and says so.

(4) Both here and throughout the book, for all that Job is prepared to argue with God, he is not prepared to write God off. Job is not the modern agnostic or atheist who treats the problem of evil as if it provided intellectual evidence that God does not exist. Job knows that God exists and believes that he is powerful and good. That is one reason why (as we shall see) he is in such confusion. Job's agonizings are the agonizings of a believer, not a skeptic.

∽

Genesis 38; Mark 8; *Job 4; Romans 8*

∾

THE FIRST SPEECH OF ELIPHAZ takes up two chapters. In the first part (**Job 4**), Eliphaz gives shape to his argument:

(1) The opening lines are seductive (4:2-4). One might almost think that Eliphaz is respectfully pursuing permission to offer helpful counsel to Job, in the same way that Job in times past has offered helpful counsel to others. But that is not it at all. Eliphaz is not asking permission; rather, he is fixing blame on Job because he is discouraged. It turns out, Eliphaz says, that the great Job who has helped others cannot cope when he faces a bit of trouble himself (4:5).

(2) The next verse transitions to the heart of Eliphaz's argument: "Should not your piety be your confidence and your blameless ways your hope?" (4:6). In other words, if Job were as pious and as blameless as many had believed, either he would not be in this fix, or else he would at least be able to live above discouragement. The disasters that have befallen Job, and Job's reactions to them, prove that Job is hiding shame or guilt that must be confronted.

(3) In brief, Eliphaz holds that in God's universe you get what you deserve (4:7). God is in charge, and God is good, so you reap what you sow (4:8).

(4) Eliphaz claims nothing less than revelation to ground his argument (4:12-21). In some sort of night vision, he says, a spirit glided by his face (4:15) and uttered words of supreme importance: "Can a mortal be more righteous than God? Can a man be more pure than his Maker?" (4:17). God is so transcendently powerful and just that even the angels that surround him are tawdry and untrustworthy in his eyes. So human beings, "those who live in houses of clay, whose foundations are in the dust" (4:19), are less significant, less reliable. The implication, then, is that a man like Job should simply admit his frailty, his error, his sin, and stop pretending that what has befallen him is anything other than what he deserves. The way Job is carrying on, Eliphaz implies, he is in danger of impugning the God whose justice is far beyond human assessment or comprehension.

We should pause to evaluate Eliphaz's argument. At one level, Eliphaz is right: God is utterly just, transcendently holy. The Bible elsewhere avers that a man reaps what he sows (e.g., Prov. 22:8; Gal. 6:7). But these truths, by themselves, may overlook two factors. First, the time frame in which the wheels of God's justice grind is sometimes very long. Eliphaz seems to hold to a rather rapid and obvious tit-for-tat system of recompense. Second, Eliphaz has no category for innocent suffering, so he is embarking on a course that condemns an innocent man.

∾

Genesis 39; Mark 9; *Job 5*; Romans 9

IN THE SECOND PART OF HIS SPEECH (**Job 5**), Eliphaz presupposes the stance he adopts in the first part (see yesterday's meditation), yet adds several new wrinkles to his impassioned presentation.

First, he says that Job's approach to God in this crisis is fundamentally flawed. By all means call on God (5:1)—but why imagine that someone as exalted as God will answer? Meanwhile, Job's attitude is what is killing him: "Resentment kills a fool, and envy slays the simple" (5:2). Eliphaz speaks out of his own observation: he has seen such fools prospering in the past, but suddenly they are uprooted. The implication is that Job's former prosperity was the prosperity of a "fool," and his current loss is nothing but his due. Somewhat inconsistently, Eliphaz adds that human suffering is a function of the human condition: "Man is born to trouble as surely as sparks fly upward" (5:7).

Second, rather self-righteously Eliphaz tells Job what he would do if he were in a similar situation (5:8-16). He would appeal to God and lay his case before him—not with Job's attitude, which Eliphaz finds insufferable, but with humility and contrition. After all, God reigns providentially and is committed to humbling the arrogant and the crafty and exalting the poor and the needy. So Eliphaz would approach God as a suppliant.

Third, Eliphaz insists that at least one of God's aims in bringing about loss and disaster is discipline: "Blessed is the man whom God corrects; so do not despise the discipline of the Almighty. For he wounds, but he also binds up; he injures, but his hands also heal" (5:17-18). Those who recognize this point discover that God quickly restores their life and prosperity. They find themselves secure in every trial. Job cannot miss the implication: if he feels he has suffered unjustly, not only is he insufficiently humble, but he fails to recognize the gracious, chastening hand of God Almighty, and therefore he remains under God's rod instead of finding mercy. "We have examined this," Eliphaz concludes rather pompously, "and it is true. So hear it and apply it to yourself" (5:27).

What Eliphaz says carries some measure of truth. God does indeed chasten his children (Prov. 3:11-12; Heb. 12:5-6). But this presupposes that they need it; God certainly does not chasten his children when they do not need it. Eliphaz thus presupposes that Job deserves God's chastening; readers of chapter 1 know he is mistaken. True, God saves the humble and abases those whose eyes are haughty (Ps. 18:27); but Eliphaz mistakenly assumes that Job must be haughty, or he would not be suffering. So here is a lesson: *false or improper application of genuine truth may be heartless and cruel—and, as here, it may say false things about God.*

Genesis 40; Mark 10; *Job 6; Romans 10*

JOB'S RESPONSE TO ELIPHAZ TAKES UP two chapters. In **Job 6** he argues as follows:

(1) In the opening verses (6:1-7) Job insists he has every reason for bemoaning his situation: his anguish and misery are beyond calculation (6:2-3). Nor does Job flinch from the obvious: in God's universe, God himself must somehow be behind these calamities—"The arrows of the Almighty are in me . . . God's terrors are marshaled against me" (6:4). Not even a donkey brays without a reason (6:5), so why should Job's friends treat him as if he is complaining without a reason?

(2) Job utters his deepest request: that God would simply crush him, "let loose his hand and cut me off" (6:9). This is more than a death wish: "Then I would still have this consolation—my joy in unrelenting pain—that I had not denied the words of the Holy One" (6:10). From this, three things are clear. (a) Despite his agony, Job is still thinking from within the framework of a committed believer. His suffering is not driving him to agnosticism or naturalism. (b) More importantly, his primary desire is to remain faithful to God. He sees death not only as a release from his suffering but as a way of dying before the intensity of his suffering should drive him to say or do something that would dishonor God. (c) Implicitly, this is also a response to Eliphaz. A man with such a passionate commitment to remain faithful to "the words of the Holy One" (6:10) should not be dismissed as a light and frivolous prevaricator.

(3) Eliphaz's position depends on the assumption that if Job acts as Eliphaz advises, all his wealth and power will be restored to him. Job insists he is well beyond that point: he has no hope, no prospects. He cannot conduct himself in such a way as to finagle blessings from God (6:11-13).

(4) Meanwhile, Job reproaches Eliphaz and his colleagues (6:14-23). "A despairing man should have the devotion of his friends, even though he forsakes the fear of the Almighty" (6:14); that is what real friendship is like. Job analyzes the real reason why his friends have proved "as undependable as intermittent streams" (6:15): they have seen something dreadful and they are afraid (6:21). Their neat theological categories have been blown away by Job's suffering, since they had believed he was a righteous man. They must now prove him to be unrighteous, deserving of his sufferings, or they too are under threat.

(5) Job ends with a wrenching plea (6:24-30). As far as he is concerned, his own integrity is at stake; he will not fake repentance when he knows he does not deserve this suffering. "Relent, do not be unjust" (6:29), he tells his friends.

Genesis 41; Mark 11; *Job 7*; Romans 11

∽

IN THE SECOND PART OF HIS RESPONSE TO ELIPHAZ, Job addresses God directly
(**Job 7**), though we are meant to understand that this agonizing prayer is uttered
in such a way that Eliphaz and his friends overhear it. In fact, as we shall see, there
is a tight connection between chapters 6 and 7.

The first ten verses of moving complaint, full of descriptions of sleepless
nights and festering sores, are focused on "reminding" God how brief human life
is. "Life is hard, and then you die" is the contemporary expression; more prosaically, Job asks, "Does not man have hard service on earth? Are not his days like
those of a hired man?" (7:1). Physically, he will not last much longer.

"Therefore," Job argues, "I will not keep silent; I will speak out in the anguish
of my spirit, I will complain in the bitterness of my soul" (7:11). To God, Job
says, in effect, I am not a monster—so why pick on me? My life is without meaning (7:16); I would rather be strangled to death than continue to live as I am now
living (7:15).

Why should God make so much of a mere mortal as to pay him the attention
God is obviously paying Job (7:17-18)? Though he is unaware of any sin in his
life that has attracted such suffering, Job knows he is not sinless. But why should
that attract so much suffering? "If I have sinned, what have I done to you, O
watcher of men? Why have you made me your target? Have I become a burden
to you?" (7:20).

Now it should be easier to see how this chapter is tied to the argument at the
end of chapter 6. There Job protests to Eliphaz that his (Job's) integrity is at stake.
The thrust of Eliphaz's argument was that Job must be suffering for wrongdoing
he had never confessed; the way ahead is self-abnegation and confession. But Job
replies to the effect that his friends should still be his friends; that they are condemning him because they themselves cannot bear the thought that an innocent
person might suffer; that their rebuke calls into question his lifelong integrity. In
chapter 7, when Job turns to address God, his stance is entirely in line with what
he has just told Eliphaz. Far from confessing sin, he tells God that he is being
picked on. Or if he has sinned, he has not done anything to deserve this sort of
minute attention and painful judgment. Indeed, Job comes within a whisker of
implying that God himself is not quite fair. Thus Job maintains his integrity.

So the drama of this book builds. The way ahead is still to be explored.
Meanwhile, meditate on Job 42:7.

∽

Genesis 42; Mark 12; *Job 8; Romans 12*

⟨⟩

BILDAD THE SHUHITE IS SCANDALIZED BY Job's response to Eliphaz and offers his own searing rebuttal (**Job 8**).

"How long will you say such things?" Bildad asks. "Your words are a blustering wind" (8:2). We would say they are nothing but hot air. From Bildad's perspective, Job is charging God with perverting justice. "Does the Almighty pervert what is right?" (8:3). But Bildad cannot let the point linger as a merely theoretical point to be debated by theologians. The implications of his rhetorical question Bildad now drives home in a shaft that must have pierced Job to the quick: "When your children sinned against him, he gave them over to the penalty of their sin" (8:4). In other words, the proper explanation of the storm that killed all ten of Job's children (1:18-19) is that they deserved it. To say anything else would surely mean, according to Bildad, that God is unjust, that he perverts justice. So the way forward for Job is "to look to God and plead with the Almighty" (8:5). If Job humbles himself and is truly pure and upright, God will restore him to his "rightful place." Indeed, all the fabulous wealth Job formerly enjoyed will seem like a mere piffle compared with the rewards that will come to him (8:6-7).

For his authority Bildad appeals to longstanding tradition, to "the former generations." The opinions he and his friends express are not newfangled ideas but received tradition. Bildad and his friends, regardless of how old they are, can only have learned by experience what can be tasted in one lifetime. What they are appealing to, however, is not the experience of one lifetime, but accumulated tradition. That tradition says that the godless and those who forget God perish like reeds without water; they enjoy all the support of those who lean on spiders' webs (8:11-19). Conversely, "Surely God does not reject a blameless man or strengthen the hands of evildoers" (8:20).

Of course, this is roughly the argument of Eliphaz, perhaps somewhat more bluntly expressed; and while Eliphaz appealed to visions of the night, Bildad appealed to received tradition. Once again, parts of the argument are not wrong. At one level, on an eternal scale, it is right to conclude that God vindicates righteousness and condemns wickedness. But as Bildad expresses the case, he claims to know more about God's doings than he really does (neither he nor Job knows the behind-the-scenes setup in chapter 1). Worse, he applies his doctrine mechanically and shortsightedly, and ends up condemning a righteous man.

Can you think of instances where premature or unbalanced application of biblical truth has turned out to be fundamentally mistaken?

⟨⟩

Genesis 43; Mark 13; *Job 9; Romans 13*

∿

"LET NO DEBT REMAIN OUTSTANDING, except the continuing debt to love one another, for he who loves his fellowman has fulfilled the law" (**Rom. 13:8**). Some Christians have used this verse to argue that all debt is wrong and condemned by God. Pay your way as you go. "Let no debt remain outstanding." The strongest voices argue that it is wrong to take a mortgage for a house or for a church building.

The flow of the passage, however, argues against such an interpretation. The opening verses exhort Christians to submit to the civil authorities, not only because they are constituted by God, but also because, when they function properly, they enforce what is right and punish what is wrong (13:1-4). So it is important to submit to such authorities, not only so as to avoid punishment, "but also because of conscience" (13:5): Christians want to keep a clear conscience by doing what is right. That is also why we pay taxes. The civil authorities are "God's servants, who give their full time to governing" (13:6). Like others of God's servants, they are sometimes disobedient and foolish, but in God's ordering of society taxes are God's means of supporting those whose task it is to govern. So we should pay what we owe: "If you owe taxes, pay taxes; if revenue, then revenue" (13:7).

More broadly yet, pay whatever is owed: "If respect, then respect; if honor, then honor. Let no debt remain outstanding, except the continuing debt to love one another" (13:7-8).

"Debt," then, in this context, has only a secondary reference to financial obligation. The passage has everything to do with the ongoing obligations of personal relationships in a society ordered by God. Moreover, insofar as finances are concerned, some financial obligations, such as taxes, are paid again and again; as they come due, we pay them. In precisely the same way, in a contracted mortgage, as the payments come due, we pay them. For all kinds of reasons it may be best to avoid fiscal debt of all kinds. But that is scarcely the point the apostle is making here.

The way Paul talks about love as "the continuing debt" reinforces the point. Some "debts," such as taxes, recur; the debt of love does not so much recur as continue: it is ever with us. The commandments that bear on horizontal relationships (what today we would call social relationships) may be summed up in this one rule: "Love your neighbor as yourself" (13:9; Lev. 19:18). Love is thus the "fulfillment" of the Law (13:10)—that is, love is that to which the Law points, in this time of eschatological fulfillment (13:11-14), and this we always owe.

∿

Genesis 44; Mark 14; *Job 10; Romans 14*

∾

JOB 10 IS THE SECOND PART OF JOB'S response to Bildad the Shuhite. Bildad has argued that God cannot pervert justice (Job 8; see meditation for February 9). In chapter 9 Job replies, rather impatiently, that he knows all that: "Indeed, I know that this is true" (9:2). Job does not doubt that he too, like other mortals, cannot stand up beside the matchless righteousness of God: "But how can a mortal be righteous before God?" (9:2). So Job argues that that is precisely the problem: in this particular case, Job insists he is blameless (9:21), free from any evil that should have attracted the miseries inflicted upon him, but God remains unanswerable. Job is certainly not more evil than many contemporaries who are unscathed by the passing years. But how can a mere mortal plead his case before the Almighty? "He is not a man like me that I might answer him, that we might confront each other in court" (9:32). There is not even available a suitable arbitrator (9:33). As for Job's "friends," they increase his suffering, for they will not admit that he is innocent (9:28); they are more than eager to drop him into the nearest slime pit to prove that he is dirty (9:30-31).

Job now turns to address God (chap. 10). He wants to know what charges God has against him (10:2). Full of self-acknowledged bitterness (10:1), Job asks, "Does it please you to oppress me, to spurn the work of your hands, while you smile on the schemes of the wicked?" (10:3). Certainly Job is prepared to acknowledge that God shaped him in the womb, carefully nurtured him, gave him life, and providentially watched over him (10:8-12). But now, it seems, there is another side: God will not only hunt him down if he sins, but even if Job is innocent he finds he cannot answer this God or compete against the pressures God is able to bring to bear (10:13-17). So why did God bring him to life in the first place? Or why did Job not die as soon as he was born, carried from the womb to the grave (10:18-22)?

This is the rhetoric of anguish and despair. We still await God's answer. But **Romans 14** may have something to say to Job's miserable "friends": "Let us therefore make every effort to do what leads to peace and to mutual edification" (14:19). Of course, in the context of Romans 14, Paul is focusing on Christian self-restraint for the sake of others, especially in the matter of eating food offered to idols (as in 1 Cor. 8; see vol. 1, meditation for September 3). Yet the broad principle applies nonetheless to Job's friends: do they speak out of passionate commitment to "mutual edification" or out of frightened self-justification?

Genesis 45; Mark 15; *Job 11*; *Romans 15*

∾

I SHALL COMMENT BRIEFLY on the two readings set for the day.

Zophar's speech (**Job 11**) carries forward the unfolding drama of the book of Job. Like Bildad, Zophar begins by condemning Job's addresses (11:2-3). To him, it sounds as if Job is claiming personal perfection: "You say to God, 'My beliefs are flawless and I am pure in your sight'" (11:4). Job has been wishing that God would answer him. Well and good, responds Zophar: "Oh, how I wish that God would speak" (11:5). No less than Job, he would love it if God would reply—and he is quite certain that, were God to do so, he would powerfully rebuke Job.

Just for a moment, Zophar seems to take a healthy turn. He begins to deal with the fathomless knowledge and wisdom of the Almighty, far beyond human capacity. If that had been all Zophar had said, he would have anticipated part of the answer of God himself later in the book (chaps. 38—41). Sadly, however, Zophar immediately turns this in a mischievous direction, following the same path as Eliphaz and Bildad: a God so great in knowledge can certainly recognize deceitful men, "and when he sees evil, does he not take note?" (11:11). Once again, the argument degenerates to a fairly mechanical theory of recompense. There is no category for innocent suffering. Job must be very wicked, for he is suffering much; the only reasonable option for him is to turn from the sin that must obviously be engulfing him (11:13-20).

The second passage is of a very different sort. Consider the way Paul here exhorts the Romans to pray: "I urge you, brothers, by our Lord Jesus Christ and by the love of the Spirit, to join me in my struggle by praying to God for me. Pray that I may be rescued from the unbelievers in Judea and that my service in Jerusalem may be acceptable to the saints there, so that by God's will I may come to you with joy and together with you be refreshed. The God of peace be with you all. Amen" (**Rom. 15:30-33**). Note: (a) What Paul asks for is prayer for himself. (b) If the Romans respond by praying, they will by their prayer be joining Paul in his struggle. (c) The particular struggle Paul has in mind is his relationship with unbelievers in Judea; he wants his service for the poor there to be so acceptable that he will be able to leave quickly and make his way to Rome. (d) Within the context of the chapter, this trip to Rome is part of his plan to evangelize Spain. In short, Paul asks for prayers that will further the Gospel in various ways.

What do you characteristically pray for?

∾

Genesis 46; Mark 16; *Job 12; Romans 16*

∾

THE CLOSING THREE VERSES OF ROMANS are extraordinary (**Rom. 16:25-27**). Formally they constitute a doxology—a word of praise to God. God is introduced as the One "who is able to establish you by my gospel" (16:25), and he is reintroduced into the structure in verse 27: "To the only wise God be glory forever through Jesus Christ! Amen." So in this context the wisdom of God, presupposed in the expression "the only wise God," is displayed in God's ability to establish the Roman Christians by Paul's gospel.

This gospel is further described in the intervening lines, and here God's wisdom is particularly stunning. God establishes people, we are told, by the Gospel, by "the proclamation of Jesus Christ, according to the revelation of the mystery hidden for long ages past" (16:25). There is a sense in which the sweep and focus of the Gospel was not clear. It remained hidden until the coming of Jesus Christ. Even when he was here, his own disciples did not grasp, before the cross and resurrection, that he, the Messiah, would also be the suffering servant and would die an odious death to redeem lost sinners.

Yet if this Gospel was hidden in "long ages past," it is "now revealed and made known through the prophetic writings by the command of the eternal God" (16:26). Here it sounds as if this Gospel has been disclosed "through the prophetic writings," that is, through the Scriptures. So on the one hand, the Gospel has been hidden in ages past but is now revealed; and on the other, the Gospel has been prophesied in ages past and is now fulfilled. How can both of these things be simultaneously true?

Part of the answer lies in the ways in which the Gospel is predicted in the Old Testament. So many of the predictions are wrapped up in "types" or models of what is to come. After the fact, we can see how Jesus is the true temple, the ultimate meeting-place between God and his sinful image-bearers; how he is the true Passover lamb; how he is the ultimate priest; how he is the ultimate "Son of God"; how he is the ultimate Davidic king. Indeed, we discover many clues distributed along the way. For instance, we read the prophecies of a new covenant, and reflect on how such announcements render the old covenant obsolete in principle and drive us to expect a new configuration. The fact remains, however, that no one expected the same person to fulfill all these images and types in himself. Indeed, some Jews in the first century expected two messiahs, one Davidic and the other priestly. But we see Jesus and his Gospel—comprehensively predicted, yet hidden for long ages past, and now disclosed "so that all nations might believe and obey him" (16:26).

∾

Genesis 47; Luke 1:1-38; *Job 13; 1 Corinthians 1*

∾

JOB'S RESPONSE TO ZOPHAR TAKES UP three chapters (Job 12—14), the first of which was part of yesterday's reading. There Job accuses Zophar and his friends, in scathing language, of mouthing traditional platitudes and thinking their utterances are profound: "Doubtless you are the people, and wisdom will die with you!" (12:2). Job adds: "But I have a mind as well as you; I am not inferior to you. Who does not know all these things?" (12:3)—that is, the things to do with God's sovereignty, greatness, and unfathomable power and wisdom. So Job spends most of chapter 12 reviewing and deepening this vision of God's greatness.

But here in **Job 13,** Job takes the argument a step farther. The common ground he shares with these three friends is plain enough: "My eyes have seen all this, my ears have heard and understood it. What you know I also know; I am not inferior to you" (13:1-2). The question is what to make of God's transcendent sovereignty. His friends use this base to argue that such a God can certainly sniff out evil and punish it; Job himself now turns the argument in a different direction.

First, far from prompting him to cringe in fear, reflection on who God is prompts Job to want to speak with the Almighty, to argue his case with God (13:3). His conscience really is clear, and he wants to prove it. He is convinced that if he could get a hearing, at least God would be fair and just.

Second, by contrast, the miserable friends merely smear him with lies (13:4). They are "worthless physicians"—i.e., they do nothing to help Job in his pain.

Third, and worse, Job insists that they "speak wickedly on God's behalf," that they "speak deceitfully for him" (13:7). They cannot find concrete evidences of gross sin in Job's life, yet they think they are speaking for God when they insist Job must really be evil. Thus in their "defense" of God, they say things that are untrue and unfair about Job: they "speak wickedly on God's behalf." How can God be pleased with their utterances? Ends do not justify means. It is always important to speak the truth and not fudge facts to fit our theological predispositions. Far better to admit ignorance or postulate mystery than to tell untruths.

Fourth, Job himself, for all that he wishes to enter into dialogue with God, is still not speaking as an agnostic. True, Job wants his day in the divine court. But for him, God is still God, and so he confesses, "Though he slay me, yet will I hope in him" (13:15). Even the alternative reading (NIV footnote—the issues are complex) acknowledges that God is God: the difference is in Job's response.

∾

Genesis 48; Luke 1:39-80; *Job 14; 1 Corinthians 2*

∾

SOME HAVE TAKEN 1 CORINTHIANS 2:1-5 to suggest that the way Paul preached in Athens (Acts 17:16-31) was a mistake, and that by the time he arrived at Corinth, Paul himself had recognized his error. In the passage before us he tells us how he "resolved to know nothing" while he was with them "except Jesus Christ and him crucified." So away with the quasi-philosophical preaching of the Areopagus address in Acts 17. Just stick to the simple Gospel.

There are good reasons for rejecting this false reading:

(1) This is not the natural reading of Acts. As you work your way through that book, you do not stumble upon some flag or other that warns you that at this point Paul goofs. This false interpretation is achieved by putting together an unnatural reading of Acts with a false reading of 1 Corinthians 2.

(2) The theology of the Areopagus address is in fact very much in line with the theology of Paul expressed in Romans.

(3) The Greek text at the end of Acts 17 does not say that "a few men" believed, as if this were a dismissive or condemning assessment, but that "certain people" believed. This expression is in line with other summaries in Acts.

(4) In Athens Paul had already been preaching not only in the synagogue to biblically literate folk, but to people in the marketplace who were biblically illiterate (Acts 17:17). What he had been preaching was "the good news" (Acts 17:18), the Gospel.

(5) Transparently Paul was cut off in Acts 17 before he was finished. He had set up the framework in which alone the Gospel is coherent: one transcendent God, sovereign, providential, personal; creation; fall into idolatry; the flow of redemptive history; final judgment. He was moving into Jesus' resurrection, and more, when he was interrupted.

(6) Paul was not a rookie. He had been through twenty years of tough ministry (read 2 Cor. 11), much of it before pagan biblical illiterates. To suppose that on this occasion he panicked and trimmed the Gospel is ridiculous.

(7) Acts 17 shows that Paul thinks "worldviewishly." Even after 1 Corinthians 2, Paul *still* thinks worldviewishly: 2 Corinthians 10:5 finds him *still* striving to bring "every thought" into submission to Christ—and the context shows this refers not simply to isolated thoughts but to entire worldviews.

(8) 1 Corinthians 2:1-5 does not cast Paul's resolution to preach nothing but the cross against the background of Athens (as if he were confessing he had failed there), but against the background of Corinth, which loved eloquence and rhetoric above substance. The apostle does not succumb to mere oratory: he resolves to stick with "Jesus Christ and him crucified."

∾

Genesis 49; Luke 2; *Job 15; 1 Corinthians 3*

∾

THE BOOK OF JOB NOW STARTS ON a second cycle of arguments from Eliphaz, Bildad, and Zophar, with responses in each case from Job (Job 15—21). In many ways the arguments are repeated, but with deepened intensity. Almost as if they are aware of the repetition, the three friends say less this time than in the first round.

Here we briefly follow the line of thought of Eliphaz's second speech (**Job 15**):

(1) Eliphaz begins in attack mode (15:2-6). From Eliphaz's perspective, Job cannot be a wise man, for he answers with "empty notions" and "fill[s] his belly with the hot east wind," uttering speeches "that have no value" (15:2-3). The result is that he even undermines piety and hinders devotion to God (15:4). Anyone who does not think that God fairly metes out punishment, Eliphaz thinks, is shaking the moral foundations of the universe. The cause of such renegade sentiments can only be sin: "Your sin prompts your mouth; you adopt the tongue of the crafty" (15:5).

(2) Without responding to any of Job's arguments, Eliphaz then returns to the authority question. Job has insisted that he is as old and experienced and wise as any of his attackers; Eliphaz rather sneeringly replies, "Are you the first man ever born? Were you brought forth before the hills?" (15:7). At most, Job is one old man. But a panoply of old men share the opinions of Eliphaz (15:10). Worse, in wanting to die, in wanting to justify himself before God, Job is declaring that God's consolations—all the consolations that the three comforters have been gently advancing—are not enough for him (15:11). It is as if Job wants to put God on trial.

(3) But how can this be? God is so holy that even heaven itself is not pure in his eyes (15:14-15): "How much less man, who is vile and corrupt, who drinks up evil like water!" (15:16). So Eliphaz repeats the heart of his argument again (15:17-26): the wicked person suffers torments of various kinds all the days allotted to him, all "because he shakes his fist at God and vaunts himself against the Almighty, defiantly charging against him with a thick, strong shield" (15:25-26).

(4) Eliphaz says that where there are apparent exceptions to this rule, time will destroy them (15:27-35). Such wicked people may be fat and prosperous for years, but eventually God's justice will hunt them down. The implication is obvious: Job is not only wicked, but his former prosperity was nothing but the calm before the storm which has broken and exposed his wretched evil.

Reflect on what is right and wrong with this argument.

∾

Genesis 50; Luke 3; *Job 16—17*; *1 Corinthians 4*

∾

WHEN JOB RESPONDS TO ELIPHAZ'S second speech, his opening words are scarcely less tempered than those of his opponents—though doubtless with more provocation (**Job 16—17**): "I have heard many things like these; miserable comforters are you all!" (16:2). Ostensibly they have come to sympathize with him and comfort him (2:11), yet every time they open their mouths their words are like hot, bubbling wax on open sores. From Job's perspective, they make "long-winded speeches" that "never end" (16:3). Job insists that if their roles were reversed he would not stoop to their level; he would bring genuine encouragement and relief (16:4-5).

There is a way of using theology and theological arguments that wounds rather than heals. This is not the fault of theology and theological arguments; it is the fault of the "miserable comforter" who fastens on an inappropriate fragment of truth, or whose timing is off, or whose attitude is condescending, or whose application is insensitive, or whose true theology is couched in such culture-laden clichés that they grate rather than comfort. In times of extraordinary stress and loss, I have sometimes received great encouragement and wisdom from other believers; I have also sometimes received extraordinary blows from them, without any recognition on their part that that was what they were delivering. Miserable comforters were they all.

Such experiences, of course, drive me to wonder when I have wrongly handled the Word and caused similar pain. It is not that there is never a place for administering the kind of scriptural admonition that rightly induces pain: justified discipline is godly (Heb. 12:5-11). The tragic fact, however, is that when we cause pain by our application of theology to someone else, we naturally assume the pain owes everything to the obtuseness of the other party. It may, it may—but at the very least we ought to examine ourselves, our attitudes, and our arguments very closely lest we simultaneously delude ourselves and oppress others.

Most of the rest of Job's speech is addressed to God and plunges deeply into the rhetoric of despair. We are unwise to condemn Job if we have never tasted much of his experience—and then we will not want to. To grasp his rhetoric aright, and at a deeper level than mere intellectual apprehension, two things must line up: First, we should be quite certain that ours is innocent suffering. In measure we can track this by comparing our own records with the remarkable standards Job maintained (see especially chaps. 26—31). Second, however bitter our complaint to God, our stance will still be that of a believer trying to sort things out, not that of a cynic trying to brush God off.

∾

Exodus 1; Luke 4; *Job 18; 1 Corinthians 5*

∼

THE SECOND ROUND OF BILDAD the Shuhite (**Job 18**) has a note of desperation to it. When the argument is weak, some people just yell louder.

Bildad begins by telling Job, in effect, that there is no point talking with him until he adopts a sensible stance (18:2). Job is worse than wrong: he is perverse or insane. In Bildad's view, Job is willing to overturn the very fabric of the universe to justify himself: "You who tear yourself to pieces in your anger, is the earth to be abandoned for your sake? Or must the rocks be moved from their place?" (18:4).

The rest of the chapter is given over to a horrific description of what happens to the wicked person—destroyed, despised, trapped, subject to calamity and disaster, terrified, burned up, cut off from the community. "The memory of him perishes from the earth; he has no name in the land" (18:17). People from the east and from the west alike are "appalled at his fate" (18:20)—and of course this means he serves as an admirable moral lesson for those with eyes to see.

Up to this point, the three "miserable comforters" have united in agreeing that Job is wicked. Unless the last verse of the chapter is mere parallelism, the charge now seems to be ratcheted up a notch: "Surely such is the dwelling of an evil man; such is the place of one who knows not God" (18:21). Job, in short, is not only wicked, but utterly ignorant of God.

It is time to reflect a little on this sort of charge. At one level, what Eliphaz, Bildad, and Zophar keep saying is entirely in line with a repeated theme of the Scriptures: God is just, and justice will be done and will be seen to be done. Everyone will one day acknowledge that God is right—whether in the reverent submission of faith, or in the terror that cries for the rocks and the mountains to hide them from the wrath of the Lamb (Rev. 6). The theme recurs in virtually every major corpus of the Bible. The alternative to judgment is appalling: there is no final and perfect judgment, and therefore no justice, and therefore no meaningful distinction between right and wrong, between good and evil. Not to have judgment would be to deny the significance of evil.

But to apply this perspective too quickly, too mechanically, or as if we have access to all the facts, is to destroy the significance of evil from another angle. Innocent suffering (as we have seen) is ruled out. To call a good man evil in order to preserve the system is not only personally heartless, but relativizes good and evil; it impugns God as surely as saying there is no difference between good and evil. Sometimes we must simply appeal to the mystery of wickedness.

∼

Exodus 2; Luke 5; *Job 19; 1 Corinthians 6*

∿

OUR TWO PASSAGES ARE linked in a subtle way.

Job's response to Bildad (**Job 19**) is striking in its intensity. It is almost as if he is willing to spell out the tensions and paradoxes in his own position. There are four essential planks to it. *First,* Job continues to berate his miserable comforters for their utter lack of support. Even if he had "gone astray" (19:4), it is not their business to humiliate him. *Second,* Job puts into concrete form what he has been hinting at all along: if he is suffering unjustly, and if God is in charge, then God has wronged him (19:6). Once again, a string of verses colorfully describes the way God has torn him down, blocked his way, shrouded his paths in darkness. *Third,* Job provides some graphic descriptions of his suffering. His breath is offensive to his wife; he is loathsome to his own brothers (19:17). In a culture where youth should respect their seniors, he finds that even little boys scorn him. His health has vanished; his closest friends display no pity or compassion. But *fourth,* the most paradoxical component is that Job still trusts God. In a passage renowned for its exegetical difficulties (19:25-27), Job affirms that he knows his "kinsman-redeemer" lives: this is the word that is used of Boaz in the book of Ruth (Ruth 2:20), and probably here carries the overtone of "defender." Despite the evidence of his current sufferings he affirms that God his defender lives, and "that in the end he will stand upon the earth" (in light of the next verse, this may be an eschatological reference, or it may refer to the end of Job's suffering with God standing on Job's grave). Job himself will see God with his own eyes, and for this his heart yearns within him.

The integrity and faithfulness of the man is astounding. He refuses to "confess" where there is nothing to confess, but he never stops acknowledging that God alone is God. Satan is losing his bet.

Interestingly, Paul, too, calls the Corinthian Christians to a certain kind of integrity (**1 Cor. 6**). The sad dimension of this chapter is that at least some of the Corinthians were compromising their integrity for no greater reason than the usual temptations plus a subliminal desire to act like the surrounding culture. They were not at all facing the kinds of pressures that confronted Job. They needed to learn that lawsuits between Christian brothers, trying to win against another, already signaled defeat (6:7); that Christian freedom is never an excuse for license, since believers pursue what is beneficial and they know that their bodies belong to another (6:12-20). These things Job already knew.

∿

Exodus 3; Luke 6; *Job 20*; *1 Corinthians 7*

∿

WHEN PAUL BEGINS TO RESPOND to the questions raised by the Corinthians ("Now for the matters you wrote about," 1 Cor. 7:1), the first thing he treats is marriage, divorce, and related issues (1 Cor. 7). And the first part of his discussion deals with sex within Christian marriage (**1 Cor. 7:1-7**).

(1) Typical of many of his responses to this divided church, Paul here displays his "Yes . . . but" pastoral sensitivity. "It is good for a man not to marry. But . . . each man should have his own wife, and each woman her own husband" (7:1-2). "I wish that all men were as I am. But each man has his own gift from God" (7:7). In short, Paul must answer not only their questions but their extremes. Ideally he must do so by bringing the factions together, commending each for whatever light it brings to the subject, while nevertheless helping each side perceive that it does not have all the truth on the matter and is in fact distorting wisdom.

(2) The NIV reads, "It is good for a man not to marry" (7:1). The Greek literally reads: "It is good for a man not to touch a woman." The NIV translators assume this is a euphemism for marriage. But more recently scholars have shown that this is not the case. Apparently there were Christians in Corinth who advanced an ascetic agenda. Paul is prepared to say there is merit in that perspective: after all, later in the chapter he points out the advantages of being single in gospel ministry. But asceticism is not the only value; indeed, it may become an idol, or a way of disparaging God's good gifts, or of refusing to recognize the diversity of gifts God bestows on his people. After all, marriage relieves sexual pressure; to deny sexual pressure and cling desperately to celibate asceticism may lead to gross sexual sins (as it often has). The societal answer, biblically speaking, is not open sex or lasciviousness, but marriage. That is not the only value of marriage, of course, but it is a real one.

(3) Notice how, in the arena of marriage, Paul insists that sexual privileges and responsibilities are reciprocal: e.g., "each man should have his own wife, and each woman her own husband"—which is a long way from treating the woman like chattel. How many reciprocal statements are found in this paragraph?

(4) Within marriage, neither partner is to deprive the other of normal sexual intercourse except under three conditions: (a) by mutual consent; (b) for the purpose of devoting themselves to prayer; (c) and even then only temporarily. Thus, according to Scripture, sex must never be used as a weapon, offered as a bribe, or withheld as a punishment.

∿

Exodus 4; Luke 7; *Job 21; 1 Corinthians 8*

$\sim$

THE SECOND SPEECH OF ZOPHAR (JOB 20) brings to a conclusion the second round from the three "miserable comforters." Job's response (**Job 21**) brings the cycle to a close.

If they cannot give him any other consolation, Job says, the least they can do is listen while he replies (21:2). When he is finished, they can continue their mocking (21:3).

The heart of Job's response is thought-provoking to anyone concerned with morality and justice: "Why do the wicked live on, growing old and increasing in power?" (21:7). Not only is there no obvious pattern of temporal judgment on the transparently wicked, but all too frequently the reverse is the case: the wicked may be the most prosperous of the lot. "Their bulls never fail to breed; their cows calve and do not miscarry" (21:10). They have lots of healthy children, they sing and dance. While they display total disinterest in God (21:14), they enjoy prosperity (21:13). It is rare that they are snuffed out (21:17). As for popular proverbs such as "God stores up a man's punishment for his sons" (21:19), Job is unimpressed; the truly wicked do not care if they leave their families behind in misery, provided they are comfortable themselves (21:21). That is why the wicked need to "drink of the wrath of the Almighty" (21:20) themselves—and that is not what usually happens. True, God knows everything; Job does not want to deny God's knowledge and justice (21:22). But facts should not be suppressed. Once the rich and the poor have died, they face the same decomposition (21:23-26). Where is the justice in that?

Even allowing for Job's exaggerations—after all, some wicked people do suffer temporal judgments—his point should not be dismissed. If the tallies of blessing and punishment are calculated solely on the basis of what takes place in this life, this is a grossly unfair world. Millions of relatively good people die in suffering, poverty, and degradation; millions of relatively evil people live full lives and die in their sleep. We can all tell the stories that demonstrate God's justice in this life, but what about the rest of the stories?

The tit-for-tat morality system of Job's three interlocutors cannot handle the millions of tough cases. Moreover, like them, Job does not want to impugn God's justice, but facts are facts: it is not a virtue, even in the cause of defending God's justice, to distort the truth and twist reality.

In the course of time it would become clearer that ultimate justice is meted out *after* death—and that the God of justice knows injustice himself, not only out of his omniscience, but out of his experience on a cross.

$\sim$

Exodus 5; Luke 8; *Job 22; 1 Corinthians 9*

∾

1 CORINTHIANS 9:19-23 IS ONE OF THE most revealing passages in the New Testament regarding Paul's view of the Law.

On the one hand, Paul states that to evangelize Jews he has to become like a Jew; more precisely, to "those under the law" he has to become like one under the Law, even though "I myself am not under the law" (9:20). Thus although Paul certainly recognizes himself as a Jew as far as race is concerned (see, for instance, Rom. 9:3), at this point in his life he does not see himself as being under the law-covenant. When he sets himself the task of winning his fellow Jews, however, he wants to remove any unnecessary offense, so he adopts the disciplines of kosher Jews; in this sense he becomes like a Jew, like one under the Law.

On the other hand, when he sets himself the task of evangelizing Gentiles, he becomes like "those not having the law." Recognizing that this stance could be understood as simple lawlessness, Paul adds, in a parenthetical aside, that this does not mean he is utterly lawless. Far from it; he writes, "I am not free from God's law but am under Christ's law" (9:21).

So on the one hand, Paul is not himself under law; on the other, he is not free from God's law, but is under Christ's law. What does this mean?

(a) The "law" under which Paul sees himself cannot be exactly the same as Torah (the Pentateuch), or more generally the demands of God from the Old Testament Scriptures. True, Paul elsewhere says, "Keeping God's commands is what counts" (1 Cor. 7:19). But these are not simply the commands found in the Old Testament. After all, the previous line reads: "Circumcision is nothing and uncircumcision is nothing. *Keeping God's commands is what counts.*" The thoughtful Jew would reply, "But circumcision is one of God's commands." Not, however, for Paul: keeping God's commands or obeying God's law is not, for him, the same thing as adhering to the Mosaic Law.

(b) What binds Paul and establishes the limits of his flexibility as he strives to evangelize Jews and Greeks alike is "Christ's law" (9:21). His statements make no sense if "Christ's law" is exactly identical to God's law as found in Torah. He must flex from his "third position" (the position of the Christian) to become like a Jew or like a Gentile.

(c) What the relationship is between the Mosaic "Law of God" and "Christ's law" is complex and glimpsed, in Paul, in Romans 3:21-26 (see meditation for January 31). Here it is enough to observe that the motive for all of Paul's magnificent cultural flexibility is that he may "win as many as possible," "so that by all possible means I may save some" (9:22).

∾

Exodus 6; Luke 9; *Job 23; 1 Corinthians 10*

∿

WE HAVE HEARD TWO FULL ROUNDS of speeches from the three "miserable comforters," plus responses from Job. There is one more round, a truncated and imbalanced one. Eliphaz speaks and Job replies (Job 22—24); Bildad speaks very briefly, and Job responds at great length (Job 25—31), with extraordinary sweep and fervor. The comforters have nothing new to say, and are winding down. Job's persistent defense of his integrity, though it does not convince them, grinds them into sullen silence.

Eliphaz's last speech (Job 22), though it extends the limits of his poetic imagery, does not extend the argument; it merely restates it. God is so unimaginably great, says Eliphaz, that he cannot derive any benefit from human beings. So why should Job think that the Almighty is impressed with his righteousness? That same greatness guarantees that God's knowledge and justice are perfect. If so, Job's sufferings are not groundless: God has winkled out Job's hidden sins—sins that Eliphaz tries to expose by shots in the dark.

While he responds with some arguments he has used before, Job embarks on a new line of thought (**Job 23**). He does not now charge God with injustice but with absence, with inaccessibility: "If only I knew where to find him; if only I could go to his dwelling!" (23:3). This is not a longing to escape and go to heaven; it is a passionate and frustrated desire to present his case before the Almighty (23:4). Job is not frightened that God will respond with terrifying power and crush him (23:6); he is frightened, rather, that God will simply ignore him. However, no geographical search Job can undertake will find God (23:8-9).

Job's words are quite unlike the modern literary protest that God is so absent that he must be dead. Job is not "waiting for Godot." His faith in God is at one level unwavering. He is perfectly convinced that God knows where Job is, and knows all about the fundamental integrity of his life (23:9-11). This integrity is not the bravado of a self-defined independent; Job has carefully followed the words of God, cherishing them more than his daily food (23:12).

That is why God's absence is not only puzzling, but terrifying (23:13-17). Job's continued confidence in God's sovereignty and knowledge are precisely what he finds so terrifying, for the empirical evidence is that, at least in this life, the just can be crushed and the wicked may escape. The "comforters" claim that Job should be afraid of God's justice; Job himself is frightened by God's absence.

When such days come, it is vital to remember the end of the book—the end of the book of Job, and the end of the Bible.

Exodus 7; Luke 10; *Job 24; 1 Corinthians 11*

∼

IN THE SECOND PART OF HIS REPLY TO Eliphaz's last speech, Job begins (**Job 24**) with a pair of rhetorical questions: "Why does the Almighty not set times for judgment? Why must those who know him look in vain for such days?" (24:1). The argument is not that God never rights the books, but that meanwhile a great deal of evil takes place without any prompt accounting, and righteous people suffer without any prompt vindication.

So Job begins another long list of representative evils, frequently unrequited in the short haul, yet commonly observed; and of public injustices (24:2-17). The wicked move boundary markers, steal cattle, abuse the poor and needy, put the poor into indentured slavery, rebel against the light, and feed their sexual lust. Meanwhile the poor barely get by, eking out a living from the wasteland. They glean in the vineyards of the wicked, they are often cold and wet, they carry the sheaves of others and go naked themselves. "The groans of the dying rise from the city, and the souls of the wounded cry out for help," Job contends. "But God charges no one with wrongdoing" (24:12).

The next big section of this chapter (24:18-24) is something of a puzzle. At first glance Job seems to be advancing the kind of argument his miserable comforters prefer: God answers the wicked in kind. Some scholars have suggested the passage has been misplaced; others think Job is deploying massive irony and means exactly the reverse. Yet perhaps the explanation is simpler. Job is not denying that justice will be done someday. To do that he really would have to change his view of God in very substantial ways. But Job acknowledges that the wicked will finally face judgment. They die; they are not remembered. God is not blind; he "may let them rest in a feeling of security, but his eyes are on their ways" (24:23). So in a while they are gone (24:24). All this Job acknowledges: "If this is not so, who can prove me false and reduce my words to nothing?" (24:25). But in the context of the first part of the chapter, the question remains: "Why does the Almighty not set times for judgment?" In other words, why does he wait until the end? Granted that he is the God of justice and that justice will finally be done, why wait so long for it, the wicked becoming more wicked and the victims still suffering?

It is a searing question. Part of the answer emerges later in the book. But at the very least we should acknowledge that instant judgment on every sin would have most of us in pretty constant pain, yelping like Pavlovian dogs to avoid the hurt, but without inner transformation. Do you really want what Job seems to be asking for?

∼

Exodus 8; Luke 11; *Job 25—26; 1 Corinthians 12*

∾

1 CORINTHIANS 12 BEGINS A three-chapter unit on tongues, prophecy, and other "grace gifts" (*charismata*) and their relation to love, which is the supreme "way" (not a gift) for the Christian. We may at least follow the flow of thought.

First, 1 Corinthians 12:4-6 affirms that there are diversities of gifts but one source. The implicit Trinitarian reference is striking: different gifts, given by the same *Spirit;* different kinds of service, but the same *Lord [Jesus];* different kinds of working, but the same *God.* This does not mean Paul is parceling these things up absolutely, as if, for instance, the gifts came from the Spirit but not from Jesus and not from God. Rather, this is a preacher's device for insisting that however diverse the gifts and graces, there is but one source: the triune God.

Second, Paul enlarges upon this principle of unity tying together diversity (12:7-12). The various gifts mentioned—the message of wisdom, the message of knowledge, faith, gifts of healing, and so forth—are not only manifestations of the one Spirit, but their primary purpose is the common good (12:7). So both in source and in purpose, they serve unity in their diversity. Moreover, although Paul will shortly say that Christians are to pursue the greater gifts (12:31), here he insists that in the final analysis the Spirit distributes them as he sees fit—which means there should never be pride in having this or that gift, nor covetousness toward another who has a gift you desire.

Third, the theme of the chapter is driven home in an analogy (12:12-20). The body is one, but it is made up of many parts that must function together. The analogy is apt, for Christians were all baptized by Christ in one Spirit (the Spirit here is the medium in which Christians are baptized, not the agent doing the baptizing, who is Christ) *into one body,* the church. Transparently, all the body parts are needed: it would not do for the body to be nothing but one giant eyeball, for instance. So the diversity and distribution of gifts in the church is to be cherished.

Fourth, it follows further that no part of the body has the right to say to any other part of the body that it is neither wanted nor needed (12:21-27). Indeed, in some ways the least presentable parts of the body should be accorded the highest honor precisely because they otherwise lack it. There ought to be so much empathy among the diverse parts that if one part is honored, all are honored; if one part suffers, all suffer.

Even though the applications to the church are obvious, Paul takes care to spell them out (12:27-31).

∾

Exodus 9; Luke 12; *Job 27; 1 Corinthians 13*

∿

THE LAST SPEECH FROM JOB'S "miserable comforters" is that of Bildad (Job 25), and it is pathetically short because even he now recognizes that he has nothing new to say, and neither do his friends. Job's answer is long and complex (chaps. 26—31), as if he is determined to drive his friends into silence. Some of it is mere review. The opening chapter (yesterday's reading, Job 26) finds Job mocking these "comforters" for their callousness, the sterility of their counsel in the face of suffering like Job's. It also finds him agreeing with them regarding God's unfathomable power. After a breathtaking review of God's powerful deeds, Job concludes, "And these are but the outer fringe of his works; how faint the whisper we hear of him! Who then can understand the thunder of his power?" (26:14). While the "comforters" charge Job with reducing God to impotence, Job so insists on God's transcendent power that he entertains the view that God is distant.

That brings us to **Job 27**. Here are all the tensions in Job's position. Job puts himself under an oath ("As surely as God lives") to make his point. He will never admit his opponents are right, for this would mean denying that he has lived his life with integrity: "Till I die, I will not deny my integrity. I will maintain my righteousness and never let go of it; my conscience will not reproach me as long as I live" (27:5-6). But ironically, the God by whom Job swears, whose greatness Job has praised in chapter 26, the God who provides the very breath in Job's nostrils (27:3), is also, Job insists, the God "who has denied me justice, the Almighty, who has made me taste bitterness of soul" (27:2-3).

More irony: this does not mean that God is corrupt or unjust. Job recognizes that God calls unjust and wicked people to account (27:7-10)—often in this life (27:11-23), but finally in death.

This is not Job's final position, of course; the drama is not yet over. But we may reflect on the place we have reached so far.

First, it is always best to be honest in our reflections on God, to avoid positions that distort facts (the folly of the three "comforters"), to remain transparent before God. He knows what we think anyway. Hope of advance is possible where there is honesty, but almost impossible where deceit reigns.

Second, this means that at various stages of a believer's pilgrimage there may be times when opponents will see in him or her conspicuous ironies or profound mysteries. One should not glory in contradictions, of course, but in matters relating to God, mysteries are inevitable. In time, some of these edge toward resolution, but almost always accompanied by the unfolding glory of new depths.

∿

Exodus 10; Luke 13; *Job 28; 1 Corinthians 14*

∾

A SUBTLE THEMATIC CONNECTION links **Job 28** and **1 Corinthians 14**.

People do not often understand just how rare real wisdom is. According to chapter 28, Job understands. The chapter is a poetic reflection on this very theme: "But where can wisdom be found? Where does understanding dwell?" (28:12). Job lists the places wisdom is not found and concludes, "It is hidden from the eyes of every living thing, concealed even from the birds of the air. Destruction and Death say, 'Only a rumor of it has reached our ears'" (28:21-22). Where then is wisdom found? "God understands the way to it and he alone knows where it dwells, for he views the ends of the earth and sees everything under the heavens" (28:23-24). And what is God's own summary? "The fear of the Lord—that is wisdom, and to shun evil is understanding" (28:28).

Doubtless in the context of the book of Job this chapter accomplishes several things. It pricks the pretensions of the "comforters" who think themselves so wise. It demonstrates that despite his protests, Job is still profoundly God-centered in all his thinking. Even while he publicly raises questions about God's fairness in his own case, Job insists that all wisdom finally rests in God. Moreover, because such wisdom is irretrievably tied to shunning evil, Job demonstrates by his poetic utterance that not only does he retain humility of mind before the Almighty, but his commitment to righteous living is profoundly tied to his faith in God's wisdom, to his own sheer God-centeredness.

There is no direct tie between this passage in Job and 1 Corinthians 14, of course. Wisdom is not specifically an issue in 1 Corinthians 14. Nevertheless, when one reads 1 Corinthians 14 after reflecting on Job 28, it is hard not to see how Paul's wise counsel regarding the use of the grace-gifts in the congregation taps into this larger picture of sheer God-centeredness. The first part of 1 Corinthians 14 compares and contrasts prophecy and tongues. The apostle's argument is that the key criterion is intelligibility. One can overhear the argument in the background. Some Corinthian Christians *like* to engage in a display of gifts that inevitably promotes someone's reputation. But Paul insists that intelligibility is at stake, both for believers and for unbelievers who may be present. In other words, godly wisdom in this matter concludes that the good *of others* is paramount; that entails lowliness of mind. The aim is not to gain a reputation for spiritual power, but to encourage others to conclude that God is truly present (14:25)—and that demands intelligible communication. Even the instructions to limit tongues and evaluate prophecies disclose a stance that is self-denying, honoring to God, God-centered. In short: it is wise.

∾

Exodus 11:1—12:20; Luke 14; *Job 29; 1 Corinthians 15*

∼

THE SUMMARY OF THE APOSTOLIC GOSPEL at the beginning of **1 Corinthians 15** is set out in a few points: Christ died for our sins according to the Scriptures, he was buried, he was raised on the third day according to the Scriptures. The last point is then expanded upon: after his resurrection, Jesus Christ appeared to Peter, to the Twelve, to more than five hundred at the same time (some of whom have subsequently died, though at the time of writing most are still alive and thus able to bear witness), to James, to all the apostles, and finally to Paul. The list is not meant to be exhaustive, but broadly comprehensive, with special focus on the official bearers of the Christian tradition and on Paul himself as one of them. Something of the significance of the resurrection is then unpacked in the following verses.

Some preliminary observations:

First, "the Gospel" is not in the first instance about something God has done for me, but about something God has objectively done in history. It is about Jesus, especially about his death and resurrection. We have not preached the Gospel when we have told our testimony and no more, or when we have conveyed an array of nice stories about Jesus, but not reached the *telos* (the goal or end) of the story told in the four Gospels.

Second, the primary events of this Gospel unfolded "according to the Scriptures." The precise way in which the Scriptures predicted these events— often by typology—is not our immediate concern; rather, it is the simple *fact* of the connection with Scripture that is so stunning. No one in the early church saw the significance of Jesus as something brand new, or standing in isolation from all that had come before. Rather, they saw him as the capstone, the culmination, the glorious goal, the climax of all of God's antecedent revelation in holy Scripture.

Third, this Gospel saves us (15:2). A great deal of theology is already presupposed by these few words: in particular, what we are saved *from.* Embedded here are Paul's understanding of human beings made in the image of God, the awfulness of sin and the curse of God that has separated us from our Maker, our inability to make ourselves over. The Gospel saves us—and always we must bear in mind exactly what it is that we are saved from.

Fourth, Paul makes clear not only the object of this saving faith (namely, the Gospel), but also the nature of this faith: it is faith that perseveres, that holds firmly to the word preached by the apostles. "Otherwise, you have believed in vain" (15:2)—a point often made in the New Testament (e.g., John 8:31; Col. 1:23; Heb. 3:14; 2 Pet. 1:10).

∼

Exodus 12:21-50; Luke 15; *Job 30;* 1 Corinthians 16

∾

IN DRAMATIC MOMENTS IN THE LIFE of Paul he is led by some intervening revelation. What we sometimes overlook is how much of his ministry is a function of planning, instruction, pastoral judgments, even uncertainties—much like our own ministries.

In **1 Corinthians 16**, Paul tells the Corinthians about his travel plans (16:5-9). He does not want to see them immediately, on his way to Macedonia, and make only a passing visit. Rather, he intends to go to Macedonia first, and then "perhaps" he will stay with the Corinthians a while, or even spend the winter (when it was unsafe to travel on the Mediterranean). "I hope to spend some time with you," Paul writes, "if the Lord permits" (16:7). Before embarking on any part of this trip, however, the apostle intends to stay for a while longer in Ephesus, "because a great door for effective work has opened to me, and there are many who oppose me" (16:9). In other words, he still has some unfinished ministry in that great city. Clearly there is uncertainty in Paul's plans, but he is trying to lay out the next few months of his service in ways that will be of maximum benefit for the promotion of the Gospel and the good of God's people.

The next two short paragraphs (16:10-12) suggest that the movements of Timothy and Apollos were not always entirely predictable either, though in both instances Paul provides the Corinthians with information covering certain eventualities.

Moreover, the first paragraph (16:1-4) finds Paul instructing the Corinthians to plan ahead in their giving. The "collection" that Paul mentions is a project to help poor Christians in Judea. He knows that if the Corinthian believers start collecting money only when he shows up, they will give little. Faithful, regular giving, set aside "on the first day of every week" (when Christians met for corporate worship, encouragement, and instruction), would ensure that a considerable sum would be raised. Of course, in those days money could not be electronically transferred; someone would have to transport it personally. Paul wants the Corinthians to choose men they themselves approve, and he will provide them with letters of introduction to the leaders in Jerusalem. He may even go with them. Clearly, these sorts of arrangements would vitiate any hint of financial impropriety on the part of the apostle. In this case, too, there is evidence of careful, godly, wise planning, and encouragement to the Corinthians to engage in the same.

Today there is a form of ethereal "spirituality" that wants to wait for explicit guidance for every decision, that regards a phrase like "if the Lord wills" as a sanctimonious cop-out. That was not Paul's perspective, and it should not be ours.

∾

Exodus 13; Luke 16; *Job 31; 2 Corinthians 1*

∿

ONCE AGAIN WE MAY USEFULLY reflect on both designated readings.

Job 31 is the final chapter of Job's last response to the three comforters. The closing three chapters of this address (chaps. 29—31) are dominated by two themes. First, Job now bemoans not so much his physical suffering as his loss of face and prestige in the community. He has been a man of dignity and honor; now he is treated with scorn, even by young men from contemptible families (e.g., 30:1). Second, although all along Job has protested that he is suffering innocently, now he discloses the habits of his life that explain why the opening chapter describes him as "blameless and upright," a man who "feared God and shunned evil" (1:1).

Indeed, one of the reasons why Job had been so honored in the community was that his righteousness and generosity were well known: he rescued the poor and the fatherless, assisted the dying, and helped widows (29:12). So also in the present chapter: almost in desperation because of the charges brought against him, Job lays out the evidence of his innocence. He made a covenant with his eyes "not to look lustfully at a girl" (31:1). He constantly remembered God's all-seeing eye (31:4), and therefore spoke the truth and dealt honestly in business (31:5-8). He avoided adultery; he dealt equitably with any grievance from his menservants and maidservants, knowing that he himself must one day face God's justice, and that in any case they are as human as he (31:13-15). Out of the fear of God, he was especially generous with the poor (31:16-23). Despite great wealth, he never trusted it (31:24-28), nor allowed himself to gloat over the misfortunes of others (31:29-30). So the chapter ends with Job maintaining his reputation for integrity, and finding no comfort.

Paul also suffers—not only the loss of possessions, family, and health, but the peculiar pressures of front-line ministry, and, worse, overt persecution (**2 Corinthians 1:1-11**). Of course, the circumstances are radically different. Paul knows, as Job did not, that he has been *called* to suffer (e.g., Acts 9:16). Moreover, Paul lives and serves this side of the cross: he self-consciously follows one who suffered unjustly for the sake of others. Perhaps most importantly, Paul knows that the encouragement he has received from "the Father of compassion and the God of all comfort" (1:3) he is able to pass on to others. He knows God "comforts us in all our troubles, so that we can comfort those in any trouble with the comfort we ourselves have received from God" (1:4). Pity those who have never been comforted; they never give comfort either.

∿

Exodus 14; Luke 17; *Job 32*; *2 Corinthians 2*

DESPITE HIS INTENTIONS, PAUL did not visit the Corinthians as he had hoped. He may have visited them on his way to Macedonia; he certainly did not do so, as he had expected, after leaving Macedonia (2 Cor. 1:16; see meditation for March 1). Apparently some of the Christians in Corinth held this against him, accusing him of being fickle. Paul replies that he is not the sort of person who says yes when he means no, or the reverse (1:17). The reason he did not go to Corinth, as he intended, was to spare them (1:23). How so?

The answer to that question is found at the beginning of **2 Corinthians 2**, which provides dramatic insight into the relations between the apostle and one of the more prominent churches he founded. The reason Paul did not fulfill his intention to visit Corinth is that he became convinced it would be "another painful visit" (2:1). An earlier visit, possibly on his way to Macedonia, had proved disastrous. Either before or after that visit (the sequence is not quite clear) Paul also sent a letter, writing "out of great distress and anguish of heart and with many tears" (2:4). The purpose of that letter was not to grieve them, but to assure them of the depth of his love for them (2:4). Apparently the substance of that letter was a strong exhortation that they impose sanctions on someone within the church who was sinning grievously.

It has often been argued that that tearful letter is 1 Corinthians, and that the man Paul wants disciplined is the man who is sleeping with his stepmother (1 Cor. 5). Certainly that is a possible interpretation. On the whole, however, 1 Corinthians does not sound like the letter Paul briefly describes in 2 Corinthians 2:4. It is more probable that he is referring to another letter, of which we have no other knowledge, one that insisted that the Corinthian church take action. At least some at Corinth have given Paul a very hard time over the issue. Now, however, good sense has prevailed, along with submission to the apostle (2:9). The church has punished the recalcitrant sinner, who duly repented, and now Paul encourages the believers to bring the sanctions to an end and forgive the man (2:5-10). Too severe a judgment may itself tempt the church to harshness, thereby falling into another of Satan's many ruses for outwitting believers and destroying them.

It is enormously encouraging to recognize in these interactions the vibrant vitality of early Christian relationships. Staid maintenance of the *status quo* may not be a sign of life; it may even be a sign of death. Where there are many new converts, there will be problems—and life.

Exodus 15; Luke 18; *Job 33*; *2 Corinthians 3*

∾

ONCE THE EXCHANGES BETWEEN JOB and the "miserable comforters" have ground to a halt, a new figure appears on the scene. Elihu's speech takes up chapters 32—37. He is a young man who has not spoken until now because the etiquette of the day demanded that the older men speak first. Elihu comes across as a rather bumptious individual who up to this point has only just barely restrained himself from speaking. But now he pours forth words like a torrent (as he himself acknowledges, 32:18-21) and vows that he will treat no one with corrosive flattery (32:22).

The substance of Elihu's address first takes form in **Job 33**. Once one allows for his slightly defensive pomposity, Elihu nevertheless has some important things to say. At several points he skirts very close to what the others have said, yet he veers away from their most egregious errors so that the total configuration of his utterance is quite different.

In this chapter he addresses Job; later he will address the "comforters." To Job he drives home two primary points.

First, Elihu asserts that although Job has acknowledged God's greatness—indeed, Job has insisted on God's greatness—he has gone over the top by so insisting on his own righteousness that he has made God out to be some sort of ogre. "I tell you, in this you are not right" (33:12). Wisely, Elihu stops there. He does not go on to say, as did the three "comforters," that Job should also admit to being thoroughly guilty. Job's sole guilt, so far as Elihu is concerned, is in charging God with guilt.

Second, Elihu asserts that God is not as distant and as inaccessible as Job makes him out to be (33:14ff.). God may come to a person in some strange dream of the night that warns him or her to abandon some evil path (33:15-18). Or—more to the point—God may actually speak in the language of pain, forestalling arrogance and independence (33:19-28). He may do these things more than once to someone, thereby turning back his soul from the grave (33:29-30). Elihu has thus opened up questions as to the purpose of suffering not entertained by either Job or his antagonists. He is certainly not saying that Job deserves all the suffering he is facing; indeed, Elihu insists that he wants Job to be cleared (33:32).

Apart from the importance of the issue itself—that suffering may have for its purpose something other than deserved punishment—the entire discussion reminds us of an important pastoral lesson. Of course, it is not invariably so; but sometimes *when two opponents square off and neither will give an inch, neither has adequately reflected on the full parameters of the topic.*

∾

Exodus 16; Luke 19; *Job 34; 2 Corinthians 4*

∾

IN JOB 34, AT FIRST BLUSH ELIHU seems to be repeating the arguments of the three "comforters." He summarizes Job's argument (34:5-9): Job says that he is guiltless, that he has done no wrong, and that God denies him justice. The implication is that there is no advantage, no "profit," in trying to please God (34:9). At this point Elihu sides with Job's three interlocutors. "Far be it from God to do evil, from the Almighty to do wrong" (34:10), Elihu insists; and again, "It is unthinkable that God would do wrong, that the Almighty would pervert justice" (34:12).

The following verses pile up more arguments along the same lines, and for a while it appears that Elihu will tumble into the same traps of reductionistic merit theology that devoured those he is rebuking. But then he adds an element that once again puts his speech in a framework a little different from theirs. Elihu leaves place for mystery. While he insists that God is utterly just, he does not conclude, as the three "comforters" do, that this means every case of suffering must be the direct result of God's just punishment. Elihu can ask, "But if [God] remains silent, who can condemn him? If he hides his face, who can see him?" (34:29). While Job flirts with the idea that God's silence opens him to a charge of unfairness, Elihu assumes God's justice, even if he (Elihu) does not draw out the inferences followed by the three miserable comforters. Elihu allows room for mystery, for divine silence that is nevertheless just silence.

Parts of Elihu's speech are hard to take. But in the framework of the book of Job, two factors stand out. *First,* when God finally responds, Job is corrected (as we shall see), and the three "miserable comforters" are roundly rebuked because, God says, they "have not spoken of me what is right, as my servant Job has" (42:7)—but no charge at all is laid against Elihu. That may reflect the fact that he is a bit player; but it also reflects the fact that his basic stance is right, even if the tone is a tad self-righteous. *Second,* in his hinted suggestions that there may be in God mysterious realties and hidden reasons to which we do not have access, Elihu anticipates some of God's own arguments when he speaks out of the storm in the closing chapters of the book (chaps. 38—41).

Biblical revelation provides us with many things to understand, some of which will require a lifetime of learning. But it also reminds us that God has not disclosed everything (Deut. 29:29). At some point God demands our trust and obedience, not merely our evaluation and understanding.

∾

Exodus 17; Luke 20; *Job 35*; *2 Corinthians 5*

∽

THINGS ARE NEVER QUITE AS GOOD as they might be. Or if for a brief moment they are as good as you can imagine them, if for a while you seem to suck in the nectar of life itself with every breath you breathe, you know as well as I do that such highs cannot last. Tomorrow you go back to work. You may enjoy your job, but it has its pressures. Your marriage may be well-nigh idyllic, but in a sour mood you may marvel at how much you cannot or will not share with your spouse. The warm west wind that tousles your hair metamorphoses into a tornado that destroys your home. One of your parents succumbs to Alzheimer's; one of your children dies. There is so much around you to enjoy, yet just as you begin to chew on a filet mignon that your children have bought for you for your birthday, you remember the millions who starve every day. There is no escape from the brute reality that, however wonderful your experiences in this broken world, others suffer experiences far more corrosive, and you yourself cannot ever believe that what you are experiencing is utterly ideal.

That restlessness is for our good. It is a design feature of our makeup, of our nature as creatures made in the image of God. We were made to inhabit eternity; by constitution we know that we belong to something better than a world (however beautiful at times) awash in sin.

Paul understands this point perfectly (**2 Corinthians 5:1-5**). He anticipates the time when "the earthly tent" (our present body) will be destroyed, and we will receive "an eternal house in heaven, not built by human hands" (5:1)—our resurrection body. "Meanwhile we groan, longing to be clothed with our heavenly dwelling" (5:2). It is not that we wish to "shuffle off our mortal coil" and exist in naked immortality: that is not our ultimate hope, for "we do not wish to be unclothed but to be clothed with our heavenly dwelling, so that what is mortal may be swallowed up by life" (5:4).

Then Paul adds: "Now it is God who has made us for this very purpose and has given us the Spirit as a deposit, guaranteeing what is to come" (5:5). God made us for this purpose, i.e., for the purpose of resurrection life, secured for us by the death of his Son. Moreover, in anticipation of this glorious consummation of life, already God has given us his Spirit as a deposit, a kind of down payment on the ultimate inheritance.

Small wonder, then, that we groan in anticipation and find our souls restless in this temporary abode that is under sentence of death.

∽

Exodus 18; Luke 21; *Job 36; 2 Corinthians 6*

~

ONE OF THE MOST MOVING VISIONS of apostolic ministry is found in **2 Corinthians 6:3-10**. It takes little knowledge of his letters to perceive that Paul is unwilling to compromise the Gospel. He is more than willing to bear the offense of the cross. But equally obvious is his willingness to put up with any personal inconvenience or suffering in order to get the message across. "We put no stumbling block in anyone's path," he writes, "so that our ministry will not be discredited" (6:3). By maintaining what he calls "our ministry," Paul is concerned to sustain not his personal reputation, but his credibility as an ambassador of Jesus Christ, as a servant of God. So he goes on, "Rather, as servants of God we commend ourselves in every way" (6:4).

This last sentence could be misleading, both in Paul's day and in ours. For a minister of the Gospel today to "commend himself in every way" sounds a bit like an ugly piece of self-promotion. One's imagination runs riot: the church bookstall selling T-shirts with "I love my Pastor Bob" emblazoned across the front, a stirring fanfare whenever he enters the pulpit, and so forth. The world of Corinth would also misconstrue Paul's words. So many itinerant teachers were profoundly self-promoting. That was how they gained students—by commending themselves, explicitly and implicitly, as the best at what they did.

But Paul's self-commendation suddenly takes a turn that neither the self-promoting types of ancient Corinth nor their smooth echoes in the modern Western church would want to follow. The framework of self-commendation Paul adopts, as a servant of God, is nothing like the framework of ordinary self-promoters, ancient or modern. Paul and other servants of God commend themselves "in great endurance; in troubles, hardships and distresses; in beatings, imprisonments and riots; in hard work, sleepless nights and hunger" (6:4b-5). Hard work? Ancient teachers were supposed to think and teach, not work hard with their hands. Riots? Are Christian apostles supposed to commend themselves as servants of God by the way they conduct themselves in riots!

Paul presses on: they are also to commend themselves "in purity, understanding, patience and kindness; in the Holy Spirit and in sincere love; in truthful speech and in the power of God; with weapons of righteousness in the right hand and in the left" (6:6-7).

Then there are all the projections people have of you: servants of God are to commend themselves "through glory and dishonor, bad report and good report" (6:8). Doubtless they are genuine, but many will view them as imposters. Indeed, Paul winds up his list with a litany of startling paradoxes (6:9-10).

Christian leadership, anyone?

~

Exodus 19; Luke 22; *Job 37; 2 Corinthians 7*

∽

SOMETIMES PEOPLE PRESENT PAUL as if he were a cold intellectual. Why "cold" should be connected with "intellectual," I am not sure. It certainly does not fit Paul. Obviously, God gave Paul a first-class mind. But he was also a man of passionate intensity.

In **2 Corinthians** 7 Paul testifies that, on the one hand, his joy knows no bounds (7:4); on the other hand, this joy has resulted from some news of the Corinthians that Paul received when he went to Macedonia. For on his first arrival in Macedonia, Paul had experienced no rest, but was "harassed at every turn—conflicts on the outside, fears within" (7:5). But then his fears and conflicts turned to joy when he received the good news about the Corinthians

What prompted this vast transformation in the apostle's outlook?

(1) Whatever the mechanics, Paul recognizes that the transformation was brought about by God, "who comforts the downcast" (7:6). In this case God brought comfort to Paul by restoring Titus to him, who brought with him some news of the Corinthians.

(2) The news Titus brought was that the Corinthians, however much they had been wounded by Paul's previous visit and by the painful letter he had sent, had regained their equilibrium. They now longed to see Paul and expressed "ardent concern" for him (7:7). Titus brought the news that the sorrow evoked by Paul's letter turned out to be a "godly sorrow" in that it led to repentance (7:8-10). Sorrow that generates repentance "leads to salvation and leaves no regret, but worldly sorrow brings death" (7:10). All this news of the Corinthians' reactions has filled Paul with joy and encouragement.

This indicates, of course, that Paul is intimately involved in the lives of the people to whom he ministers. His own emotions may go up and down as a function of how they relate to him. But what is striking is that Paul avoids two very common traps. (a) Obviously, he avoids the kind of professional distance projected by some ministers as a protective shield. (b) Although his own joys and sorrows are clearly tied to what the Corinthian Christians think of him, that link is not primarily a *personal* link. When that is the case, the minister loses his prophetic voice and will say and do only what he thinks will maintain the affection of the flock. Paul has felt duty-bound to reprimand the Corinthians, in person and in writing; he has not flinched from that responsibility. His joy that they have returned to him is thus inseparable from his joy that they have returned to faithful allegiance to the Gospel—the heart of his unbounded delight.

∽

Exodus 20; Luke 23; *Job 38; 2 Corinthians 8*

∾

AS WE APPROACH THE END OF THE DRAMA, God addresses Job directly for the first time (**Job 38**); he will continue to address Job through chapter 41. Elsewhere God speaks to Elijah in a still, small, voice (1 Kings 19); here God speaks to Job out of a storm (38:1), for he wants even the form of his communication, or its venue, to substantiate the large points he wishes to make.

God's first words are terrifying: "Who is this that darkens my counsel with words without knowledge? Brace yourself like a man; I will question you, and you shall answer me" (38:2-3). This opening salvo might lead the unwary to think that Job is the one with whom God is primarily displeased, and that the three miserable comforters have got off rather lightly. But like a drama that teeters back and forth between this perspective and that, this book is not finished yet. After all, the opening chapter records God's estimate of Job, and nothing in these chapters reverses that estimate. Further, I have already drawn attention to 42:7, where God says he is angry with the three friends (something he never says about Job), because they did not speak what was right about God (as God's servant Job did). God's terrifying challenge to Job in these four chapters must be placed within the larger framework of the book, if we are to make sense of the whole.

Job has repeatedly said that he wishes to question God. Now God says that he will question Job (38:3). Yet the nature of the barrage of rhetorical questions God raises in these chapters is scarcely the kind of questions Job wants to address. Job wants to talk about his own sufferings, about the justice of them, about God's role in sanctioning such sufferings, and the like. He wants to do this not least because he desires to maintain his justifiable reputation for integrity and righteousness. But God's questions focus on a much bigger picture. God asks, in effect: "Job, were you present at the dawn of creation? Do you have intimate knowledge of the entire world, let alone of the heavens? Do you control the course of the constellations—Pleiades and Orion, let us say? Were you the one who constructed the human mind, so that you can explain how it works? Does your word exercise the kind of providential sway that grants food to hungry ravens or to a hunting lioness?"

At one level, of course, this response does not at all answer the kind of questions Job was raising. At another level, it does. It warns Job that his capacity to understand is more limited than he thinks. It prepares us for the conclusion that God wants something more from us than mere understanding.

∾

Exodus 21; Luke 24; *Job 39; 2 Corinthians 9*

∽

THE SEPTEMBER 20 MEDITATION IN volume 1 worked its way through **2 Corinthians 9**. Nevertheless I want to come back to that passage.

Paul's carefully worded exhortation to the Christians in Corinth—to have ready for him the money they pledged to send to the poor in Jerusalem (chaps. 8—9)—need not be reviewed again. What I shall focus on for today's meditation is how Paul's exhortation about giving and money is tied to the Gospel.

In chapter 8 Paul invokes the example of Christ's self-giving: "For you know the grace of our Lord Jesus Christ, that though he was rich, yet for your sakes he became poor, so that you through his poverty might become rich" (8:9). Here in chapter 9 Paul says that, if the Corinthians come through with their promised gift, people "will praise God for the obedience that accompanies *your confession of the gospel of Christ,* and for your generosity" (9:13, italics added). In any case Paul never lets Christians forget that all our giving is but a pale reflection of God's "indescribable gift" (9:15), which of course lies at the heart of the Gospel.

So much of basic Christian ethics is tied in one way or another to the Gospel. When husbands need instruction on how to treat their wives, Paul does not introduce special marriage therapy or appeal to a mystical experience. Rather, he grounds conduct in the Gospel: "Husbands, love your wives, just as Christ loved the church and gave himself up for her" (Eph. 5:25). If you are looking for maturity, beware of any "deeper life" approach that sidesteps the Gospel, for Paul writes, "So then, just as you received Christ Jesus as Lord, continue to live in him, rooted and built up in him, strengthened in the faith as you were taught, and overflowing with thankfulness" (Col. 2:6-7). Of course, there is "deeper life" in the sense that Christians are exhorted to press on toward greater conformity to Christ Jesus and not to be satisfied with their present level of obedience (e.g., Phil. 3). But none of this is an appeal to something that leaves the Gospel behind or that adds something to the Gospel.

We must avoid the view that, while the Gospel provides a sort of escape ticket from judgment and hell, all the real life-transforming power comes from something else—an esoteric doctrine, a mystical experience, a therapeutic technique, a discipleship course. That is too narrow a view of the Gospel. Worse, it ends up relativizing and marginalizing the Gospel, stripping it of its power while it directs the attention of people away from the Gospel and toward something less helpful.

∽

Exodus 22; John 1; *Job 40*; *2 Corinthians 10*

∿

HALFWAY THROUGH HIS LONG SPEECH to Job, God gives him an opportunity to respond. Following a rhetorical question ("Will the one who contends with the Almighty correct him?"), God says, "Let him who accuses God answer him!" (**Job 40:2**).

It is vital for the understanding of this book that we do not misunderstand this challenge. God is not withdrawing his initial estimate of Job (1:1, 8). Even under the most horrible barrage from Satan and from the three "miserable comforters," Job has not weakened his fundamental integrity nor lost his basic loyalty to the Almighty. He has not followed the advice of his suffering wife to curse God and die; he has not followed the advice of his friends and simply assumed he was suffering for sins hitherto unrecognized and therefore turned to repentance. But he *has* come within a whisker of blaming God for his sufferings; or, better put, he has certainly insisted that he wants his day in court, that he wants to justify himself to God. Implicitly, and sometimes explicitly, Job has accused God of being unjust, or of being so removed that the just and the unjust seem to face the same ends. In his better moments Job steps back from the least restrained parts of his rhetoric, but he certainly feels, to say the least, that God owes him an explanation.

But now God is saying, in effect, that the person who wants to "contend" with God—to argue out some matter—must not begin by assuming that God is wrong or by accusing the Almighty of not getting things right. That has been the thrust of the rhetorical questions (chaps. 38—39): Job has neither the knowledge nor the power to be able to stand in judgment of God.

By this point Job has apparently absorbed the lesson: "I am unworthy—how can I reply to you? I put my hand over my mouth. I spoke once, but I have no answer—twice, but I will say no more" (40:4-5). But the question arises, Is Job really convinced that he was out of line? Does Job now really believe that, however righteous he may have been, he really does not have the right to talk to God that way? Or, devout man that he is, has he simply been cowed into quiescence?

God takes no chances: he presents Job with two more chapters (40—41) of unanswerable rhetorical questions. Once more Job is told to "brace [himself] like a man"—and then God begins: "Would you discredit my justice? Would you condemn me to justify yourself?" (40:8). It is as if God wants something more from Job, something that Job recognizes only in the last chapter of the drama.

∿

Exodus 23; John 2; *Job 41; 2 Corinthians 11*

∾

LIKE THE PREVIOUS THREE CHAPTERS, much of Job 41 is designed to help Job come to terms with his limitations. If Job admits what he does not know and cannot do—all of which God knows and can do—then perhaps he will be less quick to accuse God.

One verse, **Job 41:11**, demands further reflection. God speaks: "Who has a claim against me that I must pay? Everything under heaven belongs to me."

Is God's immunity from prosecution built on nothing more than raw power? We imagine the lowliest citizen in Nazi Germany trying to sue Hitler, and Hitler's brutal response: "Who has a claim against me that I must pay? Everything in the Third Reich belongs to me." Coming from Hitler, this would have seemed a distinctly immoral declaration. So why should God avail himself of its cosmic analog?

First, if this were God's only declaration about himself, it would not be a very good one. But this declaration comes within the context of the book of Job, and within the larger context of the canon of Scripture. Within the book of Job, there is common ground between Job and God: both acknowledge that in the last analysis God is just. Job is not a modern skeptic searching for reasons to dismiss God; God is not a Hitler. But if God and Job agree that God is just, at some point Job must also see that God is not a peer to drag into court. Trust in God is more important than trying to justify yourself before God—no matter how righteous you have been.

Second, within the context of the entire canon, God has repeatedly shown his patience and forbearance toward the race of his image-bearers, who constantly challenge him and rebel against him. He is the God who with perfect holiness could have destroyed us all; he is the God who on occasion has demonstrated the terrifying potential for judgment (the Flood; Sodom and Gomorrah; the exile of his own covenant people). Above all, despite the Bible's repeated insistence that God could rightly condemn all, he is the God who sends his own Son to die in place of a redeemed new humanity.

Third, within such frameworks Job 41:11 is a salutary reminder that we are not independent. Even if God were not the supremely good God he is, we would have no comeback. He owns us; he owns the universe; all the authority is his, all the branches of divine government are his, the ultimate judiciary is his. There is no "outside" place from which to judge him. To pretend otherwise is futile; worse, it is part of our race's rebellion against God—imagining he owes us something, imagining we are well placed to tell him off. Such wild fantasy is neither sensible nor good.

∾

Exodus 24; John 3; *Job 42*; *2 Corinthians 12*

THREE REFLECTIONS ON **Job 42**:

(a) Job's response to the Lord (42:1-6) is not, "Now I get it. Now I understand," but hearty repentance. He even summarizes God's argument back to him: "You asked, 'Who is this that obscures my counsel without knowledge?'" (42:3). Without a trace of self-justification, Job responds, "Surely I spoke of things I did not understand, things too wonderful for me to know" (42:3). Job is now certain that in the last analysis none of God's plans can be thwarted (42:2). In fact, God's massive self-disclosure in words to Job has revealed so much more of God that Job contrasts his present *seeing* of God with what he had only *heard* about him in the past—which of course reminds us that very often in Scripture God enables us to "see" him by disclosing himself in words. "Therefore I despise myself and repent in dust and ashes" (42:6). *This is not saying that the three friends were right after all.* Job is not now admitting to large swaths of hidden guilt that ostensibly brought on his suffering, but to the guilt of demanding that God provide him with a thorough explanation.

(b) The three friends are forgiven for all the false things they said about God only because of Job's intercession (42:7-9). This eminently suits the crime: they have been condemning Job, but only Job's prayers will suffice for their own forgiveness. What they have said that is not right about God (42:7, 8) can only be their simplistic tit-for-tat merit theology. They have allowed no mystery and grandeur; implicitly, they have allowed no grace.

(c) The drama ends with a massive vindication of Job. His wealth is restored (and doubled), he is given a new family, and all of the old honor in which he was held is restored and increased. Many a contemporary critic finds this fanciful, or even a secondary ending that some dumb editor has tacked on to the end of a more nuanced book. Such skepticism is profoundly mistaken. One of the points of the book is that in the end the people of God are vindicated. God *is* just. Similarly, Christians are not asked to accept suffering without vindication, death and self-denial without promise of heaven. Evil may now be mysterious, but it will not be triumphant. We are not spiritual masochists who can only be fulfilled by suffering. If there is any sense in which we delight in sufferings, it is that we delight to follow the Lord Jesus who suffered. Even he did not delight in sufferings. The pioneer and perfecter of our faith was the one "who *for the joy set before him* endured the cross, scorning its shame, *and sat down at the right hand of the throne of God*" (Heb. 12:2, italics added). So "let us run with perseverance the race marked out for us" (Heb. 12:1).

∾

Exodus 25; John 4; *Proverbs 1; 2 Corinthians 13*

BEFORE EMBARKING ON **PROVERBS 1**, I must say a little about "wisdom" in the Old Testament. For us, wisdom means something like sagacity. The wise person is insightful, perceptive, even shrewd, able to apply knowledge to diverse people and circumstances. One can understand why T. S. Eliot, in one of his more prescient anticipations of the digital age, asked where wisdom is now that it has been lost in knowledge, and where knowledge is now that it has been lost in information.

But wisdom in the Old Testament, though its meaning sometimes overlaps with modern English use, has a flavor all its own. At one level, it is a broad concept that embraces the structure of everything in God's universe, both substance and relationships, even before anything exists (cf. 8:22). The glory of God is manifested in such wisdom; it may even be manifested by his resolve to hide such wisdom (25:2). Yet at another level, wisdom in the Old Testament is simply a skill of one kind or another. (1) It may be the skill to survive, which is why ants and lizards are said to be extremely wise (30:24-28). (2) It is the skill to get along with people, what we call "social skills"—how to get along with friends, employers, rulers, spouse, and above all with God. Intuitively one glimpses how this practical "wisdom" or skill is related to the fundamental wisdom, i.e., to how things really are in God's universe. This use of "wisdom" is strikingly common in Proverbs. (3) Wisdom may refer to some technical skill or other (e.g., Ex. 28:3). In today's categories, one might have the "wisdom" to run a lathe or program a computer or sew a fine garment. One of these practical skills, one that overlaps with the second entry, is administrative skill, administrative wisdom. This includes judicial insight. It involves not only the mechanics of administration, but being able to listen attentively and penetrate to the heart of a matter (e.g., Deut. 1:15). This, of course, was the "wisdom" for which Solomon prayed (1 Kings 3); it is the wisdom that characterizes the Messiah (Isa. 11:2).

The proverbs of this book, then, are set out "for attaining wisdom and discipline; for understanding words of insight; for acquiring a disciplined and prudent life, doing what is right and just and fair" (1:2-3). The opposite of wisdom is therefore not only "folly" in some intellectual sense, but "folly" understood to be little short of sin. So the "son" of this chapter is exhorted to follow the instruction of Mum and Dad (1:8), or more generally, to pursue wisdom (1:20ff.); the alternative is to be enticed by sinners into some other path (1:10ff.).

Exodus 26; John 5; *Proverbs 2; Galatians 1*

∾

PERHAPS NOWHERE IS IT CLEARER than in **Proverbs 2** that the antonym of Old Testament wisdom is sin.

Solomon addresses his "son"—perhaps his immediate son and heir to the throne, or perhaps a more general reference. Solomon wants this son to "store up" his father's commands, to turn his ear to wisdom and his heart to understanding (2:1-2). If that is his passion, then (Solomon tells him) "you will understand the fear of the LORD and find the knowledge of God. For the LORD gives wisdom, and from his mouth come knowledge and understanding" (2:5-6). Such pursuit of wisdom will not make a person cunning or shrewd in a crafty sense. Far from it: "Then you will understand what is right and just and fair—every good path. For wisdom will enter your heart, and knowledge will be pleasant to your soul. Discretion will protect you, and understanding will guard you. Wisdom will save you from the ways of wicked men, from men whose words are perverse" (2:9-12).

We should reflect a little on such an understanding of wisdom. The cynical might condescendingly say that this vision of wisdom is too small. It is nothing but the parochial advantage of religious people. Genuine wisdom in our world is often associated with the kind of "sophistication" that moves comfortably, and with equal lack of commitment, around secularists, Christians, Buddhists, Muslims, pagans— taking from each a bit, rejecting other things, all in the name of a cosmopolitan wisdom. Alternatively, wisdom might be linked with the kinds of "people smarts" that enable you to run a large corporation and make your way in the business world or in the arts. Certainly it has nothing necessarily to do with religion.

Not for a moment should such gifts as "people smarts" be despised. But *by itself*, such "wisdom" would be judged raw folly in the Bible's view of things. From God's perspective, what advantage is there in gaining the plaudits of a culture that disowns God? Does not Jesus ask, "What good is it for a man to gain the whole world, yet forfeit his soul? Or what can a man give in exchange for his soul?" (Mark 8:36-37). If this is God's universe, if he is our Maker and Judge, why on earth (or beyond the earth, for that matter!) should anything be called "wise" that ignores him? How much less should it be called "wise" if it indulges in actions or attitudes forbidden by him? Far from the Old Testament wisdom being confined or too religious, for the Christian, who knows the living God, it is the only view of wisdom that makes sense. Any other stance is necessarily rather sad and frequently merely self-serving.

∾

Exodus 27; John 6; *Proverbs 3; Galatians 2*

∾

PROVERBS 3 INCLUDES SEVERAL well-known passages. Many Christians have been told not to be wise in their own eyes (3:7). The passage that likens the Lord's discipline of believers to a father's discipline of the son he delights in (3:11-12) reappears in the New Testament (Heb. 12:5-6). Growing up in a Christian home, I was frequently told, "Blessed is the man who finds wisdom, the man who gains understanding. . . . She [wisdom] is more precious than rubies; nothing you desire can compare with her" (3:13, 15). Wisdom is either God's plan or the personified means of establishing the entire created order (3:19-20).

But first place should go to 3:5-6, enshrined on many walls and learned by countless generations of Sunday school students: "Trust in the LORD with all your heart and lean not on your own understanding; in all your ways acknowledge him, and he will make your paths straight." Observe:

(1) The first part of this familiar text attacks the independence at the root of all sin. Our own understanding is insufficient and frequently skewed. The only right path is to trust in the Lord. Such trust in the Lord is not an ethereal subjectivism; it is the kind of whole-life commitment ("with all your heart," Solomon says) that abandons self-centered perspectives for the Lord's perspectives. In the context of biblical religion, that means learning and knowing what the Lord's will is, and obeying it regardless of whether or not it is the "in" thing to do. Far from being an appeal to subjective guidance, this trusting the Lord with your whole heart entails meditating on his word, hiding that word in your heart, learning to think God's thoughts after him—precisely so that you do not lean on your own understanding. Joshua was required to learn that lesson at the beginning of his leadership (Josh. 1:6-9). The kings of Israel were supposed to learn it (Deut. 17:18-20), but rarely did.

(2) The second couplet, "in all your ways acknowledge him, and he will make your paths straight," demands more than that we acknowledge that God exists and that he is in providential control, or some such thing. It means we must so acknowledge him that his ways and laws and character shape our choices and direct our lives. In all your ways, then, *acknowledge* him—not exclusively in some narrow religious sphere, but in all the dimensions of your life. The alternative is to disown him.

Thus the second couplet is essentially parallel to the first. The result is a straight course, directed by God himself.

∾

Exodus 28; John 7; *Proverbs 4*; *Galatians 3*

∿

"ABOVE ALL ELSE, GUARD YOUR HEART, for it is the wellspring of life" (**Proverbs 4:23**).

(1) In contemporary Western symbolism, the heart is the seat of emotions: e.g., "I love you with all my heart." But in the symbol-world of Scripture, the heart is the seat of the whole person. It is closer to what we mean by "mind," though in English "mind" is perhaps a little too restrictively cerebral.

(2) So "guard your heart" means more than "be careful what, or whom, you love"—though it cannot easily mean less than that. It means something like, "Be careful what you treasure; be careful what you set your *affections and thoughts* on."

(3) For the "heart," in this usage, "is the wellspring of life." It directs the rest of life. What you set your mind and emotions on determines where you go and what you do. It may easily pollute all of life. The imagery is perhaps all the clearer in this section of Proverbs because the ensuing verses mention other organs: "Put away perversity from your *mouth*; keep corrupt talk far from your *lips*. Let your *eyes* look straight ahead. . . . Make level paths for your *feet*" (4:24-26, italics added). But above all, guard your heart, "for it is the wellspring of life." It is the source of everything in a way that, say, the feet are not. Jesus picks up much the same imagery. "You brood of vipers," he says to one group, "how can you who are evil say anything good? For out of the overflow of the *heart* the mouth speaks. The good man brings good things out of the good stored up in him, and the evil man brings evil things out of the evil stored up in him" (Matt. 12:34-35, italics added). So guard your heart.

(4) Make this duty of paramount importance: "*Above all else*, guard your heart." One can see why. If the heart is nothing other than the center of your entire personality, that is what must be preserved. If your religion is merely external, while your "heart" is a seething mass of self-interest, what good is the religion? If your heart is ardently pursuing peripheral things (not necessarily prurient things), then from a Christian perspective you soon come to be occupied with the merely peripheral. If what you dream of is possessing a certain thing, if what you pant for is a certain salary or reputation, that shapes your life. But if *above all else* you see it to be your duty to guard your heart, that resolve will translate itself into choices of what you read, how you pray, what you linger over. It will prompt self-examination and confession, repentance, and faith, and will transform the rest of your life.

∿

Exodus 29; John 8; *Proverbs 5; Galatians 4*

∾

ALL OF **PROVERBS 5** IS A WARNING, in wisdom categories, against succumbing to an adulteress—a warning that keeps returning in the opening chapters of this book (e.g., 6:20-35; 7:1-27). Sometimes it appears that prostitution is in view; sometimes it is simple adultery.

In an age of heightened sensibilities about stereotypes, some have taken umbrage that the person doing the tempting is invariably an adulteress. In the real world, isn't the tempter at least as often the male, an adulterer?

Many things could be said, but four brief comments will suffice. (a) In part the warning is against an adulteress because it is offered to "my son" (5:1), following up on the fundamental structure of the genre (1:8; see meditation for March 15). (b) Even so, the "son" who goes off with an adulteress is certainly not shielded from blame. The errant son in this chapter is portrayed as more than a victim. This is the son who "hated discipline" and whose heart "spurned correction" (5:12). It is said of him, "The evil deeds of a wicked man ensnare him; the cords of his sin hold him fast" (5:22). He is guilty of "great folly" (5:23). (c) In this book, both wisdom and folly will later be personified as women (Prov. 9; see meditation for March 22). In other words, there is no univocal connection between women and evil. Men are often evil, and so are women. Both are called to pursue "Lady Wisdom." (d) In any case, in the larger canon there are many places where the primary blame for sexual misconduct is clearly laid at the man's door. That is true, for instance, of Judah's affair with Tamar, of Amnon's rape of his half-sister, of David's seduction of Bathsheba.

Adultery itself is wrong, or foolish, or sinful, or short-term, or undisciplined—whatever the category Proverbs deploys—and not just the adulteress. The chapter not only articulates warnings, but offers an alternative: a marriage that is cherished, developed, nurtured, not least in the sexual arena (5:18-19). But beyond all the immediate and cultural reasons for sexual fidelity in marriage is one of transcendent importance: "For a man's ways are in full view of the LORD, and he examines all his paths" (5:21). There are, of course, several similar verses in Scripture—e.g., "Nothing in all creation is hidden from God's sight. Everything is uncovered and laid bare before the eyes of him to whom we must give account" (Heb. 4:13). But in the context of Wisdom Literature, there is an additional overtone. Not only does God see everything, including any sexual misconduct, but it is the part of wisdom, the wisdom of living out life in God's universe in God's way, to please our Maker.

∾

Exodus 30; John 9; *Proverbs 6; Galatians 5*

∾

THE BEGINNING AND THE ENDING OF **Galatians 5**, taken together, tell us a great deal about the Gospel that Paul preaches.

In the first part, Paul is still trying to persuade his Gentile Christian readers in Galatia that adding Jewish heritage and ritual to their Christian faith does not add something to it, but subtracts something from it. In particular, if they submit to circumcision, then "Christ will be of no value" to them at all (5:2). Why not? What harm could arise from being circumcised? Paul explains that the Gentile who allows himself to be circumcised "is obligated to obey the whole law" (5:3). That was the symbol-significance of circumcision: it was the mark of submission to the law-covenant. But to take that step betrays a massive failure to understand the true relationship between the law-covenant and the new covenant that the Lord Jesus Christ introduced. The former prepares for the latter, announces the latter, anticipates the latter. But to commit oneself to obeying the terms of the law-covenant is to announce that the new covenant Jesus secured by his death is somehow inadequate. These Galatians, who have in the past clearly understood that men and women are justified by grace through faith, are now "trying to be justified by law," and in so doing "have been alienated from Christ"; it means nothing less than falling away from grace (5:4). The ultimate righteousness will be ours at the end, when Jesus returns. Meanwhile, "by faith we eagerly await through the Spirit the righteousness for which we hope" (5:5). To understand the crucial significance of Christ this way means that those who believe in Christ Jesus—what he has accomplished for us in his central place in redemptive history—know full well that circumcision itself is neither here nor there (5:6). But circumcision actually *subtracts* from Christ if one undergoes it out of a desire to submit to a covenant that in certain respects Christ has made passé.

While in the first part of the chapter Paul talks about the work of Christ, he slips in a brief mention of the Spirit: "By faith we eagerly await *through the Spirit* the righteousness for which we hope" (5:5, italics added). Already the Spirit is given to believers, consequent upon Christ's work. Christians, then, are those who "keep in step with the Spirit" (5:25), who display the lovely fruit of the Spirit: "love, joy, peace, patience, kindness, goodness, faithfulness, gentleness and self-control" (5:22-23). Pursue those things; there is no law against them, and they stand over against the wretched acts of our sinful nature (5:19-21; cf. **Prov. 6:16-19**) against which the Law pronounced but which it could not overcome.

∾

Exodus 31; John 10; *Proverbs 7; Galatians 6*

∾

IN AN EARLIER MEDITATION (vol. 1, September 30), I reflected on the flow of thought in Galatians 6. Here I want to focus on elements of **Galatians 6:1-5**.

On the face of it, there is a formal contradiction between 6:2, "Carry each other's burdens," and 6:5, "for each one should carry his own load." One could guess at a pastoral resolution. Christians should be concerned to help others; at the same time, they should not invert this concern and so depend on the help of others that they become nothing but freeloaders. In other words, 6:2 makes abundant sense when it is understood to forbid isolationism and to mandate compassion; 6:5 makes abundant sense when it is understood to forbid sponging and to mandate personal responsibility.

But the context of the paragraph in which both sayings are embedded enables us to go a little farther. The passage begins by exhorting Christians to restore, gently, a brother or sister who is caught in a sin (6:1). More specifically, Paul says that "you who are spiritual" ought to undertake this task. In light of the preceding verses (see yesterday's meditation), those who are "spiritual" are Christians who manifestly "keep in step with the Spirit" (5:25) and thus produce the fruit of the Spirit. This responsibility is laid on all Christians, but obviously some Christians are a little farther along in their fruit-bearing than others. So Christians who produce the fruit of the Spirit, as mandated of all Christians, should take primary responsibility for gently restoring a believer caught in a sin.

This should be a gentle restoration, not least because thoughtful Christians will recognize how they too may be tempted by this or some other evil (6:1b). By helping one another in this way—with encouragement, prayer, moral support, companionship, accountability, whatever—we thereby "carry each other's burdens" (6:2). This, of course, is equivalent to fulfilling the law of Christ, who not only taught that the greatest commandments are to love God and to love your neighbor as yourself, but gave us his "new commandment"—to love one another as Jesus himself loved them (John 13:34-35).

In such a regime, self-promotion is ugly, futile, and self-deceiving (6:3). Pride goes before a fall. It vitiates the quiet self-examination that is ruthlessly and patiently honest (6:4). Community-destroying, soul-deceiving pride is displayed when Christians compare their service records in order to put the other person down. Honest self-evaluation engenders a godly thankfulness and a legitimate pride that never puts another person down, for "each one should carry his own load" (6:5).

∾

Exodus 32; John 11; *Proverbs 8; Ephesians 1*

∽

IN GREEK, EPHESIANS 1:3-14 is one long sentence. Perhaps that is one of the reasons why even the best English translations are a little condensed and not simple to unpack. Here I shall focus on the first part, **Ephesians 1:3-10**, and reflect on how three themes come together: God's predestining sovereignty, God's unqualified grace, and God's glorious purposes.

The passage is a doxology, a word of praise, "to the God and Father of our Lord Jesus Christ"—and the following verses provide the reasons why we should praise this God and why his Son Jesus Christ is integral to his praiseworthy deeds. This God, Paul immediately says, is the One "who has blessed us in the heavenly realms with every spiritual blessing in Christ" (1:3). The "us" refers to Christians; the blessings we have received are "in Christ"; and the sphere of these spiritual blessings is "the heavenly realms." In Ephesians, "the heavenly realms" or "the heavenlies" refers to the heavenly dimension of our ultimate existence, *experienced in some measure right now.* So already we are being introduced to the third theme, God's glorious purpose.

If the description of God in 1:3 already exposes the reader to at least some of the reason why God is to be praised, the "for" at the beginning of verse 4 introduces the formal reason: even before the world was created, God chose us in Christ (God's predestining sovereignty) "to be holy and blameless in his sight" (God's glorious purpose). Indeed, "In love he predestined us" (God's unqualified grace and his predestining sovereignty) "to be adopted as his sons through Jesus Christ" (God's glorious purpose), "in accordance with his pleasure and will" (God's predestining sovereignty)—all of this "to the praise of his glorious grace" (both God's glorious purpose and his unqualified grace), "which he has freely given us in the One he loves" (God's unqualified grace). "In him we have redemption through his blood, the forgiveness of sins" (God's glorious purpose), "in accordance with the riches of God's grace that he lavished on us with all wisdom and understanding" (God's unqualified grace) (1:4-8).

Read through the rest of this passage and work out these themes (and there are others) for yourself.

The themes hang together in important ways. The more clearly one sees how sovereign is God's choice, the more clearly does his unmerited grace stand out. But sovereign "*pre*destination" is irrational without a "destination": God's purposes in his sovereign sway are thus inescapably tied to his sovereignty and his grace. The more we glimpse God's wonderfully good purposes, the more we shall be grateful for his sovereign sway in bringing them to pass.

∽

Exodus 33; John 12; *Proverbs 9*; Ephesians 2

∿

IN REAL LIFE, MOST OF US ARE A MIX of wise and foolish, prudent and silly, thoughtful and impulsive. Nevertheless it helps us to see what the issues are by setting out the alternatives as a simple choice. That is what **Proverbs 9** does for us. It pictures two women, Wisdom and Folly, calling out to people. In some ways, this drive toward a simple choice—wisdom or folly, good or evil, the Lord or rebellion—is typical of Wisdom Literature. It is a powerful, evocative way of getting across the fundamental issues in the choices we make.

Let us begin with Folly (9:13-18). The way Folly sits in the door of her house reminds the reader of a prostitute. She calls out to those who pass by, to those who otherwise "go straight on their way" (9:15). She is "undisciplined and without knowledge" (9:13). What she offers is never fresh: it is warmed over, stolen stuff, garnished with promises of esoteric enjoyment—not unlike the promise of illicit sex (9:17). Those who are snookered by her do not reflect on the fact that her seductions lead to death (9:17).

Wisdom, too, builds a house and calls people in (9:1-6). But her house is stable and well-built (9:1). Like Folly, Wisdom calls "from the highest point of the city," where she can be heard (9:3, 14); but unlike Folly, Wisdom has prepared a delicious and nourishing meal (9:2, 5). The "simple," i.e., those who do not yet have wisdom but are willing to acquire it, may come and feast, and learn to "walk in the way of understanding" (9:6).

Of course, to speak of informing or correcting the simple immediately draws attention to how the counsel of Wisdom will be received. There is a sense in which someone who accepts wisdom is already proving wise; the person who rejects wisdom is a mocker or wicked. Hence the powerful contrast of the next verses (9:7-9): "Do not rebuke a mocker or he will hate you; rebuke a wise man and he will love you" (9:8)—with the two alternatives fleshed out in the verses on either side of this one (9:7, 9).

The high point in the chapter comes with 9:10-12: "The fear of the LORD is the beginning of wisdom, and knowledge of the Holy One is understanding" (9:10). Normally, there are blessings even in this life for those with such priorities and commitments (9:11-12). Above all, this definition of "the beginning of wisdom" powerfully shows that the wisdom held up in Proverbs is neither esoteric insight nor secular intellectual prowess; rather, it is devotion to God and all that flows from such devotion in thought and life.

∿

Exodus 34; John 13; *Proverbs 10; Ephesians 3*

∾

PROVERBS 10 OPENS A NEW SECTION of the book of Proverbs, titled "Proverbs of Solomon" in most of our English Bibles (compare the sectional headings before chapters 25, 30, and 31). People who study these chapters debate over the extent to which each of these sections is organized, as opposed to preserving loose collections of proverbs. Almost all agree, however, that very frequently certain themes dominate a section. For instance, it is worth reading through chapter 10 and highlighting every word related to human speech: mouth, lips, chattering fool, tongue, and so forth. Proverbs 10:19 is choice: "When words are many, sin is not absent, but he who holds his tongue is wise."

Instead of pursuing this theme, today I want to reflect on what a proverb is. A proverb is not case law, i.e., a piece of legislation that covers a particular case. Nor is it unbridled promise. This affects how one interprets proverbs. Consider, for instance, 10:27: "The fear of the LORD adds length to life, but the years of the wicked are cut short." If this is unqualified promise, it follows that righteous people will invariably live longer than unrighteous people. Find someone who dies relatively young, and you know you are dealing with a wicked person. Someone who lives to the age of one hundred must be a righteous person.

But we know perfectly well that the world is not like that. Godly young people sometimes die of cancer. Having worked our way through Job, we are painfully aware that sometimes reprobates live to a ripe old age. And what shall we say of people who die unexpectedly in accidents, or in storms and other "acts of God," or in persecution?

Does this mean, then, that Proverbs 10:27 is robbed of all meaning? No, of course not. But it is a proverb, not an unqualified promise. A proverb is a wise saying, an aphorism. Most of the proverbs in this book provide wise, generalizing conclusions about how the world works under God's providential rule. The fear of the Lord really does add years to one's life: on the whole, a life lived in this way will adopt fewer bad habits, will learn to trust and therefore reduce stress, will honor hard work offered up to the Lord, will cherish family and friends, and so forth—and in God's universe all of these things have effects. None of this means that a godly person cannot die younger than an ungodly person. It does mean that, in a particular group of people, on the whole those who fear the Lord will live longer than those who do not. This is the blessing of God; the Lord has constructed the universe this way and continues his providential rule over it.

∾

Exodus 35; John 14; *Proverbs 11; Ephesians 4*

∽

I WISH TO DRAW ATTENTION TO three proverbs, or kinds of proverbs, in **Proverbs 11**:

(1) Like Proverbs 10, this chapter includes several proverbs that focus on the tongue, on human speech. The entire section 11:9-14 deals with one aspect or another of how the mouth may prove to be either a blessing or a curse. Among the more interesting elements is the twin mention of the fact that sometimes the most godly thing a mouth may do is keep silent: "a man of understanding holds his tongue. . . . a trustworthy man keeps a secret" (11:12, 13). Another striking feature of this section is its insistence that the mouth can either bless an entire city (and, in principle, a nation), or destroy it (11:10, 11, 14). The one tongue offers sage counsel, prophetic rebuke, strategic planning, utter integrity in matters of government and jurisprudence, a respectful humility in dealing with others, and transparent encouragement to walk in the fear of the Lord. The other tongue is pretentious, deceitful, happy to corrupt both legislative and judicial processes, self-serving, and manipulative.

(2) "Like a gold ring in a pig's snout is a beautiful woman who shows no discretion" (11:22). Structurally, the Hebrew is simple parallelism without predication: "A ring of gold in the snout of a pig / A beautiful woman without discretion." To make the Hebrew's subtle comparison explicit (since English poetry is not as dependent on parallelism as Hebrew poetry is), the NIV has constructed a simile. But the point is the same, and the imagery wonderfully evocative. The large, half-wild pigs of the ancient world had rings in their noses to control them. Never were those rings made of gold! The obvious silliness of the image would for the Jew carry a touch of repulsiveness, since pigs were unclean animals. On the same scale, but in a different dimension, the excellence of beauty in a woman is demeaned, debased to the level of a repulsive joke, when the woman herself shows no discretion. There is a great deal in our culture, and not just in Hollywood, that could profit from this proverb.

(3) "One man gives freely, yet gains even more; another withholds unduly, but comes to poverty" (11:24). Paradox is another feature of many proverbs. This sort of utterance is far more powerful than a simple exhortation, "We ought to be generous," or a simple slogan, "Generosity pays," or the like. The way our providential God has ordered the universe, the generous hand, as a rule, has much to give. Very often the selfish miser ends up in bitter penury. Can you think of examples?

∽

Exodus 36; John 15; *Proverbs 12; Ephesians 5*

❧

IN THE CONTEMPORARY CLIMATE, a straightforward reading of **Ephesians 5:21-33** is increasingly unpopular. Without descending to details, I shall venture my understanding of the flow of the passage.

(1) Oddly, the NIV prints 5:21 ("Submit to one another out of reverence for Christ.") as a separate paragraph. In the original, this is the last of a string of participial expressions that fill out what it means to be filled with the Spirit (5:18): functionally, being filled with the Spirit means everything in 5:19-21. Moreover, the words "submit to one another" should not be taken in a mutually reciprocal way, as if exhorting all Christians to submit to one another reciprocally. For: (a) the verb "to submit" in Greek *always* refers to submission in some sort of ordered array, *never* to mutual deference; (b) the idea is then picked up in the following "household table" of duties: wives submit to husbands, children to parents, and slaves to masters (5:22—6:4); (c) the same vision of submission is repeated in the New Testament (Col. 3:18-19; Titus 2:4-5; 1 Pet. 3:1-6); (d) the Greek pronoun rendered "one another" is often not reciprocal (e.g., Rev. 6:4).

(2) Nevertheless, certain things must be said about the wife's submission to her husband (5:22-24). (a) It is not to be confused with certain pathetic stereotypes—groveling, self-pity, unequal pay for equal work (as if God were the God of injustice), and the like. (b) This submission is modeled on the church's responsibility to submit to Christ. This brings up large issues of typology that cannot be explored here. But practically, it ought to reduce nagging, belittling one's husband, browbeating manipulation, and the like. (c) This submission does *not* deny equal worth (both are made in the image of God) or perfect functional equality in many domains (e.g., sexual rights, in 1 Cor. 7).

(3) Husbands are to love their wives as Christ loved the church (5:25-33)—which at the very least means loving their wives self-sacrificially and for their good. More explicitly, the husband's love for his wife must mirror Christ's love for his church (a) in its self-sacrifice (5:25); (b) in its goal (5:26-28a), seeking her good and her holiness; (c) in its self-interest (5:28b-30)—for there is a kind of identification that the husband makes with his wife, as Christ identifies himself with his church; (d) in its typological fulfillment (5:31-33)—which again introduces huge typological structures that run right through the Bible.

The responsibilities of *both* husband and wife are dramatically opposed to self-interest.

❧

Exodus 37; John 16; *Proverbs 13; Ephesians 6*

∽

THE PARALLELISM IN THE Bible's Wisdom Literature is diverse. Understanding this helps us to reflect more accurately on Scripture. It is easy to illustrate the point with two or three kinds of parallelism drawn from **Proverbs 13**.

Some instances of parallelism are simple opposites. "He who walks with the wise grows wise, / but a companion of fools suffers harm" (13:20). The second line is almost the opposite of the first, and the two lines together remind readers that they will be shaped by the company they keep and by the advice they listen to. "He who spares the rod hates his son, / but he who loves him is careful to discipline him" (13:24). The first line may employ a touch of hyperbole, but the contrast between the two lines makes the lesson of the whole verse clear enough.

In some cases the second line is not the opposite of the first line, but an extension of it. "The teaching of the wise is a fountain of life, / turning a man from the snares of death" (13:14). Of course, there is a contrast between "life" and "death," nevertheless the thought of the second line is not the opposite to what is expressed in the first line, but a further exposition of it. This is sometimes called "step parallelism."

Perhaps the proverbs that demand the most focused reflection are those in which the two lines are obviously meant to be opposites, and yet the categories do not, on first reading, quite line up. Such proverbs are gently provocative. Each of the two lines is subtly shaped by the other.

Here are two examples. "Pride only breeds quarrels, / but wisdom is found in those who take advice" (13:10). Merely formal parallelism might have preferred, "Pride only breeds quarrels, / but humility generates peace." But the text of Scripture invites more profound analysis. "Wisdom" is contrasted with "pride"— which gently discloses what wisdom is, while implicitly saying that pride is folly. The quarrels of the first line are generated by the arrogant refusal to listen to another point of view, to take advice.

Or again, "Every prudent man acts out of knowledge, but a fool exposes his folly" (13:16). A simple contrast would have preferred: "Every prudent man acts out of knowledge, / but a fool acts out of ignorance [or folly]." But the second line says that the fool exposes his folly. The two lines become mutually clarifying. The prudent man who acts out of knowledge (line 1) thereby displays his wisdom; the fool acts out of folly, and thereby exposes it for all to see. In this light, reflect on Psalm 14:1!

∽

Exodus 38; John 17; *Proverbs 14; Philippians 1*

$\backsim$

WHAT DOES IT MEAN TO "conduct yourselves in a manner worthy of the gospel of Christ" (Philippians 1:27)? The expression is striking. It is also adverbial—that is, it describes the manner of our conduct, not us. Paul does not say that we ourselves are worthy of the Gospel, for that would be a contradiction in terms: the Gospel, by definition, is good news to people who are not worthy of it. But once we have received the Gospel, however unworthy we may be, we are to conduct ourselves in a manner worthy of it.

The way Christians are to do this (**Philippians 1:27-30**) is by standing firm together ("in one spirit," 1:27), "contending as one man for the faith of the gospel without being frightened in any way by those who oppose [them]" (1:27-28). People who have benefited from the Gospel are certainly not conducting themselves in a way worthy of the Gospel if they are ashamed of it (Rom. 1:16). Of course, in a time when the surrounding culture ridicules Christians or even persecutes them, it takes courage to stand together in bold and transparent witness to the power of the Gospel. But there, too, another element of what it means to conduct oneself in a manner worthy of the Gospel comes into play. "For it has been granted to you on behalf of Christ not only to believe on him, but also to suffer for him" (1:29).

What a remarkable notion! Paul does not say that these Christians have been *called* to suffer as well as to believe, but that it has been *granted* to them to suffer as well as to believe—as if both suffering for Christ and believing in Christ were blessed privileges that have been graciously granted. That, of course, is precisely what he means. We often think of *faith* as a gracious gift of God (Eph. 2:8-9), but *suffering*?

Yet that is what Paul says. On reflection, it is easy to see why. The Gospel of Jesus Christ is that in God's good purposes Jesus suffered on our behalf, bearing our guilt and shame and atoning for our sin. Surely it should be no surprise, then, that conduct that is worthy of such a Gospel includes suffering for Jesus. In fact, that theme is part of what makes this paragraph transitional. For on the one hand, it looks back to the example of the apostle Paul (1:12-26). He ends the paragraph by referring to his own "struggle" (1:30), of which his Philippian readers have just read—a "struggle" so severe he was not certain he would survive. And on the other hand, the chapter ahead is one of the most powerful New Testament descriptions of Jesus' humiliation and death. We are to conduct ourselves in a manner worthy of that kind of good news.

$\backsim$

Exodus 39; John 18; *Proverbs 15; Philippians 2*

∾

FEW PASSAGES HAVE AS MUCH THEOLOGY and ethics in them as **Philippians 2**. We can pick up on only a few of its wonderful themes:

(1) Scholars have translated 2:5-11 in all kinds of creative ways. In large measure the NIV has it right. Christ Jesus, we are told, "did not consider equality with God something to be grasped [or possibly "exploited"], but made himself nothing, taking the very nature of a servant, being made in human likeness" (2:6-7). All that is quite wonderful, a glorious description of the incarnation that prepares the way for the cross. I might reword the translation in the first line of verse 6: "Who, being in very nature God." At the level of raw literalism, that is a perfectly acceptable translation. But Greek uses participles far more frequently than does English, and Greek adverbial participles, such as the word *being* in this line, have various logical relations with their context—relations that must be determined by the context. Probably most English readers mentally paraphrase this passage as, "Who, although he was in very nature God . . ." Certainly that makes sense and may even be right. But there are good contextual reasons for thinking that the participle is causal: "Who, *because* he was in very nature God." In other words, because he was in very nature God, not only did he not consider equality with God something to be exploited, but he made himself a nobody: it was divine to show that kind of self-emptying, that kind of grace.

(2) "Your attitude should be the same as that of Christ Jesus" (2:5), who did not regard his rights as something to be exploited, but who humbled himself and died a death of odious ignominy so that we might be saved—and was ultimately vindicated (2:6-11). The exhortation of 2:5 thus supports the string of exhortations in 2:1-4. Reflect on how this is so.

(3) The verses following the "Christ hymn" (as it is often called) of 2:6-11 emphasize perseverance. "Therefore" at the beginning of verse 12 establishes the connection. Christ made himself a nobody and died a shameful death but was finally and gloriously vindicated, and therefore we too should take the long view and "work out" our salvation "with fear and trembling" (2:12). Of course, there is all the more incentive when we recall that "it is God who works in [us] to will and to act according to his good purpose" (2:13). We reject utter passivity, "letting go and letting God"; rather, we work out our salvation. Yet at the same time we joyfully acknowledge that both our willing and our doing are evidence of God's working in us. And he will vindicate us.

∾

Exodus 40; John 19; *Proverbs 16; Philippians 3*

∾

IN PAUL'S LETTERS HE OFTEN, implicitly or explicitly, tells his readers not only to understand and follow what he teaches, but to imitate him. Nowhere is this theme stronger than in **Philippians 3**, reaching a climax in 3:17: "Join with others in following my example, brothers, and take note of those who live according to the pattern we gave you." Not only does Paul instruct believers to imitate him; he has been building up a cadre of leaders who exemplify the pattern of life he has been teaching, so that they can serve as models for others to follow. Some reflections:

(1) Almost certainly one of the reasons why Paul provides so many details about Timothy and Epaphroditus (2:19-30) is so that they may serve as models to be admired and emulated. Paul says of Timothy, "I have no one else like him, who takes a genuine interest in your welfare. For everyone looks out for his own interests, not those of Jesus Christ" (2:20-21). He expects the more godly among his readers to react instinctively and resolve to become like Timothy. Paul is even more explicit with respect to Epaphroditus. After detailing the man's Christian courage, Paul adds, "Welcome him in the Lord with great joy, and honor men like him" (2:29)—not only "him," but "men like him," for Paul teaches patterns of life that should be admired and imitated.

(2) Paul's suggestion that the Philippians imitate Timothy and Epaphroditus, and his instructions that they follow his own example and the pattern of living Paul had regularly taught (3:17), is proffered in part as an antidote to the alternative models that surround us. The assumption is that we inevitably imitate someone. There is always an abundant supply of bad models. Paul warns against "those dogs" (3:2) who were trying to impose observance of Jewish covenantalism. Doubtless they appeared wonderfully pious. The apostle similarly warns against the "enemies of the cross of Christ" (3:18) who, judging by the context, are almost certainly professing Christians who do not really grasp what the Gospel is about and who do not really live with eternity's values in view. They too must have had some plausibility, or Paul would not have warned against them. Christians must be *intentional* in choosing whom they should imitate, or else they may drift toward poor models.

(3) Paul's strong exhortation that the Philippians follow his example is saved from self-righteousness and religious cant by his insistence that he himself has not arrived, but is still on a pilgrimage (3:7-16).

So follow someone who follows Christ; follow a pilgrim who insists that you live up to what you have already attained, and then press for more.

∾

Leviticus 1; John 20; *Proverbs 17; Philippians 4*

∾

FOUR MORE KINDS OF proverbs appear in **Proverbs 17**:

(1) Several proverbs offer an evaluative comparison introduced by the word *better*. "Better a dry crust with peace and quiet / than a house full of feasting, with strife" (17:1). "Better to meet a bear robbed of her cubs / than a fool in his folly" (17:12). The first of these two provides a value judgment to be observed and cherished; the second makes an important assessment of the "fool," with an implied warning to avoid such company. There are many of these "better" proverbs in other chapters—e.g., "Better to be lowly in spirit among the oppressed / than to share plunder with the proud" (16:19); "Better to live on a corner of the roof / than to share a house with a quarrelsome wife" (21:9).

(2) A few proverbs take the form of rhetorical questions. "Of what use is money in the hand of a fool, / since he has no desire to get wisdom?" (17:16). This one is quite wonderful. It suggests that using money in ways that do not make you "wise" is so unprofitable that you would be better off without money.

(3) Some proverbs seem quite simple, but include an unexpected element that prompts the reader to ponder what is being said. "A wicked man listens to evil lips; / a liar pays attention to a malicious tongue" (17:4). One might have expected "A wicked man speaks with evil lips; / a liar deploys his malicious tongue." That would be true, but comparatively prosaic. The evil lips and the malicious tongue in 17:4 are doubtless wicked, but the writer does not pause to argue the point. Rather, he focuses on the character of those who *listen* to evil lips, on those who pay attention to the malicious tongue. Perhaps the worst punishment of liars is not that they are not believed, but that they do not believe truth but prefer lies—both their own and the lies of others. And what does this proverb say about a culture that loves juicy sleaze, or comforting half-truths, or squalid, vacuous violence? Who buys the porn and the cash register "newspapers"? Such organs cannot stay in business if there is no market. How could local church gossips keep in business if they did not find ready ears—wicked ears, according to this proverb?

(4) A surprising number of proverbs tell us explicitly what the Lord does. Often we are told what the Lord loves or detests, to help us form our own values; but sometimes it is something else, such as, "[T]he LORD tests the heart" (17:3); "Acquitting the guilty and condemning the innocent—the LORD detests them both" (17:15). For other examples, read 15:8, 9, 25, 26, 29; 16:4.

∾

Leviticus 2—3; John 21; *Proverbs 18; Colossians 1*

∾

A NUMBER OF PROVERBS in this book bear on the matter of disputes. Some deal with the judicial level—e.g., "It is not good to be partial to the wicked or to deprive the innocent of justice" (18:5). Again, "The first to present his case seems right, till another comes forward and questions him" (18:17)—a proverb that has application in wider settings than the courtroom. This judicial element is scarcely surprising, since of course Solomon himself was the final court of appeal in his kingdom. But many of these proverbs about disputes have little to do with the judicial system (although even the most private of disputes may go to court—and it may well be that Solomon's reflections even about private disputes were stimulated by some of the things he saw dragged into court). There are two such proverbs here: **Proverbs 18:13, 18.**

(1) "He who answers before listening—that is his folly and his shame" (18:13). This, of course, invites wide application. We think of those exasperating, aggressive conversationalists who rarely let you finish a sentence or a thought before they interject their own viewpoint. How much worse is the situation when neither side in a dispute really listens to the other side. In rare cases, of course, there is literally nothing to be said in favor of one particular side. But almost always there is at least *something* to be said for a contrary position, even if on balance it is not all that defensible. But how can you find out if you do not really listen? How can you hope to convince the other party of what you are saying if you cannot give that party the grace of courteous listening? In most disputes, tensions will improve if one party takes the initiative to lower the volume, slow the pace, cool the rhetoric, and humbly try to *listen* and discover exactly what the other side is saying.

(2) "Casting the lot settles disputes and keeps strong opponents apart" (18:18). "Casting the lot" might refer to the priestly function of appealing to the Urim and Thummim for guidance (e.g., Ex. 28:30). But I suspect not. Some disputes become so vicious or so complex that the simplest way of sorting them out is to flip a coin—provided, of course, that both parties will agree to abide by the outcome. Some disputes cannot and should not be resolved in this manner. But where both sides, deep down, acknowledge that their dispute is six of one and half a dozen of the other, this might be the simplest way forward.

Inescapably clear from all this is the Bible's profound commitment to truth, to integrity in listening and speaking, and to peace as much as to justice.

∾

Leviticus 4; Psalms 1—2; *Proverbs 19; Colossians 2*

AT AN EARLY STAGE, I WORKED through Proverbs and categorized most of the individual proverbs according to topic. Some fitted into more than one topic. I recognized that there was a disadvantage in this approach: I would lose the thematic connections in some large blocks of material. Still, there was also a gain. I could see at a glance all that Proverbs had to say about poverty, for instance, or about the family, or about human speech.

One of the themes thus clarified is God's sovereignty, worked out in sometimes mysterious providence. There is one verse on this topic in this chapter: "Many are the plans in a man's heart, but it is the LORD's purpose that prevails" (**Proverbs 19:21**). By itself, of course, this might mean no more than that the Lord proves to be a superb chess player! Yet this verse is linked to an important set of passages (e.g., 20:24) that demand we think more deeply than that. For instance:

(1) "The LORD works out everything for his own ends—even the wicked for a day of disaster" (16:4). We should not seek to evade the sweep of this utterance. This is not a dualist universe in which two autonomous principles operate, one good and one evil. While there is a basic distinction between good and evil, yet God's sovereignty reigns, through whatever mysterious means, so that even the wicked serve his purposes—not least his purposes in judgment. Paul reflects on the same theme (Rom. 9:22).

(2) "In his heart a man plans his course, but the LORD determines his steps" (16:9). Human beings are responsible for what they choose and what they do; the entire book of Proverbs maintains this perspective, for otherwise the fundamental chasms between wisdom and folly, good and evil, the fear of the Lord and haughty arrogance, could not be sustained. Yet at the same time, even with all the plotting in the world a mere human cannot escape the sweep of divine sovereignty. Elsewhere we are told, "The king's heart is in the hand of the LORD; he directs it like a watercourse wherever he pleases" (21:1).

(3) "The lot is cast into the lap, but its every decision is from the LORD" (16:33). This is a bit like saying that you can throw the dice as many times as you like, but which numbers come up is determined by the Almighty. This is why Christians have spoken of "the mystery of providence." One cannot determine the moral excellence of an occurrence by the mere fact that it happens, since God's providence rules over both good and evil, over every number that comes up. For moral distinctions, one needs God's own pronouncements, his words, his law.

Leviticus 5; Psalms 3—4; *Proverbs 20; Colossians 3*

∾

THE CONTRASTS IN COLOSSIANS 3 are so stark they are haunting. On the one hand, the sins in 3:5-9 are foul: sexual immorality, impurity, lust, evil desires, greed, anger, rage, malice, slander, filthy language, lying. Greed is labeled "idolatry" (3:5). One can see why. In effect, one worships what one most desires. If greed lies at the heart of our deepest desires, then acquisitiveness has become our god, and we are idolaters.

On the other hand, the virtues briefly spelled out in 3:12-17 have always been associated with genuine Christian character. Here I wish to focus on the last two verses: "Let the word of Christ dwell in you richly as you teach and admonish one another with all wisdom, and as you sing psalms, hymns and spiritual songs with gratitude in your hearts to God. And whatever you do, whether in word or deed, do it all in the name of the Lord Jesus, giving thanks to God the Father through him" (3:16-17).

(1) The "word of Christ" is not exactly the Scriptures. It is the Gospel—but the primary access we have to that Gospel is the Scriptures. The expression "word of Christ" is sufficiently flexible that it can mean either the word that Christ taught or the word about Christ. Insofar as the Gospel itself was both proclaimed by Jesus Christ and so embodied in his person and ministry that it is also what the apostles say about him, "the word of Christ" embraces both meanings.

(2) This is what is to dwell in us richly. It is to fill our memories, occupy our horizons, constitute our priorities. We are so to reflect on it, as we turn it over in our minds and learn how it applies in every area of our lives, that, far from occupying a little religious corner of our experience, it will dwell in us richly.

(3) This must take place not only in the privacy of personal study and reflection but also in our mutual instruction and admonition. Whatever teaching takes place within the local church, it must be full of the Gospel and its rich, life-transforming implications and applications.

(4) Over against all that is foul and all that is idolatrous, Christians are to be characterized by gratitude. We have been called to peace, the apostle says. "And be thankful" (3:15). The singing of psalms and hymns and spiritual songs is to be done "with gratitude in your hearts to God" (3:16). Indeed, the apostle concludes, "Whatever you do, whether in word or deed, do it all in the name of the Lord Jesus, *giving thanks to God the Father through him*" (3:17, italics added).

∾

Leviticus 6; Psalms 5—6; *Proverbs 21*; *Colossians 4*

∾

HERE I SHALL FOCUS ON THREE of the several themes that surface in **Proverbs 21**:

(a) "To do what is right and just is more acceptable to the Lord than sacrifice" (21:3). The prophets say something similar (e.g., Hosea 6:6), and so does the LORD Jesus (Matt. 9:13; 12:7). Every generation must remember that integrity and righteousness are more important than religious ritual. It should come as no surprise that religious people may sometimes cheat on their income tax, abuse their children, covet their neighbor's car, and love nothing so much as personal pleasure. Their religion may actually serve as a cloak to cover their sin with a veneer of respectability. This chapter includes another relevant proverb: "The sacrifice of the wicked is detestable—how much more so when brought with evil intent!" (21:27). The religious observance of wicked people is simply detestable in God's sight; it is unimaginably revolting to him when the wicked person is less a wicked dupe than a self-conscious charlatan using his religion to deceive people. Implicitly, of course, this means that the religion of the Bible is more about character than choirs, more about real transformation than religious tradition, more about God and the Gospel than about leadership and glitz.

(b) Poverty may come about because of abuse and oppression by the strong and powerful. But it may also come about because of a character flaw such as laziness or love of self-indulgence. So it is in this chapter: "He who loves pleasure will become poor; whoever loves wine and oil will never be rich" (21:17). "In the house of the wise are stores of choice food and oil, but a foolish man devours all he has" (21:20). "The sluggard's craving will be the death of him, because his hands refuse to work" (21:25). "All day long he craves for more, but the righteous give without sparing" (21:26). By contrast, "The plans of the diligent lead to profit as surely as haste leads to poverty" (21:5). The wise will not pursue pleasure as one of the great goals of life, but will prove provident, generous, hardworking, faithful, and just—precisely the kind of qualities that make good employers and good employees.

(c) "Haughty eyes and a proud heart, the lamp of the wicked, are sin!" (21:4). "The proud and arrogant man—'Mocker' is his name; he behaves with overweening pride" (21:24). The heart of all wickedness is this vaulting self-focus that deludes itself into thinking we are self-determining, such that God himself can never be more than an accessory. Small wonder that gospel transformation begins with repentance.

∾

Leviticus 7; Psalms 7—8; *Proverbs 22; 1 Thessalonians 1*

∾

SEVERAL OBSERVATIONS ON **Proverbs 22**:

(1) A break occurs after 22:16, with a new heading. We now leave behind the proverbs of Solomon and begin the "Sayings of the Wise." These must have been collected and perhaps circulated independently of the next section, "Further Sayings of the Wise" (24:23-34), which is then followed by more of Solomon's proverbs (25:1ff.). Several cultures in the ancient Near East cherished and collected proverbs, and of course this fostered the rise of groups of "wise men" whose best utterances were preserved for posterity.

(2) The proverb "Train a child in the way he should go, and when he is old he will not turn from it" (22:6) is so well known that it cries out for comment. Recall that a proverb is neither case law nor unqualified promise (review meditation for March 23). When children go wrong, very often the careful observer can spot familial reasons that have contributed to the rebellion. But this is not always the case. Sometimes young people from evidently wonderful families kick the traces. Some return years later; some never do. Good families may produce prodigal sons. This proverb must not be treated as if it were a promise that fails periodically. Rather, it is a proverb: it tells how God has structured reality, and what we should do to conform to it. This is the *principle* of how families work; it includes no footnotes and mentions no exceptions.

(3) Proverbs 22:29 provides an instance of wisdom that is simply technical skill (see meditation for March 14).

(4) Once more it is worth reflecting on how many proverbs focus on social dynamics of one sort or another and on the desirability of peace, self-control, and restrained speech. "Drive out the mocker, and out goes strife; quarrels and insults are ended" (22:10). "Do not make friends with a hot-tempered man, do not associate with one easily angered, or you may learn his ways and get yourself ensnared" (22:24-25).

(5) Several verses in this chapter encourage the reader to remember that biblical proverbs are more than good common sense of a secular sort, with a little piety thrown in. They are deeply grounded in devotion to the living God and to all the revelation he has given. Sometimes the way of framing a proverb makes this reality sing. "Rich and poor have this in common: The LORD is the Maker of them all" (22:2). The wise saying is grounded in the doctrine of creation. "The mouth of an adulteress is a deep pit; he who is under the LORD's wrath will fall into it" (22:14). The sexual sin everywhere condemned in this book is now seen as evidence of God's sovereign wrath.

∾

Leviticus 8; Psalm 9; *Proverbs 23; 1 Thessalonians 2*

∾

PAUL WRITES TO THE THESSALONIANS, "But, brothers, when we were torn away from you for a short time (in person, not in thought), out of our intense longing we made every effort to see you. For we wanted to come to you—certainly I, Paul, did, again and again—*but Satan stopped us*" (**1 Thess. 2:17-18**, italics added). The hindering work of Satan and his minions is attested to elsewhere in Scripture. In Daniel 10:13, for instance, the "prince of the Persian kingdom" is almost certainly some malevolent angel who delays the response to Daniel's prayer by three weeks, and would have delayed it further but for the intervention of Michael.

Some have taken passages like this as evidence that God is finite, that the struggle between good and evil in the Bible is between a finite good God and a finite wicked Satan. When bad things happen to people, this is the work of Satan, and God has very little to do with it, except to oppose it—though not very satisfactorily in this instance.

Yet the God of the Bible is not finite and not so limited. If he were, the entire book of Job (as we have recently seen) would not make sense. The apostle Paul himself can describe his delays in categories other than "Satan stopped us." For example, he tells the Corinthians, "I do not want to see you now and make only a passing visit; I hope to spend some time with you, *if the Lord permits*" (1 Cor. 16:7, italics added; see meditation for March 1). Nor is this an isolated example. The Lord Jesus tells us of a time of such terrible destruction that, "*If those days had not been cut short,* no one would survive" (Matt. 24:22, italics added). That really cannot mean anything other than that God intervenes to cut short those days. That in turn means he has the power to do so. The question it raises is why he did not do so earlier. Strictly speaking, the answer is not disclosed. Doubtless it is intertwined with other biblical themes: God sometimes allows evil to run its course, or much of its course, to expose its degradation; he is forbearing, leaving much time for repentance; he may have his own reasons, largely hidden, as in the book of Job. But always he is God, and his sovereignty is never truncated.

Paul frankly admits that Satan stopped him; in another frame, he might speak of the same event in terms of the Lord's permission. He is not embarrassed by either description, and we must not be embarrassed either. Daniel can speak of a three-week delay; elsewhere he speaks of God's unbridled sovereignty (e.g., Dan. 4:34-35). For him, the two are compatible.

∾

Leviticus 9; Psalm 10; *Proverbs 24; 1 Thessalonians 3*

∽

MANY OF THE VERSES IN **PROVERBS 24** seem to be set in a time of danger when evil is strong and the outcome uncertain:

(1) "If you falter in times of trouble, how small is your strength!" (24:10). That may be an uncomfortable thought, but it needs saying. Anyone can bulldoze ahead when the course is downhill. And of course, our strength often really is small. How often Christians discover, with Paul, that God's strength is perfected in our weakness (2 Cor. 12:1-10).

(2) As I write this a horrible case has come to light. A university student peeked over the wall in a public lavatory and saw his friend abusing and beating a very young girl, and he walked away and did nothing. Later the friend told him that he had killed the girl, who was found the next morning stuffed in the toilet. Still the university student did nothing. This is a microcosm of those who glimpsed something of the horrors of the holocaust and did nothing. So hear the word of the Lord: "Rescue those being led away to death; hold back those staggering toward slaughter. If you say, 'But we knew nothing about this,' does not he who weighs the heart perceive it? Does not he who guards your life know it? Will he not repay each person according to what he has done?" (24:11-12).

(3) "Do not fret because of evil men or be envious of the wicked, for the evil man has no future hope, and the lamp of the wicked will be snuffed out" (24:19-20). The believer must take the long view. If we judge everything by who wins and who loses in the short span of our own lives, we will often be frustrated. But God the Judge has the last word.

(4) Suppose, then, that the wicked, or at least your enemy whom you take to be wicked, faces horrible reverses, even in this life. Here too there is a right way and a wrong way of proceeding. "Do not gloat when your enemy falls; when he stumbles, do not let your heart rejoice" (24:17). Why not? Because you have descended to his level, and "the LORD will see and disapprove and turn his wrath away from him" (24:18)—and quite possibly toward you. As "the wise" put it, "Do not say, 'I'll do to him as he has done to me; I'll pay that man back for what he did'" (24:29). Christians cannot fail to hear in these words an anticipation of the "golden rule," an utterance by the Lord Jesus himself: "So in everything, do to others what you would have them do to you, for this sums up the Law and the Prophets" (Matt. 7:12).

Leviticus 10; Psalms 11—12; *Proverbs 25; 1 Thessalonians 4*

∾

SOMETIMES THE BIBLE PROVIDES A GLIMPSE of the means God graciously used to produce the Bible. For instance, Luke 1:1-4 lays out some of the research the third evangelist did. Here in the opening lines of **Proverbs 25**, we catch another glimpse: "These are more proverbs of Solomon, copied by the men of Hezekiah king of Judah" (25:1)—who of course lived two centuries after Solomon. Apparently some individual proverbs were passed down and finally collected by some scholars who worked during Hezekiah's administration. That means that the entire book of Proverbs, which coalesces several collections, is even later. And at every step God was guiding the developments.

Sometimes the book of Proverbs serves as a quarry for quotations in the New Testament. We have already come upon a few instances (e.g., 3:11-12 quoted in Heb. 12:5-6—see meditation for March 16). Here there are two more: 25:7, adapted by the Lord Jesus in Luke 14:7-10; and 25:22, quoted by Paul in Romans 12:20.

But the theme on which I wish to focus attention today is self-restraint or self-control, which keeps resurfacing in this chapter. "Do not exalt yourself in the king's presence, and do not claim a place among great men" (25:6). The scramble for the top is ugly self-promotion. Far better to be self-restrained and develop integrity. Someone may yet say, "Come up higher."

"Through patience a ruler can be persuaded, and a gentle tongue can break a bone" (25:15)—far different from the bluster and splutter of the uncontrolled. Self-control and tact often achieve what a blunderbuss merely destroys. Self-control should also inform the degree to which you lean on others (25:17).

"If you find honey, eat just enough—too much of it, and you will vomit" (25:16). This proverb has application to more foods than honey, and to more pleasures than food. Lack of self-control, far from multiplying pleasure, brings vomit and self-loathing. Another "honey" proverb tweaks the thought a little. "It is not good to eat too much honey, nor is it honorable to seek one's own honor" (25:27). The same sense of nauseating disgust that accompanies eating too much honey accompanies self-promotion. Others feel as much revulsion, the proverb tells us, in the one case as in the other.

And the opposite of self-restraint? "Like clouds and wind without rain is a man who boasts of gifts he does not give" (25:14). "Like a city whose walls are broken down is a man who lacks self-control" (25:28). The fruit of the Spirit includes self-control (Gal. 5:23; 1 Thess. 5:6; 2 Tim. 1:7).

∾

Leviticus 11—12; Psalms 13—14; *Proverbs 26; 1 Thessalonians 5*

∽

FAITH, HOPE, AND LOVE are often called the Pauline triad. They crop up again and again in Paul's correspondence, in various combinations and structures of thought. Doubtless the best-known passage is 1 Corinthians 13:13: "And now these three remain: faith, hope and love. But the greatest of these is love." It may be that the reason love is the greatest of these three cardinal Christian virtues is that love is the only one that God exercises. Elsewhere the Bible says that God is love (1 John 4:8); it never says that God is faith or that God is hope.

In the epistle before us, the Pauline triad first crops up in chapter 1: "We continually remember before our God and Father your work produced by *faith,* your labor prompted by *love,* and your endurance inspired by *hope* in our Lord Jesus Christ" (1:3). Sometimes only two elements of the triad are present: e.g., "We ought always to thank God for you, brothers, and rightly so, because your *faith* is growing more and more, and the *love* every one of you has for each other is increasing" (2 Thess. 1:3). Sometimes the three are linked in particular ways: "We always thank God, the Father of our Lord Jesus Christ, when we pray for you, because we have heard of your *faith* in Christ Jesus and of the love you have for all the saints—the faith and love *that spring from the hope* that is stored up for you in heaven and that you have already heard about in the word of truth, the gospel that has come to you" (Col. 1:3-6). Although love may be "the greatest" of the three, in this passage hope is the foundation or even the motivation of faith and love—though that arrangement is far from invariable (e.g., Eph. 1:15, 18).

If the Pauline triad occurs at the beginning of 1 Thessalonians, so it recurs at the end: "But since we belong to the day, let us be self-controlled, putting on *faith and love* as a breastplate, and the *hope* of salvation as a helmet" (**1 Thess.** 5:8, italics added). These variations suggest that faith, hope, and love were not, for Paul nor for the early Christians, a cluster of tired words always deployed in some boring formula. Rather, they were the quintessential Christian virtues that they thought about and pursued, so that their reflections and experience prompted them to describe these virtues in many different ways. Here we find the metaphor of the armor of God, but not with the associations found in Ephesians 6:10-17— once again demonstrating that these were fresh and living forms of speech, not clichés emptied of all power except comforting repetition.

∽

Leviticus 13; Psalms 15—16; *Proverbs 27; 2 Thessalonians 1*

∾

IN REFLECTING ON **PROVERBS 27**, I shall draw attention to five independent proverbs:

(1) "Wounds from a friend can be trusted, but an enemy multiplies kisses" (27:6). This is one of a substantial number of proverbs scattered throughout the book that despise flattery and insist that wise people not only administer rebuke in a kind and thoughtful way, but accept it and learn from it. For instance: "Do not rebuke a mocker or he will hate you; rebuke a wise man and he will love you. Instruct a wise man and he will be wiser still; teach a righteous man and he will add to his learning" (9:8-9). "He who listens to a life-giving rebuke will be at home among the wise" (15:31). This is a very different world from a culture in which people are simply encouraged to find themselves or express themselves.

(2) A number of proverbs, one of them in this chapter, value loyalty: "Do not forsake your friend and the friend of your father" (27:10). That sort of value is social; it transcends the "me first" mentality of individualism run amuck, and thus comports well with the New Testament emphasis on the corporate wholeness of the church.

(3) "As iron sharpens iron, so one man sharpens another" (27:17)—which again is impossible where rabid individualism holds sway. Pastors and scholars know their thinking is sharper if they take time for honest interaction with their peers.

(4) "Death and Destruction are never satisfied, and neither are the eyes of man" (27:20). Few sentences sum up so briefly and so evocatively the bottomless acquisitiveness of fallen human beings, the lust for things and power, the drive for possession, control, and novelty. A moment's reflection, and Death and Destruction become not only the standard of what it means never to be satisfied, but also what characterizes "the eyes of man."

(5) "The crucible for silver and the furnace for gold, but man is tested by the praise he receives" (27:21). This could simply mean that after a person has gone through the crucibles of affliction, the approval rating, as it were, is assigned by the valuation of his or her peers at the other end. But it is more likely that *praise itself* is in some respects the ultimate test of character. You can tell as much about people (and maybe more) by how they respond to praise as you can by how they respond to adversity. Ask football heroes, movie stars, and people in church too rapidly promoted. Perhaps this is the ultimate crucible. It does not destroy us; it exposes what is there, and very often it is not much.

∾

Leviticus 14; Psalm 17; *Proverbs 28; 2 Thessalonians 2*

∾

ON **PROVERBS 28**, I WISH to make two observations:

First, this chapter, typical of others in this book, devotes considerable attention to rulers. "When a country is rebellious, it has many rulers, but a man of understanding and knowledge maintains order" (28:2). This acknowledges the joint responsibility of ruler and people. "When the righteous triumph, there is great elation; but when the wicked rise to power, men go into hiding" (28:12; cf. also 28:28). The skills of ruling are never *merely* administrative and personal, but are tied to the deepest questions of public justice. "Like a roaring lion or a charging bear is a wicked man ruling over a helpless people" (28:15). This puts a similar thought in highly dramatic form. "A tyrannical ruler lacks judgment, but he who hates ill-gotten gain will enjoy a long life" (28:16). This reflects the danger of corruption in any government, especially one that is unconstrained by competing branches and electoral limitations. Indeed, this passage puts into proverbial form something more comprehensively set out in Deuteronomy 17:18-20.

Second, people sometimes charge that the Bible's Wisdom Literature seems so cut off from the rest of the Bible's plot-line that they do not know how to integrate it with the whole. Sermons and Bible studies on Proverbs or Ecclesiastes are always in danger of degenerating into thin moralizing that could easily be slotted into some other religious framework. One understands the problem, but there are more links between Wisdom Literature and the rest of the canon than is sometimes acknowledged. From this chapter I mention three:

(1) Rather exceptionally, three times this chapter refers to the Law of God. "Those who forsake the law praise the wicked, but those who keep the law resist them" (28:4)—which illustrates the social implications of law-keeping. "He who keeps the law is a discerning son, but a companion of gluttons disgraces his father" (28:7)—a contrast both startling and suggestive. "If anyone turns a deaf ear to the law, even his prayers are detestable" (28:9)—which demonstrates that under the terms of the old covenant, faithfulness to God was shown in obedience to the Law.

(2) "He who conceals his sins does not prosper, but whoever confesses and renounces them finds mercy" (28:13)—with dramatic echoes and advances in 1 John 1:9.

(3) "A rich man may be wise in his own eyes, but a poor man who has discernment sees through him" (28:11); "A greedy man stirs up dissension, but he who trusts in the LORD will prosper" (28:25). Read James.

∾

Leviticus 15; Psalm 18; *Proverbs 29; 2 Thessalonians 3*

∼

FROM **PROVERBS 29** I SHALL pick up four themes:

(1) "An evil man is snared by his own sin, but a righteous one can sing and be glad" (29:6). This is profoundly insightful. The results of sin include distortions to your own personality, falling afoul of your own evil, fear of being exposed, subjective guilt, and much more: you are ensnared by your own sin. By contrast, the person committed to righteousness not only avoids such snares, but is in consequence relatively carefree. He or she "can sing and be glad."

(2) "Bloodthirsty men hate a man of integrity and seek to kill the upright" (29:10; cf. 29:27). Although this is a general truth, it is supremely manifested in Jesus. He could tell some of his opponents, "As it is, you are determined to kill me, a man who has told you the truth that I heard from God" (John 8:40). It is precisely *because* Jesus tells the truth that they do not believe him (John 8:45). By contrast, "If anyone chooses to do God's will, he will find out whether my teaching comes from God or whether I speak on my own" (John 7:17). "Bloodthirsty men hate a man of integrity and seek to kill the upright"; it is not surprising therefore that the most upright man who ever lived, with the greatest integrity, was hung on a cross to die.

(3) Corruption may run from the bottom up or from the top down. When it starts at the bottom, it is pretty repulsive, and it may take a lot of work on the part of those above to root it out, or at least to bring it under control. But when it runs from the top down, it is both repulsive and impossible to reform piecemeal; drastic change is required. If the people at the top are corrupt, or even if they merely tolerate corruption with a wink and a nod, the situation is desperate. One form of this top-down corruption, superficially more benign, is the ruler who is soothed by lies, who surrounds himself or herself with underlings who will say only what he wants to hear. The wise understand: "If a ruler listens to lies, all his officials become wicked" (29:12).

(4) Older English versions rendered the first line of 29:18, "Where there is no vision, the people perish" (KJV), or the like, which became a call for visionary leadership. But the NIV has it right, and the issue is even more important: "Where there is no revelation, the people cast off restraint; but blessed is he who keeps the law." Where there is no revelation from God, grasped and obeyed, people "cast off restraint"—an apt and terrifying description of contemporary Western culture (cf. Judg. 21:25).

∼

Leviticus 16; Psalm 19; *Proverbs 30; 1 Timothy 1*

❧

SEVERAL TIMES IN THIS BOOK there is a formula of the sort, "For x things such-and-such, and for x+1 this-and-that." For instance, Proverbs 6:16-19 begins, "There are six things the Lord hates, seven that are detestable to him." Then the list begins: "haughty eyes, a lying tongue, hands that shed innocent blood, a heart that devises wicked schemes, feet that are quick to rush into evil, a false witness who pours out lies and a man who stirs up dissension among brothers"—seven items, always the "x+1" number of items. This way of introducing a list with two lines—the first with a number one less than the number of items in the list; the second with the precise number of items in the list—builds anticipation and is part of the Hebrew parallelism that does not like to have exactly the same thing in both lines.

Proverbs 30 has several instances of this formula. It is not *necessary* to use the formula if a list is being introduced (30:24), but it is common (30:15b, 18, 21, 29). The five lists in this chapter are grounded in thoughtful observation of highly diverse phenomena, and each of the five makes a different point. Here I reflect on two of them.

The first is the list (without introductory formula) of small things that are extremely "wise": ants, coneys (probably rock badgers), locusts, and lizards (30:24-28). This use of "wise" is bound up with the skill to survive (see meditation for March 14). An individual ant is nothing, easily crushed, without intelligence, yet ants store up food for the winter and survive. Rock badgers are small and relatively defenseless, yet they have the ability to make their homes in crags where others could not live. Lizards are so slow and stupid that children can catch them in their hands, and yet they have whatever it takes to live even in palaces. All these skills, all this "wisdom," God has graciously granted. In the larger context of the book, the lesson is obvious. We too are like stupid little ants or lizards, yet God has graciously given us the wisdom to survive. Two more thoughts are not far behind: (a) our wisdom, like that of the ant, is derived from God; (b) it is shockingly rebellious not to acknowledge him with gratitude as the source of our life.

The second list itemizes the thing Agur the author does not understand: "the way of an eagle in the sky, the way of a snake on a rock, the way of a ship on the high seas, and the way of a man with a maiden" (30:18-19). Thus sex is a created function, gloriously mysterious, to be treated with respect and neither cheapened nor abused.

❧

Leviticus 17; Psalms 20—21; *Proverbs 31; 1 Timothy 2*

PROVERBS 31 FOCUSES, IN TWO different ways, on women.

In the *first* part (31:1-9), the text offers us the "Sayings of King Lemuel" (of whom we know very little)—but although these sayings are "of King Lemuel" in the sense that he authorized them or made them known, they are alternatively described as "an oracle his mother taught him" (31:1).

These sayings touch on three subjects. (a) Lemuel's mother strongly encourages her son to avoid fornication. He must not spend his vigor "on those who ruin kings"—and presidents, for that matter. In addition to the ordinary lusts of the flesh, those in power doubtless have additional opportunities to satiate those lusts, along with additional responsibilities. So the right resolve must be taken as a matter of principle early in life. (b) She tells Lemuel to avoid intoxication. In an age before morphine, beer and wine were fine to help those dying or in terrible anguish (31:6), but the "help" provided is of the sort that makes you forget yourself and even lose consciousness. Rulers have no right to opt for such escapism, for they are responsible for upholding the law and assisting the oppressed (31:4-5). (c) That brings the queen mother to her last theme: King Lemuel must "Speak up for those who cannot speak for themselves" (31:8). High officials should not use their office to feather their nest and grow detached from ordinary people, but to administer fairly and especially to help the neediest and poorest members of society.

The *second* part of chapter 31 (vv. 10-31) is well known and describes a "wife of noble character." (It would be easy to show that the book of Proverbs also says quite a bit about the husband of noble character, but the relevant proverbs are not drawn together into one place, as here.) This woman of noble character is someone in whom her husband has full confidence (31:11) and who constantly seeks his good (31:12). She is industrious, so much so that she contributes to family income and has more than enough left over to help the poor and needy (31:13-22). She plans for the long haul, speaks with wisdom, and manages the household well. In the end she is the praise of her children and husband alike. But above all, and beyond the culturally specific descriptions (e.g., she works with wool and flax, and as a farmer's wife considers a field and buys it), she fears the Lord, which is the beginning of wisdom and knowledge. "Charm is deceptive, and beauty is fleeting; but a woman who fears the LORD is to be praised" (31:30).

Leviticus 18; Psalm 22; *Ecclesiastes 1; 1 Timothy 3*

∾

THE AUTHOR OF ECCLESIASTES IS (in transliterated Hebrew) Qoheleth, pronounced Ko-*hel*let or Ko-*hel*leth. The word is connected with the idea of assembling, and "Qoheleth" probably means something like "leader of the assembly" or even "one who addresses the assembly." Probably the assembly was religious (we would say "ecclesiastical"), yet Qoheleth is also an academic, collecting and formulating sayings (12:9-12). As a result, some Bibles render the expression "the Preacher"; the NIV supports "the Teacher." One commentator suggests "the Professor."

Qoheleth refers to himself as "king over Israel in Jerusalem" (1:12). But which king? He claims, "I have grown and increased in wisdom more than anyone who has ruled over Jerusalem before me" (1:16), which seems to rule out everyone but Solomon. On the other hand, it would be very strange for Solomon to write such words, since there was only one Davidic king over Jerusalem before him. So while some commentators think Qoheleth is Solomon, others point out that Solomon is not named and suggest this may be a religious leader who, as part of the dramatic argument he sets forth, stylizes himself as a super-Solomon: the wisest conceivable man, on a search for self-fulfillment, would still return destitute, crying out that everything is meaningless (1:2).

Just as many parts of Job cannot be insightfully or wisely read without grasping the flow of the book as a whole, so also with Ecclesiastes. Qoheleth sets himself to explore the significance of everything "from below," looked at from the vantage point of fallen humanity. In short, his stance is "under the sun" (1:9) or "under heaven" (1:13). He is a defender neither of naturalism nor of atheism, but he ruthlessly explores what can be said of various ostensibly "good" things when looked at one by one, "under the sun." His theme is set out in the introduction (**Eccl. 1:1-11**). "'Meaningless! Meaningless!' says the Teacher. 'Utterly meaningless! Everything is meaningless!'" (1:2). This gets at the heart of the expression traditionally rendered "Vanity of vanities . . . all is vanity" (KJV). The word suggests a wisp of air, the merest vapor, utterly without significance. In this book the Teacher probes domain after domain of life, domains that so many people value and cherish and even worship, and concludes, from his stance "under the sun," that everything is meaningless. By the end of the book, after scraping away the detritus of life, he hits bedrock—God himself. And here and there along the way he allows us glimpses of a divine perspective that transcends meaninglessness. But he takes his time getting there, for we must feel the depressing weight of all questing visions that do not begin with God.

∾

Leviticus 19; Psalms 23—24; *Ecclesiastes 2; 1 Timothy 4*

∾

BEFORE PROBING THE ARGUMENT OF **Ecclesiastes 2**, I must pick up one line from chapter 1. Setting himself to explore by wisdom "all that is done under heaven," the Teacher concludes, "What a heavy burden God has laid on men!" (1:13). Some might think this utterance springs more from bitterness than from faith, but at least it demonstrates that Qoheleth never descends into atheism. Yet those who read Ecclesiastes within the framework of the whole Bible cannot fail to see something more. This side of the Fall, God has indeed imposed on the created order an intentional discipline, a purposeful curse. Paul understands this and may be thinking of Ecclesiastes when he writes, "For the creation was subjected to frustration [or futility, or vanity, or meaninglessness], not by its own choice, but by the will of the one who subjected it, in hope that the creation itself will be liberated from its bondage to decay" (Rom. 8:20-21).

So now the Teacher begins his exploration of various domains:

(a) He pursues pleasure and wine (2:1-3). It is not that pleasure is never pleasurable, but that the more you chase it the more it disappears before your face, and you are "chasing after the wind" (1:17). It is such an ephemeral and unsatisfying thing for people to pursue "during the few days of their lives" (2:3).

(b) So he turns to building a vast estate, with all the pleasures tied to success and money. He is honest enough to testify that his heart took delight in his work, and this delight was the reward of his labor (2:10). Yet he looks back on his projects, at everything he had "toiled to achieve" (2:11), and he knows they have no eternal significance; they too are "meaningless, a chasing after the wind" (2:11). He has to leave them all behind, whether his heir is a wise man or a fool (2:19).

(c) Even the pursuit of wisdom seems futile (2:12-16). Both the wise and the fool end up dead; neither will be remembered very long after death. Qoheleth does not deny that wisdom is better than folly (2:13), but insists that death swamps both. Wisdom and folly do not exist by themselves; there are only wise human beings and foolish human beings, and all human beings die.

Yet the preliminary evaluation at the end of the chapter (2:24-26) anticipates arguments still to come. There is God-given pleasure in work and food and drink. Part of the problem lies in trying too hard, in trying to extract from these pleasures more significance than they can provide. They are genuine pleasures from God, and to "the man who pleases him, God gives wisdom, knowledge and happiness," while the sinner's life is profoundly meaningless.

∾

Leviticus 20; Psalm 25; *Ecclesiastes 3*; *1 Timothy 5*

NOW QOHELETH, THE TEACHER, looks at time (**Eccl. 3:1-17**). In isolation, verses 2-8 could be taken in several different ways. They might relativize everything: there is a time to kill and a time to heal, a time to love and a time to hate, and so forth. For some this means that no moral distinctions are to be made. Others might hope to shape their own "times." But in the context, it is better to read these verses as a mark of futility for those who live only "under the sun," and a mark of God's sovereignty for those who embrace a broader perspective.

The reader who has followed the book as far as 3:8 might well think that the poetical section of 3:1-8 is another way of saying, "Meaningless! Meaningless! Everything is meaningless" (cf. 1:2). The seasons pass away and return; so much of what we experience is generated by the situations we face, so few of which we control. The happy person loses a spouse and dissolves in tears; the peaceful nation finds itself at war; the bereft mourner marries again and dances at her wedding. We preach love, and learn of the Holocaust, and insist that justice demands that we hate. And it is all part of the same meaningless fabric: "There is a time for everything, and a season for every activity under heaven" (3:1). This is nothing but "the burden God has laid on men" (3:10).

But the rest of the passage suddenly changes the flavor. The Teacher will not allow us to remain in this miasma. God "has made everything beautiful in its time" (3:11). We see so little of the huge tapestry God is weaving. Qoheleth is not thereby relativizing evil. He of all people knows this is a broken and fallen world. But he insists that, far from meaningless repetition and boring cycles, what takes place "under the sun" can be seen instead as a reflection of God's design, with a "beginning" and an "end" (3:11) to the pattern. We sometimes glimpse the spectacular, kaleidoscopic glory, but our horizon is so small and our trust in God so paltry that such visions are rare. But God "has also set eternity in our hearts." Unlike dogs or chimpanzees, we know we are immersed in eternity, and we long to see more of the pattern than we can; we "cannot fathom what God has done from beginning to end" (3:11). Meanwhile, it is a "gift from God" to eat and labor and find satisfaction in one's own patch, all the while happily aware "that everything God does will endure forever" (3:13-14). The cycles that the unbeliever finds meaningless and despairing incite the believer to faithfulness and worship.

Leviticus 21; Psalms 26—27; *Ecclesiastes 4; 1 Timothy 6*

ᨘ

ONE OF THE INTRIGUING FEATURES OF **1 Timothy 6:3-19** is the way Paul's argument cuts back and forth. There are four blocks. In the first (6:3-5), Paul warns
against those who teach false doctrines and describes the character of the false
teachers with whom he is dealing. One of their motives is "financial gain" (6:5):
they are less interested in the Gospel and in genuine godliness than in sporting
an assumed "godliness" to rake in a good living. That introduces the second block
(6:6-10), which warns against the love of money. It is "a root of all kinds of evil"
(6:10). The proper Christian attitude should be committed contentment, for
"godliness with contentment is great gain" (6:6); moreover, at the end of our lives
we take out exactly what we brought in (6:7). Focusing on the transient things
of this life serves only to plunge people into "ruin and destruction" (6:9). By contrast, Paul tells Timothy what sort of man he should be: that is the third block
(6:11-16). The apostle then moves to the fourth block (6:17-19) and tells Timothy
to command those who are rich how to conduct themselves. They are to repudiate arrogance, to put no confidence in wealth "which is so uncertain" (6:17), but
to put their confidence in God, "who richly provides us with everything for our
enjoyment" (6:17). They must use their wealth to do good, to be generous, to
share. In this way they will really be laying up treasure for themselves in heaven
(6:19), as the Lord Jesus taught us (Matt. 6:20). Thus Paul insists not on asceticism but on committed generosity as the best Christian response to greed.

So the four blocks deal with, respectively, false teachers and their conduct, the
dangers of wealth, a true teacher and his conduct, and the dangers of wealth again.
Thus the section that tells Timothy what kind of man he should be (6:11-16) must
be seen, in part, as an antidote to both false teaching and greed.

What is striking about this paragraph is what Paul places over against false
doctrine and love of materialism. Paul tells Timothy, in effect, that a focus on eternal things will drive a far healthier Christian ambition. If Timothy is to *flee* from
"all this" (6:11)—from the crass materialism Paul has just condemned—he must
set himself to *pursue* "righteousness, godliness, faith, love, endurance and gentleness" (6:11). While he maintains his "good confession"—as Christ maintained
his—(6:12-13), he is to take hold of "eternal life" and persevere until "the appearing of our Lord Jesus Christ" (6:12, 14)—living and serving in the glory of God's
unapproachable light (6:14, 16).

Leviticus 22; Psalms 28—29; *Ecclesiastes 5; 2 Timothy 1*

∾

THE TEACHER PAUSES IN HIS ARGUMENT to offer some reflections and home truths regarding how to live in the world as we find it, including the religious world. His argument now takes a pragmatic turn that runs from Ecclesiastes 4:9 to 5:12. Here we focus on **Ecclesiastes 5:1-12**, which can be divided into two blocks of material.

In the *first,* Qoheleth describes and condemns the merely pious man. His target is not the full-blown hypocrite so often denounced by the prophets, but the subtler hypocrite who likes to participate in worship services, chatters piously, and who rarely keeps his promises or performs what he has volunteered to do for God. "Go near to listen rather than to offer the sacrifice of fools" (5:1), the Teacher counsels. "Do not be quick with your mouth, do not be hasty in your heart to utter anything before God. God is in heaven and you are on earth, so let your words be few" (5:2). But if you do make a vow to God, "do not delay in fulfilling it. He has no pleasure in fools; fulfill your vow. It is better not to vow than to make a vow and not fulfill it" (5:4-5). "Much dreaming and many words are meaningless. Therefore stand in awe of God" (5:7).

Corporate worship is not a time for daydreaming, a retreat for mental scribbling. This is the worship of a fool. All the pious words and corporate expressions and confessions of faith are reduced to meaninglessness. As you pick your way through the apparent meaninglessness of life, remain steady at least on this point: stand in awe of God.

The *second* block warns against the meaninglessness of riches. In a fallen and broken world, we should not be surprised by corruption that rips off the people at the bottom of the pecking order (5:8-9). Of course, we should support government administration; officialdom is better than anarchy. Nevertheless in many cultures corruption is so endemic that the predators higher up the ladder are constantly scrambling to grab bigger and bigger pieces of the pie. The Teacher's comments are dry and entirely in line with cynical secularism.

The sad fact is that love of money creates greater love of money (5:10). Inevitably it attracts a range of parasites, people who fawn over you, whom you cannot really trust (5:11). And at the end of the day, money leaves you with sleepless nights—unlike the nights of the laborer, who works his shift, tires himself out, and enjoys a good night's sleep (5:12).

The arguments are pragmatic as the Teacher works his way through life pictured from below.

∾

Leviticus 23; Psalm 30; *Ecclesiastes 6; 2 Timothy 2*

∽

IN ECCLESIASTES 5:13—6:12, the Teacher enlarges upon two or three grievous evils "under the sun." Here we focus on those described in **Ecclesiastes 6**.

One of life's immense frustrations involves people who receive from God "wealth, possessions and honor" (6:2) such that they lack nothing their heart desires—yet they lack the ability to enjoy these things. The power to enjoy things (first introduced in 5:19) is itself a great gift from God. To have so many other gifts and not this one is immensely troubling. The Teacher does not spell out what exactly has foreclosed on the ability to enjoy all the other gifts. It might be a business failure (5:13-15). But it might be chronic illness, or war, or the evil manipulation of someone more powerful, or even some form of insanity. One might die prematurely, and a "stranger" will enjoy all the things one has accumulated (6:2). Or perhaps a person will die not only unfulfilled and barely noticed, but unlamented ("not receiv[ing] proper burial," 6:3). Qoheleth insists that "a stillborn child is better off than he" (6:3). Such a child "comes without meaning, it departs in darkness, and in darkness its name is shrouded" (6:4). But even if someone should live ten thousand years and yet never enjoy all the prosperity God has graciously given him (6:6), his life is meaningless. And in the end he goes to the same place as the stillborn child (6:6).

The chapter ends with a series of blistering rhetorical questions, all designed to substantiate the thesis that, under the sun, everything is "utterly meaningless" (1:2). We work to eat, and eating gives us the strength to go on working: what is the point? (6:7). But if someone replies that a person may not only work and eat, but become a "wise man" (6:8), is it all that clear that the wise are better off than fools? After all, much wisdom may simply bring much frustration and grief, as Qoheleth has already pointed out (1:18). Moreover, isn't it better to be satisfied with the material world—with what one can touch and hear and see and feel, with "what the eye sees"—than to pursue "the roving of the appetite," i.e., all the things hidden from view that we hanker after? For this, too, "is meaningless, a chasing after the wind" (6:9).

Is this too wretchedly pessimistic to be realistic? But for those who are "under the sun" (6:12) and nothing more, what else is there? We talk too much and know too little (6:11-12). God help us! We need a deliverer from outside our myopic horizons.

∽

Leviticus 24; Psalm 31; *Ecclesiastes 7; 2 Timothy 3*

∿

IN ECCLESIASTES 7, THE BOOK'S FORM changes, taking on the more typical structure of Wisdom Literature: a string of proverbs. But these proverbs do not, by and large, adopt the stance of the person who holds that the fear of the Lord is the beginning of wisdom (cf. Prov. 9:10). Rather, Qoheleth maintains his quest, searching out the meaning of things explored "from below." These "common sense" proverbs are touched with an edge of cynicism that is brutally honest but not leavened with godly faith.

The first six are provocatively gloomy. Nothing in the first line prepares the reader for the rabbit punch of the second: e.g., "the day of death [is] better than the day of birth" (7:1b). This is not the confession of faith as in Philippians 1:21, 23. The most positive thing that could be said about this proverb is that it is bluntly realistic, and all of us would benefit from learning to live in light of the fact that we too must die—as the second part of verse 2 makes explicit: "for death is the destiny of every man; the living should take this to heart" (cf. Ps. 90:12). The line of thought to the end of verse 6 is similarly cheerless, but its brutal frankness has cautionary value.

The proverbs in 7:7-22 are harder to categorize. There is a kind of practical attempt to make sense of the world, but it is the attempt of the worldly person. Verses 8 and 9 are doubtless good counsel in the life of the believer, but in this context they have a merely pragmatic tinge. "Do not say, 'Why were the old days better than these?' For it is not wise to ask such questions" (7:10). This annihilates self-indulgent nostalgia, for the Teacher is unlikely to be impressed by the hazy glow that surrounds the past: he has already shown his hand on this point (see 1:9). True, Qoheleth praises wisdom (7:11-12), but with a cool affirmation of its utilitarian value—it has advantages, just as money does. In this mood Qoheleth can fluctuate between pious resignation (7:12) and outrageous cynicism (7:13-18)—what F. Derek Kidner labels "the shabby and self-regarding side of common sense." So also verse 18 is moral cowardice tarted up with stoicism.

The ultimate failure of such wisdom, which does not begin with the fear of the Lord, is acknowledged in the closing verses of the chapter (7:23-29). The Teacher is determined to be wise, but his brand of wisdom "from below" leaves him unable to glimpse much of the real meaning of life; true wisdom is still beyond him (7:23-25), and his own wisdom is clothed with a cynicism regarding human relationships that says more about him than about the people he describes (7:27-28). Only when he returns to the pattern of Creation and Fall (7:29) does he begin to approach a more stable answer.

∿

Leviticus 25; Psalm 32; *Ecclesiastes 8; 2 Timothy 4*

∾

FEW PASSAGES HAVE PROVED more popular at evangelical ordination services than, "Preach the Word; be prepared in season and out of season; correct, rebuke and encourage—with great patience and careful instruction" (**2 Tim. 4:2**).

We reflect, *first,* on the charge itself. It may be broken down into four components. (a) The focus of the charge: "Preach the Word." This is central to all gospel ministry—the heraldic declaration of the content of God's gracious self-revelation. (b) The urgency of the charge: "be prepared in season and out of season." It is one thing to be prepared for the stated meetings, the ordinary scheduled obligations to speak, to preach; it is another to be ready to declare the whole counsel of God at the drop of a hat. Paul demands both kinds of readiness. (c) The scope of the charge: "correct, rebuke and encourage." Preaching the Word means more than the mere conveying of information. There is information, of course, but it is so shaped and applied that it functions in one or more of these *transforming* ways. Thus the minister of the Gospel is necessarily a spiritual diagnostician, discerning the ailment and knowing what remedies to apply. Pity the minister of the Word who applies encouragement when rebuke is called for, or the reverse. (d) The manner of fulfilling the charge: "with great patience and careful instruction." Paul's view of the ministry demands a focus on the long haul, on personal patience, on great care with the substance of what is preached. This is not simply a job to be done, a job by which to support yourself and your family. This demands strong Christian character traits and a mind devoted to thinking through and implementing all that is embraced by "careful instruction."

In the second place, we observe some of the themes surrounding this charge. (a) This charge to preach the Word Paul solemnly delivers in the name and presence of God and in the light of Christ's return to judge the living and the dead and to consummate his kingdom (4:1). It is difficult to imagine a weightier introduction. (b) Paul delivers this charge in the expectation that many "will not put up with sound doctrine," but will prefer teachers who say what they want to hear. There are more "itching ears" (4:3) within evangelicalism than we would like to admit. The proper response is to "keep your head in all situations, endure hardship, do the work of an evangelist, discharge all the duties of your ministry" (4:5). (c) Paul's charge is uttered in a context that insists on how important godly mentors are (3:10-11), how bad the world can be (3:12-13), and how unshakable the Scriptures are that must be preached (3:15-16).

∾

Leviticus 26; Psalm 33; *Ecclesiastes 9; Titus 1*

∾

THE LAST THREE CHAPTERS OF Ecclesiastes bring together a reflective parenthesis (chap. 10) and a positive conclusion (chaps. 11—12). First, however, **Ecclesiastes 9** strips us of any final illusions if our vantage point is "under the sun" (9:3).

The Teacher has come to the conclusion that "the righteous and the wise and what they do are in God's hands" (9:1). But what kind of a God is he, when you look at things only "from below," from "under the sun"? Considering all the morally ambiguous things that happen in this world, does God love us or does he hate us (9:1)? Does he accept us or does he reject us? The world overflows with both beauty and ugliness, with warm intimacy and cruel terror. How can those who think only from below sort this out?

The Teacher lays out three vicissitudes that make certainty impossible for such people—yet he sets out the case as far as they can take it:

(1) We all face *death* (9:2-10). The case is put most baldly in 9:2-3: the just and the unjust, good people and sinners, face the same end. Qoheleth himself protests that this is not right; this is an evil that happens under the sun (9:3). He is not yet ready to provide any answer. But even from this perspective, there is a robust common sense conclusion to be pursued: even though life here may be hard and ambiguous, most of us concur that it is better than death (9:4-6). From this "under the sun" vantage point, verses 7-10 tell us how we should attack life, knowing that life is better than death. One hears the tension in a verse like 9:9: "Enjoy life with your wife, whom you love, all the days of this meaningless life that God has given you under the sun—all your meaningless days. For this is your lot in life and in your toilsome labor under the sun." The problems of coherence, self-fulfillment, and meaning have not been resolved; but pragmatic conclusions, even by the worldly person who lives exclusively "under the sun," quickly pile up and drive us toward robust and even grateful living—if the only alternative is a meaningless death.

(2) We all face *time and chance* (9:11-12). Apart from a God who tells us more, there is such a randomness to life that thoughtful human beings must not count on too much.

(3) We all face the *fickle folly of other human beings* (9:13-18). Even when genuine wisdom is offered, the masses are more likely to be impressed by wealth than by wisdom.

Qoheleth is frank and honest. But we cry for God's perspective.

∾

Leviticus 27; Psalm 34; *Ecclesiastes 10; Titus 2*

∾

IN 2 TIMOTHY 4 PAUL EXHORTS HIS READER to preach sound doctrine (see meditation for April 21); here in **Titus 2** he exhorts them to teach "what is in accord
with sound doctrine" (2:1).

The ensuing verses show us what this means. By what is "in accord" with
sound doctrine Paul means how to live in accordance with sound doctrine. From
the apostle's perspective, Christian leaders must teach not only what to think but
how to live in the light of what to think.

Thus older men are to be taught "to be temperate, worthy of respect, self-
controlled, and sound in faith, in love and in endurance" (2:2). That means more
than simply telling them those words from time to time. Each of these points
needs to be applied and illustrated and pressed home. Similarly, in this passage
there are practical things to be taught to older women (2:3), younger women (2:4-
5), young men (2:6-8), and slaves (2:9-10).

Yet these things are not separate education tracks for different groups of people or something to be added to the Gospel. Far from it: what is being laid on these
diverse groups is merely the outworking of the Gospel. The next paragraph makes
this clear (I have italicized some of the words more traditionally associated with
salvation): "For *the grace of God* that brings salvation has appeared to all men. It
teaches us to say 'No' to ungodliness and worldly passions, and to live self-
controlled, upright and godly lives in this present age, while we wait for the
blessed hope—the glorious appearing of our great God and Savior, Jesus Christ,
*who gave himself for us to redeem us from all wickedness and to purify for himself a
people that are his very own,* eager to do what is good" (2:11-14).

The logic is transparent enough. If Jesus gave himself to redeem us from sin
and to live godly lives in this present evil age, we must devote ourselves to deter-
mining what godly lives look like, and to living such lives. Such lives involve
many common elements for all groups of Christians, but the practicalities of life
mean that there are certain temptations that beset certain groups—old men,
young men, and so forth. Some months before he died, my aged father wrote in
his diary, "Oh God, save me from the sins of old men"—as I at the moment need
to be saved from the sins of middle-aged men.

So we must teach and live what is *in accord* with sound doctrine. "These, then,
are the things you should teach. Encourage and rebuke with all authority. Do not
let anyone despise you" (2:15).

∾

Numbers 1; Psalm 35; *Ecclesiastes 11*; *Titus 3*

∾

"WARN A DIVISIVE PERSON ONCE, and then warn him a second time. After that, have nothing to do with him" (**Titus 3:10**). It is worth reflecting a little on what this does and does not mean, and how it fits into broader streams of biblical theology.

First, the passage is written to a church leader responsible for maintaining church discipline. It does not sanction a personal vendetta: Christian X decides that Christian Y is rather divisive and therefore decides to have nothing further to do with Y. (Indeed, that itself would exemplify a divisive spirit!) This is written to a Christian who has responsibility for leading and disciplining the church.

Second, the passage focuses on discipline at the local level; it is not introducing infinitely broad approval of all ecumenical thrusts—a kind of condemnation of anyone who does not approve the latest inter-church project or confession. Of course, there may be implications for the broader work of the Gospel, but we must above all grasp what force the text has in its own context.

Third, the immediate evidence of a divisive spirit, in this context, is an unrepentant argumentativeness about peripherals: Christians must "avoid foolish controversies and genealogies and arguments and quarrels about the law, because these are unprofitable and useless" (3:9). Undoubtedly there is some common understanding between Paul and Titus on these matters that is a little difficult to probe. Paul is certainly not saying, for instance, that every question about the Law is a waste of time; he himself elsewhere discusses the subject. But controversies calculated to divide Christians without producing any gospel strength or moral improvement are "unprofitable and useless." One begins to suspect that those who are stirring up such strife have invested so much of their own egos in their eccentric positions that they can neither be corrected nor back down.

Fourth, if "have nothing to do with him" entails excommunication from the local church (as I think it does), we should reflect on the categories of sin that call forth this sanction in the New Testament. One is major doctrinal aberration, especially among teachers; a second is major moral defection, such as the case described in 1 Corinthians 5; and the third is here—a loveless, untransformed stance that refuses to see the centrality and glory of the Gospel but proves so divisive, despite repeated warnings, that the only solution is to cut the canker from the body. These three categories are the inverse of the patterns of life set out as the three primary tests of genuine Christianity in 1 John: doctrinal probity, moral conformity, *and love for the brothers and sisters.*

∾

Numbers 2; Psalm 36; *Ecclesiastes 12; Philemon*

ALTHOUGH THE TEACHER NEVER arrives at the fullness of perspective that characterizes the writers of the new covenant Scriptures, his skepticism now shrinks
as he encourages some fundamental stances that depend absolutely on a just God
who knows the end from the beginning, even if we do not. In this vein, he has
already told his readers two things: (a) refuse to live just for today; boldly invest
in the future, remembering that this world is God's (11:1-6); (b) live gratefully
and joyfully with the good gifts you have received (11:7-10).

In **Ecclesiastes 12**, Qoheleth offers one final exhortation: be godly, beginning
in your youth; for whether or not we find meaning "from below," we may be certain that God brings everything to judgment. "Remember your Creator in the days
of your youth" (12:1), the Teacher writes. To "remember" God is not simply to
recall the bare fact of his existence, but to abandon all illusions of independence
and self-sufficiency as God regains his rightful centrality in our lives. God made
everything, he alone sees the entire pattern, he is the One who has put eternity
into our hearts (3:11). He is the One who made everything good, and we are the
ones who have done so much damage with our schemes (7:29).

So remember him, Qoheleth exhorts us, "before the days of trouble come"
(12:1)—and then in graphic terms he spells out what old age looks like. In
advanced years we may no longer find pleasure in our days (12:1). We reach the
winter of life (12:2); we become like an old, decaying house, falling apart, with
only a few relics left (12:3). Our hearing fades (12:4b); instead of robust walking
or skipping over rocks, we are afraid of heights and fearful of being jostled in the
streets. The almond tree has a dark head in winter and turns white with spring
blossoms, just as our hair turns white (12:5). Suffering from arthritis and worn-
out joints, we hobble along like an ungainly grasshopper (12:5). The silver cord
is probably the spinal cord, the golden bowl the skull; the pitcher is the heart:
everything decays, and we return to the dust from which we sprang—as God himself, this side of the curse, has said we would (Gen. 3:19). It is far from clear that
by "our eternal home" (12:5) and "the spirit returns to God who gave it" (12:7)
Qoheleth means everything that New Testament writers mean by such expressions, yet even he is now quite certain that "God will bring every deed into judgment, including every hidden thing" (12:14). So, "Fear God and keep his
commandments, for this is the whole duty of man" (12:13).

Numbers 3; Psalm 37; *Song of Songs 1; Hebrews 1*

$\backsim$

ALTHOUGH (OR PERHAPS BECAUSE) the Song of Songs is one of the most difficult of biblical books, it has been extraordinarily popular with both Jews and Christians. It has called forth a large number of commentaries and sermons. Space here is far too limited for a discussion, but perhaps I should record my tentative conclusions on four matters before reflecting on **Song 1**.

(1) Although some have denied that this book is about sexual love in any primary sense, but is an allegory of either the love between Yahweh and Israel or between Christ and the church, I doubt it. So many details of Song of Songs are so explicitly human and sexual (all the more so when the ancient Semitic symbolism is appreciated) that to argue that the *meaning* of the text is allegorical is unlikely. Moreover, there are many parallels in other love poetry in ancient near eastern Wisdom Literature, so that one must conclude the genre was well known.

(2) On the other hand, *after* fully acknowledging the human and sexual love that this book celebrates—for God has made us human and sexual, and Wisdom Literature often focuses on the glory of the created order—we may not be far off the mark if we *also* see, within the canonical framework, a typological connection with God and Israel, with Christ and the church. For that is a theme repeatedly picked up in both Testaments (see, for instance, Hosea, or Rev. 21).

(3) Some have seen *three* principal figures in this book: the woman, her shepherd-lover, and the lascivious king who is trying to add the woman to his harem. On balance, it seems better to see only two primary parties, the woman and the king-shepherd-lover. The "daughters of Jerusalem" who keep reappearing (e.g., 1:5) are the woman's female companions.

(4) Although it is reasonably clear that consummation takes place in 3:6—5:1, complete with wedding song, this does not mean there are no sexual overtones earlier in the book. Yet far from endorsing promiscuity (as a few commentators have suggested), the book is committed to exclusive, monogamous love. What is less clear is that the thought is sequential, merely linear.

The "beloved," the woman, often takes the initiative (1:2ff.). Yet she is unsure of herself. Her long exposure to the sun, apparently imposed on her by brothers (Is her father dead?) who insist that she tend the vines, means she is a sun-darkened country lass (1:5-7). Her friends reassure her (1:8)—as does her lover (1:9-11). After her sensual soliloquy (1:12-14), a series of bantering exchanges between the beloved and her lover bring the section to a close (1:15—2:2). One remembers Proverbs 30:19.

$\backsim$

Numbers 4; Psalm 38; *Song of Songs 2; Hebrews 2*

∾

OCCASIONALLY WE HAVE OVERLOOKED the theological significance of Jesus' humanity. That is one of the important themes of **Hebrews 2**.

Both the one who makes human beings holy—Jesus himself—and the human beings who are made holy are of the same family. That is why Jesus is not ashamed to call us brothers (2:11). Since we have flesh and blood, he shared in our humanity (2:14)—which of course implies that this was something not intrinsically his, but something he had to take on (the eternal Word "became flesh," John 1:14). He did this so that by his death (something he could never have experienced if he had not donned flesh and blood) "he might destroy him who holds the power of death . . . and free those who all their lives were held in slavery by their fear of death" (2:14, 15). Jesus did not don the nature of angels (2:16—which shows that Jesus was not a merely angelic being). Rather, he became a human being, a human being with a genuine lineage—the lineage of Abraham (2:16). If he was to serve as mediator between God and human beings, "he had to be made like his brothers in every way" (2:17—which presupposes that he already was like *God* in every way). So it was entirely "fitting," then, that God should make the author of our salvation "perfect through suffering" (2:10). The idea is not that Jesus gains through suffering a moral perfection he otherwise would have lacked, but that the perfection of his identification with us depended on participating in our common currency, which is suffering.

The author of Hebrews has already hinted at the problem that Jesus came to resolve. Originally human beings were made to be God's vice-regents over the entire creation, a point not only made by the creation accounts (Gen. 1—2) but reiterated in the superb poetry of Psalm 8 (cited in Heb. 2:6-8). But as the author of Hebrews points out, we do not yet see everything under our feet, as Genesis 1 and Psalm 8 envisage. Of course not: the Fall has intervened, and death takes its unvarying toll. But what do we see? "[W]e see Jesus, who was made a little lower than the angels, now crowned with glory and honor because he suffered death, so that by the grace of God he might taste death for everyone" (2:9). The point is not exactly that Jesus is the "man" envisaged in Psalm 8, as if he were being prophetically described, but that by his mission, by his identification with us, and by his death, he becomes the first human being to be crowned with such glory and honor, as he brings many sons—a new humanity—to glory.

∾

Numbers 5; Psalm 39; *Song of Songs 3; Hebrews 3*

☙

IF THE END OF SONG 2 FINDS the beloved and the lover fervently expressing their mutual devotion to each other and the exclusiveness of their love each for the other, **Song 3** begins with the woman, the beloved, almost frantically searching for her lover. Many commentators have suggested that chapter 3, and perhaps the entire unit of chapters 3—6, is a dream sequence. That may be right: "*All night long on my bed* I looked for the one my heart loves" (3:1, italics added), the beloved says. In the first panel (3:1-5), the beloved searches for her lover, and simply assumes that because she knows the man for whom she is looking, everyone else should too—including the night police officers ("the watchers"). She finds him and brings him to her mother's bedroom (3:4), signaling official consummation.

The coherence of the next panel (3:6-11) is disputed. The best guess is that "this" in 3:6 (feminine Hebrew pronoun) refers to the woman. She is being brought up from her dwelling in the country to the court—and in Solomon's carriage, a gloriously designed and luxurious vehicle. Solomon himself is present, and "the daughters of Zion" watch and "ooohh and aaahh" as the couple make their way to their new home. This then leads to the extravagant language of the lover in chapter 4.

Whether or not this is a dream sequence (I am inclined to think it is), one thing abundantly clear is that the language of love is the language of mutual praise and mutual invitation. Anything less will stifle love. If the language of praise and invitation operates only one way, for instance, it will tire in time or leave the speaker feeling servile or perhaps desperate. If the language of love is the language of praise but not of invitation, it may never breed intimacy—a good relationship but not good sex; if it is the language of invitation but not of praise, it may degenerate into mutual gratification but not mutual edification—good sex but not a good relationship.

Many of us who are married and who reflect on the language of Song of Songs are slightly embarrassed at its sensual abandon. But that may say more about who we are than about what God wants us to be. Like everything else that God made good, marriage and sex and intimacy can be trivialized and sensationalized and brutalized. But God made them good. Believers are bound, so far as their transformed natures can take them this side of the new heavens and the new earth, to display God's goodness in every arena to which he calls us. We who are married ought, *intentionally,* to develop the language of mutual praise and invitation.

☙

Numbers 6; Psalms 40—41; *Song of Songs 4; Hebrews 4*

∿

HEBREWS 3:7—4:11 CONSTITUTES A sustained argument. We may briefly summarize what 3:7-19 says and focus attention on **Hebrews 4:1-11**.

The author of Hebrews quotes Psalm 95:7-11 (Heb. 3:7-11), which finds the Holy Spirit (3:7), the ultimate author of Scripture, saying, in effect, "*Today* do not harden your heart as your forefathers did at Kadesh Barnea, when they first approached the Promised Land. The majority of the spies gave a faithless report, with the consequence that the covenant people spent the next forty years wandering around the desert instead of entering into the rest that had been promised them. But *today*, do not make the same mistake. If you hear the voice of God, believe and obey—unlike the response of your forefathers." The very people whom God had saved from slavery were the ones he condemned to wander and die in the desert. So *today* the people of God should persevere in their faith and obedience, and not tumble into the unbelief (4:19) of their ancestors.

So far the argument is one of analogy. Hebrews 4 takes it much farther. If God is still offering rest to people in the time of Psalm 95, it follows that the rest provided by the Promised Land *was never meant to be the ultimate rest*. For Joshua did lead the people into the land, yet "if Joshua had given them rest, God would not have spoken later about another day" (4:8). Moreover, when God swears in his anger that the generation at Kadesh Barnea will never enter into "my rest" (Ps. 95:11; Heb. 3:11; 4:3), the thoughtful reader must ask what this "rest" of God really is. God first "rests" at the end of creation week (Gen. 2:2). That becomes a model for the covenantal Sabbath-rest. Yet neither the Sabbath-rest nor the rest in the Promised Land constitute the ultimate rest, for here in Psalm 95, "a long time later" (4:7), God still invites people to enter his rest, on the condition of persevering faith (4:2, 11).

The ultimate rest, the writer of Hebrews insists, can only be the Gospel, in which men and women cease from their works (as God rested from his at Creation). All of this argumentation depends on reading the Bible in its salvation-historical progression, that is, reading it sequentially along its story-line and observing how the bits not only hang together but point forward and anticipate greater things to come. The argument is not one of analogy but of typology. That is what is calling us to persevering faith and obedience; that is part of what makes the word of God living, active, and penetrating (4:12-13).

∿

Numbers 7; Psalms 42—43; *Song of Songs 5; Hebrews 5*

∽

SONG 5:2-16 BEGINS A NEW UNIT, with the relationship cooling and at least potentially in jeopardy. Probably the most common interpretation is that this section is
part of a dream sequence. Note the opening words: "I slept but my heart was
awake"—almost a definition of a dream. Dream or not, the intensity of the relationship is declining. In 5:2 the lover wants to come to the beloved, but her initial response is cool: "I have taken off my robe—must I put it on again? I have
washed my feet—must I soil them again?" (5:3)—scarcely the words of passionate expectation and welcome.

These and the following lines can be read on two levels. On the first, the
beloved has gone to bed and cannot even be bothered to get up and open the door;
she might get her feet dirty. The lover puts his hand through a hole in the door
and tries to raise the latch. The beloved has second thoughts. Rather belatedly she
drags herself out of bed, now with at least some anticipation, only to open the
door and find her lover gone (5:5-6). Disappointed and ashamed, she roams the
city looking for him, and this time the night policemen, the "watchers," beat her
up (5:7)—why is unclear, though some have suggested she is making such a com-
motion that this was the only way they could keep her quiet. On this reading the
"daughters of Jerusalem" (5:8-9) are not friends but city girls who are finally persuaded to join the search, which ultimately proves successful.

At the second level, there is a string of *double entendres.* "Feet" (5:3) sometimes serve as a euphemism for genitals (e.g., the Hebrew of Judg. 3:24; 1 Sam.
24:3; Isa. 7:20; Ezek. 16:25 [KJV; the NIV translation loses the word *foot* in each
instance]; and the parallelism between "wash your feet" and "lie with my wife"
in 2 Sam. 11:8, 11). English Bibles often use "latch-opening" or the like in 5:4,
but that is certainly not mandated by the relatively rare original—and the rest of
the verse, and the next two, suggest a different opening, and arousal on the part
of the woman. But by this time the lover, for whatever reason—impatience? disappointment?—is gone.

What shall we make of this? *First,* all marriages, even the best of marriages,
sometimes go through periods of coolness or reserve which, unchecked, could
destroy them. *Second,* dream sequence or not, the way forward is a mutual pursuit of the lover and the beloved, a renewed commitment to the language and self-
giving of love. *Third,* Paul is scarcely less explicit, though more prosaic, when he
insists that married Christians, apart from explicit exceptions, are not to deprive
their spouses sexually (1 Cor. 7:5; see meditation for February 20).

∽

Numbers 8; Psalm 44; *Song of Songs 6; Hebrews 6*

THE "APOSTASY" PASSAGE, **Hebrews 6:4-6** (compare 10:26-31) has historically been the focus of considerable theological and pastoral dispute.

The nub of the question is, can genuine believers lose their salvation? Some Christians reply affirmatively, though it is hard to square such affirmations with, for instance, the "golden chain" of Romans 8:29-30 or the unqualified assertions of John 6:39-40, 44. Some Christians have therefore suggested that what Hebrews envisages is not falling away from eternal life but falling away from useful service. On the face of it, the language of Hebrews 6 and 10 is sterner than that. Others postulate that the warning is merely hypothetical or even beneficial—a means of grace that guarantees believers will *not* apostatize. But if we know that, it is difficult to take the warning seriously, for we are assured in advance that the set of apostates is an empty set—and that makes the warning slightly ludicrous and not the desperately serious thing that the author of Hebrews thinks it is. Still others argue that elsewhere the New Testament may teach the perseverance and the preservation of the saints, but here it presupposes that some will fall away—and we must simply live with the tension, not to say contradiction.

My own view is that the issue turns on two points, with an important pastoral implication. *First,* it is not as if Hebrews teaches one thing and Paul and John another. Paul entreats Christians to examine themselves to see if they are in the faith (2 Cor. 13:5), yet constructs the golden chain. John warns that branches in Christ (the true vine) may be cut off (John 15:1-8), yet insists that Christ will preserve all those the Father has given him. There is therefore nothing useful to be gained by pitting Hebrews 6 against, say, John. It aligns very well with one element in John and Paul. *Second,* one must ask if the individual descriptions ("enlightened," "tasted of the heavenly gift," etc.) in Hebrews 6 and 10 require us to think of genuine Christians. The answer to this question is tied to our theology of conversion and to what is meant by "genuine Christian." The New Testament gives many instances of people who taste enough of God's grace to turn their lives around and join the visible church, *even though they do not have the kind of grace that enables them to persevere.* Even Hebrews 3:6, 14 presupposes as much. Under such a "tight" definition of genuine Christian, none falls away. The question then becomes, "Will you persevere? Is your experience of grace so light that you can walk away from the cross?"

What are the pastoral implications? The reflections suggest that the Bible provides wonderful reassurance to the weak and fainthearted, but threatens the openly defiant with a stern probing of the genuineness of their profession of faith.

Numbers 9; Psalm 45; *Song of Songs 7; Hebrews 7*

IN VOLUME 1 (MEDITATION FOR JANUARY 13), we reflected on the place of Melchizedek in Genesis and, by way of anticipation, in the rest of the canon. Here in Hebrews 7 we may reflect on Melchizedek again, this time looking backwards. I shall focus on some of the turning points in the line of thought in **Hebrews 7:11-28**.

(1) In the previous verses the author establishes that Melchizedek was greater than Abraham, and therefore greater than Abraham's descendant Levi (since in Hebrew culture the father was always superior to the son). So historically the priest Melchizedek was greater than the priest Levi; in principle, then, the Melchizedekian priesthood, as an institution, is superior to the Levitical priesthood.

(2) When one reads the Old Testament documents sequentially, it is striking that, several centuries after the Mosaic Law that established the Levites as priests, God announces in Psalm 110 (Heb 5:6; 7:17, 21) that he is raising up a messianic figure who is a priest forever according to the order of Melchizedek, *not Levi*. (See vol. 1, meditation for June 17.)

(3) In principle, such a promise announces the obsolescence of the Levitical priesthood. It cannot last. In Psalm 110 God through David announces that the Levitical priesthood will be superseded by the Melchizedekian priesthood.

(4) That in turn means there must be a change in the law-covenant given at Sinai. We are sometimes tempted to think that the Law was primarily about "morality," with a little bit of religious ceremony and some other things tacked on. If that were right, the law-covenant could remain largely intact when the priesthood changes. But that is not the argument of Hebrews. Here we are told that the Levitical priesthood, far from being tacked on, was the very basis of the Law (7:11). In other words, in certain respects the ceremonial functions of the Law lie at the heart of its covenantal structure. So with the coming of a non-Levitical priesthood, "there must also be a change of the law" (7:12; cf. 7:17-19), i.e., of the law-covenant. That in turn suggests that it was not the function of the Mosaic Law to establish a pattern of worship and a religious framework valid for God's people for all time, but that the Law was part of a pattern that *pointed forward* to a still greater priest and to the ultimate covenant. Inevitably there are points of continuity between the Sinai covenant and the new covenant, but the fundamental change must be grasped to see how the Bible hangs together.

(5) That leads to the wonderful picture in this chapter of the perfection and finality of Jesus as Melchizedekian priest. Meditate on 7:23-25.

Numbers 10; Psalms 46—47; *Song of Songs 8; Hebrews 8*

SONG 7:9B—8:4 PICTURES RENEWED CONSUMMATION. The Song of Songs depicts several cycles of estrangement, pursuit, consummation. But in the closing verses (**Song 8:5-14**) the cycles are no longer in view. All the participants in the book—the woman (the beloved), her lover, the daughters of Jerusalem, King Solomon, the mother, the brothers—reappear, as the joy and commitments of the lovers are reaffirmed.

The "friends," apparently the daughters of Jerusalem, ask the question, "Who is this coming up from the desert leaning on her lover?" (8:5a) The "leaning" is not because she is weak or ill, but is an index of intimacy. Probably there is a glance back at the theme of the country girl who has become the happy bride.

The Hebrew pronouns show that in the second half of verse 5 the bride herself, the beloved, speaks, addressing her lover. I know of no completely satisfactory explanation of 8:5b. Perhaps the woman is looking back to her first meeting with the one who would become her lover, and perhaps it was on the same spot where his mother conceived him and bore him. If so she is signaling a kind of familial link, an inter-generational connection. Couples may think they are the first to fall in love, but this woman is shrewd enough to grasp the cohesiveness of human love and life. For her, "love is as strong as death" (8:6). When death calls, none can stop it; when love calls, the same is true. In this light, "jealousy" (8:6) is not the green-eyed monster, but passionate, righteous claims of possession (as in Ex. 20:5). Genuine love can be neither quenched nor bought (8:7).

Commentators dispute who is speaking in 8:8-9, but it sounds like the brothers (cf. 1:6). The "little sister" of whom they speak is either the beloved herself, whom they do not consider ready for marriage, and to whom she gives a robust reply (8:10); or, more probably, the younger sister of the beloved and her brothers, who is not yet quite sexually mature. The point of their comment is then twofold: to hint at yet another oncoming generation that will fall in love, repeating the cycle all over again; and to serve as a foil to the maturity and delight of the beloved in her consummated relationship with her lover.

If the metaphorical value of "vineyard" persists (8:11-12; cf. 2:15), the beloved insists that Solomon may have a large harem, but the only one who can give away the beloved's "vineyard" is the beloved herself. He cannot command her love, whether for himself (the thousand shekels) or for others (the two hundred shekels—the percentage of the profit of a vineyard shared by the laborers); she gives it. The closing verses are a reprise of consummated love.

Numbers 11; Psalm 48; *Isaiah 1; Hebrews 9*

∾

THE OPENING VERSE OF **ISAIAH 1** introduces the massive sweep of the book. It announces a vision that Isaiah saw, a vision that runs through the reigns of the four kings of Judah from King Uzziah on.

The first section (1:2-9) displays how far the nation has fallen. God himself raised up the nation of Israel (1:2)—indeed, he "reared" them, brought them up like children; and like rebellious children they have turned against him. An ox or a donkey knows more of its true home than Israel knows of hers. The heavens and earth are invited to listen in on the rebuke (1:2), both as a measure of the intensity of the rebellion and because there is a sense in which the well-being of the entire universe depends on whether God's people obey or disobey his word. The description of the devastation in the land (1:5-9) is not metaphorical: probably what is being described is the bloody carnage that accompanied the invasion of Judah by Sennacherib's Assyrian forces (701 B.C.)—a foretaste of judgment to come.

From here to the end of the chapter, the thought runs in three movements:

(1) Israel is excoriated for her corrupt and hypocritical worship (1:10-17). In dripping sarcasm, God addresses his covenant people as Sodom and Gomorrah. They maintain the stipulated sacrificial system and high feast days, but God insists he cannot bear their "evil assemblies" (1:13); he hates them (1:14). God will not even listen to his people when they pray (1:15), for oppression of the weak and corruption in the administration have reached such proportions that he must act in line with the Sinai covenant (Deut. 21:18-21). He can ignore these violations no longer.

(2) Nevertheless Israel is still being invited to forgiveness and cleansing: "'Come now, let us reason together,' says the LORD. 'Though your sins are like scarlet, they shall be as white as snow; though they are red as crimson, they shall be like wool'" (1:18-20). It is not cultic observance that triggers such forgiveness, but repentance: "If you are willing and obedient, you will eat the best from the land" (1:19). The alternative is judgment (1:20). Later in the book the basis for such forgiveness will be set forth; the devastating judgment of oppression and exile was not necessary, but so often we prefer sin to salvation, greed to grace.

(3) Yet Zion (representing the people of God) will one day "be redeemed with justice, her penitent ones with righteousness" (1:27). There is no final redemption that ignores justice and righteousness; only judgment awaits the impenitent (1:28, 31).

∾

Numbers 12—13; Psalm 49; *Isaiah 2; Hebrews 10*

∾

THE FIRST SECTION OF **ISAIAH 2** (vv. 1-5) simultaneously looks backward and forward. The first line reminds the reader of 1:1. When the two introductions, 1:1 and 2:1, are taken together, we are afforded a comprehensive glimpse of this book. Much of it focuses on the days of Uzziah and the other kings mentioned in 1:1, but the vision is so comprehensive that it includes "the last days" (2:2). It deals with Judah and Jerusalem, but it anticipates the Zion that is to come.

These opening verses also link up with the blessings promised in the final verses of chapter 1. Now, however, the vision is openly eschatological. One holy mountain, the mountain of the Lord, will reign supreme. In one sense this vision is exclusive; in another, it is comprehensive, for "all nations will stream to it," and "[m]any peoples" will say, "Come, let us go up to the mountain of the LORD" (2:2, 3). In terms that have become proverbial in the English language, Isaiah depicts universal peace (2:4). Although he roundly denounces the injustice of his day, he never loses sight of the fact that our ultimate hope is not political reform but the final intervention of God.

These opening verses also point forward in the text. Before the "last days" of 2:2-5, the Lord has another "day" in store (2:6-22, especially 2:12). The prophet knows judgment is impending, for what is going on in the nation means God has already in some measure abandoned his people (2:6). They have adopted religious superstitions from the East, and they now practice divination like the Philistines (who lived in the West). In other words, they pursue idolatry wherever they can find it. Material blessings have made them unbearably arrogant (2:7-9). But when judgment falls, the "eyes of the arrogant man will be humbled and the pride of men brought low; the LORD alone will be exalted in that day" (2:11). Some will hide among rocks and caves, fleeing invaders whom God has brought on his people (2:10, 19-21; compare Rev. 6:12-17). When in "the splendor of his majesty" God "rises to shake the earth" (2:21), there is no place to hide.

How much more do large swaths of the confessing church in the West stand under similar judgment? "Their land is full of silver and gold; there is no end to their treasures" (2:7). But we are not a people characterized by great humility and zeal for the Lord's glory. The solution is the same as in Isaiah's day: "Stop trusting in man, who has but a breath in his nostrils. Of what account is he?" (2:22).

∾

Numbers 14; Psalm 50; *Isaiah 3—4; Hebrews 11*

∾

MOST OF ISAIAH 3—4 IS GIVEN OVER to specific judgment, in a kind of ABB'A' construction (3:1—4:1), which is followed by glorious hope for the future (4:2-6).

At the core of the condemnation is the Lord as Judge, indicting "the elders and
leaders [literally, 'princes'] of his people" (3:13-15). Royal family and local leaders ("elders") alike have descended to corruption and oppression. But the next
two verses condemn the "women of Zion" as well (3:16-17). The men are condemned primarily for oppression, the women for their vanity and ostentation.
Surrounding these verses are two longer sections unfolding what the men are
being condemned for (3:1-12) and what the women's judgment will be like
(3:18—4:1).

God will bring siege and famine upon the people (3:1), resulting in the elim-
ination of community leaders, whether by deportation or death (3:2-3). The entire
society will break down, signaled not least by a desperate willingness to appoint
almost anyone as leader (3:5). This vision was literally fulfilled a century and a
half later (2 Kings 25:1-12), but there were adumbrations within Isaiah's lifetime
of what the judgment would be like: what Assyria began (Isa. 39:5-7), Babylon
completed. For the culture was largely corrupt (3:8-11), the cause lying in the
leadership, which was as weak as it was oppressive (3:12).

The siege will not be kind to the ostentatious women either (3:18—4:1). All
their finery is to be snatched away (3:18-23). Instead of the delightful fragrances
on which they have spent so much money, there will be stench. There will be dis-
ease (3:17a), sexual abuse (3:17b—the RSV is probably right: "the Lord will lay
bare their secret parts," i.e., subject them to the sexual assaults so common in
war), and bereavement (3:25). Some will end up throwing themselves at any male
available in the desperate hope for refuge and home (4:1)—but the slaughter of
males will be so terrible that there will not be enough to go around.

Often in Old Testament prophecy there is a "foreshortening" of visions of the
future that runs back and forth between the near future and something much farther away. If the day of the Lord brings horrendous judgment (3:6—4:1), it also
brings glory (4:2-6). Later, "Branch" (4:2) will clearly be a way of referring to
Messiah (11:1; 53:2; cf. Jer. 23:5; 33:15; Zech. 3:8; 6:12), but here it seems to refer
to the people and purposes of God in glorious fruitfulness. In language that calls
forth images of the Exodus, God promises to wash away the filth of his people
and manifest his glory as a protective shield over them (4:4-6).

∾

Numbers 15; Psalm 51; *Isaiah 5; Hebrews 12*

∽

IT IS NEVER EASY TO GET ACROSS a message of impending judgment (**Isa. 5**) to people who are convinced they are not all that bad, especially when the ruling elite are enjoying good times. So Isaiah resorts to an attention-grabbing song. He picks up the ancient equivalent of a guitar and begins to sing a simple ballad about his true love. His audience is hooked—and then they cannot help but feel the hammer-blows.

In the ballad Isaiah begins by referring to God as "the one I love. . . . My loved one" (5:1). Because God has not yet been identified, doubtless the language instantly captures the audience. But it also reflects what Isaiah feels: he is not a dispassionate observer but a prophet deeply in love with the being and ways of the living God. Not to love him wholly is already part of the problem, whether under the old covenant or the new (cf. Rev. 2:1-7). Israel is often pictured as the Lord's vine, so it will not be long before Isaiah's hearers begin to get the point. Isaiah does not restrict himself to subtle allusions, however; he delivers both God's threatening speech and his own explanation of his ballad-parable.

The people have produced only useless wild grapes, bad fruit. The nature of that fruit is described in the string of woes (5:8-25). In a nutshell, the social justice demanded by the covenant has been observed in the breach. Against the specific covenantal insistence that the land is the Lord's and is to be parceled out fairly, land-grabbing has become the norm, squeezing out the little people (5:8-11). The wealth among the elite in Uzziah's day has fueled wanton arrogance and drunkenness (5:11-12) and sneering defiance of God (5:18-19). Ultimately the land has overflowed with moral relativism and confusion, doubtless pitched as sophisticated thought, but actually nothing more than a commitment "to call evil good and good evil" (5:20). At bottom there is arrogance (5:21) and corruption in the administration and the courts (5:22-23). The Lord's judgment is implacable (5:24-25).

None of this means that God is checkmated. In the final section of the chapter (5:26-30), God says what he will do. Punishment, the destruction of God's "vineyard," will come by foreign invasion—the metaphorical language of these verses is frankly terrifying. But the foreign invaders are not merely fortunate opportunists with a powerful army. God himself whistles them up, like someone calling for a dog. Despite the ruinous guilt of the people, Isaiah never doubts that God is sovereign over history and can dispose of nations in judgment as well as in mercy. That theme will grow stronger in this book.

∽

Numbers 16; Psalms 52—54; *Isaiah 6; Hebrews 13*

∾

PROBABLY ISAIAH'S VISION OF God and his commission (**Isa. 6**) took place at the beginning of his ministry, but it is reported only here, for thematic reasons. After the series of "woes" pronounced on the people, Isaiah pronounces one on himself (6:5), which shows that his stance as a prophet has never been self-righteous. Moreover, the sequence of his own call—seeing God (6:1-4), deep awareness and confession of sin (6:5), cleansing (6:6-7) and commissioning (6:8-13)—is precisely the sequence that Israel must experience if they are to return to their proper role as servant of the living God. It is the sequence we must follow too. Moreover, several elements in Isaiah's call are then picked up in the ensuing chapters (as we shall see), making this placement of the narrative of his vision of God highly strategic. Some notes:

(1) It was when King Uzziah died that Isaiah saw the Lord *seated on a throne*—as if the earthly king had to die before Isaiah could begin to grasp the awesomeness of the divine King.

(2) The seraphs, a high order of angelic beings, enhance the throne by their adoration and praise. God is the "thrice holy" God. In its core usage, "holy" is almost an adjective for God, and embraces both his transcendence and his righteousness (5:16).

(3) When the finite, the unclean, and the mortal comes into contact with the infinite, the pure, and the immortal, there must be, there ought to be, a profound sense of inadequacy. To begin to see God is to begin to see how awful and desperate our plight is. The holiness of God discloses our rebellious and dirty nature to us in a way that mutual comparisons among the members of the rebel race never can. Here Isaiah condemns himself, for in the presence of God degrees of sin seem superfluous.

(4) Only the cleansing provided by the altar that God himself has prescribed will suffice to take away Isaiah's sin.

(5) For the first time in this vision, God speaks, and looks for volunteers (itself a gracious act of condescension). When Isaiah responds, it is less the cry of the hero than the petition of the pardoned. It is as if he is begging, "Here! Please! Will I do? Is there any way I can help? Will you please use me?"

(6) The substance of the commission Isaiah receives is to preach on until the irrevocable judgment falls. There is no prospect of revival. It is too late. The preaching will serve only to harden the people. The only hint of hope—a hint powerfully developed later in the book (11:1)—is that out of the stump of the destroyed nation new life will spring, and through this remnant the promised seed (6:13b).

∾

Numbers 17—18; Psalm 55; *Isaiah 7; James 1*

❧

THE INTERPRETATIONS OF **ISAIAH 7** are legion. In my view only two are plausible.

The setting is clear enough (7:1-12). King Ahaz of Judah is terrified of the northern kingdom of Israel forming an alliance with Syria and destroying the southern kingdom. He is therefore unwilling to join them in their pact against the regional superpower, Assyria. In fact, he thinks that by becoming a vassal state of Assyria he might gain some security against the northern kingdom and Syria. The Lord tells Isaiah to take his son Shear-Jashub (which can mean either "a remnant shall return" or "a remnant shall repent") and meet King Ahaz at the end of the aqueduct; apparently the king is inspecting the water supply in anticipation of a long siege. Isaiah has a radical alternative plan to propose from the Lord: trust no one but God, and God will protect Jerusalem and Judah. But under a pretense of piety Ahaz refuses to do this (7:12), and therefore judgment must follow: Judah will shortly be attacked and overrun by the very Assyria Ahaz courts for protection (7:17-20).

Uncertainty arises over the Immanuel prophecy. On one view, the end of Isaiah 6, which anticipates the rise of a righteous remnant, is tied to the name of Isaiah's son: at least a remnant will repent, and Ahaz is invited to join that remnant. Zion, pictured as a young woman, gives birth to the faithful remnant who will emerge from her sufferings. This "son" is given the name "Immanuel" precisely because God is with us, the faithful remnant. Note the change from "your God" (7:11) to "my God" (7:13). Before this "son" reaches the age of moral discernment (not more than a few years), the land will have been devastated by Assyria (7:17)— for the Lord himself will whistle up the opponents. Even before this (7:16a), the lands of Israel and Syria will be laid waste. From the righteous remnant springs the Messiah—which is why Matthew 1:23 can apply Isaiah 7:14 to Jesus.

By the alternative view, Ahaz, despite his pious language (7:12), has utterly rejected the Lord's demand that he trust the Lord and abandon any thought of an alliance with Assyria. So the "sign" promised in 7:13-14 is not a sign inviting repentance but a sign confirming divine condemnation (as in, e.g., Ex. 3:12; 1 Sam. 2:34; Isa. 37:30). Judging by the high expectations of verse 11, the sign must be spectacular, not merely a time-lag before a young woman becomes pregnant. Despite arguments to the contrary, the word rendered "virgin" really should be taken that way. In this light, the "Immanuel" prophecy really is messianic. The title, "God with us," anticipates "mighty God" applied to the Davidic Messiah in Isaiah 9:2-7. His coming retrospectively confirms all the judgment that has been pronounced.

❧

Numbers 19; Psalms 56—57; *Isaiah 8:1—9:7; James 2*

&

"FOR WE MAINTAIN THAT A MAN is justified by faith apart from observing the law" (Rom. 3:28). So writes the apostle Paul. "You foolish man," argues James, "do you want evidence that faith without deeds is useless? . . . You see that a person is justified by what he does and not by faith alone. . . . As the body without the spirit is dead, so faith without deeds is dead" (**James 2:14-26**, especially vv. 20, 24, 26).

The formal contradiction between Paul and James is so striking that it has called forth relentless discussion across the centuries. Many contemporary critics, skeptical that God has really spoken in the Bible, think the passages are irreconcilable, and that together they demonstrate that from the beginning there were disparate branches of Christianity with distinctive and even mutually contradictory interpretations. Others think that the real secret to the relationship between Paul and James lies in very different meanings of "works" or "deeds."

Several explanatory syntheses have been offered, but they cannot be evaluated here. It may be helpful, however, to reflect on the following points:

(a) Paul and James are facing very different problems. Paul is facing those who want to say that works, whether good or bad, make a fundamental contribution to whether one becomes a Christian (see one of his responses in Rom. 9:10-12). His answer is that they do not and cannot: God's grace is received by faith alone. James is facing those who argue that saving faith is found even in those who simply affirm (for instance) that there is one God (James 2:19). His answer is that such faith is inadequate; genuine faith produces good works, or else it is dead faith.

(b) Issues of sequence are thus at stake. Paul argues that works cannot help a person become a Christian; James argues that good works must be displayed by the Christian. But on this point, Paul would not disagree; see, for instance, 1 Corinthians 6:9-11.

(c) Paul's dominant usage of "justification" has to do with that act of God by which, on the basis of Christ's work on the cross, he declares guilty sinners acquitted and just in his eyes. Such justification is entirely gracious (Rom. 3:20; Gal. 2:16). James focuses rather more on "justification" before peers (James 2:18) and even on final judgment. A genuinely Christian life, says James, must be a transformed life. Again, Paul does not disagree: "For we must all appear before the judgment seat of Christ, that each one may receive what is due him for the things done while in the body, whether good or bad" (2 Cor. 5:10). The allotment of rewards may be of grace, for even our good deeds finally spring from God's grace—but the deeds are not therefore less necessary.

&

Numbers 20; Psalms 58—59; *Isaiah 9:8—10:4; James 3*

ISAIAH 9:8—10:4 RETURNS TO THE theme of judgment, but this time it is directed not against the southern kingdom of Judah (as in 5:8-25) but against the northern kingdom of Israel (characterized as "Ephraim" and "Samaria," 9:9). The passage is broken into four sections, each ending with the same refrain: "Yet for all this, his anger is not turned away, his hand is still upraised" (9:12, 17, 21; 10:4). This refrain answers the question, "What will God do with a people who will not seek him even in a situation of social collapse and threatening devastation?" These are already marks of God's judgment on the nation, but still there is no sign of repentance. So what will God do? The answer is that, even though God's judgment is gradually being ratcheted up, transparently it is not yet enough—so his anger is not turned away; his hand is still upraised. God has already sent a "message" against Jacob (9:8), but they have not attended to it; "the people have not returned to him who struck them, nor have they sought the LORD Almighty" (9:13). What is left is the "day of reckoning" (10:3).

There is another rough progression of thought running through the four sections. The first two sections tend to emphasize the moral decay: "everyone is ungodly and wicked, every mouth speaks vileness" (9:17). But wickedness burns and devours like a forest fire (9:18). Soon there is social disintegration and cultural collapse (9:20—10:4). Ultimately the Assyrians will obliterate the northern kingdom. (Syria fell to Assyria in 732 B.C., Israel in 722. Judah was devastated by Assyria in 701, but not totally destroyed; that awaited the Babylonians a century later.)

Once again this section of Isaiah, for all that it condemns the populace of the northern kingdom for their wanton sin and failure to heed God-given warnings, lays primary responsibility on the leaders. The Lord "will cut off from Israel both head and tail. . . . [T]he elders and prominent men are the head, the prophets who teach lies are the tail. Those who guide this people mislead them, and those who are guided are led astray" (9:14-16). "Woe to those who make unjust laws, to those who issue oppressive decrees, to deprive the poor of their rights and withhold justice from the oppressed of my people, making widows their prey and robbing the fatherless. What will you do on the day of reckoning, when disaster comes from afar? To whom will you run for help? Where will you leave your riches?" (10:1-3).

Numbers 21; Psalms 60—61; *Isaiah 10:5-34; James 4*

∽

THE THRUST OF ISAIAH 10:5-34 is clear enough. At the beginning and the end (10:5-19, 28-34), the emphasis is on the fact that mighty Assyria will herself be crushed after God has used her to punish his own covenant people. In the central section (10:20-27), the people of God are encouraged neither to fear nor to rely on Assyria, but to rely on the Lord alone.

I shall begin with this central section (10:20-27). One of its great themes is "the remnant." Judgment will fall, but the people of God will not be wiped out: there will be a remnant. This "remnant of Israel" (10:20) probably does not refer to the remnant from the northern kingdom of Israel, but to the remnant of Israelites from the south as well as the north (note the parallel "house of Jacob," the common ancestor, and "remnant of Jacob," 10:20, 21). "Destruction has been decreed, overwhelming and righteous" (10:22), against "the whole land" (10:23). But a remnant will return, not just to a place, but "to the Mighty God" (10:21). In the light of such promises, the people of the southern kingdom, God's "people who live in Zion" (10:24), should not be afraid of the Assyrians, even though they are beaten by them. God's wrath against Israel will end; indeed, it will in short order turn against the Assyrians themselves (10:25-27).

That brings us to the sections on either side of 10:20-27. At one level the theme is plain enough. The God who uses Assyria to punish his wayward covenant community nevertheless holds Assyria responsible for her own sins, and will ultimately destroy them. The empire that is nothing more than a battle ax in the hand of God, wielded against a rebellious nation (10:15), will itself ultimately be axed down by God (10:34). The pronouncement of this judgment is designed to foster faith and perseverance on the part of the remnant.

There is an important subsidiary theological theme in this chapter; the biblical tension between God's sovereignty and human responsibility surfaces in powerful ways. God uses mighty Assyria as if it were nothing but a tool in his hands (10:5, 15). He himself dispatches Assyria to punish Israel (10:6). Assyria, of course, is totally unaware of God's control. Nevertheless, she is held responsible for her own actions and attitudes, not least her arrogance and pride (10:7-11, 13-14). So God will punish her (10:12). This tension between God's sovereignty and human responsibility is not to be despised or rejected, but seized with gratitude, for it will preserve us both from denying the reality of evil and from imagining that evil could ultimately triumph. Meditate on Acts 2:23; 4:27-28.

∽

Numbers 22; Psalms 62—63; *Isaiah 11—12; James 5*

∾

ISAIAH 1—12 FORMS THE FIRST major division of the book; **Isaiah 11—12** closes that division with a picture of the ideal king and the changes he will bring, with the Lord being praised in Zion.

There is a rapid move from the destruction of Assyria in Isaiah 10 to the establishment of the kingdom of God in Isaiah 11. The two are obviously connected theologically: it is God's initiative that effects both. Nevertheless, there is in Isaiah's prophecy a massive foreshortening of the historical process.

In the vision by which he was called to prophetic ministry, Isaiah saw a seed springing from the stump, the remnant of Israel (6:13). Now Assyria falls like a mighty forest before the ax of God (10:33-34)—and a shoot springs from the stump of Jesse (11:1), i.e., from the Davidic dynasty. If in 4:2 the Branch referred to the remnant, or to the Lord's saving work through the remnant, here it explicitly refers to the Messiah. "Messiah" simply means "anointed one," so every anointed king in the Davidic line was in this sense a "messiah." But only the ultimate Messiah could fill the slot described here. Uniquely empowered by the Spirit of God (11:2-3a; cf. John 3:34), his rule is impeccably righteous (11:3b-5), the antithesis of the corruption in the nation that has attracted God's judgment. So perfect and absolute will be Messiah's rule that death and destruction will die: the ultimate state he introduces will be ideal (11:7-9).

Verses 10-16, the second part of chapter 11, unpack some of the symbolic elements of the preceding verses. God's covenant people are regathered to him (11:11-16), but surrounding them are the nations who will also rally to him (11:10). The banner raised over this vast assembly (11:10, 12) marks Messiah's rule, "and his place of rest will be glorious" (11:10). At one level, the "remnant" thus regathered refers to the survivors of historic Israel (11:12), but in the prophetic foreshortening they are also the generation of the elect and faithful people of God in the last days.

The praise of chapter 12 is directed toward "the Holy One of Israel," one of Isaiah's titles for God. In chapter 11 the Messiah is among his people and his reign has begun; in chapter 12 God is among his people and is praised. It is hard not to see that the presence of the Messiah and the presence of God are one and the same, just as in Isaiah 9:2-7 the Davidic king is also the mighty God. Here is the consummation of salvation. "The LORD, the LORD, is my strength and my song; he has become my salvation. With joy you will draw water from the wells of salvation" (12:2-3).

∾

Numbers 23; Psalms 64—65; *Isaiah 13; 1 Peter 1*

∾

THE SECOND MAJOR SECTION OF Isaiah, chapters 13—27, focuses on the nations. This word of the Lord through Isaiah is not actually delivered to the nations; it is pronounced *against* the nations but in the ears of the people of Judah and Jerusalem. In a general sense the message is similar to that in the first part of Isaiah (chaps. 1—12): salvation belongs only to the Lord, so he alone is the One to be trusted. The denunciation of the nations therefore includes comforting asides to Judah (e.g., 14:1-2) and ends with the deliverance of the people of God (chaps. 26—27).

Isaiah 13 is an oracle against Babylon. Because in Isaiah's time the primary military threat was Assyria and not Babylon, many critics think that this chapter is a later interpolation, written a century and a half later (about 550 B.C.) when Babylon had not only risen to supremacy but was already in decline, threatened by the rising Medo-Persian Empire (see 13:17). But that view is too skeptical. The introduction to the oracle unambiguously affirms that Isaiah, son of Amoz, saw this vision (13:1). Moreover, Isaiah 39 shows that even in Isaiah's day, though Babylon was not an immediate threat like Assyria, it was already a rising power. Perhaps more important yet, Babylon's history went back all the way to the Tower of Babel (Gen. 10:9-10; 11:1-9) and thus could serve as a symbol of all nations that defy the God of Israel—a symbolism that persists even in the New Testament (e.g., Rev. 17—18), long after historic Babylon is in eclipse. The ultimate collapse of "Babylon" takes place when "Babylon the Great, the Mother of Prostitutes and of the Abominations of the Earth," who is "drunk with the blood of the saints, the blood of those who bore testimony to Jesus" (Rev. 17:5-6), is obliterated in the triumphant dawning of the reign of the Lord God Almighty (Rev. 19:6), the rule of him who is called "Faithful and True" and whose name is "the Word of God" (Rev. 19:11, 13).

Note three features of this oracle. (a) Once again the "day of the LORD" (Isa. 13:6) is bound up not only with the Lord's coming, but with his coming in judgment. For those opposed to the living God, it is "a cruel day, with wrath and fierce anger" (13:9). (b) Typical of Hebrew poetry, this day is associated with celestial signs; it is as if all nature has to join in with these events, for their significance is no less than cosmic (13:10; cf. Acts 2:20). (c) The heart of the sin that must be overthrown is arrogance (13:11, 19).

∾

Numbers 24; Psalms 66—67; *Isaiah 14; 1 Peter 2*

∿

THE SHORT PARAGRAPH **1 PETER** 2:13-17 is filled with moral admonitions found elsewhere in the New Testament. In today's meditation I shall briefly clarify the main points and observe the supporting themes around the paragraph.

First, like Paul in Romans 13, Peter tells his readers to submit to every properly constituted human authority, and to do so "for the Lord's sake" (2:13-14). Implicitly, Peter acknowledges that such human authorities were set up by God, and their proper function (or at least one of them) is to foster justice. *Second,* it is always God's will that Christians by doing good "should silence the ignorant talk of foolish men" (2:15). Behavior stamped by courtesy, respect, and integrity is not itself preaching the Gospel, but it wins a hearing for the Gospel, simultaneously preparing a way for it and authorizing it. *Third,* our freedom from the law-covenant must never become an excuse for licentiousness: "live as servants of God" (2:16). *Finally,* it is always right and good to show proper respect to everyone. Everyone is made in the image of God. But what "proper" means may take on different overtones with different ranks: "Love the brotherhood of believers, fear God, honor the king" (2:17).

The surrounding verses provide support for this outlook. (a) Christians are "a chosen people, a royal priesthood, a holy nation, a people belonging to God," their very existence designed to declare the praise of the One who called them "out of darkness and into his wonderful light" (2:9). The transformation of Christians' conduct is the attestation that they really do belong to God (2:10, 25). (b) This also means that we no longer belong to the world. Here we live "as aliens and strangers" (2:11). If we do not think in those terms, but are frankly comfortable with the world and its ways, we ought to question whether or not we really belong to the "people belonging to God." This is the assumption Peter makes when he writes, "Live such good lives among the pagans that, though they accuse you of doing wrong, they may see your good deeds and glorify God on the day he visits us" (2:12). (c) If any of this involves hardship or suffering—as it especially did in the case of slaves who belonged to cruel and unjust masters—we can never forget that we follow a Master who himself suffered most unjustly. No moral value attaches to suffering what we deserve; we show ourselves to be followers of Jesus Christ when we suffer unjustly and endure it faithfully. "To this you were called, because Christ suffered for you, leaving you an example, that you should follow in his steps" (2:21).

∿

Numbers 25; Psalm 68; *Isaiah 15; 1 Peter 3*

∾

ONE OF THE STRIKING THINGS ABOUT 1 Peter is how Christian conduct is tied to winning a hearing for the Gospel. We saw that theme in yesterday's meditation. Christians are to live in such a way that even the pagans will be forced to glorify God (1 Pet. 2:12). It is God's will "that by doing good you should silence the ignorant talk of foolish men" (2:15). The same theme is developed in chapter 3. Wives with unbelieving husbands should so adorn themselves with a gentle and quiet spirit that their husbands "may be won over without words by the behavior of their wives, when they see the purity and reverence of [their] lives" (3:2).

Similarly in **1 Peter 3:8-22**. This passage includes one of the most difficult texts in the New Testament (3:18b-21), one I cannot hope to broach here. But it also once again connects Christian conduct with Christian suffering and therefore with Christian witness. This does not mean that Christian conduct has a merely utilitarian function. Christians are not to act in godly ways simply because it increases their credibility for propagandistic purposes. There are many reasons for doing good. We were "called" to it (3:9); doing good is constitutive of our very identity. Moreover, such behavior inherits blessing from God (3:9-12). Apart from the horrible exceptions that arise out of corrupt regimes and renegades (all too many of them), a citizen doing good does not have to fear oppression from those in charge of criminal justice systems (3:13). We ourselves ought to keep a clear conscience before the living God (3:16). Above all there is the example of Jesus Christ (3:17-18).

But in addition to all these reasons for living godly lives, Peter again connects conduct with witness. Even if we suffer unjustly, we will not live our lives in fear, as pagans must (3:13). Rather, in our tears we will "set apart Christ as Lord" (3:15); we will "sanctify" or "consecrate" Christ as Lord. And in this context, we will hear the apostolic injunction: "Always be prepared to give an answer to everyone who asks you to give the reason for the hope that you have" (3:15). This is similar to Paul's "be prepared in season and out of season" (2 Tim. 4:2). Of course such readiness presupposes a heart attitude eager to bear witness and a commitment to grow in apologetic competence. As in so many other areas of life, we learn best how to do it by doing it. But Peter's immediate point is that as we bear witness, we must do so "with gentleness and respect . . . so that those who speak maliciously . . . may be ashamed of their slander" (3:15, 16).

∾

Numbers 26; Psalm 69; *Isaiah 16; 1 Peter 4*

∾

1 PETER 4 CONTINUES THE THEME of Christian conduct, including unjust suffering. This theme is now increasingly tied to identification with Christ (e.g., 4:14), to final judgment (4:5-6, 7, 17), and above all to the will of God: "So then, those who suffer according to God's will should commit themselves to their faithful Creator and *continue to do good*" (4:19, italics added).

But what does it mean to "do good"? This is spelled out in part in **1 Peter 4:7-11**:

(a) We must be "clear minded and self-controlled so that [we] can pray" (4:7). Self-control is an element of the fruit of the Spirit (Gal. 5:22-23). Minds clouded by the heated pursuit of hedonism are not minds that can pray.

(b) We must "love each other deeply, because love covers over a multitude of sins" (4:8). Peter assumes, realistically, that various breaches will occur in the Christian assembly—just as they occur in a family. But in a mature family, the love of each family member for the others covers over the breaches. So also in the church. This does not mean that there are no sins to expose and discipline; the whole New Testament stands against such reductionism. On the other hand, we must face the fact that sins will be committed—and be prepared to cover them over with love. For there is no way back to the innocence of Eden—certainly not by probing each blemish and letting it all hang out, going over the same sins and failures again and again. There is no way back; there is only a way forward—through the cross, to forgiveness and forbearance. Christians must love each other deeply, "because love covers over a multitude of sins." Mature Christians know their own hearts well enough to realize that they need such love and need to display it.

(c) We must "[o]ffer hospitality to one another without grumbling" (4:9). Loving has more to it than forbearing with another's faults; it has more to it than positive activity such as showing hospitality: it includes how we show such hospitality—not in a grumbling or resentful fashion, but eagerly, graciously, generously.

(d) We must use whatever gifts we have received to serve others (4:10-11). Peter gives some examples, but his list is not exhaustive. If one is called to speak in the church (for example), it is not a time for showing off or for amusing the goats, but for feeding the sheep, and that means speaking "as one speaking the very words of God" (4:11). Meditate on Romans 12:6-8.

Everything is to be done in such a way "that in all things God may be praised through Jesus Christ" (4:11).

∾

Numbers 27; Psalms 70—71; *Isaiah 17—18; 1 Peter 5*

ↄ

IN CHAPTERS 14—16 ISAIAH records oracles against Philistia (to the west of Jerusalem) and against Moab (to the east). Now (**Isaiah 17—18**) he speaks against Syria to the north (with its capital Damascus) and Cush to the south. Ancient Cush was made up of modern Ethiopia, Sudan, and Somaliland, i.e., a large area south of the fourth cataract of the Nile River. By the late eighth century B.C., Cush had merged with Egypt, which is still in view in chapters 19—20. Indeed the twenty-fifth dynasty, which ruled this huge region, were Ethiopians.

Recall that the crisis King Ahaz of Judah faced in Isaiah 7 was an alliance between Syria and Israel, designed to thwart Assyria; Syria and Israel tried to force Judah to join their alliance. So this oracle is against Damascus (17:1) the capital of Syria, and includes Ephraim (17:3—another name for the northern kingdom of Israel). Syria and Israel, so threatening to Judah, would soon be destroyed by Assyria. Damascus fell in 732, Samaria ten years later. After their destruction they would be like an emaciated man (17:4), like a field after harvest with only a few stalks left (17:5), like a grove of olive trees in which the fruit has been plucked and beaten with only a few olives left (17:6). The ultimate cause of the destruction of these nations is their idolatry (17:7-8), bound up with fertility cults (17:10-11).

The means for destroying Syria and Israel is depicted in 17:12-18—almost certainly Assyria, which is in turn destroyed. Yet Isaiah speaks of "many nations" (17:12): once again we have stumbled across prophetic foreshortening, Assyria serving as a model both of all the means of temporal judgment that God uses, and of the fact that he brings all nations to account, even those his providence has deployed as the club of his wrath (cf. 10:5).

If there is no help for Judah and Jerusalem in the nations of Israel and Syria (and still less in Assyria), there is also no help in the other regional power, Egypt/Cush (chap. 18). Egypt sends its ambassadors to Judah (and doubtless to other minor states) to try to woo them into their camp (18:1). Isaiah speaks to them (18:2)—almost certainly he actually speaks to the king in a prophetic oracle about the ambassadors, rather than addressing them directly—and in brilliant rhetoric describes the destruction of their nation. Yet he also heralds a time when Egyptians, just one of the many "people of the world" (18:3), will see the banner the Lord raises and bring gifts to "Mount Zion, the place of the Name of the LORD Almighty" (18:7).

Why fawn over pagan nations (and thinkers!) when the Lord himself will judge them, and when they will one day bow to him?

ↄ

Numbers 28; Psalm 72; *Isaiah 19—20*; *2 Peter 1*

ISAIAH 19—20 CONTINUES THE prophecies regarding Egypt/Cush. Here I shall outline the flow of thought and then draw out an important lesson for the contemporary world.

Isaiah 19 is divided into two parts. The first is poetic in form (19:1-15) and pronounces judgment on Egypt. The details are not sufficiently specific for us to be certain which historical assault on Egypt is in view. Egypt was seized by Esarhaddon (671 B.C.), Ashurbanipal (667), Nebuchadnezzar (568), Cambyses (525), and Alexander the Great (332). Probably the "cruel master" or "fierce king" (19:4) is representative of all of them. The lesson for Isaiah's fellow citizens is the one constantly repeated in this book: do not make alliances with foreign powers; trust God alone. When God acts against Egypt, her religion will not save her (19:1-4), nor will the Nile (normally her lifeblood, 19:5-10), nor her counselors (19:11-15).

The second part of Isaiah 19 is in prose (19:16-25). The words "in that day" recur (19:16, 18, 19, 23, 24)—a sign of the collapsing of the ultimate horizon, the final day of judgment, into the impending historical horizon, much closer to the prophet's immediate context. Using the categories of the day, Isaiah depicts the time when all of Egypt—even a city like Heliopolis (19:18 fn.), formerly the center of the sun-god, Ra—will come under the reign of God. And not Egypt alone: other pagan powers, here represented by Assyria, will unite in common worship of Israel's God, and there will be peace (compare 2:2-5). Here is another adumbration of gospel power that draws in men and women from "every tribe and language and people and nation" (Rev. 5:9), in line with God's gracious promise to Abraham (Gen. 12:3b).

The setting of Isaiah 20 is more specific: the Egyptian-backed Philistine revolt against Assyria (713—711 B.C.; cf. 14:28-31). The passage predicts the destruction of Ashdod, a major city of Philistia. During these three years, Isaiah was told by God to be dressed (or undressed!) like a captive, "stripped and barefoot" (20:2), for at least part of each day, until Ashdod fell—and then he gave a stunning interpretation of his action: he was depicting the destruction and captive status, not of Philistia *but of Egypt* (20:4-6). The lesson is obvious: do not trust your future to Egypt; she is a broken reed.

One lesson to learn turns on the fact that this destruction of Egypt did not take place *until forty years later* (671). Often we demand immediate answers from God. But God took twelve years to bring down Hitler, seventy to bring down the Russian empire, two centuries to humble the British Empire. Reflect on the implications.

Numbers 29; Psalm 73; *Isaiah 21; 2 Peter 2*

∾

IN **2 PETER 2:1-3**, AND THROUGHOUT much of the rest of the chapter, Peter warns against false teachers.

(1) These false teachers emerge *from within* the believing community—in precisely the way that the most dangerous false prophets in Old Testament times were those who emerged *from within* the old covenant community (2:1). False teachers and false prophets are a lot easier to spot when they stand outside the fellowship of God's people and criticize. A David Hume or a Bertrand Russell seduces far smaller numbers of God's people than many popular "televangelists." Even on a smaller scale, the most dangerous false teachers in a local church are those with either little biblical grasp or perverse biblical grasp who in the name of the Gospel twist the community into their particular mold. Expect such people. All of the Bible attests the frequency of their attacks and the tragic damage they cause.

(2) What they "secretly introduce" are "destructive heresies, even denying the sovereign Lord who bought them" (2:2). They never describe their teaching in such terms, of course, nor do they stand in the pulpit and say something like "I disown Jesus" or "I deny that Jesus fully redeemed me from my sin." If they did, they would be turned out. Their approach is almost always to relativize Jesus, diminish his significance, or allow him to stand as part of the background noise while they direct the attention of believers to their own agenda—legalism, perhaps, or endless self-help, or sentimentalized therapy, or a Jesus who is no more than one of many options. Thus by their teaching they disown the Jesus whose death potentially embraced all, not least these false teachers who nominally submit to him but who in reality domesticate him or reinvent him.

(3) Very often these false teachers are popular (2:2). In fact, their popularity has two painful effects. In the eyes of many, it legitimizes these teachers—and then their ostensible legitimacy destroys the credibility of genuine Christianity, for their conduct brings "the way of truth into disrepute."

(4) Quite commonly these false teachers "exploit you" (2:3). Sometimes this exploitation is blatantly fiscal: always watch where the money goes. At least as commonly it is manipulative: they shape your mind and direction by their fluent storytelling.

(5) God has the last word; the condemnation of these false teachers is inevitable (2:3). As the following verses (2:4-10) make clear, God is perfectly capable of saving the righteous remnant and of bringing these false teachers to condemnation.

For each of the preceding five points, think of two examples, one drawn from the Bible and one from Christian history, recent or otherwise.

∾

Numbers 30; Psalm 74; *Isaiah 22; 2 Peter 3*

∽

PETER URGES HIS READERS TO "wholesome thinking" (**2 Peter 3**, especially v. 1), in particular about the Lord's return. This presupposes that unwholesome thinking about the Lord's return was circulating. Today even more forms of unwholesome thinking about this event exist than in the first century. Peter stresses that:

(1) In every generation there will be scoffers who sneer at the notion of Christ's return (3:3). Sometimes this scoffing will be grounded in a profoundly anti-Christian worldview. In our own day, philosophical naturalism obviously has no place for the ultimate supernatural visit to Planet Earth, nor even for an end of history brought about by God himself. The stance may be tied to some uniformitarian perspective (3:4). Never should we forget that such perspectives often have moral dimensions to them. It is so much more convenient, for those who cherish their own moral autonomy, to deny that there is a final accounting (3:3).

(2) We should never overlook the fact that God has not left himself without witness in this regard. Not only has he imposed massive judgments on powerful nations and empires (often by "natural" means), but two events in the record of the earth's existence testify to God's cataclysmic intervention: Creation, and the destruction of the Deluge (3:5-7). Here our society suppresses, for example, the extremely articulate forms of the argument from design: we "deliberately forget" what God has done. Our evaluation of these matters is tied to our *moral* and *spiritual* alienation from God our Maker.

(3) The delay before Christ's return reflects not only God's very different view of the pace of events (3:8), but his matchless forbearance: "He is patient with you, not wanting anyone to perish, but everyone to come to repentance" (3:9). Paul says something similar: "Or do you show contempt for the riches of his kindness, tolerance and patience, not realizing that God's kindness leads you toward repentance?" (Rom. 2:4).

(4) When Christ does return at the end, however, his return will be sudden, unmistakable, and cataclysmic (3:10). It will mark the end of the universe as we know it. During the 1950s, when residents of North America were sometimes asked to build nuclear bomb shelters to shield themselves from the holocaust that threatened, I asked my dad if we should build one. He quietly replied, "Why? When Jesus comes, the very elements will be destroyed [cf. 3:10, 12]. Be ready for him, and fear nothing else."

(5) And that is the point. In light of all this, "what kind of people ought you to be? You ought to live holy and godly lives as you look forward to the day of God and speed its coming" (3:11-12). The test of eschatology is ethics.

∽

Numbers 31; Psalms 75—76; *Isaiah 23; 1 John 1*

IN THIS SECTION OF ISAIAH'S PROPHECY (chaps. 13—27), the city-state of Tyre (**Isaiah 23**) is the last region to attract an oracle of God against it. If Babylon became proverbial for its imperial might and for its cultural and aesthetic achievements, Tyre was famous throughout the Mediterranean world for its wealth.

The historical setting of this oracle is reasonably clear. Babylon has recently been destroyed by the Assyrians (23:13)—a reference to either the attack of Sennacherib (710 B.C.) or the pillaging destruction under Sargon (689). This was before Babylon rose to become a superpower in its own right, one that would eventually destroy and replace Assyria. At this juncture in history, the recent destruction of Babylon serves as the model and threat of what will happen to Tyre.

Tyre made its money as the premier trading center of the Mediterranean world. The ships of Tarshish (Spain, at the other end of the Mediterranean) wail at the reports of Tyre's destruction (23:1, 14). These reports reach Cyprus (23:1), just off the coast, and then Sidon (23:2-4). Egypt, the bread-basket of the Mediterranean, weeps because of the effect on her trade in grain (23:5). The fall of Tyre affected the Mediterranean the way the crash of Wall Street in 1929 affected the world.

Whatever the historical pressures that brought about Tyre's destruction, Isaiah wants us to know that it was the Lord's doing (23:8-12)—and it is he who restores the city-state again, even if all she does with her new lease on life is return to her old "prostitution" (23:15, 17). Yet her sin, finally, is not money, but pride: "The LORD Almighty planned it, to bring low the pride of all glory and to humble all who are renowned on the earth" (23:9). There is no *necessary* connection between wealth and pride (witness Job), but the link is frighteningly common. Great wealth often fosters a spirit of arrogant self-sufficiency. What steps should Christians in the relatively prosperous West take against this dreadful sin?

In the spirit of prophetic foreshortening, the last verses (23:17-18) dance from history to eschatology. Eventually the wealth of the earth, even if it is gathered by great commercial traders like Tyre, will all be set apart for the Lord: he is the One who gave it, and all things return to him. And all such wealth will go to "those who live before the LORD." Here is another adumbration of a reconstituted universe, no longer crippled by all that is vile, where God's people delight in him and his gifts forever.

Numbers 32; Psalm 77; *Isaiah 24; 1 John 2*

∾

ISAIAH 24—27, WHICH CULMINATES the long section of chapters 13—27, is sometimes called "the Isaiah apocalypse." Here Isaiah moves from oracles against particular nations to an apocalypse (an "unveiling") regarding the entire world. The thought is not so much sequential or literalistic as a series of provocative images that tell their own story. **Isaiah 24** primarily describes the devastation that must fall on the whole earth. This is followed by three chapters of songs and even feasting, joyously offered up to the Lord for the triumph that is finally and irrefragably his.

Most of chapter 24 is taken up with the sheer devastation of the final judgment, its thoroughness and terror. In a series of shocking images, cities lie desolate (24:10), vineyards are fruitless (24:13), terror and traps rise everywhere (24:18), and the whole earth is broken up while the heavens unleash cataclysmic floods (24:18-19)—or, alternatively, in a mix of metaphors, the earth withers under devastating drought (24:4). Yet there are two sub-themes that also capture the attention of the reader.

First: "The earth is defiled by its people; they have disobeyed the laws, violated the statutes, and broken the everlasting covenant. Therefore a curse consumes the earth; its people must bear their guilt" (24:5-6). Probably the reference to "covenant" has in view the covenant God established with Noah and his descendants after the Flood (Gen. 9:8-17), which echoes the structure of obligations coming from creation itself. If so, the "laws" and "statutes" that have been violated are the fundamental standards of right behavior implicit and sometimes stipulated in a universe where God is absolutely central and where human beings, God's image-bearers, are rightly and lovingly related to him. The sad reality is that we have "broken the everlasting covenant" (24:5). Our horrible breach has attracted the righteous curse of God (24:6). The apocalyptic vision of final judgment in this chapter is the consequence.

Second: twice in this chapter the glory that accompanies judgment, or that awaits beyond it, breaks through the otherwise unrelenting gloom. In 24:14-16a, Isaiah pictures people coming from the west and the east, acclaiming the majesty of the Lord, raising their voices in joyous praise, singing from the ends of the earth, "Glory to the Righteous One"—which simultaneously signals that the judgment is over and that God has been righteous in dispensing it. The last verse in the chapter (v. 23) is like a prelude to the closing vision of the Bible. The ultimate glory of the new Jerusalem is so brilliant that no sun is needed: "the glory of God gives it light, and the Lamb is its lamp" (Rev. 21:23).

∾

Numbers 33; Psalm 78:1-39; *Isaiah 25; 1 John 3*

～

ISAIAH 25 IS DIVIDED INTO three parts. In the center is a festive banquet (25:6-8). On either side is a song. The first is sung by a solitary singer, doubtless Isaiah himself (25:1-5); the second is a communal song of praise (25:9-12).

At the feast (25:6-8) the food is the finest, and free—"a feast of rich food for all peoples." The "shroud" or "sheet" that "covers all nations" (25:7) is death itself, the result of the curse mentioned in the preceding chapter. This feast is a celebration because God "will swallow up death forever" (25:8). Indeed, all the results of the curse will be obliterated: "The Sovereign LORD will wipe away the tears from all faces" (25:8; compare Rev. 21). Indeed, the blessings depicted in this verse are secured by Jesus (see Luke 14:15-24), who vanquishes death (1 Cor. 15:25-26, 51-57; 2 Tim. 1:10). This feast is for "all peoples" (25:6)—another of the many Isaianic prefigurings of the universal application of the Gospel—yet they must come to "this mountain" (25:7); for salvation, as Jesus insists to the Samaritan woman, is "from the Jews" (John 4:22). When Isaiah adds that God will remove the disgrace of "his people" from all the earth, the reference is slightly ambiguous: this may be a reference to Israel, or it may be a reference to those drawn from "all peoples" who truly prove to be his people on the last day.

The song of the lone singer (25:1-5) abounds in exuberant praise to God because he is perfectly faithful. This faithfulness is demonstrated both in the devastating judgments he has brought about and in God's perennial care for the poor and needy (25:4). In short, God is praised for the faithful *justice* of his judgments. The final communal song (25:9-12) finds God's people collectively praising him: "Surely this is our God; we trusted in him, and he saved us." (25:9). But here, too, the inverse activity of God is to be praised: God has brought judgment on those full of pride. Moab is singled out as an example of such waywardness. So at the end, there will be two communities: God's people at the festal banquet where God himself is host and death is destroyed; and the utterly proud, who will not bend the knee but whom God brings down "to the very dust" (25:12). One commentator (Barry G. Webb) writes, "Either repentance will bring you to the feast or pride will keep you away, and the consequences will be unsullied joy or unspeakably terrible judgment. The alternatives which the Gospel sets before us are as stark as that."

Numbers 34; Psalm 78:40-72; *Isaiah 26; 1 John 4*

IN HIS SONG OF PRAISE, ISAIAH celebrates the Lord's impending triumph and demonstrates what it means to wait for him to act (**Isaiah 26**). The opening verses offer anticipatory praise (26:1-6), offered to the God who makes the ultimate Jerusalem the rampart of security (26:2) and preserves in peace the minds of all the individuals within it—all who trust in the living God (2:3-4).

Most of the chapter is devoted to reflections on what it means to wait for that ultimate triumph (26:7-21). "Yes, LORD," Isaiah writes, "walking in the way of your laws, we wait for you; your name and renown are the desire of our hearts" (26:8). But while the righteous yearn for the living God (26:9a), the shocking reality is that the people who do not know him never learn anything from the grace that God shows them (26:9b-10). And so eventually the people of God cry out that God might come and impose his righteousness (26:11)—very much as in Revelation 6:10.

Meanwhile, the faithful remnant live with ambiguity and disappointment (26:12-18). Idolatry flourishes in the land where the living God established peace (26:12-13). The remnant remains faithful while the culture succumbs (26:13). What is described in the next verses is almost the cyclical pattern of Israel's history. God responds to the infidelity with judgment. In due course he returns with grace, enlarges the nation, and extends his own glory. And yet, when all is said and done, what is the outcome? The nation is like a woman writhing in the pains of childbirth—and when she finally brings forth her offspring, all she has produced is wind (26:18). "We have not brought salvation to the earth; we have not given birth to people of the world" (26:18). Where is the great hope bound up with Israel's identity, with the promise to the patriarch that in Israel's seed all the nations of the earth would be blessed (Gen. 12)?

Yet the chapter ends with hope. There is even hope for those who have died during the wearisome cycles of frustration, failure, futility, and judgment: they neither waited nor died in vain, for they will rise from the dead and share in the joy of victory (26:19)—a promise of life briefly glimpsed in 25:8, demonstrated in the resurrection of Jesus, and ultimately fulfilled at the end (1 Cor. 15; 1 Thess. 4:13-18). Meanwhile, those who are still alive must wait in patience for the wrath of God to pass (26:20-21). More clearly than Isaiah, we know that "our light and momentary troubles are achieving for us an eternal glory that far outweighs them all" (2 Cor. 4:17-18; cf. Rom. 8:18).

Numbers 35; Psalm 79; *Isaiah 27; 1 John 5*

∾

MOST PEOPLE WHO HAVE READ 1 John a few times know that John discusses a number of evidences (some commentators call them "tests" or "tests of life") that clarify who truly is a Christian. Most people see three tests: (a) a test of truth, in particular the truth that Jesus is the Son of God; (b) a test of obedience, in particular obedience to the commands of Jesus; (c) a test of love, in particular love for our brothers and sisters. The danger lies in thinking that these "tests" somehow make independent contributions, as if a person might hope to pass two out of three. But toward the end of this epistle, not least in 1 John 5:1-5, these three tests come together in such a way that they are not independent at all. They all hang together.

This paragraph begins with the truth test, with the person "who believes that Jesus is the Christ" (5:1). That person is born of God—a point repeatedly reiterated in John's writings. But everyone who is born of God will surely love others who have been born of God—spiritual siblings, as it were (5:1). Thus the truth test is linked, through the new birth, to the love test. How then do we know that we really do love the children of God? Well, first of all, by loving God himself, and then in consequence carrying out his commands (5:2). Indeed, it is ridiculous to claim to love God and not obey him. So obvious is this that one might go so far as to say that "love for God" is "to obey his commands" (5:3). Of course, John has already reminded his readers that one of Jesus' central commands, his "new commandment," is that his disciples love one another (2:3-11; 3:11-20; cf. John 13:34-35). Thus the love test is tied to the obedience test at several levels.

One must not think that Christianity is nothing more than tough-minded obedience. The truth is that Jesus' commands "are not burdensome" (5:3), for in the new birth God has given us the power to perform what Jesus commands, the ability to overcome "the world" (5:4-5; cf. 2:15-17). Who, then, has this power to overcome the world? Those who are born again, those who have genuine faith, of course—and genuine faith is defined in terms of faith's object, namely the truth that Jesus truly is the Son of God. Thus the test of obedience, and with it the test of love, is tied back to the truth test.

The glorious reality is that, in the Christian way, truth and ethics are tied together. Creedal confession and transformed living go hand in hand. Any other alternative is either superstition or humbug.

∾

Numbers 36; Psalm 80; *Isaiah 28; 2 John*

∾

EVEN A CURSORY READING OF **2 John** shows that the background to this short epistle overlaps in some measure with the background to 1 John. In both epistles there is a truth question tied to the identity of Jesus Christ. "Many deceivers, who do not acknowledge Jesus Christ as coming in the flesh, have gone out into the world" (2 John 7). These particular deceivers denied "Jesus Christ as coming in the flesh"—which, interpreted paraphrastically, means they denied that Jesus was Christ come in the flesh. They introduced a hiatus between the flesh-and-blood Jesus and the "Christ" who came upon him. Thus they denied the essential oneness of Jesus Christ, the God/man, the one who was simultaneously Son of God and human being. There were many sad implications.

The reasons for this doctrinal aberration were bound up with widespread cultural pressures. Suffice it to say that these "deceivers," these "errorists" (as some have called them), thought of themselves as advanced thinkers, as progressives. They did not see themselves as evaluating the Christian faith and choosing to deny certain cardinal truths, picking and choosing according to some obscure principle. Rather, they saw themselves as providing a true and progressive interpretation of the whole, over against the conservatives and traditionalists who really did not understand the culture. That is why John speaks of them, with heavy irony, as running ahead of the truth: "Anyone who runs ahead and does not continue in the teaching of Christ does not have God; whoever continues in the teaching has both the Father and the Son" (9). John's stance is much like the old minister who hears some newfangled doctrine and opines,

> You say I am not with it.
> My friend, I do not doubt it.
> But when I see what I'm not with,
> I'd rather be without it.

The crucial issue, of course, is not whether one is "progressive" or not, or a "traditionalist" or not: one could be a progressive in a good or a bad sense, and a traditionalist in a good or a bad sense. Such labels, by themselves, are frequently manipulative and rarely add much clarity to complex matters. The real issue is whether or not one is holding to the apostolic Gospel, whether or not one is continuing in the teaching of Christ. That is the perennial test.

Which contemporary movements fail this test, either because they rush "ahead" of the Gospel in their drive to be contemporary or because they have become encrusted with traditions that domesticate the Gospel?

∾

Deuteronomy 1; Psalms 81—82; *Isaiah 29; 3 John*

∾

IN THE THIRD MAJOR SECTION of his book (chaps. 28—35), Isaiah focuses on the central issue that the Jerusalem monarch faces. Will the southern kingdom turn to Egypt as it seeks to withstand the aggression of Assyria, or will it trust the Lord? The nature of the crisis and the abysmal voices circulating in the court occupy chapters 28—29. Chapters 30—31 pronounce woes on all who rely on Egypt: in that direction lies only disaster. Chapters 32—33 depict the godly solution: trust the living God who reigns as King in the midst of his people. The last two chapters of the section, 34 and 35, display respectively the scorched earth of judgment that will result from trusting pagan nations, and the garden of delight that awaits those who trust the Lord.

Isaiah 29, then, is part of the description of the crisis. Jerusalem is addressed as "Ariel" (29:1, 2, 7). We know this stands for Jerusalem, because it is described as "the city where David settled" (29:1). The coinage is almost certainly Isaiah's; there is no record of any earlier use of this word for Jerusalem. "Ariel" is a pun on "altar hearth"—the flat surface on the altar where the fire consumed the sacrifices (cf. Ezek. 43:15). God says he is going to "besiege Ariel," which will be to him "like an altar hearth" (29:2): God will ignite the fires of judgment under Jerusalem.

The tragedy of the situation lies in the sheer blindness of the people. This is simultaneously their perversity and God's judgment (29:9-10). No matter what God discloses through Isaiah, the people simply blank out when they hear his words. The truth they cannot fathom; they have no categories for it, for their hearts are far removed from God's ways (29:13). For them, all that Isaiah says remains like words sealed up in a scroll they cannot read (29:11-12). Even their worship becomes little more than conformity to rules (29:13b). So when God does finally break through, it will be with "wonder upon wonder," all designed to overthrow the pretensions of the "wise" and "intelligent" (29:14) who counsel the king to do what God forbids.

The ultimate fulfillment of this pattern takes place in gospel times. Paul understands perfectly well how the person without the Spirit of God finds the truth of the Gospel largely incoherent, how the "wise" and "intelligent" broach many schemes, none of them consistent with the Gospel (1 Cor. 1:18-31; 2:14). Here, too, God destroys the wisdom of the wise (1 Cor. 1:19; Isa. 29:14), for his own way is what none of the wise had foreseen: the sheer "foolishness" of the cross.

∾

Deuteronomy 2; Psalms 83—84; *Isaiah 30; Jude*

∾

ISAIAH 30—31 STAND TOGETHER AS A stern denunciation of all who pursue an alliance with Egypt. Both chapters open with formidable opposition to this alliance (30:1-5; 31:1-3). But **Isaiah 30** concludes with the grace of God, while Isaiah 31 ends in a mighty call to repentance. Striking parallels emerge between Isaiah 30 and today's second highlighted reading, **Jude**.

The first half of Isaiah 30 denounces the leaders in Judah who are aggressively pursuing the help of Egypt. Already their envoys have reached cities in Egypt's Nile delta (30:4). Donkeys and camels, burdened with wealth to buy Egypt's support, are crossing the Negev on their way south. From God's perspective this proves that they are covenantally unfaithful. They are "obstinate children," "deceitful children" (30:1, 9), literally "rebellious sons"—instead of being the faithful son God expected (Ex. 4:22-23). They are more like the proverbial "rebellious son" of Deuteronomy 21:18-21, utterly unteachable and finally to be condemned. And the reason is disheartening: they do not want to listen to revelation—whether the ancient covenantal stipulations that forbade any return to Egypt (Ex. 13:17; Deut. 17:16) or the visions of their contemporary prophets and seers (30:10). Their criterion for acceptable sermons is painfully simple: "Tell us pleasant things, prophesy illusions. Leave this way, get off this path, and stop confronting us with the Holy One of Israel" (30:10-11). That sounds desperately reminiscent of much of the quest for "spirituality" in our day, inside and outside the church, and for much of "therapeutic Christianity," for much of ecumenical Christianity, for much of the health and wealth gospel. There are huge differences among these movements, of course, but what is characteristically missing in them is the powerful theme of impending judgment wherever there is no unqualified submission to God's gracious revelation.

Our hope is the grace of God (30:17-33). He longs to be gracious to his people (30:18)—whether as their Teacher (30:18-22), the One who heals their land (30:23-26), or the Warrior who defends them (30:27-33). Here are the fundamental alternatives: grace (30:18) or Topheth (30:33), the fire pit that anticipates hell itself. Jude understands this. In his own day false teachers leading the people astray are "godless men . . . who suffer the punishment of eternal fire" (Jude 4, 7). By contrast, "To him who is able to keep you from falling and to present you before his glorious presence without fault and with great joy—to the only God our Savior be glory, majesty, power and authority, through Jesus Christ our Lord, before all ages, now and forevermore!" (24-25).

∾

Deuteronomy 3; Psalm 85; *Isaiah 31; Revelation 1*

$\sim$

ALTHOUGH ISAIAH 31 BEGINS ON a historical plane, as so often in this prophecy the text holds up a more distant horizon and a more extensive hope.

At one level Isaiah is still pronouncing divine woes on "those who go down to Egypt for help, who rely on horses, who trust in the multitude of their chariots . . . but do not look to the Holy One of Israel, or seek help from the LORD" (31:1). Isaiah resorts to sarcasm: God, too, "is wise and can bring disaster" (31:2). He resorts to metaphor: God can be likened to a lion perfectly able to fight (31:4), or to a flock of birds perfectly able to protect its own (31:5). That brings the reader to the pivotal verses of this chapter, the only ones written in prose: "Return to him you have so greatly revolted against, O Israelites. For in that day every one of you will reject the idols of silver and gold your sinful hands have made" (31:6-7).

There is no alternative to repentance, no other way to experience the blessing of the Lord. The nature of repentance in Scripture precludes the nonsense of partial repentance or contingent repentance. Genuine repentance does not turn from one sin while safeguarding others; partial repentance is as incongruous as partial pregnancy. Loyalty to God in selective areas is no longer loyalty, but treason. To repent of disloyalty in select areas, while preferring disloyalty in others, is no repentance at all. God does not ask us to give up this or that idol while permitting us to nurture several others; he demands, rather, that we abandon idolatry itself and return to the God against whom we have "so greatly revolted." For God is more than able to defend his people against the might of Assyria, to unleash a sword "not of mortals" (31:8). The literal fulfillment of this promise is 37:36 (see meditation for June 5).

Yet the hints of a still greater deliverance in the more distant future are not hard to find. Once again Isaiah predicts what will happen "in that day" (31:7), that pregnant expression that so commonly signals prophetic foreshortening. Although the loss of almost two hundred thousand Assyrian troops, referred to in 37:38, occurred in 701 B.C., the final collapse of Assyria and its capital Nineveh, described in the closing verses of this chapter, would not take place for another century (612). Moreover, references to the fire of God in Zion (31:9) call to mind 4:2-6 and 29:5-8—visions of the destruction of all of Zion's foes and of the Lord's future reign.

$\sim$

Deuteronomy 4; Psalms 86—87; *Isaiah 32; Revelation 2*

༄

IF ISAIAH 30—31 EXPOSE THE PROBLEM and the dangers of relying on Egypt, Isaiah 32—33 provide the alternative: a good government led by a righteous King. Although Isaiah expects such government to dawn only in the future (e.g., 32:1, 15-16; 33:5-6, 17-22), his stance is not wholly eschatological: he is addressing the crisis of his own day, a day of complacency (32:9-11), when the diplomats have failed and the leaders are desperate (33:7-8), a day when the arrogant Assyrians, "those people of an obscure speech" (33:19), are still in the land. Historically, this probably refers to King Hezekiah's futile attempt to buy off Sennacherib with extraordinary tribute (2 Kings 18:13-16). But Sennacherib is not appeased. His envoys "with their strange, incomprehensible tongue" (33:19) demand that Hezekiah throw open the gates of Jerusalem. When Hezekiah refuses, the siege begins. Now the people of Jerusalem can see the consequences of a government that follows nothing but the empty futility of merely human wisdom. Isaiah offers the only alternative: the kingship of God. Happily, Hezekiah seizes this alternative in the nick of time (2 Kings 19:14-19). But what Isaiah looks for is the time when God's kingship is fully accepted by people and rulers alike.

Isaiah 32, then, begins this vision by showing what such divine government looks like, what it would produce (32:1-8). The identity of this king who reigns in righteousness (32:1) is not as clear as in 11:1-9 (where he is the Messiah) or as in 33:22 (where he is the LORD). From the Christian's perspective, there is no tension in these dual claims: the ultimate King is simultaneously the Anointed One from the line of David and the living God (as in Isa. 9 and Ezek. 34). Here (Isa. 32), the focus is less on the king's identity than on his passion for righteousness. The transformation of the realm is so complete that "the eyes of those who see will no longer be closed, and the ears of those who hear will listen" (32:3)—the reverse of 6:9-10.

But at this juncture there is no way to reach such glory except through judgment. Only a year will slip by before a crushing destruction of the harvest (32:10)—probably when Sennacherib moves in his mighty army after the extravagant tribute fails to placate him. Worse, the city itself will be destroyed (32:14)—an event still a century off. But beyond all that is the pouring out of the Spirit (32:15-20)—God's doing, powerfully transforming the people of God—effected at Pentecost in the wake of the resurrection and exaltation of Jesus the Messiah (Acts 2:16-18) and consummated at his return (Rev. 11:15-17).

༄

JUNE 1

Deuteronomy 5; Psalm 88; *Isaiah 33; Revelation 3*

∽

IF THE LORD RULES, ONE OF THE things he does is destroy the enemies of his people. In **Isaiah 33**, the opening "Woe" is now pronounced, not against the erring people of God (as in 28:1; 29:1, 15; 30:1; 31:1), but against the "destroyer," the Assyrian horde. They are the "traitor" (33:1), doubtless because they accepted the extortionate tribute (see yesterday's meditation) and then attacked anyway. But the betrayer will be betrayed (33:1); probably this refers to the fact that Sennacherib, after returning home, was assassinated by his own sons (37:38).

At this juncture the people of God cry out for his help: "O LORD, be gracious to us; we long for you" (33:2)—an overdue reversal of the callousness they displayed in chapters 29—30. After the extraordinary death of almost two hundred thousand Assyrian troops in 701 B.C., the citizens of Jerusalem were able to leave the city and strip the slain army of vast quantities of plunder (33:4; 37:36).

Once again, the historical picture is cast in terms that anticipate the final judgment of the "nations" (33:4—plural!) and the ultimate blessedness of Zion (33:5-6; cf. 33:17-24). What will prevail is "justice and righteousness" (33:5). God himself "will be the sure foundation" for such times, "a rich store of salvation and wisdom and knowledge; the fear of the LORD is the key to this treasure" (33:6)—showing how the prophetic literature of the Old Testament overlaps with the Wisdom Literature (cf. Prov. 1:7).

The rest of Isaiah 33 expands on these themes. The lament of 33:7-9 demonstrates that the strategies of the rulers and diplomats had to fail before the authorities turned to the Lord in desperation. But that is when God arises (33:10). God himself is able to consume the chaff. Even the enemies "who are far away" (33:13) hear what God has done. But if God is the sort of God who destroys sinners, will not the sinners in Zion likewise be consumed (33:14)? "Who of us can dwell with the consuming fire? Who of us can dwell with everlasting burning?" (33:14). That is why the promise of the Lord's deliverance is always simultaneously a massive call to repentance (33:15-16).

The closing verses (33:17-24) offer a retrospective, a time to reflect on the destruction of all who cherish evil. Such judgment generates a time of peace and stability (33:20). But above all, it is a time of sheer God-centeredness. "Your eyes will see the king in his beauty" (33:17); "the LORD will be our Mighty One" (33:21); for "the LORD is our judge, the LORD is our lawgiver, the LORD is our king; it is he who will save us" (33:22).

∽

Deuteronomy 6; Psalm 89; *Isaiah 34; Revelation 4*

∽

REVELATION 4 IS TO REVELATION 5 what a setting is to a drama. Revelation 4 is a description, in apocalyptic symbolism, of the throne room of Almighty God; Revelation 5 plays out a drama in that setting.

John identifies the voice he hears as the voice he first heard speaking to him like a trumpet (4:1)—the voice of the exalted Lord Jesus (1:10-16). John is called up through an open door into heaven to see the elements of the spectacular vision that unfolds in the ensuing verses. Immediately he is "in the Spirit" (4:2)—perhaps some Spirit-imparted trance or vision, or perhaps, like Paul (2 Cor. 12:1-10), John does not really know the nature of his movement. But what he sees is clear enough:

(a) John sees the centrality and ineffable majesty of the Almighty (4:2b-3). He does not let his readers forget that above all temporal thrones, some of them responsible for appalling persecution, stands the ultimate throne, the throne of God. He describes the blazing glory of light refracting over precious gems, like the crown jewels in the Tower of London. One cannot come away from this vision and draw God. This dazzling, fiery beauty commands awe but permits no replicas (cf. Ezek. 1:28).

(b) John sees the divine throne enhanced by spectacular heavenly beings (4:4). Although it is possible to take the "elders" as representing believers from both old and new covenants, it is better to take them as a high order of angels. They offer the prayers of God's saints to God (5:8), an angelic function (8:3). Believers sing a new song that the elders cannot sing (14:3). In the visions of 7:9-11 and 19:1-4 the elders are found in concentric circles between angels and the four living creatures (the highest order of angelic beings). An elder frequently interprets what is going on (e.g., 5:5)—a common angelic function in apocalyptic literature. Here they enhance the throne and participate in worship.

(c) John sees the holy separateness of the Almighty. That is the point of the three vignettes in 4:5-6a. The massive storm reminds the reader of Sinai (Ex. 19:16). The sea serves as a symbol for the entire fallen order; that is why in the new heaven and the new earth there is no more sea (21:1). John is distanced from the Almighty by these and related phenomena.

(d) John sees the four living creatures, described in terms drawn from Isaiah 6 and Ezekiel 1 and 10. They are the highest angelic beings, orchestrating the praise of the Almighty and reflecting his transcendent administration (4:6b-11). God alone is to be worshiped, for he alone is the Creator (4:11), and all other authority derives from his (4:10).

∽

Deuteronomy 7; Psalm 90; *Isaiah 35; Revelation 5*

∽

THE SETTING OF REVELATION 4 gives way to the drama of **Revelation 5**. In the right hand, the hand of power, "of him who sat on the throne"—the transcendent, awesome God described in chapter 4—there is "a scroll with writing on both sides." This scroll contains all of God's purposes for justice, judgment, and blessing. Most people wrote on only one side of a scroll, the side with the horizontal strips of papyrus. Those who wrote on both sides were perhaps too poor to afford another blank scroll—or, as in this case, they had a great deal to say and wanted it to remain within the confines of one scroll. So this scroll in the hand of the Almighty embraces the fullness of God's purposes for judgment and blessing—that is why it has writing on both sides. Yet the scroll is sealed: this means that the purposes of God recorded in this scroll will not be enacted until the seals are broken.

The angel's dramatic question (5:2) is fundamental to all religion: Who is the agent who has attributes so rich, life so pure, capacities so unexcelled, as to be able to approach this God—the God before whom even the highest order of angels hide their faces—and to take the scroll from his right hand and bring to fruition all of God's purposes? When no one is found who is worthy, John weeps and weeps (5:3-4). His tears stem not from frustration at being unable to see into the future, but from his awareness that, in the symbolism of this vision, God's purposes will never be carried out. There will be no justice in the universe, and no salvation. This is the despair of concluding that history is meaningless, that God is dead.

But an interpreting elder consoles John (5:5). The Lion of the tribe of Judah has "prevailed" (5:5, KJV) to open the scroll: the verb suggests a horrendous struggle, but the Lion has won. This Lion is the king of the Davidic line. So John looks up and sees—a Lamb. The Lion is announced, and what John sees is a Lamb. This is not a separate animal. Apocalyptic literature delights in mixed metaphors. Here the Lion is the Lamb—at that, a slaughtered, sacrificial lamb, yet one with a perfection of kingly power (the seven horns). Here is the Messiah, the utmost in self-giving, the utmost in power, emerging from the very center of the throne. He alone brings to pass all of God's purposes. Small wonder that the entire universe explodes with a new song, the song of redemption (5:9-14). The triumph of the Lord God and of the Lamb is what stands behind the transformation of **Isaiah 35**.

∽

Deuteronomy 8; Psalm 91; *Isaiah 36; Revelation 6*

∾

ISAIAH 36—39 IS LESS A HISTORICAL excursus than the hinge on which the book turns. To change the metaphor, these chapters constitute the bond that holds together the two large parts on either side. Not only do they provide the historical setting of much of the book (especially of many of the first thirty-five chapters), they put in historical form the fundamental question the book addresses: whom shall we trust? Or, in the pagan outlook of Sennacherib's field commander, "On whom are you depending?" (36:5). **Isaiah 36** begins the drama.

King Hezekiah had led the nation in anti-Assyrian rebellion and then looked to Egypt for help. Sennacherib of Assyria was not in a forgiving mood. Proud of his unbroken string of successes (36:18-20), Sennacherib determined to crush Jerusalem and teach an unforgettable lesson. He captured town after town in Judah, until only two were left, Lachish and Jerusalem. Here we find Sennacherib's field commander trying to undermine the remaining forces, speaking in the Hebrew the people of Jerusalem would understand instead of in his own Aramaic (36:11-12).

Perhaps what we should observe most closely from this chapter is the example of Satanic half-truths, the methods of sowing doubt, the arguments calculated to diminish faith in the living God. Know your enemy, not least his lies, and he is diminished and less credible. So here are his weapons:

Much of the speech is raw taunt. By this point, Judah was so desperately short of warriors that even if Sennacherib had provided the horses, Hezekiah could not have provided the men (36:8). The field commander insists he is here at the Lord's command (36:10)—which was of course partially true and even resonated with Isaiah's own teaching (10:5). Yet it was totally false in any sense that presupposed Assyria was the Lord's obedient servant as opposed to an instrument used in the mystery of providence. A conscious attempt to undermine the confidence of the people in Hezekiah (36:13-15) is finally met only by silence (36:21), but the psychological damage must have been considerable. Even the threat of deportation to a strange land is made to sound like a jolly good move to a better location (36:16-17)—a bit like making sin delightful and hiding the shame, loneliness, and death. Of course, if Yahweh can be reduced to the status of pagan deities, it will be easier to dismiss him (36:18-19). And if the field commander misunderstands the significance of Hezekiah's destruction of pagan shrines (36:7), nevertheless he is probably right in sensing the disaffection of many of the people.

What similar lies and half-truths do powerful voices in our society endlessly repeat so as to demoralize the people of God?

∾

Deuteronomy 9; Psalms 92—93; *Isaiah 37; Revelation 7*

∼

HEZEKIAH IS BESIDE HIMSELF (**Isa. 37**). He has disobeyed the Lord and defied Assyria. Mercifully, at this juncture he does the right thing: in desperation he turns to the Lord in importunate and passionate prayer, and to the Lord's prophet Isaiah for intercession and guidance (37:1-4). Isaiah promptly reports a visionary word from the Lord (37:5-7). God sees the stance of Sennacherib as profoundly blasphemous: he has treated the living God as if he were some local pagan deity. God promises that Sennacherib will hear a report that will make him withdraw, and in due course he will be cut down in his own country.

The sequence of events is at this point unclear: we do not have enough information. The next verses suggest that Lachish has proved more difficult to conquer than Sennacherib had anticipated (though he ultimately seizes it), and that he has moved to Libnah. While he is there he hears a report that Egypt (the Cushites, 37:9) is moving against him, and he warns Hezekiah not to think that this will be more than a temporary reprieve. Since Sennacherib shortly resumes his siege of Jerusalem (37:33ff.), perhaps Egypt sent no more than harrying contingents.

In any case, the bleak prospects for Jerusalem drive Hezekiah to prayer (37:14-20), the high water mark of this king's life. Hezekiah does not address God as if he were just a tribal deity. God is the Maker of heaven and earth, the sovereign Creator who alone is "God over all the kingdoms of the earth," and the Almighty God of Israel who is "enthroned between the cherubim" in the Most Holy Place, the God of the covenant (37:16). At the end of his resources, Hezekiah casts himself upon God's mercy, not only so that the tiny nation might be spared, but "so that all kingdoms on earth may know that you alone, O LORD, are God" (37:20).

God answers Hezekiah's prayer. Through the prophet Isaiah, God pronounces an oracle of judgment against Sennacherib (37:22-29), provides a reassuring sign for Hezekiah (37:30-32), and stipulates that Sennacherib will not be permitted to take Jerusalem (37:33-35). God will defend Jerusalem, not for Hezekiah's sake, but for his own sake and for the sake of his servant David. Hezekiah prays, and God answers, but he is saved, not for his own sake, but for the sake of another.

The result is briefly told (37:36-38). The slaughter of the soldiers may have been the result of God-ordained bubonic plague; other similar catastrophes are known from ancient sources. And twenty years later, Sennacherib's sons did cut him down in his own temple, while the temple of the Lord remained inviolate.

∼

Deuteronomy 10; Psalm 94; *Isaiah 38; Revelation 8*

∾

ONE OF THE MOST STRIKING of the symbol-laden images in the book of Revelation is found in **Revelation 8:3-5.**

It has various roots. One goes back to passages like Psalm 141:2: "May my prayer be set before you like incense; may the lifting up of my hands be like the evening sacrifice." David wants his prayers to be as pleasant to God, as acceptable to God, as the incense burned before him in the tabernacle, as the sacrifices offered to him in front of the tabernacle at the close of the day. The incense altar was ordained by the Mosaic covenant (Ex. 30:1-10). This particular kind of altar and sacrifice would have associations in the ancient world that are foreign to us. In a world before Right Guard, better homes might well burn a little incense to mask the inevitable odors, and that association would accompany the burning of incense in the tabernacle and later in the temple. Certainly this God-ordained rite was still functioning in Jesus' day (Luke 1:8-9).

The association between prayers and incense has already been used by John in Revelation 5:8. When the Lion/Lamb, the Lord Jesus, takes the scroll from the right hand of him who sits on the throne and prepares to open the seals, the angels surrounding the throne "fell down before the Lamb." They "were holding golden bowls full of incense, which are the prayers of the saints." The point of the vision is not that incense candles are a good thing in cathedrals (that would confuse symbol and reality), but something more profound. If no one were found to bring about God's purposes for justice and blessing, then all the prayers of God's people are futile. Now that the Lion/Lamb has prevailed, the prayers (symbolized by the incense because of the Old Testament simile) are wafted into the presence of God. The prayers of God's people will be heard and answered, because God's purposes for blessing and judgment are now certain to be carried out.

Here in 8:3-5, "the prayers of all the saints" are burned on the incense altar before God. "Then the angel took the censer, filled it with fire from the altar, and hurled it on the earth; and there came peals of thunder, rumblings, flashes of lightning and an earthquake" (8:5)—all signs, in the context, of the terrifying presence and judgment of God. God's judgment responds to the prayers of his people.

Why should this be thought strange? The souls of martyrs call for justice (Rev. 6:10). The entire church cries, "Come, Lord Jesus" (22:20), knowing that this will bring down final justice. Followers of Jesus pray, "Your kingdom come"—not a sentimental notion in the context of a broken, rebellious world.

∾

Deuteronomy 11; Psalms 95—96; *Isaiah 39; Revelation 9*

∾

IN VOLUME 1 (MEDITATION FOR NOVEMBER 7) I commented on the near-fatal illness of King Hezekiah, and on his recovery and subsequent folly with the
Babylonian emissaries (an account similar to Isa. 39—40 is found in 2 Kings 20).
Death is not the thing most to be feared. Had Hezekiah died from his illness,
instead of living for fifteen additional years, he would not have succumbed to
some of his worst sins of pride and callousness (**Isa. 39:5-8**). But here I shall focus
on something more prosaic: the chronology of the events. For there are lessons
to be learned.

There is considerable dispute over the dating of Hezekiah's reign. What is reasonably clear is that Sennacherib's invasion (Isa. 36:1) occurred in 701 B.C. This
was in the fourteenth year of Hezekiah's reign, which means he came to the throne
in 715 (701 + 14). But 2 Kings 18:1 insists that Hezekiah's accession took place
in the third year of King Hoshea of Israel (the northern kingdom), i.e., approxi-
mately 727. Probably Hezekiah was co-regent with his father Ahaz from 727 to
715, when Ahaz died, and thereafter ruled alone. (Co-regencies were common
among the kings of Judah and Israel.) So the invasion of 701 occurred in either
the fourteenth or the twenty-sixth year of Hezekiah's reign, depending on whether
or not one includes the co-regency years. But 2 Kings 18:1 also specifies that
Hezekiah reigned for twenty-nine years from the onset of his co-regency, which
places his death in 698. If his illness occurred fifteen years earlier (Isa. 38:5), it
happened in 713. The visit of Babylon's emissaries was apparently shortly after
this, in 712 or 711—more than a decade before the Assyrian invasion under
Sennacherib. The phrase "In those days" (38:1) must then be a general reference
to the time of Hezekiah's life and reign rather than something more specific.

What this means is that we should not interpret the events of Isaiah 38—39
as taking place after Sennacherib's invasion, as if this is a relapse following the
heroic and faithful intercession and obedience described in chapters 36—37. The
situation is more complex. Following fruitful years of administration (2 Kings
18), Hezekiah falls ill and is miraculously restored. His boasting to Babylon's emissaries follows (Isa. 39), and may well have been part of Hezekiah's plan to rebel
against Assyria. Hezekiah only learns to trust the Lord a decade later, when
Assyria almost crushes him. He dies three years after that invasion. If this chronology is correct, Hezekiah's extraordinarily selfish and calloused stance in Isaiah
39:8 accurately reflects his ambivalence toward God and toward God's prophet—
until driven by desperation.

When and how do we learn to trust the Lord?

∾

JUNE 8

Deuteronomy 12; Psalms 97—98; *Isaiah 40; Revelation 10*

∽

THREE OBSERVATIONS TO PREPARE THE WAY: (a) If Isaiah was about thirty when he was called to be a prophet in the year that King Uzziah died (6:1), then he was sixty-nine at the time of the Assyrian invasion in 701 and seventy-two in 698 when Hezekiah died. Tradition outside the Bible says that he lived a little longer, into the reign of the wicked King Manasseh, who resolved to kill him. Fleeing Manasseh, the elderly Isaiah hid in a hollow tree in the forest, only to be found by Manasseh's men, who cut down the tree with a saw, Isaiah still inside. There may be an echo of this in Hebrews 11:36-37. (b) On this chronology, Isaiah had foreseen the Babylonian invasion as early as 712 B.C. (39:5-7). Nevertheless the Assyrian invasion of 701 doubtless captured most of his attention until it was behind him. Judging by what appears in these next chapters, Isaiah then spent the few remaining years of his life in a ministry of comfort designed to help the faithful remnant in the still darker days that were ahead. Perhaps this ministry was public and oral for the remaining three years of King Hezekiah's life. Under the brutally repressive regime of Manasseh, however, Isaiah's ministry was more likely to the smaller circle of his disciples (8:16-17) and in the written page that they would preserve until a new generation was again ready to listen to the words of God conveyed through him. (c) Thematically, this next section embraces chapters 40—55, which are full of comfort grounded in the astounding greatness of God and in the immeasurable atonement for sin that he provides.

The comfort provided in the opening overture (**Isa. 40:1-11**) has at least five elements. (a) These are still God's people, "my people" (40:1). Despite the devastating prediction in the preceding verses of Jerusalem's destruction and the transportation of its people, God will comfort Jerusalem again (40:2—clearly parallel with "my people"). (b) Their sins have been forgiven. Since it was their sins that attracted judgment, this is marvelous news. "Your sin has been paid for! Your hard service has been completed!" How this was accomplished is not fully unveiled until chapter 53, but the overture anticipates the symphonic splendor. (c) In consequence of their forgiveness, God himself will bring home the exiles, smoothing their way (40:3-4), gathering his flock like a shepherd (40:11), thereby disclosing his glory to *the entire human race* (40:5); the missionary theme recurs. (d) However fickle people may be, God's word is utterly reliable (40:6-8). (e) The good news shouted from Zion/Jerusalem is "Here is your God"—for "the Sovereign LORD comes with power" (40:9, 10). Small wonder, then, that the remaining verses of the chapter dwell on the sheer majesty of God.

∽

Deuteronomy 13—14; Psalms 99—101; *Isaiah 41; Revelation 11*

THE THEOLOGICAL POWER OF **Isaiah 41** becomes clearer if we grasp something of the underlying history.

In line with the prediction of 39:6-7, Jerusalem was finally destroyed in 587 B.C., her temple razed and her people killed or transported. This was the most shattering event Israel faced in Old Testament times. But far from thinking that this proved that God was losing control, Isaiah not only foresaw the event but insisted that it was God's doing. Now he addresses those who would suffer Babylonian aggression and who would wonder if there was any hope for them at all. Isaiah has already reminded them that as far as God is concerned the nations are no more significant than a drop in the bucket or dust on the scales (40:15-17). Now he predicts that God himself will end the aggression of the Babylonian Empire. He will raise up the Persian king Cyrus (41:2-4, 25-27; Cyrus is actually named in 44:28; 45:1).

Cyrus, king of the Persian city of Anshan, ascended to power in 559, when Persia was still subject to Media. Ten years later he killed the Median king Astyges and founded the Persian Empire. In less than a decade, he subdued territory to the west as far as modern Turkey (conquering the legendary King Croesus on the way), and to the east as far as northwest India. Babylon fell in 539. Cyrus reversed the policy of previous empires. Far from transporting subdued peoples, he encouraged exiles to go home—including Israel (Ezra 1:2-4; see meditation for January 1).

Isaiah 41, then, makes two important points. *First,* God alone is the One who summons nations before him, controlling their destinies, calling on them to accomplish his will—and this includes Cyrus, whom God has "stirred up" for the tasks allotted him. Where is the evidence of this bold claim? It is found in the fact that *God predicts the entire sequence of developments a century and a half in advance* (41:21-29). This is something the pagan idols could not possibly do. "See, they are all false! Their deeds amount to nothing; their images are but wind and confusion" (41:29). Such predictions are the exclusive domain of "Jacob's King" (41:21), for he alone writes history in advance. *Second,* Israel must understand that they are collectively God's servant (41:8-20), the descendants of Jacob and of Abraham before him, themselves the servants of God. None of this means that they are intrinsically great: God addresses them as "O worm Jacob, O little Israel" (41:14). But they do have a great God, their Redeemer, the Holy One of Israel (41:14). They may abandon fear (41:10) and rejoice in him (41:16).

JUNE 10

Deuteronomy 15; Psalm 102; *Isaiah 42; Revelation 12*

∽

ISAIAH HIMSELF IS GOD'S SERVANT (20:3), and so is Hezekiah's chief steward Eliakim (22:20). Israel collectively is God's servant (41:8-20). Who is the servant of the Lord in **Isaiah 42:1-9**?

Some argue that it is still Israel. In that case, God's words, "Here is my servant" (42:1) are uttered before the nations, a kind of defense of his people before the mighty powers that are nothing to him. But this reading of Isaiah 42 is unlikely. "Here is my servant" sounds like the introduction of a new figure. More importantly, God's servant Israel was described in the preceding chapters as complaining (40:27), fearful, and dismayed (41:10). By the end of this chapter, God's servant Israel is deaf, blind (42:18-19), and sinful (42:23-24). By contrast, the servant of the Lord in 42:1-9 neither falters nor is discouraged (42:4), delights in God (42:1), is gentle, persevering, and brings forth justice in faithfulness (42:3). This is an ideal Servant, one who embodies all that Israel failed to be. In this light, the announcement "Here is my servant" is made to Israel. The Servant is introduced to them not only because he is an ideal to which they should aspire, but because he is an individual who will rescue them, as Isaiah will make clear.

This servant song is divided into three parts. (a) In 41:1-4 God addresses Israel and introduces the Servant, who will bring "justice" to the nations. The Hebrew term includes more than the English word. It embraces putting into effect all of God's purposes. But when the Servant does this, he is quite unlike Cyrus or some other imperial leader. He is gentle: he does not shout or cry out or raise his voice in the streets (42:2). He neither breaks the bruised reed nor snuffs the smoldering wick (42:3)—a passage explicitly applied to Jesus in Matthew 12:15-21. (b) In 41:5-7, the Servant himself is addressed (note v. 6: "I the LORD, have called you [*sing.*] in righteousness"), and Israel is allowed to overhear what is said. Here the God who gives breath to all people (42:5) now makes this Servant "to be a covenant for the people and a light for the Gentiles" (42:6), undoing all the degrading effects of sin (42:7). (c) In 42:8-9, the Lord again addresses Israel, once again summarizing the mission of the ideal Servant and insisting that these are "new things" graciously announced in advance.

Small wonder that this song issues in profound praise to the Lord (42:10-17), and contrasts once again the depth of the moral culpability of God's servant Israel (42:18-25) which only the ideal Servant can resolve.

∽

Deuteronomy 16; Psalm 103; *Isaiah 43; Revelation 13*

∾

ALTHOUGH GOD HAS AN IDEAL Servant who will be his perfect agent to bring to pass all his purposes (Isa. 42:1-9), Israel is also God's servant. In **Isaiah 43** and on into chapter 44, Isaiah encourages Israel, God's servant (43:10; 44:1). Here I shall pick up on elements of this encouragement and then draw attention to an important clause picked up by the Lord Jesus in the New Testament.

In the first section (43:1-7), God tells Israel not to be afraid (43:1)—not because she will not go into exile, but because when she passes through the waters God will be with her, and when she passes through the fire the flames will not utterly destroy her (43:2). Moreover, she will not face extinction or assimilation: God himself will gather her children from the four points of the compass (43:5-6). Despite the most appalling circumstances, the living God declares Israel to be precious and honored in his sight, and much loved (43:4). Paul reasons analogously with respect to Christians in Romans 8:31-39.

More briefly: (a) Israel should be encouraged because her return after exile will bear witness to God and testify that it was God alone who knew of these stupendous events and brought them to pass (43:8-13). (b) Babylon will be destroyed. The nation of conquerors will become a tumult of fugitives (43:14-15). (c) Israel is used to reflecting on God's mighty deeds to redeem his people at the time of the Exodus (43:16-17), but now God will do a new thing (43:18-21). So do not dissolve into the past and whine your way to defeat. Be courageous, for God is about to do a new thing, to effect a new cycle of spectacular delivery. (d) Above all, the Israelites' massively compromised worship and multiplied offenses (43:22-24) are not the last word. The first line of 43:22 in Hebrew might better be rendered: "It was not me you called upon, O Jacob"—for the Israelite worship was so corrupt, such a distortion of the covenant, that the true God was not really being worshiped at all. But God himself is the One who blots out their transgressions for his own sake (43:25)—a further anticipation of Isaiah 53.

God wants his servant Israel to understand "that I am he" (43:10; cf. 41:4; 48:12). The Hebrew conjures up associations with Exodus 3:14; the Greek rendering of this phrase is precisely the expression that Jesus repeatedly applies to himself in John 8 (e.g., John 8:58, "I am"). How then does Isaiah 43 shape how we must think of Jesus?

∾

Deuteronomy 17; Psalm 104; *Isaiah 44; Revelation 14*

WE HAVE ALREADY LEARNED THAT God told Israel, "You are my witnesses" (Isa. 43:10, 12). For the Israelites were to testify that God and God alone had predicted all these things, and had thus given evidence that he had done them, since he alone is the sovereign God. In **Isaiah 44:6-23**, these themes are summarized (44:6-8). Yahweh alone is "Israel's King and Redeemer, the LORD Almighty" (44:6). God says, "I am the first and I am the last; apart from me there is no God" (44:6). As for his people: "Do not tremble, do not be afraid. Did I not proclaim this and foretell it long ago? You are my witnesses. Is there any God besides me? No, there is no other Rock; I know not one" (44:8). But if God alone is God, all pretenders are idols. So the summary of this theme introduces one of the most damning indictments of idolatry in the Bible.

From God's perspective, idolatry is always repulsive. In one sense, it is the fundamental sin, for it dethrones God and replaces him with something or someone else. That is why greed is idolatrous (Col. 3:5): we pursue what we covet, and what we pursue most ardently becomes our god. The historical context of this denunciation is critical, for idolatry was practiced not only by all the little nations around Israel, but also by the regional powers and by the succession of superpowers. Inevitably, Egyptians and Assyrians and Babylonians all credited their success to the power of their own deities. Yet here is the God of little Israel— crushed, defeated, exiled, pathetic little Israel—claiming to be the only God, the sovereign Lord, the mighty Creator and providential Ruler over all the kingdoms of the earth. And he is expecting his covenant people to bear witness to this truth instead of succumbing to the idolatry around them which, sadly, they find perennially attractive.

The question of power God will handle on the long haul. Here, the focus is on making idolatry absurd and thereby destroying its plausibility (44:9-20). What initially seems attractive is shown to be ridiculous. The idolatry that is profoundly offensive to God is also profoundly stupid.

The solution is twofold. (a) Israel is called to *remember* what God has said, what God has done (44:21), not least the fact that God has constituted Israel and made Israel his privileged servant. (b) Israel is called to *return* to God, for he has redeemed them (44:22). These must be the constant priorities of God's people: remember all that God is, all that he has said and done; and when we stray, return to him immediately and promptly (1 John 1:7-9).

Deuteronomy 18; Psalm 105; *Isaiah 45; Revelation 15*

∾

THE RICHES OF ISAIAH 45 cannot be summarized in brief compass. It ends with a stunning missionary passage (45:14-25), with echoes reverberating into the New Testament (e.g., 45:23; cf. Phil. 2:10-11). It begins in the closing verses of chapter 44 and the opening lines of chapter 45, where the Persian king Cyrus is introduced by name. Here God calls him "my shepherd" (44:28), and Isaiah labels him the Lord's "anointed" (i.e., "messiah," a title usually restricted in the Old Testament to Saul or to one of the Davidic kings).

This is not the only place in the Old Testament where God identifies someone by name long before that person is born (cf. 1 Kings 13:1-3). What is striking is that, after the blistering denunciation of idolatry in Isaiah 44 (see meditation for June 12), God should refer to a pagan idolater as his anointed. Yet the point is important. God denounces idolatry, but his providential rule may use an idolater, or anyone else, for his own good purposes. It is always wrong to argue from providence to ethics, or to establish who is "right" by who wins in a particular context, or to doubt that God may sovereignly use an evil person to accomplish a great good without thereby exonerating or justifying all the evil in his or her life.

Transparently, Israel herself found this word of God hard to accept. One can imagine the exiles torn by doubt and troubled by fear. If God calls the pagan Cyrus his "messiah," does that mean he has rejected the Davidic dynasty? Can the prophet's word be accepted when it says such daft things? Anticipating the skepticism, God responds with a robust defense of his sovereignty and righteousness (45:8-13). "Woe to him who quarrels with his Maker" (45:9). The people who had so persistently defied God that they landed in exile now wish to defy his chosen means of getting them home. But they have no more right to question God's ways than clay has to question the potter, or a newborn has to question his or her parents (45:9-10). "This is what the LORD says—the Holy One of Israel, and its Maker: 'Concerning things to come, do you question me about my children, or give me orders about the work of my hands?'" (45:11). God is the sovereign Creator, and in the perfection of his righteousness he will raise up Cyrus to rebuild Jerusalem (45:13—itself evidence that the Davidic line was not being supplanted) and set his exiles free. All this comes as a step to the glorious invitation: "Turn to me and be saved, all you ends of the earth; for I am God, and there is no other" (45:22). Reflect on **Revelation 15:3-4**.

∾

Deuteronomy 19; Psalm 106; *Isaiah 46; Revelation 16*

∾

THERE ARE THREE SECTIONS TO **Isaiah 46**, and each advances a distinct argument that implicitly or explicitly calls Israel to faithfulness toward the living God.

(1) In the first two verses, Isaiah mocks Babylonian gods. "Bel" means "lord" and is equivalent to Baal as a title. It was applied to Marduk, the chief god of the city of Babylon. "Nebo" was the son of Bel-Marduk. He was the patron of writing and wisdom. At the New Year festival, Bel-Marduk and Nebo were carried through the streets in a great procession to the Esagila shrine. It was the greatest religious event of the year. But Isaiah foresees a time when Bel-Marduk and Nebo bow and stoop, and the exhausted beasts of burden that have to carry them fall and stagger off into captivity (46:1-2). This was not literally fulfilled when the Persians took over in the sixth century, for Cyrus preserved and even enhanced the status of the Babylonian gods. On the long haul, of course, Bel-Marduk and Nebo slipped into oblivion. No one worships them today. But millions of men and women still worship the God of Israel.

(2) In the next section (46:3-7), God continues his denunciation of idolatry. Now there is a slightly novel development. God says, in effect, that idolaters have to carry their gods, and even their beasts of burden get tired; but with the true God, it is the other way around: he carries his people. It is hard not to perceive a contrast between two religions. In the one, the people do all the heavy lifting; in the other, God does it, and his people are carried by him.

(3) In the last section (46:8-13), God rebukes his covenant people in blunt, not to say brutal, terms. They are rebels, and they have forgotten all of God's gracious and powerful ways with them when the nation was born at the time of the Exodus. There are important things for the believer to remember (46:8-9). Probably part of their hang-up is still Cyrus. They still find it difficult to imagine that God will use a pagan king like that, rather than simply destroy him. But God insists he will summon from the east "a bird of prey" (46:11)—almost certainly a reference to Cyrus. Whatever his purpose and plan, he will be sure to bring it to pass. The implication, of course, is that God is both sovereign and good—so stop trying to second-guess him, and trust him. "Listen to me, you stubborn-hearted, you who are far from righteousness. I am bringing my righteousness near, it is not far away; and my salvation will not be delayed" (46:12-13).

∾

Deuteronomy 20; Psalm 107; *Isaiah 47; Revelation 17*

∾

AT ONE LEVEL, ISAIAH 47 is pretty straightforward; at another, it is subtly symbol-laden and prepares the way for the development of some biblical symbolism in the New Testament.

At the obvious level, this chapter depicts the fall of Babylon that the accession of Cyrus will bring about. Babylon is a pathetically proud and arrogant city. She is the "queen of kingdoms" (47:5); she thinks she will last forever (47:7)—not unlike Hitler's thousand-year Reich. She is so confident of her own security she cannot envisage becoming a widow or losing her children (47:8). Proud of her wisdom and knowledge (47:10) and her devotion to astrology, she thinks she can control her future (47:12-13). Her self-deification is frankly repulsive: the repeated "I am, and there is none besides me" (47:8, 10) is a direct challenge to God's identical claim (45:5). But God has had enough. The "queen of kingdoms" will sit in the dust (47:1); she will become a slave (47:1-3). This "mother" will suddenly be widowed and bereaved (47:8-9). Astrology will prove futile to save her (47:12-13), and sorcerers and magicians will be of no avail (47:12). God himself is out to destroy Babylon.

But this text hints at another level. Chapters 47 and 48 are tied together, constituting one large unit. Isaiah 47 condemns Babylon for its defiant arrogance and promises her doom; Isaiah 48 is addressed to the captives, who (as we shall see in tomorrow's meditation) are rousingly told to leave Babylon and return to Jerusalem. Empirically they live in one city, Babylon; theologically, they belong to another city, Jerusalem. At the level of brute history, of course, the captives *could not* return to Jerusalem at this stage. They could do so only after Cyrus came to power and granted permission to return. But theologically, the exiles must see themselves as belonging to Jerusalem and not to Babylon. Thus just as "Jerusalem" sometimes refers to the ancient city by that name, and sometimes, as we have seen, anticipates the new, eschatological Jerusalem, so also "Babylon" not only may refer to the ancient city that reached the pinnacle of its splendor about the sixth century B.C., but becomes a symbol—a symbol that anticipates every proud city or culture that imagines it will live forever and arrogantly measures all things by the standards of its own sins and presuppositions. Historic Babylon becomes the symbol of many Babylons.

John understands these things. That is why in **Revelation 17** he describes Rome as "Babylon the Great, the Mother of Prostitutes and of the Abominations of the Earth" (Rev. 17:5), a woman drunk with the blood of the saints. What Babylons have arisen since then?

∾

Deuteronomy 21; Psalms 108—109; *Isaiah 48; Revelation 18*

IT IS ONE THING FOR GOD TO RAISE UP a Cyrus who will permit the Jews to return to Jerusalem. But will the Jews be willing to go? And if they are willing to return physically and rebuild Jerusalem, are they spiritually prepared to abandon the sin that sent them into exile in the first place? (**Isa. 48**).

It does not look good. Formally, they take their oaths in the name of the Lord, "and invoke the God of Israel—but not in truth or righteousness" (48:1). True, the captives still call themselves "citizens of the holy city" (48:2), Jerusalem, which by the sixth century was a pile of rubble. But one of the reasons why God predicted these things, including the return of the people, is that he well knew that many of the Jews would become so enmeshed in Babylonian idolatry that they might be tempted to credit their idols with their return (48:3-6). Like their forefathers they can be stubborn (48:4), treacherous, and rebellious (48:8). The "furnace of affliction" (48:10) has taught them so little that the only reason God does not wipe them out entirely is because he wishes to preserve the honor of his own name (48:9-11). The world must know that Babylon does not rule; God does. So he will press on, though the terrible problem of sin among his people has not been resolved, even by the exile.

The tragedy is that even in exile God's people have been unwilling to listen (48:1, 12, 16, 17-18). Their entire history would have been dramatically different, filled with untold blessings, if only they had paid attention to God's commands (48:18-19). Their "peace would have been like a river," their "righteousness like the waves of the sea" (48:18). Even now what they most need is to leave Babylon (48:20-21)—not yet physically, of course, for Cyrus has not yet arisen and sanctioned it; but morally, spiritually. But if the people remain in their sin even after release from Babylon, they will poison their new freedom: "'There is no peace,' says the LORD, 'for the wicked'" (48:22)—a perennial warning no less applicable in our own day.

So God's servant Cyrus will not provide the final answer. He may free the Jews from exile, but he cannot free them from their sin. That sets the stage for the reintroduction of the ideal Servant of the Lord, who returns in chapter 49. Indeed, he probably appears rather enigmatically in 48:16, for the one who speaks there has the Spirit upon him (as in 42:1) and is called by God (as in 49:1). But there is no doubt of his presence in Isaiah 49. In this Servant of the Lord is the only lasting succor for God's people.

Deuteronomy 22; Psalms 110—111; *Isaiah 49; Revelation 19*

∾

IN THE FIRST SIX VERSES OF **Isaiah 49** the Servant of the Lord speaks. Who is he? He is unnamed, but we can draw some inferences from the description provided by the text. Like the prophet Jeremiah, he was called by God before he was born (49:1; cf. Jer. 1:5); like him, he meets opposition that drives him to despair, though he faithfully perseveres (49:4; cf. Jer. 4:19-22, etc.). God has made his mouth "like a sharpened sword" (49:2), which rather suggests prophetic ministry.

But what is most striking about this Servant is something that at first appears to be a striking confusion. God addresses him in these terms: "You are *my servant, Israel,* in whom I will display my splendor" (49:3, italics added)—so the Servant is Israel. Yet the Lord calls this Servant "to bring Jacob back to him *and gather Israel* to himself" (49:5, italics added)—which distinguishes this Servant from Israel and represents him as Israel's savior. Why?

As in Isaiah 42, this Servant embodies all that Israel should have been. This Servant is an ideal Israel, God's perfect Servant—and thus a figure different from empirical Israel, and one that is able to save empirical Israel. In part, the identity of this Servant is still hidden at this point in the book: "[God] made me into a polished arrow and concealed me in his quiver" (49:2), says the Servant. God does insist, however, that it is "too small a thing for you to be my servant to restore the tribes of Jacob and bring back those of Israel I have kept. I will also make you a light for the Gentiles, that you may bring my salvation to the ends of the earth" (49:6). Indeed, even when the Lord uses this Servant "to bring Jacob back to him and gather Israel to himself" (49:5), surely this envisages something more than a return to the land or to Jerusalem. After all, the servant Cyrus accomplishes that for Israel. This Servant, however, brings Israel to God; the restoration is not so much to a place as to the living God.

Isaiah 49 is too long and complex to permit an adequate summary here. But I draw attention to two themes. *First,* in 49:8-12, the "returning" people are not Israelites only, but Gentiles, and the return is primarily to God. Israelites would return from the north, but these come from everywhere. *Second,* although God has promised some fine things, Zion (standing for the people of God) complains that the Lord has forsaken and forgotten her. But God replies with moving commitment: "Can a mother forget the baby at her breast . . . ? Though she may forget, I will not forget you" (49:15). In stagnant, discouraging times, remember God's long-range commitments, and reflect on Romans 8:31-39.

∾

Deuteronomy 23; Psalms 112—113; *Isaiah 50; Revelation 20*

∾

ISAIAH 50 HAS A TRANSITIONAL importance that belies its brevity. In 50:1-3 God addresses the children of Israel in exile, especially those who think he has utterly abandoned them. He hasn't. He has neither divorced their mother, i.e., Zion, nor sold them into slavery to pay off some creditor—so the way back to him is still open. In this light, the last two lines of 50:1 should be read as irony: if the children were "sold" or the mother "sent away" in any sense, it was because of their sin, not because of some final legal action on God's part. Moreover, the sovereign Creator is certainly capable of bringing them back (50:2b-3). The real question is, why did none of them come to him when he called? (50:2a).

Then the Servant speaks (50:4-9), more to himself than to others, but so as to be overheard (50:10-11). Who is he? There have been many suggestions: Isaiah, or a sixth-century disciple of Isaiah; Jeremiah; Israel, personified as an abused and suffering person (cf. Ps. 129:1-3). As the book unfolds, Isaiah will make the Servant's identity clear. Even now, observe his characteristics: This Servant is a gifted counselor. His words sustain the weary, for he himself has an ear for all the Sovereign Lord says, and he has not been rebellious (50:4-5—unlike Israel). Thus he is a perfect disciple, but of the Lord, not of Isaiah (compare John 5:18ff.). He does not draw back from obedience (50:5), even in the face of implacable abuse (50:6; cf. Matt. 27:30; Mark 14:65; 15:19). The Sovereign Lord sustains him in his mission, so he sets his face like a flint to complete the task assigned him (50:7; cf. Luke 9:51), confident that God will finally vindicate him (50:7-9; cf. Phil. 2:9-11).

How, then, does the second part of this chapter relate to the first? Surely in this way: those who are addressed in 50:1-3 still seem alienated, distant, unresponsive, cynical, while here in 50:10-11 a line is drawn in the sand, and this line concerns the Servant. On the one side is the person who "fears the LORD *and obeys the word of his servant*," who despite the terrible darkness that now engulfs him "trust[s] in the name of the LORD" (50:10, italics added). On the other side is the person who tries to provide his or her own light, who lights fires of rebellion; God says to such a person, "This is what you shall receive from my hand: You will lie down in torment" (50:11). Thus the identity of "the people of God" is undergoing subtle redefinition. In 49:8-12 they embrace both Israelites and Gentiles; here one element that defines them is that they obey the word of the Lord's Servant.

∾

Deuteronomy 24; Psalms 114—115; *Isaiah 51; Revelation 21*

∾

IN THE LIGHT OF THE ABSOLUTE alternatives set out at the end of Isaiah 50—either fear the Lord and obey his Servant and know his blessing, or light your own fire and lie down in torment—Isaiah 51:1-11 opens with words of encouragement to the faithful remnant. The passage climaxes with a grand vision of returning to the Lord, of entering Zion with singing (51:11). The words evoke the pilgrimages the godly undertook when they were in the land. In the best of circumstances these were joyful occasions, full of singing, full of personal and family memories, full of joyous expectation as the people of God wended their way to Zion, to the temple of the living God. But the pilgrimage that the prophet has in mind eclipses any other. The old pilgrimages occurred three times a year for the prescribed feasts. Here the language of pilgrimage is retained, but we are given a glimpse of the End: "They will enter Zion with singing; everlasting joy will crown their heads. Gladness and joy will overtake them, and sorrow and sighing will flee away" (51:11). We have returned to the ultimate hope expressed in 2:1-5 and 11:1-16.

But the people are not there yet. If they are discouraged by their small numbers and reduced circumstances, they should remember their origins, the rock from which they were cut: Abraham started off as one man, but God "blessed him and made him many" (51:2). So here: "The LORD will surely comfort Zion and will look with compassion on all her ruins" (51:3). Indeed, God's salvation will last forever, and his righteousness will never fail (51:6). Meanwhile, God's people must listen to him. They have God's "law" in their hearts (51:7): the word properly means "instruction," and may here include not only the Law of Moses but all the instruction of God mediated through prophets and priests alike. If this word is what anchors you, the next injunction is manageable: "Do not fear the reproach of men or be terrified by their insults" (51:7). On the long haul, they will perish like a moth-eaten garment, while God's righteousness and salvation "will last forever . . . through all generations" (51:8).

Some manuscripts preserve (probably rightly) a slightly different reading in verse 4. Instead of "my people" and "my nation," read "peoples" and "nations." That means that 51:4-6 addresses another group of pilgrims, in addition to the Israelites—all those drawn in from around the world. All of these, together with the remnant of Israelites, constitute "the ransomed of the LORD" (51:11; cf. Rev. 5:9-10).

∾

Deuteronomy 25; Psalm 116; *Isaiah 52; Revelation 22*

∿

WE MAY USEFULLY DIVIDE **Isaiah 52** into three unequal parts.

(1) In the first six verses, the tone is of tender reassurance. So much that has happened to Israel (even though her sin has brought it on) has crushed her. She has been "sold for nothing" (52:3) and "taken away for nothing" (52:5); she has been defiled (52:1), chained (52:2), "oppressed" (52:4), and mocked (52:5). But now she is to wear "garments of splendor" (52:1) and "sit enthroned" (52:2) like a queen in Jerusalem. Though she was sold for nothing, in God's eyes she is still beyond price (52:3). God still calls Israel "my people" (52:4). Moreover, he attaches his own name to what has happened to them: his name has been "constantly blasphemed" (52:5). Now they can take comfort: the God who foretold their destruction has foretold their restoration (52:6).

What is striking about this list of opposites—the crushing defeat and denigration of Israel on the one hand, and the rapturous categories that the Sovereign Lord uses of her on the other—is that the first set is generated (according to the running argument of the book) by Israel's own sin, while the second set is generated by God's gracious goodness and faithfulness in pursuing her and delivering her from the punishment that he himself has imposed.

(2) In the next four verses (52:7-10) the good news that God is reversing the sanctions imposed on Israel is to be carried to the ends of the earth. Not only are the ruins of Jerusalem commanded to burst into songs of joy, but "[t]he LORD will lay bare his holy arm in the sight of all the nations, and all the ends of the earth will see the salvation of our God" (52:9-10).

(3) The last two verses (52:11-12) call on the exiles to depart, to leave their captivity behind. At the historical level, of course, this could not happen until Cyrus granted his permission. But Isaiah's prophecy must have stirred anticipation and helped to prepare the people. The language itself is redolent of the Exodus, but the difference in emphasis is striking. When the Israelites left Egypt they were told to bring with them whatever they could get from the Egyptians—valuable jewelry and clothing. Here, however, the people are warned not to touch anything, but to come out "from there" and be pure. This suggests that the ultimate goal is not geographical Jerusalem, but the new Jerusalem, and what must be left behind is more than Babylon, but all that Babylon represents. That reflection enables us to understand how and why Paul uses this passage in 2 Corinthians 6:14-18, and how we should use it today.

∿

Deuteronomy 26; Psalms 117—118; *Isaiah 53; Matthew 1*

∿

NOW THE IDENTITY OF THE perfect Servant comes into sharp focus. **Isaiah 53**, or better, Isaiah 52:13—53:12, is the fourth of five Servant songs that describe him. "See, my servant" (52:13), God says, echoing the introduction to this Servant in 42:1. The "arm of the LORD," God's saving power, has been promised in 51:9 and 52:10. Now the question becomes, "[T]o whom has the arm of the LORD been revealed?" (53:1). The implicit answer in this high point of Isaiah's prophecy is that God's saving power is nowhere more clearly seen than in the work of the Servant. In the previous chapters God has repeatedly promised forgiveness to his people, but its basis has not been established. Here all becomes clear: "my righteous servant will justify many . . . he will bear their iniquities" (53:11). He is a priest, sprinkling the unclean (52:15); he is a guilt offering, removing their iniquities (53:10).

The *first* of five sections (52:13-15) anticipates the whole: "My servant will act wisely," God says, anticipating the conclusion. Beginning with the Servant's exaltation (52:13), this stanza descends to his appalling suffering (52:14) and ends with the "sprinkling" of many nations and the stunned reaction to it. "Sprinkling" with blood, oil, or water is in the Old Testament bound up with cleansing, i.e., with making a person or thing fit to come before God. Normally this has reference to Israel or its institutions, but not here: this is for "many nations" (52:15). The stunned reaction testifies that God's wisdom overthrows and confounds all human wisdom (cf. 1 Cor. 1:18—2:5).

In the *second* and *third* stanzas (53:1-3, 4-6) the speakers are witnesses. God has repeatedly called on his people to bear witness to him (43:10, 12; 44:8), but they have been blind and deaf. Now, not only do they attest that the Lord alone is God (43:12), but they bear witness to what God has done through his suffering, vindicated, exalted Servant. At first, reactions to him are cautious, and then negative (53:1-3). He grew to be despised and rejected by men: "we esteemed him not," the witnesses say. Indeed, when he was barbarically killed, many thought it God's providential judgment (53:4)—and they spoke better than they knew. But the witnesses come to grasp that "he was pierced for our transgressions, he was crushed for our iniquities"—a substitutionary lamb (53:5-7). In the *fourth* stanza (53:7-9) Isaiah reflects on the Servant's silent suffering and ambivalent death and burial (Had God accepted his work?), to end in the *fifth* (53:10-12) with resounding affirmation of the purposes of God. God's Servant will act wisely (52:13); "by his knowledge" he will (literally) cause many to become righteous, "and he will bear their iniquities" (53:11). Reflect on **Matthew 1:21**. Hallelujah! What a Savior!

∿

Deuteronomy 27:1—28:19; Psalm 119:1-24; *Isaiah 54; Matthew 2*

∽

REPEATEDLY ISAIAH'S PROPHECY has anticipated "peace," the total well-being that flows from a right relationship with the living, Sovereign Lord. Early on he tells us that the Messiah would be "the Prince of Peace" (9:6), introducing a reign of everlasting peace (9:7). Ultimately it is the Lord who establishes peace (26:12). But while this is good news (52:7), such peace is reserved for those who trust him (26:3). "There is no peace . . . for the wicked" (48:22). Those who trust God become witnesses who fully and gladly recognize that their reconciliation with God has been accomplished by the Servant: "the punishment that brought us peace was upon him, and by his wounds we are healed" (53:5). The result, in Isaiah 54—55, is great peace for Zion's children (54:13), a "covenant of peace" that will never be removed (54:10), a great procession of God's people who "will go out in joy and be led forth in peace" (55:12).

In Isaiah 54, this glorious prospect is heralded as a "covenant of peace" (54:10) that in some ways fulfills three other great covenants:

First, the covenant with Abraham comes into view (54:1-3). References to the "barren woman," the "tent," and promised "descendants" who dispossess the nations call it to mind. God will overcome Zion's desperate circumstances during the exile as readily as he overcame Sarah's barrenness. Abraham's descendants eventually dispossessed the nations in the land of Canaan; the returning exiles will do the same—or is there a hint that the children of this new covenant of peace will ultimately dispossess nations more comprehensively as they "spread out to the right and to the left" (54:3)?

Second, the Sinai covenant enters the picture, with the reminders of the shame of Israel's youth (the slavery in Egypt, 54:4), of Israel's "Maker" as her "husband" (54:5), and of her widowhood in exile (54:5-8). But now God discloses himself as their Redeemer still, though now in the light of the great redemption secured in 52:13—53:12: "with everlasting kindness I will have compassion on you" (54:8), he declares, establishing the direction of the Sinai covenant's continuity.

Third, the covenant with Noah is probed (54:9-17), temporally out of sequence but entirely appropriate, as it was a covenant made not with Israel but with the entire human race. The exile is likened to the Flood, and Zion's children to Noah's descendants. They will not be destroyed; indeed, the "servants of the LORD" (54:17) follow the pattern of the Servant of the Lord in suffering and ultimate vindication.

∽

Deuteronomy 28:20-68; Psalm 119:25-48; *Isaiah 55; Matthew 3*

∽

HERE I REFLECT ON BOTH **Isaiah 55** and **Matthew 3**, for they overlap.

(1) In the light of the Servant's triumph in Isaiah 53 and the covenantal promises of peace in Isaiah 54, Isaiah 55 opens with a wonderful invitation. The thirsty and the hungry are invited to a glorious banquet where the fare is free (55:1-3a). The theme of covenant continues: these blessings are bound up with "an everlasting covenant" (55:3b) that the Lord enacts with his people—and this time the covenant is seen as the fulfillment of promises to David (see meditation for June 22). God made David "a witness to the peoples, a leader and commander of the peoples" (55:4); he conquered the nations around him and subjugated them to his rule, and thus to the rule of the Lord. Restored to the land, Israel does something similar: they "summon nations . . . because of the LORD your God, the Holy One of Israel" (55:5). Their summoning of the nations is not by military prowess, but because of what the Lord is doing in their midst. Moreover, this covenant has a confirming sign. The Noahic covenant had the sign of the rainbow; the Abrahamic, circumcision; the Sinai covenant, the sprinkled blood. The everlasting covenant has as its eternal sign a transformed universe (55:12-13; cf. 2:2-5; 11:1-16).

(2) Matthew affirms that John the Baptist sees himself as a "voice of one calling in the desert, 'Prepare the way for the Lord, make straight paths for him'" (Matt. 3:3), citing Isaiah 40:3. In the meditation for June 8, I briefly explained that passage as the Lord's (metaphorical) smoothing of the way for the people of God to return to the land, part of a passage of rich comfort. The return of the people of God displays the glory of God. But it is possible to read the passage a slightly different way, no less concerned for the glory of the Lord. On this view it is not the people who cross the wilderness, but the sovereign Lord himself who "comes with power" (Isa. 40:10) like a potentate whose path his underlings smooth for him. John the Baptist claims that function: he prepares the way "for the Lord"— which in his setting identifies Jesus as the sovereign Lord.

(3) John calls the people of his day to radical repentance, making repentance, not literal descent from Abraham, critical for membership in God's people (Matt. 3:7-10). Similarly in Isaiah 55, the promised covenantal blessings are for those who forsake their wicked ways and thoughts and turn to the Lord for mercy and free pardon (55:6-7). For our thoughts are not God's thoughts (55:7-8)—a confession that admires God's thoughts not for their transcendence but for their lofty purity.

∽

Deuteronomy 29; Psalm 119:49-72; *Isaiah 56; Matthew 4*

∽

THE LAST SECTION OF ISAIAH (chaps. 56—66) focuses primarily on the period after the return of the first exiles from Babylon. This, too, was an enormously troubled period, as other Scriptures attest (especially Ezra, Nehemiah, Haggai, and Zechariah). But some of Isaiah's vision extends beyond the early years of return to the ultimate hope—the new heaven and the new earth (e.g., 65:17). In some ways the situation of the people described in these chapters mirrors our own: we live between the "already" and the "not yet," between the glory of what God has already accomplished and what God has not yet done but has promised to do.

The opening verses (**Isa. 56:1-8**) emphasize two themes:

First, the Lord says that those who wait for his salvation, which is "close at hand" (56:1), must "[m]aintain justice and do what is right" (56:1). The reason, he says, is that his "righteousness will soon by revealed." In other words, one of the fundamental motives for the righteous behavior of believers is that it anticipates the consummated righteousness that is still to come. Unlike so many of our contemporaries, who live for the day with little serious thought devoted to the future, we are committed to living in a way that anticipates the future. That is part of what it means to "[keep] the Sabbath without desecrating it" (56:2). Isaiah's readers will not then simply be keeping a rule, however divinely authorized, but will be demonstrating two further things: (a) their allegiance to the Mosaic covenant (and therefore to the God of the covenant), and (b) their living out of patterns of rest that are simultaneously tied to God's rest (Gen. 2; Ex. 20) and to the rest to come (cf. Heb. 3:7—4:11).

Second, the Lord promises that the blessings to come are open to people whom many have systematically excluded. After all, there were passages in the Law of Moses that excluded the emasculated and the foreigner (especially Moabites and Ammonites), e.g., Deuteronomy 23:1-6 (and cf. Lev. 22:24-25, and the parallel with animals). Still, it is hard to believe that these laws were meant in every case to exclude genuine converts, or the accounts of Rahab and Ruth (the latter a Moabite) would make little sense (Josh. 6:24-25; Ruth 1—4). On the one hand, the community cleansed by the suffering Servant is to touch no unclean thing and come out from "Babylon" and be pure (52:11); on the other, the Lord here insists that the eunuchs and foreigners are to be admitted (56:3-8). The difference, of course, is conversion, in which God gives them "an everlasting name" (56:5), such that they hold fast to his covenant (56:4).

∽

Deuteronomy 30; Psalm 119:73-96; *Isaiah 57; Matthew 5*

∿

THE PARAGRAPH MATTHEW 5:17-20 begins the body of the Sermon on the Mount. It is a complex but enormously evocative section.

Jesus says, "Do not think that I have come to abolish the Law or the Prophets; I have not come to abolish them but to fulfill them" (5:17). These lines have called forth some popular but doubtful interpretations. (a) Some think that the verb "fulfill" must mean the opposite of "abolish," since the last clause demands an obvious opposition ("not . . . to abolish . . . but to fulfill"). So they take Jesus to mean, "I have not come to abolish the Law but to *maintain* it or *preserve* or *keep* it." But does Jesus really see his mission in such terms, especially if the *maintaining* or *keeping* of the Law is understood simply in terms of its demands and prescriptions? Even in some of the antitheses that follow (5:21-48), does it not sound as if Jesus is introducing at least some modifications? Does not Jesus introduce some changes to the food laws in Matthew 15:1-20 (cf. Mark 7:1-23)? (b) Some therefore argue that Jesus has only the moral law in mind. But it is far from clear that first-century Christians distinguished moral from civil and ceremonial law as readily as we do. In any case, 5:18 ("not the smallest letter, not the least stroke of a pen") sounds too comprehensive to allow such a restriction. (c) Still others want "to fulfill" to mean something like "to intensify" or even "to show the true meaning of." But the verb never carries that meaning.

The most common meaning of the verb "to fulfill" in the New Testament has to do with eschatology. In the past God predicted something; now he "fulfills" his word; he brings to pass what he promised. That is *always* what Matthew means by the verb (which he uses frequently). So here Jesus says, in effect, that he has not come to abolish the Law, but to do something quite different: to bring to pass all that the Law predicted. Such fulfillment will go on until everything predicted by the Law is accomplished, to the very end of the age (5:18). All of this presupposes (a) that the Law has a predictive function (a commonplace in the New Testament); (b) that Jesus does show the true meaning of the Law and Prophets, not in some abstract sense, but in their prophetic fulfillment, the true direction in which they point; and (c) that Jesus interprets his own mission as prophetic fulfillment of the promises inherent in the Law and the Prophets. He thinks of himself neither as someone who destroys all that has come before and starts over, nor as someone who simply maintains the antecedent tradition. Rather, all previous revelation points to him, and he brings its expectations to pass.

∿

Deuteronomy 31; Psalm 119:97-120; *Isaiah 58; Matthew 6*

$\sim$

HOW SELF-DECEIVED WE HUMANS ARE when it comes to matters religious. So many things that start off as incentives to repentance and godliness develop into vicious idols. What starts as an aid to holiness ends up as the triple trap of legalism, self-righteousness, and superstition. So it was with the bronze snake in the wilderness. Although it was ordered and used by God (Num. 21:4-9), it became such a religious nonsense in later times that Hezekiah destroyed it (2 Kings 18:4).

So it sometimes is with other forms of religious observance or spiritual discipline. One may with fine purpose and good reason start "journaling" as a discipline that breeds honesty and self-examination, but it can easily slide into the triple trap: in your mind you so establish journaling as the clearest evidence of personal growth and loyalty to Christ that you look down your nose at those who do not commit themselves to the same discipline, and pat yourself on the back every day that you maintain the practice (legalism); you begin to think that only the most mature saints keep spiritual journals, so you qualify—and you know quite a few who do not (self-righteousness); (c) you begin to think that there is something in the act itself, or in the paper, or in the writing, that is a necessary means of grace, a special channel of divine pleasure or truth (superstition). That is the time to throw away your journal.

Clearly, fasting can become a similar sort of trap. The first five verses of **Isaiah 58** expose and condemn the wrong kind of fast, while verses 6-12 describe the kind of fast that pleases God. The first is bound up with hypocrisy. People maintain their fasts, but quarrel in the family (58:4). Their fasts do not stop them from exploiting their workers (58:3b). These religious people are getting restless: "We tried fasting," they say, "and it didn't work" (58:3). At a superficial level they seem to have a hunger for God and his way (58:2). The truth is that they are beginning to treat the fast as if it were a bit of magic: *because I've kept the fast, God has to bless me.* Such thinking is both terribly sad and terribly evil.

By contrast, the fast that pleases God is marked by genuine repentance (58:6-12). Not only does it turn away from self-indulgence but it actively shares with the poor (58:7), and intentionally strives "to loose the chains of injustice," "to set the oppressed free and break every yoke" (58:7), to abjure "malicious talk" (58:9). This is the fast that brings God's blessing (58:8-12).

$\sim$

Deuteronomy 32; Psalm 119:121-144; *Isaiah 59; Matthew 7*

∾

ISAIAH 59 IS DIVIDED INTO THREE PARTS. If taken out of its context in the book, it could be taken to describe the descent into sin and degradation that characterized many periods of Israel's history, and that still characterizes many periods of the church's experience. But both its position in the book and the closing two verses suggest that the prophet has in view the community of the people of God after they have returned from exile. They are still characterized by sin, and there is no hope but one.

The *first* section (59:1-8) describes the people in their desperation. The reason for their plight, the prophet insists, is not some inadequacy in God: "the arm of the LORD is not too short to save" (59:1). Their plight turns on their own sin: "But your iniquities have separated you from your God; your sins have hidden his face from you, so that he will not hear" (59:2). The wearisome list follows: injustice, want of integrity, violence, conspiracies. At the heart of it all is human character: the evil emanates from within. "Their thoughts are evil thoughts; ruin and destruction mark their ways. The way of peace they do not know; there is no justice in their paths. They have turned them into crooked roads; no one who walks in them will know peace" (59:7b-8). Small wonder that the apostle Paul quotes several of these lines in his own indictment of the human race (Rom. 3:15-17). What can be done with a brood so persistently sinful? Even the enormous trauma of the exile proves insufficient to transform them.

In the *second* section (59:9-15a), the verbs become first person plural. The language is that of communal lament. These mourners (compare 57:19) grieve for their sins. The language is brutally honest. Like Isaiah himself, like a Daniel or an Ezra, they confess not only their own sins but the sins of their people (6:5; Dan. 9:4-19; Ezra 9:6-15). They know their situation is desperate. And that itself, of course, is a mark of grace. The people of God are farthest from reformation and revival when they are smugly content, like the church in Laodicea (Rev. 3:14-22). There is hope when by God's grace they writhe in an agony of honest confession, horribly aware of the insidious and pervasive power of sin in their lives and their culture.

The *third* section (59:15b-21) provides the relief. Only God is adequate to this situation—and he is more than adequate. God saw there was no one else who could save the people, "so his own arm worked salvation for him" (59:16). And once again, this vision of hope and promise ends in apocalyptic proportions and in the categories of the new covenant (59:20-21).

∾

Deuteronomy 33—34; Psalm 119:145-176; *Isaiah 60; Matthew 8*

∾

IF ISAIAH 59 IS EXTRAORDINARILY BLEAK, **Isaiah 60** blazes with glory. Here Zion returns—not the Jerusalem that the returning exiles gradually rebuilt, but the ultimate Zion, the kingdom of God coming to earth. If much of the symbolism still springs from the historical city, that is no surprise. Yet the vision transcends any merely earthly hope. As evidence, we note that there is no longer any sun or moon, "for the LORD will be your everlasting light, and your God will be your glory" (60:19; cf. Rev. 21:23). Here the sovereign Lord himself arises, infinitely more glorious than any earthly sunrise: "Arise, shine, for your light has come, and the glory of the LORD rises upon you" (60:1). The previous chapter establishes the desperate need of the people, the raw evidence that they cannot really transform themselves. This chapter picks up on that dark picture and introduces the only possible solution: "See, darkness covers the earth and thick darkness is over the peoples, but the LORD rises upon you and his glory appears over you. Nations will come to your light, and kings to the brightness of your dawn" (60:2-3).

Three further observations:

(1) This Zion is home to nations and foreigners and kings, to "islands" (a way of referring to people a long way off), to people from countries that have nothing to do with the Promised Land (60:3, 9-10, 14). Gentiles will join Jews in this kingdom, honoring those of the faithful Israelites who belonged to Zion before them. The light dawns in Jerusalem and spreads to all nations.

(2) All who refuse this glory face judgment: "For the nation or kingdom that will not serve you will perish; it will be utterly ruined" (60:12). The text offers no hope that the final Zion embraces all without exception; rather, it embraces all without distinction, provided they embrace "the Holy One of Israel" and "the City of the Lord" (60:14).

(3) Above all, there is a glorious prospect of eternal longevity to what this kingdom brings. "I will make peace your governor and righteousness your ruler," God says. "*No longer* will violence be heard in your land . . . but you will call your walls Salvation and your gates Praise" (60:17-19, italics added). Follow the temporal terms: the sun will *no more* be your light; the LORD will be your *everlasting* light; your sun *will never set again;* your days of sorrow *will end;* the people will possess the land *forever* (60:19-21). The cycles of rebellion and repentance will end; the cycles of blessing and cursing will be no more. "I am the LORD; in its time I will do this swiftly" (60:22). Even so, come, Lord Jesus.

Joshua 1; Psalms 120—122; *Isaiah 61; Matthew 9*

∾

HERE I REFLECT ON TWO THINGS: first, the place of **Isaiah 61** in the developing argument; and second, its contribution to biblical theology.

(1) Isaiah 60 made it clear that the present order of things cannot go on forever: a time is coming that will be characterized by both unqualified blessing (60:19-21) and irremediable judgment (60:12). This bifurcation is picked up in Isaiah 61: here is proclamation both of "the year of the LORD's favor" and of "the day of vengeance of our God" (61:2). The vengeance theme is not developed until chapter 63. Immediately at hand is "the year of the LORD's favor" (chaps. 61—62). Isaiah 61 opens with someone proclaiming that the Spirit of the Lord is upon him to accomplish the Lord's redemptive purposes (61:1-6). Then the Lord himself speaks (61:7-9), proclaiming an everlasting covenant characterized by both joy and justice. The chapter ends with a solitary voice, presumably Isaiah's, exulting in the anticipated fulfillment of these promises (61:10-11).

(2) But who is the one who speaks in 61:1-6? The most important clue is in the first line: "The Spirit of the Sovereign LORD is on me," he says—and thoughtful readers recall two previous passages. Isaiah has already said that the Spirit of the Lord will rest in peculiar measure on the Messiah (11:1-2; cf. John 3:34), and has pictured God saying to the Servant, "I will put my Spirit on him" (42:1). The most obvious conclusion is that the one who speaks in Isaiah 61:1-6 is this Servant-Messiah, the superlative suffering Servant of Isaiah 40—55 and the expected Messiah of Isaiah 1—35. Small wonder, then, that in the synagogue in Nazareth, the Lord Jesus reads these lines from the Isaiah scroll and deliberately applies them to himself (Luke 4:17-19).

This Spirit-anointed Servant-Messiah brings in "the year of the LORD's favor" (61:2), almost certainly an allusion to the Year of Jubilee when, according to the Mosaic covenant, slaves were freed and those forced to sell their property were to receive it back again (Lev. 25:8-55). The Servant-Messiah comes "to preach good news to the poor" and "to bind up the brokenhearted, to proclaim freedom for the captives and release from darkness for the prisoners," "to comfort all who mourn"—to bestow the "insteads": a crown of beauty *instead* of ashes, the oil of gladness *instead* of mourning, a garment of praise *instead* of a spirit of despair (61:1-3). If the initial installment of such blessing was in the return from exile and the first restoration of the ruins (61:4), the ultimate fulfillment bursts these categories (chap. 62).

∾

Joshua 2; Psalms 123—125; *Isaiah 62; Matthew 10*

∾

MUCH OF THE POETRY OF ISAIAH 62 picks up the circumstances of earthly Zion. But the language is so exalted and the promises so sweeping it soon becomes clear that much more than the restoration of empirical Jerusalem after the exile is in view.

At the end of chapter 61 Isaiah delights in the triumph of the Servant-Messiah who transforms the people of God. Here Isaiah still speaks, and then increasingly in this chapter it is the Sovereign Lord who speaks. Initially Isaiah says that, in light of the glorious promises for Zion, he "will not keep silent" until Zion's peace and glory are established. This means more than that Isaiah will continue in faithful proclamation. Intrinsic to the task of the "watchmen" posted on the walls of Jerusalem (62:6) is the warning of judgment to come where there is no repentance, or where there is thoughtless lapse into sin (cf. Ezek. 33). But if there is horizontal proclamation—i.e., preaching to the people—there is also vertical intercession: "You who call on the LORD, give yourselves no rest, and give him no rest till he establishes Jerusalem and makes her the praise of the earth" (62:6-7). Like Daniel interceding with God in light of the promises God himself had made (Dan. 9), Isaiah wants faithful men and women to pray to God, giving him no rest till all his glorious promises regarding Zion are fulfilled. Here, then, is a call for fervent and persistent intercession: "Your kingdom come, your will be done on earth as it is in heaven" (Matt. 6:10).

This Zion will be "called by a new name" (62:2, 12); it will have a new identity. It will no longer be called "Deserted" and "Desolate"; now it will be called "My Delight Is in Her" and "Married" (62:4)—picking up the massive typology found so often in the Old Testament: the Sovereign Lord is the husband; the covenant people, here represented by Zion, is the bride (cf. 62:5). Verse 12 rolls out more names: "the Holy People," "the Redeemed of the LORD" (which reminds us again how they have been transformed), "Sought After," "the City No Longer Deserted." This is far more than empirical Jerusalem after the exile. This is the covenant people themselves, and this community raises a banner "for the nations" (62:10). This is the anticipation of "the Jerusalem that is above" (Gal. 4:26-27, where Isaiah is quoted), of "Mount Zion," "the heavenly Jerusalem, the city of the living God" (Heb. 12:22), of "the Holy City, the new Jerusalem," "prepared as a bride beautifully dressed for her husband" (Rev. 21:2).

∾

Joshua 3; Psalms 126—128; *Isaiah 63; Matthew 11*

∾

WE SHOULD NOT IGNORE THE OBVIOUS: in this passage (**Matt. 11:2-19**) John the Baptist is discouraged.

He is discouraged because Jesus is failing to meet his expectations. John has announced someone who would not only baptize people with the Holy Spirit (3:11), but who would come in stern judgment, separating wheat and chaff and burning up the latter (3:12). Yet here is Jesus, preaching to vast crowds, training his own followers, performing miracles—but not obviously imposing judgment on the wicked. John the Baptist languishes in prison for the fiery way he denounced Herod's illicit marriage. Why hasn't Jesus denounced Herod and then, utilizing his astonishing power, imposed judgment?

Jesus answers (Matt. 11:4-6) by describing his ministry in terms of two crucial passages from Isaiah—35:5-6 and 61:1-2. But John the Baptist certainly knew the Isaiah scroll very well. Elsewhere he himself quotes from it (3:3, quoting Isa. 40:3). So if Jesus is going to refer to these passages (John might well ask himself), why doesn't he also mention the judgment theme in the same contexts? After all, Isaiah 35:5-6 mentions not only the lame leaping and the like, but "divine retribution" as well. Isaiah 61 talks about preaching good news to the poor, but it also anticipates "the day of vengeance of our God" (Isa. 61:2; see meditation for June 29). Why does Jesus mention the blessings without the judgments?

It is as if Jesus is saying, in effect, "John, look closely: the promised blessings of the kingdom are dawning. What I am doing fulfills Scripture exactly. If the judgment has not yet dawned, it will come, but not yet. Right now, focus on the good that is being done, and let it confirm that I am who I say I am."

Jesus takes three more steps to defend John, of which I briefly mention two. (a) He warns those who were listening in on this conversation not to suppose for a moment that John is really some fickle reed, swayed by the winds of harsh circumstances, and still less someone interested in feathering his nest (11:7-8). Far from it: (b) John's role in redemptive history makes him the one who announces the coming of the Sovereign, pointing him out, in fulfillment of a Malachi prophecy (11:10). That is what makes John the Baptist the greatest man born of woman up to that point—greater than Abraham or David or Isaiah—for he actually announces Christ and points him out explicitly. That is why the least in the kingdom, this side of the cross, is greater still (11:11): you and I point out who the Messiah is with even more immediacy and explicitness. That is where our greatness lies.

∾

Joshua 4; Psalms 129—131; *Isaiah 64; Matthew 12*

∽

IN A PREVIOUS CHAPTER, ISAIAH WROTE, "You who call on the LORD, give your-selves no rest, and give him no rest till he establishes Jerusalem and makes her the praise of the earth" (Isa. 62:6-7). Now Isaiah follows his own advice. **Isaiah 64** (more precisely, 63:7—64:12) records one of the great intercessory prayers of Scripture.

The earlier part of the prayer (63:7-19) begins with an affirmation of God's goodness, manifested especially in the rescue of Israel in the days of Moses. Isaiah does not sugar-coat the problem: the people rebelled so grievously that God himself became their enemy (63:10). But to whom else could Isaiah possibly turn? He appeals to God's "tenderness and compassion" (63:15), to God's covenantal faithfulness as the Father and Redeemer of his people (even if Abraham and Jacob might want to disown the people, 63:16).

But now in Isaiah 64, the prophet utters one of the most wrenching pleas found in Holy Scripture: "Oh, that you would rend the heavens and come down, that the mountains would tremble before you!" (64:1). That is the only hope we have: we cannot save ourselves. Nothing of our resolutions and gimmicks and religion will suffice. God himself must rend the heavens and come down. Isaiah is not denying God's immanence; rather, he is saying that God must actively inter-vene on our behalf to save us, demonstrating his power once again, or we are lost.

Three other elements of Isaiah's intercession must not be missed. *First,* no one recognizes more clearly than Isaiah that the God to whom he is appealing is also the Judge whom we have offended. "But when we continued to sin . . . you were angry. How then can we be saved?" (64:5), he asks. That is the heart of the dilemma—and the hope. *Second,* not only does Isaiah understand that sin sepa-rates us from God, he also identifies himself completely with his sinful people: "All of us have become like one who is unclean, and all our righteous acts are like filthy rags" (64:6). The greatest intercessors have always recognized that far more connects them with the common lot of sinners than what distinguishes them—and in any case they do not hesitate to plead with God on behalf of those who will not plead for themselves. *Third,* Isaiah deeply understands that if God res-cues us, he must do so out of grace, out of mercy, out of pity—not because we have any claim on him. That accounts for the moving tone of 64:8-12.

When have we last prayed with such insight and passion?

∽

~

ISAIAH HAS PRAYED, "Oh, that you would rend the heavens and come down" (64:1). Now (**Isa. 65**) God replies with two complementary perspectives.

First, God says that he is not as distant as Isaiah thinks. Throughout Israel's troubled history God revealed himself to the people again and again (65:1). He kept disclosing himself, through a long stream of prophets, to people who did not ask for him, to those who did not seek him, to a nation that did not call on his name. He was busy saying, "Here am I, here am I" (65:1)—but they proved to be an obstinate people, walking "in ways not good, pursuing their own imaginations" (65:2). Doubtless Isaiah wants God to come near, but by their persistent rebellion in every domain the people are saying, in effect, "Keep away; don't come near me, for I am too sacred for you!" (65:5). This habit of thinking oneself better than God is prevalent today. We are so interested in "spirituality" and so committed to exonerating ourselves on every side that we cannot possibly allow ourselves to submit to what God says. We judge what he says to be unreasonable; we are wiser and better than God, more sacred than he. That is what stands behind his judgment (65:6-7).

Second, notwithstanding the threat of judgment, God holds out a vastly different prospect for the chosen remnant who seek his face in contrition and faith. What he promises them is far more than a somewhat more secure empirical Zion. He holds out to them nothing less than a "new heavens and a new earth" (65:17). That is what "Jerusalem" ultimately means (65:18-19); as in Revelation 21, Jerusalem is not so much a center in the new heavens and the new earth as another way of conceptualizing the same reality. The vision is spectacular (65:17-25), akin to what was foreseen earlier (2:2-5; 11:1-16). But it is not for everyone without exception. As clearly as any in the book, this chapter distinguishes between, on the one hand, God's chosen ones (65:22), the people blessed by the Lord (65:23), those who seek him (65:10), his servants (65:9), and, on the other hand, those described in the first seven verses, who amuse themselves with notions of magic, playing their games of Fortune and Destiny (65:11). The bottom line is that when God called they did not answer, when he spoke they did not listen. "You did evil in my sight and chose what displeases me" (65:12). Nowhere is the distinction clearer than in 65:13-16. "My servants," God says, will experience unimaginably fine blessings, but the "you" whom he addresses will face utter abandonment and reprobation.

~

Joshua 6; Psalms 135—136; *Isaiah 66; Matthew 14*

∾

ALTHOUGH ISAIAH 66 ENDS on a note of apocalyptic decisiveness and hope (66:18-24), intermingled with a frankly missionary theme (66:19), the beginning of the chapter provides one more warning. This warning (**Isa. 66:1-6**) captures our attention here.

The text envisages the time when the temple in Jerusalem will be rebuilt. All along Isaiah has predicted that Jerusalem would be destroyed and with it, implicitly, the temple. He has also prophesied that a remnant would return to the city and begin to rebuild. Yet never should they forget that God cannot be reduced to the dimensions of a temple: "Heaven is my throne, and the earth is my footstool. Where is the house you will build for me? Where will my resting place be? Has not my hand made all these things, and so they came into being?" (66:1-2). Solomon understood this when he led Israel in prayer at the dedication of the first temple (1 Kings 8:27). Nevertheless it is a lesson soon forgotten as successive generations slip into a religious ecclesiasticism. Somehow they think they are good because they go through the prescribed religious motions. But God insists that offering a prescribed animal at the newly built temple when one's heart is far from the Lord is no better than offering up the sacrifice of an unclean animal—indeed, it may be as repulsive to the Lord as sacrificing a human being, for the entire exercise becomes so awesomely God-defying (66:3). These religious people finally descend to religious persecution of those who want to follow God's word (66:5). Once again the Lord threatens massive judgment (66:4, 6).

What, then, will the Lord look for among the remnant that returns from exile? "This is the one I esteem," God says: "he who is humble and contrite in spirit, and trembles at my word" (66:2). A few verses later, Isaiah directly addresses the faithful as "you who tremble at his word" (66:5). They are contrasted with those who do not answer or listen when the Lord calls and speaks (66:4). None of this is new. One of the lessons the Israelites were to learn through their years of wilderness wandering was that "man does not live on bread alone but on every word that comes from the mouth of the LORD" (Deut. 8:3). This is of perennial importance—not only careful listening to every word that God has spoken, but listening characterized by humility, contrition, and godly fear (66:2). In every generation, what ultimately distinguishes the true from the false among God's people, the blessed from the cursed, is faithfulness or unfaithfulness to the Word of God.

∾

Joshua 7; Psalms 137—138; *Jeremiah 1; Matthew 15*

JEREMIAH LIVED IN DAYS of threat and declension. Called to be a prophet in the thirteenth year of the reign of King Josiah, Judah's last reforming king (about 627 B.C.), Jeremiah served for more than forty years. The fall of Jerusalem took place in 587 (forty years after Jeremiah's call), and the prophet continued his ministry for a while after that. His ministry was doomed to apparent fruitlessness. But God had called him to speak the truth about the nation and about impending judgment, regardless of whether or not his words were well received. One senses Jeremiah's growing maturity and resolve as the years of his ministry slip past.

The call of Jeremiah occupies the first chapter (**Jer. 1**). Some important elements:

(1) Not only was Jeremiah's commission from God, but God had chosen him even before he was born (1:5). In the hours of darkest opposition and brutal treatment, that reality doubtless proved immensely stabilizing to Jeremiah.

(2) Clearly, Jeremiah was only a young man when God called him to his first commission. Jeremiah protested that he was too young, "only a child"—but God would not accept the excuse, for he is perfectly capable of equipping anyone he chooses. God himself would put words in Jeremiah's mouth and make him a prophetic voice, not only over Judah but over the surrounding nations (1:7-10).

(3) Two visionary vignettes clarify Jeremiah's call. The first is an almond branch. The Hebrew word sounds much like the Hebrew for "watching over." The almond branch was the first to bud in the spring, and thus points to the advent of spring; in the pun, God's word points to its own fulfillment, which must inevitably follow. Thus Jeremiah is encouraged to speak God's words with utter confidence that all that God says is true, and all that he predicts will take place (1:11-12): God watches over everything. The second visionary element is a boiling pot, tilting away from the north—a graphic way of indicating that the boiling cauldron of judgment, the judgment that Babylon would mete out to the tiny nation (1:13-16), would pour down on Judah from the north.

(4) Above all, God tells Jeremiah not to be afraid—a common divine word to God's servants (e.g., Abraham, Gen. 15:1; Moses, Num. 21:34 and Deut. 3:2; Daniel, Dan. 10:12, 19; Mary, Luke 1:30; Paul, Acts 27:24). God does not sugarcoat the difficulties: Jeremiah will be opposed and will at times stand alone "against the whole land" (1:18)—but they "will not overcome you," God says, "for I am with you and will rescue you" (1:19). Only such promises are sufficient to breed titanic prophetic courage.

Joshua 8; Psalm 139; *Jeremiah 2; Matthew 16*

∾

FEW PASSAGES IN THE Synoptic Gospels have been more disputed in the history of the church than Peter's confession that Jesus is "the Christ, the Son of the living God," and its aftermath (**Matt. 16:13-28**). Here we may venture only three reflections:

(1) Judging by his response, Jesus sees this confession as a significant advance, achieved by revelation from the Father (16:17). But that does not mean that before this point Peter had no inkling that Jesus is the Messiah. Nor does it mean that he understood "Messiah" in the full-fledged, Christian sense associated with the word after Jesus' death and resurrection. At this point, quite clearly, Peter was prepared to accept Jesus as Israel's King, the Anointed One from the Davidic line, but he had no idea that he must be simultaneously Davidic king and suffering Servant, as the ensuing verses show. Both Peter's understanding and his faith were maturing, but still painfully lacking. Part of Peter's coming to full Christian faith on these matters depended absolutely on waiting for the next major redemptive-historical appointment: the cross and the resurrection.

(2) Jesus' words, "[Y]ou are Peter, and on this rock I will build my church" (16:18), have been taken to be the foundation of the Roman Catholic papacy. Even on the most sympathetic reading, however, it is difficult to see how this passage says anything about *passing on* a Petrine precedence, still less about gradually developing and enhancing the papacy until in 1870 the doctrine of papal infallibility was promulgated. Offended by such extravagant claims, many Protestants have offered exegeses equally unbelievable. Perhaps Jesus said, "You are Peter" (pointing to Peter) "and on *this* rock I will build my church" (pointing to himself). Or perhaps the "rock" on which the church is built is not Peter, but Peter's confession—which scarcely accounts for the pun in Greek: "you are *petros* and on this *petra.*"

(3) It is better to see that Peter really does have a certain primacy—what has been called "a salvation-historical primacy." He was the first to see certain things, the leader gifted by God in the first steps of organization and evangelism after the resurrection (as Acts makes clear). But not only was this leadership bound up with Peter's unique role in redemptive history (so unique that it could not, in the nature of the case, be passed on), but the gospel authority extended to him (16:18-19) is extended to all the apostles (18:18). This is what we should expect: elsewhere we are told that the church is built on the foundation of prophets *and apostles* (Eph. 2:20, italics added). As the ancient formula puts it, Peter was *primus inter pares*—first among equals.

∾

Joshua 9; Psalms 140—141; *Jeremiah 3; Matthew 17*

∽

WHEN THE HUMAN AUTHORS of the Bible wrote Scripture, more often than not they had read and thought through the Scriptures that had already been written. Thus the earliest writers of the New Testament books constantly read (and cited and alluded to) what we call the Old Testament. The later writers of the New Testament read at least some of the early New Testament books (consider 2 Pet. 3:15-16). Similarly, the later writers of the Old Testament read all or some of the earlier Old Testament books.

It is very likely that Jeremiah, a sixth-century prophet, had read and reflected on the work of Hosea, an eighth-century prophet. Hosea's book develops at great length the analogy between Israel and a prostitute: apostasy is a form of spiritual prostitution. This horrible but telling analogy is teased out in a number of ways—not least in God's remarkably faithful love for his prostitute-bride. Some elements of this theme from Hosea are picked up and developed by Jeremiah (not least in Jer. 3).

The first verse alludes to Deuteronomy 24:1-4. There it is established that if a woman is divorced and marries another, she cannot divorce the second and return to the first. Sadly, the people of Judah have "lived as a prostitute with many lovers" (3:1)—and now they make noises about coming back to the Lord as if there is no problem. They think they can saunter into God's presence and nostalgically pray, "My Father, my friend from my youth, will you always be angry?" (3:4-5)—as if approaching this vastly offended God is an easy matter, as if the results were a foregone conclusion, as if whatever difficulty that remains lies with God and his unyielding anger. But God's perspective is rather different. He quietly comments, "This is how you talk, but you do all the evil you can" (3:5). Pretensions of repentance, promises of allegiance, and pretty allusions to a past relationship mean nothing to God in comparison with present performance. Religious cant often hides not only ungodly behavior, but a secret lust to do evil (3:5)—though the person doing the evil is usually so blind that he or she cannot label it as evil.

The northern nation of Israel was caught in spiritual adultery, and God gave her "a certificate of divorce" (3:6-8): she was sent off into exile in 722 B.C. under the Assyrian king, Sargon II. From this, her sister Judah learned nothing: a century later she did what her sister Israel did, but with even less excuse since she had seen what had happened to Israel (3:9ff.).

To what extent is contemporary evangelicalism selling out the Gospel, having learned almost nothing from the somewhat similar capsize of Protestant confessionalism about a hundred years ago?

∽

Joshua 10; Psalms 142—143; *Jeremiah 4; Matthew 18*

∽

MOST OF JEREMIAH 4 IS DEVOTED to depicting the devastation that will be caused by the Babylonian hordes from the north (4:5-31). Much of this prediction is on the lips of Yahweh himself. At one point there is an interlude in which Jeremiah expresses his own devastation at the prospect: "Oh, my anguish, my anguish! I writhe in pain. Oh, the agony of my heart! My heart pounds within me, I cannot keep silent. For I have heard the sound of the trumpet; I have heard the battle cry" (4:19). However faithfully he reports God's words, however much he recognizes that God's judgments are just, Jeremiah nevertheless identifies with the agony his people will endure. In this he anticipates the Lord Jesus, who condemns the sins of his day, but weeps over the city as he contemplates the judgment that must inevitably follow.

In the opening four verses of the chapter, however, the Lord demonstrates that it is still not too late. In fact, if Israel returns to him, not only will the nation be spared, but she will resume her role as a channel of blessing to the nations (cf. Gen. 12:3; Ps. 72:17). But such a return must not be a masquerade, a mere show of repentance. Israel must genuinely abandon her idols. She must swear "in a truthful, just and righteous way . . . 'As surely as the LORD lives'" (4:2). There are at least two facets to this oath. The *first* is that it constitutes, in effect, a renewal of the Sinai covenant. If the oath were not meant—i.e., not truthful, just, and righteous—then of course it would be not only false but blasphemous. The *second* facet is that it reflects the Mosaic stipulation that the oaths of the nation should be in the name of the Lord (Deut. 10:20). A nation steeped in idolatry would take its oaths in the names of the many false gods. If all in the nation take their oaths in the name of the Lord, it could only be because the Lord alone is supreme, the only God, the highest Being by whom they can swear.

Two word pictures further describe the genuineness of repentance and the sincerity of heart that God demands. (a) "Break up your unplowed ground and do not sow among thorns" (4:3). The people show no genuine receptivity to the Lord and his words. The hardness must be broken up. There is no fruitfulness in sowing where thorns choke the life out of all that is worthwhile (cf. Mark 4:1-20). (b) What God wants is more than circumcision of the foreskin, however deeply symbolic the act is. He wants circumcision of the heart (4:4)—a cutting away of all that is evil. That was so even in Mosaic times (Deut.10:16). Reflect on Paul's inferences (Rom. 2:28-29).

∽

Joshua 11; Psalm 144; *Jeremiah 5; Matthew 19*

∾

HERE I SHALL BRIEFLY REFLECT ON a number of elements of the depravity to which the citizens of Judah had succumbed (**Jer. 5**):

(1) God challenges Jeremiah to find a single honest man on the streets of Jerusalem (5:1), anticipating the search of Diogenes in the Greek world. Even one such person would have been enough, according to God, to forestall judgment on the city. But of course that is another way of saying how slippery the moral life of the city had become, how extensive the sin was, how insincerity and moral corrosion had damaged the city's children.

(2) Initially Jeremiah thinks that perhaps the negative results of his search could be laid at the door of the disadvantages of the lower classes. Of course, even the poor were supposed to know and keep the Law of God, but it is compassionate to make allowances. So Jeremiah goes off to examine the sophisticated, the privileged, the articulate—and finds no less moral rot there than elsewhere (5:4-5). Intelligent sinners use their intelligence to sin; sophisticated sinners concoct sophisticated reasons for thinking sin is not sin; upper-crust sinners indulge in upper-crust sin. "But with one accord they too had broken off the yoke and torn off the bonds" (5:5).

(3) The common stance toward God is that he is absent or ineffective (5:12); the common stance toward genuine prophets is that they are windbags (5:13). So God will bring about catastrophic judgment to show his power, and he will speak to the people in the words of a foreign language (5:14-17). They so much love to serve foreign gods in their own land; they will henceforth serve foreigners in a land not their own (5:19).

(4) By and large, the people have learned nothing from God's wise and generous providential care (5:24). Equally they have learned nothing from the times when God has chastened them by depriving them of harvest (5:25). Whether he is gentle or firm, whether he is generously forbearing or promptly just, they ignore him or rebel against him. What is he to do? Sooner or later he must respond to the violence, deceit, and corruption in the coinage of punishment (5:26-29).

(5) There may be hope for the people of God when their leaders call them back to faithfulness and integrity, or when the people try to check and remove errant leaders. But what do we have here? "A horrible and shocking thing has happened in the land: The prophets prophesy lies, the priests rule by their own authority, and my people love it this way [cf. 2 Tim. 3:1-7]. But what will you do in the end?" (5:31).

How many of these elements are playing out today?

∾

Joshua 12—13; Psalm 145; *Jeremiah 6; Matthew 20*

∾

SOME REFLECTIONS ON the warnings of **Jeremiah 6**:

(1) Benjamin (6:1), which with Judah remained loyal to the Davidic dynasty and therefore had not been transported by Assyria along with the other ten tribes, lay to the north of Jerusalem. So when marauding hordes loomed "out of the north," one might think that Jeremiah would advise them to flee south to Jerusalem, the best-defended city in the entire region. But Jeremiah tells Benjamin to flee *away* from Jerusalem—essentially a prediction that Jerusalem itself will be utterly destroyed and that no one should expect to find refuge there.

(2) The Hebrew of verse 4 literally reads, "Sanctify battle against her!" All war was "sacred" in the ancient Near East. The mighty pagan armies were accompanied by staff astrologers and fought under the patronage of various deities. The following lines depict a typical battle. Combatants began in the morning after both sides had made preparations, and then continued all day, with both sides normally retiring from the field about dusk. But here the enemy continues the attack at night (6:5)—suggesting a battle of uncharacteristic ruthlessness and ferocity.

(3) The heart of the charge against the citizens of Jerusalem and Judah is that they care nothing for the word of the Lord. When the prophet issues warnings, their ears are "closed"—literally, "uncircumcised" (6:10) "so that they cannot hear" (see yesterday's meditation). Why? What is the problem? They are not literally deaf, but, "The word of the Lord is offensive to them; they find no pleasure in it" (6:10). Meanwhile the prophets and priests, according to the Lord, "dress the wound of my people as though it were not serious. 'Peace, peace,' they say, when there is no peace" (6:14). In other words, most of the religious leaders are not addressing the sins of the age and seeking to reform the people of God. Rather, they give soothing talks for busy people, above all avoiding themes like judgment and punishment. Their conduct is "loathsome" (6:15) because the people are being neither warned nor reformed, but the preachers, far from being ashamed, "do not even know how to blush" (6:15). Of course not: they are deluded into thinking they are doing the right thing. But the prophet of God is to "ask for the ancient paths" and "ask where the good way is, and walk in it" (6:16). This is not an appeal to boundless traditionalism, but to the inherited revelation of the covenant, of the Word of God, that is being jettisoned in favor of comforting illusion: the people said, "We will not listen" (6:17) and, God says, they "rejected my law" (6:19).

∾

Joshua 14—15; Psalms 146—147; *Jeremiah 7; Matthew 21*

∾

THIS TEMPLE ADDRESS (JER. 7), delivered in prose to the people coming through the gates "to worship the LORD" (7:2), is famous for its powerful insistence that no rite or institution or building can shield a guilty people from the wrath of God. To think otherwise is to descend to ridiculous superstition. Some notes:

(1) The merely repetitious chanting of a godly theme such as "the temple of the LORD" (7:4)—or, for that matter, "Jesus is Lord"—avails nothing. What God demands is moral renovation, repudiation of false gods, justice, and generosity (7:6-8). The shedding of innocent blood (7:6) might refer to judicial murders, for we know they were committed (26:23, under Jehoiakim).

(2) But what is offensive above all is the sheer hypocrisy. People would happily steal and murder and commit adultery and perjury, offering their worship to false gods—and then participate in temple worship, claiming shelter as if the temple's ramparts could save them from the judgment of God (7:9-11). When one reads contemporary statistics on stealing (e.g., cheating on income tax) and adultery, both outside the church and inside, it is difficult to believe that we are in a vastly different situation. We may not claim the sanctuary of temple precincts, but somehow we think that our modicum of Christian observance means that we are still "good people" and therefore safe from the judgment that falls on other nations.

(3) The time may come, as it came in the days of Jeremiah, when intercessory prayer on behalf of such people is actually forbidden by God himself (7:16). This is equivalent to saying that it is too late.

(4) Even so, God wants Jeremiah to tell the people all these things. Perhaps the sheer extremity of the threat will prompt reflection and encourage repentance. But no: "When you tell them all this, they will not listen to you; when you call to them, they will not answer. Therefore say to them, 'This is the nation that has not obeyed the LORD its God or responded to correction. Truth has perished; it has vanished from their lips'" (7:27-28). Though written to describe Judahites in the sixth century before Christ, it is difficult to imagine any passage that more accurately describes Western culture, including much of the Western church. Indeed, in our day "truth has perished" not only in the sense that integrity is at a low ebb, but as a result of postmodern sensibilities that find it difficult to see what all the fuss is about: all these religious claims are driven by sociological pressures, aren't they, and not by a divine Being who actually speaks objective truth? And so we rush to perdition.

∾

JULY 12

Joshua 16—17; Psalm 148; *Jeremiah 8; Matthew 22*

∾

AT EACH STAGE OF JEREMIAH'S description of the rebellion of God's people, some facets of their sin are reiterated while others are refined and some new ones introduced. Here I focus on two of the latter (**Jer. 8**).

First, Jeremiah focuses on the sheer unnaturalness of the people's unwillingness to learn from their mistakes and repent. The presentation of the argument turns in part on a pun: the Hebrew word for "turn" or "repent" is the same as that rendered "return." The point is that in ordinary experience someone who "turns away," i.e., who makes a mistake, eventually returns, learning from the experience. But Israel always turns away (8:4)—they never learn from their bitter experiences. That is because they cherish their sin, they "cling to deceit; they refuse to *return*" (8:5). "No one repents of his wickedness, saying, 'What have I done?'" (8:6).

First-time readers of the Old Testament sometimes wonder how people can be so thick as not to learn from the repeated cycles of rebellion and punishment. Rats in a maze learn to adapt to external stimuli; to some extent, well-brought-up children learn to conform to cultural expectations and hide their worst instincts. Why doesn't Judah learn from the history of the northern kingdom? Or even from her own checkered history? Although some behavioral modification can be achieved by training, biblical history demonstrates that the problem is bound up *with human nature.* We are a fallen breed. Sinners will sin. Creeds and covenants and vows and liturgy may domesticate the beast for a while, but what we are will not forever be suppressed. Israel's history demonstrates the point, not because Israel is the worst of all races, but because Israel is typically human—and fallen. Even people as privileged, chosen, and graced as these cannot escape downward spirals. How naive for us to think that we can!

Second, not only do many of these people foolishly think they are "safe" because they "have the law of the LORD" even though they do not obey it (8:8—a common theme in the prophets), but in this case the problem is massively exacerbated by "the lying pen of the scribes" who have "handled it falsely" (8:8). This is the first Old Testament reference to "scribes" as a class—and the people whose duty it is to study, preserve, and expound the Scriptures mishandle them. Perhaps they pick up elements they like and create a synthesis that pleases them, ignoring the whole; perhaps they deploy clever techniques to make the Law say what their presuppositions and theology demand. Sound familiar? Review the meditation for July 4.

∾

Joshua 18—19; Psalms 149—150; *Jeremiah 9; Matthew 23*

∾

ONCE AGAIN JEREMIAH CYCLES around some of the themes he has already introduced (**Jer. 9**). For instance, the closing two verses pick up on true and false circumcision (cf. 4:4). But here, too, a new facet of the sin of the people is explored
(9:23-24). About these verses I must say four things:

First, the heart of much sin is the smug self-sufficiency that boasts in its own
wisdom or strength or wealth (9:23). That is always a mark of lostness. It focuses
on *self*. Worse, it fails to recognize that all that we have (and boast about) is
derived: we do not choose our own genes, or parents, or heritage; all we have
achieved has been in function of others, of health, of gifts, of support, of situation—a thousand elements over which we have little control and which, this side
of the Fall, we do not have the right to claim. Worst of all, smug and self-suffi-
cient people leave no place for priorities outside themselves; they leave no place
for God, for they are their own gods.

Second, there is nothing in the universe more important to human beings than
to know the Lord (9:24a). He is God, not we; he is the Creator, not we; he exercises providential rule, not we. He is the Self-Existent, and we are derived and
dependent. He inhabits eternity; we are restricted to our very small segment of
time. He is utterly holy and glorious; we are massively contaminated by dirt, and
stand under his judgment. But we may know him! That is the only thing truly
worth "boasting" about. Will you doubt this point two hundred or two billion
years from now?

Third, the One we know is Yahweh, "who exercises kindness, justice and righteousness on the earth" (9:24b). "Kindness" is God's covenantal love, his covenantal mercy, bound up with his own utter reliability—a virtue that stands in stunning
contrast to the fickleness of the people in rebellion against him.

Fourth, Paul understands the universal applicability of these verses when he
alludes to them and then cites part of them in 1 Corinthians 1:26-31. He writes,
"Not many of you were wise by human standards; not many were influential; not
many were of noble birth"—the kinds of things the Corinthians were boasting
about. "Wise/wisdom" is found in both contexts; Paul interprets "strong" not in
terms of physical strength but in terms of political and social influence; he interprets the "rich" in terms of the "noble," for in the preindustrial world the two usually went hand in hand. But if Christ is our true wisdom—"that is, our
righteousness, holiness and redemption" (1 Cor. 1:30), then, "Let him who boasts
boast in the Lord" (1:31).

∾

Joshua 20—21; Acts 1; *Jeremiah 10; Matthew 24*

∾

TWO REFLECTIONS ON **Jeremiah 10**:

First, the catastrophic punishment about to befall Judah is traced to her incompetent leaders: "The shepherds are senseless and do not inquire of the LORD; so they do not prosper and all their flock is scattered" (10:21). "Shepherds" in this context includes more than "pastors" (KJV): it includes all who direct the affairs of the nation—king, priests, prophets, and other leaders.

The arena in which these leaders are incompetent is not general administration, charismatic sheen, financial acuity, or management potential. They are "senseless," and their folly is manifest in the fact that they "do not inquire of the LORD." This cannot mean that they do not go through the mere forms of seeking out the Lord's counsel, consulting the prophets and treating the prescribed rituals like a talisman that brings good luck. It means, rather, that they do not really want to do what God wants. They do not approach him with the contrition and profound reverence for his Word of which Isaiah speaks (Isa. 66). They do not treat him as if he is radically "other" and fundamentally different from the myriad false gods that surround them. Neither nations nor churches rise higher than their leaders. If our leaders are passionate about knowing and obeying the will of the Lord, our prospects are excellent; if they are dissolute and intoxicated by selfism, our prospects are dim or even desperate.

Second, in the closing verses (10:23-25) Jeremiah identifies with his people in a startling way. "I know, O LORD, that a man's life is not his own; it is not for man to direct his steps. Correct me, LORD, but only with justice—not in your anger, lest you reduce me to nothing" (10:23-24). These lines might initially be read as referring to Jeremiah the prophet, Jeremiah the individual, and nothing more. Certainly individual believers ought so to be aware of their own sins that they entreat God to spare them from the destruction they deserve. But closer inspection shows that the sins Jeremiah is confessing are the sins of the nation, in particular the smug self-determinism that refuses to acknowledge the sheer Godhood of God, the glorious truth that God alone is God and is in control. The next verse (10:25) discloses that what Jeremiah wants God to spare is "Jacob," the covenant people of God. Doubtless punishment is decreed against them, but Jeremiah pleads with God that he will not wipe out the people in his wrath, but reserve the worst measures for "the peoples who do not call on your name." Thus Jeremiah cries to God for himself, but also for his people with whom he identifies—not unlike Paul in Galatians 2:17-21 and perhaps Romans 7:7ff.

∾

Joshua 22; Acts 2; *Jeremiah 11; Matthew 25*

ᢙ

THE OPENING LINE OF **JEREMIAH 11** shows that what follows is a new prophecy, a new oracle from God, the fourth reported in this book. It is difficult to be certain exactly when it was preached. Many have suggested, plausibly enough, that it was delivered not too long after Hilkiah rediscovered the scroll of the Law, about 621 B.C. This generated something of a religious reformation under King Josiah (2 Kings 22—23). According to 2 Chronicles 34, the discovery of the scroll was preceded by a centralization of worship at Jerusalem. Inevitably this meant a decline of the rites shaped by Canaanite religion at the local shrines—and, presumably, an increase in the resentment of local religious leaders. Jeremiah certainly supported Josiah in this reformation. *If* this is the setting—and one cannot be certain, for there are other possibilities—two elements in the chapter before us take on new significance.

First, the Lord tells Jeremiah to threaten the people with judgment specifically grounded in the blessings and cursings of the Mosaic covenant (11:6-8). What is threatened is more specific than the judgments reserved for other nations, judgments grounded in God's response to unrighteousness and idolatry. Rather, what is threatened is no more and no less than what the covenant said would happen if the people fell away into disobedience (Deut. 28). The religion of the covenant people of God had apparently become so debased, so merely traditional, and so removed from any current study of the Scriptures, that such elements had largely passed from public memory, until the scroll of the Law was rediscovered. These specific covenantal threats of judgment were what caused Josiah to tear his clothes and utter, "Great is the LORD's anger that burns against us because our fathers have not obeyed the words of this book; they have not acted in accordance with all that is written there concerning us" (2 Kings 22:13). Assuming this setting for Jeremiah 11, the prophet is carefully drawing out the covenantal implications of the failure to obey.

Second, this also explains why the men of Anathoth, Jeremiah's own village, seek to do away with him (Jer. 11:18-23). Priests had lived there since the time of the settlement under Joshua (Josh. 21:18). Because this line had participated in the revolt against David, Solomon excluded them from temple service (1 Kings 2:26-27). Doubtless they were heavily invested in local shrines and resented the centralized worship in the Jerusalem temple, where they were not allowed to serve. So in addition to the animus against a local (a prophet is without honor in his home town, Luke 4:24), these men may have especially hated Jeremiah's support for Josiah's reformation. Where there is no passion for the Word of God, other passions take over.

ᢙ

JULY 16

Joshua 23; Acts 3; Jeremiah 12; Matthew 26

∽

IN THE EIGHTH CENTURY BEFORE CHRIST, Hosea experienced the terrible betrayal of a woman joined to him by the covenant of marriage who was tragically committed to prostitution. He learned thereby something of how God perceives the spiritual prostitution of the people to whom he was covenantally linked. In a somewhat similar vein, Jeremiah has suffered rejection by his friends and relatives (11:18-23—yesterday's meditation). His anguish and anger over the situation sets the stage for God to explain his own response to the people who have rejected him (Jer. 12).

The question Jeremiah raises is prompted by his experiences in the immediately preceding verses. He has been doing his bit to foster reformation, yet his life is threatened by the relatives and people of his own village. Although he still affirms the righteousness of God, Jeremiah protests, "Yet I would speak with you about your justice: Why does the way of the wicked prosper? Why do all the faithless live at ease?" (12:1). Plunged into despair and flooded with a sense of the sheer inequity of it all, Jeremiah in the opening verses of this chapter asks God why he does not simply root out the wicked and do away with them.

God does not directly respond to Jeremiah's question (12:5-6). Instead, he tells the prophet, in effect, that he hasn't seen anything yet. If Jeremiah stumbles so painfully in his own village, how will he fare in the far more complicated and perverse atmosphere of Jerusalem? "If you have raced with men on foot and they have worn you out, how can you compete with horses?" (12:5). If you stumble in the relatively safe arena of Anathoth, "how will you manage in the thickets by the Jordan?" (In the preexilic period, the Jordan's flood-plain was covered with luxuriant vegetation that protected many wild animals, including the Asiatic lion.) Many Christian leaders have had to learn that initial sufferings merely prepare the way for much more of the same.

At least Jeremiah is a little better able to understand what God means when he says, "I will forsake my house, abandon my inheritance; I will give the one I love into the hands of her enemies. My inheritance has become to me like a lion in the forest. She roars at me; therefore I hate her" (12:7-8). So the following verses depict the judgment that must inevitably ensue.

Even here, however, God's graciousness shines through. After God has "uprooted" them, he will bring them back to their own inheritance (12:14-15). If exile is inevitable because of their sin, restoration will follow because of God's compassion. Even pagan nations will join in the blessing of the Lord, wherever they repudiate the Baals and swear by the living God (12:16).

∽

Joshua 24; Acts 4; *Jeremiah 13; Matthew 27*

∾

MATTHEW TELLS US THAT AT THE moment Jesus died, "the curtain of the temple was torn in two from top to bottom" (**Matt. 27:51**). The immediate cause was apparently the earthquake that accompanied Jesus' death. Yet it is impossible for the thoughtful Christian not to nestle this brief and cryptic observation into the bigger picture—the account of what the curtain had already come to mean in the history of Israel and how it plays out in the later books of the New Testament, such as Hebrews and Revelation, where the first generation of Christian writers explain to their readers just what the cross achieved. Along this axis, the tearing of the curtain was a symbol-laden act of great significance. Four reflections:

(1) Neither the curtain nor the tearing of the curtain make any sense unless we see that, this side of the Fall, we have no right to come into the presence of a holy God. After their calamitous rebellion, Adam and Eve are expelled from the garden (Gen. 3). When the rescued Israelites construct their golden calf in the desert, God not only sends judgment, but threatens not to manifest himself among them, lest they be destroyed (Ex. 32—33). In narrative and oracle alike, the biblical writers drive home this truth: sin separates us from our transcendentally holy Maker. We do not have right of access to the most holy.

(2) That reality was symbolized in the construction of the tabernacle and later the temple. One third of the structure, called the Most Holy Place, had the dimensions of a cube. It was separated from the rest of the building by a heavy curtain. Here God manifested himself in glory. Only the high priest could enter—and only once a year, bearing the blood of the prescribed sacrifices, offered up for his own sins and for the sins of the people. All others were excluded under pain of death.

(3) The tearing of the curtain at the moment of Jesus' death therefore symbolizes that Jesus' death has gained access for sinners into the very presence of God. He is our great high priest; he is our atoning sacrifice. Nor does he have to slip into the Most Holy Place every year, once a year. He dies once for all and satisfies the holy demand of God, so that in principle the curtain can come down.

(4) Small wonder, then, that the "new Jerusalem," one of the images for the final abode of God's people (Rev. 21—22), is shaped like a perfect cube. Already Christians have access to the throne of God by the merit of Jesus Christ; in the consummation, however, we will stand unafraid and overwhelmed by joy and adoration in the unshielded splendor of his holiness.

∾

Judges 1; Acts 5; *Jeremiah 14; Matthew 28*

∾

THIS CHAPTER, JEREMIAH 14, oscillates between poetry and prose, and between God's speech and Jeremiah's response. The occasion is the calamitous drought devastating the country. Some reflections:

(1) A disaster may be no more than the effluent of the Fall, and not God's specific judgment on a people. Even then it reminds us of our mortality and our lostness, and calls for repentance (Luke 13:1-5). Nevertheless, a specific disaster *may* be the immediate and direct judgment of God on a people. Therefore disasters demand self-examination and a humble heart. In exactly the same way, a crippling illness *may not be* the direct consequence of a specific sin (John 9). But it *may be* (John 5).

(2) Again and again in the Old Testament, God punishes the covenant community for their sins by using the recurrent banes of the ancient world: sword (i.e., war, and sometimes exile with it), famine, and plague (14:11-12). This three-fold combination is brought together seven times in the prophecy of Jeremiah. Ezekiel 14 adds a fourth: wild beasts. These are either "natural" phenomena (famine and plague) or are brought about by wicked human conduct (war, and sometimes famine and plague).

(3) Because our own culture tries so hard to detach from God what happens in the "natural" world, reserving for him only private or distantly "spiritual" things, we rush to give naturalistic explanations for our wars and famines and plagues instead of at least trying to learn the lessons providence may be teaching us. I am not suggesting that it is easy to read providence. We have seen that Scripture itself warns us against trying to infer too much too quickly (Luke 13:1-5). Nevertheless, not to draw any moral and spiritual lessons from disasters may be nothing more than an index of how far we have sold ourselves to the forces of secularization. We resolutely refuse to "hear" what God says when he speaks to us in the language of judgment—*exactly* the response of ancient Israel. Indeed, according to this chapter there was a hearty collection of religious leaders who *denied* any connection between disaster and divine judgment (14:14). It is ever so. So not only will prophets be held accountable for what they say and teach, but the people are responsible for what they choose to listen to. Shall we not learn any moral and spiritual lessons in this bloody twentieth century from two world wars, the arms race, economic collapses, the Nazis, Stalin, Mao, Pol Pot, Biafra, the Balkans, Rwanda, Vietnam, wretched totalitarian regimes of left and right, famines, slavery, the Sudan, racism, AIDS, abortion? Kipling was right: "Lord God of hosts, be with us yet / Lest we forget; lest we forget."

∾

Judges 2; Acts 6; *Jeremiah 15; Mark 1*

∾

JEREMIAH 15 PROVIDES SOME OF the most haunting insights into the inner life and thought of the prophet Jeremiah:

(1) Jeremiah has been interceding with God on behalf of the covenant people (Jer 14). God tells Jeremiah to stop, that he will not listen (14:11-12). Indeed, he now says that even if Moses and Samuel were to stand before him and intercede for the people, he would not spare them (15:1). Centuries earlier Moses and Samuel had successfully interceded for Israel (Ex. 32:11-14; Num. 14:13-24; Deut. 9:18-20, 25-29; 1 Sam. 7:5-9; 12:19-25)—though it is important to remember that they also secured, in some measure, the willingness of the people to return to the Lord with contrition and renewed obedience. This Jeremiah has not been able to achieve. Now God is telling him that he will not achieve it: the people will go into captivity. The iniquity and idolatry under Manasseh have been the last straw (15:4; see 2 Kings 21:10-15; 23:26; 24:3).

(2) In 15:10, Jeremiah frankly wishes he had never been born. The entire nation "strives and contends" with him. Everyone curses him, not because he has been corrupt in business, but because he faithfully conveys the word of the Lord. The Lord reassures him (15:11-14; the best iron came "from the north," from the Black Sea area, so this is a way of saying that Israel's arms would be no match for those of the Babylonians). But that is part of Jeremiah's anguish. One part of him wants justice, wants retribution for his persecutors (15:15). That same part utterly delights in God's words (15:16a). Yet on the other hand, his allegiance to God and his words is precisely what isolates him from the people: "I sat alone because your hand was on me and you had filled me with indignation" (15:17b). Some of his most virulent foes were his own relatives (cf. Matt. 10:36). Jeremiah is sometimes tempted to think that it is God who has failed, like an intermittent spring (a wadi, 15:18) that flows at times with life and blessing, and at other times provides nothing.

God's response (15:19-21) is that if Jeremiah proves utterly faithful in conveying his words, he will continue as God's spokesman and will be preserved from the evil machinations of his opponents. But one point is nonnegotiable: "Let this people turn to you, but you must not turn to them" (15:19b).

The deep tension between faithfulness to God and alienation from one's own people is an unvarying constant in the ministry of faithful preachers assigned to a declining culture.

∾

Judges 3; Acts 7; *Jeremiah 16*; *Mark 2*

෴

THREE OBSERVATIONS ON **Jeremiah 16**:

(1) The opening section of this chapter probably occurs quite early in Jeremiah's ministry. He is forbidden to marry, not merely because women and children will within a few decades face an extraordinarily difficult time under siege warfare and subsequent exile, but as a symbolic way of anticipating the enforced asceticism that judgment will bring. In a culture in which almost all males married, his celibacy was doubtless a powerful symbol.

(2) One of the most striking features of this chapter is that the people really do not seem to be aware of their guilt. They cannot see why they *should* face judgment. "Why has the LORD decreed such a great disaster against us?" they ask. "What wrong have we done? What sin have we committed against the LORD our God?" (16:10). One of the most terrible indices of how far a people have strayed from righteousness is the degree to which they can no longer perceive their own guilt. Men and women who truly love righteousness and integrity are invariably aware when they breach it. The most holy people are the first to confess their sin with shame and contrition. The most guilty people are blissfully unaware of their corruptions and idolatries. So we must ask ourselves: where on this sort of spectrum are our churches found? Or our culture? Are we characterized by profound contrition, or by a frank inability to think that we have really done anything all that wrong? What does that say of us? What does that say about the Lord's stance toward us?

(3) Although the Lord promises judgment, there are two hopeful elements. The *first* is that God will one day bring the people out of exile with so dramatic and unexpected a rescue that it will eclipse the glory of the Exodus (16:14-15). The *second* is that part of the purpose of this judgment is pedagogical. The people have cherished false gods. "Therefore I will teach them—this time I will teach them my power and might. Then they will know that my name is the LORD" (16:21). The exile was to reduce if not eliminate the chronic idolatry of the covenant people. At least at the level of formal idolatry it turned out to be remarkably effective in this respect. The history of the Jews after the return from exile is far different in this respect than what it was before. Despite horrible lapses, postexilic Jewish history displays far less polytheism and syncretism than preexilic history. Of course, for Jew and Gentile alike, the snare of idolatry is much more subtle and corrosive than the attractions of formal polytheism.

෴

Judges 4; Acts 8; *Jeremiah 17; Mark 3*

AMONG THE CHORUSES I learned as a boy in Sunday school were these two:

> *These are the names of Jacob's sons:*
> *Gad, and Asher, and Simeon,*
> *Reuben, Issachar, Levi,*
> *Judah, Dan, and Naphtali—*
> *Twelve in all, but never a twin—*
> *Zebulun, Joseph, and Benjamin.*

> *There were twelve disciples Jesus called to help him:*
> *Simon Peter, Andrew, James, his brother John,*
> *Philip, Thomas, Matthew, James the son of Alphaeus,*
> *Thaddaeus, Simon, Judas, and Bartholomew.*
> *He has called us, too; he has called us, too!*
> *We are his disciples, I am one, and you.*
> *He has called us, too; he has called us, too!*
> *We are his disciples; we his work must do.*

I am grateful that I was brought up at a time when many of the songs we learned gave us some facts, some data, some reasons for things. Many Christians today could not name either the twelve patriarchs or the twelve apostles, and are dismally ignorant of a lot of other elementary data that the least informed Sunday school student a generation ago mastered by the age of six or ten. Of course, the acquisition of mere data does not necessarily make a Christian. On the other hand, ignorance of Scripture almost always ensures a painful immaturity.

Nevertheless, the chorus of the second piece quoted above is slightly misleading. True, we are called to be disciples of Jesus, i.e., followers of Jesus. That is the calling of all Christians. Nevertheless, there were unique elements to the calling of the twelve apostles (**Mark 3:13-19**). Here I mention only one: these were appointed "that they might be with him" (3:14). This was important for at least two reasons: (a) They were trained by him, and a major component of their training was what we today would call "mentoring"—not merely the impartation of a message and a commission, but shaping people by example as well as precept as to how they should live. (b) These twelve were able to bear witness to the facts concerning Christ from the first days of his public ministry. Peter understood the importance of this point (Acts 1:21-22), for the revelation of Jesus Christ was not some private mystical experience but a unique, historical event that demanded witnesses.

Judges 5; Acts 9; *Jeremiah 18; Mark 4*

THE IMAGERY OF THE POTTER and the clay (**Jer. 18**) recurs in Scripture (e.g., Rom. 9:19ff.). Slightly different emphases are brought forward in the different passages, though all of them emphasize God's sovereign sway over the people who are likened to the clay. The emphases here may be clarified by the following observations:

(1) The potter's wheel was a common sight in the ancient Near East, not so much a hobby item as an essential element in the manufacture of vessels both useful and aesthetically pleasing. The word *wheel* is in the dual form in Hebrew: two circular stones were fitted onto a vertical axis; the lower one was spun by the potter's foot while the upper one served as the platform for the work.

(2) Often in the shaping of a pot some defect or other would become obvious—a defect in size or shape or in the texture of the clay or in some pollutant. The potter might then squash the developing pot into an amorphous blob of clay and begin all over again. It rather misses the point to ask if the potter is responsible for the defect. In the real world of pottery-making, of course, the potter might well be responsible or might be proceeding by trial and error. Certainly no one is suggesting that the clay itself, in the real world of pottery-making, bears some sort of moral responsibility for the way it turns out. But the point of the extended metaphor is not to assign blame for the defect: that is another subject. To try to read any such lesson here is to make the imagery walk on all fours. Moreover, in the context of the chapter at large—i.e., outside the world of the extended metaphor—God clearly holds the people of Israel responsible for the behavior that is calling forth his judgment (e.g., 18:13-15).

(3) What, then, is the point of this imagery? Perhaps there are two points. *First*, God has the *right* to destroy this pot and begin again. Whatever the cause of the defects, he has every bit as much right as the potter has to squash the pot and begin again. In other words, the people are not nearly as autonomous and self-determining as they think they are. That means their present course of conduct and disobedience is a recipe for unmitigated disaster. *Second*, just as a competent potter may well begin again because he or she is dissatisfied with the way a pot is developing, so God begins again because he is dissatisfied with the way his covenant people are developing. Are God's standards lower than those of the village potter?

God has the right, and he has the standards. What sense does it make to buck him?

Judges 6; Acts 10; *Jeremiah 19; Mark 5*

∾

THE HEALING OF THE Gerasene man who was demonized by a "legion" of demons (**Mark 5:1-20**) calls for explanations and reflection at many points. To pick up on six:

(1) The setting is Gentile territory on the east side of Lake Galilee, in the region of the Decapolis (5:20), the Ten Cities of largely Gentile constitution. That point is clear even from the herd of pigs, something that no self-respecting Jew would keep.

(2) The poor man described in these verses was subject to some sort of cyclical attack. At times he was docile enough to be chained, and then the attack would be so desperately strong that he could tear the chains apart and free himself. Banished from home and hearth, he lived among the tombs, where he cried out and lacerated himself, a man in the final throes of destruction by demonic powers (5:5). We should not assume that every case of what is today called insanity is the result of demonic activity; neither should we adopt the reductionism that reduces all demonism to chemical imbalances in the brain.

(3) The words addressed to Jesus (5:6-8), though on the lips of the man, are the product of the "evil spirit." This spirit knows enough (a) to recognize who Jesus is, and (b) to live in horrible anticipation of the ultimate doom that awaits him.

(4) This exchange between Jesus and the "evil spirit" has two elements not found in any other exorcism in the canonical Gospels. *First,* the strange interplay between the singular and plural—"My name is Legion, . . . for we are many"—suggests an ambiguity in certain demonic activity. Moreover, as Jesus hints elsewhere, multiple invasion by unclean spirits is a "worse" condition to be scrupulously avoided (Matt. 12:45). *Second,* these demons do not wish to leave the area, and they do wish to be embodied (5:10, 12). Jesus accedes to both requests. Presumably this reflects in part the fact that the final hour for their banishment has not yet arrived.

(5) While it is essential to reflect on Jesus' absolute mastery over these evil spirits, one must add that he does not call forth these spirits one by one, solicit their names, enter into conversation with them, or a host of other things commonly practiced by some who are given to "deliverance ministries."

(6) The responses to this deliverance are striking. The delivered man wants to follow Jesus, and is commissioned to bear witness, in his Gentile world, to how much the Lord has done for him and how he has shown him mercy (5:18-20). The people of the region beg Jesus to leave (5:17): they prefer pigs to people, their financial security to the transformation of a life.

∾

Judges 7; Acts 11; *Jeremiah 20; Mark 6*

∽

THE CHAPTER BEFORE US (JER. 20) provides insight both into Jeremiah's external circumstances at this stage of his ministry, and into his inner turmoil.

(1) *Jeremiah's external circumstances:* the priest Pashhur son of Immer is the "chief officer" in the temple, presumably the chief security officer, serving under the current high priest. The prophetic actions and words Jeremiah has delivered in the previous chapter, announcing the destruction of Jerusalem and its temple, have been interpreted as something near treasonous, if not blasphemous, the more so because Pashhur has been among those who have "prophesied lies" (20:6) to the effect that God would never let this city fall to the pagans (cf. 14:14-15). So he has Jeremiah arrested and beaten, presumably with the legal limit of forty stripes (Deut. 25:3—that number was reduced by one in Paul's day to ensure that the limit was not accidentally exceeded, 2 Cor. 11:24). Jeremiah spends a night in the stocks, devices guaranteed to cause the terrible pain of cramped muscles. By the next morning Pashhur has second thoughts and lets Jeremiah go. If he thinks this leniency will reduce the prophet to cowering jelly, he is mistaken: Jeremiah uses the occasion to assign Pashhur a new name meaning "terror on every side" (20:3-4)—another picturesque anticipation of the judgment sure to fall, when all of Pashhur's false prophecies will be exposed for what they are.

(2) *Jeremiah's inner turmoil:* if the prophet is outwardly courageous, the following verses (20:7-18) disclose something of his personal anguish. By this point Jeremiah has been predicting judgment for decades, and it has not yet fallen. It has become progressively easier to dismiss him and mock him. The Lord's forbearance becomes an excuse for cynicism (as in 2 Pet. 3:8-9). Jeremiah temporarily resolves on silence, but so strong is the prophetic word burning within him that he cannot hold it in (20:9). So he speaks, and his erstwhile "friends" listen with sneering condescension, hoping he will say something that will enable them to report him to the authorities and get this silly man into trouble (20:10). Jeremiah oscillates between a focused and brilliant faith utterly confident that the Lord will finally vindicate him (20:11-13), and a debilitating despair that frankly wishes he had never been born and wallows in understandable self-pity (20:14-18).

Perhaps there are some servants of the Lord who have never experienced such highs and lows. But they are rare. Certainly those who serve in hard places almost invariably mirror Jeremiah's experiences in some degree. Pray for Christian leaders, especially those whose patch is profoundly discouraging.

Judges 8; Acts 12; *Jeremiah 21; Mark 7*

∾

JERUSALEM BECAME A VASSAL TO Babylon from 605 B.C. on, after Babylon defeated Egypt at the Battle of Carchemish. Jerusalem revolted and was defeated in 597, when most of the royal family, along with the nobility, the wealthy, and the skilled craftsmen were transported to Egypt, leaving behind Zedekiah as caretaker monarch. Zedekiah was an uncle of the young King Jehoiachin, who was taken into exile. Despite God's strong warnings through Jeremiah that Israel should not rebel again against the Babylonians, the Jerusalem authorities preferred to listen to the false prophets. When Judah rebelled, Babylon's retaliation was implacable. Nebuchadnezzar's troops destroyed Judah and besieged Jerusalem, which was finally destroyed in 587.

The prophecy of **Jeremiah 21** takes place under Zedekiah, when the Babylonian troops are gathering for the final siege, probably 589 or 588. The Pashhur whom Zedekiah sends to consult Jeremiah is not the Pashhur introduced in 20:1. Massive destruction threatens, just as Jeremiah has been predicting for more than three decades. Desperate, Zedekiah consults with anyone he can, including Jeremiah, hungry for the slenderest thread of hope. Will the Lord perhaps do great miracles again, as he did in the past—at the time of the Exodus, for instance, or when the Assyrians were turned back during the reign of Hezekiah—and spare Jerusalem? God's answer through Jeremiah is in three parts:

First, far from sparing the city, God is determined to destroy it (21:3-7). He will fight on the side of the Babylonians. "I myself will fight against you with an outstretched hand and a mighty arm in anger and fury and great wrath" (21:5). Zedekiah and his entourage will not be spared.

Second, it follows that the only wise course is to surrender. Under the well-understood terms of siege warfare, the city that defended itself against a siege could expect no mercy. Those who surrendered might be enslaved or otherwise sent into exile, but at least their lives would be spared. These are the two ways that God sets forth (21:8-10): the way of life and the way of death. This choice is not exactly like other "two ways" choices in Scripture (e.g., Deut. 30:15, 19; Matt. 7:13-14), but it is like them in distinguishing between obedience and disobedience and their respective consequences.

Third, like so many of God's promises of judgment, there is a way out—provided there is an immediate return to the social justice and personal righteousness at the heart of the Mosaic covenant (21:11-14). Without swift reformation, however, the little nation is doomed. And tragically, of reformation there is none—not the last time when somber warnings go unheeded.

∾

Judges 9; Acts 13; *Jeremiah 22; Mark 8*

ALL SERIOUS READERS OF JEREMIAH know that the various oracles are not given in chronological sequence. Sometimes the sequence of the oracles is perplexing; sometimes it is clearly thematic. In **Jeremiah 22**, we find a series of utterances regarding the final kings of Judah, but the list is not in chronological order. Perhaps the most important thing about these utterances is that collectively they provide a foil for the prospect of a far more fruitful king, introduced in the next chapter.

(1) The first nine verses continue the warning to Zedekiah, the plea to return to the covenantal stipulations to ward off imminent disaster.

(2) Jeremiah 22:10-12 deals with Shallum, otherwise known as Jehoahaz. He was one of the sons of the last reforming king, Josiah, who was killed at Megiddo in 609 B.C. Shallum reigned a mere three months before he was deposed by Pharaoh Neco (during the final years when Judah was still a vassal of Egypt, before Babylon took over the role of regional superpower in 605: cf. yesterday's comments). Transported to Egypt, Shallum never returned to Israel—the first of the Davidic kings to die in exile.

(3) Shallum's older brother Jehoiakim succeeded him (22:13-23). Jehoiakim was forced to pay a heavy tax to Egypt, but laid on additional loads for his own glorification. He was oppressive, covetous, greedy, and foolish (cf. 2 Kings 23:35). Worst of all, he reversed all the reforming policies of his father Josiah, and sanctioned pagan rites, even those of the oppressing power, Egypt. His exploitation of workers defied the Mosaic covenant (Lev. 19:13; Deut. 24:14). Jeremiah's denunciation is scathing: "Does it make you a king to have more and more cedar? Did not your father have food and drink? He did what was right and just, so all went well with him" (22:15). The consequence of Jehoiakim's disastrous and evil policies was the destruction of the nation. As for himself, he would die an ignominious death, and his corpse would be taken out with the garbage (22:19). "I warned you when you felt secure," God says, "but you said, 'I will not listen!'" (22:21).

(4) His son Jehoiachin (also called Jeconiah [24:1, note] or Coniah [37:1, note]) took over in December, 598, when Jehoiakim died. By this time Jerusalem was already under siege. Jehoiachin was a mere lad, eighteen years old. He ruled for three months. Then Jerusalem fell, and he was taken to Babylon, where he lived out the rest of his years—in prison until 561, and then in the Babylonian court. None of his children or his grandchildren would sit on the throne of David (22:30). "O land, land, land, hear the word of the LORD!" (22:29).

Judges 10; Acts 14; *Jeremiah 23; Mark 9*

∾

MUCH OF JEREMIAH 23 IS A denunciation of the "shepherds" destroying and scattering the sheep of God's pasture (23:1; compare Jer. 10 and meditation for July 14). The long section denouncing the lying prophets (23:9-40) is one of the most penetrating presentations of the differences between true prophets and false in all of holy Scripture. Its pathos is deepened by the asides of the prophet Jeremiah, asides that not only disclose some element of the true prophet but expose Jeremiah's own heart: "My heart is broken with me; all my bones tremble. I am like a drunken man, like a man overcome by wine, because of the LORD and his holy words" (23:9). The blistering condemnation of dreams that are enthusiastically passed around the circles of the prophets, while these same prophets fail to speak God's word faithfully (23:25-39), has a contemporary relevance that only the blind could miss.

But here I want to focus on the first six verses. In the light of the abysmally immoral and idolatrous kings condemned in the previous chapter, and in the light of the destructive shepherds introduced in this chapter, God presents the ultimate solution. It has three components:

(1) God will destroy the destructive shepherds (23:2). That is a theme we have seen before, and one that takes up a fair bit of this chapter.

(2) More importantly, God himself will gather the remnant of the flock from where they have been scattered, and he will bring them back to their pasture. "I will place shepherds over them who will tend them, and they will no longer be afraid or terrified, nor will any be missing" (23:4), the Lord declares. In other words, the promise of an end to the exile and a return of the remnant is now cast in the categories of a scattered flock being returned to its pasture. But there is also an element of expectation that transcends the historical end of the exile: the Lord himself will provide a quality of "pastors" (i.e., "shepherds") who will transcend what the people have experienced in the past.

(3) In particular, God "will raise up to David a righteous Branch" (23:5). The Davidic line will be little more than a stump, but a new "Branch" will grow out of it, "a King who will reign wisely and do what is just and right in the land" (23:5). His days will bring safety and salvation for the covenant people of God. "This is the name by which he will be called: The LORD Our Righteousness" (23:6). Just so: for by him, God will be both just and the One who justifies the ungodly, vindicating them by the life and death of the Branch from David's line (Rom. 3:20-26).

∾

Judges 11; Acts 15; *Jeremiah 24; Mark 10*

∾

THE VISION OF THE TWO BASKETS of figs (**Jer. 24**), one "very good figs, like those that ripen early" (24:2—the early ones ripened in June and were viewed as a delicacy, cf. Isa. 28:4) and the other basket full of figs "so bad they could not be eaten" (24:2), is plain enough. The good figs point to the Israelites who have already been sent away into exile in "the land of the Babylonians" (24:5). God will watch over them and bring them back. He will give them a heart to know the Lord. "They will be my people, and I will be their God, for they will return to me with all their heart" (24:7). By contrast, the poor figs point to Zedekiah and his officials and the remainder of the people in Jerusalem. They will become "a reproach and a byword, an object of ridicule and cursing" (24:9). They will not remain in the land. They will be banished, and God will follow them with "sword, famine and plague" (24:10).

This analogy calls forth two reflections. *First,* it is a reversal of popular expectation, both in Jerusalem and in the exilic community in Babylon. The Jerusalemites were tempted to think that they were the elite, since they had been spared: God had not sent them into exile. The exiles were the rubbish; those left in the land were the faithful remnant. The exiles were tempted to think the same thing. They did not want to contemplate the destruction of Jerusalem and the temple, for then there would be no "home" to go home to. So they tended to idealize the people who were left behind, praying that God would one day restore the exiles to the faithful remnant in Jerusalem. But God here says that the real situation is precisely the reverse. Those left behind in Jerusalem are disgusting and will be destroyed. The good figs are in exile, and God will bring them back to the land. In short, the remnant is in exile. The same theme (without the imagery of the figs) is developed in Babylon by Jeremiah's contemporary, Ezekiel: e.g., Ezekiel 11:14-21.

Second, this is such an astounding reversal of popular expectations that it prompts the reader to think of a host of other reversals in the Bible. One thinks of the mighty Egyptian empire against the Israelite slaves; of the rich man and Lazarus; of the beatitudes of Jesus that promise the kingdom to the poor in spirit. Think of as many such reversals as you can, both within the pages of Scripture and in later history. God delights to exalt the humble and to humble the exalted. After all, our Redeemer died on a cross. So why should thoughtful Christians scramble for power and position, instead of for humility and faithfulness?

∾

Judges 12; Acts 16; *Jeremiah 25; Mark 11*

∾

THE PROPHECY OF JEREMIAH 25 is dated to the fourth year of Nebuchadnezzar, i.e., 605 B.C., the year when the Babylonians defeated the Egyptians at Carchemish, forcing Judah to switch its allegiance to the new and rising power. By this time Jeremiah has been prophesying for twenty-three years—from the reign of the last good king, Josiah, to this day (25:3).

The onset of Babylonian supremacy is an appropriate occasion for Jeremiah to reiterate some of his principal themes: a review of the chronic disobedience of the people, a review of the warnings not to follow other gods, the refusal of the people to listen to the words of the Lord (25:4-8). But there are several elements in this chapter that either have not been mentioned before or have been given relatively light treatment up to this point.

First, in language reminiscent of that found in Isaiah, Nebuchadnezzar is designated God's "servant" (25:8). This is a way of saying that it is God himself who will be behind the destruction of Jerusalem, even though the temporal power that is doing the work is Babylon and its king.

Second, service to the king of Babylon will endure "seventy years" (25:11). There are different ways of calculating the duration of the exile. This one is a rounded-off figure that begins with the ascendancy of Babylon in 609 and runs either to the defeat of Babylon by the Persians (539) or, perhaps, from the first transportation of leaders in 605 to the first return of the Jews to the land under the regime of King Cyrus of Persia (536; cf. 2 Chron. 36:20-23; Zech. 1:12).

Third, reminiscent of what God says he will do with the Assyrians after he has used them to chasten the northern kingdom (Isa. 10:5ff.), God here says that he will punish Babylon "for their guilt . . . and will make it desolate forever" (25:12). "I will bring upon that land all the things I have spoken against it, all that are written in this book and prophesied by Jeremiah against all the nations" (25:13).

Fourth, in the following verses, Jeremiah is required, in a visionary experience, to compel the nations to drink the cup "filled with the wine of [God's] wrath" (25:15; compare Rev. 14:10). The God of the Bible is not some mere tribal deity; he holds all the nations to account. Judgment may begin with the covenant community, but it finally embraces all communities without exception. "You will not go unpunished, for I am calling down a sword upon all who live on the earth, declares the LORD Almighty" (25:29). And where shall we flee to escape judgment, except to the refuge that he alone provides?

∾

Judges 13; Acts 17; *Jeremiah 26; Mark 12*

∼

BECAUSE DEVOUT READERS THINK of the biblical writers as heroes of the faith, they sometimes overlook the fact that in their own day many of these writers were despised, treated as outsiders, viewed with contempt. Of course, some who contributed to the canon of Scripture grew rich or famous or both: Solomon comes to mind. Some who were powerful at one point in their life faced extraordinary difficulties and malice at other points: one thinks of David. But many of the prophets were despised; some of them lost their lives. As the Lord Jesus said, "Blessed are you when people insult you, persecute you and falsely say all kinds of evil against you because of me. Rejoice and be glad, because great is your reward in heaven, *for in the same way they persecuted the prophets who were before you*" (Matt. 5:11-12, italics added).

Already we have seen that Jeremiah's lot was not a happy one. From here on (**Jer. 26**), the dismal picture becomes clearer. To his most robust critics, Jeremiah's message, especially his constant insistence that unless the people repented Jerusalem and its temple would be destroyed, sounds perilously close to treason garnished with blasphemy: treason because Jeremiah could be charged with demoralizing the people and therefore making them less able to withstand the Babylonian onslaught; blasphemy because he is saying in effect that God either could not or would not preserve his city and temple. So the officials try to organize a judicial execution.

What saves Jeremiah, humanly speaking, is his strong insistence that if they kill him they will bring down severe judgment on their own heads. For "in truth the LORD has sent me to you to speak all these words in your hearing" (26:15). Some therefore want to give him the benefit of the doubt; others recall that Micah of Moresheth (the biblical Micah) uttered similar words of denunciation. (The chronology of the prophets makes it probable that some of the oldest people standing before Jeremiah had actually heard Micah.) So Jeremiah is reprieved.

Not so his colleague Uriah son of Shemaiah. We know nothing of Uriah except what is recorded in these verses (26:20-23). Jeremiah was not the only prophet faithfully proclaiming God's word. When Uriah, like Jeremiah, was threatened with death, unlike Jeremiah he fled to Egypt. At this point Israel was still a vassal state of Egypt, and some sort of mutual extradition treaty pertained. Uriah was hauled back and executed. His flight had convinced his accusers that he really was some kind of traitor. So reflect again on Jesus' words, cited above.

∼

Judges 14; Acts 18; *Jeremiah 27; Mark 13*

∽

IF THE PROPHECY IN JEREMIAH 27 takes place early in the reign of Zedekiah (27:1), there are still years to go before Jeremiah is vindicated. At this point King Jehoiachin and the aristocracy have already been transported to Babylon, leaving behind Zedekiah and a ruling remnant. But far from being warned by these recent setbacks, Zedekiah and the ruling oligarchy want to be heroes and take on the Babylonian might. God instructs Jeremiah to provide both a verbal warning and an object lesson, not only to Zedekiah but also to the emissaries of the surrounding little nations and city-states (27:1-3, 12). They are all in the same boat: if they submit to the Babylonian superpower, they will be spared; if they rebel, they will be crushed and destroyed. The God of Israel is sovereign over all the nations; the pagan states would do better listening to him than to all of their own diviners, pagan prophets, and mediums (27:9-10). Of course, most listened to their own religious establishment. Nevertheless, after the tragic events unfolded, doubtless some individuals were a little more impressed by the God of Israel than before these events. He was the only one who had gotten the future right.

For some years I have been keeping odd essays and books that predict the future. These are written by astrologers, various futurologists, and self-proclaimed prophets. Of course, they do not all work on the same premises. Futurologists tend to project current trends into the future and infer what will take place. The best of them also make some allowances for reactions to current trends. Astrologers and self-proclaimed prophets claim some sort of external perspective. I have been keeping these projections for enough years to know that their track record is not good. Inevitably they get some things right—they make many predictions, and they cannot always be wrong. Nevertheless, picking an essay at random out of my files, I consult what one expert predicted in 1968 regarding the state of religion in Canada in twenty-five years, i.e., 1993. Among his predictions: the Catholic Church will be ordaining women; church attendance in the nation will be down by about 60 percent; a new Billy Graham will appear, "more charismatic, more hypnotic in his sway over the masses, than Graham himself"; the crucial public ethical issue will not be abortion or capital punishment but sterilization of the mentally retarded and brain transplants. And much more of the same. Many of us are familiar with the widely disseminated prophecy that predicted massive revival in the West by a set date (now long past).

Brothers and sisters, do not fear them, listen to them, or respect them. Fear and hear the words of the Lord.

∽

Judges 15; Acts 19; *Jeremiah 28; Mark 14*

∽

EVENTUALLY THE CLASH BETWEEN Jeremiah and the false prophets becomes con-cretized in one particular contest—that between Jeremiah and Hananiah (**Jer. 28**). The issue could not be clearer. Jeremiah insists that unless Judah repents, its cap-ital city Jerusalem will be destroyed, most of its population will perish, and the remainder will be sent into captivity. Hananiah insists that within two years of his utterance, i.e., within two years of 594 B.C. (still seven years before the ultimate destruction took place), there would be a miraculous deliverance from God. The rightful king, Jehoiachin (who had already been in exile for three or four years), would be restored to his throne, and the treasures that had been taken from the temple would be returned. Both prophets speak in the name of the Lord. Whom should the people believe, and why?

In this case, there are two useful time markers by which to test things. *First,* Hananiah stipulates that his prophecy will be fulfilled within two years (28:3). When that does not occur, there are still about five years to the final catastrophe—plenty of time for the people to repent. *Second,* we are told that shortly after the dramatic confrontation between Jeremiah and Hananiah in the temple, the word of the Lord comes to Jeremiah regarding Hananiah's impending death, imposed by God himself: "This very year you are going to die, because you have preached rebellion against the LORD" (28:16). Seven months later, Hananiah dies (28:17). Should not the entire nation take notice and turn to the Lord?

In fact, there is a more dramatic marker for those with eyes to see. Jeremiah insists: "From early times the prophets who preceded you and me have prophe-sied war, disaster and plague against many countries and great kingdoms. But the prophet who prophesies peace will be recognized as one truly sent by the LORD only if his prediction comes true" (28:8-9). This is a remarkable insight. Jeremiah does not deny that a faithful and godly prophet, in a particular historical circum-stance, might prophesy peace. But he treats the possibility as so improbable that implicitly he advocates a certain healthy skepticism until the predicted peace has actually come to pass. By contrast, the normal and expected themes of faithful prophets have to do with prophesying "war, disaster and plague against many countries and great kingdoms." This is not because prophets are a dour and mor-bid lot. It is because faithful prophets deal with sin and its horrible consequences, and call people to flee from the wrath to come. Jeremiah insists that this lies at the heart of genuinely prophetic ministry. Does it lie at the heart of yours?

∽

Judges 16; Acts 20; *Jeremiah 29; Mark 15*

∾

MORE THAN THREE THOUSAND people were transported to Babylon (including King Jehoiachin) in the deportation of 597 B.C. (Jer. 52:28). Doubtless many of these people earnestly hoped for a speedy return to Jerusalem. Their longings made them easy prey for "prophets" who kept their hopes alive by promising them the sorts of things they wanted to hear. The prophet Ezekiel, himself an exile, repeatedly denounced these false prophets (as we shall see in the meditations for September). Back home in Jerusalem, Jeremiah heard of these developments and resolved to write a letter (**Jer. 29**), which was duly hand-delivered (29:1-3).

This letter begins with an exhortation to settle down, to seek the good of the city where the exiles are located (the largest settlement was close to Nippur, near the Kebar canal). "Pray to the Lord for it, because if it prospers, you too will prosper" (29:7). This is linked to a warning not to be deceived by the false prophets. Jeremiah then sets out the destiny of three groups:

(1) Those already in captivity (29:10-14): God plans to restore them to Jerusalem after the seventy years of Babylon's ascendancy. This is bound up with a transformation of heart: "Then you will call upon me and come and pray to me, and I will listen to you. You will seek me and find me when you seek me with all your heart. I will be found by you . . . and will bring you back from captivity" (29:12-14).

(2) Those still in Jerusalem (29:15-19): Far from being the means of the salvation of the exiles, they themselves will be punished. They are the "poor figs" (29:17; cf. chap. 24). Those who are not destroyed will be scattered into exile themselves (29:18). Location near the temple is inadequate protection. Regardless of their location and religious ritual, they will be destroyed, because "they have not listened to my words . . . words that I sent to them again and again by my servants the prophets" (29:19). And then a warning for the recipients of the letter: "'And you exiles have not listened either,' declares the LORD" (29:19).

(3) The false prophets in Babylon (29:20-23): Two are specifically named: Ahab son of Kolaiah and Zedekiah son of Maaseiah. We know nothing more of them than what is written here. They are not to be confused with other Ahabs and Zedekiahs in Scripture. As is commonly the case, their false message about God went hand in hand with immorality in their lives. And God knows; he always knows (29:23).

∾

Judges 17; Acts 21; *Jeremiah 30—31; Mark 16*

JEREMIAH 30—31 INTERRUPTS THE biographical material on Jeremiah with a group of utterances about the restoration of Israel and Judah. Sometimes both of the kingdoms are named (30:3); sometimes both are subsumed under "Jacob" (30:7) or "Israel" (30:10; 31:1). As in the prophecy of Isaiah, only the context determines whether "Israel" refers to the northern kingdom, already in exile for more than a century, or to all of "Jacob" (or, more precisely, that part that hears and returns to the land). The "incurable" wound and "injury beyond healing" that they have suffered is the result of their sin (30:12-14)—an invariable reality this side of the Fall. "'But I will restore you to health and heal your wounds,' declares the LORD" (30:17). Two high points:

(1) *Jeremiah 31:15:* Rachel, one of the matriarchs, whose tomb was near Ramah about five miles north of Jerusalem (1 Sam. 10:2-3; Josh. 18:25), is here pictured weeping for her "children" who were transported in 722 B.C. (when the northern tribes went into exile) and again in 587 (when what was left of the southern kingdom was transported, Jer. 40:1). Matthew 2:17-18 insists these words are "fulfilled" (typologically) when mothers weep again in the wake of the slaughter of the innocents connected with Jesus' birth. For although the exiles returned to Jerusalem during the Persian period, the most magnificent features surrounding the end of the exile did not begin to unfold until the coming of the Messiah.

(2) *Jeremiah 31:29ff.:* This promise of a new covenant is extraordinarily penetrating. Because of the tribal, representative nature of the old covenant, the people had coined a proverb: "The fathers have eaten sour grapes, and the children's teeth are set on edge" (31:29). Under the Mosaic covenant, special people—prophets, priests, kings, and a few other individuals—were especially endowed with the Spirit, and had the task of representing the people to God, and God to the people. "Know the Lord," they exhorted them. And because of this tribal, representative structure, when the leaders fell into sin ("have eaten sour grapes"), the entire nation fell into corruption and suffered destruction ("the children's teeth are set on edge"). But under the new covenant the proverb will no longer apply (31:30ff.). *All* those under the new covenant will know the Lord: God will put his law in their minds and write it on their hearts (31:33). There will no longer be mediating teachers, for all will know him (31:34); teachers will merely be part of the body, not mediators with an "inside" knowledge of God. And the forgiveness of sins will be absolute (31:34).

Identify where these themes are picked up in the New Testament.

Judges 18; Acts 22; *Jeremiah 32; Psalms 1—2*

∾

AT ONE LEVEL, PSALM 2 CAN BE understood entirely within the framework of the life of a Davidic king—even of David himself. He has conquered the surrounding nations. If they rebel, they are plotting together "against the LORD and against his Anointed One" (2:2), i.e., his "messiah," an expression that can refer to any anointed king of Israel, or to the ultimate Messiah. If they try to throw off the fetters of their obligations to Israel (2:3), they must reckon with God: "The One enthroned in heaven laughs; the Lord scoffs at them" (2:4). He rebukes them in his anger, for he is the One who has installed his King on Zion (2:5-6).

Now the king himself speaks. He testifies to this same installation, i.e., to his own installation as king, using forms of speech common in the ancient Near East. At the king's installation, he becomes the "son" of the god who extends primary sovereignty over that people. Yahweh himself uses that language: the king of Israel becomes God's "son" at his installation, committed to seeking his "Father's" glory and good, reflecting his character and will (2:7). God is so much in control of all nations that the Davidic king need only ask, and God will give him absolute sovereignty over the nations (2:8-9). The kings ought therefore to be wise, and warned (2:10). "Serve the LORD with fear. . . . Kiss the Son [i.e., the Davidic king], lest he be angry" (2:11-12).

But there are at least two elements that warn us against thinking the psalm's meaning is exhausted in one of the ancient Davidic monarchs. *First,* early in the life of the Davidic dynasty David became a type or model of the ultimate "messiah" from this line, the ultimate "David." One can easily find explicit references to this figure centuries later (e.g., Isa. 9; Ezek. 34). Typological reasoning might run like this: if the historical King David was God's agent to rule over the nations that surrounded him, how much more will great David's greater Son, the Davidic king *par excellence,* rule over the nations? *Second,* there are several hints in the psalm that suggest something more than an early Davidic king. He subdues the "kings of the earth" (2:2), which sounds pretty comprehensive (though it *could* mean "the kings of the land"); this "Son" is promised "the nations" and "the ends of the earth" as his possession—a lot harder to dismiss. The final blessing (2:12) sounds vaguely pompous for anyone other than the ultimate Messiah. Each of these expressions can be "explained" (or "explained away"): they might, for instance, be examples of hyperbolic language. But taken together, they do not so much point away from the historic David as point beyond him. Reflect on Acts 4:23-30.

∾

Judges 19; Acts 23; *Jeremiah 33*; Psalms 3—4

∾

IN THE VISION OF RESTORATION provided by Jeremiah 33, the last half of the chapter focuses on the restoration of the Davidic throne and related matters (**Jer. 33:14-26**). Some observations:

(1) Verses 15-16 largely repeat 23:5-6 (see meditation for July 27). The words are described as God's "gracious promise" (33:14), i.e., the promise he made to Israel a little earlier through Jeremiah, and to which he again draws attention now that Jeremiah is imprisoned in the courtyard and the doom of the city is not long delayed. The destruction of the city is imminent, the exile of the people all but inevitable—and God wants both Jeremiah and the people to look beyond the impending disasters and contemplate his promises that await sure fulfillment. That is a substantial part of what it means to walk by faith.

(2) On the whole, Jeremiah does not disclose as much about the coming of the Messiah as does Isaiah—or, more accurately put, what he discloses is more diffuse and less focused. Nevertheless he depicts the coming one as the good shepherd (23:4; 31:10), the righteous Branch (23:5; 33:15), and as David the king, the Lord's servant (30:9; 33:21, 26).

(3) The certainty of God's covenant with David is tied to the certainty of God's covenant with the day and the night (33:19-21)—in other words, to the utter reliability of God to maintain his ordered universe. The stability of the Davidic monarchy is not likened to the morning mist that passes away, but to the daily cycle, whose regularity depends on the faithfulness and reliability of a powerful, providential God. Although all that will be seen of the Davidic dynasty for a while will be a poor stump, yet God himself will make "a righteous Branch sprout from David's line" (33:15).

(4) Slightly more surprising, and certainly rarer among the prophets, is the promise that the Levites will not fail to have a man stand before God and offer the prescribed sacrifices (33:18, 21). This may refer to the postexilic years when the temple was rebuilt and the Levitical sacrifices were reconstituted. But this same Jeremiah has also foreseen a new covenant, an announcement that makes the Mosaic covenant obsolete in principle (Heb. 8:13). Indeed, four centuries before Jeremiah, David foresaw the rise of a Melchizedekian priesthood (Ps. 110) that anticipated the end of the Levitical system and a change in the Law (Heb. 7:11-12). From a canonical perspective, perhaps the ultimate typological fulfillment of this passage is in the kingdom of "priests" arising from the work of the great David (1 Pet. 2:5; Rev. 1:6).

∾

Judges 20; Acts 24; *Jeremiah 34; Psalms 5—6*

∾

BOTH INDIVIDUALS AND LARGER communities sometimes vow, under the pressure of desperation, to reform themselves and devote themselves to pleasing God. When the pressure abates, they rescind their promises and return to their self-centered sin. Their fickleness becomes transparent. The judgment or disaster threatening them does not really teach them the ways of righteousness or instruct them to turn from sin. They simply want relief, and if a vow before the Lord can achieve it, why, then they will vow. But that does not mean they really try to *keep* their vows.

That is the sort of pathetic drama that unfolds in **Jeremiah 34**. Nebuchadnezzar is at the gates of Jerusalem (34:1). Motivated by sheer desperation, King Zedekiah leads the people in a covenant that proclaims freedom for all slaves (34:8). The Mosaic covenant had in principle greatly ameliorated slave conditions by limiting servitude to six years (34:14; Ex. 21:2; Deut. 15:1, 12). A stream of prophets—Amos, Hosea, Isaiah, Micah—excoriated the covenant people for their callousness, for their mercenary defiance of God's Law, especially in the matter of slavery. And now Zedekiah leads the Jerusalemites in this major reform.

From other sources (see meditation for August 9) we know that news reached the armed forces of Babylon to the effect that an Egyptian army was advancing to relieve Jerusalem. So far as we know, this report was untrue. Nevertheless the Babylonian army withdrew to face this new threat from the south. To the citizens of Jerusalem, this must have seemed like almost miraculous relief. Stupidly, sinfully, wickedly, the former slave-owners "changed their minds and took back the slaves they had freed and enslaved them again" (34:11). Their real hearts are thus completely exposed.

Inevitably, the Babylonian forces discover there is no threat from Egypt, and the siege closes in again. There is no hope of relief this time. Who will believe any of their acts of "repentance" now? God declares, "But now you have turned around and profaned my name; each of you has taken back the male and female slaves you had set free to go where they wished. You have forced them to become your slaves again" (34:16). They have not "proclaimed freedom" to their "fellow countrymen" (34:17). So the only "freedom" they themselves will experience is the freedom to fall by sword, plague, and famine (34:17).

What hope is there for people who put on a show of "repentance" calculated to earn some mercy, but who return like a dog to its vomit and like a pig to its muck (2 Pet. 2:20-22)?

∾

Judges 21; Acts 25; *Jeremiah 35; Psalms 7—8*

∾

PSALM 8 IS A PRICELESS JEWEL that celebrates the glory and goodness of God disclosed in creation. With a wonderful brevity, David provides a heady mixture of awe and barely restrained joy. Without overlooking the evil in the world (8:2), he focuses on elements of the created order that reflect God's majesty. Even the heavens are inadequate to the task (8:1b), yet God has ordained that his praise should be on the lips of children and infants (8:2). "O LORD, our Lord, how majestic is your name in all the earth!" (8:1, 9); appropriately, the psalm begins and ends with God himself.

In large part, the psalm focuses on the place of human beings in this God-constructed, God-centered universe. The central rhetorical question is, "[W]hat is man that you are mindful of him, the son of man that you care for him?" Variations of this question carry different overtones, depending on the context. The question may beg for respite (Job 7:17), hide in shame in the face of human sin (Job 25:6), or undermine human arrogance (Ps. 144:3-4). In the context of Psalm 8, the question expresses stunned awe as the psalmist glimpses the surpassing greatness of the universe and reflects on human smallness and massive significance: astonishingly, God is "mindful" of "man," which means much more than that he "remembers" us (as if Omniscience could forget!). Rather, the word has overtones of compassion, as the parallel line shows: he cares for us. What is glorious is the relationship. Indeed, here is one of these human beings addressing this great and majestic God personally: "that you are mindful . . . that you care." One commentator reminds us that the appropriate inference Isaiah draws from the glory of God's ordered heavens is not his remoteness but his "eye for detail" (Isa. 40:26ff.). The universe was not designed to be vast and meaningless, but to be a vast home for God's people (Isa. 45:18; 51:16). Indeed, the vision of Psalm 8 harks back to the creation account (Gen. 1—2). This creature, this small being, this God-blessed human, is designed to serve as God's co-regent over the entire created order of this planet (8:6-8).

Two further reflections: *First,* this account of human beings is vastly removed from contemporary visions that picture us as the accidental byproducts of cosmogony, neither significant nor intrinsically good or evil. *Second,* the Epistle to the Hebrews, reflecting on Psalm 8, recognizes how far short we human beings fall from our purpose in creation, and finds hope in the fact that we see Jesus as the prototypical Man of the consummated order still to come (Heb. 2:5-13).

∾

Ruth 1; Acts 26; *Jeremiah 36, 45; Psalm 9*

∽

THESE TWO CHAPTERS, JEREMIAH 36, 45, provide valuable insights into two realms: the relationship between Jeremiah and Baruch, and how Jeremiah's prophecies came to be written down.

(1) Baruch, son of Neriah (36:4) and brother of Seraiah, who was a staff officer serving King Zedekiah (51:59), first appears in this book in chapter 32, where he serves as a legal witness. It now transpires that Baruch was Zedekiah's amanuensis (his scribe, more or less his secretary).

(2) Clearly at some point Baruch thought that being attached to a prophet like Jeremiah would contribute to his advancement. He is deeply disappointed to find things not working out that way (Jer. 45). The import of the messages he has been transcribing sinks into his own soul, and he is terribly depressed. Jeremiah responds in two ways. (a) He rebukes the young man for thinking so narrowly of his own future when the entire nation is going down. That is a rebuke that many in the individualistic West need to hear. (b) He provides him with some assurance: despite the catastrophe about to fall on the city, Baruch will survive.

(3) We are not always provided precise information as to how the revelation God gave to particular prophets reached the written form we have in the Bible. Here the information is wonderfully specific. God himself instructs Jeremiah to write the words down, and Jeremiah carefully dictates them to Baruch, who transcribes them. Since this was the fourth year of Jehoiakim's reign (36:1), it was 605/604 B.C., the year of the Battle of Carchemish when Babylon replaced Egypt as the regional power.

(4) It appears that, at least at first, the written form of Jeremiah's prophecies carried more weight with the authorities than the oral form for which Jeremiah was incarcerated (36:8-19). Even today a public medium—newspapers, radio, television—is more likely to be believed than mere word of mouth from a friend. The tragedy is that when the king hears the words read to him, he responds with cynical defiance, cutting up the scroll section by section and throwing it into the fire. His action provides an ugly foil to the response of King Josiah when the rediscovered law scroll was read to him (2 Kings 22:11). Worse yet, if what he is destroying really is the scroll of God's words, how utterly stupid to think that God's words can be overthrown and destroyed so easily. Is God's memory so short that he cannot remember what he has said? Can he not raise up human servants who will transcribe the material afresh and even include fresh revelation (36:27-32)? So too with all the efforts across history to destroy the Scriptures: is God so impotent that he cannot defend his words and destroy those who mock them?

∽

Ruth 2; Acts 27; Jeremiah 37; Psalm 10

～

WE HAVE SEEN AGAIN AND AGAIN that the flow of the book of Jeremiah is rarely chronological. Here we jump from the reign of Jehoiakim in chapter 36 to Zedekiah (**Jer. 37**), the puppet monarch installed after the last legitimate king of Judah, Jehoiachin, was transported to Babylon in 597 B.C. The date is 589—588. The two incidents described in this chapter reflect the further degeneration of the leadership and illustrate yet again God's forbearance.

(1) The first incident (37:1-10) is apparently precipitated by the fact that Pharaoh Hophra of Egypt made a show of marching out to confront the Babylonians and relieve Jerusalem. The report was sufficiently troubling to the Babylonians that they temporarily lifted the siege of Jerusalem and turned to this new threat. Zedekiah sends some emissaries to Jeremiah, asking for his intercession—presumably to make this temporary respite permanent. Jeremiah responds with the words of 37:7-10: the reprieve is temporary, the Babylonians will return, Jerusalem will be destroyed. So do not be deceived into thinking otherwise.

(2) During the reprieve, Jeremiah tries to leave the city by the Benjamite gate, apparently with the intention of inspecting his newly acquired property in Anathoth (37:11-21; cf. 32:9). But he is arrested, beaten, and imprisoned under a charge of desertion. The officials do not believe a word the prophet says, so he remains incarcerated in an underground dungeon in the home of the secretary of state. The officials are very different from their predecessors under Jehoiakim (26:19; 36:19), who seemed to be open to Jeremiah but who were under the thumb of a stubborn and wicked monarch. Here the officials are contemptuous of Jeremiah and frankly cruel to him, while King Zedekiah, more out of desperation and fear than principle, tries to keep in contact with Jeremiah and finally makes his incarceration less painful.

All this suggests that in any hierarchy, including government and church, there are many different ways for things to go wrong. Sometimes there are a lot of weak, indecisive, but not profoundly amoral underlings being manipulated by a wicked leader. Sometimes there is an indecisive leader who is being controlled by a packet of incompetent, unfaithful, evil underlings.

Reflect: "Why, O LORD, do you stand far off? Why do you hide yourself in times of trouble? In his arrogance the wicked man hunts down the weak, who are caught in the schemes he devises. He boasts of the cravings of his heart; he blesses the greedy and reviles the LORD. In his pride the wicked does not seek him; in all his thoughts there is no room for God" (**Ps. 10:1-4**).

～

Ruth 3—4; Acts 28; *Jeremiah 38; Psalms 11—12*

∿

IT IS NOT EASY TO SEE HOW the events of **Jeremiah 38** are tied to the events of Jeremiah 37:11-21. Some think they are two entirely separate episodes in the life of the prophet; others think Jeremiah 38 is an expansion of the previous chapter. However one resolves the issue, the final exchange in this chapter between Jeremiah and King Zedekiah demands serious reflection.

The events themselves are easily understood. For several decades Jeremiah has been preaching the imminent destruction of Jerusalem. For the most part, he has been ignored or mocked. With Nebuchadnezzar's troops all around the walls, however, Jeremiah's credibility is doubtless at an all-time high. So when he reports that the Lord says that anyone who remains in the city will die by sword, famine, or plague, while those who surrender will survive (38:2), he is much more likely to be believed than he would have been five years previously. The city's officials, however, not believing that these words are from the Lord, see this religious God-talk as nothing more than treason—treason with the pernicious effect of undermining the confidence of the remaining troops.

The punishment Jeremiah faces is unpleasant. Most dwellings in Jerusalem in this period had cisterns, often bottle-shaped, for retaining drinking water. This one was unused, but had thick mud in its bottom. Left for very long in this place, probably without food and water, Jeremiah would die.

What saves Jeremiah, humanly speaking, is the fact that King Zedekiah still seeks his counsel. Jeremiah does not pull any punches. Though it is politically inexpedient, Jeremiah tells the king that he should obey the Lord and submit to the Babylonians: the alternative is the route to disaster (38:20-21). Perhaps Zedekiah found this hard to believe for historical reasons: the pattern of siege warfare meant that because he had resisted even this far, he was slated for execution even if he surrendered. Doubtless he also found Jeremiah's words hard to believe for another reason: he was still far too dependent upon his "friends"—who, Jeremiah insists, would one day be mocked as useless allies who led the king into the mud (38:22).

The juxtaposition of chapters 37 and 38 (yesterday's meditation and today's) is no accident. Leadership of God's people can go disastrously wrong at the top, with the underlings being better but too weak or afraid to effect the desperately needed change (Jer. 37). Or leadership may be weak or corrupt throughout the hierarchy, with the top figure too indecisive or too much of a wimp to clean things up. Saddest of all are the Christian institutions where weakness or corruption prevails at both levels.

∿

1 Samuel 1; Romans 1; *Jeremiah 39; Psalm 13—14*

෨

A FRIEND OF MINE ONCE GAVE a university evangelistic address under the title, "Atheists Are Fools and Agnostics Are Cowards." Needless to say, he drew a considerable crowd, even if the crowd was pretty hostile. Whether or not this was the tactically wise thing to do in that setting may, I suppose, be debated. What should not be debated is that my friend was being faithful to Scripture: "The fool says in his heart, 'There is no God'" (**Ps. 14:1**). Indeed, if anything, the text of Scripture is stronger than the English suggests. The word rendered "fool" is in Hebrew a term of moral opprobrium suggesting perversity, churlish and aggressive perversity. Paul certainly understood the point: "Although they claimed to be wise, they became fools" (Rom. 1:22). After all, "what may be known about God is plain to them, because God has made it plain to them" (Rom. 1:19); and "since they did not think it worthwhile to retain the knowledge of God, he gave them over to a depraved mind" (Rom. 1:28). The Bible's view is that in the last analysis atheism is less the product of misguided searching, a kind of intellectual mistake, than a defiant and stubborn rebellion.

The fact that atheism is not widely seen that way is itself an index of our depravity. In fact, the best-informed atheists commonly acknowledge the connection between morality and belief, between immorality and unbelief. There is a famous passage in Huxley that acknowledges that one of the driving forces behind atheistic naturalism is the desire to tear away any sort of moral condemnation of otherwise condemned behavior. In a passage scarcely less famous, Michel Foucault, one of the theoreticians behind postmodernism, frankly acknowledges that it became important for him to destroy traditional notions of truth and morality because he wished to justify his own sexual conduct. A few years ago, Foucault died of AIDS.

We must not misapply this text. Within the framework of their own presuppositions, there are many honest atheists. But the framework itself is wrong. That framework is never established by a single individual. It is built up piece by piece until certain beliefs are culturally possible, then probable, then almost inevitable—and each generation, each individual, has contributed to this massive rebellion, this lust for autonomy that refuses to recognize the rights of our Maker and our obligations to him. Atheism becomes not simply an individual choice but a social degeneracy. The ultimate result is the sweeping condemnation of Psalm 14:2-3. Compare Romans 3:10-18: sin is not merely ubiquitous but universal, and results in massive social damage (Psalm 14:4-6). At the end of the day, there is no help but in the Lord (14:7).

෨

1 Samuel 2; Romans 2; *Jeremiah 40*; Psalms 15—16

∾

WHEN JERUSALEM FELL IN 587 B.C. (Jer. 39), Zedekiah was punished horribly, though leniently by the standards of siege warfare of the day. As for Jeremiah, probably the reports of his prophecies about the fall of Jerusalem soon filtered through the captives to Nebuchadnezzar (who was not himself at Jerusalem, but maintained regional headquarters at Riblah, leaving the final assault to his commander Nebuzaradan). In consequence the emperor gave orders that Jeremiah was to be well-treated (39:12). Initially that order was carried out, and Jeremiah was turned over to Gedaliah (39:13-14), who became the new governor of the region after the imperial troops had withdrawn, taking countless captives into exile.

That sets the stage for **Jeremiah 40**. The framework of the story is simple enough; the closing verses of the narrative evoke reflection on a terribly important theme. First, the framework: Those who were to be transported to exile were gathered at Ramah, which served as a rallying point about five miles north of Jerusalem. Despite Nebuchadnezzar's instructions to leave Jeremiah with Gedaliah, somehow the prophet was swept up in this group (40:1). Anyone familiar with the confusion of war understands how easily this could have happened. The commander Nebuzaradan freed him and offered to take him to Babylon; probably it would have added to the commander's prestige back home to be the patron of a great prophet who had predicted Babylon's success. But Jeremiah was free to make his own decision, and he opted to stay with the remnant in Judah. Nebuzaradan provided him with food and a gift (40:5)—one more instance of the principle that a prophet is often honored by everyone except those closest to him (cf. Matt. 13:57).

But the account rushes on to describe the early stages of Gedaliah's governorship. On almost all fronts he did the right thing. He encouraged the poor to settle down and till the land and gather the harvest. He drew in the Jewish "army officers still in the open country" (40:13), a potentially dangerous guerrilla force that might have broken out in the kind of anarchy that would have angered Babylon again. Even those who had fled to nearby countries began to return home (40:11-12), reassured by the moves Gedaliah was making to ensure stability. But Gedaliah's great weakness was that he could not believe ill of people. Despite all the evil of the previous years, he still did not believe that evil happens, that evil people do evil things, that leadership must sometimes oppose evil. On so many fronts he was a good man. But he paid for his Pollyannish optimism with his life.

∾

1 Samuel 3; Romans 3; *Jeremiah 41*; *Psalm 17*

∾

THE ACCOUNT OF GEDALIAH'S assassination and its aftermath (**Jer. 41**) is brutal and ugly.

(1) The man responsible for Gedaliah's death, Ishmael son of Nethaniah (40:8; 41:1), was a man of royal blood, and may have been incensed because he was not the one the Babylonians appointed to rule the people. It is always shocking to see people scrambling for power even when there is nothing more than disaster and poverty over which to exercise power.

(2) The depth of Ishmael's perfidy is powerfully portrayed. To kill people at a meal you are sharing was far more shocking in the sixth century B.C. than in our own, inured as we are by Agatha Christie novels and the like. Moreover, Ishmael's rage boils over so that others are assassinated, including the Babylonian troops left behind to keep an eye on things. The motive impelling the next atrocity (41:4-7) is uncertain: Ishmael may still have been suspicious of anyone interested in serving Gedaliah (41:6). Or in the still terribly unstable political situation following the war, he may have been intent on robbery and mayhem. The latter view is favored by the fact that some of the pilgrims save their lives by telling Ishmael of a food cache (41:8).

(3) Johanan son of Kereah was the one who first warned Gedaliah of Ishmael's conspiracy (40:13-14). Now he is equally quick to put together a band and go after Ishmael and his men and those they have taken captive (41:11-12). Even though Ishmael and eight of his men escape, the captives are rescued (41:14-15).

(4) Now Johanan must ask himself what to do. He and those with him are afraid that when the murder of Gedaliah and the others is reported back to Babylon, Nebuchadnezzar will be so filled with rage that he will send back powerful army units and kill everyone who is left. So Johanan starts south, heading for Egypt, stopping near Bethlehem (just south of Jerusalem) to gather together those who want to escape with him.

(5) Theologically, all of this is part of the utter devastation befalling Judah. The city and temple have been destroyed. The Davidic dynasty has ended. All of the leaders, craftsmen, priests, and the like have been deported in waves (see 52:28-30). And now, just when it seems that a good man, Gedaliah, might somehow nurse this broken nation back through slow recovery to real economic and political health, he is assassinated, and the few remaining leaders fear the Babylonians and plan to flee to Egypt. Unaware of what they are doing, they thus bring to perfect fulfillment the prophecies of utter doom that Jeremiah has pronounced for four decades.

∾

1 Samuel 4; Romans 4; *Jeremiah 42; Psalm 18*

∾

THERE IS AN OLD JOKE about a reprobate who absorbs just enough religion to think he should try to get his life in order. He goes to a minister, who tells him that the best thing he can do is turn away from his whiskey, his women, and his gambling. The old boy looks thoughtful for a few moments and then says, "You know, I don't think I deserve the best. What's second best?"

One might have thought that in the wake of the disastrous destruction of Jerusalem, long predicted by Jeremiah, the prophet would have enormous credibility among the survivors. The sad reality is that he has enough credibility for them to consult him, but no more (**Jer. 42**). What they want is divine approval for the plan they themselves have already concocted. They do not want God's best, or God's will, but God's approval of their will. Jeremiah carefully seeks God, and ten days later (42:7) the word of the Lord comes to him. The substance of the message is this: stay in Judah, and God will protect you; fly to Egypt, and God will take this as a further sign of rebellion, and God's wrath will pursue you and destroy you there, just as it recently destroyed so many in and around Jerusalem. Even as he is delivering this message, Jeremiah sees that it is not going down very well, and that the hostility against it—and against him—is deep. The next chapter (Jer. 43) records the sneering skepticism and the resolve of the leaders to disregard Jeremiah and his messages, to dismiss his words as outright lies, and to collect the remnant of the people and travel to Egypt. That is what they do, bringing Jeremiah with them.

Most movements that spring up from the fertile soils of Christendom appeal, in one way or another, to the will of God. Few probe the will of God very deeply. God is for evangelism; therefore he is for the way we are proposing to do evangelism, and we invoke his will to sanction our methods. God is love; therefore he is against church discipline except in the most egregious cases (which either never arise, or, if they do, by the time they do they too are covered by the love of God), and we invoke God's will to sanction our determined niceness. God wants his people to be separate and holy; therefore we must withdraw into huddled isolationism and lob hateful barbs against all who disagree with us, and we invoke God's will to authorize our tearless harshness and ruthless condescension. These wretched pits are terribly easy to fall into. All it takes is resolution, and no more real interest in the will of God than what we need to sanction our preferences.

1 Samuel 5—6; Romans 5; *Jeremiah 43*; *Psalm 19*

∾

PSALM 19 IS ONE OF THE precious gems of the Psalter. It has three sections. The first delights in the wordless disclosure of God in the universe (19:1-6); the second exults in the clarity, perfection, and wealth of God's written revelation (19:7-11); after a transitional verse (19:11), the third section portrays the appropriate response of the believer, a response full of self-examination and godly resolve.

If ancient Israel was sometimes inclined to worship the created order—sun, moon, stars—our generation is more inclined to marshal arguments that make them the product of impersonal forces and nothing more. Both stances are abominations. Owing to our culture's prevalent philosophical commitment to naturalism, the powerful evidence of intelligent design is marginalized until we can no longer see the obvious: "The heavens declare the glory of God; the skies proclaim the work of his hands" (19:1). The paradox of wordless utterance is delightful, as is the vision of irrepressible speech: "Day after day they pour forth speech; night after night they display knowledge. There is no speech or language where their voice is not heard. Their voice goes out into all the earth, their words to the ends of the world" (19:2-4).

But it is in connection with his written self-disclosure that the covenant name of God, Yahweh ("the LORD" in many of our English Bibles), appears seven times (19:7-11). The six predications (19:7-9) overlap somewhat, but together they project a vision of written revelation that anticipates the even fuller exposition of Psalm 119. One of the striking things about these six affirmations is that several of them are not merely abstract. The text not only says something about the words of God, but about their function in the lives of those who absorb them and follow them. For instance: "The statutes of the LORD are trustworthy" (19:7): that is so, but the psalmist does not leave things there. Precisely because the LORD's statutes are trustworthy, they serve to make wise the simple. Again: "The precepts of the LORD are right" (19:8)—a point strengthened in the next verse: "The ordinances of the LORD are sure and altogether righteous" (19:9). But that is precisely why they give joy to the heart (19:8): we are dealing with the Lord's righteous precepts and ordinances, so they are never corrupt or manipulative.

What these two spheres of revelation demand is more than awe in the face of transcendent power, and more than personal delight in the personal, talking God—but both. Indeed, the appropriate response is repentance and faith, and zealous prayer that God himself would purify us within and make our words and meditations pleasing in his sight (19:12-14).

∾

1 Samuel 7—8; Romans 6; *Jeremiah 44; Psalms 20—21*

∾

SO FAR AS WE KNOW, JEREMIAH 44 contains Jeremiah's last prophecy. The prophecy of the next chapter is explicitly dated to an earlier period, and probably the miscellaneous prophecies against the nations, found in chapters 46—51, all stem from an earlier period as well. So far as the record goes, the words before us are Jeremiah's last public utterance.

One cannot say that Jeremiah's ministry ended on a high note. We are all called to be faithful; some are called to be faithful in troubled and declining times. One dare not measure Jeremiah's ministry by how many people he convinced, how many disasters he averted, or how many revivals he experienced. One must measure his ministry by whether or not he was faithful to God, by whether or not God was pleased with him. And so, finally, it is with each of us. I doubt that many of us living in the West have fully come to grips with how much the success syndrome shapes our views of ourselves and others—sometimes to make us hunger at all costs for success, and sometimes, in a kind of inverted pseudospirituality, to make us suspicious at all costs of success. But success is not the issue; faithfulness is.

What we find in this chapter is irretrievable rebellion. The Jews in Egypt—both those who have just descended there, and those who apparently had settled there earlier in an attempt to escape the troubled times back home—have merely replaced the Canaanite gods they used to worship at home with the Egyptian gods all around them. Their reading of their own history is entirely different from Jeremiah's. They hark back to the time when they "stopped" their pagan worship (44:17-18): probably they are thinking of the reform under King Josiah. All the disasters that have befallen them have taken place since then. So what they must do, they reason, is serve the Queen of Heaven and the other pagan deities, and they resolve on this course.

There are two important lessons to be learned. *First,* you can always read history to make it prove almost anything you want. This does not mean that we are not to learn anything from history, for God himself tells the people what they should have learned. It means that what the people of God should learn from history must be shaped by the lens of God's written revelation, by his prophetic word, by our covenantal vows. We cannot expect pagans always to agree with our reading of history. *Second,* this chapter demonstrates, in the harshest terms, that there is no hope for the covenant race, none at all, apart from the intervention of grace.

1 Samuel 9; Romans 7; *Jeremiah 46*; Psalm 22

∽

A COMMON THEME AMONG THE biblical prophets is that God is sovereign over all nations. To most who read these pages that seems obvious. But in the ancient world, most nations had their own gods. So when a nation went to war, the people prayed to their own gods; if a nation was defeated, so were their gods. Clearly they were not as strong as the gods of the ascendant nation.

But the God of Israel keeps telling her that he is the God over all the universe, over all the nations. He is not a tribal deity in the sense that they own him or that he is exclusively theirs. That is why in many chapters of Isaiah and Jeremiah God insists that he himself is the One who is raising up Assyria or Babylon to punish the people. In other words, the defeat of Israel does not signal the defeat of God. Far from it: this God keeps insisting that if Israel is defeated and punished, it can only be because he has ordained it—and he does this by utilizing the very nations Israel fears.

But there is another side to the story. If God uses these various pagan nations, so also does he hold them to account. Of course, they cannot be expected to submit to the entire Law of Moses—after all, they are not part of the covenant community. Nevertheless God holds pagan nations to standards of decency and basic righteousness. So after using Assyria to chasten the northern kingdom of Israel, God turns around and chastens Assyria for her arrogance (Isa. 10:5ff.; see meditation for May 12). In the same vein, some of Israel's prophets pronounce words of judgment and warning, and sometimes of hope, against the surrounding nations over which their own God is utterly sovereign. That is what is found in Jeremiah 46—51 and elsewhere (e.g., Isa. 13—23; Ezek. 25—32; Amos 1:3—2:3).

The chapter before us (**Jer. 46**) opens the larger section with a word from the Lord concerning Egypt. The first part (46:2-12) details Egypt's decisive defeat at the battle of Carchemish in 605 B.C., when the Babylonians rose to supremacy in the region. The second part (46:13-26) anticipates a further defeat of Egypt at the hands of Babylon, this time under Nebuchadnezzar. This almost certainly refers to the same assault predicted in 43:10—part of the reason why the Jews remaining in Judah were not to go down to Egypt (as they did, about 586). That assault is not reported in Scripture, but inscriptional evidence records that Nebuchadnezzar invaded Egypt in a punitive expedition in 568—567.

Why is this chapter included in the book at this point?

∽

1 Samuel 10; Romans 8; Jeremiah 47; Psalms 23—24

∾

THOUGH A SHORT CHAPTER, JEREMIAH 47 is full of interest. It begins with a prophecy regarding the destruction of the Philistine city-states along the coast, and ends with one of the most thought-provoking bits of anguish in the latter part of this book.

First, the prophecy (47:1-5). Its precise timing is a trifle obscure: it came to Jeremiah "before Pharaoh attacked Gaza" (47:1). This may have taken place when Pharaoh Neco of Egypt marched north to attack Haran in 609 B.C. Gaza, one of the Philistine city-states, was on the route. But although this shows the prophecy came to Jeremiah before the days of Egyptian ascendancy were past, it did not concern Egyptian aggression, but Babylonian: the waters that "overflow the land and everything in it" rise "in the north" (47:2)—the direction from which the Babylonian might would come. The word picture of the subsequent destruction is not pretty. Panic will be so acute, Jeremiah insists, that fathers will abandon their children (47:3). Verse 4 may be improperly translated. The Hebrew is literally "to cut off Tyre and Sidon," and the expression may mean that any help from these Phoenician cities is prevented from reaching the Philistine cities farther down the coast. In any case it is the Lord who destroys the Philistines, whatever the agency (47:4). Gaza and Ashkelon (47:5) were two of their principal cities. "Caphtor" (47:4) is the ancient name for Crete, from which the original Philistines came—so to say that the Lord is about to destroy "the remnant from the coasts of Caphtor" is a poetic way of saying that the Lord is about to destroy the Philistines.

Second, the final thought-provoking anguish (47:6-7). In colorful imagery, Jeremiah pictures the Philistines (according to the NIV) addressing the sword of the Lord: "'Ah, sword of the LORD,' you cry, 'how long till you rest? Return to your scabbard; cease and be still'" (47:6). This supposes that the Philistines recognize that it is Israel's God, the Lord himself, who has brought judgment on them at the hands of the Babylonians. Although it is possible to understand the Hebrew that way, strictly speaking the words "you cry" are not found in the text: they have to be inferred. But if they are simply omitted, then it is Jeremiah himself who is addressing the sword of the Lord. The Philistines may be pagans, and they may often have oppressed Israel, but now they are about to get pounded—and by the Babylonians, Judah's premier enemy. So Jeremiah intercedes for the Philistines. But the final verse shows that he understands perfectly well that he cannot command God's sword. The Lord himself has commanded it, the God of just judgment, and it will do its work. So also on the last day.

∾

1 Samuel 11; Romans 9; *Jeremiah 48; Psalm 25*

ONE OF THE STRIKING FEATURES OF the Psalms, especially the psalms of David, is the theme of enemies. This makes some Christians nervous. Does not the Lord Jesus tell us to love our enemies (Matt. 5:43-47)? Yet here David prays that God will not let his enemies triumph over him (**Ps. 25**, especially v. 1), calls them "treacherous" (25:3), and complains that they have increased and fiercely hate him (25:19). It is inadequate to ascribe the two stances to differences between the new covenant and the old.

Preliminary reflections include:

(1) Even Jesus' teaching that his followers love their enemies presupposes that they *have* enemies. Jesus' requirement that we love our enemies must not be reduced to the sentimental notion that we all become so "nice" that we never have any enemies.

(2) New Testament believers may have enemies who must at some level be opposed. The apostle Paul, for instance, says that he has handed Hymenaeus and Alexander over to Satan to teach them not to blaspheme (1 Tim. 1:20). Both 2 Peter 2 and Jude deploy pretty colorful language to denounce fundamental enemies of the Gospel. Even if his language belongs to hyperbole, Paul can wish that the agitators in Galatia would emasculate themselves (Gal. 5:12). The Lord Jesus himself—the same Jesus who, while dying on the cross, cries, "Father, forgive them, for they do not know what they are doing" (Luke 23:34)—can elsewhere denounce his enemies in spectacularly colorful language (Matt. 23). It is difficult to avoid the conclusion that, unless we are to accuse the apostles and Jesus of hypocritical inconsistency, the demand that we love our enemies must not be reduced to the sentimental twaddle that merely smooths enemies out of existence.

(3) A very good case can be made for the view that the primary concern of Matthew 5:43-47 is to overthrow personal retaliation, to eschew the vendetta, to overcome the evil we receive by the good we perform, to absorb the hatred of an opponent and return love. But none of this denies for a moment that the other person is an enemy. Moreover, those in leadership may, out of love, feel obligated to protect the flock by chasing out a wolf in sheep's clothing, by exposing the charlatan, by denouncing the wicked—without succumbing to personal venom.

(4) One measure of whether one's response is the hatred of vengeance or something more principled that cherishes God's holiness and leaves room for forbearance and love, is the set of associated commitments. In David's case, these include trust (25:1-3, 4-5, 7b, 16, 21), repentance and faith (25:7, 11, 18), and covenantal fidelity (25:10).

1 Samuel 12; Romans 10; *Jeremiah 49; Psalms 26—27*

∾

PSALM 27 SHARES SOME THEMES with its nearest neighbors (Pss. 26, 28) but is more exuberant than either.

(1) The Lord is my light (27:1-3). Light is an evocative figure for almost everything good: truth, knowledge, joy, moral purity, revelation, and more. Here the word is linked with "salvation" and "stronghold" (27:1); light is associated with security. David faces enemies who attack him like a pack of wolves, but if the Lord is his light and salvation, David will not be afraid. With a God this sovereign, this good, this self-revealing, this delightful, how will he not also be our security?

(2) The Lord is my sanctuary (27:4-6)—in the double sense that the word has in English. On the one hand, the theme of the first three verses continues: God is David's sanctuary in the sense that he is David's protection, his stronghold: "in the day of trouble he will keep me safe in his dwelling" (27:5). But on the other hand, this "sanctuary" spells infinitely more than mere political security: "One thing I ask of the LORD, this is what I seek: that I may dwell in the house of the LORD all the days of my life" (27:4). This does not mean that David entertains a secret, impossible desire to become a Levite. Rather, he has a profound passion to live his life in the presence of the living God. That is the locus of security.

(3) The Lord is my direction (27:7-12). David does not envisage his relation with God as something static, but as his lifelong pursuit. Moreover, he understands that this pursuit simultaneously shapes him. If he seeks God's face as he ought (27:8), if he begs for mercy so that God will deal with him in compassion and not in wrath (27:9-10), then he will also learn God's ways and walk in a straight path (27:11). This cannot be said too strongly or too often: *to claim that one is pursuing God without concomitant reformation of life and growing conformity to the ways of God is wicked and dangerous nonsense.*

(4) The Lord is my hope (27:13-14). However true it is that God is the believer's refuge, sometimes in this broken and fallen world it does not feel like it at the moment. The truth is that God's timetable is rarely the same as ours. Often he demands that we wait patiently for him: his timing is perfect. His vindication of his people often takes place in history (27:13), but rarely as soon as we want; nevertheless his ultimate vindication is priceless. "Wait for the LORD; be strong and take heart and wait for the LORD" (27:14).

∾

1 Samuel 13; Romans 11; *Jeremiah 50; Psalms 28—29*

∿

THE CLOSING VERSES OF **Psalm 28** bring together several themes prominent in biblical theology:

(1) The first and most obvious one is the unrestrained praise in 28:7: "The LORD is my strength and my shield; my heart trusts in him, and I am helped. My heart leaps for joy and I will give thanks to him in song." Here is no faith of mere resignation; here, rather, is a faith that wells up from (or produces?) a heart that "leaps for joy" and expresses itself in thankful song. One cannot read the Psalms without recognizing that genuine faith does not produce a merely stereotypical emotional response. Given different sets of circumstances, genuine faith may be tied to an almost desperate trust and anguished petition, to quiet confidence and steadfastness, to praise that bursts the borders of exuberance into spectacular spontaneity. In this passage faith is closest to the latter, for the Lord has *already* heard David's cry for mercy (28:6).

(2) Throughout the first seven verses of the psalm, David's petitions and praises are in the first person singular; they arise from his status as an individual. The last two verses focus on God's "people" (28:8-9), his collective "inheritance" (28:9). So far as language goes, this is effected in part through David's meditation on God's "anointed one" (28:8), the word that ultimately generates our "messiah." As the king, David himself is of course the royal "anointed one," the royal "messiah." But as God has heard his prayers, shown him mercy, and called forth his joyous praise, so his individual experience ought to be a paradigm for the covenant community at large. He represents them, and there is a profound sense in which they are collectively God's "anointed one," his "son" (cf. Ex. 4:22—another title applied both to Israel at large and distinctively to Israel's king). The expression "anointed one" in a Davidic psalm inevitably prompts us to think of the king; the parallelism in verse 8 shows that the expression here refers to Israel: "The LORD is the strength *of his people,* a fortress of salvation *for his anointed one*" (italics added). The thoughtful reader reflects on the ways in which David and the people are linked—and on the ways in which Jesus the Messiah (i.e., Jesus the Anointed One) not only springs from David's line, but shows himself to be both the ultimate Davidic king and the ultimate embodiment of Israel.

(3) The last line calls to mind a delightful truth: "Save your people and bless your inheritance," David writes; *"be their shepherd and carry them forever"* (28:9, italics added). Reflect on such passages as Psalm 23; Ezekiel 34; Luke 15:1-7; John 10; 1 Peter 5:1-4.

∿

1 Samuel 14; Romans 12; *Jeremiah 51; Psalm 30*

∾

MANY A CHRISTIAN HAS experienced the almost ineffable release of being transported from despair or illness or catastrophic defeat or a sense of alienated distance from God, to a height of safety or health or victory or spiritual intimacy with our Maker and Redeemer. Certainly David had such experiences. **Psalm 30** records his pleasure during one of those transports of delight.

The psalm divides into three parts. In the *first* (30:1-5), David depicts the marvelous transformation. In the *second* (30:1-6) he describes the complacency that drove him down in the first place, whether prior to the first five verses or in another cycle of the same thing. In the *last* section (30:11-12), he concludes with the same exuberant joy he displays in the first five verses, as he bursts the boundaries of language to depict the glorious transformation when wailing is turned into dancing, and sackcloth into the garments of joy.

The list of contrasts in the psalm captures the heart and the imagination. Here we may reflect on one pair of such contrasts: "For his anger lasts only a moment, but his favor lasts a lifetime; weeping may remain for a night, but rejoicing comes in the morning" (30:5).

David is writing from his perspective as a member of the covenant community. Almighty God is linked by solemn oath and covenant with them. If they sin, God does not write them off: "his anger lasts only a moment"; his punishments, however severe, are temporary. His basic stance toward them is gracious: "his favor lasts a lifetime." And since the earlier verses show that David is thinking not of the nation but of his individual experience, what is true for the people of God as a whole is true for him in particular: God may punish him for various reasons, but God's fundamental stance toward him is merciful and gracious, lasting a lifetime. Basking in the conscious presence and blessing of God, David looks back on his recent experience and exults in the fact that "weeping may remain for a night, but rejoicing comes in the morning."

There are many such contrasts in Scripture, not a few of them bound up with the new covenant. The apostle Paul can speak of "our light and momentary troubles" (though by our comfortable Western standards his troubles were neither light nor momentary!). These achieve for us "an eternal glory that far outweighs them all" (2 Cor. 4:17)—and on such a scale they truly are light and momentary. Paul is merely following Jesus, "who for the joy set before him endured the cross, scorning its shame, and sat down at the right hand of the throne of God" (Heb. 12:2).

∾

1 Samuel 15; Romans 13; *Jeremiah 52*; *Psalm 31*

∽

THE HISTORICAL APPENDIX TO the prophecy of Jeremiah (**Jer. 52**) imposes a "spin" on the book as a whole. Without it, certain points would be left hanging—that is, they would still be there within the body of the book, but they would not be high-lighted as powerfully as they are with this appendix to flesh them out.

First, it may be useful to offer notes on several of the historical details of this report. It is rather surprising that no mention is made of Nebuchadnezzar's instructions for the protection of Jeremiah. But in fact, the interest lies in the large historical movement, not in Jeremiah's personal circumstances. Some of the details complement the historical account provided by 2 Kings 25. Second Kings, for instance, does not mention Zedekiah's imprisonment (Jer. 52:11). Seraiah the chief priest (52:24), one of the leaders who were executed, was grandson of Hilkiah, the high priest under Josiah, who traced his descent from Aaron (cf. 1 Chron. 6:13-15). The report of the numbers transported (52:28-30) is much lower than the figures given in 2 Kings 24. Probably the figures in Kings reflect the total, while the figures here refer to adult males or adult males of a certain rank. The variation in dates between 2 Kings 25:8 and Jeremiah 52 reflects, respectively, the Judean and the Babylonian methods of reckoning years of reign. Nebuchadnezzar's son, Evil-Merodach (52:31—Amel-Marduk in Babylonian sources) reigned only one year (561—560 B.C.). Babylonian records confirm that Jehoiachin was among those who enjoyed this emperor's largess.

Second, we should isolate the theological effects of reading this chapter at the end of the book. Two elements stand out. (a) The historical details remind the reader that everything predicted by Jeremiah came to pass. Because Jeremiah is not named, the flavor is stronger yet: everything that God said he would do, he did. The sin of the people was persistent, unrepented, corroding, perverse. Far from softening the people, the promise of judgment, which God out of mercy delayed and delayed, merely bred hardness of heart. But the promised judgment finally fell. One is reminded of the reasoning in 2 Peter 3. (b) The closing verses of the chapter (52:31-34) describe how the legitimate Davidic king was finally released from his imprisonment and treated with honor during the closing years of his life. Of course, he never returned to Jerusalem or to any part of the land of Israel. But thoughtful readers cannot help reflecting on the fact that the book does not finally *end* in judgment. There is still the whisper of hope. God is not yet fin-ished with the Davidic dynasty. The first adumbration of the promises of the prophecy of Jeremiah fall across the horizon.

∽

1 Samuel 16; Romans 14; *Lamentations 1; Psalm 32*

∾

BEFORE SAYING SOMETHING ABOUT **Lamentations 1**, I should offer a few observations on the book as a whole.

(1) In Hebrew, the first word of the book means "Oh, how [deserted is the city]," and this first word becomes the title in the Hebrew Bible. Later Jewish writers referred to the book either by this word or by another Hebrew word that means "lamentations."

(2) Early Greek and Latin translations of this short book assign it to Jeremiah the prophet. This is entirely possible, but strictly speaking, the work is anonymous.

(3) Lamentations is made up of five poems, five dirges, each occupying one chapter. The first four are acrostics: i.e., the twenty-two consonants of the Hebrew alphabet introduce, respectively, each of the twenty-two stanzas in each poem (though there are slight irregularities in chapters 2, 3, and 4). In the first three poems, each stanza is normally made up of three lines in some kind of parallelism (with two exceptional four-line stanzas, 1:7; 2:19). In the third poem, each *line* of each stanza begins with the same Hebrew consonant that introduces that dirge. The fourth poem has only two lines for each stanza. Though it is poetry, the fifth lament is not an acrostic, but consists of twenty-two lines that resemble some psalms of corporate lament (e.g., Pss. 44, 80).

(4) No linear flow of thought sweeps through each chapter or through the entire book. Certain themes keep reappearing, of course, but by and large the book is impressionistic, full of powerful images that reinforce a small number of burning truths.

If Job deals with the calamity that befell a righteous man, and thus with the problem of innocent suffering, Lamentations deals with the calamity that befell a guilty nation. Those who sow the wind will reap the whirlwind. While honestly and powerfully portraying the suffering of the nation, these poems vindicate God: God, not human beings, is in control of history, and God will not be mocked. Justice ultimately will prevail in the drama of history, because God is just.

Two final challenges. (a) Read through this first chapter and identify each of the powerful images the writer casts up, asking what it contributes to the chapter and how it is related to other biblical passages (if at all). For instance, verse 10 calls to mind that only the high priest could enter the Holy Place—and now raw pagans not only have entered but have ravaged the temple. Theologically, this is tied to the fact that the glory of God abandoned the temple (cf. Ezek. 8—11), demonstrating, among other things, that the presence of God is more to be sought than the building. (b) What is godly about 1:21-22?

∾

1 Samuel 17; Romans 15; *Lamentations 2; Psalm 33*

∾

THIS DELIGHTFUL HYMN OF PRAISE (**Ps. 33**) focuses on what God is and what he does. It is so wonderfully fecund that here I can do no more than draw attention to some of its evocative themes.

(1) The Lord is righteous, and "it is fitting for the upright to praise him" (33:1). Faithful and thoughtful worship turns in part on adoration of God *for his character.* Those who reflect the same character, however feebly, will most hungrily worship him for his perfections. Thus godly praise is tied to the moral transformation of the worshiper.

(2) The psalmist envisages creativity in music, consummate skill on the instruments, and fervor (33:3)—a combination fairly rare in evangelical corporate worship.

(3) God's character and God's work cannot be separated from his word (33:4-9). This is not only because God's word is as righteous, true, reliable ("faithful"), and loving as he is, but because God's word is effective—something nowhere more clearly seen than in creation: "By the word of the LORD were the heavens made, their starry host by the breath of his mouth" (33:6).

(4) God is utterly sovereign. He foils the plans of the nations; no one ever foils his plans (33:10-11): "the plans of the LORD stand firm forever, the purposes of his heart through all generations."

(5) Although God is sovereign over the entire human race, and is the judge of all, yet he is peculiarly the God of his own covenant people (33:12-15).

(6) Nations are never saved by mere might, apart from the blessing and sanction of God. Of course, God might well use the big guns, and his sovereign providence operates even in the preparation of the mighty empires that chastened his own people. But to trust the big guns is to forget who gives strength and wealth and blessing. Moreover, the Lord is perfectly capable of overturning any nation of any size, of spiking the big guns. "A horse [or a tank] is a vain hope for deliverance; despite all its great strength it cannot save" (33:17). The ultimate hope is in the Lord: "But the eyes of the LORD are on those who fear him, on those whose hope is in his unfailing love" (33:18).

(7) Granted that this is the sort of God who is really there, that this is the God we worship, the three closing verses are as inevitable as they are jubilant. Here is the proper grounding for godly hope: "We wait in hope for the LORD; he is our help and our shield. In him our hearts rejoice, for we trust in his holy name. May your unfailing love rest upon us, O LORD, even as we put our hope in you" (33:20-22).

∾

1 Samuel 18; Romans 16; *Lamentations 3; Psalm 34*

∾

IT IS DIFFICULT TO DECIDE whether the first part of **Lamentations 3** describes the experience of an individual (perhaps Jeremiah), or if the individual is a figure representing the entire nation as it has been forced into catastrophic defeat, poverty, and exile. Several lines favor the former view (e.g., 3:14, where the individual has become the laughingstock "of all my people" rather than of the surrounding peoples). The book as a whole, and the plural "we" that dominates most of the second half of this chapter, slightly favor the second view.

But more important than deciding this issue is the striking way in which hope or confidence twice break out in the midst of the most appalling distress. The *first* instance is in 3:22-27. Despite the horrible devastation, the writer says, "Because of the LORD's great love we are not consumed, for his compassions never fail" (3:22). Their sins merit more judgment than they are facing. They might have been wiped out. Only the Lord's mercy prevented that from happening. However great their sufferings, the fact that they still exist testifies to the Lord's graciousness toward them. God's mercies renew themselves in our experience every day (3:23). Besides, the faithful will surely insist that what they want the most is not the Lord's blessings but the Lord himself: "I say to myself, 'The LORD is my portion; therefore I will wait for him'" (3:24). This is a moral stance: it signals the end of the self-sufficiency and self-focus that thought it could thumb its nose at God. For this writer, the chastening is having its desired effect: it is driving people back to God.

The *second* block of hope is a retrospective on the preliminary ways in which the Lord has already answered (3:55-57), and which then becomes a plea for vindication (3:58-64). The stark simplicity of the first of these two passages is profoundly compelling, the heritage of many believers who have passed through dark waters: "I called on your name, O LORD, from the depths of the pit. You heard my plea: 'Do not close your ears to my cry for relief.' You came near when I called you, and you said, 'Do not fear'" (3:55-57). The prayer for vindication that follows (3:58-64) must not be reduced to bitter vengeance. If God is just, then in the same way that he has chastened his own covenant people, he must mete out justice to those who have cruelly attacked others—even if it is that very attack that God has providentially deployed to chasten his own people. God himself elsewhere insists on this same point (e.g., Isa. 10:5ff.).

∾

1 Samuel 19; 1 Corinthians 1; *Lamentations 4; Psalm 35*

∾

THE FOURTH DIRGE (LAM. 4) again casts up a variety of mental pictures to depict the suffering of the final siege of Jerusalem and beyond. It also lays out some of the reasons why the judgment was imposed, and ends in a whisper of hope.

The dirge opens by likening the people of Jerusalem to gold that has lost its luster (4:1). Like gold, they started off precious, but now they are treated like the cheapest clay pots (4:2). Under conditions of siege and transportation, food becomes so scarce that mothers can no longer nurse their children; even baby jackals are better treated (4:3-4). Proverbial for wickedness, Sodom was destroyed in a quick holocaust, "in a moment" (4:6). But the punishment of the poet's people "is greater than that of Sodom" (4:6); siege warfare is a wretched, drawn-out affair, and the exile that follows it goes on and on. The theological assumption, of course, is that there are degrees of guilt: those with most knowledge of God's ways have least excuse, and so they can expect severest judgment (e.g., Matt. 11:20-24). As for the nobility, they are as emaciated, degraded, and dirty as the rest, and therefore indistinguishable from the rest (4:8-9)—which is another way of saying that the leadership of the little nation has been destroyed. They are so filthy that they are physically and ceremonially unclean, like lepers who must eke out their existence where no one wants to have contact with them (4:14-15). "The LORD's anointed" (4:20)—here a reference to King Zedekiah—proves to be of no help. "We thought that under his shadow we would live among the nations" (4:20)—that is, secure in the knowledge that he was in the Davidic line, the Lord's anointed. But as the Lord has destroyed the city and the temple, so also has he removed the Davidic descendants from the throne.

Why did the Lord do this? "[I]t happened because of the sins of her prophets and the iniquities of her priests" (4:13). The writer does not mean to suggest that these were the only sinners, but that the religious leaders, who should have been doing the most to preserve the nation in covenantal faithfulness, led the nation instead in corruption and infidelity. Because of their own positions, far from staying the national decline, they abetted it and hastened it. Where is that true today?

The story does not end here. In mocking derision the writer tells nearby pagans that they might as well delight in the moment, for their turn will come. God's justice will be imposed on them as well as on Israel—and one day the covenant community, though afflicted now, will put behind them every trace of the exile (4:21-22). The Lord's Anointed will give them rest.

∾

1 Samuel 20; 1 Corinthians 2; *Lamentations 5; Psalm 36*

∾

IN THIS INFORMATION-RICH AGE, many of us have learned to be as brief as possible. That was one of the areas in which my own doctoral supervisor helped me a great deal: though my prose style is still too rambling, whatever leanness and precision it has owes a great deal to his thorough correcting of my work a quarter of a century ago. Efficient managers learn to be brief; computer programmers are rated on how briefly they can write precise code to do what needs to be done. Only a few contemporary authors (e.g., Tom Clancy and James Michener) get away with long, rambling books—and even then the editors have drastically trimmed them.

Yet here we are, quietly reading through Isaiah, Jeremiah, Lamentations, with Ezekiel to go, and we find ourselves circling around the same handful of themes again and again: sin in the covenant community, threatened judgment, then enacted judgment, first for the northern tribes, then for Judah. We recognize the subtle differences, of course: history, apocalyptic, oracle, lament, prayers. Here in **Lamentations 5**, the fifth dirge is cast as a long prayer: "Remember, O LORD, what has happened to us; look, and see our disgrace" (5:1). But haven't you caught yourself saying to yourself more than once, "I know this is the Word of God, and I know it is important, but I think I understand now something of the history and the theology of the exile. Couldn't we get on to something else?" We live in an age burgeoning with information, we cry for brevity, and the Bible at times seems terribly discursive. So we scan another chapter as rapidly as possible because we already "know" all this.

But that is part of the problem, isn't it? Read through this chapter again, slowly, thoughtfully. Of course, it is tied to Israel six centuries before Christ, to the destruction of her cities and land and temple, to the onset of the exile. But listen to the depth and persistence of the pleas, the repentance, the personal engagement with God, the cultural awareness, the acknowledgment of God's sovereignty and justice, the profound recognition that the people must be restored to God himself if return to the land is to be possible, let alone meaningful (5:21). Then compare this with the brands of Christian confessionalism with which you are most familiar. In days of cultural declension, moral degradation, and large-scale ecclesiastical frittering, is our praying like that of Lamentations 5? Have the themes of the major prophets so burned into our minds and hearts that our passion is to be restored to the living God? Or have we ourselves become so caught up in the spirit of this age that we are content to be rich in information and impoverished in wisdom and godliness?

∾

1 Samuel 21—22; 1 Corinthians 3; *Ezekiel 1; Psalm 37*

∾

EZEKIEL WAS JEREMIAH'S contemporary. Though he was born into a priestly family, Ezekiel was removed from the temple. In March, 597 B.C., he, young King Jehoiachin, the Queen Mother, the aristocracy, and many of the leading priests and craftsmen were transported seven hundred miles to Babylon. The young king was in prison or under house arrest for thirty-seven years. The exilic community, impoverished and cut off from Jerusalem and the temple, dreamed nostalgically of home and begged God to rescue them. They could not conceive that in another decade Jerusalem would be utterly destroyed. On the banks of the Kebar River— probably an irrigation canal swinging in a loop southwest from the Euphrates— the exiles tried to settle. And here, according to **Ezekiel 1**, when he was thirty years old and in the fifth year of his exile (i.e., about 593, still six years before the destruction of Jerusalem), Ezekiel received an extraordinary vision.

Detailed explanation of this apocalyptic vision demands more space than I have here. But some observations are crucial:

(1) In general terms, what Ezekiel sees is a vision of a mobile throne, the mobile throne of God. (I once preached on this passage to some hearing-impaired folk, and more than one thought I was saying it deals with the mobile phone of God!)

(2) The throne is made up of four "living creatures," each with wings outstretched to touch the adjacent two at the wingtips, so that together the four creatures make a huge, hollow square. Inside this space there are torches, flashes of lightning, and fire. Each of the four living creatures has four faces—probably a way of signaling that God's throne is intelligent (the human face), royal (the lion), strong (the bull), and compassionate (the eagle, cf. Ex. 19:4; Isa. 40:31). Beside each creature is a pair of wheels, intersecting each other so that they cannot fall over. The entire structure moves in straight lines, like a cursor on a monitor only in three dimensions, propelled by the wheels and additional wings of the living creatures, directed cohesively by the Spirit. Above the heads of the creatures, and supported by them, is a platform like a giant wok, sparkling like ice or hoarfrost. Above that is the throne of God.

(3) The importance of this mobile throne becomes clear later in the book. Here we must grasp two things: (a) The closer the vision gets to God himself, the more distantly he is described. The culmination—"This was the *appearance* of the *likeness* of the *glory* of the LORD" (1:28)—elicits not an artist's conception, but worship. (b) More broadly: visions of God always induce brokenness, humility, and worship (cf. Isa. 6; Rev. 1, 4—5).

∾

1 Samuel 23; 1 Corinthians 4; *Ezekiel 2; Psalm 38*

∾

IN SOME WAYS THE FIRST three chapters of Ezekiel hang together to describe Ezekiel's early call and commission—the commission of a prophet called to serve in declining times. In the Old Testament, not all prophetic calls are the same. Elisha served as an apprentice to Elijah; Amos was called while he was serving as a shepherd; Samuel first heard the call of God when he was but a stripling. But prophets commissioned to serve in peculiarly declining times have some common features in their call. We cannot trace all of those features here, but one of them emerges with great strength in **Ezekiel 2**.

Here God tells Ezekiel what he is being called to do. He is being sent, God says, "to a rebellious nation that has rebelled against me" (2:3). He is being sent to the nation of Israel, at least that part of it that is in exile with him—and that part, of course, comprised the most gifted, the most learned, the most noble, the most privileged. From God's perspective, they are merely "obstinate and stubborn" (2:4). Ezekiel is to tell them, "This is what the Sovereign LORD says" (2:4). So far God has not told Ezekiel what he is to say, i.e., the *content* of what the Sovereign Lord says. Rather, the rest of this chapter is devoted to making sure that Ezekiel understands that his ministry turns absolutely on one thing: passing on to this rebellious house the words of God. "You must speak my words to them, whether they listen or fail to listen" (2:7).

Of course, it is always important for prophets and preachers to speak God's words faithfully. But it is especially urgent in declining times. In periods of revival and prosperity, the preacher may be viewed with respect, his faithfulness and insight lionized. But in declining times, those who truly speak for God will be taunted and threatened. The pressures to dilute what God says become enormous. Clever exegesis to make the text say what it really doesn't, selective silence to leave out the painful bits, hermeneutical cleverness to remove the bite and sting of Scripture, all become *de rigueur,* so that we can still be accepted and even admired. But God is aware of the danger. From his perspective, success is not measured by how many people Ezekiel wins to his perspective, but by the faithfulness with which he declares God's words. Anything less participates in the rebellion of this "rebellious house" (2:8). This calls for godly courage that drives out fear (2:6-7).

Precisely where are such faithfulness and courage most urgently demanded in the Western world today?

∾

1 Samuel 24; 1 Corinthians 5; *Ezekiel 3; Psalm 39*

∾

TWO OF THE THEMES OF **Ezekiel 3**, intrinsic to the call of Ezekiel, may usefully be elucidated:

First, the opening part shows how important it is for the prophet to empathize with God and his perspective. Trailing on from the closing lines of chapter 2 and into the beginning of chapter 3, Ezekiel in his vision is commanded to eat a scroll with "words of lament and mourning and woe" (2:10) written on both sides. Ezekiel eats it and reports that "it tasted as sweet as honey in my mouth" (3:3). Why would a scroll full of "words of lament and mourning and woe" taste sweet? The point of the vision is that God's words become sweet to Ezekiel simply because they are God's words. God really does know best; he knows what is right. Therefore even when his words pronounce judgment and calamity, there is a sense in which the prophet must be empathetic to God's perspective.

Similarly in the next verses (3:4-9): Ezekiel is not being sent to some foreign culture where the first step is to learn the local language. He is being called to speak to the people of his own heritage. Nevertheless he will find them unwilling to listen to him, precisely because they are unwilling to listen to God (3:7). So God promises: "But I will make you as unyielding and hardened as they are. I will make your forehead like the hardest stone, harder than flint. Do not be afraid of them or terrified by them, though they are a rebellious house" (3:8-9). So in this head-butting contest Ezekiel is being enabled to side with God unreservedly. God sometimes raises up strong and obstinate leaders who, regardless of personal popularity, hunger to side with God. None of this means that Ezekiel has no fellow-feeling for the exiles; both the next verses and the rest of the book contradict any such notion. Nevertheless his commission is a call to empathize with God's perspective and to be unyielding.

Second, this chapter contains a call to utter warnings and to be careful (3:16-27). The theme of the watchman (3:16-21) recurs in the book (chap. 33), and can be explored later. But in the closing verses Ezekiel is forbidden to say *anything*—courtesies, greetings, political speeches, whatever—*except* for what God gives him to say. This state of affairs endures until the fall of Jerusalem, about six years away (Ezek. 33:21-22), when his tongue is loosed. This restriction adds weight to the times he does speak. It is also a challenge to everyone who speaks for God. All of our talk and our silences should be so calibrated that when we convey God's words our credibility is enhanced and not diminished.

∾

1 Samuel 25; 1 Corinthians 6; *Ezekiel 4; Psalms 40—41*

∿

IF WE ARE TO UNDERSTAND THE reasons why Ezekiel is called to the powerful parabolic actions we find in **Ezekiel 4**, we must put ourselves in the place of the exiles. Like the people back home in Jerusalem and Judah, many of them could not imagine that the city and temple of the Great King could ever be destroyed. God simply would not allow it to happen. In general terms the exiles in Babylon respond to Ezekiel the same way that the Jews in Jerusalem respond to Jeremiah: they don't believe him. In fact, the exiles doubtless have added incentive to maintain their false hopes. As long as Jerusalem stands, they can nurture the hope that God will rescue them and bring them back home. If Jerusalem falls, there will be no "home" to which to return. One can imagine how desperately negative and even impossible Ezekiel's warnings sound to them.

But Ezekiel does not flinch.

(1) He begins by drawing a picture of Jerusalem on a large clay tablet—perhaps the profile or some other easily recognized perspective, so that onlookers can instantly see what he is doing. Around the city he erects siege works and the like, as if he were playing war games with homemade toys. Everyone perceives that this means Jerusalem will be besieged. Then he holds an iron pan over the model. As God's prophet he stands in for God, and holds the pan in such a way as to threaten to crash it down on the city and destroy it—picturing the fact that it is God himself who is threatening the city.

(2) In the next section (4:4-8), Ezekiel spends some time each day lying on his left side. (He is not there all the time, of course, as the succeeding verses show he has other actions to perform.) If his head is toward the model of Jerusalem he has made, and his body lies on an east-west axis, then when he lies on his left he is facing north, toward Israel, the ten tribes that have already gone into captivity under the Assyrians. For 390 days (more than a year!) he does this, every day. Then one day the onlookers show up and find him on his right side—facing the south and thus threatening Judah with judgment and disaster.

(3) Inside a besieged city in the ancient world, as supplies dwindled people were forced to make bread out of dried beans and lentils mixed with the tiny bit of flour that was left. They would eat their impossibly small portions (about eight ounces of "bread") and sip their tiny quota of water, and waste away. They would cook their food on cow patties (as in the slums of India), because there was no more wood. All this, Ezekiel predicts, "because of their sin" (4:17).

∿

1 Samuel 26; 1 Corinthians 7; *Ezekiel 5; Psalms 42—43*

∾

IN **EZEKIEL 5**, EZEKIEL EXTENDS BY one more his list of parabolic actions and then reports God's words as to their significance.

Ezekiel sharpens a sword and uses it as a straight razor. He shaves his head, beard and all. After tucking a few strands into his garments, he divides the rest into three piles. The first he puts into the city (i.e., onto the clay tablet that is the model of the city of Jerusalem, 4:1), and sets the hairs alight, perhaps with a live coal. Another third he scatters on the ground all around the city, and then whacks them and whacks them with his sword until only tiny pieces are left. The final third he throws up into the wind, a few hairs at a time, until they have all blown away. A few strands tucked into his garments he now takes out and throws onto the smoldering coal and ashes within the model city, and they too burst into flame and are consumed.

The significance of all this is spelled out in 5:12: a third of the people will die within the city (from the famine of the siege), a third will die by the sword in the final breakout, and the remaining third will be scattered into exile.

The entire chapter emphasizes that it is *God himself* who is going to bring down this judgment on his people: highlight every instance of "I" in 5:8-17. This is what takes place when the Lord shoots to kill (5:16). "Because of all your detestable idols, I will do to you what I have never done before and will never do again" (5:9); the formula means that this judgment is as bad as temporal judgments get. Jesus himself uses virtually the same words with respect to the impending judgment on Jerusalem in *his* century (Matt. 24:21).

God says his wrath must be poured out. Yet this wrath is not ungovernable temper. God insists that when judgment has been meted out, his wrath will subside and his anger will cease (5:13). This outbreak of wrath forms part of a list of punctuated outbreaks of wrath from the Fall on: the curse in Genesis 3, the Flood, Babel, slavery in Egypt, various judgments in the desert (including the wilderness wanderings for forty years), and so on. In cycles of judgment corresponding to cycles of particularly egregious sin, God pours out his wrath. All of this forms part of the necessary biblical theology behind Romans 3:20-26: there is no solution to the threat of God's righteous wrath upon his creatures who have rebelled against him—until in the person of his Son God himself bears the wrath we deserve, preserving his justice while justifying us.

∾

1 Samuel 27; 1 Corinthians 8; *Ezekiel 6; Psalm 44*

∾

PSALM 44 IS AN IMPORTANT FOIL for the themes we have been digesting from the prophets. The major prophets keep drawing a tight link between the sins of Israel and the destruction that God inflicted upon them: the people get what they deserve. Of course, we have come across *innocent* suffering before, especially in Job and in some Psalms. But here in Psalm 44 is the suffering of an innocent *nation.*

There were defeats and even deportations (44:11) before the exile (see Amos 1:6, 9), so we cannot be certain when this psalm was written. Defeat was not unknown even to good kings (e.g., Ps. 60). Here the psalmist begins by reviewing the past. When the nation was called into existence, everything depended on God's strong intervention: "it was your right hand, your arm, and the light of your face, for you loved them" (44:3). The psalmist is not looking back to national heroes and bemoaning their contemporary absence. He looks back to God's power in the past, and insists the nation still relies on God (44:6-8). So why the disastrous defeats (44:9-16)? Unlike the gross sin denounced by Isaiah, Jeremiah, and Ezekiel, here fidelity still triumphs: "All this happened to us, though we had not forgotten you or been false to your covenant. Our hearts had not turned back; our feet had not strayed from your path" (44:17-18).

At least two hints toward the end of the psalm, though they do not provide "solutions," invite the reader to reflect on the direction taken by later biblical writers. (1) Sometimes God's apparent sleep, his withdrawal (44:23ff.), is not overt wrath poured out on our sin, but his own timing. He refuses to be hurried, and his "unfailing love" (44:26) will triumph in the end. The ebbs and flows of Christian history support the same stance: they do not always correspond with differing degrees of loyalty or different methods. As one commentator (F. D. Kidner) has finely put it, "Although its picture of the sleeping Lord may seem naive to us, it was acted out in the New Testament, to teach a lesson which we still find relevant: cf. verse 23 with Mark 4:38." (2) More stunningly, the psalmist says it is "*for your sake* [that] we face death all day long" (44:22, italics added). That point is not fully developed until Paul quotes the verse (Rom. 8:36ff.). But already it embraces the notion that some suffering is not the result of our sin but simply the result of being faithful to God in a world at war with him. In such cases suffering is not a sign of defeat but a badge of fidelity and fellowship, even of victory: we are "more than conquerors through him who loved us" (Rom. 8:37).

∾

1 Samuel 28; 1 Corinthians 9; *Ezekiel 7; Psalm 45*

AT ONE LEVEL **PSALM 45** is a royal wedding song. The opening verse affords a glimpse of the psalmist's passions as he composes his lines (cf. similar introductions in 39:1-3; 49:1-4). The rest of the psalm is broken down into five sections.

The *first* (45:2-5) depicts the king's majesty and stature. "Gird your sword upon your side, O mighty one; clothe yourself with splendor and majesty" (45:3)—and pursue truth, humility, and righteousness, even while displaying "awesome deeds" and military prowess (45:4-5). In the *second* (45:6-9), the psalmist reflects on the monarch's person and state, and addresses him as God (45:6). The psalmist is *not* turning away from the monarch to address God. The next verse (45:7) proves he is still addressing the king, and is perfectly able to distinguish between the king as "God" and God himself: "therefore God, your God, has set you above your companions." Thus the address of verse 6 is extravagant: "Your throne, O God, will last for ever and ever"—in the first instance referring to a Davidic king, as the rest of the psalm demonstrates. In the *third* section the psalmist addresses the bride and encourages her lifelong allegiance (45:10-12). That entails "forgetting" her father's house (the counterpart of Gen. 2:24), and focusing her affections and loyalty on her husband. The *fourth* briefly describes the bridal party (45:13-15) leading up to the wedding itself, the details signaling the importance of the occasion. Scripture never trivializes marriage, least of all the marriage of a Davidic king. In the *fifth* section (45:16-17), the psalmist returns to the king (the Hebrew pronouns are masculine). The focus is on the fruit of the marriage: heirs who displace their fathers. This demonstrates that the psalmist is thinking in terms of ordinary procreation and succession. This is not an oracular messianic psalm.

Nevertheless Hebrews 1:8-9 quotes 45:6-7 to prove Jesus' essential superiority over mere angels. Only the Son is directly addressed as "God." Why does the writer of Hebrews feel he can use Psalm 45 in this way? The surrounding verses show he has reflected long and hard on several passages and themes: 2 Samuel 7 (see vol. 1, meditation for September 12), which promises an eternal Davidic dynasty; several passages that link the Davidic king to God as his "son" (2 Sam. 7; Ps. 2—on which see meditation for August 4); an entire pattern or "typology" in which David is understood to be a shadow, a type, an adumbration of a still greater "David" to come. If Scripture (and thus God) addresses an early Davidic monarch as "God," how much more deserving of this title is the ultimate David?

1 Samuel 29—30; 1 Corinthians 10; *Ezekiel 8; Psalms 46—47*

∾

EZEKIEL 8—11 CONSTITUTES one long vision.

The opening verse of **Ezekiel 8** establishes the time at exactly fourteen months after the prophet's inaugural vision, and therefore *after* the 390 days when he was lying for some part of each day on his left side denouncing the northern tribes already taken into captivity, and *during* the 40 days when he was lying on his right side denouncing the sins of Judah and Jerusalem. By this point he has established his credentials as a prophet, so the elders of the exilic community come and consult him (8:1). Probably they are troubled by his symbol-laden actions, and are asking him what will happen to Jerusalem, and if and when they will get home.

Ezekiel does not respond off the top of his head. Rather, he waits, and is granted another vision, the content of which he ultimately transmits to the exiles (11:25). In this vision, he sees something of God in categories reminiscent of those in the inaugural vision (chap. 1). Within the visionary world, Ezekiel is transported by the Spirit to Jerusalem, near the north gate. He is shown several horrible examples of idolatry and syncretism.

First, he witnesses the idol that provokes God to jealousy (8:3-6). If it is by the north gate, it is by the gate the king and his retinue would use on their way to the temple. The king whose responsibility it is to lead the people in covenantal faithfulness is the leader in compromise and syncretism—and in line with his covenantal conditions, God is rightly jealous (see Ex. 20:1-17). *Second*, Ezekiel sees seventy elders actually worshiping creatures that were, according to the Mosaic covenant, unclean even for eating and touching (8:7-13). *Third*, he sees women profoundly engaged with Tammuz (8:14-15). The Tammuz cult was a fertility cult, ascribing agricultural bounty to a dying and rising god. Some of these cults were also terribly promiscuous. *Finally*, Ezekiel sees priests (for only they could be between the portico and the altar) with their backs to the temple, worshiping the sun—not only cherishing the created thing above the Creator (Rom. 1:25), but violating the covenant (Deut. 4:19), influenced perhaps by the Egyptian sun god Ra.

Modern forms of idolatry are different, of course. Most of us have not been caught mourning for Tammuz. But do our hearts pursue things that rightly make God jealous? Do we love dirty and forbidden things? Do we ascribe success to everything but God? We may not succumb to fertility cults, but doesn't our culture make sex itself a god?

Corrupt worship invariably replaces and relativizes God and ends up dulling moral vision (8:17).

∾

1 Samuel 31; 1 Corinthians 11; *Ezekiel 9; Psalm 48*

∾

IF EZEKIEL 8 DESCRIBES THE CORRUPT worship that was going on in Jerusalem in the years leading up to her destruction in 587 B.C., **Ezekiel 9** describes something of what God does about it.

There is both a negative component and a positive element. In his vision, Ezekiel hears God call for "the guards of the city" (9:1)—more precisely, the executioners of the city. Six men arrive, "each with a deadly weapon in his hand" (9:2). A seventh man, clothed in linen, has a writing kit at his side. God commissions him to put an identifying mark on the foreheads of those who will escape slaughter; he commissions the executioners to go through the city "and kill, without showing pity or compassion" (9:5), beginning at the sanctuary itself. "So they began with the elders who were in front of the temple" (9:6).

As they proceed with their grisly task, Ezekiel cries out, "Ah, Sovereign LORD! Are you going to destroy the entire remnant of Israel in this outpouring of your wrath on Jerusalem?" (9:8). The Lord responds with a devastating indictment (9:9-10) that includes a word-play: the people of Israel insist the Lord does not "see" (or "look"), so the Lord resolves not to "see/look" on them with pity or spare them. He is resolved to "bring down on their own heads what they have done" (9:10).

The positive element has already been alluded to. Not everyone is destroyed. The seventh man, the man with the writing kit, goes through the city putting a mark on the foreheads "of those who grieve and lament over all the detestable things that are done in it" (9:4). The executioners are strictly forbidden to harm these people (9:5). Note well: those who are spared are not those who simply sit on the sidelines, but those who actively grieve over the spiritual degradation of the city. They may not have the power to effect change, but they have not sunk into the lassitude of careless indifference. And God spares them.

Of course, all that is described here takes place within Ezekiel's visionary world. In the real world, we are not to think that all the righteous and only the righteous escaped all of the sufferings associated with Nebuchadnezzar's siege: the Bible is full of stories in which *righteous* people suffer (e.g., Naboth the vineyard owner). What this vision *does* mean is that God himself ordains the judgment, and God himself vindicates those who are covenantally faithful. Similar symbolism is picked up at the end of Revelation 13 and the beginning of Revelation 14 (see vol. 1, meditation for December 23).

∾

2 Samuel 1; 1 Corinthians 12; *Ezekiel 10*; Psalm 49

∾

IN LIGHT OF THE TERRIBLE JUDGMENTS pronounced against Jerusalem in Ezekiel
8-11, with the beginning of the withdrawal of the glory of the Lord in **Ezekiel 10**,
we should think through the bearing of such sins in our own framework:

> *Why do we choose what can last but an hour*
> *Before we must leave it behind?*
> *Why do possessions exert brutal power*
> *To render us harsh and unkind?*
> *Why do mere things have the lure of a flower*
> *Whose scent makes us selfish and blind?*
> > *The cisterns run dry, and sour is our breath;*
> > *We dwell in the valley of death.*

> *Why is betrayal attractive to us*
> *Who often are hurt and betrayed?*
> *Why barter faithful devotion for lust,*
> *Integrity cast far away?*
> *Why do our dreams, then our deeds, beggar trust,*
> *Our guilt far too heavy to pay?*
> > *The cisterns run dry, and sour is our breath;*
> > *We dwell in the valley of death.*

> *Why do we stubbornly act out a role,*
> *Convincing the world that we've won?*
> *Why for mere winning will we sell our soul,*
> *In order to be number one?*
> *Why sear our conscience so we're in control—*
> *Despairing of what we've become?*
> > *The cisterns run dry, and sour is our breath;*
> > *We dwell in the valley of death.*

> *O Jesus—*

> *Why do you promise to quench all our thirst,*
> *When we have despised all your ways?*
> *Why do you rescue the damned and the cursed,*
> *By dying our death in our place?*
> *Why do you transform our hearts till they burst*
> *With vibrant expressions of praise?*
> > *The well flows with life—and we're satisfied—*
> > *The fountain that flows from your side.*

∾

2 Samuel 2; 1 Corinthians 13; *Ezekiel 11*; *Psalm 50*

∾

THERE ARE TWO HIGHLY SYMBOLIC actions in **Ezekiel 11**, one of them beginning in Ezekiel 10, the other entirely within the chapter at hand:

(1) Although it is difficult to trace exactly the movement of the glory of the Lord, it is reasonably clear that this glory, once associated with the temple—especially with the Most Holy Place and the ark of the covenant over which the cherubim stretched their wings—abandons the temple and hovers over the mobile throne. The same mobile throne Ezekiel had seen in Babylon is now parked by the south entrance to the temple. The four living creatures, now identified as cherubim, transport the glory of the Lord to the east gate (10:18-19), and then to the mountain east of the city (11:23). Thus the presence of God judicially abandons the temple and the city. Nothing stands in the way of their destruction.

(2) The picture of the cooking pot (11:3-12) conjures up the false sense of security that a strong, walled city could engender among its inhabitants. The Jerusalemites thought of themselves as the good meat within the "pot" of the walled city, nicely surrounded and protected. But God himself will drive them out (11:7). This city will not be a "pot" for them at all (11:11). The truth of the matter is that the Jerusalemites, whom the exiles were inclined to lionize because they were still *there in Jerusalem,* were extraordinarily arrogant. While the exiles pinned their hopes on them, the Jerusalemites themselves saw the exiles as so much rubbish, people rejected by God and transported far away from the land and the temple (11:14-15). Indeed, God says there is going to be a mighty reversal. True, God did scatter the exiles among the nations. But while they have been away, God himself has been their sanctuary (11:16)—which shows that the temple is not strictly needed for God to be present among his people, to be a "sanctuary" for them. Thus while the Jerusalemites will be destroyed (even as they dismiss the exiles as of no account), God will gather together a remnant from among them (11:17). Ultimately he will put into place a new covenant that will transform them (11:18-20). These themes are taken up in more detail later in the book (e.g., chap. 36).

The vision of chapters 8—11 ends with Ezekiel transported back to Babylon, telling the people everything he has seen and heard. The first strands of hope in this book have been laid out, but not in the categories expected. Jerusalem will be destroyed, and God's purposes for the future center on the exiles themselves. How often in Scripture does God effect his rescue, his salvation, through the weak and the despised!

∾

2 Samuel 3; 1 Corinthians 14; *Ezekiel 12*; *Psalm 51*

∾

THE SUBSTANCE OF **EZEKIEL 12** is easy to understand.

One can imagine the power in Ezekiel's symbol-laden actions. In full view of the exiles, he packs his meager belongings in exactly the same way he would if he were a Jerusalemite preparing for a seven-hundred-mile march into exile. What he could bring would have to be carried on his shoulders. At night he digs through the mud-brick walls of his own house. Probably this symbolizes the futile attempt at breakout made by Zedekiah and those immediately around him (2 Kings 25:4; Jer. 39:4): they fled, but they could not escape. All of this Ezekiel does without saying a word, and then the next morning he delivers his message: "I am a sign to you. As I have done, so it will be done to them. They will go into exile as captives" (12:11)—with further explanations following (12:12-16).

The second symbol-laden action adds a layer to something already in place. So far as his public eating is concerned, Ezekiel is still restricted to the starvation rations imposed in 4:9-17. Now as he eats them, he shudders and puts on a display of terror and despair (12:17-20).

And then the stunning application. The people have heard a lot of prophets, and they have grown so cynical that they are circulating a couple of proverbs: "The days go by and every vision comes to nothing" (12:22); "The vision he sees is for many years from now, and he prophesies about the distant future" (12:27). After all, not only are there false prophets around, but even the true prophets like Ezekiel and (in Jerusalem) Jeremiah keep promising the destruction of the city while years pass with its mighty walls intact. Jeremiah has been at it for decades. Doubtless God sees the long delay as powerful evidence of his forbearance and mercy, providing multiplied opportunities for repentance; the people simply grow cynical. So judgment will certainly fall, Ezekiel says—and the popular proverbs will be destroyed.

Peter applies the same point to Christians, drawing from another Old Testament account. After the warnings began, the Flood was decades coming, and no one was ready for it except Noah and his family. So it is not surprising that in the "last days"—the days between the first and second comings of Christ, the days in which we live—new generations of scoffers arise and make a virtue of the same wretched cynicism: "Where is this 'coming' he promised? Ever since our fathers died, everything goes on as it has since the beginning of creation" (2 Pet. 3:3-4). But the Flood came. And so will the fire.

∾

2 Samuel 4—5; 1 Corinthians 15; *Ezekiel 13; Psalms 52—54*

IN ALMOST EVERY GENERATION there are both true voices and false. How can one discern between the two?

The question cannot be comprehensively answered by referring to only one passage. For instance, Deuteronomy 13 provides one framework that should be carefully thought through, but it is not the only one. Here in **Ezekiel 13** the matter is cast not so much as a set of points to help the righteous discern between true prophet and false, but as a denunciation of all that is false. In so doing God provides at least a partial profile of false prophets.

(1) False prophets speak out of their own spirit, out of their own imaginations. They may think they have something from the Lord, but they do not. "Their visions are false and their divinations a lie" (13:6). This is not so much a principle that the onlooker can use, as a warning to the false prophets themselves. False prophets may deceive other people; they never deceive God. And it is to God that we will one day have to give an account (13:8-9).

(2) They do not deal with the fundamental issues of sin, corruption, injustice, and covenantal faithlessness. To use the metaphor of a walled city, instead of repairing the "wall" they merely cover it with whitewash, so that it looks sturdy enough to the casual observer even though it is hopelessly compromised. "You have not gone up to the breaks in the wall to repair it for the house of Israel so that it will stand firm in the battle on the day of the LORD" (13:5), Ezekiel writes. A good storm strips away the whitewash and discloses the horrible weakness. The false prophets deal in omens and end-times fancies and promises of revival, but they do not declare the holiness of God and the odiousness of sin; they fail to bring people to repentance, faith, and obedience.

(3) They are more interested in auguries, telling personal fortunes, serving as "prophetic" personal hope-spinners, than in conveying the word of the Lord. They are not really serious people—except for their seriousness when it comes to getting paid (13:17-19).

(4) One of the larger effects they have is to discourage the genuine people of God. Too many false voices in a culture and many people become confused, disheartened, disoriented. Instead of maintaining a moral standard that reinforces righteousness, builds character, and encourages godliness, these people pronounce their curses and taboos on people God himself has not condemned, and exonerate the wicked so that they do not turn from their evil ways and so save their lives (13:20-23).

Where in our culture do these characteristics thrive? Where do they thrive in the professing church?

2 Samuel 6; 1 Corinthians 16; *Ezekiel 14; Psalm 55*

∿

THREE OBSERVATIONS FROM **Ezekiel 14**:

First, the peculiar expression "set up idols in their hearts," repeated several times with minor variations in 14:1-8, reeks of duplicity. Publicly there may be a fair bit of covenantal allegiance, but heart loyalty simply isn't there. To set up idols in the heart is to separate oneself from the living God (14:7).

That danger is no less treacherous today than in Ezekiel's time. Somehow we manage to adhere to our creedal profession, but if anything goes wrong our undisciplined rage shows that we maintain little real trust in the living God: our secret idol is comfort and physical well-being. We attend church, but rarely do we pray in private or thoughtfully read the Word of God. We sing lustily at missionary conventions, but have not shared the Gospel with anyone for years. And deep down we are more interested in our reputation, or in sex, or in holidays, than we are in basking in the awesome radiance and majesty of God. Meditate on 14:8, and ask for forgiveness and grace to become more consistent.

Second, those who set up idols in their hearts are the very people most likely to seek out a prophet or a preacher to keep up appearances and secure a little help along the way. But God says, "I the LORD will answer [them] myself in keeping with [their] great idolatry" (14:4). He will "entice" the prophets (14:9-11)—the word might better here be rendered "deceive." God's "deception" of the prophets is part of his judicial sentence. Yet it is a peculiar "deception," for God's revelation is already there in public Scriptures to be read and studied; moreover, he now openly tells the prophets of his judicial hand upon them. If they had an iota of spiritual sensibility, the warning would drive them to self-examination and repentance. But no: the sentence is pronounced, and they are deceived. Such prophets lie to the people, and the people like the lies and listen to them (cf. 13:19).

Third, sometimes judgment becomes so inevitable that not even the presence of the most righteous would delay it any longer (14:12-23). The reasoning presupposes the theology of Genesis 18: God may spare a wicked city or nation for the sake of the just who reside there. But where wickedness overflows, not even the presence of Noah (spared from the Flood), Job (declared "blameless" and "upright," Job 1:1), and Daniel (Ezekiel's contemporary, serving in the Babylonian courts, renowned for his piety) will stay the disaster that God ordains. Indeed, when the exiles see the revolting conduct of the new refugees, they will realize how right God was (14:22-23).

∿

2 Samuel 7; 2 Corinthians 1; *Ezekiel 15*; *Psalms 56—57*

∾

THE SUPERSCRIPTION OF **Psalm 57** specifies that this psalm was written when David "had fled from Saul into the cave" (cf. 1 Sam. 22:1; 24:3). What we find, then, is something of the emotional and spiritual tone of the man when he could say, in effect, that "there is only a step between me and death" (1 Sam. 20:3). Some reflections:

(1) Even as he cries for mercy, David expresses his confidence in God's sovereign power. The language is stunning: "I cry out to God Most High, to God, who fulfills his purpose for me" (57:2). The title "God Most High" is not very common in the Psalms. Perhaps David is thinking of another man without a home, Abraham, who was more familiar with this way of addressing God. Certainly David does not think that somehow circumstances have slipped away from such a God. He begs for mercy, but he recognizes that God, the powerful God, fulfills his purposes in him. This mixture of humble pleading and quiet trust in God's sovereign power recurs in Scripture again and again. Nowhere does it reach a higher plane than in the prayer of the Lord Jesus in the garden: "My Father, if it is possible, may this cup be taken from me. Yet not as I will, but as you will" (Matt. 26:39). In some measure or another, every follower of Jesus Christ will want to learn the anguish and the joy of that sort of praying.

(2) The refrain in 57:5 and 11—"Be exalted, O God, above the heavens; let your glory be over all the earth"—finds David not only in reverent worship, but affirming something believers easily forget, not least when they are under duress. Perhaps the clearest New Testament equivalent lies in the prayer the Lord Jesus taught us: "[H]allowed be your name" (Matt. 6:9). Here David meditates not on God's sovereign power, but on God's sovereign importance. More important, *for David*, than whether or not he gets out of the cave, is that God be exalted above the heavens. The passionate prayer that willingly submerges urgent personal interests to God's glory breeds both joy and stability: "My heart is steadfast, O God, my heart is steadfast; I will sing and make music" (57:7).

(3) Rather striking is David's glance at the orbit where he intends to bear witness: "I will praise you, O LORD, among the nations; I will sing of you among the peoples. For great is your love, reaching to the heavens; your faithfulness reaches to the skies" (57:9-10). No truncated vision, this. And today as countless millions sing these words, David's vow has been fulfilled far more extensively than even he could have imagined.

∾

2 Samuel 8—9; 2 Corinthians 2; *Ezekiel 16; Psalms 58—59*

∾

IF EZEKIEL 15 PICTURES JERUSALEM as a useless vine (imagery that shows up else-where, e.g., Ps. 80; Isa. 5), **Ezekiel 16** pictures Jerusalem as a prostitute.

The language is shocking, horrible—and it is meant to be. The long analogy begins as a rather extreme version of *My Fair Lady*: absolutely everything this woman enjoys, not least life itself, is the direct result of God's gracious interven-tion. But quite unlike *My Fair Lady*, in which the man proves to be an unthink-ing and self-centered manipulator until the "lady" he has created out of a street urchin rebukes him, here God is the One who proves indomitably faithful. Moreover, he is hurt by the ingratitude and betrayal implicit in this lady's constant pursuit of other lovers—i.e., other gods. She proves to be not only "weak-willed" but "brazen" (16:30). Worse, while prostitutes receive a fee for their services, this woman pays others so that she can sleep with them. Israel has not so much been seduced by idolatry or somehow been paid to engage in idolatry, as she has taken the active role and has paid quite a bit so that she can indulge in idolatry, precisely because that is what she *wants* to do.

The analogy is extended to talk about the older sister (the northern tribes, who went into captivity more than a century earlier because of *their* spiritual adul-tery). The Judahites like to think of themselves as superior not only to places like Sodom (proverbial for wickedness) but to the northern tribes; God says that Judah is so bad that by comparison the other two "sisters" look good (16:49-52).

The analogy works for four reasons. (a) It exposes the emotional horror of apostasy. Apostasy as adultery is seen for the betraying, despicable, hurtful, self-ish conduct it really is. The issue is not freedom of religion (any more than adul-tery is freedom from sexual narrow-mindedness), but self-love and inconstancy. (b) Marriage can be seen as a covenantal relationship. Thus breaking the marriage covenant is inevitably reminiscent of breaking the covenant between God and the people he redeemed from slavery in Egypt. In both cases the apostasy/adultery is a flagrant defiance of solemn vows. (c) The imagery taps into a large biblical-theological theme that runs almost the entire way through Scripture: Yahweh is the bridegroom of the bride Israel; Christ is the bridegroom of the church; the ulti-mate consummation is the marriage supper of the Lamb. (d) All covenant-keeping requires the right sort of diligent remembering: re-read 16:43, 60, 61, 63—and reflect on 1 Corinthians 11:23-26.

∾

2 Samuel 10; 2 Corinthians 3; *Ezekiel 17; Psalms 60—61*

∾

A PASTORAL COLLEAGUE OF MINE, Dr. Roy Clements, has preached through a number of psalms under the series title "Songs of Experience." The title is insightful. Though they are full of doctrine, the psalms are not summaries of doctrine. Many of them are, quite literally, songs of experience. In the Psalms, not a few doctrines become firmly planted in our minds, or their implications are worked out in our lives, precisely because they are heated up in the cauldron of experience. To put the matter another way, the existential value of many doctrines is best seen in the way they are worked out in human lives. So there are psalms of hope, of fear, of doubt, of exuberant joy, of forgiveness, of disappointment, of danger, of despair, of solitude, of contemplation. Many psalms plunge from one mood to another.

One of the psalms before us, **Psalm 61**, finds David hungering for the security that only God can give. When the psalm opens, David is apparently suffering from exhaustion or depression (61:2). Perhaps when he penned these lines he was a long way from home: "From the ends of the earth I call to you" (61:2). On the other hand this may simply be a poetic way of expressing how alienated he feels, how far removed from the living God. What he wants, then, is "refuge" (61:3), "a strong tower against the foe" (61:3)—or, in the line that has been incorporated into many hymns, he begs God, "[L]ead me to the rock that is higher than I" (61:2). This conjures up competing images: a rock that will provide shelter to a person beaten down by the sun, a rock that is a craggy redoubt—something far more secure than the man himself can be.

But the following verses show that the security David longs for can never be reduced to physical strength, "a strong tower"—a Maginot Line, a nuclear deterrent, a carrier task force. "I long to dwell in your tent forever and take refuge in the shelter of your wings" (61:4). The prayer for security has become immensely personal: David hungers above all for the presence and assurance of God himself. This God protects his own—and his own are those who have been granted the glorious heritage of fearing God's name (61:5). It is almost as if the precise nature of the security God affords gradually dawns on David. Each verse adds an ever-deepening grasp of the true ground of the believer's security, culminating in this prayer for the king: "May he be enthroned in God's presence forever; appoint your love and faithfulness to protect him" (61:7). No greater security is possible. Small wonder David ends his reflection in unbounded praise (61:8)—as must we.

∾

2 Samuel 11; 2 Corinthians 4; *Ezekiel 18*; Psalms 62—63

∾

THE CASE FOR INDIVIDUAL RESPONSIBILITY is perhaps nowhere in the Bible put more strongly than in **Ezekiel 18**. Yet it is important to understand the passage within its historical and theological context, before attempting to apply it to our own day.

The proverb quoted in verse 2, "The fathers eat sour grapes, and the children's teeth are set on edge," is also found in Jeremiah 31:29, so it must have circulated both in Jerusalem and among the exiles. Apparently some people were using the saying as a cop-out: there was little they could do with their miserable lot, they were saying, since they were suffering for the sins of their fathers, about which they could do nothing. So instead of pursuing justice and covenant renewal, they were using the proverb as an excuse for moral indifference and tired fatalism.

Yet if it is not turned to such sad ends, the proverb does in fact convey some truth. In various ways, corporate responsibility *does* cross generational lines. At the giving of the Law, God himself declares that he punishes the children for the sin of the fathers to the third and fourth generation of those who hate him— though of course this presupposes that these later generations continue to hate him. The preaching of Isaiah, of Jeremiah, and of Ezekiel himself threatens suffering and exile because of the persistent rebellion and idolatry of both preceding generations and the current crop of Israelites. We ourselves know that sin is often social in its effects: for instance, children from backgrounds of abuse often become abusers, children from arrogant homes often become arrogant themselves, or turn out to be broken and bitter. Sin is rarely entirely private and individualistic. The proverb is not entirely wrong.

When Jeremiah counters this proverb, the alternative he presents is eschatological—that is, the proverb will be overthrown in the last days, with the dawning of the new covenant (see meditation for August 3). Ezekiel's point is a little different. God is concerned with every individual: "For every living soul belongs to me, the father as well as the son" (18:3). Moreover, whatever social consequences there are to sin, one must never use the proverb as an excuse to cover current sin. Individual responsibility *always* prevails: "The soul who sins is the one who will die" (18:4). That is the importance of the accounts of behavioral change in this chapter. They are not establishing some simple scheme of works righteousness. Rather, they insist that genuine religion is transforming, and no excuses (hidden perhaps behind a proverb) will suffice. The practical conclusion is found in 18:30-32, which deserves to be memorized.

∾

2 Samuel 12; 2 Corinthians 5; *Ezekiel 19*; *Psalms 64—65*

∾

THE LAMENT FOR ISRAEL'S PRINCES (**Ezek. 19**) is at one level pretty straightforward. The lioness in the opening verses of the psalm is the nation as a whole, which gave birth to the kings. Then as now, the lion was the king of beasts, and so it readily served as a symbol for the royal Davidic line (e.g., Gen. 49:9; Mic. 5:8). In 19:10-14 the nation is the vineyard.

The kings Ezekiel has in mind in each section are pretty obvious. Jehoahaz is the first in view. He was captured and taken to Egypt in 609 B.C. (19:4). Jehoiakim is skipped, but the fate of Jehoiachin is made clear in 19:5-9. He was taken to Babylon in 597 (19:9). The fate of Zedekiah is played out in 19:10-14. If this poem was written about the same time as the surrounding chapters (i.e., about 592 or 591), then of course Zedekiah had not yet been destroyed (587). In that case, this section of the poem is predictive. Alternatively, Ezekiel may have completed the lament after the events of those days.

It is striking that the words do not simply portray the overthrow of a minor power by superior force, but the decline of the line *and even the decline of the nation*. That is part of the picture of the vine in 19:12-14. The nation itself became pathetically weak: "No strong branch is left on it fit for a ruler's scepter" (19:14). The worst irony is that the fire that consumed the vine's fruit "spread from one of its main branches": the allusion is to Zedekiah's rebellion, which in turn attracted the punitive expedition of the Babylonians. This not only put an end to the Davidic line, but virtually destroyed Israel's national identity for many years. Within the theology of Ezekiel's prophecy as a whole, of course, the ultimate cause of Israel's overthrow was God himself, acting in judgment. But here it is clear that the mediate cause of the nation's destruction was within itself.

That is neither the first nor the last time that a nation or an institution was destroyed from within. Readers of history may call to mind the Roman Empire, the Russian years under Communism, certain local churches, Christian universities, confessional seminaries, and on and on. They know that human institutions can never be so safely constructed that outcomes are guaranteed. For the heart of the human dilemma is so deeply rooted in personal sin that no structure can finally reform it. The lament for Israel's princes becomes a lament for the human race, which desperately needs a solution far deeper and more effective than princes, presidents, and structures can ever provide.

∾

2 Samuel 13; 2 Corinthians 6; *Ezekiel 20*; Psalms 66—67

∾

AS IN EZEKIEL 8, WHERE THE elders of the exilic community consult with the prophet, so here in **Ezekiel 20**. As in the earlier instance, God gives Ezekiel something to say to the elders and to the community they represent.

Part of what Ezekiel conveys has been said before. The Sovereign Lord is not too eager to let them consult him when he finds their hearts so distant (20:2-4, 31; cf. chaps. 13—14). There follows a survey of Israel's history of rebellions. But there are two or three themes in this chapter that have either not been introduced before or have been barely mentioned.

The *first* is the sheer glory of God: that is one of God's driving concerns behind the judgments that have fallen and are about to fall. For the sake of his own name God has done what would keep his name "from being profaned in the eyes of the nations in whose sight [he] had brought them out" (20:14; cf. 20:22). This theme is further developed in chapters 36 and 39. It is so central in Scripture that we are in danger of overlooking it precisely because of its familiarity. For instance, when Jesus goes to the cross we are accustomed to thinking about God's love for us in sending so stupendous a gift, or about Jesus' love for us in that he bore our guilt and punishment in his own body on the tree. Well and good. But the Scriptures also insist that the exaltation of Christ is the product of the Father's commitment that all should honor the Son even as they honor the Father (John 5:23; cf. John 12:23). When Jesus goes to the cross, in part he is acting out of sheer loving obedience to his Father (John 14:31; cf. 15:9-11). God's awesome plan of redemption is to the praise of his glory (Eph. 1:3-14). This must shape our understanding of God—and thus our prayer lives and our priorities.

That is also why, in the *second* place, God will not permit his people to be comfortable in their sin. The law was given so that the one who obeys it will "live by" it (20:11, 21, 25; cf. Lev. 18:5)—in this context this means that the one who obeys the Law will prosper. When the people disobey and hunger to be "like the peoples of the world," God vows that what they have in mind "will never happen" (20:32). Instead, God will protect his name, invoke "the bond of the covenant" (20:37) and pour out his wrath (20:33) so that the people will not "live by" the evil statutes they choose: they will not prosper. Years of God's forbearance (whether then or now) must ultimately issue either in transformation or in judgment.

∾

2 Samuel 14; 2 Corinthians 7; *Ezekiel 21; Psalm 68*

∾

PSALM 68 IS ONE OF THE MOST exuberant and boisterous psalms in the Psalter. The opening lines mingle praise and petition that focus on God's justice and compassion (68:1-6). The next verses (68:7-18) picture the march of God from Sinai on—probably on to Jerusalem as the place where the tabernacle would be sited. Some have argued that this psalm was composed to be sung for the joyous procession that brought the ark from the house of Obed-Edom to the city of David (2 Sam. 6:12). Probably verses 24-27 lay out the cavalcade of participants in the procession as they come into view, bringing the ark up to Jerusalem (compare the list with 1 Chron. 13:8; 15:16-28). So great is the glory of the Lord reigning in Jerusalem that all the other nations are envisaged as coming to do homage to him. The psalm ends with an explosive fanfare of praise (68:32-35): "You are awesome, O God, in your sanctuary; the God of Israel gives power and strength to his people" (68:35).

But here I wish to reflect a little further on 68:11: "The Lord announced the word, and great was the company of those who proclaimed it." In the context of this psalm, the "word" that the Lord announced is the word of victory. We are to envisage some such scene as 2 Samuel 18:19ff., where a victorious general announces his victory—only here the victory belongs to the Lord, and he is the One who announces the word. The result is as in 1 Samuel 18:6-7: the streets fill with people who are dancing and singing for joy at the victory. When the Lord announced the word, "great was the company of those who proclaimed it"—and what they proclaimed is found in the following verses.

All of the Lord's victories deserve our praise and our proclamation. That is why the victories envisaged here become a pattern for things to come. When the Lord announces that he will reverse the sanctions imposed on Israel, the good news is to be carried to the ends of the earth: the fleet messengers who convey such good news have beautiful feet (Isa. 52:7; see meditation for June 20). Small wonder, then, that the apostle Paul quotes Isaiah 52:7 with respect to the Gospel (Rom. 10:15): the ultimate end of the exile, the ultimate triumph of God, lies in the Gospel itself. As in the case of the beautiful feet pounding across the mountains to bring the good news, and as in the case of the company of those who proclaimed the word the Lord announced, so also with us (and how much more so!): the only right response to the word of the glorious victory of God in the cross of Jesus Christ is that there be a great company to proclaim it.

∾

2 Samuel 15; 2 Corinthians 8; *Ezekiel 22*; *Psalm 69*

MY CALL TO THE MINISTRY WAS bound up with **Ezekiel 22:30-31**: "I looked for a man among them who would build up the wall and stand before me in the gap on behalf of the land so I would not have to destroy it, but I found none. So I will pour out my wrath on them and consume them with my fiery anger, bringing down on their own heads all they have done, declares the Sovereign LORD."

We should first reflect on this passage in its own textual and historical context. Ezekiel 22 condemns the sins of Jerusalem, this "infamous city, full of turmoil" (22:5). In particular, it focuses on the sins of the leaders—the kings and princes, the priests, the prophets—and shows the ways in which their sins have brought ruin to the people as a whole. In any declining culture much of the declension comes about by leaders and preachers who are self-serving or even rapacious, corrupt, and perhaps vicious, people who are far more interested in retaining power than in serving, people who devote more attention to the "spin" they will give to public answers than to the truthfulness of their answers. Pretty soon the entire fabric of the culture unravels. Corruption is soon tolerated, then expected. Cynicism becomes the order of the day. More and more people do more and more of what they think they can get away with. Integrity becomes so rare it is newsworthy.

That is what happened to the ancient kingdom of David. When God says he sought for a man to build up the wall and stand in the gap before him on behalf of the land so that he would not have to destroy it (22:30), in part he is picking up the imagery already deployed in chapter 13 with respect to the false prophets (see meditation for September 10). But he is also looking for a mediator, a leader like Moses to intercede for the people when they sin (Ex. 32—33), a leader called and equipped to establish righteousness and justice. In Israel at the beginning of the sixth century, he found none. Of course, God had Jeremiah in Jerusalem and Ezekiel among the exiles. But these men were to declare God's word in declining times. Theirs was not the task of rebuilding the wall, of standing in the gap, of averting the wrath of God.

Superficially, of course, one might say that Nehemiah rebuilt the wall, that Ezra reestablished righteousness. But ultimately, only one Mediator would suffice to stand in the gap.

And my call, more than thirty-three years ago? It was complex. I did not understand this passage very well. But the Spirit of God hit me hard with it, and I knew only that I wanted to stand in the gap before him for his people.

2 Samuel 16; 2 Corinthians 9; *Ezekiel 23; Psalms 70—71*

∿

OLD AGE. IT IS NOT SOMETHING our generation likes to talk about very much, at least not in realistic categories. We talk about preparing for retirement, but only with the greatest reluctance do we prepare for infirmity and death. Very few talk about these matters openly and frankly—without, on the one hand, dwelling on them (which shows they are frightened by them), or, on the other hand, suppressing them (which again shows they are frightened by them).

It is much more responsible to learn how to age faithfully, to learn how to die well. This the psalmist wanted. "Do not cast me away when I am old; do not forsake me when my strength is gone. . . . Even when I am old and gray, do not forsake me, O God, till I declare your power to the next generation, your might to all who are to come" (**Ps. 71:9, 18**). From his youth, he knew, God had taught him (71:17). Now he prays against abandonment in old age.

At one level, the psalmist is primarily asking that God will protect him against outside attacks when he is too old and infirm to resist (71:10ff.). This would be a special concern if the author of this particular psalm is David or some other Davidic king. A nearby nation that would not dare attack Israel when David was forty might be emboldened when David was pushing seventy. Though most of us are not kings, it is right and good to ask God for special protection when we grow. so elderly and infirm that it is easy for others to take advantage of us.

But David's vision is more comprehensive than mere protection. He wants so to live in old age that he passes on his witness to the next generation. His aim is not to live comfortably in retirement, but to use his senior years "to declare your power to the next generation, your might to all who are to come." That is a prayer eminently worth praying. Should not senior saints be praying for grace to pass on what they have learned to a new generation? Perhaps this will be one on one, or in small groups. Perhaps one of them will take under his or her wing some young Christian or abandoned waif. Perhaps some experienced prayer warrior will teach a young Christian leader how to pray. And when there is too little strength even for these things, we shall pray that God's grace will so operate in our weakness that God will be glorified in us: perhaps we shall teach younger Christians how to persevere under suffering, how to trust in the midst of pain, and how to die in the grace of God.

∿

2 Samuel 17; 2 Corinthians 10; *Ezekiel 24; Psalm 72*

∽

THE SECOND PART OF EZEKIEL 24 (**Ezek. 24:15-27**) is perhaps the most wrenching passage in the entire book. Elsewhere we catch glimpses of Ezekiel the faithful prophet, Ezekiel the stern witness to the truth of God, Ezekiel the man prepared to act out extraordinary symbol-laden parables. Here we read of Ezekiel the husband. Some observations:

(1) A tiny hint of how Ezekiel viewed his wife peeps through the expression that God uses: "the delight of your eyes" (24:16). If Ezekiel was thirty years of age in the fifth year of the exile (1:1-2), then now in the ninth year (24:1) he could not have been more than thirty-four or thirty-five, and probably his wife was no older. Ezekiel is not the only leader of God's people to suffer devastating personal bereavement. Here he is told in advance that the blow will come (to know in advance is both a blessing and an agony), but he is also commissioned not to grieve: his silence on such an occasion, in a society known for its uninhibited expressions of grief, becomes another symbolic prophetic action.

(2) One can almost feel the massive restraint in the terse words, "in the evening my wife died. The next morning *I did as I had been commanded*" (24:18, italics added). His silence might have been misunderstood as callousness, but in this case not for long. The people know what sort of man he is, and discern that his utter self-restraint carries a message for them (24:19).

(3) Ezekiel conveys to the people the significance of his silence (24:20-24). The delight of their eyes, their heart's desire, that on which they still pin their hopes, is the city of Jerusalem. From there, they have thought, God will break out and rescue them. But Jerusalem will be taken away, just as Ezekiel's wife has been taken away. And when this happens, they are not to weep any more than Ezekiel has mourned the death of his wife.

What does this mean? (a) Some think this is a condemnation of the people: they are so callous and insensitive that they will not bother to mourn the fall of the city. This interpretation is entirely out of tune with the book as a whole. (b) Others think that the tragedy of Jerusalem's destruction is too deep for any expression of grief to be appropriate. That is possible, but Ezekiel is not silent because of the depth of his loss but because of the command of God. (c) It may be, then, that the people are here *commanded* not to grieve for the fall of the city, since the judgment is so richly deserved (cf. 14:22-23; 1 Sam. 16:1).

Regarding 24:25-27, reflect on 3:26-27 and 33:21-22.

∽

2 Samuel 18; 2 Corinthians 11; *Ezekiel 25; Psalm 73*

∾

EZEKIEL 25—32 PRESERVES Ezekiel's oracles against the nations. If Yahweh is the God of the whole earth, it is not surprising if he has things to say to individual nations other than Israel, quite apart from what he says to all nations without distinction. Certainly there is ample evidence that God holds all nations responsible for the sins they commit on the grand scale—he may not hold them responsible for the details of the Law of Moses, but he is certainly ready to impose judgment where there is arrogance, cruelty, aggression, covenant breaking, and rapacity. Always that proverb is true: "Righteousness exalts a nation, but sin is a disgrace to any people" (Prov. 14:34).

Four more preliminary observations will orient us to these chapters. (a) The number of nations treated is seven: Ammon, Moab, Edom, Philistia, Tyre, Sidon, and Egypt. The same number of nations appears in Amos. These oracles may have been uttered over an extended span of Ezekiel's ministry, but their gathering in this way into seven, and only seven, suggests the number itself is symbolic: God speaks to all the nations. (b) Intriguingly, Babylon is not included. Probably that is because Babylon is God's agent in crushing all of these nations. (c) By far the majority of the space is given over to the condemnation of Tyre, at that point a powerful city-state made awesomely wealthy by her trade. After Nebuchadnezzar finished with Jerusalem, the next city he successfully besieged was Tyre—and that siege lasted thirteen years. Undoubtedly the exiles would be interested to hear whether or not a city like Tyre would be held accountable in the same way that Jerusalem was. (d) From a literary point of view, the collection of these oracles into one group, squeezed between chapter 24 and chapter 33 (when the news of Jerusalem's fall arrives in Babylon), has the effect of heightening the dramatic tension. The first two dozen chapters of Ezekiel colorfully specify what God will do. Then, before unveiling the outcome, this book records that God's justice will be meted out on all the nations. And then comes the report of what has happened to Jerusalem.

The burden of **Ezekiel 25**, with its oracles against the first four nations (all of them small states around Judah) contains a salutary lesson. When the mighty Babylonian army finally attacked and destroyed Jerusalem, these nearby states joined in the final assault. Probably in part they were trying to win the favor of Babylon. They were also trying to demolish Judah. Their heartless gloating and arrogant vengeance is an abomination to the Lord, and they will pay for it. Reflect on the implications.

∾

2 Samuel 19; 2 Corinthians 12; *Ezekiel 26; Psalms 74*

∾

IT IS APPROPRIATE TO REFLECT ON **Psalm 74** at this stage of our reading of the major prophets. It sounds as if it was written at a time of national disaster, perhaps the devastation of 587 B.C. (compare Pss. 79, 137; Lam. 2:5-9). The worst blow of all is that all the prophets are silent (74:9). Then suddenly in the midst of the gloom and havoc is a breath of praise (74:12-17), before the darkness descends again (74:18-23). The interruption is dramatic, and reinforced by a sudden switch from the first person plural ("we," "us") to the first person singular: "But you, O God, are *my* king from of old" (74:12). Noteworthy features include:

(1) The anguish of this chapter emerges out of faith, not skepticism, still less cynicism. These people know God, but cannot see what he is doing. They are not so much protesting his punishment of them as its duration: they act as if they know the punishment is deserved, but is it open-ended? Is there no relief? "Why have you rejected us *forever,* O God?" (74:1). "Turn your steps toward these *everlasting* ruins" (74:3). "*How long* will the enemy mock you, O God? Will the foe revile your name *forever*?" (74:10).

(2) There is a powerful emphasis on God's "remembering"—or, more precisely put, on appealing to God to remember. It is not as if the psalmist thinks something may have slipped God's mind, and that he must be reminded of a few basics which, under the press of ruling the universe, he may have accidentally overlooked. The appeal to God to remember is explicit in 74:2, 18, 22 and implicit often—e.g., "Have regard for your covenant" (74:20). These passages provide some insight into what this "remembering" means: it is an appeal to God to act in the light of his ancient covenantal association with his people, the people he "purchased of old" (74:2), the tribe of his inheritance that he himself redeemed (74:2). It is a plea that, in the midst of wrath, he would "remember" mercy.

(3) Verses 4-8 sound as if they arise from an eyewitness view of the temple being destroyed, from a memory indelibly etched with sorrow. This was the place, the psalmist tells God, "where you met with us" (74:4). The following verses are nauseous with grief.

(4) Now, perhaps, we are better placed to reflect on the role of verses 12-17 in the psalm. Precisely when there seems little hope, it is most important for individual believers to recall the power of God both in creation (74:16-17) and in redemption (74:13-15). How should such a stance work out in our lives?

∾

2 Samuel 20; 2 Corinthians 13; *Ezekiel 27*; *Psalms 75—76*

∽

THE STRUCTURE OF PSALM 76 has an elegant simplicity, with a theological lesson I shall spell out at the end of this meditation. The first six verses recall a great deliverance, a concrete historical event; the final six verses paint a picture on a cosmic scale, with every prospect that God will triumph no less in this domain.

The historical particularity of the first six verses is clear in the first two: "In Judah God is known; his name is great in Israel. His tent is in Salem [an alternative name for Jeru*salem*, Gen. 14:18; Heb. 7:2], his dwelling place in Zion [the fortress on the hilltop that David captured]" (76:1-2). The focus, then, is on Jerusalem, the city where God disclosed himself. The reference to "tent" may suggest that the tabernacle was still standing, the temple not yet built. Alternatively, the temple was built, but "tabernacle" language was still being used of it because that was the terminology used in the Mosaic covenant. This city, in any case, was where God "broke the flashing arrows" (76:3, literally, "thunderbolts," cf. 78:48) and other weapons of war. Verses 4-6 suggest a dramatic and sudden rescue like that when Sennacherib's army was destroyed overnight by the angel of the Lord (Isa. 37:36; see meditation for June 5). God himself declared, "He will not enter this city or shoot an arrow here" (Isa. 37:33). Compare: "[N]ot one of the warriors can lift his hands."

The rest of the psalm paints with a broader brush. Now God reigns not from Jerusalem, but from heaven (76:8). The lessons from the first six verses are universalized: "You alone are to be feared. Who can stand before you when you are angry?" (76:7). Verse 10 is notoriously difficult to translate. The "wrath" of the first line could either be God's (hence the NIV), or that of the people (hence NIV footnote). The two notions may not be that far apart. If it is the "fierceness of man" (Coverdale) that turns to the praise of God, it does so in this context because God has the last word and replies in judgment—though it is also true that God operates with such providential wisdom that he can turn the wrath of human beings to serve him even under the most extraordinary conditions (Acts 2:23). What is clear from the closing verses is that God rules over all, and none can stand against him.

Thus the structure of the psalm mirrors in some respects the structure of the entire biblical plot-line, authorizing contemporary readers to see in old covenant narratives of grace and judgment portraits of the ultimate self-disclosure of God in grace and judgment.

∽

2 Samuel 21; Galatians 1; *Ezekiel 28*; *Psalm 77*

∾

THE LONG PROPHECY AGAINST THE city-state of Tyre culminates in this prophecy against Tyre's king (**Ezek. 28:1-19**). Historically, the king in question was Ithobal II. Yet it is clear from the chapter before us that the focus is not so much on a particular monarch as on all he represents.

The charge constantly repeated is that the king of Tyre says in his heart, "I am a god" (28:2, 6, 9). The context shows that the issue is not that the individual monarch is making some sort of monstrous personal and ontological claim, as that the king, typifying the attitude of Tyre as a whole, is immensely self-confident, proud of fabulous commercial success and, in consequence, fiercely independent. There is no sense of personal weakness or need, still less any lingering sense of dependence upon the God who made them and who providentially rules over them. The heart of the issue is easily summarized: "By your great skill in trading you have increased your wealth, and because of your wealth your heart has grown proud" (28:5).

The iniquitous dimensions of the arrogance are highlighted by the many allusions back to Genesis 2—3 (clearer in Hebrew than in English translation). They thought of themselves as being in Eden, the garden of God (28:13), as being God's guardian cherub (28:14), but they will be expelled (28:16). In other words, their sin is of a piece with that of Adam and Eve. They, too, wanted to be like God, independent, knowing good and evil themselves without anyone (not even their Maker!) to tell them. In both cases the result is the same: ruinous disaster, death, catastrophic judgment. There is but one God, and he rightly brooks no rivals.

This is a pretty obvious summary of the passage. But we must think through what this says to any culture or country or church that is hooked on wealth today. Of course, very poor people can be materialistic, in the sense that material possessions are what they most want. Materialism is not the exclusive preserve of the rich. But the focus here is on the wealthy, whose possessions have made them proud. They are above the common folk, above other nations that are impoverished or dispossessed. At what point does the famous line of the Lord Jesus bite into us hard: "You cannot serve both God and Money" (Matt. 6:24)?

The fact that America is the sole surviving superpower has bred more than a little arrogance. Countless pundits have argued, reasonably enough, that the moral indifference to presidential lying is to be attributed to a strong economy more than to anything else. So how far and how long will God let us go if there is not broad and deep repentance?

∾

2 Samuel 22; Galatians 2; *Ezekiel 29*; *Psalm 78:1-39*

∾

IN SOME WAYS THE PROPHECY AGAINST Egypt (**Ezek. 29**) is akin to the prophecies against other nations mentioned in this section of Ezekiel (chaps. 25—32). The repetition of themes should signal us as to how important God judges them to be, e.g., the wickedness of arrogant self-confidence and the boasting of independence (29:3, 9). But in addition there are several fresh elements here worth pondering.

(1) Egypt is charged with being "a staff of reed" that could not provide the support she promised. When people tried to lean on her, the reed splintered and tore their flesh (29:6; cf. Isa. 36:6 = 2 Kings 18:21). Neither individuals nor nations should promise what they cannot deliver.

(2) Like Israel (and a lot of other nations, for that matter), Egypt would be defeated and a significant part of its population would go into exile (29:12). Just as the Israelites would be permitted to return to their homeland under the more lenient policies of the Persians, so also a lot of other exiles would be permitted to return to their respective homelands. Not least among them would be the Egyptians (29:13). This is Yahweh's doing: "I will gather the Egyptians from the nations where they were scattered."

(3) Nevertheless, God insists that Egypt will never again be a great power (29:14-16). If he is the God who can raise up nations and put them down, he has every right to make these assignments. Some ancient powers have virtually or entirely disappeared: the Hittites, the Assyrians, the Babylonians. The Egyptians are still here, but God says he will make them weak so that they will "never again rule over the nations" (29:15)—and will never be relied on by nations like Israel (29:16).

(4) One of the most intriguing "behind-the-scenes" reasonings is found in 29:17-20. Nebuchadnezzar of Babylon is going to succeed against Tyre, but it will be a hard campaign and with little profit. So God will give Egypt to Babylon, in part to pay off Babylon for its long and costly years against Tyre. "I have given him Egypt as a reward for his efforts because he and his army did it for me, declares the Sovereign LORD" (29:20). Not for a moment should one think that any of the nations acted out of conscious obedience to the Lord (cf. Isa. 10:5ff!). But the Lord is no one's debtor, and these are the arrangements that Almighty God is making.

We would not know these things apart from revelation, of course. But they warn us against pontificating too loudly about what is going on in our day, when we see so little of the big picture as to what God himself is doing.

∾

2 Samuel 23; Galatians 3; *Ezekiel 30*; Psalm 78:40-72

∾

THE MAY 25 MEDITATION IN the first volume of this two-volume set focused on **Psalm 78:40-72**, especially on verses 40-41: "How often they rebelled against him in the desert and grieved him in the wasteland! Again and again they put God to the test; they vexed the Holy One of Israel" (cf. also 78:56). The repeated failures of the covenant community were cumulatively a defiance of God that put him to the test, until he responded in anger: "He was very angry with his inheritance" (78:62). That is a powerful theme in the psalm. But there is another side to this theme that one should think about.

The closing verses of the psalm (78:65-72) picture the Lord rousing "as from sleep" (78:65), beating back his enemies. What did he do? He did not choose "the tents of Joseph" (though Joseph had been the governor of Egypt). Rather, "he chose the tribe of Judah." "He chose David his servant and took him from the sheep pens" (78:70); indeed, he chose "Mount Zion, which he loved. He built his sanctuary like the heights, like the earth that he established forever" (78:69). "And David shepherded them with integrity of heart; with skillful hands he led them" (78:72).

But you and I are today reading these lines while at the same time reading Ezekiel, and we know that David's line provided little enduring stability. Within two generations the Davidic dynasty lost the northern ten tribes, and its history from that point to the exile turned out to be as fickle and as repulsively wicked as anything described in this psalm, which scans the period from the Exodus to the beginning of the Davidic dynasty. In other words, this psalm looks back on the debris of failure and the well-deserved wrath of God, but sees the appointment of David and the choice of Zion as spectacular marks of God's grace and goodness, an encouraging basis for stable faithfulness in the years ahead. But when we look back from the perspective of Ezekiel or Jeremiah, we find a still longer string of failures and still more well-deserved wrath. So is Psalm 78 simply naive?

At each stage of the Bible's plot-line, in the midst of wrath God intervenes in mercy. The human race was sliding into a miasma of sin, so God chose Abraham. In the debauchery of the twelve sons, God chose Joseph. In the abyss of Israelite slavery, God chose Moses. In desperate cycles of rebellion, God raised up the judges. Each step marked glorious hope. And now God raises up David. But living as we do three millennia later than David, we look back and breathe our profound thanks for how God disclosed himself "in these last days" (Heb. 1:1-4)—in the finality of his Son.

∾

2 Samuel 24; Galatians 4; *Ezekiel 31*; Psalm 79

∾

ON THE FACE OF IT, PSALM 79 depicts the outrage bound up with the fall of Jerusalem in 587 B.C. Before we reflect on a few of its themes, we should pause to ask how both Psalm 78 and Psalm 79 can purport to come from Asaph. Psalm 78 was clearly written at the beginning of the Davidic dynasty; Psalm 79 was apparently written four-and-a-half centuries later, at the destruction of Jerusalem. So how can they both be psalms of Asaph? The Asaph we know was a contemporary of David.

The best guess is that the dozen psalms attributed to Asaph were variously written either by him or by the choir he founded. Just as some psalms are attributed to "the sons of Korah" (presumably another musical foundation), so also in this case.

Here Asaph does not question the justice of God's burning "jealousy" (79:5), but (as in Ps. 74; see meditation for September 23) its duration: "How long, O LORD? Will you be angry forever?" (79:5). Note how some of Asaph's themes mesh with what we find in the prophets.

(1) "Pour out your wrath on the nations that do not acknowledge you, on the kingdoms that do not call on your name" (79:6). But the major prophets insist, as we have repeatedly seen, that the pagan nations will also be held accountable by God. They are not given a free pass. Meanwhile believers should always recall God's words to his people through Amos (3:2): "You only have I chosen of all the families of the earth; *therefore I will punish you for all your sins*" (italics added). In a world under the curse, Christians too must grasp that punishment that steers us back toward repentance can only be a good thing (cf. Heb. 12:4-13).

(2) "Do not hold against us the sins of the fathers" (79:8): review Ezekiel 18 (see meditation for September 15).

(3) "[M]ay your mercy come quickly to meet us, for we are in desperate need" (79:8). Such a plea simultaneously asks for the only help that can save us, *and reflects the attitude of dependence and trust so utterly lacking in the defiant rebellion and self-reliance that brought down the judgment in the first place.*

(4) "Help us, O God our Savior, for the glory of your name; deliver us and forgive our sins for your name's sake" (79:9). Once again there is no attempt to whitewash the sins. The appeal is to God's glory, so that pagan nations will not conclude that God is too weak or fickle to save his people (79:10). How much of the driving force behind contemporary evangelical praying is motivated by a passion for the glory of God?

∾

1 Kings 1; Galatians 5; *Ezekiel 32; Psalm 80*

∾

PROBABLY PSALM 80 WAS WRITTEN BY Asaphite singers at another time of national disaster—when the Assyrians captured the northern kingdom, destroyed its capital, and exiled many of its people. The shock felt by the godly remnant in Judah must have been considerable. It accounts for the refrain, "Restore us, O God" (80:3, 7, 19; cf. v. 14).

Perhaps the most striking feature of this psalm is the peculiar use it makes of the extended vine imagery (80:8-18):

(1) We have often seen Israel portrayed as a vine: see, for instance, the meditation for May 7 (on Isa. 5). In the most dramatic of these passages, Israel is a vine that God carefully planted and nurtured, but sadly it produced only bad fruit. The vine ultimately proved so disappointing that in due course God resolved to destroy it.

(2) But here the emphasis is not on the terrible quality of the vine's fruit (though that is presupposed), but on the wretched condition of the vine now that the Lord himself has broken down the protecting wall he had built around it. God himself brought the vine out of Egypt, planted it, nurtured it, and watched it spread from the (Mediterranean) Sea to the (Euphrates) River (80:8-11). "Why have you broken down its walls so that all who pass by pick its grapes?" (80:12). Even the wild beasts from the forest trample it and ravage it (80:13).

(3) So the appeal is that God would have compassion on his own vine. Without dwelling on *why* God broke down the protecting wall—though Asaph recognizes that it is God's smoldering anger (80:4), God's righteous rebuke (80:16)—the psalmist makes a frankly emotional appeal to God to protect the vine that he himself has nurtured and protected: "Watch over this vine, the root your right hand has planted" (80:14-15).

(4) Interlaced with this theme is a reference to the "son" God raised up for himself (80:15). The Hebrew word can refer to a branch or a bough (as in Gen. 49:22), but in this poem it is also preparing the way for 80:17. Probably in the first instance we are to detect a reference to Israel, a reference stemming from Exodus 4:22: "Israel is my firstborn son, and I told you, 'Let my son go, so he may worship me.'" The psalmist pleads for compassion for God's "son." Even in verse 17 the "son of man" and the man at God's right hand, i.e., God's firstborn, envisage, in the first instance, Israel.

In the larger horizon, the ultimate answer to these petitions of Asaph would come when the true vine (John 15), the ultimate Son of Man, emerged from Israel.

∾

1 Kings 2; Galatians 6; *Ezekiel 33*; *Psalms 81—82*

∾

EZEKIEL 33 MARKS A TURNING POINT in the book. Chapters 33—37 record oracles related to the fall of Jerusalem. Although the warnings and calls for repentance continue, one now hears a rising note of comfort. As long as the exiles found it difficult to believe that Jerusalem *could* fall, Ezekiel was full of warning. Once the fall has taken place, God in his mercy gives Ezekiel words that will comfort the exilic community, nurture their faith, and steel their minds and wills.

Before that turning point arrives, the first half of the chapter returns to a theme first introduced in 3:16-21: Ezekiel the watchman. The theme returns because Ezekiel now begins a new phase in his ministry. In a sense, he is being recommissioned. At the same time, the news he is about to deliver regarding the fall of Jerusalem provides the people with a new opportunity to repent and trust God. So the first half of the chapter (33:1-20) divides naturally into these two themes. On the one hand, God reminds the prophet of his awful responsibility as a watchman (33:1-9). He is committed to standing somewhat apart from his fellow exiles. He must keep a vigil, listen to God, and proclaim faithfully what God tells him to say, warning of judgments to come and eliciting faith in God's faithfulness. On the other hand, the people are called to respond to the watchman's warnings (33:10-20). They are neither to trust their own righteousness nor to slide into fatalism. The appropriate response is *always* to heed God's watchman, for God himself is the One who declares, "As surely as I live . . . I take no pleasure in the death of the wicked, but rather that they turn from their ways and live. Turn! Turn from your evil ways! Why will you die, O house of Israel?" (33:11).

So the news arrives: Jerusalem has fallen (33:22). Ezekiel is now released from the silence God earlier imposed: he can converse openly and can say things other than what was given to him as a prophet. But all that he says in the rest of this chapter are more words from the Lord. He has two themes. (a) Regarding the people left among the ruins of Jerusalem, they are ever the optimists. They think they will reestablish themselves, even though they have not renounced their sins. So God will continue his chastening until there is only desolation, so that they will learn that he is the Lord (33:23-29). (b) As for the exiles whom Ezekiel addresses directly, they have learned to enjoy listening to him, as one enjoys listening to a gifted orator—but they have not learned to repent.

Where are the closest analogies to such stances today?

∾

1 Kings 3; Ephesians 1; *Ezekiel 34; Psalms 83—84*

∾

"SHEPHERD" WAS A COMMON METAPHOR for "king" in the ancient Near East, not least in the Old Testament (cf. Isa. 44:28; Jer. 10:21; 23:1-6; Mic. 5:4, 5; Zech. 11:4-17). The shepherd provided not only care and nurture for the sheep, but leadership, medical attention, and defense against foes. Doubtless it was an excellent metaphor to apply to hereditary monarchs who might be tempted to think of their calling in terms of power and privilege but not in terms of responsibility. Conversely, when David confesses that the Lord is his shepherd (Ps. 23:1), the metaphor includes the notion that God is king. The sheep pass under the rod (Ps. 23:4—the same word used for royal scepter).

The chapter (**Ezek. 34**) begins with a scathing denunciation of the shepherds who have been leading Israel (34:1-10). The charges are basically two. (a) They have been greedily fleecing the sheep, exploiting the flock to make themselves comfortable and rich, but they have not nurtured and cared for the sheep entrusted to them (34:2-4). (b) Far from protecting the sheep by keeping them in one flock, the conduct of the shepherds has led to the sheep being "scattered" (34:5-6)—a term that signals the exile. So what God will do is ensure that these false and dangerous shepherds will never have charge of the sheep again (34:7-10). It is difficult not to detect in these lines the demise of the Davidic dynasty as then understood, along with the Levitical priesthood.

What God will put in their place is—himself. He will himself come to shepherd his sheep. Read the moving lines from verse 16 on, and count the number of times God says "I will . . ." or "I myself will . . ." Not only will he protect the flock (34:10-16), he will also exercise judgment *within* the flock (34:17-22), for inevitably some sheep are corrupt or bullies. The flock will be purified not only of its greedy leadership but also of its wicked members, not least the "fat" sheep who butt the others away from plenty.

Suddenly the language changes. All along God has been declaring that he himself will shepherd his flock. Now he says, "I will place over them one shepherd, my servant David, and he will tend them; he will tend them and be their shepherd. I the Lord will be their God, and my servant David will be prince among them. I the LORD have spoken" (34:23-24). Indeed, the promised reformation will bring a transforming new covenant (34:25-31). This covenant will be effective (that is what "covenant of peace" suggests).

A transforming shepherd who is both Yahweh and someone in David's line? Meditate on John 10.

∾

1 Kings 4—5; Ephesians 2; *Ezekiel 35; Psalm 85*

∾

ONE MIGHT WELL ASK WHY EDOM should be specially denounced in **Ezekiel 35**. Doesn't this material belong in chapters 25—32? Shouldn't this passage be connected with the brief denunciation of Edom in 25:12-14? The easiest solution, of course, is to suppose that this is a late interpolation (which is what some critics allege). But that simply knocks the question back: why was the interpolator such an idiot? Moreover, if we can find reasons why the location of this chapter makes sense, then of course it makes sense if placed here in the original text.

Formally, Ezekiel 35 preserves some of the structure of the denunciations in chapter 34: "because . . . therefore" (e.g., 35:5-6, 10-11). More importantly, of all the neighboring nations Edom was in one respect a special case. The nation of Edom was descended from Esau, and the old rivalry between Jacob and Esau was passed down into the rivalry between Israel and Edom, two nations of relatives divided by a common animus. Edom is not specifically mentioned in this chapter, of course; the reference instead is to Mount Seir (35:2)—i.e., the mountain region east of the Arabah, the valley running south from the Dead Sea. There they harbored their "ancient hostility" (35:5). But the four references to "blood" in this chapter (Hebrew *dam*) may be a deliberate pun on the unmentioned word *Edom,* as a way of pointing out that Edom's callous treachery was all the more repugnant because of the degree of kinship they sustained with Israel. When Jerusalem was on the verge of collapse, Edom hoped that it could profit from the destruction of the "two nations" (35:10, Israel and Judah) for territorial aggrandizement. Probably they tried to trade support for Nebuchadnezzar for the promise of territorial gain. Above all, their gloating over their fallen rivals (35:12-15) is in God's perspective nothing less than defiance of the Lord himself: "I the LORD was there" (35:10), God declares; "You boasted against me and spoke against me without restraint, and I heard it" (35:13), God warns. In fact, part of the restoration of Israelite exiles to the land will involve making it safe for them: the land must be rid of the "wild beasts" (34:25) that have ravaged it. If this subtly alludes to the surrounding tribes that tried to move in, this prophecy of the destruction of Edom is suitably placed here (see also tomorrow's meditation.)

Thus quite apart from implicit warnings against nurtured bitterness and feud-like vendettas, this chapter also implicitly reassures the covenant people of God of his continuing commitment to their good—including the destruction of their enemies. What New Testament passages preserve the same tune, transposed to the key of the new covenant?

∾

1 Kings 6; Ephesians 3; *Ezekiel 36; Psalm 86*

∾

JUST AS IN CHAPTER 35 God through Ezekiel addresses Mount Seir (the region of the Edomites), so in **Ezekiel 36** he addresses the mountains of Israel (36:1-15). This rhetorical device has the effect of linking chapters 35 and 36 together, not least since Edom is again specifically singled out (36:5; see yesterday's meditation). The first part of the address to the mountains of Israel condemns the enemies who have ravaged and plundered them, not least Edom (36:1-7); the second half (36:8-15) foresees a time when the mountains will be prosperous again. The promise that the mountains will once again be fertile and densely populated is exactly the opposite of the curse pronounced against Edom (35:3, 7, 15).

As if thus addressing the mountains of Israel brings with it the danger that the Israelites will start thinking of themselves as mere victims and not as sinners calling down devastation on themselves, God provides a short historical review (36:16-21). Its purpose is to reiterate that God poured his wrath on the land because the covenant people themselves were so wicked. They themselves "defiled it by their conduct and their actions" (36:17).

But to a watching pagan world it looked as if the God of Israel was not able to protect his own people. So because God is committed to showing his holiness among the nations of the world, before whom the covenant people have profaned it, God will take action. He will not do so for the sake of the house of Israel (36:22)—i.e., as if they deserved it—but for his own name's sake (36:22-23). And what action will he take to vindicate his glory? *First,* he will physically return the exiles to their native land (36:24). *Second,* he will follow this up with powerful moral and spiritual changes. The sprinkling with clean water (36:25) means more than forgiveness of sins. The language derives from ritual washings (Ex. 30:17-21; Lev. 14:52; Num. 19:17-19), but here it is tied to cleaning up the people from the dirt of idolatry. The gift of a "new heart" and a "new spirit" does not suggest mere aspects of human personality, but the transformation of all of human character. This is the equivalent of Jeremiah's promise of a new covenant (Jer. 31:31ff.); its language is taken up by the Lord Jesus in his description of the new birth (John 3); the transformation is described by Paul (e.g., Rom. 8). This is what drives genuine repentance (Ezek. 36:31-32).

1 Kings 7; Ephesians 4; *Ezekiel 37*; *Psalms 87—88*

∾

SINCE THE ANNOUNCEMENT OF the fall of Jerusalem, Ezekiel has been promising new leadership, a restoration to the land, and moral and spiritual transformation. But just as his earlier announcement of the fall of Jerusalem was met with considerable skepticism, so now his announcement of blessings to come meets with the same. Their nation is shattered, their cities destroyed, and many of their people are scattered abroad, living as exiles in foreign lands. It is hard to detect even a glimmer of hope. They cry, in effect, "Our bones are dried up and our hope is gone; we are cut off" (37:11). In **Ezekiel 37**, God provides a vision and an object lesson to engender and nurture that hope.

The *first* is the vision of the valley of dry bones (37:1-14). Ezekiel is shown these "very dry" bones and is asked, "Son of man, can these bones live?" (37:3). The bones represent the Israelites in exile. The northern tribes have been in exile for a century and a half. The exilic community in Babylon where Ezekiel is living has been there a decade. The bones are very dry indeed. First Ezekiel is told to prophesy *to the bones*. Miraculously, the bones come together and are covered with flesh and skin—but we have moved only from skeletons to corpses. Then Ezekiel is told to prophesy to the "breath"(*rûah*, which equally means "Spirit" and "wind"). Now the corpses come to life and stand on their feet—"a vast army" (37:10). In other words, although preaching of itself effects some changes, what is required is the sweeping power of the Spirit of God. Within the metaphorical world, this is nothing less than resurrection from the dead (37:12). The meaning of the vision, however, is that God will pour out his Spirit, and the exile will end (37:14).

The *second* part of the chapter is devoted to the object lesson of the two sticks (37:15-28). The first stick represents Judah; the second represents the northern tribes of Israel. Ezekiel stands for God. As he puts the two sticks together, so God declares that in the promised restoration there will no longer be two kingdoms, but one. "There will be one king over all of them and they will never again be two nations or be divided into two kingdoms" (37:22). Once again, the promise of inner transformation surfaces: "They will no longer defile themselves with their idols and vile images or with any of their offenses, for I will save them from all their sinful backsliding, and I will cleanse them. They will be my people, and I will be their God" (37:23). Most important of all, the promised Messiah will lead them: "My servant David will be king over them, and they will all have one shepherd" (37:24).

∾

1 Kings 8; Ephesians 5; *Ezekiel 38*; Psalm 89

∽

CHAPTERS 38—39 OF EZEKIEL are among the most difficult chapters in the entire book. In many ways they stand apart from what comes before and after. Perhaps the simplest explanation is the following. Chapters 40—48 are so much later than most of the book (the twenty-fifth year of exile, 40:1) that they are almost like an appendix to the rest of the visions and oracles. If so, then chapters 38—39 must be seen as a conclusion to the preceding thirty-seven chapters, but not necessarily as a bridge to chapters 40—48. Precisely how this prophecy against Gog serves as a conclusion to all that comes before it in Ezekiel depends very much on how these two chapters are interpreted. Even to catalog the possibilities would turn these brief meditations into a commentary, so I must largely restrict myself to some tentative conclusions.

It cannot have escaped notice that in several previous chapters I chose not to comment on certain sections. In part this was nothing more than selectivity based on my restricted space. But in part these passages belong to the same genus, and can usefully be thought about together. For instance, 37:25-28 anticipates the time when Israel, under God's servant David, will live in the land "forever," and "David my servant will be their prince forever." God's "sanctuary is among them forever." Such language must either be taken at face value—a temple in Jerusalem, with a Davidic king, the throne and temple enduring forever—or it points beyond itself. For reasons that will become clearer, I am inclined to think that these and similar prophecies look forward to the glorious messianic future, but are largely cast in terms of the familiar categories of the old covenant. These same categories, the New Testament writers insist, have a predictive function fulfilled in Jesus the son of David and all that he brings.

Along similar lines, **Ezekiel 38** begins by denouncing "Gog, chief prince of Meschech and Tubal" (38:3). The suggestion that these names refer to Moscow and Tobolsk is without linguistic merit. The pair of names appears elsewhere (Gen. 10:2; 1 Chron. 1:5; Ezek. 27:13; 32:26) and refers to the known tribes of Moschoi and Tibarenoi. Gog is perhaps to be identified with Gyges, king of Lydia (called *Gûgu* in some ancient records). More importantly, this anticipated horde of opponents to God's people comes from the "far north" (38:6)—which is the direction from which the worst of Israel's foes always came. The chapter ends in apocalyptic imagery (38:18-23)—which begins to make the scene feel like an idealized and final outbreak against the people of God, in which God vindicates his name and his cause. Thus all previous outbreaks anticipate, and are concluded by, this final apocalyptic struggle.

∽

1 Kings 9; Ephesians 6; *Ezekiel 39; Psalm 90*

∽

EZEKIEL 38 BEGINS THE ORACLE against Gog; **Ezekiel 39** continues it. Here Gog's overthrow is narrated again, but in different terms. This is typical of Hebrew semi-poetry. We are not dealing with a separate account of the same thing, which has somehow been stitched onto the first account. Hebrew rhetoric loves to loop around and enlarge on previous statements, even if this conflicts with our Western sense of sequence. Two observations:

(1) There are plenty of hints that these two chapters have moved from a literal or largely prosaic description of battle to the apocalyptic description of the ultimate battle. This does not mean that the ultimate battle is not real. It means that its shape and details cannot be read off the surface of the text. The war implements are the implements of Ezekiel's time ("shields, the bows and arrows, the war clubs and spears," 39:9)—but this battle certainly did not take place in any literal sense in Ezekiel's time, and if it were taking place at the end of history these would not be the instruments of war. Typical of apocalyptic literature, we now have nicely stylized periods of time: seven years (39:9), seven months (39:12, 14). The triumphant Israelites end up eating the flesh and drinking the blood of the mighty men and princes of the earth, who are sacrificed like rams and lambs, goats and bulls (39:17-19). To say that this is merely an evocative way of saying that the opponents will all be defeated is to concede my point: the language is visceral and symbol-laden, and one must proceed with care.

(2) It is God himself who sovereignly brings Gog and his might from the "far north" (39:2) to lead them to destruction. This is both like and unlike an important theme in the major prophets that we have already noticed. The prophets keep saying that the mighty powers (Assyria, Babylon) that chasten Israel and Judah do so under God's powerful sway, even though they are held accountable for their brutality (e.g., Isa. 10:5ff.). The picture here affirms God's sovereignty over these pagan nations, but now he is not using them to chasten the covenant community but to bring them to their own destruction. The biblical book with this theme most clearly worked out is Revelation. Believers are to take encouragement from the fact that even in this world of horrible cruelty and injustice, God will ultimately bring the perverse to final judgment. Justice will not only be done but will be seen to be done. So we do not lose heart. We cherish and nurture the apocalyptic vision, not because it is a prosaic roadmap of impending history, but because it signals the ultimate triumph of God.

1 Kings 10; Philippians 1; *Ezekiel 40; Psalm 91*

∽

APART FROM EZEKIEL 29:17-21, the nine chapters before us, Ezekiel 40—48, take place later than the other visions and oracles that constitute the book. As the book began with a vision, so now it ends with one. Although this vision is sufficiently cut off from the rest of the book that some have labeled it an appendix, nevertheless there are some dramatic connections. In the vision of 8:1—11:25 Ezekiel saw the glory of God abandon the temple; now he witnesses the glory returning and filling the new temple (43:5). In the years following the catastrophic sack of Jerusalem Ezekiel has been comforting the people by the promise of a return to the land and to God; in some ways this vision of a temple must have lent encouragement and hope.

But that does not make this vision an easy one to understand. Today I shall lay out, rather superficially, the flow of thought not only in **Ezekiel 40** but through these nine chapters. Tomorrow I shall lay out four principal lines of interpretation, and indicate the one I think is closest to what this Scripture says.

In the twenty-fifth year of his exile (by which time he was about fifty), Ezekiel in a visionary experience is transported to "a very high mountain" (40:2) near what turns out to be the holy city. Probably Mount Zion is intended. An angelic figure gives him a tour around the temple area, measuring everything as he goes. He begins with a detailed study of the east gate to the outer court (40:6-16). This is followed rapidly by the outer court itself, two other gates to the outer court (north and south), then gates to the inner court (40:17-37). There are no gates on the west, because the temple itself is situated there. After a brief tour of the sacrificial equipment and of the rooms reserved for the sacrificing priests (40:38-47), Ezekiel is given a fairly detailed description of the temple (40:48—41:26), followed by a survey of the temple area with special attention devoted to the rooms for the priests (42:1-20). The glory of God enters the temple, and Ezekiel is told what he must do with this information (43:1-12). The rest of chapter 43 deals with the altar of sacrifice and how it is to be used (43:13-27). Chapters 44 and 45 give regulations for the ordering of the temple (not least with respect to Levites and Zadokites), and then with the distribution of land around the temple. More ritual regulations follow (45:18—46:24). Ezekiel 47:1-12 describes a flow of water from the sanctuary bringing life to the barren Dead Sea valley. The rest of the vision divides up the land for the twelve tribes and specifies the gates of the city.

∽

1 Kings 11; Philippians 2; *Ezekiel 41*; *Psalms 92—93*

∾

ALTHOUGH **EZEKIEL 41** (or, more precisely, 40:48—41:26) is devoted to the description of the temple within the great vision of chapters 40—48, I shall focus attention here on how this chapter, indeed all nine of these chapters, should be interpreted. I shall survey two of the more important options here, and two more tomorrow.

(1) Some hold that this is Ezekiel's vision of what should in fact be built once the exile has ended and some of the people return to the land. In that case chapter 41 provides specifications for the building. The strength of this view is that it follows up on the many passages in this book telling that the exile will end. Nevertheless one has to say that, read as building specs, this chapter is pretty thin (much less detailed, for instance, than the specifications either for the tabernacle or for the Solomonic temple). Moreover, chapter 41 must be read within the framework of chapters 40—48, and as we shall see, there are numerous features that cannot be taken literally. Certainly there is little evidence that those who built the second temple thought they were bound to follow Ezekiel's guidelines.

(2) The mid-twentieth-century form of dispensationalism argued for a similar literalism, but held that the construction of the temple and the return of blood sacrifices and Levitical and Zadokite priesthood will take place in the millennium. The sacrifices would look back to the sacrifice of Christ in the same way that the Old Testament sacrifices looked forward. But it is very difficult to square this view with the theology of Hebrews. Moreover, there are many hints that these chapters should not be taken literally. The division of land (chaps. 47—48) is all but impossible for anyone who has seen the terrain. The impossible source and course of the river (47:1-12) strains credulity—and in any case both the temple and the river of life are given quite different interpretations in Revelation, the last book of the Bible. With the best will in the world it is difficult to see how the prescribed tribal purity of Levitical and Zadokite lines could be restored. Intervening records have been lost, so that no one could prove his descent from Aaron. Presumably a dispensationalist could argue that God could reveal the necessary information. But the point is that the tribes have been so mixed up across the centuries that they *cannot* be unscrambled. The problem is not one of information, but of mixed lines. Thus this interpretation, precisely because it deals with something at the end of time when the tribal lines are no longer differentiable, is even less credible than the previous one.

How, then, shall we interpret these chapters?

∾

1 Kings 12; Philippians 3; *Ezekiel 42; Psalm 94*

∾

THE DESCRIPTION OF THE TEMPLE (Ezek. 41) is followed by a description of rooms reserved for priests (**Ezek. 42**). But I shall press yesterday's discussion a little farther and briefly discuss two more of the ways these chapters have been interpreted.

(3) Many older commentators argued that chapters 40—48 are straightforward symbols of what is fulfilled in the Christian church. There is some truth to this view. It is given impetus when one observes, for instance, that John's vision of the holy city in Revelation is drawn in substantial part from the language of Ezekiel. But the same passages in Revelation spell the weakness of this interpretation. When John uses the language of Ezekiel (or of Daniel or some other Old Testament writer), he regularly transmutes it, or picks up its words and phrases without putting it to exactly the same use. Although John's description of the holy city leans heavily on Ezekiel, John's city has no temple, for the Lord God and the Lamb are its temple (Rev. 21:1—22:5). In that sense, Revelation is not a direct and immediate fulfillment of a string of symbols.

(4) It is better, but messier, to take these chapters as belonging to the borderlands of apocalyptic literature and typology. The symbolism includes numerical features; its future-orientation springs not from mere verbal prediction or simplistic symbolism, but from structures of patterns and events that point forward. We have already glimpsed this sort of thing in chapters 38—39, depicting the final battle, when God sovereignly moves to destroy all his foes. Read this way, chapters 40—48 envisage the messianic future, but in the symbolic categories of Ezekiel's present. The temple is a kind of enactment or incarnation of the presence and blessing of God in the age for which pious Israelites yearned. On this view, the theological themes and pastoral comforts of these chapters include: (a) God's presence remains continuously as the fount of all blessing. (b) God's people are perfectly restored, the perfection of his plan and of their experience bound up with the perfection of symmetry in the building. (c) Because God is perfectly present, fullness of life and fruitfulness flow from God's presence to all the barren places of the earth. This is a transformed universe. (d) The worship of God is central, and undertaken exactly as God demands. (e) Justice and righteousness are the order of the day, seen in the perfect allotment of land and responsibilities.

If this is largely right, the ultimate hope lies at the very end of history—but that end has already invaded history itself, in these last days. The consummation is not yet, but the kingdom has dawned.

∾

1 Kings 13; Philippians 4; *Ezekiel 43; Psalms 95—96*

∾

ALMOST TWENTY YEARS HAVE elapsed since the visionary experience in which Ezekiel saw the glory of the Lord abandoning the temple (Ezek. 10:18-22; 11:22-24). Here in **Ezekiel 43:1-12** he witnesses the Lord's return.

Numerous phrases and clauses remind us that the glory Ezekiel now sees is to be identified with the glory he first saw in the mobile throne vision in Ezekiel 1—3, and with the glory that abandoned the temple and the city in the vision of chapters 8—11. Ezekiel makes the point explicit: "The vision I saw was like the vision I had seen when he came to destroy the city and like the visions I had seen by the Kebar River, and I fell facedown" (43:3).

Within the symbol-structure of the vision, this means that God is manifesting himself among his people once more. They are to respond by being ashamed of their sins (43:10-11) and by conforming perfectly to whatever he prescribes (43:11).

The culmination of this vision *within the book of Ezekiel* is found in the last verse of the book: "And the name of the city from that time on will be: THE LORD IS THERE" (48:35). That is wonderful. Wherever the Lord is, is holy. "Therefore, prepare your minds for action; be self-controlled; set your hope fully on the grace to be given you when Jesus Christ is revealed. As obedient children, do not conform to the evil desires you had when you lived in ignorance. But just as he who called you is holy, so be holy in all you do; for it is written, 'Be holy, because I am holy'" (1 Pet. 1:13-16). John saw a vision of "the Holy City, the new Jerusalem, coming down out of heaven from God" (Rev. 21:2). The voice cried, "Now the dwelling of God is with men, and he will live with them. They will be his people, and God himself will be with them and be their God" (Rev. 21:3).

We must always remember that: The Gospel is not admired in Scripture primarily because of the social transformation it effects, but because it reconciles men and women to a holy God. Its purpose is not that we might feel fulfilled, but that we might be reconciled to the living and holy God. The consummation is delightful to the transformed people of God, not simply because the environment of the new heaven and the new earth is pleasing, but because we forever live and work and worship in the unshielded radiance of the presence of our holy Maker and Redeemer. That prospect must shape how the church lives and serves, and determine the pulse of its ministry. The only alternative is high-sounding but self-serving idolatry.

∾

1 Kings 14; Colossians 1; *Ezekiel 44; Psalms 97—98*

∞

IN THE ANGLICAN *BOOK OF COMMON PRAYER,* **Psalm 98** is known as the *Cantate Domino* ("Sing to the Lord") and is placed between the evening Old Testament reading and its New Testament counterpart. It overflows with exhilarating worship and joy.

The psalm has three stanzas. The *first* (98:1-3) celebrates the "salvation" of God (found in each verse). The word is perhaps more comprehensive than the way it is used today. It includes victory over enemies: this "salvation" or victory was effected by the Lord's "right hand and his holy arm" (98:1). But it also includes what we mean by salvation: God reconciles people to himself and transforms them by his grace. While God "has remembered his love and his faithfulness to the house of Israel" (98:3), the glorious truth is that he "has made his salvation known and revealed his righteousness to the nations" (98:2); "all the ends of the earth have seen the salvation of our God" (98:3). Small wonder, then, we must sing to the Lord "a new song" (98:1). The expression signals not so much a new composition, written for the occasion perhaps, as a fresh response to new mercies showered upon us.

The *second* stanza (98:4-6) responds to the first. The first celebrates God's coming in power and salvation, the second responds to every act of God in exhilarated worship. Indeed, because the full salvation briefly described awaits the consummation, all our acts of worship are an anticipation of the end. We "shout for joy before the LORD, the King" (98:6) as a prelude and an announcement of the consummation of his reign. The instruments listed here were regularly used as part of temple worship (cf. 1 Chron. 16:5-6) or on joyous occasions such as the accession of a new king (e.g., 1 Kings 1:39).

If the praise of the second stanza is carefully put together in orchestrated singing, the praise of the *third* stanza (98:7-9) is inarticulate. But it is no less powerful for being artless. Even now the whole universe declares the glory of God. But if various Old Testament passages anticipate a vast renewing of the created order (Ps. 96:11-13; Isa. 2; 11; 55:11-12), Paul not only anticipates the same but recognizes that the fulfillment depends on the transformation of human beings at the end: "The creation waits in eager expectation for the sons of God to be revealed. For the creation was subjected to frustration, not by its own choice, but by the will of the one who subjected it, in hope that the creation itself will be liberated from its bondage to decay and brought into the glorious freedom of the children of God" (Rom. 8:19-21).

∞

OCTOBER 12

1 Kings 15; Colossians 2; *Ezekiel 45; Psalms 99—101*

∾

SOME OF THE PSALMS ARE grouped into collections. Psalms 93—100 celebrate the kingship and coming of the Lord. Thematically, however, they range from the exuberant exhilaration of Psalm 98 (yesterday's meditation) to a more subdued but profoundly submissive awe. After the unrestrained joy of Psalm 98, there follows in **Psalm 99** a profound reverence. We have moved from a festival of praise to a cathedral.

The psalm divides into two parts. The theme of the *first* is established by the repeated line, "he is holy" (99:3, 5). This does not mean something as narrow as saying that God is good or moral (though it does not exclude such notions). The emphasis is on the sheer "Godness" of God—what makes him different from human beings, what makes him uniquely God. The two instances of the clause "he is holy" are meant to be statements summarizing in each case the preceding lines. (a) The Lord reigns; he is exalted above the mighty cherubim (99:1). Though he manifests himself in Zion, he is no tribal deity: "he is exalted over all the nations" (99:2). "Let them praise your great and awesome name" (99:3)—and then the summarizing refrain, "he is holy." (b) If he reigns over all, he is, supremely, the King (99:4). He is not only mighty, he loves justice and fairness. This has been eminently displayed in his own covenant community: "in Jacob you have done what is just and right" (99:4). There is only one appropriate response before such a God: "Exalt the LORD our God and worship at his footstool" (99:5)—and again the summarizing refrain, "he is holy."

The *second* part of the psalm contemplates the truth that, however exalted and holy he is, God chose to disclose himself to human beings. We may be tempted to think of Moses and Aaron and Samuel as almost superhuman. But the psalmist carefully places them *among* the priests and *among* those who called on his name: they were not fundamentally different from others. Moreover, they were frail and flawed like the rest of us. According to verse 8, God was to them (not "to Israel": the NIV footnote is correct) "a forgiving God," even though he "punished their misdeeds" (here follow the NIV text, not the footnote).

Thus the theme of God's holiness does not end in mere transcendence, but in an unimaginably great God graciously disclosing himself to human beings—even when they rebel against him. We stand in their company. If his holiness is disclosed both in mercy and in wrath, then we are neither to despair of it nor to presume upon it. "Exalt the LORD our God and worship at his holy mountain, for the LORD our God is holy" (99:9).

∾

1 Kings 16; Colossians 3; *Ezekiel 46*; *Psalm 102*

∽

PSALM 102 IS SOMETIMES WRONGLY labeled a penitential psalm. It sounds far more like the cry of a person whose sufferings are unexplained (like those of Job). At the beginning the sorrows are private and personal; later they are eclipsed by a growing concern for Zion. Progress toward Zion's glory seems slow. This fosters a contrast between the psalmist's restricted and fleeting "days" (102:3) and the Almighty's eternal "years" (102:27).

But here I shall focus attention on the final verses of the psalm. Regular Bible readers will recognize that verses 25-27 are quoted in Hebrews 1:10-12, with God addressing the Messiah, in effect giving him divine status. One may well ask how the writer of Hebrews construed the Old Testament text in this way.

The answer turns in part on the fact that the original Hebrew of the Old Testament was composed with what today we call consonants. Vowels were not included. They were added much later—indeed, the most common vowel system was added to the Hebrew text about one thousand years into the Christian era. Usually this presents no problems. Once in a while, however, it is possible to read the Old Testament consonantal text with a slightly different vowel choice, yielding a different meaning. In this instance there is no question at all about the consonants. But the ancient Greek translation of the Old Testament, the Septuagint, shows how those translators understood the Hebrew—and in this passage they understood it exactly as the Epistle to the Hebrews takes it. The traditional vowel placement, preserved in our English versions, understands verses 23-24 much as in the NIV. The thought is parallel to verses 11-12. But the LXX and Hebrews read it as follows: "He answered him in the way of his strength, 'Declare to me the fewness of my days. Do not bring me up [i.e., summon me to action] in the middle of my days; your years are for generations on end. In the beginning you, Lord, laid the foundation of the earth. . . .'" The implication of this rendering is that God is addressing the psalmist, whom God addresses as Lord and Creator. That is how Hebrews takes it. On this view, the entire psalm is messianic, an oracular psalm like Psalm 110 (see vol. 1, meditation for June 17). Try rereading Psalm 102 that way; it makes sense. Compare the use of Psalm 45 in Hebrews 1 (see meditation for September 4): the Davidic king is addressed as God, and this too is cited in Hebrews 1. But even if the traditional Hebrew vowel assignments are correct, the inferences drawn by Hebrews 1 are not far away, though they must be drawn on quite different grounds.

∽

1 Kings 17; Colossians 4; *Ezekiel 47; Psalm 103*

∾

ONE OF THE LOVELIEST OF THE PSALMS IS **Psalm 103**. I reflected on it in volume 1 (meditation for June 11). Here I want to return to several of its themes:

(1) "The LORD is compassionate and gracious, slow to anger, abounding in love" (103:8). That truth is often expressed in the Old Testament. For example, when the Lord passes before Moses while the latter is hiding in a cleft in the rock, he intones, "The LORD, the LORD, the compassionate and gracious God, slow to anger, abounding in love and faithfulness . . ." (Ex. 34:6). Yet that is not the impression that many readers of the Old Testament have of God. Somehow they think he runs on a short fuse, never very far off from an outburst that can wipe out a nation or two. Why do they have that impression?

Probably in part because they do not read the Old Testament very closely. Or perhaps they read the Old Testament impressionistically: there are all those passages in the prophets where the Lord is threatening judgment, and they can leave a sour taste and a smell of sulfur. But should we not see the Lord's mercy in them? He *delays* judgment, which may be postponed for years or even decades. On the first signs of genuine repentance, he turns from wrath, for the Lord is "slow to anger, abounding in love." Strict justice would be immediate—an easy thing for Omniscience! The truth is that God "does not treat us as our sins deserve or repay us according to our iniquities" (103:10).

(2) "As a father has compassion on his children, so the LORD has compassion on those who fear him; for he knows how we are formed, he remembers that we are dust" (103:13-14). It is almost as if this God is looking for reasons to be as forbearing as possible. But it is also true that a human father is likely to be far more compassionate and forbearing with a son or daughter who "fears" him and basically respects him. Then each confusion or failure or mistake is likely to be treated with more forbearance than the conduct of the son or daughter who is profoundly anarchic. In any case, this heavenly Father knows us better than we know ourselves. Who better than he can tell us what we are made of?

(3) In our guilt before a holy God, what we need most is to be forgiven all our sins (103:3), to have them removed far from us: "as far as the east is from the west [a distance without limit, unlike north to south], so far has he removed our transgressions from us" (103:12). With that assurance, all other blessings of any worth will one day be ours; without the forgiveness of sins, any other blessing we have received is worse than worthless: it may be deceptive.

∾

1 Kings 18; 1 Thessalonians 1; *Ezekiel 48; Psalm 104*

∾

"O LORD MY GOD, YOU ARE VERY GREAT; you are clothed with splendor and majesty." So we read in the opening verse of **Psalm 104**. In this psalm the evidence of the Lord's greatness is bound up with the created order. Some reflections:

(1) In the opening verses (104:1-4) the string of metaphorical touches is revealing. God wraps himself in light; he stretches out the heavens like a tent; he makes the clouds his chariot; he rides on the wings of the wind; he makes winds his messengers. Pantheism merges god with the universe; robust Christian theism not only makes God separate from the universe as Creator is to creation, but in these metaphors suggests that God delights in what he has made. The mood is not only exalted, but almost playful. If pantheism is ruled out, equally there is no scope for deism. The created order is alive with God's presence as he delights in what his hands have made.

(2) In this psalm there is a strong emphasis on the way all of life depends on the sustaining providence of the Almighty. God makes springs pour water down ravines, and in consequence the beasts of the field drink, trees grow, birds of the air nest in the branches (104:10-12). God is the One who makes grass grow for the cattle, and makes other plants for human consumption (104:14). The lions roar and seek their food from God (104:21). As for the sea, with its teeming millions of life forms, "These all look to you to give them their food at the proper time" (104:27). The sheer abundance and diversity of life forms testifies to God's imagination, power, wisdom, and incalculable wealth. Life itself is sustained by God's sanction. If he takes away their breath, they die (104:29-30). The assumption is not the animism of the pagan world. There is an orderliness to the whole (note the rhythm of light and dark, 104:19-24) that makes science possible. But God never withdraws from active, providential rule over every single element of the universe's operation, with the result that it is not only appropriate but essential to confess that all of life is daily dependent on God for its quotidian supply of food.

(3) All the created order elicits delighted and faithful praise from the unnamed psalmist (104:33). There is just a hint that we *ought* to be thinking about God in these terms; we *want* our meditation to be pleasing to him (104:34). And before the closing lines of praise, there is a quiet reminder that despite the glory and beauty of the created order, sin has made this more of a war zone than a museum or a choir (104:35).

∾

1 Kings 19; 1 Thessalonians 2; *Daniel 1;* Psalm 105

ᔀ

"[T]HE THIRD YEAR OF THE REIGN OF Jehoiakim king of Judah" (Dan. 1:1) is calculated on the Babylonian reckoning; the corresponding calculation in Judah would have made it his fourth year, i.e., 605 B.C. The first round of deportations took place, then, in 605, and swept up Daniel; the second, including Ezekiel, Jehoiachin, the Queen Mother, the aristocracy, and skilled craftsmen, occurred in 597. The final crushing destruction of Jerusalem was in 587.

Almost twenty years before that took place, then, a number of aristocratic young Jewish men had been transported to Babylon. According to **Daniel 1**, they were well-treated. The imperial policy was not only generous, it was clever. The empire would pull in these gifted and well-bred young men and give them the best education and social formation in the world, with a string of perquisites to make the prospect still sweeter. In due course they would enter government service, intensely loyal to their benefactors while contributing their youth, skills, and knowledge of the imperial frontiers. The four Hebrew young men mentioned here would eventually become so Babylonian in their outlook that they would forget even their birth names: Daniel would become Belteshazzar, Hananiah would become Shadrach, and so forth.

But Daniel drew a line in the sand. It could have cost him his life. He did not object to the change in his name, nor to royal service on behalf of the Babylonian Empire. But he would not "defile" himself (1:8) by eating food prepared in the royal kitchens. He knew that if he partook, he would almost certainly eat things from time to time that the Law of God strictly forbade. For him it was a matter of obedience, a matter of conscience. In the providence of God, the chief to whom he was responsible, Ashpenaz, was an understanding sort, and the result is reported in this chapter.

For many of us today, Daniel's stand is vaguely quixotic, but certainly not something to emulate. Why die over sausages? Come to think of it, is there *anything* worth dying for? Probably not—if all there is to life is found in our brief earthly span, and all that is important is what happens to me. But Daniel's aim was to please God and to conform to the covenant. His values could not be snookered by Babylon; on this point he was prepared to die. The trouble is that when a culture runs out of things to die for, it runs out of things to live for. A colleague in the ministry (Dr. Roy Clements) has often said, "We are either potential martyrs or potential suicides; I see no middle ground between these two. And the Bible insists that every believer in the true God has to be a potential martyr."

ᔀ

1 Kings 20; 1 Thessalonians 3; *Daniel 2; Psalm 106*

∽

NEBUCHADNEZZAR'S DREAM (DAN. 2) could usefully occupy us for many pages. It provides insight not only into Daniel and his times, but into our times as well.

(1) The pagan Babylonian Empire had its share of astrologers and other fortune tellers. Like thoughtful people in every generation, Nebuchadnezzar had his suspicions about their competence, and put them to this rather brutal test. Anecdotal accounts of "magical" insight cannot withstand this level of analysis.

(2) Daniel's bold approach to the king claims nothing for himself and ascribes everything to God, who knows our thoughts and our dreams. That took courage. Here is the next stage in the development of Daniel's character. The courageous and unshakable old man that Daniel became (Dan. 6) was formed by a young man who obeyed God even in what he ate, and who was so honest that he would not take any credit where none was due. He was committed to faithfulness, humility, courage, and integrity. He has few successors in high places.

(3) Doubtless contemporary psychiatrists would speculate that the colossus in Nebuchadnezzar's dream betrays profound personal insecurity. Megalomaniacal ambition to rule the world may suggest secret doubts about whether or not one has feet of clay. Whatever the means, God uses the vision to disclose something more profound—the future of forthcoming empires.

Most liberals have argued that the four metals—gold, silver, bronze, and iron—represent, respectively, Babylon, Media, Persia, and Greece. After the death of Alexander the Great, the Greek Empire disintegrated into four territories squabbling among themselves—hence the feet of clay. Certainly the later chapters of this prophecy focus not a little attention on that period, and picture the dawning of the messianic kingdom succeeding it. Nevertheless that view is tied up with the theory that at the very least the later chapters of Daniel were written pseudonymously in the second century B.C. Most evangelicals find little evidence to support that stance. Moreover, they point out that there never really was a Median Empire. It is better to speak of the Medo-Persian Empire; the Median element was not much more than a transition team. On that view the four empires are Babylon, Medo-Persia, Greece, and Rome—and during the latter the messianic kingdom delivers the mighty blow that ultimately fells the colossus. That seems to be what Jesus held (Matt. 24:15).

(4) This vision reminds us that in this broken and ambiguous world the people of God nurture a hope for what God will do in the end. Little in the Christian way makes sense without such hope; little in our culture makes much sense without a shared vision toward which to press, a vision that transcends personal fulfillment and selfism.

∽

1 Kings 21; 1 Thessalonians 4; *Daniel 3*; *Psalm 107*

∾

THE IMAGE NEBUCHADNEZZAR SET UP (DAN. 3) was doubtless designed to unify the empire. That is why he ordained that all "peoples, nations and men of every language . . . must fall down and worship the image of gold" (3:4-5). Living as he did in a pluralistic culture where people could with impunity add gods to their personal pantheon, Nebuchadnezzar saw no reason but rebellion or intransigent insubordination for anyone to refuse to worship the image. The threat of the furnace, from his perspective, guaranteed conformity, and the potential political gain was incalculable. Furnaces in Babylon were primarily for the firing of bricks (cf. Gen. 11:3), widely used because suitable building stone was so scarce. Some large brick kilns have been dug up outside the ruins of ancient Babylon. Certainly Nebuchadnezzar would have had no scruples about burning people to death (Jer. 29:22).

The striking exchange in this chapter is between Nebuchadnezzar and the three young men, Shadrach, Meshach, and Abednego, after their first refusal to bow before the image (3:13-18). The emperor's final taunt almost dares any god to come forward: "Then what god will be able to rescue you from my hand?" (3:15). Of course, as a pagan, he lived in a world of powerful but definitely finite gods, and in some instances he certainly felt that he was their equal or even their superior. From the perspective of biblical theism, this is monstrous arrogance.

But it is the answer of the three men that deserves memorizing and pondering: "O Nebuchadnezzar, we do not need to defend ourselves before you in this matter. If we are thrown into the blazing furnace, the God we serve is able to save us from it, and he will rescue us from your hand, O king. But even if he does not, we want you to know, O king, that we will not serve your gods or worship the image of gold you have set up" (3:16-18). Observe: (a) Their basic courtesy and respect are undiminished, however bold their words. (b) They are completely unwilling to apologize for their stance. The wise believer never apologizes for God or for any of his attributes. (c) They do not doubt God's ability to save them, and they say so: God is not hostage to other gods, or to human beings, emperors or otherwise. (d) But whether or not God *will* save them they cannot know—and the point is immaterial to their resolve. Faithfulness is not dependent upon an escape hatch. They choose faithfulness because it is the right thing to do, even if it costs them their lives.

The courage we need in this anti-Christian age is courteous and steadfast. It never apologizes for God. It joyfully believes that God can do anything, but it is prepared to suffer rather than compromise hearty obedience.

∾

1 Kings 22; 1 Thessalonians 5; *Daniel 4; Psalms 108—109*

ONE OF THE REASONS WHY the narratives of **Daniel 4** and Daniel 5 are put side by side, even though they clearly come from two quite different periods of Daniel's life, is that each serves as the foil of the other. Both are accounts of rich, powerful, arrogant men. The first, mercifully, is humbled and therefore spared and transformed; the second is simply destroyed.

Many critics doubt that the account of Daniel 4 is anything more than pious fiction to encourage the Jews. They note that there is no record of Nebuchadnezzar's insanity in the surviving Babylonian records, and they doubt that the empire could have held together had the emperor himself gone mad for a period of time. Neither argument is weighty. Official records would not have talked much of Nebuchadnezzar's period of insanity, and in any case records from the latter part of his life have not so far come to light. Moreover, we do not know exactly how long Nebuchadnezzar was insane: it is uncertain what "seven times" (4:16) means. Certainly the Roman Empire survived under Caligula, whose insanity no one doubts.

In our short space, we may reflect on the following:

(1) Nebuchadnezzar's dream reflects his megalomania. He has a narcissistic personality: he is corroded by his own greatness yet is so insecure that his grandiose fantasies must be nurtured by incessant self-admiration. Unlike the egotist, who is so supremely self-confident that he does not care a rip what anyone thinks of him or her, the narcissist is often hypersensitive and emotionally fragile. Regardless of all psychological speculations, the man's arrogance before God is unrestrained (despite the experience of chaps. 2 and 3), and God resolves to humble him.

(2) Daniel's approach to Nebuchadnezzar, once he has heard the dream, should be studied by every Christian preacher and counselor. On the one hand, he is deeply distressed to grasp what Nebuchadnezzar is going through, or going to go through (4:19). On the other hand, once he is prevailed upon to give the interpretation of the dream, he does so with admirable clarity and forthright truthfulness. He neither maintains professional detachment nor resorts to mealy-mouthed indirection.

(3) The psychotic breakdown is probably a form of lycanthropy (which today is subdued by antipsychotic drugs). But once his sanity is restored (4:36), Nebuchadnezzar articulates the lesson he has learned: God is sovereign, he raises and abases whom he wills, none can withstand him, and every virtue or strength we possess we derive from him. To think otherwise is to invite rebuke, for "those who walk in pride he is able to humble" (4:37).

2 Kings 1; 2 Thessalonians 1; *Daniel 5; Psalms 110—111*

∽

AFTER NEBUCHADNEZZAR DIED, the Babylonian Empire rapidly declined. In violent coups, several members of the dynasty succeeded each other. Nabonidus eventually imposed some stability, though various vassal states broke away. Nabonidus himself became a religious dilettante. He abandoned the worship of Marduk (chief god in the Babylonian pantheon) and ended up, apparently, excavating buried shrines, restoring ancient religious rituals, and fostering the worship of the moon god Sin. Probably he was on one of these strange religious quests at the time of **Daniel 5**. As a result he had left the care of Babylon itself in the hands of Belshazzar his son. (The NIV footnote, 5:2, 11, 13, 18, rightly observes that Nebuchadnezzar was Belshazzar's "father" only in the sense that he was his "ancestor" or possibly "predecessor"—a common use of the Semitic word, not unlike the usage in 2 Kings 2:12.)

The account makes it clear that the Persian army was outside the walls of the city, but Belshazzar obviously felt that the city was impervious to assault. The bacchanalia he ordered up was worse than an orgy of self-indulgence. Bringing out the golden goblets that had been taken from the temple in Jerusalem was more than a whim. In the sequence of the two chapters, Daniel 4 and 5, it is hard not to see that this was a repudiation of what Belshazzar's "father" Nebuchadnezzar had learned about the living God. Perhaps Belshazzar thought that Babylon's fortunes had declined because of the relative neglect of the pagan deities. Nebuchadnezzar had learned to revere the God of Israel; Belshazzar was happy to spit in his eye. So they drank from the goblets and "praised the gods of gold and silver, of bronze, iron, wood and stone" (5:4). Daniel sees the connection between the two emperors, and this forms part of his stinging rebuke: Belshazzar knew what "the Most High God" had done to Nebuchadnezzar, and how Nebuchadnezzar had come to his senses and acknowledged "that the Most High God is sovereign over the kingdoms of men and sets over them anyone he wishes"—and yet he set himself up "against the Lord of heaven" and refused to "honor the God who holds in his hand your life and all your ways" (5:18-24). Somehow Belshazzar thought he could ignore or defy the God who had humbled the far greater Nebuchadnezzar.

So what have we learned? Have we absorbed the lessons of history—that God will not, finally, be mocked or defied? That we are utterly dependent creatures, and if we fail to acknowledge this simple truth our sins are compounded? That God can humble and convert the most unlikely, like Nebuchadnezzar, and destroy those who defy him, like Belshazzar?

∽

2 Kings 2; 2 Thessalonians 2; *Daniel 6*; *Psalms 112—113*

∾

FROM THE ACCOUNT OF DANIEL in the lions' den (**Dan. 6**), we observe a man about eighty years of age as faithful at the end of his life as he was at the beginning. Some notes:

(1) Despite his advanced years, Daniel's administrative abilities and his passion for integrity make him highly valuable to a relatively enlightened ruler such as Darius. The same virtues make him a target of envy to lesser men, who are happy to engage in a dirty-tricks campaign to bring him down. Dirty tricks were not invented by Nixon; they stretch back to the Fall. Blessed is the Christian whose life is so transparent, who is "trustworthy and neither corrupt nor negligent" (6:4), so that the only way he or she can be destroyed is by making Christian conduct and conviction a crime.

(2) Daniel serves as a model of how a Christian may serve in a government that is itself in no way Christian. He offers no comfort to those who withdraw not only from sin but from responsibility and godly influence.

(3) The expression "laws of the Medes and the Persians, which cannot be repealed" (6:8) was probably a badge of honor in the empire. Probably the policy was designed to discourage favoritism, corrupt exceptions, shifting pragmatism. But no legal system can ensure consistent justice. Corrupt people will always find ways of exploiting the system to oppress others and advance themselves. Hidden behind the slogan is a deeper issue. Historically there has long been a tension between *positive law* theory, in which the only law to be obeyed is that enacted by government, and *natural law* theory, in which some fundamentals are thought to be discoverable by human beings. In the name of equity and justice, British courts, until fairly recently, would sometimes set aside positive law in favor of natural law where it was pretty obvious an injustice was otherwise being committed. Both in Britain and in the United States, such considerations are now rare. In Britain, what must be obeyed is what Parliament says; in the United States, what must be obeyed is what the Supreme Court says. In both instances, positive law largely prevails, as in ancient Persia. The matter has become increasingly difficult here since Western states have come to think they have a therapeutic role in society, defining the "illnesses" that must be confronted and the "therapies" that must be imposed as they go along. The potential for injustice and inequity multiplies.

(4) In the crisis precipitated by this unjust law, Daniel remains consistent, neither flaunting his independence nor hiding his convictions and habits. The outcome he leaves with God—very much as in Jesus' prayer ("Your will be done") and example (Matt. 6:10; 26:39). Such maturity may well become a cherished model for us.

∾

2 Kings 3; 2 Thessalonians 3; *Daniel 7; Psalms 114—115*

∾

DANIEL NOT ONLY INTERPRETED the dreams of others, on occasion he himself had dreams that needed interpretation. The one described here (**Dan.** 7) took place in the first year of Belshazzar (7:1), i.e., more than fifty years since Daniel had first been deported to Babylon. Not all revelation is given at once. From now to the end of the book, Daniel writes in the first person (with the exception of the note at 10:1).

(1) Although the four beasts representing four kingdoms or empires are in some measure sequential (and to that extent probably to be identified with specific historical kingdoms—see below), the initial observation that these *four* beasts came out of the sea (proverbial for chaos and wickedness) churned up by the *four* winds (i.e., from the four points of the compass, or everywhere) may hint that they also represent all kingdoms that oppose God.

(2) The evocative nature of these beasts must not be overlooked. The lion combined with the eagle suggests dominion, speed, and strength. The brown Syrian bear may weigh up to six hundred pounds and has a voracious appetite. The leopard is known for its extraordinarily sudden, rapid attacks; its four heads show it to be rapacious in all directions, wanting dominion everywhere. The last beast is "terrifying and frightening and very powerful . . . it crushed and devoured its victims and trampled underfoot whatever was left" (7:7). Horns represent kings or kingdoms or dominion; this beast has ten of them, five times more than the natural two horns. The best identification is that the four beasts represent, respectively, the Babylonian, Medo-Persian, Greek, and Roman Empires.

(3) The expression "son of man" is a Semitic way of saying "human being." The other kingdoms are beastly and inhuman; here the reins of power rest in the hands of a human being as God meant a human being to be. Because of the parallels between verse 14 and verses 18 and 27, some have argued that "son of man" is merely a symbol for the "saints of the Most High" (7:18). But the matter is not so simple. If "son of man" in verses 13-14 were merely a symbol of the people of God, why should the authority be given to one who is *like* "a son of man"? The figure in verse 12 is an *individual* figure, yet he has a *representative* role (like the Old Testament priest, cf. Ex. 19:6). He comes "with the clouds of heaven," a common association with the glory of deity. And by using "son of man," the vision simultaneously signals a kingship that extends beyond Israel to all of humankind and prepares the way for the incarnation. Cf. Matthew 19:28; Mark 13:26; 14:62; Revelation 1:13-16.

∾

2 Kings 4; 1 Timothy 1; *Daniel 8*; *Psalm 116*

∾

TWO YEARS AFTER THE VISION OF CHAPTER 7, Daniel had his vision of the ram and the goat (**Dan. 8**). The text from 2:4 to the end of 7 was written in Aramaic (a cognate of Hebrew, widely used in the late Babylonian and Persian Empires). Both chapter 2 and chapter 7 provide visions that sweep through from the Babylonian period to the dawning of the kingdom of God; both of these chapters also provide some identification of the referents of the figures in their respective visions. None of the remaining chapters in the book of Daniel includes the same sweep, including the chapter before us. Here the focus is on just two beasts/kingdoms, which turn out to be the middle two of the four specified in chapters 2 and 7. Some observations:

(1) The ram has two horns, one more prominent than the other. The ram represents the Medo-Persian Empire (8:20); the more prominent horn, of course, is Persia. This has a bearing, you may recall, on how chapter 2 is interpreted (see meditation for October 17). The shaggy goat is Greece. Philip of Macedon united the Greek city-states, and his son Alexander the Great (referred to as "the first king" of Greece, 8:21) established the Greek Empire, expanding its limits to the borders of India. Along the way he prevailed against Persia. Upon his premature death, the empire was divided up under his four most powerful generals (8:8, 22). Only two of them affect biblical history, the two that established the dynasties between which little Israel, "the Beautiful Land" (8:9), was squeezed: the Ptolemies in Egypt to the south and the Seleucids based in Syria to the north. In the second century B.C., the Seleucids prevailed, and one particular Seleucid king, Antiochus IV Epiphanes, became extraordinarily brutal and oppressive. He made the observance of Jewish religion a capital offense, defiled the rebuilt temple, and for three-and-a-half years (roughly 1,150 days, embracing 2,300 morning and evening sacrifices, 8:14), 167—164 B.C., wreaked havoc in the land until the guerrilla warfare led by the Maccabees forced him out of Israel and back to Syria.

(2) The vision presents itself as dealing with the "distant future" (8:26), i.e., almost four centuries after Daniel's time. It deals with "the time of the end" (8:17). That expression means different things in different contexts. The "end" can refer to the end of the Lord's forbearance at a particular time in history (e.g., Ezek. 7:2-3); here, the "end" is probably with respect to the question asked in verse 13.

(3) The last verse of chapter 8 testifies that deep dealings with God, and the reception of genuine revelation, may exact a physical toll.

∾

2 Kings 5; 1 Timothy 2; *Daniel 9; Psalms 117—118*

DANIEL'S GREAT INTERCESSORY PRAYER (**Dan. 9:1-19**) cries out for prolonged meditation. The date is 539 B.C. Daniel "understood from the Scriptures, according to the word of the Lord given to Jeremiah the prophet" (9:2; cf. Jer. 25:11; 29:10), that the seventy years were up—which on the face of it shows that Jeremiah's writing quickly circulated *as Scripture*. Some reflections:

(1) The "seventy years" have occasioned some dispute. There were different ways of calculating the period of exile (see, for example, the figures in Ezek. 4). Some argue that seventy years is merely an idealized fixed term for God's wrath (cf. Zech. 1:12; 2 Chron. 36:21). If (as is more likely) this refers to seventy literal years, the best judgment is that the beginning of the seventy is 609, when the Babylonians beat the Egyptians at the battle of Carchemish, with the result that Judah for the first time became a vassal state in service to Babylon.

(2) When Daniel becomes aware from Scripture just when the close of the exile would take place, far from resting and waiting for the promises to come true, he prays for such fulfillment. The peculiar dynamic between God's sovereignty and human responsibility in the Bible never retreats to fatalism. The promises of God are incentives to intercession.

(3) Daniel's confession is general, not personal: "*we* have sinned and done wrong. . . . *We* have been wicked and have rebelled; we have turned away . . ."—and so forth. Here Daniel reminds us of Isaiah, who joins together personal and general confession (Isa. 6:6). It is doubtful that we can fruitfully pray for our church and our culture without confessing our own sin.

(4) The heart of the confession is that Daniel and his people have turned away from God's commands and laws (9:5), have not listened to God's servants the prophets (9:6), have not obeyed the laws God gave through his servants the prophets (9:10), have transgressed the Law (9:11), and have not sought the favor of the Lord their God by turning from their sins and giving attention to his truth (9:13). Note carefully: the heart of the matter, as Daniel sees it, is neglect of what God said or disobedience to what he said. That is always the heart of the issue. Conversely, genuine sanctification comes through adherence to God's words (Ps. 1:2; John 17:17). *That is why the rising biblical illiteracy within confessional churches, let alone the culture at large, is the most distressing and threatening symptom among us.*

(5) Daniel recognizes that the judgments that have befallen God's people are both just and perfectly in line with Scripture (9:7, 11b-14). What bearing does this have on us today?

(6) What are the grounds of Daniel's appeal for relief?

2 Kings 6; 1 Timothy 3; *Daniel 10; Psalms 119:1-24*

THE LAST THREE CHAPTERS OF Daniel are largely given over to the final vision, a vision of a heavenly messenger and his revelation (Dan. 10:1—12:13). This chapter (**Dan. 10**) establishes the setting. The date is 537 B.C. The first group of exiles have returned to Jerusalem. The reminder that Daniel's assigned name is Belteshazzar, and the mention of Cyrus, tie this chapter to 1:7, 21. The setting includes several remarkable features:

(1) The heavenly messenger is more radiant than Gabriel and mightier than Michael (the only named angels in all of Scripture), and has power to strengthen Daniel.

(2) Far from being exhilarated by the experience, Daniel is so drained of energy and even speech and consciousness that three times he must be revived by the visitor from God. Cf. Deuteronomy 5:26; Acts 9:8; 22:11. All this, Joyce Baldwin writes, "is a salutary reminder of the majesty of our God and of the amazing condescension of the incarnation."

(3) Daniel is a man highly esteemed by God (10:11, 19). The thought is stunning. What serious Christian would not give everything for a similar encomium? Does not Jesus teach, in effect, that we *ought* to pursue the "Well done, good and faithful servant!" (Matt. 25:21)?

(4) The three-week delay (10:12-14) unveils conflict in the heavenlies. The prince of the Persian kingdom is apparently some angelic being connected with Persia; similarly for the prince of Greece (10:20). Michael, "one of the chief princes" (10:13), is "your [Israel's] prince" (10:21). The hierarchy of angelic beings is not governed by the relationships of their earthly counterparts. As there is war between good and evil on earth, so is there war in heaven. In the same way that observing earthly people and powers might lead the unwary to conclude that God is not really in control, so also this delay in the movements of angels has caused the unwary to conclude that God is not really in control in heaven either—since clearly there are many contingencies of which we are not normally aware. But that is to draw a conclusion that Scripture rules out of order. Nebuchadnezzar learned the lesson well: God "does as he pleases *with the powers of heaven* and with the peoples of the earth" (Dan. 4.35, italics added). There is a terrible war going on, but this takes place under God's sovereignty; in its affirmation of God's utter dominion the text insists, "All the peoples of the earth are regarded as nothing. . . . No one can hold back his hand" (4:35). So there is space for conflict, resolve, perseverance—and for faith and utter confidence.

2 Kings 7; 1 Timothy 4; *Daniel 11*; *Psalm 119:25-48*

∾

THE ACTUAL CONTENT OF THE VISION disclosed by the heavenly messenger to Daniel occupies **Daniel 11** and the first part of Daniel 12. Although the meaning of many of the details is not easy to sort out, the main lines of thought are reasonably clear.

The Persian Empire is in view in 11:2. The standpoint of the vision, according to 10:1, is the reign of Cyrus. Who are the other four kings? The Persian Empire lasted two more centuries and produced nine kings (not counting usurpers between Cambyses and Darius I). Are the four the most prominent? The ones mentioned in Scripture (Cyrus, Darius, Xerxes [=Ahasuerus], Artaxerxes)? We do not know.

The Greek conqueror (11:3-4) is Alexander the Great, and the four kingdoms into which his empire was broken up have already been mentioned (Daniel 8; see meditation for October 23). The running struggles between the king of the south (the Ptolemies) and the king of the north (the Seleucids) found Jews squeezed between the two. Eventually the north prevailed (11:5-20). The one who sent out the tax collector (11:20) is almost universally recognized to be Seleucus IV, who died in 175 B.C. The "contemptible person" (11:21-39 [or possibly 21-45]) is undoubtedly Antiochus IV Epiphanes, a Seleucid monarch we have met before (October 23).

Readers of this book who love history should read Josephus, I Maccabees and II Maccabees, and contemporary reconstructions of the dramatic events of that period. There is no space here to survey that turbulent history. Yet we must ask why Scripture devotes so much space to it. From certain perspectives, Antiochus IV Epiphanes was not very significant. So why all this attention?

There are at least two reasons. *First,* at one level Antiochus attempted something new and profoundly evil. The oppression the Jews had suffered up to this point was diverse, but it was not like this. The ancient Egyptians had enslaved them, but did not try to impose their own religion on them. During the period of the judges, the Israelites were constantly running after pagan deities; when the pagans prevailed they imposed taxes and cruel subjugation, but not ideology. With the exception of one brief experiment by Nebuchadnezzar (Dan. 3), Assyria and Babylon did not forcibly impose polytheism. But here is Antiochus IV Epiphanes outlawing Israelite faith, killing those found with any part of Torah in their possession, militarily *imposing and coercing* a pagan worldview. The people suffer, and God eventually saves them. *Second,* canonically this brutal period of history becomes a model, a type, of ideological oppression, suffering, and martyrdom against the church. What New Testament passages reflect this?

∾

2 Kings 8; 1 Timothy 5; *Daniel 12; Psalm 119:49-72*

∽

REGARDING THE LAST CHAPTER OF Daniel (**Dan. 12**):

(1) The chapter division (which was not part of the original text) obscures the flow of the passage. Daniel 11:40-45 should be read with 12:1-4. As is pretty common in Hebrew prophecy, a vision of future history (11:2-39) suddenly slips over into a longer perspective. The expression "At the time of the end" (11:40) is ambiguous: it could refer to the end of the oppression of Antiochus IV Epiphanes, but several elements in the paragraph stretch way beyond his brief years—and 12:1-4 announces resurrection at the end of history, before which a period of terrible distress must take place. This confirms the canonical importance of the preceding chapter (see yesterday's meditation): in Daniel, the people of God learn to suffer for no other reason than their allegiance to the Word of God. In the closing verses of the chapter (12:5-13), there again seems to be anticipation of another like Antiochus IV Epiphanes. The reference to "time, times, and half a time" (12:7) probably means "a year, [two] years, a half a year"—i.e., three-and-a-half years, just as in 8:14 with respect to the cruel rage of Antiochus. It has thus become a conventional way of speaking of a shortened period of extreme suffering through which the people of God must go before God relieves them—and this is in anticipation of the final suffering at the end (12:1).

(2) The closing up and sealing of the scroll until the time of the end (12:4, 9) does not signal esoteric knowledge. Partly it has to do with preserving the scroll intact. It also suggests that the full sweep of its anticipatory and prophetic truth will not be grasped until the events to which it refers arrive on the scene. Even when the events break out, some will not see—just as some did not "see" what Jesus was saying in his parables (Matt. 13:14-15), and some do not "see" what the Gospel is all about (1 Cor. 2:14).

(3) In verse 7 the man swears "by him who lives forever." There are two elements in what this "man clothed in linen" says. *First,* the tone (attested by the oath) combined with the assertion that "all these things will be completed" shows that in the last analysis there are no contingencies with God: he knows the end from the beginning, and can guarantee outcomes. *Second,* the final relief will come when "the power of the holy people has been finally broken" (12:7). It was not broken under Antiochus IV Epiphanes. This *must* be referring to something at the end, making the reign of Antiochus a ghastly advance shadow of what was to come.

(4) Meditate on 12:1-3.

∽

2 Kings 9; 1 Timothy 6; *Hosea 1; Psalm 119:73-96*

෴

THE FIRST VERSE OF HOSEA 1 establishes that this prophecy came during the eighth century, which also witnessed the prophets Jonah and Amos (mainly, like Hosea, in the northern kingdom of Israel), and Micah and Isaiah (in Judah in the south). Early in the century both kingdoms, materially speaking, were doing pretty well, but both sank into decadence and moral and religious indifference. While Hosea appears in the canon immediately after Daniel, it thus deals with a period centuries earlier. Nevertheless the canonical association is helpful. If Daniel's prophecy constantly discloses a God who is in sovereign control, Hosea discloses a God who is passionately moved by his fickle people. We need to nurture both portraits of God—God the transcendent sovereign, God the passionate person—if we are to be faithful to what the Bible says about him.

When the Lord first speaks to Hosea, his language is blistering. The NIV is too tame; the *Jerusalem Bible* is closer to the Hebrew: "Go, marry a whore, and get children with a whore, for the country itself has become nothing but a whore by abandoning Yahweh" (1:2, JB). So Hosea marries Gomer. On the face of it, she was a prostitute when he married her, and soon returned to her wanton ways. Alternatively, it is possible that the Lord's command leaps forward to what she becomes, and Gomer was not a prostitute when Hosea married her.

Regardless of her background, the next chapters make clear what she became. Her children capture the attention in this chapter. Jezreel is a name that can be associated with a particular meaning (cf. 2:23), but above all it was the name of a town where the house of Jehu formerly massacred so many people. It would be like naming a child Chernobyl or Hiroshima or Soweto: everyone knows the connections. The Jehu massacre occurred about a century earlier, but the nation was still responsible, for it never repudiated the violence. At least Gomer bore this son to *Hosea* (she "bore *him* a son," 1:3, italics added). That is not said of the next two: likely Hosea was not the father. The first is called "Not Loved" or "Not Pitied"; the second is called "Not My People." The lessons are explicit: God will no longer love or pity Israel, and he will declare, "[Y]ou are not my people, and I am not your God" (1:9). God will break Israel's bow (i.e., break her armed might) in the Valley of Jezreel (1:5). Historically, that took place in 733, just over a decade before Israel was finally destroyed; Assyria marched in and removed the defenses (2 Kings 15:29).

Astonishingly, despite these three shattering oracles, the chapter ends with stunning hope (1:10-11). That tells where this book is going—both this book of Hosea and this Bible.

෴

2 Kings 10—11; 2 Timothy 1; *Hosea 2*; *Psalm 119:97-120*

∾

IN HOSEA 1, APOSTATE ISRAEL IS likened to a brood of children characterized by violence and mayhem (Jezreel, 1:4) or born out of wedlock (1:6-9). Although the "children" briefly reappear at the beginning and end of **Hosea 2**, here the focus is on apostate Israel as a fickle wife.

The verb translated "rebuke" in the NIV (2:2) is better rendered "plead," as in a legal setting: "Plead my cause" (NEB), God begs of the children. The next two lines are better taken as a question: "Is she not my wife and I her husband?" (NEB). The entire book insists that God will not finally go back on his marriage vows, but that he will pursue her. If the words are taken as a statement (NIV), then they must mean that the heart of the marriage has gone out of it, not that God himself is finally ending it.

The next verses (2:3-4) demand radical repentance, not a merely formulaic "I'm sorry." The alternative is that God will force Israel to face the consequences of her sin (2:5-13). The picture is perhaps worse than we think: the false gods after whom Israel lusted were often fertility gods, and she was constantly tempted to think that they provided her wealth (2:5), the way sex provides a prostitute's resources. A culture with fertility religions glamorizes sex—as does our culture, if for different reasons. God sometimes seemed so remote or confined that Israel did not recognize that he alone provides all good things (2:8), just as Hosea provided for all of Gomer's needs. Sooner or later, at all costs, the sheer horror of the apostasy must be exposed, the apparent glamour stripped of its false aura, the deceit and perfidy recognized, and the consequences experienced (2:10-13). There is both heartbreak and anger in God's words: Israel "decked herself with rings and jewelry, and went after her lovers, but me she forgot" (2:13).

But if God threatens judgment, he will also woo the Israel he loves and allure her with his charms. He calls to mind the "courting" days in the desert: he will court her all over again, this whore who has betrayed him (2:14). The marriage will be preserved and strengthened (2:16), and God will guarantee that all the blessings of material prosperity will be provided (2:17-22). Violence will be swallowed up by prosperity; the valley of Jezreel will no longer be associated with Jehu, but with planting (the allusion depends on Hebrew etymology). The new covenant bride (2:18), dressed in wedding clothes, promises righteousness, justice, love, compassion, and faithfulness (2:19-20). And alienated, illegitimate children will belong to God (2:23)—which Paul sees as a foretaste of the grandest proportions (Rom. 9:25-26).

∾

2 Kings 12; 2 Timothy 2; *Hosea 3—4; Psalm 119:121-144*

∾

HOSEA 1 IS TO HOSEA 2 WHAT Hosea 3 is to Hosea 4. The first member of each pair of chapters is written in prose and focuses on Hosea and Gomer; the second is written in poetry and focuses on the parallel relationship between Yahweh and Israel.

In the pair of chapters before us (**Hosea 3—4**), Hosea begins with a restrained, first-person account of what happened next in his marriage. This chapter brings the account of his marriage to an end. Hosea is charged with loving his wife, who has apparently returned to her harlotry and now "belongs" to some other man (presumably a pimp). Hosea discloses none of his feelings as he buys Gomer back; actions are more important anyway (something our generation has all but forgotten). Yet at the same time he charges Gomer, now returned to him, to be faithful to him.

This exactly mirrors God's situation. In theory he could righteously dismiss his "bride" and forget about her. Instead, he is committed to getting her back, to paying whatever is necessary to do so—but he also expects his bride, newly returned, to be faithful to him. God still loves his elect. He will pursue them, even after the most horrible rebellion and chastening, and he will buy them back. Indeed, the last verses of chapter 3 envisage an exile which on the long haul will do good: it will establish a time when the remnant will truly "seek the LORD their God and David their king" (3:5).

In Hosea 4 God addresses apostate Israel. "There is no faithfulness, no love, no acknowledgment of God in the land" (4:1). The long list of sins is profoundly depressing. The people "are destroyed from lack of knowledge" of God's Word (4:6). Otherwise put, "A spirit of prostitution leads them astray; they are unfaithful to their God" (4:12). The corruption is now endemic. Sarcasm boils to the surface: why should God punish daughters and daughters-in-law for prostitution, when the men love to consort with harlots (4:14)?

God is deepening his people's sense of shame and guilt. The scorn is palpable: "Do not go to Gilgal; do not go up to Beth Aven" (4:15). Gilgal and Bethel were two of the most important shrines for the covenant people of God. The second, Bethel, means "house of God," but the prophet recasts it as "Beth Aven," i.e., "house of wickedness," for that is all that goes on there. "Ephraim is joined to idols; leave him alone!" (4:17). Go to church with this lot, and all you are doing is participating in disgusting idolatry and self-seeking, with no attention devoted to learning God's Word. Better to stay home; this sort of "church" will merely corrupt you.

∾

2 Kings 13; 2 Timothy 3; *Hosea 5—6; Psalm 119:145-176*

∾

SOMEONE HAS SAID THAT THE entire book of Hosea can be understood as a study of what it means to turn back to God. Here there are no glib nostrums; merely verbal apologies are not acceptable. And yet hope is held out for people who display the kind of return that the Lord *does* accept. Nowhere is that tension clearer than in **Hosea 5—6**.

Hosea 5 opens with an indictment of Israel, especially the leaders. Nothing about them is unknown to God (5:3; cf. 7:2; Heb. 4:13). Their problem is not merely an intellectual one, but is profoundly moral: "Their deeds do not permit them to return to their God. A spirit of prostitution is in their heart; they do not acknowledge the LORD" (5:4; cf. John 3:19). Worse, when they do formally "seek" the Lord, their pursuit is so false that he withdraws from them, for God is not the prisoner of his own sacrificial system (5:5-6). In bringing judgment upon them, God's purpose is not only retribution but inducement to repentance: "Then I will go back to my place until they admit their guilt. And they will seek my face; in their misery they will earnestly seek me" (5:15).

The opening verses of chapter 6 (vv. 1-3) can be understood in two ways. (1) They may be a moving plea from Hosea to his own people to repent and turn to the Lord. He wants them to move away from religion as sacrificial observance to religion as genuine acknowledgment of the Lord. The same God who has chastened the people will then gladly bind up their wounds. "As surely as the sun rises, he will appear" (6:3). (2) They may be the words of the people themselves—and in that case the context in which they are embedded suggests that, although they sound very good, in reality they mean little (cf. Ps. 78:34, 36-37). Such repentance is mere presumption, and God sees through it and dismisses it, for their "love is like the morning mist, like the early dew that disappears" (6:4)—like Gomer's love. Either of these two ways of taking 6:1-3 makes sense; in both instances the fickleness in God's covenant people is deeply repugnant. If I have to choose between the two, I tilt toward the first. Hosea 6:1-3 sounds rather more like genuine repentance that is urged but not followed, than like the empty words of insincere hypocrites.

Whatever the interpretation, clearly God is not impressed with mere words and religious observance: "For I desire mercy, not sacrifice, and acknowledgment of God rather than burnt offerings" (6:6; cf. Matt. 9:13; 12:7). A generation that lustily sings God's praises while lustily sleeping around had better expect the blistering judgment of God.

∾

2 Kings 14; 2 Timothy 4; *Hosea 7; Psalms 120—122*

∽

AMONG THE SONGS OF ASCENT (see vol. 1, meditation for June 29) is the delightful **Psalm 122**. Here the psalmist joyfully accompanies those heading to Jerusalem for one of the high feasts: "Let us go to the house of the LORD" (122:1). Already in verse 2 the pilgrims have arrived: "Our feet are standing in your gates, O Jerusalem."

Two themes dominate the remaining verses of the psalm.

First, verses 3-5 emphasize the unity of God's people, brought about by their common worship in Jerusalem of the true God and by their common submission to the rule and justice of the house of David. There was of course diversity—not only the diversity common to all collections of human beings, but the diversity implicit in the twelve "tribes" (122:4), each with its own marked character. The unity was more profound than blood ties. It was based on a common covenant with the one God. These were "the tribes of the LORD" (122:4). Small wonder, then, that when the northern ten tribes revolted, the leader, Jeroboam, greatly feared that Jerusalem and its temple would become the rallying point for renewed unification (1 Kings 12:26ff.).

Yet unity was merely the byproduct of the festive ascents to Jerusalem. The purpose of the ascents was "to praise the name of the LORD according to the statute given to Israel" (122:4). When God becomes the means to the end, unity is never achieved; when God himself is the end, the glorious byproducts of unity and peace are never far behind. The sheer God-centeredness of biblical religion is one of the things that regularly distinguishes it from paganism, which commonly sees religion as a means to certain ends (cf. Hosea 2:5).

Second, in another distinction between means and ends, David exhorts people to pray for the peace of Jerusalem, not for the sake of an abstract ideal or for the sake of the city *per se,* but for the sake of people (122:8) and above all for the sake of "the house of the LORD our God" (122:9). To pursue political peace and forget people is a sham. Indeed, the exhortation to pray for the "peace" of "Jerusalem" (122:6) includes a pun: we are to pray for the *shalom* of Jerusalem; the Hebrew consonants are the same, and remind us that Jerusalem rightly conceived holds out the fullness of "well-being" to people. To pursue merely physical benefits for people and forget the presence and purposes of the Lord God is at best short-term thinking and at worst a route to disaster and to hell itself. "For the sake of the house of the LORD our God," David writes, "I will seek your prosperity" (122:9).

Reflect on how to transpose these two points to the Christian antitype (Heb. 12:22-24), not least in detailed application (Heb. 12:28—13:13).

∽

2 Kings 15; Titus 1; *Hosea 8; Psalms 123—125*

PERHAPS THE SINGLE ELEMENT that holds together the various sins condemned in **Hosea 8** is human self-reliance. The "eagle" in 8:1 is probably a vulture. A "[vulture] . . . over the house of the LORD" is a way of saying that Jerusalem is as good as dead: the carrion eaters are already gathering for their feast. The people might be living in relative prosperity and peace, but the ominous signs were there for those with eyes to see. Evidences of sinful self-sufficiency include:

(1) A hypocritical allegiance to the covenant (8:1-3). What makes it hypocritical is that Israel cries out, "O our God, we acknowledge you!" (8:2) while breaking the covenant and rebelling against God's law (8:1). This is the rejection of what is good—and there are consequences (8:3). Cf. 1 John 2:4.

(2) Defiant alternatives to the Davidic dynasty (8:4). That is what is meant by the charge, "They set up kings without my consent; they choose princes without my approval." The Lord set his seal on the Davidic dynasty, but to preserve their independence from Jerusalem the northern ten tribes, now constituted as Israel, opted for their own monarchs. They were not "chosen" in any democratic sense; frequently they succeeded one another in bloody coups. But they were the choice of the northern tribes nonetheless, insofar as they preferred these to allegiance to David's line. It is always the case that unless the Lord builds the house, those who labor do so in vain (Ps. 127:1); here the sin is compounded by the alienation from the messianic line.

(3) The development of idols, of the culture's choice of religion (8:4-6, 11-13). Initially two golden calves were set up, one in Dan and one in Bethel, to offset the draw of Jerusalem's temple (1 Kings 12:27-30). Moreover, people in Israel would not have to travel so far. Thus, although they formally preserve the altars for sin offerings, these have become "altars for sinning" (8:11).

(4) The constant dependence on expensive and tricky allies (8:8-10). Instead of trusting the Lord, they think their clever diplomacy with regional superpowers will save the day. God is demeaned, and Israel ("Ephraim") is further seduced by idolatry.

(5) Reliance on wealth and military strength (8:14). Israel (the north) has its palaces; Judah (the south) fortifies many towns—forty-six of them, in fact. But God will destroy them (8:14b). When Assyria vanquished Israel (722 B.C.), it also took all the walled cities of Judah except Jerusalem (2 Kings 18:13), which was spared until the rise of Nebuchadnezzar more than a century later.

What signs of self-reliance characterize our culture? What will God do about them?

2 Kings 16; Titus 2; *Hosea 9*; *Psalms 126—128*

∾

"THE DAYS OF PUNISHMENT ARE COMING, the days of reckoning are at hand. Let Israel know this" (9:7). This chapter (**Hosea 9**) spells out some of the connections between sin and judgment.

(1) The language of prostitution continues: "For you have been unfaithful to your God; you love the wages of a prostitute at every threshing floor" (9:1). Both politically and religiously, Israel flirted continuously with alien gods and foreign powers. All the ceremony of religion she dearly loved. But the days are coming when she will be scattered, forced to abandon "the LORD's land" (9:3, 17). Israel will return to "Egypt" (9:3); some Israelites did end up there, but Egypt is also a cipher for any alien, oppressive country. Ephraim (= Israel) will "eat unclean food in Assyria" (9:3). Not just the ceremonial uncleanness of the food is in view, but the prospect of forced exile. All the offerings for her much loved festivals and ceremonies will dry up (9:5); the punishments are tied to the sins.

(2) Systematic denigration of the prophets means that the people cannot hear God's warnings—and so their cynicism ensures that they stumble into the judgments against which the prophets warn. "Because your sins are so many and your hostility so great, the prophet is considered a fool, the inspired man a maniac. The prophet, along with my God, is the watchman over Ephraim, yet snares await him on all his paths, and hostility in the house of his God" (9:7-8). How well does this apply today?

(3) The history of Israel swings from really wonderful connections with the living God—from God's perspective it was "like finding grapes in the desert" (9:10)—to abominable degradation. The incident of Baal Peor (9:10; cf. Num. 25) is telling, for it combines both physical and spiritual unchastity: the Moabite women seduced the men of Israel, and the local Moabite Baal attracted their worship. Our culture follows sex as avidly and sometimes connects it with the self-fulfillment of new age spirituality. The result with us will be what it was at Baal Peor: the people "became as vile as the thing they loved" (9:10). What you worship you soon resemble (Ps. 115:8); more, you identify with it, defend it, make common cause with it—and if it is an abomination to God, soon you are an abomination to him. So the "glory" departs (9:11), whether in the sense of reputation, or self-respect, or moral leadership, or, finally, the very presence of God (Ezek. 8:6; 11:23).

To defend a king or a president because of his economic policies when the moral core has evaporated means we have become as vile as the things we love.

∾

2 Kings 17; Titus 3; *Hosea 10; Psalms 129—131*

∾

MANY HAVE OBSERVED THAT PSALM 131 anticipates the teaching of Jesus in Matthew 18:1-4, where he asks, "Who is the greatest in the kingdom of heaven?"—and calls a little child to stand among his disciples. In certain respects, the follower of Jesus must be childlike, and this psalm makes its own contribution to that theme. Yet childlikeness is not childishness; simplicity is not simple-mindedness; humility is not servility. The psalm will speak with greater power if we reflect on some of its features:

(1) According to the superscription, this is a psalm of David. One may well ask during what period of his career he wrote it. More than one writer has suggested it springs from an early period, before the successes of his middle and later years bred a certain arrogance that would have made it impossible for him to write, "I do not concern myself with great matters or things too wonderful for me" (131:1). That is possible, of course. Nevertheless a very young man who has not yet had the opportunity to concern himself with great matters would not be very likely to write these words—or if he did, they would sound vaguely pretentious, a bit like a pompous excuse for not tackling the tough issues. One cannot finally prove the point, but I suspect this psalm is easier to understand if it springs from the end of David's life, after he has been humbled by such matters as Bathsheba and Uriah, and by the revolt led by his son Absalom. Humbled, less quick to imagine he alone understands, slower to take umbrage, and more impressed by the wise providence of God, David (one imagines) now quietly writes, "My heart is not proud, O LORD, my eyes are not haughty; I do not concern myself with great matters or things too wonderful for me" (131:1).

(2) Some commentators (and even translations) picture the child of verse 2 as nursing at the breast. But that is not what the text says. David pictures himself "like a weaned child with its mother." This child, like David, no longer cries for what it formerly found indispensable. This too suggests that David is mature enough now to be giving something up—namely, in the light of verse 1, the confident questing to understand everything, borne of more than a little arrogance. The immaturity he abandons is like a little child squealing to get hold of its mother's breast. But David has eclipsed that point. He is weaned, and he is content. Cf. Philippians 4:11ff.

(3) The maturity David has reached is grounded not in escapist retreat from life's complexities, but in trust in the Lord (131:3), whose perfect knowledge is a bulwark for our hope.

∾

2 Kings 18; Philemon; *Hosea 11; Psalms 132—134*

∾

IN HOSEA 9, GOD SAYS OF HIS covenant people, "Because of all their wickedness . . . I hated them there. Because of their sinful deeds, I will drive them out of my house. I will no longer love them; all their leaders are rebellious" (9:15). Yet here in **Hosea 11** God declares, "My heart is changed within me; all my compassion is aroused" (11:8). How shall we put these two passages together?

First, this emotional turmoil is the language of the jilted husband: in this book, Almighty God plays the role of the cuckolded husband. Make all the allowance you like for anthropomorphism, this is as truly the way God presents himself in Scripture as the passages where his utter sovereignty is affirmed. It is the juxtaposition of such themes that has driven orthodox confessionalism to insist that God is simultaneously, on the one hand, sovereign and transcendent, and, on the other, personal and interactive with his image-bearers.

Second, the juxtaposition of God's wrath and God's love makes it unnecessary to pull verses out of two chapters (9 and 11). Within chapter 11 the tension is already almost unbearable. The chapter opens with a brief historical review. God saved Israel out of Egypt at the time of the Exodus (11:1) and taught her to walk, leading her "with cords of human kindness, with ties of love" (11:4). But the more he lavished on Israel the more they turned away (11:2), and they utterly refused to repent (11:5). So God will come at them with great wrath: "Swords will flash in their cities. . . . Even if they call to the Most High, he will by no means exalt them" (11:6-7). It sounds as if it is too late. And then suddenly, almost as if God is talking with himself, he asks how he can possibly give them up (11:8).

What is the answer? The answer lies in the very character of God. He is not *exactly* like a cuckolded husband. "For I am God, and not man—the Holy One among you. I will not come in wrath" (11:9). Or, more precisely, as the next two verses demonstrate, he will not *finally* come to them in wrath. They *will* go into captivity, but he will roar again with the lion's royal sway and call his children from the west, from Egypt, from Assyria, and they will be settled again. Indeed, within the larger canonical framework, the fact that God is God and not a mere mortal, the fact that both his wrath and his love must be satisfied, means that wrath and love will rush forward together—until they meet in the cross, the cross of the man who was also called out of Egypt by God to be the perfect son, the perfect anti-type of Israel (11:1; Matt. 2:15).

∾

2 Kings 19; Hebrews 1; *Hosea 12; Psalms 135—136*

∾

SOME PSALMS GIVE US A glimpse of ancient Israelite worship, and **Psalm 136** is one of them. Probably this was sung antiphonally: either a restricted part of the choir, or one part of the congregation in the temple would sing the lead line of each cycle, and the whole congregation would burst out and respond with "His love endures forever." Comparing 136:18-22 with 135:10b-12 suggests that some other psalms were sung this way too. In Jewish tradition this psalm is known as the Great Hallel, "the Great Psalm of Praise." The refrain itself celebrates God's "love": the Hebrew word is *hesed,* notoriously difficult to render consistently by one English word. The King James Version opts for "steadfast love." It is bound up with God's faithfulness to the covenant, and in various contexts might properly be rendered "grace," "love," even "covenant-fidelity"—with overtones of a reciprocal obligation.

What makes this psalm so thought-provoking is not the compactness of the refrain but its connection with a vast grounding of evidence—evidence that God's love endures forever. The psalm speaks of God's character (136:1), the sweep of his sovereignty (136:2-3), his creative power (136:4-9), the extraordinary displays of his might when he redeemed his people from Egypt (136:10-22), and his mercy displayed alike to his elect and to every creature under heaven that needs food (136:23-25). Contrast this specificity with more than a few contemporary praise choruses that endlessly exhort us to praise the Lord, without telling us *why* we should praise the Lord, or perhaps giving us only a reason or two. In the choruses, the emphasis tends to be on worship; here, the emphasis is on the One who is worshiped, such that the worship has the flavor of being no more than the inevitable response to so great a God. The one focuses on what we do, the other on who God is and what he has done.

Some final reflections: (1) The expression "Give thanks" that opens the first three verses and the last suggests more than a casual "Thanks a lot." It has to do with "confessing" (in the old-fashioned sense), "acknowledging" (with thoughtful God-centeredness), with grateful worship. (2) This God brooks no rivals. He is the God of gods, the Lord of lords (136:2, 3). (3) Informed as they are by pluralism, our ears find it strange to append the refrain "His love endures forever" to such lines as "who struck down great kings" and "[h]e swept Pharaoh and his army into the Red Sea." But these actions were expressions of God's elective love for his chosen people. The notion that God loves all people exactly the same way and in every respect finds little support in Scripture.

∾

2 Kings 20; Hebrews 2; *Hosea 13; Psalms 137—138*

∽

IT IS APPROPRIATE THAT **Hosea 13** should be read in conjunction with **Psalm 137**. Hosea 13 brings the prophet's promises of judgment to their climax. God is going to destroy proud Samaria (Ephraim). Similar warnings were repeatedly thundered against Judah, but they showed no sign of repentance. In 587 B.C., God destroyed Jerusalem and the last great wave of people were transported into exile. Here in Psalm 137, the captives from that catastrophe voice their utter despair, and almost all of their focus is on the secondary agents—their captors, the Edomites, the people of Babylon. *And both perspectives are valid and complementary.*

Here I shall reflect on the four sections of Psalm 137.

(1) The first (137:1-3) is so vivid it sounds like eyewitness recollection. A relief from the Assyrian palace of Sennacherib in Nineveh pictures three prisoners of war playing their lyres while a soldier marches them along; doubtless this also happened in Babylon. The "rivers of Babylon" was a system of canals connected with the Tigris and Euphrates river systems. The "harps" (lyres) were instruments of joy. In the symbolic language of Revelation 5, when the lion who is also the lamb takes the scroll from the right hand of the Almighty, signaling that he is worthy to open the scroll and bring about all of God's purposes in blessing and judgment, all the "harps" break out; it is a moment of ineffable joy, the opposite of this paragraph.

(2) But the exiles refuse to sing (137:4-6). All of the associations of the songs of the Lord are tied to Jerusalem and the temple. For them, their staunch refusal, even to their tormenting captors, was a sign not only of pathos and heartbreak (v. 4) but also of passion and fidelity (vv. 5-6).

(3) The Edomites had obviously delighted in the destruction of Jerusalem and perhaps helped it along. On this point the prophet Ezekiel has more to say (Ezek. 35; see meditation for October 2). God hates smugness and a vengeful spirit. The judgment on Jerusalem came, ultimately, from God—but he would also judge those who delighted in and contributed to Jerusalem's fall. One of the ugliest recent evidences of that smug vengefulness within the ranks of professing evangelicalism was the slogan "no tears for queers" after a young gay man had been beaten to death.

(4) At the end of a siege, victorious soldiers might pick up small children by their ankles and kill them by bashing their heads against a wall. What such barbarism demands, strictly speaking, for justice to prevail, is similar suffering. These white-hot lines are not cool policy statements, but the searing cries of moral indignation. We must hear the anguish, before we also hear God insisting that vengeance is his (Rom. 12:19).

∽

2 Kings 21; Hebrews 3; *Hosea 14; Psalm 139*

∾

THE FINAL CHAPTER OF THE PROPHECY, **Hosea 14,** has a gentler tone. It is almost as if the thunder of rebellion and judgment has exhausted itself, and grace triumphs. The chapter begins and ends with exhortation from Hosea. In between there are, first, the words of the people (or, more precisely, the words the prophet instructs the people to say), and then the words of God. I shall reflect briefly on each of these four sections.

(1) Hosea begins with repentance: "Return, O Israel, to the LORD your God" (14:1). "Return" is perfectly answered by "your God": the prophet is not calling for some new and hazardous spiritual journey, but for a turning away from the rebellion, a turning back to the Lord they have long known. They must come to terms with the heart of the problem: "Your sins have been your downfall!" (14:1). There is never any way back without coming to grips with this fundamental reality. Moreover, what the prophet wants is not a mere return to formal adherence to a code of law. He wants them to "take words" with them when they return (14:2). Words, of course, can be empty: sometimes actions speak louder than words. But often genuine repentance demands not only begrudging conduct, but words—not a sullen return to prescribed ritual and church attendance, but the kind of repentance that bubbles up in words that disclose what is in the heart.

(2) And what words should they say? Hosea tells them (14:2b-3). They must ask for the forgiveness of sins; they must ask that God would receive them; they must renounce their political allegiances, implicitly acknowledging that such ties distracted them from trust in God; they must put aside their idolatry and place their hope in the living God. Precisely how should such petitions find echoes in our own lives?

(3) The Lord's words (14:4-8) are lovely. "I will heal their waywardness and love them freely, for my anger has turned away from them" (14:4). Then in a series of images God describes the blessings he will be to Israel and provide for Israel. The closing lines of the section reinforce the theological point of the entire chapter: "I am like a green pine tree; your fruitfulness comes from me" (14:8). God has all the "greenness," the constancy, of the evergreen, and all the nourishment and prosperity of a fruit-bearing tree (cf. Ps. 1:3).

(4) Hosea concludes the book: "Who is wise? He will realize these things. Who is discerning? He will understand them. The ways of the LORD are right; the righteous walk in them, but the rebellious stumble in them" (14:9).

∾

2 Kings 22; Hebrews 4; *Joel 1*; *Psalms 140—141*

∽

THE PROPHECY OF JOEL IS anomalous on several grounds. Most canonical Old Testament prophecies are introduced by prophets who identify the period of their ministry with reference to the reigns of kings (e.g., Hosea 1:1). Joel does nothing of the kind. Nor do we have any idea who his father Pethuel is. Estimates of the date of composition of the book vary from the ninth century B.C. to the second century B.C. Clearly the temple is in operation (e.g., 1:13), but it is uncertain whether this is the first temple (built in Solomon's reign) or the temple built after the exile.

In some ways this open-endedness is an advantage. While we lose the specificity that characterizes much Old Testament prophetic writing, we gain in a kind of timeless feel that perhaps makes application easier. Almost certainly what precipitated the crisis was a plague of locusts (though some think of the locusts as symbols for a mighty army). That experience has become the template the prophet uses to call the people to repentance in the light of judgment both past and portending. It is also the background for some of the most stirring prophecies of the future, fulfilled in the coming of the Gospel, found in all of the Old Testament canon (see especially tomorrow's meditation).

The locust plague pictured in **Joel 1** is a phenomenon well known in some parts of the world today. Once locusts have swarmed, they are almost impossible to stop. Really terrible plagues of locusts were recognized for what they were: the judgment of God. That is why Solomon in his prayer at the dedication of the temple includes the possibility that God would chasten his people with locusts—and he prescribes what to do about it (1 Kings 8:37). Joel is doing it. He invites the priests especially ("you who minister before the altar," 1:13) to put on sackcloth, mourn, and declare a holy fast, calling a sacred assembly, summoning the elders to the temple to cry out to the Lord (1:13-14). Joel himself ends the chapter with the cry, "To you, O LORD, I call" (1:19).

This is a good place to reflect for a moment on how we should think about disasters. We should not adopt the stance of fatalists. If we can stop locusts today (satellites can sometimes spot incipient swarms that are then stopped by trucks with pesticides), then we should do so—in exactly the same way that we should try to stop war, plague, AIDS, famine, and other disasters. But in a theistic world where God is sovereign, we must also hear the summoning judgment of God calling his image-bearers to renounce sin's selfism and cry to him for mercy.

∽

2 Kings 23; Hebrews 5; *Joel 2; Psalm 142*

∾

THE OPENING VERSES OF JOEL 2 provide a stunning picture of the advancing hordes of locusts. The last verse of the section (2:11) makes it clear that these locusts are the Lord's army. The fact of the matter is that "the day of the Lord" in the Old Testament, i.e., the day when the Lord manifests himself, is as often a day of judgment as of blessing and light: "The day of the LORD is great; it is dreadful. Who can endure it?" (2:11). Transposed to the ultimate day of the Lord, the same thing is true: it is very great and dreadful. Who can endure it? Only those who have fled for protection to the security that only God himself provides will be able to proclaim on the last day, when the wrath of God is fully displayed, "I need no other argument / I need no other plea; / It is enough that Jesus died / And that he died for me" (L. H. Edmonds).

Two highly memorable passages follow:

First, in Joel's exhortation to return to the Lord comes this remarkable verse: "Rend your heart and not your garments. Return to the LORD your God, for he is gracious and compassionate, slow to anger and abounding in love, and he relents from sending calamity" (2:13). The habit of wearing sackcloth or of rending one's garment at times of great distress or as a sign of repentance was well known. Like all outward manifestations, however, it could be aped. Instead of being an outward manifestation of inward repentance, it could easily become one more piece of religious cant. God wants a change that stems from within, not an external display that hopes it can wheedle blessings from him. This also suggests, in strong terms, that deep repentance involves not only a turning away from sinful behavior but an emotional, visceral response—a rent heart, a deeply shamed repugnance at previous engagement with sin. It does not produce people who try to negotiate a new contract with God, but men and women who, convicted by the Spirit, cry out in desperation, "What shall we do?" (Acts 2:37).

Second, the closing verses of the chapter (2:28-32) tell us what God will do "afterward," i.e., after the blessings that he promises to pour out on the people in terms of their homeland and harvest. He will pour out his Spirit on all people (2:28) so mightily that all will have the knowledge of God, all will enjoy the prophetic Spirit. These verses are quoted by Peter as being fulfilled on the day of Pentecost (Acts 2:17-21); they are parallel to various promises of the new covenant (Jer. 31; Ezek. 36). See the meditation for July 15 in volume 1, and, in this volume, for August 3 and October 3.

∾

2 Kings 24; Hebrews 6; *Joel 3*; *Psalm 143*

∾

TRADITIONALLY, PSALM 143 IS classified as the last of seven penitential psalms, doubtless because verse 2 admits to universal guilt. Yet regardless of how important that truth is in the Bible as a whole, in this psalm only in the one verse does this theme surface. Most of the psalm is devoted to the troubles David is facing, occasioned by enemies (143:1-6), and David's growing resolve as he focuses on following God's way, regardless of what his enemies may do. Some observations:

(1) David's initial appeal is to God's faithfulness and righteousness (143:1). This is entirely appropriate, in exactly the same way that the goodness of a potentate or the integrity of a judge is welcomed by those trying to redress a wrong. The difficulty, of course, is that as we sinners appeal to the righteousness of God for vindication, it is easy to remember that we ourselves are horribly soiled compared with the clean glory of the unshielded holiness of the Almighty. Hence verse 2: David acknowledges that "no one living is righteous before you." This is a tension not finally resolved until the cross (Rom. 3:21-26; cf. 1 John 1:9).

(2) If verses 3-4 wallow in the slough of despond, verses 5-6 find David beginning to climb out. On first reading the line "I remember the days of long ago," a reader might think that David is succumbing to nostalgia, remembering "the good old days." But he is not so foolish, as the rest of the verse shows: he commits himself instead to thinking of all the things that God has done—in other words, he meditates on all of God's creative and chastening and redemptive acts in the past; he sets himself to meditate on the God of the Bible. Nor is this a merely intellectual exercise, like reviewing lists for an impending exam. David knows that this focus on what God has done is a God-given means of connecting with the living God himself, and that is what he wants: "I spread out my hands to you; my soul thirsts for you like a parched land" (143:6).

(3) Three times in verses 8-10 David prays for guidance. Each petition has a slightly different focus. "Show me the way I should go" (143:8) reflects David's confusion, but also hints that there are unique and individual elements to the guidance he needs (as there are individual callings in the church, John 21:21-22). "Teach me to do your will" (143:10a) now focuses entirely on God's agenda ("for you are my God"). Knowing and doing God's will is the very stuff of guidance. "[M]ay your good Spirit lead me on level ground" (143:10b) is to admit that we may trip as well as rebel, stumble as well as stray—and always we need help.

∾

2 Kings 25; Hebrews 7; *Amos 1*; Psalm 144

∾

THE PROPHECY OF AMOS CALLS the people of God back to the behavior stipulated by the covenant. But since so much of Israel's misbehavior is bound up with *social* injustice, not exclusively individualistic sins, this prophecy includes some of the most incisive denunciation of social injustice found anywhere.

Some preliminary reflections on **Amos 1**:

(1) Unlike Ezekiel, who was a trained priest before he became a prophet, and unlike Isaiah and Jeremiah, who seem to have been prophets all their lives, and unlike Daniel, whose work was in the "secular" arena but whose training was first-class, Amos was neither a professional religious leader nor a scholar. He was a shepherd (1:1)—as Elisha was a farmer and our Lord was a carpenter.

(2) Unlike the book of Joel, this book specifies the reigns under which Amos preached: under Uzziah king of Judah and Jeroboam II of Israel (1:1). We do not know the date of the earthquake to which Amos alludes, but the two kings in question enjoyed long reigns in the first half of the eighth century B.C., the former from about 790 to 740 B.C., the latter from about 793 to 753 (including co-regencies with their respective fathers). During that time Assyria, the regional power, was not expansionist, so the two kingdoms of Judah and Israel were not oppressed from the outside, and grew politically and militarily strong. (Assyria did not become a threat until after 745, when Tiglath-Pileser III ascended the throne.)

(3) Amos was a missionary, i.e., a cross-cultural preacher of the word of God. He was a shepherd from Tekoa, in Judah, but his ministry took place in Israel. During that time, Jeroboam II, an able man, extended the boundaries as far as Solomon had done. But despite all the prosperity and expansionism, the wealth settled into the hands of a very few. Combined with moral decay and continuing idolatry, this meant that the nation was heading for destruction—and apart from Amos, very few detected the dangers.

(4) Regal king that he is, the Lord "roars" like a lion from Zion, threatening judgment (1:2). His forbearance is running out. That is why one popular Amos commentator (J. Alec Motyer) titles his book *The Day of the Lion*, and another (Roy Clements) *When God's Patience Runs Out*.

(5) The formula "For three sins of X, even for four" (1:3, 6, 9, 11, 12) is a poetic way in Hebrew of specifying four sins. In Amos 1, the sins are the sins of Israel's neighbors: the God who chastens his own covenantal people is nevertheless Judge of all the earth—a truth both somber and encouraging.

∾

1 Chronicles 1—2; Hebrews 8; *Amos 2; Psalm 145*

∾

WOE TO CHINA. IN THIS CENTURY she has butchered fifty million of her own people in the name of equality. Proud and haughty, she maintains an officially atheistic stance, persecuting the church while that church, nurtured by the blood of the martyrs, has in half a century multiplied fifty times.

Woe to Russia. In the second decade of this century she embarked on a massive social experiment that resulted in the deaths of more than forty million people. She subjugated nation after nation, so certain was she that the tide of history was on her side. She became excellent at producing the "revolutionary man," but could not produce the promised "new man" of Marxist thought, and so hid behind illusions and lies until her economic incompetence brought her down.

Woe to Germany. Privileged to serve as home to some of the greatest Reformers, she became extraordinarily arrogant intellectually, and in this century started two world wars that wreaked death and havoc, including the horrors of the Nazis, on countless millions. Today she builds excellent BMWs but has a materialist soul, worshiping nothing greater than the deutsche mark.

Woe to Great Britain. At one time ruler of one-quarter of the world's population; inheritor of some of the greatest Christian thought and literature ever produced, she became ever more proud and condescending to the nations she colonized and the people she enslaved. Having repeatedly squandered a heritage of the knowledge of God, she thrashes around directionless and degraded.

Woe to Canada. She likes to think of herself as morally superior to her nearest neighbor, while hiding under the U.S. military umbrella. Sliding toward a moral abyss, her Supreme Court issues decisions that are as morally corrosive as any in the Western world, while the English-French factionalism drives toward enmity and breakup for want of courtesy and respect from both sides.

Woe to the United States. She prides herself on being the only world power left, but never reflects on how God has brought low every world power in history. Her cherished freedoms, so great a heritage, have increasingly become a facade to hide and then defend the grossest immorality and selfishness. To the nation at large, no issue, absolutely none, is more important than the state of the economy.

This is the reasoning of Amos. In Amos 1, he circles around the pagan neighbors, articulating the judgment of God. Here in **Amos 2**, he moves to Moab, Judah ("Canada"), and finally brings it home to Israel. Israelite audiences would begin with smug contentment during the early parts: how would they end up? *And understand: the sequence of my "Woes," above, could have been rearranged to end with any country—with your country.*

———

∾

1 Chronicles 3—4; Hebrews 9; *Amos 3; Psalms 146—147*

∾

HERE I REFLECT ON TWO themes from **Amos 3**:

·   (1) "You only have I chosen of all the families of the earth; therefore I will punish you for all your sins" (3:2). The basic premise is simple: privilege brings responsibility. But the matter runs deeper, along at least two lines. (a) The peculiar privilege here is being chosen to know God, being known by him—and all knowledge of this God entails proximity to holiness. Small wonder, then, that this privilege brings punishment for sins. (b) But this is in any case itself a privilege. Nurtured sin eventually brings condemnation and destruction; sin punished may bring repentance and contrition, which the Lord seeks. Certainly this text excludes the view that being chosen by God means one is exempt from obedience and faithfulness to him, or that God is a big sugar daddy in the sky. As J. A. Motyer has put it: "Special privileges, special obligations; special grace, special holiness; special revelation, special scrutiny; special love, special responsiveness . . . the church of God cannot ever escape the perils of its uniqueness."

(2) The sequence of rhetorical questions in verses 3-5 may initially seem irrelevant to Western eyes. But doubtless they were Amos's way of getting his message across to hearers who were hostile both to him and to his message. In a culture that loved riddles and proverbs, his questions drew them into his thought before they realized what was up. The point becomes clearer with each new question: events have causes. If people meet and walk together, it is because they have agreed to do so. If a lion roars, it is because it has killed its prey. If a trap is sprung, it is because some bird or animal has triggered it. If a warning trumpet sounds, it is because a dangerous enemy has been sighted. Events have causes. So Amos drives home two points. (a) If disaster strikes a city, God must be behind it (3:6). Of course, there may be many secondary causes, but ultimately God himself is behind it. Amos does not believe in coincidence, bad luck, or a finite God who slips up now and then. He believes in providence—and believing in providence means believing that in disasters God is speaking the language of warning or judgment. (b) The warnings God gives correspond with real dangers. The trumpet blows to warn of a real enemy. God may provide gracious warning through his servants the prophets (3:7)—and such warnings are not hot air, mere religious mouthings, but flags that correspond with imminent danger. So repent: "The lion has roared—who will not fear?" And don't shoot the messenger: "The Sovereign LORD has spoken—who can but prophesy?" (3:8).

∾

1 Chronicles 5—6; Hebrews 10; *Amos 4; Psalms 148—150*

∾

IN SOME WAYS AMOS 4 follows on very naturally from Amos 3. God has said that the warnings of the prophets are linked with real dangers (3:7-8). Now he highlights some of the sins that have evoked his warnings (4:1-5) and explains some of the warnings themselves and what they mean for the future if they are not taken to heart (4:6-13).

(1) The first warning is to the wealthy women of Israel (4:1-3), derogatorily described as "cows of Bashan"—proverbial for being well-fed, fat, and lazy, rather than lean and tough. These women have used their wealth and position to "oppress the poor and crush the needy" (4:1). The one-line vignette is devastating: they say to their husbands, "Bring us some drinks!" (4:1). This conjures up a picture of spoiled matrons, peremptory, decadent, interested only in being served and never in serving, lording it over their husbands, swilling down their boredoms in booze. So the Sovereign Lord swears "by his holiness" (4:2), which is akin to saying that he swears by himself, and thus by that which is immutable and than which there is nothing and no one greater. He swears that he will drag them away with hooks and chains into captivity, humiliated and degraded, in pain amid the rubble of their city (4:2-3).

(2) In the last half of the preceding chapter (3:9-15), God hammered away at three disgusting features of national life: social oppression, self-indulgence, and corrupt religion. The first two are enlarged upon in the first three verses of chapter 4, as we have just seen. The third, corrupt religion, is now treated with fine prophetic scorn (4:4-5). "Go to Bethel and sin; go to Gilgal and sin yet more"— the equivalent of saying, "Go to Canterbury and sin; go to Baptist headquarters and sin yet more." (Fill in your own denominational mecca!) The place where, historically, Israel faithfully offered stipulated sacrifices (before the temple took precedence) are still places of sacrifice, but are now characterized by fine aesthetics, religious enthusiasm, and lots of bragging. Where are contrition and the broken spirit (cf. Ps. 51:17)?

(3) In the following verses (4:6-13) God reviews some of the temporal judgments he has imposed on the people at various times as warnings of much greater judgment to come. These warnings proved ineffective: witness the dreadful refrain, "'[Y]et you have not returned to me,' declares the LORD" (4:8, 9, 10, 11). Therefore the God of Israel will meet them (4:12)—he will meet them, all right, not in the glory of theophany but in the terror of judgment.

∾

1 Chronicles 7—8; Hebrews 11; *Amos 5; Luke 1:1-38*

∾

ON FIRST READING, AMOS 5 is a bit of a muddle. It is made up of such diffuse bits—not only different themes, but different forms and literary genres. The NIV recognizes the point by putting verses 8-9 in parentheses (there are no parentheses in Hebrew). The first three verses are a lament, a funeral dirge, mournfully bemoaning the fall of Israel. Verses 4-6 and 14-15 constitute an evangelistic appeal. This is how Israel must respond if they are to be accepted by the Lord and survive. Verses 7 and 10-13 deal with the oppression and corruption in the land. The last two verses (16-17) return to lament.

It is easy enough to reflect on these distinct themes separately. For example, one might well meditate on how seeking the Lord himself (5:4-6, 14-15) is more important than the aesthetically pleasing form of worship (5:4-5), on how genuine repentance embraces a massive hatred of sin not only at some distant, theoretical level, but at the level of practical integrity and social responsibility, including justice in the courts (5:15). Does any society need to hear this more than ours, where there is less and less interest in justice and righteousness, and more and more interest in merely manipulating the duly enacted laws? And so we could work through all of the themes and forms in 5:1-17.

For some purposes, of course, such thematic analysis is helpful. It finds its extreme in the liberal critic who thinks the chapter is a mismatched pastiche of sources that can be set to rights with scissors and paste. But that misses the genius and power of the chapter. This is a collage, akin to a rapid succession of images on film that dance from war to sermon to funeral to judgment to sin to repentance. Amos's original hearers were hostile. To retain their interest he had to knock them off base, and the resulting rapid transitions give power to the whole precisely because they are jarring and unexpected. We are forced to think not only about the themes themselves, but about their interconnectedness with other themes.

The direction of the whole is exposed in the final verses of the chapter (5:18-27). For all their self-indulgence and moral ambivalence, these people retain a religious fervor that hungers for "the day of the LORD"—as many of us hunger for "revival." But God says he despises their religious feasts and hates their assemblies. What he demands is implacable: "But let justice roll on like a river, righteousness like a never-failing stream!" (5:24). Otherwise "the day of the Lord," when he truly does meet with them, will be a day of dark judgment, infinitely removed from the paradisiacal light for which they hope.

∾

1 Chronicles 9 — 10; Hebrews 12; Amos 6; Luke 1:39-80

∾

TO UNDERSTAND ARIGHT THE POWER OF **Amos 6**, it is helpful to reflect a little on two themes: complacency and the power elite.

(1) I shall begin by reminding you of a story I told in the meditation for January 15. One of my high school history teachers related how, toward the end of World War II, he had been furloughed home because of an injury. He had seen many of his buddies killed; others were still in action. He was riding a bus in a Canadian city, and he heard an obviously wealthy and ostentatious woman in the seat in front of him talking to her companion. Her husband was making a lot of money in arms production. She confided to her seatmate: "I hope this war doesn't end soon. We've never had it so good."

That is the ugly face of complacency. The picture of those "who are complacent in Zion" (6:1) is no less repugnant. There they are, strumming away on their guitars, fancying themselves to be gifted musicians like David (6:5), slurping their Chardonnay, the atmosphere charged with their perfumes and aftershaves (6:6)— but they do not grieve over all that is wrong and corrupt.

(2) Virtually every society develops an elite. An absolute monarchy or a dictatorship demonstrates this in obvious ways. Communism, theoretically classless, develops its own elite, its own rulers; the privilege of birth gives way to the privilege of party membership and political power. In a democracy, there may be relative equality of opportunity, but that is not the same as classlessness. Rather, at its best equal opportunity ensures some mobility within a more or less stratified society: outsiders can become insiders, and the elite can be penetrated by *hoi polloi*. Aristocracy and dictatorship are then replaced by meritocracy; the rule of the rich and the noble is replaced by the rule of the successful and the clever and the vicious. Of course, this is almost inevitable, as many sociologists have explained: for practical reasons, *direct* rule *by* the people is impossible. There have to be representatives, appointees, someone to make decisions and effect things—and a new power bloc is born. Perhaps the greatest benefit of democracy is that it provides a peaceful way of turning blighters out every few years, and selecting others.

But from God's perspective, leadership goes hand in hand with responsibility. Amos 6 is directed against the capitals of Judah and Israel (Zion and Samaria) and against the "notable men" (6:1). The ugly complacency of this chapter is the complacency of rulers and leaders presiding over decadence, compromise, injustice, theological perversity, and their own creature comforts. And where, in the church and in the broader culture, do leadership and complacency join hands today? At how many levels? And what does God think of it?

∾

1 Chronicles 11—12; Hebrews 13; *Amos 7; Luke 2*

∿

IN AMOS 7:1-9 THE PROPHET intercedes with God to avert two catastrophic judgments. In both cases, the Lord relents (7:3, 6). But then God deploys a plumb line to show just how crooked Israel is, and promises that he will spare the people no longer (7:6-9). Two reflections:

(1) If God were endlessly forbearing, there would be no judgment. A lot of people think of God in these terms. God is good, so he is bound to forgive us: that's his job. So argued Catherine the Great. The Bible insists that such a picture of God is hopelessly flawed. On the other hand, if God executed instantaneous justice, there would be no place for either compassion or forbearing delay. This sort of tension is bound up with many virtues. Genuine courage presupposes fear that is overcome. If there is no fear at all, there can be no courage. Similarly, if there is no wrath, forbearance is no longer a virtue; it dissolves into some strange alchemy of niceness and moral indifference. Thus a large part of what these scenes are saying to the ancient Israelites is that God's patience is running out. The reason God has not destroyed them already is that he is forbearing. But genuine forbearance presupposes that justice must sooner or later prevail: it is a call for repentance before it is too late.

(2) God here answers the intercessory prayer of Amos and relents—as in a number of other moving passages where God responds to fervent intercession (Gen. 18:23-33; 20:7; Ex. 32:9-14; Job 42:8-9). How does this square with a passage like 1 Samuel 15:29? "He who is the Glory of Israel does not lie or change his mind; for he is not a man, that he should change his mind." Indeed, if I were certain I could change God's mind in some absolute sense, I would be terrified of trying, for I know far, far less than he. Yet the "prayer of a righteous man is powerful and effective," we are told (James 5:16-18). The point, surely, is that this God is not some cold, deterministic, mechanical, force. He is a personal God who has ordained means as much as ends—means that include our intercession. If we are to pray according to God's will (1 John 5:14), then Luther was right: "Prayer is not overcoming God's reluctance. Prayer is laying hold of God's willingness." It is not so much a means of talking God into a position repugnant to him, as a God-ordained means of obtaining the blessings that God in the perfection of his virtues is willing to bestow. But that perfection of virtues also means that there may come a point when the collision of holiness and sin issues in implacable wrath that will not be diverted.

∿

1 Chronicles 13—14; James 1; *Amos 8; Luke 3*

∽

THERE ARE MANY THINGS IN AMOS 8 that one might usefully reflect on: the whining moans that religious services last too long and cut into time better used for business (8:5); the shady practices that boost profits (8:5b); the rising slavery grounded in economic penury (8:6); the bitter irony of 8:7 (if one remembers that "the Pride of Jacob" is God himself); the apocalyptic language of 8:9 (compare Joel 2:30-31 and Acts 2:19-20); the colorful imagery of the "ripe fruit" (8:1-2). But here I shall focus on verses 11-12: "'The days are coming,' declares the Sovereign LORD, 'when I will send a famine through the land—not a famine of food or a thirst for water, but a famine of hearing the words of the LORD. Men will stagger from sea to sea and wander from north to east, searching for the word of the LORD, but they will not find it.'"

This expresses a "use it or lose it" philosophy. The covenant people in Amos's day are content not to regulate their lives by God's revelation, and so they will lose it. Whether "the words of the LORD" refers to messages spoken to them through prophets such as Amos, or to the written Word of God (substantial parts of which were already available) makes little difference. The point is that the people who do not devote themselves to the words of God eventually lose them. The loss is catastrophic. The only adequate analogy is a desperate famine.

It is easy to see how this judgment works out in history. For complex historical reasons, France turned on the Huguenots and persecuted them almost out of existence, so the Bible and the Reformation never took hold in France as it did in England. Sometimes the antipathy toward the Bible has arisen from drift, rather than from persecution. In many Western countries, the public sense of morality was until a few decades ago largely tied to the Ten Commandments. Nowadays very few even know what the Ten Commandments are. The result is not freedom and integrity, but a lilting scorn that flaunts its superiority over something no longer even understood, much less respected—and what shall the end of these things be? So many Bibles, so many Bibles—and so little thoughtful reading of them. The next stage is the Bible as source of prooftexts; the stage after that is the Bible as quaint relic; the next, the Bible as antiquarian magic; the next, implacable ignorance—and all the while, a growing hunger for something wise, something stable, something intelligent, something prophetic, something true. And the hunger is not satisfied.

The only answer is the fulfillment of Jesus' prayer in John 17:17.

∽

1 Chronicles 15; James 2; *Amos 9*; *Luke 4*

∾

ALTHOUGH AMOS 9 CONTAINS some pretty dreadful threats of judgment, it ends on a positive chord in three-part harmony.

(1) The judgment will not be total, but partial. "I will not totally destroy the house of Jacob," the Lord declares (9:8). The sifting will be very thorough (9:9-10), but God will spare a remnant. From about the time of Elijah on, the remnant theme gets stronger with each passing century. Thoughtful people receive it and are greatly encouraged: God always preserves some faithful people.

(2) "In that day"—a prophetic formula that is exceedingly flexible in its referent—God "will restore David's fallen tent" (9:11). God will restore the Davidic dynasty to its former splendor—indeed, to something even greater, as the next verse suggests. Amos was warning the *northern* kingdom; at this point the Davidic dynasty, however reduced, was still intact in the south. This prophecy does not envisage the restoration of the dynasty after it has ceased for a time to exist (which is the way the later prophets speak, a century and a half after Amos). Rather, it foresees the restoration of the dynasty to its former glory, and more.

(3) The final verses of the chapter (9:13-15) portray such a time of fertility in the land that the reaper is overtaken by the plowman—a wonderful picture of almost magical fertility. The ruined cities will be rebuilt, and never again will Israel be uprooted from the land.

When are these prophecies fulfilled? The first is surely fulfilled in the events surrounding the exile, but similar events have happened many times since. God preserved a remnant then, and he has done so since. Some think that once the extravagant language of the closing verses is taken with a grain of salt, these promises were fulfilled when the people returned to the land after the exile. But the text says they would "never again" be uprooted, and of course they were. So one must conclude either that Amos goofed or that this promise was not fulfilled in the postexilic period. Certainly that period did not witness the restoration of the Davidic empire. So some foresee a literal fulfillment in the future. But Christians will remember how 9:11-12 is applied by James at the Jerusalem Council (Acts 15:16-17). He insists that Jesus is the Davidic king, that his reign fulfills this promise, that the blessings to the Gentiles hinted at here are being fulfilled in the extension of the Gospel to the Gentiles. This suggests a *typological* fulfillment of some Old Testament prophecies—an approach that has a bearing on how we read some other Old Testament prophecies as well.

∾

1 Chronicles 16; James 3; *Obadiah; Luke 5*

∽

WE EARLIER REFLECTED ON THE judgments God pronounced on Edom, the nation made up of the descendants of Esau (and thus the distant cousins of the Israelites). Ezekiel is very explicit (Ezek. 35; see meditation for October 2); Hosea is less prosaic but says similar things (Hosea 13; see meditation for November 7). Here in **Obadiah**, an entire book (albeit a short one) is devoted to this theme. The time is after the sack of Jerusalem in 587 B.C., and possibly as late as the early postexilic period when the Jews started returning to the land. The fulfillment of these prophecies took place over an extended period. Certainly by 312 the capital of Edom was firmly in the hands of the Nabatean Arabs. A coalition of Arabs had been displacing the Edomites for more than a century. In the early period they were led by King Geshem, who in about 440 was one of Nehemiah's opponents.

One must ask why the Old Testament prophets devote so much time and space to Edom.

(1) Swelling through this little book is the theme of God's justice. If Edom could get away with her triumphalism and gloating, when her own conduct was no better than that of the nation of the Jews she mocked, then there is no justice.

(2) The point can be universalized. "The day of the Lord is near for *all* nations. As you have done, it will be done to you; your deeds will return upon your own head" (15, italics added). Although in some ways Edom is unique (of the surrounding nations only she had blood ties to Israel), yet at another level she stands as an important model for *all* nations. When we see opponents fall, we had better recognize that God is the One who exacts temporal judgments—and one day all of us will face eternal judgment. Temporal judgments are thus God's prophetic announcement of what will happen to all. Jesus argues along similar lines (Luke 13:1-5) with respect to relatively small groups of individuals. Here Obadiah insists the same thing is true at the level of the nation. The Nazis fell: should we gloat and pat our backs in triumphalistic glee? Shall we not remember that Germany was a country of extraordinary education and technical competence, and it turned toward power, expansionism, and cascading evil—and fell? Should we not fear, and beg God for mercy that we might walk in integrity, honor, and love of virtue?

(3) In some ways, Obadiah is a commentary on Amos 9:12. Like Judah, Edom is cut down. Nevertheless the hope of the world lies in Judah's future, not Edom's—and that kingdom is the Lord's (17, 21). That was reason enough not to despise God's covenant people, both then and now.

∽

1 Chronicles 17; James 4; *Jonah 1*; *Luke 6*

∿

REGARDLESS OF WHEN THE BOOK OF Jonah was written, Jonah himself can be located with fair accuracy. According to 2 Kings 14:25, Jonah son of Amittai was a prophet from Gath Hepher who predicted the military successes of King Jeroboam II (about 793 to 753 B.C.). If one were to play a game and ask what verbal link comes to mind when the word *Jonah* is uttered, probably most people would reply, "big fish" or "whale" or the like. Yet we should not forget that the big fish occupies textual interest for precisely three verses—three out of forty-eight. The comment of G. Campbell Morgan is still appropriate: "Men have looked so hard at the great fish that they have failed to see the great God."

The greatness of God is highlighted by Jonah's twin confessions (1:9; 4:2). Here we reflect on the first: "I am a Hebrew and I worship the LORD, the God of heaven, who made the sea and the land" (1:9).

(1) From our perspective, as from Jonah's, this confesses that God made everything, that he is the Sovereign Lord over the entire universe. Probably the pagan sailors did not understand quite so much. For them, the gods have various domains. If this Hebrew claims that the God from whom he is fleeing is the Creator of *the sea* (whatever else he made), for them the claim would gain credibility precisely because of the storm.

(2) But for Jonah (and for us), the claim has two other overtones. *First:* not only has God made the sea, but everything; and he is in charge of everything. So there is no escaping this God. Even if Jonah were to find a way to get to shore safely, this God can track him down anywhere. Jonah painfully recognizes that there is no fleeing from this God—if "the hound of heaven" is on your trail and resolves that you will not get away. That is why he invites death. *Second:* the sheer greatness of God is what makes sense of God's determination to give the wicked city of Nineveh an opportunity to turn from its sin. If monotheism is true, if there is but one God, then in some sense this God must be God of all, not just the God of the covenant people. This Jonah could not stand. He could see that just over the horizon Assyria would become a formidable foe of his own people, the people of God—and here is God giving them ample opportunity to repent.

(3) From a canonical perspective, here once again is the missionary God—far more committed to reaching toward "outsiders" than his people are. Here too he prepares the ground, step by step, for the Great Commission that mandates believers to herald the good news of Jesus Christ throughout the whole world.

∿

1 Chronicles 18; James 5; *Jonah 2; Luke 7*

∾

TWO STAGGERING THOUGHTS COME together in **Luke 7:36-50**:

(1) The first I have mentioned before in these two volumes, but it is worth mentioning again. Who has the right to forgive sins? If someone robbed you of your life's savings or murdered your spouse, I would not have the right to forgive the perpetrator. On the human plane, the only one who can forgive is the injured party. From God's perspective, of course, regardless of how many human beings are injured, the primary offense is against God himself (cf. Ps. 51:4). Thus God can forgive *any* sin, because he is *always* the injured party. On the human plane, the sinful woman in this narrative had not injured Jesus in any way. At that level, he did not have the right to forgive her. But the narrative turns on Jesus' forgiveness of this woman (7:48)—and the other guests, a bit confused by this development, raise the question, "Who is this who even forgives sins?" (7:49). Who, indeed?

(2) The axiom Jesus develops in his interchange with Simon is puzzling. At one level the axiom is clear enough: the person who has been forgiven many things is likely to be more thankful to the benefactor than the person who has been forgiven little. As Jesus says, "[H]e who has been forgiven little loves little" (7:47). The axiom makes sense of the conduct of both the woman and the Pharisee: she is overcome with tears of sheer gratitude, while he is stuffy and supercilious.

But if this axiom is pressed too hard, would it not mean that those who have lived a relatively "good" life inevitably love God less than those who have been converted out of a life of abysmal degradation? One might then argue that there are some benefits to being degraded before conversion: one appreciates grace in proportion to the degree of depravity grace must overcome.

That misses the point. At the social level, of course, the woman's sins are much worse than the Pharisee's. But the gradations of sin that one makes at the social level are nothing compared with the awfulness of the rebellion in which each of us has indulged. Simon the Pharisee has not even got to the place where he perceives that he *needs* to be forgiven. Suppose instead that two people have both been converted, one from a socially despicable background and one from a disciplined and "righteous" background: what then? *Both* ought to pray that they may see the ugliness of their own sins, whether sins socially disapproved or those ugly sins (often condemned by Jesus) of arrogance and self-righteousness. For unless we are given grace to see the horror of our sin, it is quite certain that we shall never grasp the glory of grace, and we will love Jesus too little.

∾

1 Chronicles 19—20; 1 Peter 1; *Jonah 3; Luke 8*

～

THE CALMING OF THE STORM (**Luke 8:22-25**) as reported in Luke's gospel carries special weight:

(1) The substance of the account is straightforward, though almost obliquely it sheds light on the sheer exhaustion Jesus sometimes experienced in the course of his extensive ministry "from one town and village to another, proclaiming the good news of the kingdom of God" (8:1). Not only could he fall asleep in the boat, he could remain asleep even when the boat tossed and corkscrewed in a storm serious enough to frighten fishermen.

(2) The closing lines of this paragraph draw attention to its chief focus: who Jesus is. "Who is this?" the disciples ask. "He commands even the winds and the water, and they obey him" (8:25). Indeed, the paragraph kicks off a series of miracles. In the following verses Jesus heals a demon-possessed man (8:26-39), raises a dead girl and heals a sick woman (8:40-56), provides the Twelve with similar authority (9:1-9), and then feeds the five thousand (9:10-17)—which is then an entirely appropriate place to pause and reflect again on who Jesus is (9:18ff.). The one who controls the natural elements and the powers of the spirit-world and who can even overturn death itself is not only the promised "Christ of God" (9:20) but is transfigured before three apostles (9:28-36), who see something of the glory that his incarnate form normally shielded.

(3) But one must also ponder the strange question Jesus asks: "Where is your faith?" (8:25). This must not be misunderstood. Jesus is not berating his followers for some ostensible failure to see the goodness of the world or the inevitability of a happy ending. Storms do kill people; cancer can take out a fifteen-year-old; accidents happen; good people die. To think otherwise is to display not faith but Pollyannish optimism. The faith the disciples should have had is faith *in Jesus*—not simply faith that he could or would help them out, but rich faith in him precisely because *if* he is the promised Messiah sent by Almighty God, it is ridiculous to think that an "accidental" storm could kill him and those with him. Their fears betray less than a firm, faithful grasp of who Jesus is. (On this point see also vol. 1, meditation for February 3.)

(4) Now the contribution of 8:22-25 to the larger context is clearer: The parable of the sower looks for *hearers* of the word who persevere and produce a crop (8:10-11, 15). The next lines tell the reader, "Therefore consider carefully *how you listen*" (8:18, italics added). Jesus' real mother and brothers "are those who *hear* God's word and *put it into practice*" (8:21, italics added). So now our text: genuine disciples display their faith when they so broadly recognize who Jesus is that they trust him in all circumstances.

～

1 Chronicles 21; 1 Peter 2; *Jonah 4; Luke 9*

∾

JONAH IS TERRIBLY UPSET (**Jonah 4**) because the judgments he has pronounced against Nineveh have not taken place. The people have repented, from king to pauper, and God has relented and shown mercy to the great city. "O LORD, is this not what I said when I was still at home?" (4:2). This is stronger than an idiomatic and caustic "I told you so." The expression "what I said" is literally "my word": Jonah pits his own word against "the word of the LORD" (1:1) that he had been called to deliver. He is telling God, "See? I told you so. My word was right, and your word was at best ill thought out." He explodes, "I knew that you are a gracious and compassionate God, slow to anger and abounding in love, a God who relents from sending calamity" (4:2). This basic creedal confession is found in Exodus 34:6-7; Jonah cites it in the same form in which it is found in Joel 2:13 (which may be significant: Joel 2:14 is cited in Jonah 3:9). When the prophets want grace and mercy for themselves, they appeal to God's character; when Jonah does not want grace and mercy for others, he portrays the same attributes of God as fatal weaknesses. He has forgotten 2:1-9, where he recognizes that only God's mercy could have released him from the big fish. The ironies call to mind one of Jesus' parables in which grace is gladly received but denied to another (Matt. 18:23-35). In 4:3 Jonah pretentiously strikes a pose: his words "take away my life" are culled from Elijah (1 Kings 19:4)—but instead of continuing "for I am no better than my ancestors" (a confession of personal weakness and failure), Jonah says "for it is better for me to die than to live"— which is nothing but whining self-pity.

There follows the incident of the "vine," probably a ricinus plant, whose broad leaves provide some shelter. When it dies, Jonah repeats his whining desire to die (4:8), and God repeats the question he raised earlier: "Have you any right to be angry?" (4:4, 9). In rough language Jonah insists he has every right to be angry. What's the point of living in a world that pops up a ricinus and then cuts it down again, dead almost before it is alive? So God debunks Jonah's thinking. Jonah shows more concern for the death of a plant than for the death of a city. Yet even here, his concern for the ricinus is not deep, but provoked by self-interest. He views the Ninevites the same way—with no thought for what is good for them, but out of self-interest. It is God, the gracious and merciful God, whose compassion extends to "that great city" (4:11). Reflect on Matthew 23:37-39; 28:18-19.

∾

1 Chronicles 22; 1 Peter 3; *Micah 1*; *Luke 10*

THE OPENING LINES OF MICAH 1 show that this prophet served in the second half of the eighth century B.C. Initially, mighty Assyria was dormant, and the twin kingdoms of Israel and Judah flourished. Israel expanded its territory under Jeroboam II. This book records the vision that Micah saw "concerning Samaria and Jerusalem" (the two capital cities, 1:1). The first oracle was clearly delivered before either capital had fallen. Later in the book Samaria has fallen (722 B.C.) and Jerusalem itself, in the time of King Hezekiah, is under threat. Although Judah was overrun by the Assyrians in 701, Jerusalem itself was miraculously spared. Micah, from Moresheth Gath (a farming village southwest of Jerusalem), is called to prophesy in Judah, much as Amos was called to prophesy in Israel.

Throughout much of Micah's ministry, Judah was prosperous. The money was invested in land, with the result that a few rich and powerful operators bought up huge tracts, destroying the system of agricultural small holdings mandated by the covenant (2:2; Isa. 5:8 inveighs against the same corruption). But issues of justice and social responsibility were not high on anyone's agenda. Coming as he did from the fertile lowlands, Micah doubtless saw firsthand how ordinary people were being crushed; he was providentially prepared to utter the prophetic word of God's own indignation. He attacks the rising selfishness and the widespread abandonment of the standards of God's law, as he depicts Judah on the brink of catastrophic judgment. Writing a century or so later, Jeremiah records a fascinating report of Micah's ministry (Jer. 26:18-19); it is probably not too fanciful to conclude that Hezekiah's initial and powerful reformation owed a great deal to Micah's preaching.

Above all Micah is shocked at the perversion of true religion (2:6-9). Israel's election has come to be equated with triumphalist theology (3:11); God himself has been reduced to a grandfatherly protector of a pampered people. Micah therefore warns the people of the implications of covenantal disloyalty (6:14-15). Already in chapter 1 he makes it clear that God must punish his people if they continue in their sin: "All this is because of Jacob's transgression, because of the sins of the house of Israel" (1:5). Where is the locus of such sin? In the capital cities themselves (1:5b). The odious corruption and faithlessness have worked down from the top.

These driving themes have two critical bearings on us. *First*, they demand that we become passionate about righteousness and covenantal faithfulness in our own day. *Second*, they set the stage for Micah's vision of a promised redeemer (e.g., 5:2).

1 Chronicles 23; 1 Peter 4; *Micah 2; Luke 11*

∾

WHEN THINGS GO RADICALLY WRONG in a culture, the problems often become intertwined. Two of the strands are twisted together in **Micah 2:6-11**. The passage begins and ends with a warning against false prophets, but in the middle of the oracle is Amos's ongoing denunciation of the powerful people who are stripping bare the powerless (2:8-9).

Begin with the latter. They are so corrupt, Micah announces, that they act not like the people of the covenant, but like their enemies (2:8a). Women and children are despoiled by these brutes (2:9). Children cruelly lose their inheritance while these powerful people become richer—even though it is written, "Do not take advantage of a widow or an orphan. If you do and they cry out to me, I will certainly hear their cry. My anger will be aroused, and I will kill you with the sword; your wives will become widows and your children fatherless" (Ex. 22:22-23).

With this background in God's revelation, one might have thought that the prophets of the land would be calling the powerful to account. Instead, the powerful and the corrupt turn out to be the prophets' patrons. These prophets still preach, but what they preach is that Hosea must not preach (2:6). Micah's response is blistering: "If a liar and deceiver comes and says, 'I will prophesy for you plenty of wine and beer,' he would be just the prophet for this people" (2:11).

We must see how this happens. It is terribly easy for the preacher to shape his message to fit in with the spirit of the age. What begins as a concern to be relevant and contemporary—both admirable goals—ends up with seduction and domestication. This is especially likely when the rich and the powerful are paying our bills. At every level it is easy to fool oneself into thinking that cowardice is prudence, that silence on the moral issues of the day is a small price to pay in order to have influence in the corridors of power. Get invited to the White House (or even denominational headquarters!), and you will never inveigh against its sins. Give a lecture at a prestigious academic organ, and be sure to ruffle as few feathers as possible. Become a bishop, and instead of being the next J. C. Ryle, you sell your silence. Of course, it doesn't have to be that way. God will always have his Micah and his Amos. But it happens frequently enough that we ought to return often to God's revelation, to make sure that our message is shaped by what he has said and is neither the fruit of smart-mouthed petulance nor the oily "appropriateness" of those who cleverly say only what people want to hear.

∾

1 Chronicles 24—25; 1 Peter 5; *Micah 3*; *Luke 12*

∾

JESUS TELLS HIS "FRIENDS" not to be afraid "of those who kill the body and after that can do no more. But I will show you whom you should fear: Fear him who, after the killing of the body, has power to throw you into hell. Yes, I tell you, fear him" (**Luke 12:4-5**). The Gospel demands that we examine not only our loves, but our fears. We are to love God above all others; so also are we to fear him above all others. The reason is the same in both cases: he is God. He deserves our passionate adoration; he is not to be trifled with. His untrammeled holiness evokes our awe; it also evokes our fear. We should love him now, and we will love him without reserve in the new heaven and the new earth; we should fear him, for he has both the power and the right to exclude us from the new heaven and the new earth.

People sometimes say, unthinkingly, that it is a great blessing that so-and-so has died, for he or she was in such great pain during the last days or weeks of life on this earth. But supposing the person was an unrepentant reprobate: is he or she better off now? Not according to this passage. Again, how many of our decisions in life are shaped in part by what people think or, more precisely, by what we fear they will think? In short, we are often afraid of people—if not afraid of brutal attack, then afraid of condescension, afraid of rejection, afraid of being marginalized, afraid of being laughed at. There is very little possibility of overcoming such fear by merely trying to stop fearing. We need to fear something else more, something that will make the fear of people not only wrong but silly. If we absorb the words of these two verses, and fear God above all, the problem will largely be resolved. That is one of the reasons why it is so important to know this God and to think much about him: you will never fear God if he rarely crosses the horizon of your thought.

Lest anyone should think for a moment that the Christian's connection with Almighty God is characterized by nothing but fear, we must observe that even in this chapter Jesus tells his followers, "Do not be afraid, little flock"—of people, or circumstances, or the future—"for your Father has been pleased to give you the kingdom" (12:32). Although God is to be feared, the reason is not because he is the meanest dude of all. Far from it: his love and grace and holiness—all of his perfections—combine to provide the most glorious future possible for his own.

∾

1 Chronicles 26—27; 2 Peter 1; *Micah 4; Luke 13*

∿

SEVERAL TIMES MICAH MOVES from a long section of denunciation and warning to a relatively short, positive vision of the future. **Micah 4** includes one such vision (4:1-5), immediately followed by a description of *how* the daughter of Zion gets from here to there (4:6-13): she passes *through* severe testing and chastening, and emerges on the other side into the light of God's blessing.

The opening verses depict a time when "the mountain of the LORD's temple will be established as chief among the mountains; it will be raised above the hills, and peoples will stream to it" (4:1). Many mountains in the ancient Near East were sites for the worship of some god or other. To say that "the mountain of the LORD's temple"—i.e., Zion—is established as "chief" among them and "raised above the others" is to say that the God of Israel has now eclipsed all other gods. The result is that not only does Israel stream back to the site, but "peoples" do so as well. "Many nations" exhort one another, saying, "Come, let us go up to the mountain of the LORD, to the house of the God of Jacob. He will teach us his ways, so that we may walk in his paths" (4:2).

Then the movement of the oracle swings around from the centripetal to the centrifugal. "The law will go out from Zion, the word of the LORD from Jerusalem" (4:2b). The result is that justice prevails among many peoples, and war sinks away, swamped by peace as people, transformed by the word of God, "beat their swords into plowshares and their spears into pruning hooks" (4:3). The vision concludes with the only thing that can ensure its fulfillment: "the LORD Almighty has spoken" (4:4). So now, in his own day, Micah insists that genuine believers not be seduced by other gods, who could not possibly effect this transformation. This is the time to be faithful to the one, true God of the covenant. "All the nations may walk in the name of their gods; we will walk in the name of the LORD our God for ever and ever" (4:5).

The symbol-laden vision is cast in the categories of Micah's day: the weapons of war, for example, become plowshares and pruning hooks, not tractors and combines. Though cast in terms of the supremacy of Mount Zion, there is no mention of an Israelite hegemony over the nations, nor of the Messiah or the sacrifice he would offer. Even the geography of the oracle looks a little different from the perspective of John 4:21-24. But in the light of the Gospel, the triumph of the new Jerusalem, which brings to an end death and war and all sin (Rev. 21:1-4), is that for which all Christians pray, the fulfillment of Micah's vision.

∿

1 Chronicles 28; 2 Peter 2; *Micah 5; Luke 14*

∽

IF THE FORWARD-LOOKING VISION OF Micah 4 does not include any description of a coming Messiah, the opening verses of **Micah 5** redress the balance. The chapter begins with a sad depiction of Jerusalem and her king (5:1). Probably the historical allusion is to the invasion of the Assyrians under Sennacherib in 701 B.C. Although in God's providence Jerusalem held up, the other walled towns of Judah were breached, and King Hezekiah was humiliated and almost overthrown. Ideally, the king from David's line was to quell rebellion and disorder "with a rod of iron" (Ps. 2); he was to promote justice by striking with the rod of his mouth (Isa. 11:4). Yet here "Israel's ruler" is struck "on the cheek with a rod" (5:1).

But the dynasty survives. Without filling in the intermediate steps, Micah the prophet envisages another king from the Davidic line (5:2-4). He springs from Bethlehem Ephrathah, ancestral home of David, the birthplace of his dynasty. From this village, God says, "will come for me one who will be ruler over Israel, whose origins are from of old, from ancient times" (5:2). This wording is not affirming the eternal preexistence of this messianic figure (though of course it is not denying it). Rather, the glorious prospect is grounded in the past, in the ancient Davidic dynasty. When this king takes up the scepter, he will "shepherd his flock," not in the uncertain strength of Hezekiah or any other king who precedes him in the line, but "in the strength of the LORD, in the majesty of the name of the LORD his God" (5:4). And in due course "his greatness will reach to the ends of the earth," and the secure peace pictured in the previous chapter will be ushered in (5:4-5).

So in the fullness of time, God arranged international affairs to ensure that Jesus was born not in Nazareth, the residence of Mary and Joseph, but in Bethlehem, their ancestral home (Luke 2). It was almost as if Almighty God was going a second mile: not only would it be said that Jesus "as to his human nature was a descendant of David" (Rom. 1:3) and thus an offshoot from Bethlehem, but that he was actually born there. Indeed, when the Magi arrived in Herod's court to inquire as to where the promised King had been born, the chief priests and teachers of the Law quoted this passage in Micah 5 to settle the matter: he would be born in Bethlehem in Judea (Matt. 2:5-6). Though the village of Bethlehem was entirely unprepossessing ("small among the clans of Judah," 5:2), with such a son it could "by no means" be considered "least among the rulers of Judah" (Matt. 2:6).

∽

1 Chronicles 29; 2 Peter 3; *Micah 6; Luke 15*

∾

THERE IS IMPORTANT COMMON GROUND IN **Micah 6** and **Luke 15**. Yet I shall approach it obliquely.

One of the slogans of the Reformation was *simul justus et peccator,* a Latin phrase meaning something like "simultaneously just[ified] and a sinner." It was a way of getting at the legal nature of justification as expounded by Paul. On the ground of Christ's death, God declares guilty sinners just—not because, *from the act of justification itself,* they are in their actions and thoughts truly just or right-eous, but because they have been acquitted before the bar of God's justice. Because Christ has paid their penalty, they are just in God's eyes, even though, at the level of their very being, they are sinners still. Nevertheless, the Reformers never argued that justification stands by itself. Justification is part of salvation, but it is not all of it. The Holy Spirit brings conviction of sin and regeneration; the ultimate step is the final transformation of God's people in body and spirit at the last day. These elements and more belong together, and all who are truly saved ultimately experience all of them. So while justification *in and of itself* leaves a per-son a sinner still, justification never operates all by itself. Genuine salvation not only forgives us but transforms us.

Micah understands this. He does not so much deal with the ground of Israel's acceptance before God (which is finally tied to God's grace, Deut. 9) as insist that, if the covenantal relationship with God is genuine, it will not be soaked in idol-atry, syncretism, and injustice. So how shall I come before the Lord? Shall I sac-rifice the prescribed yearling? (6:6). How about thousands of rams? Or how about sacrificing my own son: will that pay "for the sin of my soul" (6:7)? What the Lord requires is this: "To act justly and to love mercy and to walk humbly with your God" (6:8).

Micah is not alone on this point, of course. Jesus preached something simi-lar, quoting Hosea (Matt. 9:13). Paul insists that the wicked will not inherit the kingdom of God (1 Cor. 6:9-11). He does not mean that only the perennial goody-goody will make it, for he goes on to say that some of his readers once practiced astonishing evil. But if they have been truly saved, transformation must manifest itself. That is equally true in the parable of the lost son (Luke 15:11-27). He is received by the father's grace. Yet in the complexity of the return, the son abandons his sin even as he casts himself on his father's mercy. As critically important as *simul justus et peccator* is, it must *never, never* be used to justify the practice of sin.

∾

2 Chronicles 1; 1 John 1; *Micah 7; Luke 16*

∽

THE ACCOUNT OF THE RICH MAN and Lazarus (**Luke 16:19-31**) stirs the imagination by its powerful reversal. The rich and powerful man ends up in hell; the poor man at his gate ends up by the side of Abraham. Some observations:

(1) The narrative does not make explicit the reason why Lazarus the beggar was received up into the presence of Abraham, or why the rich man was excluded from that blessedness and consigned to hell. But there are hints. Although the Bible is far from imagining that every poor person is automatically justified (read Proverbs) and every rich person automatically condemned (consider Solomon, Zacchaeus, and Philemon), nevertheless there is some kind of alignment. Elsewhere Jesus insists it is impossible to serve both God and money (Matt. 6:24). The narrative before us says that Lazarus lay ill and hungry outside the rich man's gate, and was literally dying to receive scraps of food. The rich man provided nothing. He was therefore without compassion; he was contravening even the most elementary societal expectations of courtesy and hospitality; he would not even give alms. As for Lazarus, he belongs to a long tradition in Israel going back to the Wisdom Literature that often associates the poor and the despised with the contrite and the righteous. That is simply assumed here. The reversal follows. It would be shocking to those of Jesus' hearers who were pursuing the almighty shekel.

(2) At least part of the description of the state after death must be symbolic (Is there a real chasm between Lazarus and the rich man? Can residents of the two domains converse back and forth at will?). Nevertheless some elements of this description have to be accepted at face value, or the entire account unravels. The rich man is in conscious torment (entirely in line with other passages of Scripture). Lazarus is in (literally) "Abraham's bosom"—i.e., he is with Abraham, and wherever Abraham is, there must be peace and blessing. The fixed chasm ensures that no one may pass from one abode to the other—which rather discourages the view that some people may be converted after death.

(3) Abraham's response to the rich man's concern for his surviving brothers establishes two important points. *First,* they were without excuse because they had the Scriptures ("Moses and the Prophets," 16:29). We should not think that those who will not listen to what Scripture says will listen to anything else—so why resort to gimmickry? The assumption is that Scripture is the first recourse. *Second,* even the spectacularly miraculous is not more convincing than Scripture (16:31). Those who will not be convinced by Scripture "will not be convinced even if someone rises from the dead" (16:31). And someone has.

∽

2 Chronicles 2; 1 John 2; *Nahum 1; Luke 17*

∾

FROM THE TWO DESIGNATED PASSAGES, I shall reflect on two faces of judgment.

From **Nahum 1**, we learn that sometimes God's promise of judgment on the triumphant perpetrators of evil can be an encouragement. That is a summary of the theme of this book. Nahum is called to pronounce judgment on Assyria and its capital Nineveh, but unlike Jonah he is not called to proclaim this message to the Assyrians, but to the covenant people of God. That is seen, for instance, in the way Nahum initially talks about Nineveh in the third person (1:8). When Nineveh is directly addressed (e.g., 1:11), that is merely part of the rhetoric of the oracle.

At a guess, Nahum delivered these words from the Lord sometime after 722 B.C., when Assyria destroyed Samaria, the capital city of Israel, and transported many of its leading citizens. The ten northern tribes effectively ceased to exist as a nation. But the faithful believers among those left behind and among those carried off into exile, not to mention the watching Israelites in the southern kingdom of Judah, needed to know that God does not stop reigning, or holding people to account, just because he uses them to chasten his people (cf. Isa. 10:5ff.). "The LORD takes vengeance on his foes and maintains his wrath against his enemies" (1:2). "The LORD is good, a refuge in times of trouble. He cares for those who trust in him, but with an overwhelming flood he will make an end of Nineveh; he will pursue his foes into darkness" (1:7-8). Many, many times when believers have been crushed under wicked regimes, or when innocent nations have been pulverized by brutal and powerful nations, words like these have sustained the faithful: God is just, and will hold the violent oppressors accountable, regardless of their political stance, religious affiliation, race, economics, or public image.

From **Luke 17** comes the memorable line, "Remember Lot's wife" (17:32; cf. Gen. 19:26). The picture is of "the day the Son of Man is revealed" (17:30). Judgment will be so sudden that the person on the rooftop—where people could catch some fresh, cooling breeze in the evening—should not think of going downstairs to take something with them. They should run from rooftop to rooftop and get out before the judgment falls. The imagery, of course, depends on first-century Jerusalem architecture. But the words "Remember Lot's wife," and the verse that follows, combine to show that the real issue is hesitation as to where one's heart belongs. Those who longingly look back to the City of Destruction and try to cling to its toys are destroyed with them. Press on, then; invest in heaven's stock (Matt. 6:19-21); set your sights on the New Jerusalem.

∾

2 Chronicles 3—4; 1 John 3; *Nahum 2; Luke 18*

∾

TODAY I SHALL REFLECT ON **Luke 18:31-43**. These verses are divided into two sections.

The *first* section (18:31-34) constitutes a prediction of Christ's passion. It reports one of several times when Jesus tried to warn his disciples what would happen when he went up to Jerusalem for the last time. Despite the explicitness of Jesus' language, the "disciples did not understand any of this. Its meaning was hidden from them, and they did not know what he was talking about" (18:34). From our perspective, this side of the cross, we might wonder how they could be so thick. What they suffered from was a narrow focus of vision equivalent to having blinders on. Their conception of Messiah was that he was triumphant. Certainly Jesus had the power. The kind of person who could heal the sick, raise the dead, still storms, and walk on water could certainly take on a few Roman legions; he could certainly turf out corrupt officials and impose justice on the land. Besides, couldn't all of Jesus' expressions be understood in some way other than the way Christians take them today? In the Old Testament (the disciples might have recalled) the title "Son of Man" is only rarely messianic: of whom, then, is Jesus speaking? Perhaps the handing over of this "Son of Man" to Gentiles is a temporary thing prior to his dramatic rescue in the final fight—that is, he will "rise again" (18:33).

In broader theological terms, the disciples had not come to terms with the fact that the promised king from the line of David would also be the suffering servant. Their expectations were bent; they could see only what they expected to see. On the broadest horizon, that is one of the effects of the corrosive, blinding power of sin: it so dulls our vision and disorients our perspective that it shuts off crucial parts of evidence so we cannot see the truth and the greatness and the glory of God's revelation.

The *second* section deals with the healing of the blind man sitting by the side of the Jericho road (18:35-43). Unlike the disciples in the previous verse, who doubtless thought they understood something of what was said, even though they didn't, this man knows he is blind. Others try to quiet him; he will not be silent, but calls all the more strenuously: "Son of David, have mercy on me!" (18:39). Jesus heals him; the man sees. And that is always what is needed: for men and women to admit their blindness and cry to him who alone can give sight. Otherwise, no matter how many words are spoken, their meaning will be hidden.

∾

2 Chronicles 5:1—6:11; 1 John 4; *Nahum 3; Luke 19*

∽

BY ITSELF, THE PARABLE OF THE TEN MINAS (**Luke 19:11-27**) is easy enough to understand. What makes it more challenging is the way it is bracketed—that is, how it is introduced and how it ends.

(1) The story itself depicts a nobleman who travels to a distant country to be appointed king. The picture would not be foreign: the Herods on occasion traveled to Rome to obtain or to secure their standing with Caesar. Before leaving, the nobleman entrusts ten minas, a considerable sum of money, to his servants, apparently one mina to each. On his return (and now king), he discovers that his servants have handled his money with various degrees of success. The parable does not recount each servant's rate of return, but reports representative cases. One has earned ten minas, an increase of 1,000 percent; another, five minas, an increase of 500 percent. Each is rewarded extravagantly, but in proportion to the increase. One servant merely returns to his master the mina he has been given. His excuse is that he is afraid of the master, knowing him to be a hard man. The rest of the story plays out. Probably we contemporary readers need to be reminded that the servants were not employees who could quit if they wanted to or withhold their services under union rules. They were slaves who owed their master their best effort. Hence the punishment for the irresponsible slave.

(2) But the story ends with a lengthy saying: "I tell you that to everyone who has, more will be given, but as for the one who has nothing, even what he has will be taken away. But those enemies of mine who did not want me to be king over them—bring them here and kill them in front of me" (19:26-27). The last servant has nothing by way of increase; all he "has" is the gift entrusted to him for the benefit of another. The king's servants are responsible to labor for their master's profit, and if they do not, they show themselves to be rebellious servants, no true servants at all. They are scarcely better than the enemies who defy the master's kingship altogether.

(3) All of this must be nestled into the framework of expectation created by the opening verse (19:11). Jesus tells this parable to respond to those who thought "that the kingdom of God was going to appear at once." Not so, the parable insists: the master goes away to receive a kingdom; some of the people hate the notion; even his servants vary in their faithfulness and fruitfulness, and some prove to be false servants. Those who are truly devoted slaves of King Jesus will busy themselves trying to improve their Master's assets, eagerly awaiting his return.

∽

2 Chronicles 6:12-42; 1 John 5; *Habakkuk 1; Luke 20*

∾

THE PROPHECY OF HABAKKUK—or, more precisely, the "oracle that Habakkuk the prophet received"—is cast not as something he is to deliver to others, but as a response to his own complaint before the Lord. The fact that it was written down and preserved in the canon means that in God's providence either Habakkuk or someone else thought it was so important others should read it. It should not remain a private communication (like the private revelations that Paul sometimes received, 2 Cor. 12:1-10).

The nature of Habakkuk's protest is set out in **Habakkuk 1**. The setting is apparently about the time of the final Babylonian assault (1:6). Initially Habakkuk's complaint concerns the decline of his own people and culture (1:2-5). He has cried to the Lord for help, and expects heaven-sent revival. "How long, O LORD, must I call for help, but you do not listen?" (1:2). The rest of his complaint lists the symptoms of a culture in disintegration: violence, injustice, wrong, strife, conflict, and the Law of God paralyzed.

But God answers with words Habakkuk does not want to hear. Habakkuk wants revival; God promises judgment (1:6-11). If Habakkuk is so concerned about the injustice, he should know that God is going to do something about it: he is going to punish it. God will do something astonishing: he will raise up the Babylonians, "that ruthless and impetuous people, who sweep across the whole earth to seize dwelling places not their own" (1:6). They will come "bent on violence" and "gather prisoners like sand" (1:9). God does not pretend that the Babylonians are fine folk. After describing the massive strength of their armed forces, he scathingly calls them "guilty men, whose own strength is their god" (1:11). These guilty men, intoxicated by the ferocity of their own violence, are the people God is going to deploy to chasten his own covenant people—in response to Habakkuk's prayer that God would do something about the injustice in the land.

God's response does not satisfy Habakkuk. The second complaint (1:12—2:1) goes to the heart of the issue. Granted that God is eternal and faithful to his covenant people; granted too that he is "too pure to look on evil" (1:13) and therefore must punish his own covenant community, the burning question remains: "Why then do you tolerate the treacherous? Why are you silent while the wicked swallow up *those more righteous than themselves?*" (1:13, italics added). For however wicked the Judahites are, the Babylonians are worse. How can God use the more wicked to punish the less wicked?

What other examples of this are there in history, sacred and profane?

∾

2 Chronicles 7; 2 John; *Habakkuk 2; Luke 21*

GOD'S RESPONSE (HAB. 2) TO Habakkuk's second complaint (see yesterday's meditation) answers it in part and evades it in part. More precisely, it implicitly dismisses one part of Habakkuk's question by putting all the weight on another part.
Clearly God judges his answer to be so important that he wants it circulated (2:2),
so what starts off as private communication takes the first step toward becoming
incorporated into the canon.

God describes the "typical" Babylonian (2:4-5): puffed up, with corrupt
desires, often intoxicated, arrogant, restless, greedy, violent, and oppressive. He
is precisely the opposite of what God wants a human being, a divine image-bearer,
to be: "the righteous will live by his faith" (2:4). There is a long-running dispute
over whether the word for "faith" should properly be rendered "faithfulness," not
least because this line is quoted in the New Testament (Rom. 1:17; Gal. 3:11; Heb.
10:37-38). Although there are strong voices on both sides, a good case can be
made for preserving the ambiguity. Over against the person whose wretched conduct God lists in the surrounding lines, God certainly wants people to be "faithful." On the other hand, the preceding two lines depict the wicked as "puffed up"
and with desires "not upright"—just the opposite of a person with genuine
"faith," which in the Bible depends on God and therefore cannot be either puffed
up (which presupposes independence from God) or corrupt.

Whatever the responsible way to take that line, the Babylonians themselves
are so wicked, God says, that all of their erstwhile victims will one day rise up
and taunt the oppressors with a long list of "woes" (2:6, 9, 12, 15, 19)—dramatic
curses pronounced on them because of their grievous sins. These woes should be
pondered by any nation that hungers to act justly. The last one is bound up with
idolatry: "Woe to him who says to wood, 'Come to life!' Or to lifeless stone, 'Wake
up!' Can it give guidance? It is covered with gold and silver; there is no breath in
it." By contrast: "But the LORD is in his holy temple; let all the earth be silent
before him" (2:19-20). It is as if the wickedness of the Babylonians is traced back
to their idolatry. The words are a powerful reminder that God reigns over all the
nations, and he abhors the idolatry that drives people to pant after created things
rather than the Creator who made them and to whom they owe everything (cf.
Rom. 1:18ff.).

So God has not explained how he can use a more wicked nation to chasten a
less wicked one. Rather, he has said that he knows more about Babylonian
wickedness than Habakkuk does, that he keeps accounts, that justice will one day
be meted out.

2 Chronicles 8; 3 John; *Habakkuk 3; Luke 22*

∾

HABAKKUK'S FINAL PRAYER (**HAB. 3**) is in large measure a response to the Lord's perspective in chapter 2. It is a wonderful model of how to respond to God's revelation when it says things we may not like. Dominant themes include the following:

(1) Habakkuk continues to pray for revival. Who knows whether or not this is one of the instances when God will respond to fervent intercession? In the preceding chapter God does not absolutely rule out the possibility of such a visitation. So Habakkuk prays: " LORD, I have heard of your fame; I stand in awe of your deeds, O LORD. Renew them in our day, in our time make them known; in wrath remember mercy" (3:2).

(2) In highly poetic language, Habakkuk then recalls a number of instances in the past when God *did* in fact save his covenant people by thrashing their opponents. "In wrath you strode through the earth and in anger you threshed the nations," Habakkuk recalls (3:12), clearly intimating, "So why not do it again?" After all, he adds, on those occasions, "You came out to deliver your people, to save your anointed one" (3:13—note how "anointed one" here apparently refers to the entire people of God, not just the Davidic king).

(3) Yet Habakkuk has heard what God has said on this occasion. As much as it makes his heart pound and his legs shake (3:16), he resolves to pursue the only wise course: "I will wait patiently for the day of calamity to come on the nation invading us" (3:16). In other words, he will wait for what God has promised— the righteous judgment of God upon the oppressors, even if the people of God have to suffer judgment first.

(4) Yet the loveliest and most insightful part of Habakkuk's prayer is reserved for the end. His ultimate confidence does not rest on the prospect of judgment on Babylon. At one level his ultimate confidence is utterly detached from political circumstances and from the material well-being of his own people. "Though the fig tree does not bud and there are no grapes on the vines," he writes, "though the olive crop fails and the fields produce no food, though there are no sheep in the pen and no cattle in the stalls, yet I will rejoice in the LORD, I will be joyful in God my Savior" (3:17-18).

That kind of faith can live without knowing; it can triumph when there is no revival; it can rejoice in God even when the culture is in decline. "The Sovereign LORD is my strength; he makes my feet like the feet of a deer, he enables me to go on the heights" (3:19).

∾

2 Chronicles 9; Jude; *Zephaniah 1; Luke 23*

∾

I WANT TO COME AT ZEPHANIAH 1:12-13 rather obliquely.

There is more than one way to relegate God to the sidelines of history. Some do so by arguing that God acts intermittently. When good things happen, that's God; when bad things happen, that's the devil—and there is no sense in which God remains sovereign over the devil. Others argue that God's providence arches over everything, but invariably in line with what takes place in the natural order. For instance, in the past most theistic evolutionists argued that God intervened at dramatic moments in the process of evolution. Nowadays, there is a rising number of theistic evolutionists who say that, at the level of the actual physical processes, their position is undifferentiable from that of the atheist who understands what took place exclusively in term of natural processes. The theistic evolutionists, of course, insist that God's providence was operating throughout the process. But they say that if God had actually intervened we would be returning to some discredited "God-of-the-gaps" scenario. They can be quite vehemently opposed to those who cite the rising evidence for *design* in the created order, for that simple notion would radically transform naturalistic assumptions and change the mechanisms that naturalistic scientists are forced to espouse. But are they sure they want to go down this route? Would they apply the same reasoning to the resurrection of Jesus? Would they want to propose that all the forces that brought Jesus back from the dead with a resurrection body can be explained on purely "natural" terms? Or would they say that in this case God dramatically intervened, setting aside the structures of normal physical forces to introduce a stunning miracle? And if God did so in this case, why should it be so difficult to imagine that he did so in connection with the creation—*especially* when the evidence for design, evidence *from the physical order,* is multiplying? Transparently, there are many ways of relegating God to the periphery.

But perhaps the worst is simpler and far more damaging than either of the two ways I have mentioned so far. The two that I have mentioned involve a well-thought-out scheme, a worldview. But the worst is rarely systematic or intentional. It simply ignores God. It may formally espouse providence, but in practice it thinks through none of the implications of serving and obeying a God who is irrevocably in charge. It may happily confess the resurrection of Jesus, but expects no other interventions by God. It reads history, but learns nothing that is in line with holy Scripture.

Now meditate on Zephaniah 1:12-13.

∾

2 Chronicles 10; Revelation 1; *Zephaniah 2; Luke 24*

∽

THE RESURRECTED JESUS APPEARED to his disciples on several occasions. Here we reflect on **Luke 24:36-49**.

Notwithstanding what the Bible says about the transformed nature of the resurrection body (especially 1 Cor. 15), in this section Jesus goes out of his way to demonstrate that he is not a dematerialized body or a disembodied spirit. He can be touched; the scars of the nails can be seen (that is the significance of his words, "Look at my hands and my feet. It is I myself!" [24:39]); he speaks of himself as having "flesh and bones" (24:39); he eats some food in the presence of his disciples (24:42-43). This is entirely consistent with other voices in New Testament witness. It is unimaginably glorious: death has been beaten, and the long-promised king, once crucified, is now alive.

But Jesus insists that at one level his disciples should not have been surprised. He had been predicting for some time that he would die and rise again, but they had no categories for accepting his words at face value. Now he goes further: what has happened to him has fulfilled what was written about him "in the Law of Moses, the Prophets and the Psalms" (24:44—i.e., in all three divisions of the Hebrew canon, which were often referred to in just this way). That Jesus has to explain this to them presupposes, of course, that as far as he is concerned they really have not properly understood the Scriptures up to this point. So now he opens their minds in order to overcome this deficiency (24:45). He does this by synopsizing what the Scriptures say—just as on the road to Emmaus he explained to the two disciples precisely the same thing. On that occasion he began with Moses and all the Prophets and explained "what was said in all the Scriptures concerning himself" (24:27).

Clearly Jesus read the Old Testament in an integrated way, with himself at the center of it. From the New Testament records written by Jesus' immediate disciples and heirs, we can gain a pretty comprehensive glimpse of his self-understanding in this regard. He saw himself not only as the rightful messianic king in the line of David, but also as the suffering servant who would be wounded for our transgressions. He knew he was not only the atoning sacrifice but also the priest who offered the sacrifice. He was not only the obedient Son who discharged the mission his Father assigned him, but also the eternal Word made flesh who disclosed the Father perfectly to a generation of rebellious image-bearers. And so much more. And all of these things we should see, too, and bow in solemn, joyful worship.

2 Chronicles 11—12; Revelation 2, Zephaniah 3; John 1

∾

JOHN'S PROLOGUE (JOHN 1:1-18) is one of the richest quarries in the Bible for the mining of wonderful truths about Christ. Here there is space for only the most introductory reflections.

(1) In the first verse, the one who is eventually said to become flesh, the Lord Jesus himself, is called the "Word." The label is not only intrinsically peculiar, but at first glance is especially odd because it is not taken up in the rest of the Gospel of John. But perhaps that is the first clue. If in this first verse John had used one of the titles ascribed to Christ throughout the book (son of God, Son of Man, King of Israel, Messiah, and so forth), that title would have been elevated to the place of first importance. Instead, John uses an expression that encompasses all of them. He recalls that in the Old Testament God's "word" is regularly the means by which he discloses himself in creation, redemption, and revelation. "The word of the Lord" comes to prophets; by the word of the Lord the heavens were made; God sends forth his word and heals the people. John finds it wonderfully appropriate: in the eternal "Word" that becomes flesh, God discloses himself in creation, revelation, and redemption. Even the word *Word* is evocative. We might paraphrase, "In the beginning God disclosed himself, and that self-disclosure was with God, and that self-disclosure was God."

(2) If God's "Word" was with God even in the remotest beginning, that Word was God's own fellow, and distinguishable from him. If God's "Word" was God even in the remotest beginning, that Word was God's own self, and identified with him. Here are rudimentary pieces of what comes to be called the doctrine of the Trinity. From the beginning, God has always been a complex unity.

(3) Verse 2 picks up the middle clause of verse 1, in preparation for verse 3. In other words, the fact that the Word was with God in the beginning makes it possible for him to be God's agent in the creation of everything. Moreover, the insistence that God created absolutely everything by means of the Word's agency drives the conclusion that neither God nor the Word is part of the creation; pantheism is ruled out, as well as any suggestion that the Word is a created being, an inferior god.

(4) In verse 14, John declares that the Word became flesh (i.e., a human being) and (literally) "tabernacled" among us. Readers of the Old Testament instantly see that this means that in some sense Jesus, for John, is a new tabernacle, a new temple (cf. John 2:13-25). Indeed, there are half a dozen allusions to Exodus 32—34 in John 1:14-18. Find them. What do they mean?

∾

2 Chronicles 13; Revelation 3; *Haggai 1; John 2*

∽

THE PROPHET HAGGAI IS ONE of several "postexilic prophets," i.e., prophets who addressed the covenant people of God who returned to the Promised Land after the exile. **Haggai 1** can be dated to about August 520 B.C., almost twenty years after the first groups of Jews returned home. Although initially addressed to Zerubbabel and Joshua (1:1), almost immediately it is clear that the message is intended for everyone (1:3-4), for "the whole remnant of the people" (1:14).

Zerubbabel was a grandson of King Jehoiachin, who had been taken to exile in 597. He was thus the heir apparent to the throne of David. Zerubbabel was the son of Pedaiah, Jehoiachin's third son (1 Chron. 3:19); apparently the first son, Shealtiel, was childless. Perhaps Shealtiel adopted his eldest nephew, who would thereafter be called by his name (as in 1:1). In any case, Zerubbabel was "governor of Judah." This would have allowed him very little freedom, as the relationship of his authority to that of the governor of Samaria, the provincial center, and the borders of their respective territories, were ill-defined. Joshua was son of Jehozadak the priest, who was taken captive in 587 (1 Chron. 6:15). He was responsible for the religious affairs of the community.

The burden of this first chapter, set out in the challenge of the prophet's message (1:1-11) and the response of Zerubbabel and the people (1:12-15), is that they have delayed far too long in building the new temple. They have had enough time and energy to build their own nicely paneled homes (1:4), but not enough to get on with the temple. That is the reason, God says, why the previous twenty years have been as hard as they have been. He refuses to pour out great blessings on them when they have been so short-sighted with respect to that which should have been at the very heart of their enterprise: the joyful and committed worship of Almighty God. "Give careful thought," the prophet repeats (1:5, 7), and they will find this assessment of their recent past entirely realistic. "You expected much, but see, it turned out to be little. What you brought home, I blew away. Why? . . . Because of my house, which remains a ruin, while each of you is busy with his own house" (1:9).

The fundamental issue is not one of buildings, but of priorities. Our generation faces this challenge no less than any other. Why bother to ask God to bless us unless our priorities are conscientiously aligned with his? That will affect our conduct and speech, our pocketbooks and our imaginations, our vocation and our retirement, where we live and what we do and how we do it.

∽

2 Chronicles 14—15; Revelation 4; *Haggai 2; John 3*

෴

AS WE SAW IN YESTERDAY'S MEDITATION, Haggai 1 is set in August 520 B.C. **Haggai 2** is set in the same year, but is broken up into two parts. The first oracle comes to Haggai in October (2:1-9); the second, in December (2:10-23). The first is measured encouragement to the remnant that is beginning the task of rebuilding the temple; the second promises blessing (2:10-19) and an ultimate "Zerubbabel" (2:20-23).

The first section promises that the new temple, "this house," will be filled with more glory than the first. If this "glory" is measured in terms of wealth or political influence, that simply did not happen before the temple was destroyed in A.D. 70. But if instead the glory of "this house" is bound up with the coming of the Messiah who graced its structures and who was himself the ultimate "temple" toward which it pointed, the claim is not extravagant. The expression "the desired of all nations" (2:7), taken as a singular, has often been understood to refer to the Messiah. The Hebrew, however, is plural ("the desired things," i.e., "the treasures"), suggesting a time when all nations will pay homage to the God of Israel. After all, as verse 8 reminds us, all the silver and gold are God's anyway.

The words "give careful thought" now recur (2:15, 18), reminding the reader how Haggai has used this expression in chapter 1 to call Israel to reflect on the two decades that have elapsed since their return. God's blessing on them has been restrained, almost miserly. "From this day on" (2:19), however, God will bless the people.

But the greatest blessing is still to come. God predicts that in the vague future, the prophetic "on that day" (2:23), he will overturn kings and kingdoms and make Zerubbabel "like my signet ring" (2:23). Why? Because "I have chosen you," the Lord Almighty declares. This cannot be a simple reference to the historical Zerubbabel. Too many indicators point beyond him. God is referring to "that day." Zerubbabel is not only the governor (2:21), but "my servant" (2:23)— a title used of David (Ezek. 34:23; 37:24), as well as of the "suffering servant" of Isaiah. "Servant" and "chosen" are juxtaposed in Isaiah 41:8; 42:1; 44:1. David, Judah, and Mount Zion are similarly "chosen" (Ps. 78:68-70). Recall, too (yesterday's passage), that Zerubbabel's grandfather was King Jehoiachin, so that Zerubbabel is in the Davidic line, the messianic line. So Zerubbabel (whose name still appears with honor in contemporary Jewish liturgies for Hanukkah) sets a pattern, part of a larger Davidic pattern, that points to the ultimate Zerubbabel, the ultimate David—King Jesus.

෴

2 Chronicles 16; Revelation 5; *Zechariah 1; John 4*

∾

LIKE HIS CONTEMPORARY HAGGAI, Zechariah is a postexilic prophet. If Haggai is largely responsible, under God, for encouraging the people to get going and build the second temple, Zechariah's contribution, though in some ways more significant, is harder to pin down. Here one finds searing apocalyptic, enigmatic visions, decidedly difficult passages, soaring perspective. However difficult they may be, chapters 9—14 constitute the Old Testament section most quoted in the passion narratives of the canonical Gospels, and the second most important source (after Ezekiel) for the countless Old Testament allusions in the book of Revelation. Few Old Testament prophetic books have called forth a wider diversity of "partition theories"—theories that assign chapters 9—14, or certain parts of them, to some writer other than the historical Zechariah.

This of course is not the place to address all these debates. We shall be concerned to grapple with parts of the text as they stand. For the moment, we focus on **Zechariah 1:1-17**.

The opening six verses constitute an introduction to chapters 1—8. The word of the Lord comes to Zechariah in October or November 520 B.C. The burden of this introduction is to review the catastrophic judgment of 587, when Jerusalem and the temple fell, and what led up to it and what flowed from it. "Return to me . . . and I will return to you" (1:3) is the lesson to be learned. Initially the people would not listen. But eventually they were carried off into exile and began to reflect more seriously on all the messages that had been given them. In exile they came to their senses: "The LORD Almighty has done to us what our ways and practices deserve, just as he determined to do" (1:6). The implication is obvious: the covenantal blessings and judgments still stand, and the people of God must come to him in reverence and godly fear, lest they repeat the stubbornness of their ancestors and call down judgment on themselves.

There follow eight visions (1:7—6:15), sometimes collectively referred to as "the book of visions." These eight visions have a more-or-less standard form. After an introductory expression we are told what the prophet sees. He asks the angel what these things are or mean, and the angel provides an explanation. With four of the visions there is an accompanying oracle (1:14-17; 2:6-13; 4:6-10a; 6:9-15), usually but not invariably at the end. The eight visions are thematically chiastic: the first and eighth are similar, the second and seventh, and so forth. All of them disclose something of the future of Jerusalem and Judah. What contribution is made by the first?

∾

2 Chronicles 17; Revelation 6; *Zechariah 2; John 5*

∽

THE LAST FEW VERSES OF ZECHARIAH 1 (which we did not think through in yesterday's meditation) are fairly straightforward. "Horn" represents strength or kingdom or kingly power. The four horns that scatter Judah and Israel may not be four empires, but a way of referring to all the powers that had any hand in it (as in "from the four corners of the world" or "the four winds"). But the "craftsmen" ultimately overcome them—again, four, to correspond to the four who decimate the people of God. Historically, of course, the Persians overcame and incorporated the territory of the preceding empires into their own. The general point is clear enough and is repeated in many ways in the prophets: all nations meet divine retribution, especially those that attack God's covenant people.

That sets the stage for **Zechariah 2** and the third vision. Here Jerusalem has a divine protector: it no longer needs walls. Indeed, the great number of people and livestock belonging to the city makes walls impractical. But Jerusalem is not thereby threatened. Far from it: "'I myself will be a wall of fire around it,' declares the LORD, 'and I will be its glory within'" (2:5). Parts of this vision anticipate the vision of the new Jerusalem (see especially Rev. 22:1ff.).

Elements of this vision resonate with other biblical themes. (a) The Lord will plunder the nations that have been faithless and cruel. That theme crops up in every major Old Testament corpus, and it surfaces in the preceding chapter. (b) The Lord's covenant people are "the apple of his eye" (2:8). True, to be the elect of God may mean being first in line for chastening (Amos 3:2), but it also means being loved by God from before the foundation of the earth, cherished by him, preserved by him, and finally brought into eschatological glory. (c) The missionary theme surfaces again: "Many nations will be joined with the LORD in that day and will become my people" (2:11). This should come as no surprise. The first announcement of the covenant with Abraham promises that all the nations of the earth will be blessed through him (Gen. 12:3). (d) "Be still before the LORD, all mankind, because he has roused himself from his holy dwelling" (2:13). In other words, in light of the glorious revelations God has given through Zechariah, the appropriate response is quiet reverence, hushed awe. How much more should that be our response as we contemplate the fulfillment of these promises and glimpse something of the horizon of the achievement in the Gospel and its entailments!

2 Chronicles 18; Revelation 7; *Zechariah 3; John 6*

ᔢ

ZECHARIAH'S FOURTH VISION (ZECH. 3) envisages the reinstatement of the high priest in the person of Joshua. At the same time, it envisages someone who transcends him, making Joshua a pointer along the stream of redemptive history, just as at the end of the prophecy of Haggai, Zerubbabel is a pointer along the stream of redemptive history (Hag. 2:23; see meditation for December 13).

The first three visions look at Jerusalem from the outside. This one and the next find the prophet within the temple courts. Here he finds Joshua the priest teetering, as it were, between the angel of the Lord and "Satan": the word means "accuser." Joshua is dressed "in filthy clothes" (3:3). The filth is a sign of guilt, as the second part of verse 4 makes clear. The accuser tries to destroy Joshua by the charges brought against him, and in truth Joshua is a guilty sinner (as indicated by the filthy clothes)—so how can he possibly be an effective priest? The answer is that the angel of the Lord, standing in for the Lord himself, gives him clean clothes, rich garments. The situation is akin to Isaiah's experience in Isaiah 6. When Isaiah sees the Lord, he becomes terribly aware of his sin. But God provides the means of removing the sin—in that case, a live coal from the altar. The implication here is that Joshua must walk in God's ways and keep his requirements (3:7).

So Joshua is recommissioned. But the vision says much more. Joshua and his associates (presumably other priests) are (literally) "men of good omen"—or, as the NIV puts it more prosaically, they are "men symbolic of things to come" (3:8). They point to "my servant, the Branch" (3:8). Nothing more is revealed about his identity here, but he crops up again in 6:12-13, where we shall reflect on him further (see meditation for December 19). The metaphor then changes to a stone with seven "eyes" or "facets" (or even "springs"); the precise meaning of the metaphor is disputed, but the result is that the Almighty declares, "I will remove the sin of this land in a single day" (3:9). As God removed the filth from his high priest, he does the same for his people, removing "the sin of this land in a single day." The result is utter contentment (which is the substance of the visionary ideal in 3:10).

Living this side of the cross, we have no doubt who the ultimate high priest is, and how he fully bore our sin in his own body on the tree. By God's action, the sins of his covenant people were dealt with at one decisive moment. The "men symbolic of things to come" served better than they knew: "Joshua" is the Hebrew name for the Greek form we know as *Jesus*.

ᔢ

2 Chronicles 19—20; Revelation 8; *Zechariah 4; John 7*

∾

RATHER NAIVELY, SOME OF US THINK that if Jesus were alive today, our tolerant culture would not give him a really rough time, much less crucify him. We would simply marginalize him, treat him as if he were a harmless eccentric. Is that true? Not according to John. The issues are bound up with the nature of fallenness and its response to holiness.

Nowhere is this clearer than in **John 7:7**. Jesus' brothers have been egging him on to return to Jerusalem. If he wishes to become a celebrity, they argue, he must show himself in the capital city on the high feast days. They are thinking like politicians: what will bring you public notice? But Jesus says that the "right time" for him has not yet come. They can follow their own timetable; he does and says only what the Father gives him to do and say (7:6; cf. 5:19ff.). Eventually he will go up to the Feast, but not yet (7:8). And when he does go, he goes quietly, without fanfare (7:10), refusing to draw attention to himself, with all the political fuss that would make. One important reason for this self-restraint is provided in 7:7: "The world cannot hate you," Jesus tells his brothers, "but it hates me because I testify that what it does is evil."

Four brief reflections. (a) The "because" clause is both disturbing and revealing. The assumption, of course, is that the world is not only evil, but desperately hates to have its evil exposed, shown up for what it is. Both by his flawless character and by his candid speech, Jesus makes "the world" horribly uncomfortable. How long would Jesus have lasted in Stalin's Russia? In Hitler's Germany? Or in Northern Ireland? Or the Balkans? Or in the United States? The least we would do, I imagine, is have him committed for psychiatric evaluation. (b) But I doubt that it would end there. Consider just one small arena: Some of my friends have had their lives repeatedly threatened because they publicly oppose homosexual marriages. These are not homophobes or gay bashers. Some of them have proven wonderfully fruitful and loving in their ministries to gays and straights alike. Were Jesus ministering among us today, I have no doubt that such death threats would have become assassination. (c) The implication of 7:7 is that Jesus' brothers belong to the world. That is why they fit in so well. Are we being faithful if *no one* hates us? (d) This candid exposure of the world is not smug one-upmanship, disgusting self-righteousness. Jesus *is* righteous; he *is* holy. Where sin and holiness collide, there will *always* be an explosion. And we sinners *must* come to recognize our deep sinfulness, or we will never turn to the Savior for help.

∾

2 Chronicles 21; Revelation 9; *Zechariah 5; John 8*

∾

BEFORE REFLECTING BRIEFLY on the two visions of **Zechariah 5**, I must go back and add a note on Zechariah 3—4.

Chapters 3 and 4 clearly carry messianic overtones. For Zechariah 3, see the meditation for December 16: though the primary reference is to the reconstruction of 519 B.C., the stone (3:9), the Branch (3:8), and the temple all point beyond themselves. That significance is tied in Zechariah 4 to the two "sons of oil" (i.e., "the two who are anointed," 4:14) who "serve the Lord of all the earth" (4:14). In the historical context, the two are Zerubbabel the governor, who is also the Davidic prince, and Joshua the priest. The one rebuilds the temple; the other offers the sacrifices prescribed by the covenantal sacrificial system. These two "messiahs," these two anointed ones, exercise complementary roles. Together the two point forward to the ultimate Davidic king and the ultimate priest. The people of Qumran (a monastic community by the Dead Sea, still operating in Jesus' day) actually expected two different messiahs, one Davidic and one priestly. They did not know how both the kingly and the priestly functions would come together in one man, the God-man, Jesus of Nazareth.

The two visions of chapter 5 leave aside the messianic overtones of the previous two chapters and focus on the continuing lawlessness and violence in the land. Yet the change of theme is not arbitrary. One of the functions of the Davidic king was to enforce justice (3:7; see 2 Sam. 15:2-3). Priests, too, were charged with administering justice (e.g., Deut. 17:9). The prophets foretold a time of perfect justice (Isa. 11:3-5; Jer. 23:5).

The first of the two visions (the flying scroll, 5:1-4) promises judgment on the lawless. The scroll represents the whole law, not least its sanctions on those who defy God. These are God's words, and God's words have the power to accomplish all of God's purposes. The second vision, of the woman in a basket (5:5-11), deals with the persistence of evil in the community. Because the Hebrew word for "wickedness" is feminine, it is personified in this vision as a woman—the Old Testament equivalent of the woman Babylon, the mother of prostitutes, in Revelation 17. Just as evil is often hidden, so is she—until she is exposed. The only answer is God's: she is taken away to "Babylonia" (5:11) where she belongs. Thus God removes sin from his people as far as the east is from the west (Ps. 103:11-12). He washes away the uncleanness of his people (Ezek. 36:25), and the filthy garments are replaced by clean ones (Zech. 3), or else we have no hope at all.

∾

2 Chronicles 22—23; Revelation 10; *Zechariah 6; John 9*

෩

THE LAST OF THE EIGHT VISIONS and a related oracle now unfold (**Zech. 6**). This last vision (6:1-8) is in some ways parallel to the first. In the first, there were horses but no chariots; here there are both. In the first, the setting was a valley; here, two mountains. There the horses were coming in to report; here they are sent out—indeed, they are eager to be off. In both, they are part of the Lord's worldwide patrols.

Although various explanations have been offered for the two mountains made of bronze, the most likely recalls the gigantic bronze pillars that stood on either side of the entrance to the original temple (1 Kings 7:15-22). Bronze and iron were used in defense against attack (e.g., Jer. 1:18). No one can force entrance to God's dwelling. I cannot deal here with the intricacies of the colors and destinations. Zechariah is told by the interpreting angel that the four horses/chariots are "the four spirits [= winds] of heaven, going out from standing in the presence of the Lord of the whole world" (6:5). Like the winds, they are God's messengers (Ps. 104:4), ranging over the whole world, for the whole world belongs to God. Chariots were the panzer divisions of ancient warfare. If they already control "the north country" (6:6, 8), where the mightiest pagan empires flourished, then they control everything. At the end of the vision, the angel is more than an interpreter for the prophet. The verb "He *called* [literally, 'cried'] to me" introduces a proclamation. This angel of the Lord discloses his identity, for he speaks either for or as the Lord of the whole earth. The promised rest and salvation have been achieved.

Yet the final oracle (6:9-15) leaves the chapter with a slightly different feel. The climax of God's redemptive purposes lies not in a temple or a ritual, but in a person. Asking for a share of the silver and gold recently arrived in a new caravan from the exiles in Babylon, Zechariah is to make a magnificent crown (its magnificence is hinted at in the Hebrew plural). This crown is for the head of the high priest Joshua the son of Jehozadak (6:11). That is so stunning that some contemporary commentators want to emend the text. Surely the ruler with the crown is the Davidic king, they argue, not the high priest. Others think this reflects a very much later time when the priests picked up more political power. But the truth is simpler: *here God brings together into one figure both the kingly symbolism and the priestly functions.* His name is the Branch (6:12; compare the use of this title in Isa. 4:2; Jer. 23:5; 33:15). New Testament readers cannot doubt where the fulfillment is found.

෩

2 Chronicles 24; Revelation 11; *Zechariah 7; John 10*

∾

THE LAST TWO CHAPTERS OF the first part of Zechariah are triggered by a question. The question is posed by a delegation from the exiles about liturgical observance. The Jews in Babylon wanted to remain in liturgical sync with the Jerusalemites. Their delegation is pretty early in the life of the returned community—late 518 B.C., just over twenty years since the initial restoration and only a year since the commitment to rebuild the temple, under the preaching of Haggai, had taken hold. The formal answer to their question is not given until 8:18-19. Yet the focus on fasting as a ritual to be observed calls forth sermonic material and various oracular sayings from the Lord that press beyond merely formal observance and call the people, yet again, to fundamental issues. **Zechariah 7** is the first of these two chapters, and verses 5-14 provide the first barrage of the prophetic response. We may usefully organize this material by asking three questions:

(1) *Is our religion for us or for God?* The prophet Zechariah faithfully conveys God's question to the delegates of the exiles: when across seventy years (i.e., from 587) they faithfully fasted on certain days, thinking those were the "proper" days, did they do so primarily as an act of devotion to God, or out of some self-centered motivation of wanting to feel good about themselves (7:5-7)? Fasting may be no more than self-pity, or faithfulness to a cultural mandate, or passive acceptance of tradition. How much of the religious practice was offered to God?

(2) *Does our religion elevate ritual above morality?* That is the burden of Zechariah's stinging review of earlier Jewish history (7:8-12). Implicitly, Zechariah is asking if their concern for liturgical uniformity is matched by a passionate commitment to "show mercy and compassion to one another," and to abominate the oppression of the weak and helpless in society (7:9-10). Indeed, a genuinely moral mind extends to inner reflection: "In your hearts do not think evil of each other" (7:10). Implicitly, Zechariah asks us precisely the same questions.

(3) *Does our religion prompt us passionately to follow God's words, or to pursue our own religious agendas?* "When I called, they did not listen; so when they called, I would not listen" (7:13), the Lord Almighty announces. Passionate intensity about the details of religion, including liturgical reformation, is worse than useless if it is not accompanied by a holy life. *In true religion, nothing, nothing at all, is more important than whole-hearted and unqualified obedience to the words of God.*

∾

2 Chronicles 25; Revelation 12; *Zechariah 8*; *John 11*

∾

AT THE END OF THE ACCOUNT OF the resurrection of Lazarus, John pens a short section steeped in ironies (**John 11:45-53**). All of them point unerringly to the cross.

(1) The authorities are thoroughly frustrated. No one can deny that the miracle Jesus has performed actually occurred: it was too public, and Lazarus was genuinely dead—so dead that the smell of decomposition was public and obnoxious (11:39). So how can the Sanhedrin trim Jesus' rising authority or quell the messianic fervor that is likely to erupt when the report of the miracle circulates? Eventually, they fear, "everyone will believe in him," the rebellion will become established, "and then the Romans will come and take away both our place and our nation" (11:48). There may be irony even in their mention of "our place": the peculiar expression could refer to the temple (as the NIV footnote suggests), yet it is hard to deny that their real interest is not so much the temple as their place of privilege in society. Yet there is a deeper irony. As the story unfolds, they take action against Jesus, and he is crucified. Yet this fails to preserve their "place." Within forty years, the Romans descend on Jerusalem and crush it. They destroy the temple. And the "place" of the authorities is wiped out.

(2) But that is still in the future. It is Caiaphas who first formalizes the concrete proposal to pervert justice, sacrificing judicial integrity on the altar of political expediency. "You know nothing at all!" he exclaims (11:49), his pique belittling his colleagues as, in effect, a bunch of nincompoops. "You do not realize that it is better for you that one man die for the people than that the whole nation perish" (11:50). Note: it is better *for you*—that is the real locus of interest, the political selfishness behind the political claptrap. Bump off Jesus, and the messianic fervor dies and the nation is spared: it all seems so clean, so logical—and besides, it will be good for "our place." So Jesus dies—and the tragic irony is that the nation perishes anyway. Not even A.D. 70 was the end of it. Six decades later the Bar Kochba revolt brought in the Romans again (132—135). Jerusalem was razed to the ground. It became a capital offense for any Jew to live anywhere in the environs of Jerusalem.

(3) But there is a deeper irony yet, which John detects in Caiaphas's words. Caiaphas speaks as high priest, and in God's providence he speaks better than he knows. Jesus dies for the Jewish nation, and not only for them "but also for the scattered children of God, to bring them together and make them one" (11:52).

∾

2 Chronicles 26; Revelation 13; *Zechariah 9; John 12*

∾

ZECHARIAH 9—14 CONSTITUTES A second and distinctive part of the book. With their apocalyptic images and colorful metaphors, these chapters include many units hard to understand. Usually, however, the main line of thought is clear enough. **Zechariah 9** can be divided into three sections:

(1) The first is "an oracle" (9:1-8). The peculiar word used suggests something of compulsion: this oracle is a "burden" to the prophet, and he cannot keep it in. In the past, most of Israel's enemies have come from the north. In this oracle, however, it is Yahweh himself who advances on the Promised Land from the north. The sequence of cities mentioned establishes the geography: he will conquer all the cities down the coast and come to his own house (9:8) and defend his own people. The ultimate hope of God's people resides in something more dramatic than the return from exile that they have already experienced. It resides in the supreme visitation of Almighty God.

(2) The second section depicts the arrival of the king (9:9-10). These verses are steeped in allusions to earlier Old Testament passages—to the figure pictured in Genesis 49:10-11, to the kingly deeds of Micah 5:10, to the extent of his kingdom in Psalm 72:8, and so forth. The figure, in short, is messianic, yet the preceding verses depict Yahweh himself coming to rescue his people. Thus in some respects the passage is akin to Isaiah 9:1ff.: there, too, a prophet looks forward to a Davidic king, yet one who is called "the mighty God." Matthew 21:5 and John 12:15 allude to this passage in their respective accounts of Jesus' triumphal entry into Jerusalem. Neither of them refers to verse 10, for both of these evangelists are aware that only a partial fulfillment has taken place in their day. Unqualified disarmament and unqualified peace among the nations (9:10) await the consummation. In this sort of partial quotation of an Old Testament text they follow the example of the Lord Jesus, who for exactly the same reason—that is, because the final judgment still lies in the future—cites certain parts of Old Testament passages and not others (cf. Matt. 11:2-19, and meditation for July 1).

(3) God still speaks, and he gives all the reasons for rejoicing (9:11-17). He himself will come and free the prisoners, for his covenantal faithfulness has been sealed in blood—not only in the Abrahamic covenant (Gen. 15:9-11) but in its extension in the Mosaic covenant (Ex. 24:8), and supremely in the blood of the new covenant that was shed on a hill outside Jerusalem (see Mark 14:24).

∾

2 Chronicles 27—28; Revelation 14; *Zechariah 10; John 13*

∽

THE ACCOUNT OF JESUS WASHING his disciples' feet (**John 13:1-17**) is narrated to establish several points:

(1) Walking on dusty roads in open sandals took its toll. Many homes would assign the lowest of the servants to wash the feet of visitors. On this occasion, however, Jesus and his closest disciples are on their own, and no one thinks to take on the role of the humblest servant—no one, that is, but Jesus himself. The way John marshals the facts shows that, decades later when he is writing these lines, he is still awed by the dimensions of the deed. Jesus knows that it is time for him to go to the cross, "to leave this world and go to the Father" (13:1), but he is not self-absorbed. He knows that one of those whose feet he will wash is Judas Iscariot, who, sold out as he is to the devil, is in the process of betraying him. Jesus knows whence he has come, "that he had come from God and was returning to God" (13:3). All along he has "loved his own who were in the world," and now he shows them "the full extent of his love" (13:1)—not only the foot-washing itself, but the cross, to which the footwashing points (as we shall see). Knowing all this, loving like this, "he got up from the meal, took off his outer clothing, and wrapped a towel around his waist" (13:4)—it is as if every step has been indelibly burned onto John's memory, and he can play it back, again and again, in slow motion. In the hush of the room, Jesus washes his disciples' feet.

(2) Peter balks (13:6-11). The exchange that follows is multi-layered. On the surface of things, there is a form of humility that is actually proud. In one sense, the most humbling thing to endure in this setting is Jesus washing your feet. So there is a lesson in humility. But there is something deeper: "You do not realize now what I am doing, but later you will understand" (13:7); Jesus' washing of his disciples' feet anticipates, symbolically, the washing that is accomplished by the cross, the supreme self-humiliation that is displayed in the cross. Peter will understand such things only after the events. And then, in a moment of flip-flop enthusiasm, Peter wants a bath, and a third level is peeled back to view: a person who is already clean does not need a bath, but only to have his feet washed (13:10). And in some respects the disciples, with the exception of the son of perdition, are already clean. Here, then, is a picture of the "once-for-all" element in the cross (cf. Heb. 9:11-14, 23-26); we do not need a new sacrifice, but fresh confession (1 John 1:7, 9).

(3) And always there is the demand to be like Jesus. Reflect on 13:12-17 and its bearing on us today.

∽

2 Chronicles 29; Revelation 15; *Zechariah 11; John 14*

∾

ZECHARIAH HAS ALREADY USED imagery associated with sheep and shepherd (9:16; 10:2, 3, 8-12; 11:3). Now he deploys it at length (**Zech. 11:4-17**). The passage is difficult. Probably it is an extended allegory, rather than something acted out, if only because of all the other people involved. Quite certainly its purpose is to overturn a major assumption about leadership. Many think that if a nation has the right ruler, all will be well. But here the right shepherd is hated and rejected.

(1) The "LORD my God," Zechariah says, gives the people one last chance (11:4-6). God commissions him to serve as shepherd of a flock "marked for slaughter," i.e., raised for their meat. The "sheep" are oppressed people, while their oppressors are variously their own shepherds who fatten them for the slaughter, and the traders who "slaughter them and go unpunished" (11:5). The language that describes their owners is scathing: they sell them for slaughter and say, "Praise the LORD, I am rich!" (11:5)—as if wealth were a reliable index of the Lord's favor (cf. Mark 10:23). The "buyers" in the parable are the occupying powers. Thus the "sellers," the leaders of the covenant people, are complicit in "selling out" their people. Zechariah's mission as a shepherd, to save this flock, appears doomed to failure. God himself will turn the people over to their own neighbors and their own king. They are not loyal to him, and he abandons them to their fellow citizens—and God will not rescue them (11:6).

(2) In the second section (11:7-14), the good shepherd, Zechariah, is rejected. One might have thought that the flock would turn to him for rescue, since everyone else—sellers, shepherds, buyers—are intent on selling them and profiting from them. But the flock detests the good shepherd (11:8). Eventually he abandons the sheep to follow the course they are determined to take (11:9). The staff called "Favor" or "Graciousness" is broken, as is the covenant made "with all the nations" (probably referring to the Jewish colonies scattered among many nations, as in Joel 2:6). So the merchants who provided Zechariah's salary, and who doubtless wanted him to be gone, unwittingly accomplish God's judicial will and buy off Zechariah with a final payment of thirty pieces of silver. These Zechariah is commanded to throw to the potter (a craftsman who worked with both clay and metal), presumably so that he could make a little figurine, a little godlet (11:12-13). Those who reject the good shepherd are left with idols—and disunity (12:14).

(3) In the closing lines (11:15-17) Zechariah acts out the only alternative to a good shepherd: a worthless shepherd.

How much did Jesus meditate on this chapter—the good shepherd rejected by so many of his people and dismissed for thirty pieces of silver?

∾

2 Chronicles 30; Revelation 16; *Zechariah 12:1—13:1; John 15*

∾

THE LAST THREE CHAPTERS OF Zechariah (chaps. 12—14) develop themes that appeared in chapters 9—11. But there is a rising intensity, signaled by the phrase "on that day," repeated sixteen times. The climax is in the last chapter, where God's universal kingdom is fully established.

Zechariah 12 is part of this rising intensity. The first part (12:1-9) is superficially easy to understand, but at one level its interpretation is difficult; the second part (12:10—13:1) is immensely evocative, and is cited in the New Testament.

(1) The first part pictures the formerly scattered exiles, now returned to Jerusalem, facing the onslaught of hostile nations. It appears that even Judah initially abandons Jerusalem: the NEB's translation is probably right: "Judah will be caught up in the siege of Jerusalem." Then the Lord intervenes and makes "Jerusalem a cup that sends all the surrounding peoples reeling" (12:2). God confounds the cavalry charges (12:4), and the people of Judah take courage from the steadfastness of the Jerusalemites (12:5). As a result, the fact that they are among the enemy is turned to advantage: they are like fire that ignites dry tinder (12:6). The triumph is glorious (12:7-9).

So far, so good. But of what does this speak? The question cannot be answered without recourse to other Scriptures, to an entire way of putting the Bible together. Some think that this refers to empirical Jerusalem at some point in the future, with (presumably) suitable shifts from cavalry to something more modern. Others think this is an apocalyptic vision of final assaults on the people of God, on the citizens of the new Jerusalem. Does the next section shed light on the debate?

(2) The second section is in stunning contrast to the first. The house of David and the Jerusalemites have just been powerfully encouraged. Yet now God himself pours upon them a spirit of contrition (12:10), certainly not a spirit of triumphalism. They find themselves mourning for someone put to death in the city, and being cleansed from their sin and impurity by a new fountain "opened to the house of David and the inhabitants of Jerusalem" (13:1). Who is this person, pierced through, for whom the people mourn? The most natural reading of the Hebrew is that it is Yahweh himself: "They will look on me, the one they have pierced, and they will mourn" (12:10). At one level the "piercing" can be understood metaphorically: Yahweh is "wounded" in exactly the same way that he is cuckolded in Hosea. But there is a more literal fulfillment, a more literal piercing (John 19:34, 37). What is the good of a merely military triumph unless the people of God mourn for what they have done to God—and discover that he has opened a fountain to cleanse them from their sin (13:1)?

∾

2 Chronicles 31; Revelation 17; *Zechariah 13:2-9; John 16*

∾

IN SOME WAYS ZECHARIAH 13:2-9 continues with the theme of leadership. But it has two parts, each with very distinctive emphases:

(1) In 13:2-6 God condemns the false shepherds—a common theme, of course (e.g., Jer. 23:9ff.; Ezek. 13; 34:1-10). Moreover, it fits the immediately preceding verses. There, we saw, a fountain is opened up for the cleansing of the inhabitants of Jerusalem in general, and for the house of David in particular. But if citizens and royalty alike are purified, so also must the religious leaders be purified. "On that day" (13:2), God declares, he will banish not only the idols but the false prophets from the land. So transformed will be the situation that the covenantal ideal will be in force (Deut. 13:6-11): if someone says "Thus says the Lord" when the Lord has not spoken, his closest family members will be the first to silence him. Those who in the past have been false prophets will be so ashamed of themselves that when they are challenged they will insist that they are farmers (13:4-5). If there are "prophetic scars" on their bodies (doubtless from self-inflicted wounds tied to ecstatic paganism, as in 1 Kings 18:28) they will lie through their teeth and insist that the scars were the result of some brawl or other that went on "at the house of my friends" (13:6).

The point is that in the final arrangements of things, false teaching and false prophecy will be a thing of the past. Those with ears to hear should therefore abominate all such "prophecy" already, as a mark of attentiveness to the true word of the Lord.

(2) Some have wondered if the final three verses (13:7-9) have somehow been misplaced from the end of chapter 11, where Zechariah has devoted a lot of attention to shepherds. In fact, these verses would not have made much sense there but they are admirably suitable here. Chapter 11 ends with Zechariah representing the worthless shepherd who undergoes divine disapproval. But the shepherd in 13:7-9 is one God approves. The connections with the preceding two sections are easier to demonstrate. In 12:10—13:1, Yahweh himself is wounded, pierced through; and then false prophets are denounced (13:2-9). But there is still a need for the *right* shepherd. The right one is God's shepherd, "my shepherd . . . the man who is close to me" (13:7). God *commands* the sword to strike him (reflect on Acts 4:27-28). Elsewhere, God himself is the shepherd, and so is his servant David (Ezek. 34); so here, God himself is pierced through, and so also is his shepherd. The first result is that the sheep scatter (13:7; see Mark 14:27; Matt. 26:31); the ultimate result is the purification and faithfulness of the people of God (13:9).

∾

2 Chronicles 32; Revelation 18; *Zechariah 14; John 17*

∾

FROM TIME TO TIME IN THESE two volumes I have drawn attention to the fact that the way a biblical writer uses a word may not be the same way we use it. The serious reader of the Bible will then want to take special pains to avoid reading into the Bible what it does not say.

On the night he was betrayed, the Lord Jesus prayed for his followers in these terms: "Sanctify them by the truth; your word is truth. As you have sent me into the world, I have sent them into the world. For them I sanctify myself, that they too may be truly sanctified" (**John 17:17-19**). Observe:

First, this side of the Reformation "sanctification" usually refers to the gradual growth in grace that flows out of conversion. In justification God declares us to be just, on account of the sacrifice that his Son has offered up on our behalf; in sanctification, God continues to work in us to make us more and more holy, "sanctified," maturing into conformity with Jesus Christ. There is nothing wrong with talking like that: in the domain of systematic theology, the categories are reasonably clear. And after all, whether or not the word "sanctification" is used, there are plenty of passages that depict this sort of growth in grace (e.g., Phil. 3:10ff.).

Second, that sort of use of "sanctification" makes little sense of 17:19. When Jesus says that for the sake of his disciples "I sanctify myself," he does not mean that for their sakes he becomes more holy than he was, a little more mature and consistent perhaps. Rather, in the light of John's closing chapters, he means that he totally devotes himself to his Father's will—and God's will is that Jesus go to the cross. Jesus is entirely reserved for what the Father wants; he sanctifies himself.

Third, Jesus' purpose in such obedience is that his disciples "may be truly sanctified" (17:19). Because of Jesus' self-sanctification he goes to the cross and dies for his own; in consequence of this cross-work, his disciples are truly "sanctified," i.e., set aside for God. This sounds like what systematicians call "positional sanctification": the focus is not on growing conformity to God, but on the transformation of one's position before God owing to Jesus' decisive atonement.

Fourth, what Jesus asks for in his prayer is that his Father "sanctify" his disciples by the truth, i.e., by his word which is truth (17:17). He may simply be asking that they be decisively "sanctified" by the truth of the Gospel. But if an experiential, long-term dimension is also in view, this passage tells us how to become more "sanctified"—in line with Psalm 1:2; 119:109, 111.

∾

2 Chronicles 33; Revelation 19; *Malachi 1; John 18*

∾

WE DO NOT KNOW MUCH about Malachi. He served in the postexilic period, later than the early years when the greatest crises took place. By his day, both the wall and the temple had been rebuilt. Nehemiah, Zerubbabel, and Joshua were names in the past. The returned remnant had settled down. Nothing of great significance had occurred very recently. There was no spectacular restoration of the glory of God to the temple, envisaged by Ezekiel (43:4). The ritual was carried out, but without fervor or enthusiasm.

This is the situation Malachi addresses. It makes his words peculiarly appropriate for believers living in similar days of lethargy. There is not much going on: the political situation is stable, religious freedom is secure, the prescribed rituals are carried out—but all of it lacks not only passion but integrity, life-transformation, zeal, honor in relationships and promises, the fear of the Lord. The returned Jews are characterized by a world-weary cynicism that will not be moved.

Already **Malachi 1** sets the stage:

(1) The people are not convinced that God really loves them. "How have you loved us?" they protest (1:2)—especially considering the generally sorry state of weakness and relative poverty in which they find themselves. God appeals to his love in choosing them in the first place. He chose Jacob above Esau; there was nothing intrinsic to the two men to prompt the choice. The choice is traceable to nothing more and nothing less than the electing love of God. Believers must learn to rest securely in this love, or they will be bushwhacked by every dark circumstance that comes along.

(2) In their religious practices the people perform the rituals but treat God with a distinct lack of respect. That is shown in at least two ways. (a) The law specified that those who bring a sacrifice should bring an unblemished lamb, not the weak and the crippled. Yet these people bring the worst animals from their flocks—something they would not think of doing if they were presenting a gift to an earthly monarch (2:6-9). (b) Above all, by word and deed the people treat the worship of Almighty God as a burden to be endured rather than as a delight to enjoy or at least as a happy duty to discharge. "What a burden!" (1:13), they moan, sniffing "contemptuously" (1:13).

What is at issue is that God is a great king. These people act in a way that despises him. "My name will be great among the nations, from the rising to the setting of the sun" (1:11). "For I am a great king . . . and my name is to be feared among the nations" (1:14). Do Malachi's words shame our approach to God?

∾

2 Chronicles 34; Revelation 20; *Malachi 2; John 19*

∽

ONE OF THE SIGNS THAT A culture is coming apart is that its people do not keep their commitments. When those commitments have been made to or before the Lord, as well as to one another, the offense is infinitely compounded.

There is something attractive and stable about a society in which, if a person gives his or her word, you can count on it. Huge deals can be sealed with a handshake because each party trusts the other. Marriages endure. People make commitments and keep them. Of course, from the vantage point of our relatively faithless society, it is easy to mock the picture I am sketching by finding examples where that sort of world may leave a person trapped in a brutal marriage or a business person snookered by an unscrupulous manipulator. But if you focus on the hard cases and organize society on growing cynicism, you foster selfish individualism, faithlessness, irresponsibility, cultural instability, crookedness, and multiplied armies of lawyers. And sooner or later you will deal with an angry God.

For God despises faithlessness (**Mal. 2:1-17**). Within the postexilic covenant community of ancient Israel, some of the worst examples of such faithlessness were bound up with the explicitly religious dimensions of the culture—but not all of them:

(1) The lips of the priest should "preserve knowledge" and "from his mouth men should seek instruction—because he is the messenger of the LORD Almighty" (2:7). The priest was to revere God and stand in awe of his name (2:5), convey true instruction (2:6), and maintain the way of the covenant (2:8). But because the priests have proved faithless at all this, God will cause them to be despised and humiliated before all the people (2:9). So why is it today that ministers of the Gospel are rated just above used car salesmen in terms of public confidence?

(2) As do some other prophets (e.g., Ezek. 16, 23), Malachi portrays spiritual apostasy in terms of adultery (2:10-12).

(3) Unsurprisingly, faithlessness in the spiritual arena is accompanied by faithlessness in marriages and the home (2:13-16). Oh, these folk can put on quite a spiritual display, weeping and calling down blessings from God. But God simply does not pay any attention. Why not? "It is because the LORD is acting as the witness between you and the wife of your youth, because you have broken faith with her, though she is your partner, the wife of your marriage covenant" (2:14).

(4) More generically, these people have wearied the Lord with their endless casuistry, their moral relativism (2:17).

"So guard yourself in your spirit, and do not break faith" (2:16).

∽

2 Chronicles 35; Revelation 21; *Malachi 3; John 20*

෫

PEOPLE MAY BE FAITHLESS, but the Lord does not change. That changelessness threatens judgment; it is also the reason the people are not destroyed (Mal. 3:6). Hope depends on God's gracious intervention, grounded in his changeless character (**Mal. 3**).

(1) "'See, I will send my messenger, who will prepare the way before me. Then suddenly the Lord you are seeking will come to his temple; the messenger of the covenant, whom you desire, will come,' says the LORD Almighty" (3:1). This promise sounds as if it is responding to the cynicism that set in after the second temple was built. There was the temple, but where was the glory Ezekiel had foreseen (Ezek. 43:1-5)? Only when the Lord comes will the purpose of the rebuilding of the temple be fulfilled. And the Lord will fulfill that promise. First, he will send his "messenger," a forerunner "to prepare the way before me." And then suddenly "the Lord you are seeking" will come to his temple, "the messenger of the covenant, whom you desire." Despite valiant efforts to explain the text some other way, the most obvious reading is the one picked up just a few pages later in the Bible (though actually a few centuries later). Before the Lord himself comes—the Lord they seek, the messenger of the new covenant long promised—there is another messenger who prepares the way. Jesus insists that the forerunner of whom Malachi spoke is none other than John the Baptist (Matt. 11:10).

(2) Whenever God discloses himself in a special way to his people, and not least in this climactic self-disclosure, there is wrath as well as mercy. Anticipation of the "day of his coming" (3:2) therefore calls for profound repentance (3:2-5). Such repentance covers the sweep from the ugly sins listed in 3:5 to something more easily passed over, but clearly ugly to God: robbery, robbing God of the tithes and offerings that are his due (3:6-12). Away with the cynicism that says serving God is a waste of time and money, that there is no percentage in putting God at the center, that it is "futile" to serve the Lord (3:13-15).

(3) Not a few of the Old Testament prophets faithfully discharged their ministry and saw little fruit in their own times. Others witnessed something of a revival. Haggai saw the Lord so work among the people that the temple was rebuilt. Malachi, too, saw fruit in the lives of those who heeded his message and began to live in the light of the promise yet to be fulfilled: "Then those who feared the LORD talked with each other [presumably encouraging and stimulating one another to faithfulness], and the LORD listened and heard. A scroll of remembrance was written in his presence concerning those who feared the LORD and honored his name" (3:16).

෫

2 Chronicles 36; Revelation 22; *Malachi 4; John 21*

∾

OF ALL THE RESURRECTION APPEARANCES of Jesus, doubtless the one that probed Peter most deeply is the one reported in **John 21**.

It starts off with seven disciples going fishing, catching nothing overnight, and then pulling in a vast catch at Jesus' command. It continues with a breakfast over coals on the beach (21:1-14). There follows the memorable exchange that reinstates Peter after his ignominious disowning of his master.

(1) In the interchange between Jesus and Peter (21:15-17), the interplay of two different Greek words for "love" has convinced many commentators that there is something profoundly weighty about the distinction (though the distinction itself is variously explained). For various reasons, I remain unpersuaded. John loves to use synonyms, with very little distinction in meaning. The terms vary for feed/take care/feed, and for lambs/sheep/sheep, just as they varied for "love." In 3:35, the Father "loves" the Son, and one of the two verbs is used; in 5:20, the Father "loves" the Son, and the other of the two verbs is used—and there is no distinction in meaning whatsoever. Both verbs can have good or bad connotations; everything is determined by context. If we are to probe the significance of this exchange between Jesus and Peter, we shall have to depend on something other than the interchange of the two Greek verbs. So drop the "truly" in 21:15 and 16 (which is the NIV's way of trying to maintain a distinction between the two verbs).

(2) "Simon son of John, do you love me *more than these?*" (21:15, italics added). Does "these" refer to "these other disciples" or to "these fish"? In Matthew 26:33, Peter boasts that he will never fall away, even if all the other disciples do. That boast is not reported in John's gospel, even though John records Peter's awful denials. Alternatively, since the men have just been fishing, perhaps "these" refers to the fish. But if so, why pick only on Peter, and not on all seven disciples? On balance, I suspect this passage is reminding Peter of his fateful boast, and this is one of the passages that provides a kind of interlocking of accounts between John and the Synoptic Gospels. Is Peter still prepared to assert his moral superiority over the other disciples?

(3) Three times Jesus runs through the same question; three times he elicits a response; three times he commissions Peter. As the denial was threefold (18:15-18, 25-27), so also are these steps of restoration. Peter is "hurt" by the procedure (21:17); the next verses show he still retains streaks of immaturity (see vol. 1, meditation for March 31). But while Jesus here gladly restores a broken disciple who has disowned him, he makes him face his sin, declare his love, and receive a commission.

∾

GENERAL INDEX

importance of lineage, II. Jan 2, 17
obsolescence of, II. May 2, Aug 5
ordination of, I. Apr 7
weaknesses of, I. Nov 8, 13-14
(see also high priest; Israel, twelve
tribes)
Liddell, Eric, I. May 29
Lightfoot, J. B., I. Nov 2
living sacrifice (see worship, living
sacrifice)
Lloyd-Jones, Martin, I. Feb 24
Lois and Eunice, I. Oct 29
Lord's Supper, I. Mar 1, 8, Apr 13,
Sep 6, II. Jan 20 (see also bread of
life discourse)
loyalty, II. Apr 9
Luther, Martin, I. May 8, Oct 15,
II. Nov 18
lycanthropy, II. Oct 19
lying (see sin, lying)

M'Cheyne, Robert Murray, I. x, 11-
13, II. x, 11-13
Maccabees, II. Oct 23, 26
Magnificat, I. Feb 15
Malachi, II. Dec 28-30
manna, I. May 12, Jul 3
Manasseh, I. Nov 9, Dec 29, II. Jun 8,
Jul 19
mark of the beast, I. Dec 23, 28
mark of the Lamb, I. Dec 23
marriage (see covenant, marriage;
intermarriage)
marriage supper of the Lamb,
II. Sep 13
martyrdom (see persecution)
Marxism (see worldviews, Marxism)
Mary, I. Feb 15, 22 (see also Jesus
Christ, family of)
materialism, I. Jan 6, Feb 25-26, May
28, Nov 28, II. Apr 17, Sep 25 (see
also wealth)
McGill University, II. Jan 19
mediator
Christians as, I. Dec 10
Holy Spirit as, I. Mar 24
Jesus as (see Jesus Christ, as
mediator)
Moses as, I. Mar 21, Jun 13
prophet as, I. Jun 13
Medo-Persian Empire, II. Oct 17, 22-
23, 25
Megiddo, II. Jul 26
Melchizedek, I. Jan 13, May 4,
Jun 17, II. May 2, Aug 5
merit theology, II. Mar 5, 13 (see also
faith, relation to good works)
Messiah
as an ideal king, I. May 19, Jun 12,
Jul 14, Nov 10, II. May 13, Aug
4, 21
as priest-king, II. Dec 13, 16, 18-19
as referring to Israel, II. Dec 8
as "the servant of the Lord," II. Jun
29-30 (see also servant of the
Lord)
as the Son of God, I. Nov 10, II.
Aug 4, Sep 4
as the "Branch," II. May 6, 13,
Jul 27, Dec 16, 18-19
Davidic heir as, I. Jan 29, Feb 5,

II. Jul 6, Aug 4, Oct 4, Nov 30
(see also Messiah, as the
"Branch")
divine status of, II. Oct 1, 13, Dec
22
expectations of, I. Jan 12, 22, Feb
1, Mar 6, 12, 26, 28, May 19,
Jul 22, II. Feb 13, Jul 1, Aug 3,
Dec 4, 18
messianic bridegroom, I. Jan 30,
II. Sep 13
prophecies concerning, II. May 9,
Nov 30
(see also psalms, messianic; Jesus
Christ, as Messiah)
Micah, II. Jul 30, Oct 28, Nov 26,
Dec 1
Micaiah, I. Oct 19
miracles (see God, miraculous inter-
vention of)
Miriam, I. May 5
missions (see evangelism; Great
Commission; disciples, mission of)
money (see wealth)
monotheism (see worldviews)
moral standards, I. Mar 9, Apr 8, 14,
Aug 12, Nov 1, II. Mar 10
Mordecai, II. Jan 27-30
Morgan, G. Campbell, II. Nov 22
Mormonism, I. Jun 9, Nov 6
Mosaic covenant (see covenant,
Sinai)
Moscow, II. Oct 5
Moses, I. Feb 19-21, 28, Mar 1, 7, 9,
13, 21, 23, May 8-9, 11-12, Jun 28,
II. Oct 12
motives, I. Jan 6, Aug 16 (see also
Christian leadership, motives of)
Motyer, J. Alec, II. Nov 12, 14
Mount Ebal, I. Jun 22
Mount Gerizim, I. Jun 22
murder (see sin, murder)
My Fair Lady, II. Sep 13

Nabatean Arabs, II. Nov 21
Nabonidus, II. Oct 20
Naboth, II. Sep 6
Nadab and Abihu (see judgment,
divine)
Nahum, II. Dec 3
Naomi, I. Aug 8-10
Nathan, I. May 7, Sep 16-17, Nov 22
natural law theory (see justice, natural law theory)
Nazirite vow, I. Apr 29
Nebuchadnezzar, I. Nov 11-12, II.
May 19, Jul 25, Aug 6, 10, 12, 17,
23, Sep 22, 26, Oct 2, 17-20, 25-26
Nebuzaradan, II. Aug 12
Nehemiah, II. Jan 11-12, 14-17, 23,
Sep 19
nepotism (see Christian leadership,
nepotism)
Nero, I. Dec 22, II. Jan 25
new age spirituality, II. Nov 3
new birth (see regeneration)
new covenant (see covenant, new)
new creation, I. Sep 30, Oct 4
new heaven and new earth, I. Dec 20,
30, II. Feb 1, Jun 2, 24, Jul 3, Oct
10, Nov 28

new Jerusalem, I. Jan 9, Nov 17, Dec
27, 30, II. May 23, Jun 15, 20, 30,
Jul 3, 17, Oct 10, Nov 29, Dec 15
New Testament's use of the Old
Testament
proof-texting, I. Jul 14
typology, I. Jan 13, Feb 12, 21, Mar
12, 16, May 4, 11, 17, 19, Jul
14-15, 17, Sep 5, Oct 3, 12,
Nov 13, 15, 17, II. Feb 13, 28,
Apr 29, Jun 20, Aug 3, 5, Sep 4,
Nov 20, Dec 16
use of OT imagery, I. Dec 19, 23,
26-27, II. May 14
verbal prediction, I. Jul 15, II. Feb
13, May 9
(see servant of the Lord)
Nicodemus, I. May 12
Nineveh, II. Nov 7, 22, 25, Dec 3
Noah, I. Jan 7, II. Sep 9, 11

oaths, I. Jan 21, 27, May 21, Jul 28,
Aug 7, 23 (see also Nazirite Vow)
Obed-Edom, I. Sep 11, Nov 20,
II. Sep 18
obedience, I. Jan 21, 28, Feb 22, Apr
7-8, May 15, Jun 7, II. May 26
occult practices, I. Aug 1, Sep 4
old age, II. Sep 20
Omri, I. Oct 13
Onesimus, I. Nov 5
outcasts (see poor)

pantheism (see worldviews,
pantheism)
papacy (see Roman Catholicism)
parables
lost son, II. Dec 1
of Nathan, I. May 7, Sep 16
persistent widow, I. Mar 4
Pharisee and tax collector, I. Mar 4
rich farmer, I. Feb 26
sheep and goats, I. Jan 25
shrewd manager, I. Mar 2
soils, I. Feb 1, 25, II. Nov 24
sower (see parable of soils)
ten minas, II. Dec 5
tenants, I. Mar 6
Passhur, II. Jul 24
Passover, I. Mar 1, Apr 19, May 2,
Dec 24, II. Jan 20 (see also
Jerusalem, festivals in)
Passover meal, I. Mar 1, 8
Paul
and the Law, II. Jan 21, 24, 31,
Feb 22
apostleship of, I. Sep 25
apostolic authority of (see authority, apostolic)
arrest of, II. Jan 21
before Felix, II. Jan 24
before Festus, II. Jan 25-26, 29
before Herod Agrippa II,
II. Jan 26, 29
boasting of (see boasting)
conversion of, I. Jul 22
evangelistic preaching and practices of, I. Sep 13, Oct 6, II. Jan
13, 26, Feb 15, 22
Gentile mission of, II. Jan 22
in Antioch, I. Jul 24, 26

SCRIPTURE INDEX

Italics indicate Scriptures that are the focus of discussion for that day's meditation.

Genesis

1, I. Jan 1
1–2, II. Apr 27, Aug 7
1:27-28, I. Jan 3
1:28-30, I. Jan 3
2, II. Jun 24
2–3, II. Sep 25
2:2, II. Apr 29
2:18-24, I. Jan 2
2:24, II. Sep 4
2:25, I. Jan 2
3, I. Jan 3, II. Jul 17, Sep 2
3:7, I. Jan 2
3:10, I. Jan 2
3:19, II. Apr 25
3:21-22, I. Jan 5
4, I. Jan 4, 9
4:26, I. Jan 9
5, I. Jan 5
5:22, I. Jan 9
6–8, I. Jan 5
6–11, I. Apr 18
6:3, I. Jan 5
7, I. Jan 7
9:6, I. Jan 9
9:8-17, II. May 23
9:12-17, I. Jan 9
10:2, II. Oct 5
10:9-10, II. May 14
11, I. Jan 5, Feb 10
11:3, II. Oct 18
11:1-9, II. May 14
12, I. Jan 11, Feb 16, Mar 18
12:2, I. May 19
12:3, I. Jan 15, 16, May 19, Jul 22,
   Oct 3, 5, II. May 19, Jul 8,
   Dec 15
13, I. Jan 13
14, I. May 13
14:8, II. Sep 24
14:18-20, I. Jan 13, Jun 17
15, I. Jan 14, 15, 16
15:1, II. Jul 5
15:9-11, II. Dec 22
16:8, I. Jan 15
16:9, I. Jan 15
17, I. Jan 16
17:1, 25, I. Jan 16
18, II. Sep 11
18:18, I. Jan 11
18:23-33, II. Nov 18
19:26, II. Dec 3
20:7, II. Nov 18
21, I. Jan 15
21:17, I. Jan 15
21:18, I. Jan 15
22, I. Jan 21
22:18, I. Jan 11
25, I. Jan 15
25:23, I. Jan 26
25:34, I. Jan 26
26:4, I. Jan 11

27, I. Jan 26
28, I. Jan 27, 31
28:14, I. Jan 11
28:16-17, I. Jan 31
29, I. Jan 29
30, I. Jan 29
32, I. Jan 31
32:22-32, I. Apr 20
34, I. Feb 2
35, I. Jan 29
35:1-5, I. Feb 2
37, I. Feb 6
37:19-30, I. Feb 11
38, I. Feb 6, 11
39, I. Feb 6
40, I. Feb 7
41:15, I. Feb 7
41:16, I. Feb 7
41:25, I. Feb 7
44, I. Feb 11
46:3-4, I. Feb 13
49:9, II. Sep 16
49:10-11, II. Dec 22
49:22, II. Sep 29
50:15-21, *I. Feb 17*

Exodus

1:8, *I. Feb 18*
2:11-25, *I. Feb 19*
3, I. Feb 19, *20*, Mar 3
3:5, I. Jul 3
3:12, II. May 9
3:14, I. Mar 18, May 22, II. Jun 11
3:15, I. Jul 15
4, *I. Feb 21*
4:14, I. Feb 19
4:22, II. Aug 21, Sep 29
4:22-23, II. May 29
4:24-26, I. Mar 7
7:3, I. Feb 21
7:13, I. Feb 21
7:22, I. Feb 21
8:15, I. Feb 21
8:19, I. Feb 21
8:32, I. Feb 21
11, *I. Feb 28*
12, *I. Mar 1*, May 2
12:33, I. Feb 28
12:36, I. Feb 28
13:17, I. Mar 3, II. May 29
13:21, I. Mar 3
14, *I. Mar 3*
15, I. Mar 5
15:15-16, I. Jun 30
15:22-26, I. Mar 5
16, *I. Mar 5*, 16
17:1-7, I. May 11
17:2, I. Sep 5
18, *I. Mar 7*
18:11, I. Jul 4
19:4, II. Aug 29
19:5, I. Mar 9

19:6, II. Oct 22
19:16, II. Jun 2
19:16-19, I. Mar 9
20, *I. Mar 9*, II. Jun 24
20:1-17, II. Sep 5
20:5, I. Mar 22, II. May 3
20:18-19, I. Jun 13
21:2, II. Aug 6
21:23-25, I. Mar 11, Jun 14
22, I. Apr 3
22:1-15, *I. Mar 11*
23:27, I. Jun 30
24, *I. Mar 13*
24:7, I. Mar 21
24:8, II. Dec 22
25, *I. Mar 14*
25–30, I. Mar 14
26:30, I. Mar 14
28, *I. Mar 17*
28:3, I. Oct 1, II. Mar 14
30:1-10, II. Jun 6
30:17-21, II. Oct 3
32, *I. Mar 21*
32–33, II. Sep 19
32–34, I. Mar 29, Apr 20, II. Dec 11
32:9-14, II. Nov 18
32:11-14, II. Jul 19
33, *I. Mar 22*, 23
33:20, I. Mar 13
34, *I. Mar 23*
34:5-7, I. May 22, 30
34:6, II. Oct 14
34:6-7, II. Nov 25
34:9, I. Mar 22
34:14, I. May 22
40, *I. Mar 29*

Leviticus

4, I. Apr 3
5, *I. Apr 2*
5:3, I. Apr 3
6, *I. Apr 3*
8, I. Apr 7
9, I. Apr 7
10, *I. Apr 7*
11:44-45, *I. Apr 8*
14:52, II. Oct 3
16, *I. Apr 12*
17, *I. Apr 13*
18, *I. Apr 14*
18:5, II. Sep 17
19:13, II. Jul 26
19:18, II. Feb 10
21:7, I. Aug 5
21:13-15, I. Aug 5
22:24-25, II. Jun 24
23, *I. Apr 19*
23:5-8, I. May 2
25:8-55, II. Jun 29
25:32-34, I. May 26
26, *I. Apr 22*

Numbers

3, *I. Apr 26*
6, *I. Apr 29*
8, *I. May 1*
9, *I. May 2*
12, *I. May 5*
13, *I. May 5*
14, *I. May 6*
14:13-24, II. Jul 19
16, *I. May 8*
17, *I. May 9*
18, I. May 9
18:5-7, I. May 1
18:20-26, I. May 26
19:17-19, II. Oct 3
20, I. May 31
20:1-13, *I. May 11*
21:4-9, *I. May 12,* Nov 7, II. Jun 26
21:21-35, I. Jul 4
21:34, II. Jul 5
22, *I. May 13,* 16
23, *I. May 14,* 16
23:9, I. May 16
24, I. May 16
25, I. May 16, Jul 22, II. Nov 3
27:1-11, I. May 27
30:1-2, *I. May 21*
31:16, I. May 16
35, *I. May 26*
36, *I. May 27*

Deuteronomy

1–3, I. May 31
1:3, I. May 31
1:15, II. Mar 14
1:37, I. May 31
2:25, I. Jun 30
3:2, II. Jul 5
3:23-27, I. May 31
4, *I. May 31*
4:19, II. Sep 5
4:37, I. Mar 25, Jun 6
5:26, II. Oct 25
6, *I. Jun 2*
7, *I. Jun 3*
7:6, II. Jul 4
7:7-8, I. Mar 25
8, I. Feb 13, *Jun 4*
8:3, I. ix, II. ix, Jul 4
9, *I. Jun 5,* II. Dec 1
9:18-20, II. Jul 19
9:19, I. Nov 17
9:25-29, II. Jul 19
10, *I. Jun 6*
10:16, II. Jul 8
10:20, II. Jul 8
11, *I. Jun 7*
11:2, I. Jun 8
11:29, I. Mar 14
12, *I. Jun 8*
13, *I. Jun 9,* 13, II. Sep 10
13:6-11, II. Dec 26
15, *I. Jun 10*
15:1, II. Aug 6
15:12, II. Aug 6
16:1-8, I. May 2
17, I. Aug 16
17:9, II. Dec 18
17:14-20, *I. Jun 12*
17:16, II. May 29

17:18-20, II. Mar 16, Apr 10
18:12-22, *I. Jun 13,* Jul 16
18:15-18, I. Mar 9, Jun 28
18:22, I. Jun 9
19, *I. Jun 14*
20–21, I. May 9
21:18-21, II. May 4, 29
23, *I. Jun 18*
23:1-6, II. Jun 24
24, *I. Jun 19*
24:1-4, II. Jul 7
24:14, II. Jul 26
24:16, I. Nov 1
24:19-22, I. Aug 9
25:3, II. Jul 24
27–28, *I. Jun 22*
27–30, I. Apr 22
28, II. Jul 15
28:20-68, *I. Jun 23*
29:29, *I. Jun 24,* II. Mar 5
30:4-5, II. Jan 11
30:15, II. Jul 25
30:19, II. Jul 25
31, *I. Jun 26,* 28
31:16, I. Jun 28
32, I. Jun 26
32:35, I. Apr 10, 24
32:36, I. Jul 4
33, I. Jun 28
34, *I. Jun 28*

Joshua

1:6-9, II. Mar 16
2:8-11, *I. Jun 30*
3–4, I. Jul 3
4:14, I. Jul 3
5, *I. Jul 3*
5:1, I. Jun 30
6:24-25, II. Jun 24
6:26, I. Oct 13
7, *I. Jul 5*
8:30-33, I. Jun 22
8:33, I. Mar 14
9, *I. Jul 7*
15, I. Jul 13
15:63, I. Jul 13
18–19, *I. Jul 13*
18:25, II. Aug 3
20–21, I. Jul 13
21:18, II. Jul 15
21:43-45, I. Jul 13

Judges

1, I. Jul 19
1:8, I. Jul 13
1:21, I. Jul 13
1:28, I. Jul 19
2:1-12, *I. Jul 19*
3:24, II. Apr 30
6–7, I. Jul 25
8, *I. Jul 25*
9, I. Jul 25
11:30-40, *I. Jul 28*
14, *I. Jul 31*
17, *I. Aug 3*
17:5, I. Aug 4
18, *I. Aug 4*
19, I. Jan 4, *Aug 5*
19–21, I. Aug 17

20, *I. Aug 6*
20:47-48, I. Aug 7
21, *I. Aug 7*
21:25, II. Apr 11

Ruth

1, *I. Aug 8*
1–4, II. Jun 24
1:22, I. Aug 9
2, *I. Aug 9*
2:20, II. Feb 19
3–4, *I. Aug 10*

1 Samuel

2:12-25, I. Aug 13
2:34, II. May 9
3, *I. Aug 13,* Sep 17
4, *I. Aug 14*
4:5-11, I. May 25
5–6, *I. Aug 15*
7:5-9, II. Jul 19
8, *I. Aug 16*
9, *I. Aug 17*
10:2-3, II. Aug 3
11, I. Aug 23
12:19-25, II. Jul 19
13, I. Aug 23
13:14, I. Sep 16, Oct 28
14, I. Aug 23, 28
15, *I. Aug 23*
15:14-23, I. Aug 25
15:29, II. Nov 18
16, I. Oct 28
16:1, II. Sep 21
16:1-13, *I. Aug 24*
16:13, I. Aug 25
17, *I. Aug 25*
18, *I. Aug 26*
18:1-4, I. Aug 28
18:6-7, II. Sep 18
19:4-7, I. Aug 28
20, *I. Aug 28*
20:3, II. Sep 12
21:10-15, I. May 10
22:1, II. Sep 12
23:17-18, I. Aug 28
24, I. Sep 1
24:3, II. Apr 30, Sep 12
25, *I. Sep 1*
28, *I. Sep 4*
31:9-10, I. Sep 7

2 Samuel

1, *I. Sep 7*
2:1-9, I. Sep 9
2:17-23, I. Sep 9
3, I. Jan 4, *Sep 9*
4–5, *I. Sep 10*
6, *I. Sep 11*
6:12, II. Sep 18
7, *I. Sep 12,* Nov 22, II. Sep 4
11, I. Jan 4, *Sep 15*
11–12, II. Feb 1
11:1, I. Sep 16
11:8, II. Apr 30
11:11, II. Apr 30
12, I. May 7, *Sep 16*
13, I. Sep 9, 17

14, I. *Sep 18*
15, I. Sep 18
18:19ff., II. Sep 18
24, I. Nov 25

1 Kings

1, *I. Sep 29*
1:39, II. Oct 11
1–2, I. Nov 30
2:13-22, II. Dec 19
2:26-27, II. Jul 15
3, *I. Oct 1*, II. Mar 14
8, *I. Oct 5*
8:27, II. Jul 4
8:37, II. Nov 9
9:10-19, I. Jul 1
10, I. May 30, *Oct 7*
11, *I. Oct 8*
11:1-13, I. Jul 1
11:26-40, I. Oct 9
12, *I. Oct 9*
12:8, I. Dec 11
12:26ff., II. Nov 1
12:27-30, II. Nov 2
13:1-3, II. Jun 13
15, I. Oct 13
16, *I. Oct 13*
18, *I. Oct 15*
18:13, I. Oct 16
18:28, II. Dec 26
19, *I. Oct 16*, II. Mar 9
19:4, I. Aug 21, II. Nov 25
19:10, I. Aug 21
19:18, I. Aug 21
21:19, I. Oct 19
22, I. Feb 21, *Oct 19*
22:28, II. Dec 24
23:29, I. Nov 11

2 Kings

2:12, II. Oct 20
9, *I. Oct 28*
9–10, I. Jan 4
10:28-31, I. Oct 28
11, *I. Oct 29*
14, *I. Nov 1*
14:24, I. Oct 9
14:25, II. Nov 22
15:2-3, II. Dec 18
15:29, II. Oct 28
16, *I. Nov 3*
17, *I. Nov 4*
18, II. Jun 7
18–19, I. Nov 7
18:1, II. Jun 7
18:3-4, I. Nov 7
18:4, II. Jun 26
18:13, II. Nov 2
18:13-16, II. May 31
18:21, II. Sep 26
19:14-19, II. May 31
20, *I. Nov 7*, II. Jun 7
21, I. Nov 9
21:10-15, II. Jul 19
22, *I. Nov 9*, Dec 29
22–23, II. Jul 15
22:11, II. Aug 8
22:13, II. Jul 15
23:26, II. Jul 19

23:35, II. Jul 26
24, *I. Nov 11*, II. Aug 23
24:3, II. Jul 19
25, *I. Nov 12*, II. Aug 23
25:1-12, II. May 6
25:4, II. Sep 9
25:8, II. Aug 23

1 Chronicles

1–2, *I. Nov 13*
1:5, II. Oct 5
3:19, II. Dec 12
6:13-15, II. Aug 23
6:15, II. Dec 12
13:8, II. Sep 18
13:11-12, I. Nov 20
15, *I. Nov 20*
15:16-28, II. Sep 18
16:5-6, II. Oct 11
17, *I. Nov 22*
21, I. Nov 25
21:25-27, I. Nov 26
22, *I. Nov 26*
23, *I. Nov 27*
23–26, I. Nov 27
28, *I. Nov 30*
29, *I. Dec 1*
29:10, I. Nov 30
29:20-21, I. Nov 30

2 Chronicles

5:1–6:11, *I. Dec 5*
6:12-42, *I. Dec 6*
7:1-22, *I. Dec 7*
11–12, *I. Dec 11*
12, I. Dec 13
14–15, *I. Dec 13*
15:17, I. Dec 14
16, *I. Dec 14*
17–18, I. Dec 17
19–20, *I. Dec 17*
29, *I. Dec 24*
33, I. Nov 9
34, *I. Dec 29*, II. Jul 15
36, *I. Dec 31*
36:20-23, II. Jul 29
36:21, II. Oct 24

Ezra

1, *II. Jan 1*
1:1, II. Jan 1
1:2-4, II. Jun 9
2, *II. Jan 2*
3, *II. Jan 3*
4, *II. Jan 4*
4:8, II. Jan 5
4:11-16, II. Jan 5
5, *II. Jan 5*
5:1, II. Jan 4
7, *II. Jan 7*
9, *II. Jan 9, 10*
9:6-15, II. Jun 27
10, *II. Jan 10*

Nehemiah

1, *II. Jan 11*
2, II. Jan 11, *12*

4, *II. Jan 14*
5, *II. Jan 15*
6, *II. Jan 16*
7, *II. Jan 17*
8, *II. Jan 18*
9, II. Jan 20
10, *II. Jan 20*
13, *II. Jan 23*

Esther

3, *I. Jan 26, II. 26*
4, *II. Jan 27*
5, *II. Jan 28*
6, *II. Jan 29*
7, *II. Jan 30*

Job

1, *II. Feb 2, 9*
1:1, II. Mar 2, 11, Sep 11
1:8, II. Mar 11
1:18-19, II. Feb 9
2, *II. Feb 3*
2:11, II. Feb 17
3, *II. Feb 4*
4, *II. Feb 5*
5, *II. Feb 6*
6, *II. Feb 7, 8*
7, *II. Feb 8*
7:17, II. Aug 7
8, *II. Feb 9*
9, II. Feb 11
10, *II. Feb 11*
11, *II. Feb 12*
12–14, II. Feb 14
13, II. Feb 14
15, *II. Feb 16*
15–21, II. Feb 16
16–17, *II. Feb 17*
18, *II. Feb 18*
19, *II. Feb 19*
20, II. Feb 21
21, *II. Feb 21*
22, II. Feb 23
22–24, II. Feb 23
23, *II. Feb 23*
23:12, I. ix, II. ix
24, *II. Feb 24*
25, II. Feb 26
25–31, II. Feb 23
25:6, II. Aug 7
26, II. Feb 26
26–31, II. Feb 17, 26
27, *II. Feb 26*
28, *II. Feb 27*
29–31, II. Mar 2
30:1, II. Mar 2
31, *II. Mar 2*
32, II. Feb 4
32–37, II. Mar 4
32:18-21, II. Mar 4
32:22, II. Mar 4
33, *II. Mar 4*
34, *II. Mar 5*
38, *II. Mar 9*
38–41, II. Feb 12, Mar 5
40, *II. Mar 11*
41, II. Mar 12
41:11, *II. Mar 12*
42, *II. Mar 13*

42:7, II. Feb 8, Mar 5, 9
42:8-9, II. Nov 18

Psalms

Ps. 1, *I. Apr 1*
1:2, II. Oct 24, Dec 27
1:3, II. Nov 8
Ps. 2, *II. Aug 4,* Sep 4
2:7, *I. Nov 10*
Ps. 3, I. Apr 4
Ps. 6, I. Jul 2
Ps. 7, I. Apr 4
7:15-17, *I. Apr 4*
Ps. 8, *II. Aug 7*
Ps. 9, *I. Apr 5,* Jul 10
Ps. 10, *I. Apr 6,* Jul 10
10:1-4, *II. Aug 9*
11:1, I. Jun 29
14:1, *I. Apr 8,* 25, II. Mar 26, *Aug 11*
14:2-3, II. Aug 11
14:4-6, II. Aug 11
14:7, II. Aug 11
Ps. 16, I. Apr 11
16:2, *I. Apr 9*
16:8-11, I. Jul 15
Ps. 17, *I. Apr 10,* 11
Ps. 18, *I. Apr 11*
18:27, II. Feb 6
Ps. 19, I. Jan 1, *Apr 12,* II. *Aug 15*
Ps. 23, II. Aug 21
Ps. 23:1, II. Oct 1
Ps. 23:4, II. Oct 1
Ps. 25, *I. Apr 16,* Jul 10, *II. Aug 19*
Ps. 26, II. Aug 20
Ps. 27, *II. Aug 20*
27:4-5, *I. Apr 17*
Ps. 28, II. Aug 20, *21*
Ps. 29, *I. Apr 18*
Ps. 30, *II. Aug 22*
31:21-24, *I. Apr 20*
32:1-5, *I. Apr 21*
Ps. 33, *II. Aug 25*
Ps. 34, *I. Apr 23,* Jul 10
Ps. 35, *I. Apr 24*
36:1-2, *I. Apr 25*
Ps. 37, I. Jul 10
Ps. 38, *I. Apr 27*
Ps. 39, *I. Apr 28*
39:1-3, II. Sep 4
Ps. 42, *I. Apr 30,* Jul 2
Ps. 44, II. Aug 24, *Sep 3*
Ps. 45, *II. Sep 4,* Oct 13
Ps. 46, *I. May 3*
Ps. 47, *I. May 3*
Ps. 48, *I. May 4*
49:1-4, II. Sep 4
Ps. 51, *I. May 7,* Apr 10
51:4, II. Nov 23
51:17, II. Nov 15
52:9, I. Jul 4
Ps. 56, *I. May 10*
Ps. 57, I. Jun 16, Jul 8, *II. Sep 12*
57:7-11, I. Jun 16
Ps. 60, I. Jun 16, II. Sep 3
60:5-12, I. Jun 16
Ps. 61, *II. Sep 14*
Ps. 66, *I. May 15*
Ps. 68, *II. Sep 18*
68:18, I. May 1
Ps. 69, *I. May 17,* Jul 2, 14

69:25, I. Jul 14
Ps. 71, *I. May 18*
71:9, 18, *II. Sep 20*
71:10ff., II. Sep 20
71:17, II. Sep 20
Ps. 72, *I. May 19*
72:8, II. Dec 22
72:17, I. Jan 11, II. Jul 8
Ps. 73, *I. May 20*
73:25-26, I. Apr 9
Ps. 74, *II. Sep 23,* 28
75:1-5, *I. May 22*
Ps. 76, *II. Sep 24*
Ps. 77, *I. May 23*
Ps. 78, *I. May 24,* II. Feb 1, Sep 28
78:34, 36-37, II. Oct 31
78:40-41, *I. May 25,*
78:40-72, *II. Sep 27*
78:48, II. Sep 24
78:68-70, II. Dec 13
Ps. 79, II. Sep 23, *28*
Ps. 80, II. Aug 24, Sep 13, *29*
Ps. 81, *I. May 28*
Ps. 84, *I. May 29*
84:10-11, I. Apr 17
85:2-11, *I. May 30*
86:15, I. May 30
Ps. 88, *I. Jun 1*
90:12, II. Apr 20
Pss. 93–100, II. Oct 12
Ps. 95, I. Dec 1
95:7-11, I. Jun 8, II. Apr 29
96:11-13, II. Oct 11
Ps. 98, *II. Oct 11,* 12
Ps. 99, *II. Oct 12*
Ps. 102, *II. Oct 13*
Ps. 103, *I. Jun 11,* *II. Oct 14*
103:11-12, II. Dec 18
Ps. 104, *II. Oct 15*
104:4, II. Dec 19
Ps. 107, *I. Jun 15*
Ps. 108, *I. Jun 16*
Ps. 109, I. Jul 14
109:8, I. Jul 14
Ps. 110, I. Jan 13, Jan 22, *Jun 17,*
 II. May 2, Aug 5, Oct 13
Ps. 111, I. Jul 10
Ps. 112, I. Jul 10
113:1, I. Jul 4
115:3, I. Jul 4
115:4-11, I. Jul 4
115:8, II. Nov 3
Ps. 116, *I. Jun 20*
116:19, I. Jul 4
Ps. 118, *I. Jun 21*
118:22, I. Mar 6
Ps. 119, *I. Jun 22,* 27, II. Aug 15
119:45, I. Jun 25
119:89-96, *I. Jun 25*
119:109, II. Dec 27
119:111, II. Dec 27
119:133, I. Jun 25
Ps. 120, *I. Jun 29*
Pss. 120–134, I. Jun 29
Ps. 121, *I. Jun 29*
Ps. 122, I. Jun 29, *II. Nov 1*
Ps. 127, *I. Jul 1*
127:1, II. Nov 2
Ps. 128, I. Jul 1
129:1-3, II. Jun 18
Ps. 130, *I. Jul 2*

Ps. 131, *II. Nov 4*
Ps. 135, *I. Jul 4*
135:10-12, II. Nov 6
Ps. 136, *II. Nov 6*
136:10, I. Jul 4
136:18-22, I. Jul 4
Ps. 137, II. Sep 23, *Nov 7*
138:2-3, *I. Jul 5*
Ps. 139, *I. Jul 6*
141:2, II. Jun 6
Ps. 142, *I. Jul 8*
Ps. 143, *II. Nov 11*
Ps. 144, *I. Jul 9*
144:3-4, II. Aug 7
Ps. 145, *I. Jul 10*
Ps. 146, *I. Jul 11*
147:1, I. Jul 4
Ps. 148, *I. Jul 12*

Proverbs

1, *II. Mar 14*
1:7, I. Mar 9, Apr 25, II. Jun 1
1:8, II. Mar 18
2, *II. Mar 15*
3, *II. Mar 16*
3:11-12, II. Feb 6, Apr 7
4:23, *II. Mar 17*
4:24-26, II. Mar 17
5, *II. Mar 18*
6:16-19, *II. Mar 19,* Apr 12
6:20-35, II. Mar 18
7:1-27, II. Mar 18
8:22, II. Mar 14
9, II. Mar 18, *22*
9:8-9, II. Apr 9
9:10, I. Apr 25
10, *II. Mar 23,* 24
11, *II. Mar 24*
13, *II. Mar 26*
14:2, I. Jul 18
14:34, II. Sep 22
15:31, II. Apr 9
16:4, II. Mar 30, Apr 1
16:9, II. Apr 1
16:19, II. Mar 30
16:33, II. Apr 1
17, *II. Mar 30*
18:5, II. Mar 31
18:13, 18, *II. Mar 31*
18:17, II. Mar 31
19:21, *II. Apr 1*
20:24, II. Apr 1
21, *II. Apr 3*
21:1, II. Apr 1
21:9, II. Mar 30
22, *II. Apr 4*
22:8, II. Feb 5
24, *II. Apr 6*
24:23-24, II. Apr 4
25, II. Mar 23, Apr 4, 7
25:2, I. Jun 24, II. Mar 14
27, *II. Apr 9*
28, *II. Apr 10*
29, *II. Apr 11*
29:12, II. Apr 11
30, *II. Mar 23, Apr 12*
30:19, II. Apr 26
30:24, I. Oct 1
30:24-28, II. Mar 14
31, II. Mar 23, *Apr 13*

410

413